Jesse Liberty
Bradley Jones

SAMS
Teach Yourself

C++

fung fung 2005.

in **21** Days

FIFTH EDITION

SAMS   *800 East 96th Street, Indianapolis, Indiana, 46240 USA*

Sams Teach Yourself C++ in 21 Days, Fifth Edition

Copyright © 2005 by Sams Publishing

International Standard Book Number: 0-672-32711-2

Library of Congress Catalog Card Number: 2004096713

Printed in the United States of America

First Printing: December 2004

07   06   05   04   4   3   2   1

Trademarks

All terms mentioned in this book that are known to be trademarks or service marks have been appropriately capitalized. Sams Publishing cannot attest to the accuracy of this information. Use of a term in this book should not be regarded as affecting the validity of any trademark or service mark.

Warning and Disclaimer

Every effort has been made to make this book as complete and as accurate as possible, but no warranty or fitness is implied. The information provided is on an "as is" basis. The authors and the publisher shall have neither liability nor responsibility to any person or entity with respect to any loss or damages arising from the information contained in this book.

Bulk Sales

Sams Publishing offers excellent discounts on this book when ordered in quantity for bulk purchases or special sales. For more information, please contact

U.S. Corporate and Government Sales
1-800-382-3419
corpsales@pearsontechgroup.com

For sales outside of the U.S., please contact

International Sales
international@pearsoned.com

Associate Publisher
Michael Stephens

Acquisitions Editor
Loretta Yates

Development Editor
Songlin Qiu

Managing Editor
Charlotte Clapp

Project Editor
Seth Kerney

Copy Editor
Karen Annett

Indexer
Erika Millen

Proofreader
Paula Lowell

Technical Editors
Mark Cashman
David V. Corbin

Publishing Coordinator
Cindy Teeters

Multimedia Developer
Dan Scherf

Book Designer
Gary Adair

Page Layout
Eric S. Miller
Julie Parks

Contents at a Glance

Contents

About the Authors

JESSE LIBERTY is the author of numerous books on software development, including best-selling titles in C++ and .NET. He is the president of Liberty Associates, Inc. (http://www.LibertyAssociates.com) where he provides custom programming, consulting, and training.

BRADLEY JONES, Microsoft MVP, Visual C++, can be referred to as a webmaster, manager, coding grunt, executive editor, and various other things. His time and focus are on a number of software development sites and channels, including Developer.com, CodeGuru.com, DevX, VBForums, Gamelan, and other Jupitermedia-owned sites. This influence expands over sites delivering content to over 2.5 million unique developers a month.

His expertise is in the area of the big "C"s—C, C++, and C#—however, his experience includes development in PowerBuilder, VB, some Java, ASP, COBOL I/II, and various other technologies too old to even mention now. He has also been a consultant, analyst, project lead, associate publisher for major technical publishers, and author. His recent authoring credits include *Sams Teach Yourself the C# Language in 21 Days*, a 6th edition of *Sams Teach Yourself C in 21 Days*, and now this edition of *Sams Teach Yourself C++ in 21 Days*. He is also the cofounder and president of the Indianapolis .NET Developers Association, which is a charter INETA group with membership of over 700. You can often hear his ramblings on the CodeGuru.com or VBForums.com discussion forums, and he also does the weekly CodeGuru newsletter that goes out to tens of thousands of developers.

Dedication

Jesse Liberty: This book is dedicated to the living memory of David Levine.

Bradley Jones: Dedicated to my wife and our future family.

Acknowledgments

JESSE LIBERTY: A fifth edition is another chance to acknowledge and to thank those folks without whose support and help this book literally would have been impossible. First among them remain Stacey, Robin, and Rachel Liberty.

I must also thank my editors at Sams for being professionals of the highest quality; and I must especially acknowledge and thank Michael Stephens, Loretta Yates, Songlin Qiu, Seth Kerney, and Karen Annett.

I would like to acknowledge the folks who taught me how to program: Skip Gilbrech and David McCune, and those who taught me C++, including Stephen Zagieboylo. I would like to thank the many readers who helped me find errors and typos in the earlier editions of this book.

Finally, I'd like to thank Mrs. Kalish, who taught my sixth-grade class how to do binary arithmetic in 1965, when neither she nor we knew why.

BRADLEY JONES: I would also like to thank Mark Cashman, David Corbin, Songlin Qiu, and a number of readers from the previous editions.

In this fifth edition, we made an extra effort to ensure accuracy; we focused on honing the content of this book for technical accuracy with an eye on the latest specifications for the C++ language. Although we still might have missed something, chances are good that we didn't thanks to Mark and David and their close scrutiny of the technical details.

We Want to Hear from You!

As the reader of this book, *you* are our most important critic and commentator. We value your opinion and want to know what we're doing right, what we could do better, what areas you'd like to see us publish in, and any other words of wisdom you're willing to pass our way.

As an associate publisher for Sams Publishing, I welcome your comments. You can email or write me directly to let me know what you did or didn't like about this book—as well as what we can do to make our books better.

Please note that I cannot help you with technical problems related to the topic of this book. We do have a User Services group, however, where I will forward specific technical questions related to the book.

When you write, please be sure to include this book's title and author as well as your name, email address, and phone number. I will carefully review your comments and share them with the author and editors who worked on the book.

Email: feedback@samspublishing.com

Mail: Michael Stephens
         Associate Publisher
         Sams Publishing
         800 East 96th Street
         Indianapolis, IN 46240 USA

For more information about this book or another Sams Publishing title, visit our website at www.samspublishing.com. Type the ISBN (excluding hyphens) or the title of a book in the Search field to find the page you're looking for.

Introduction

This book is designed to help you teach yourself how to program with C++. No one can learn a serious programming language in just three weeks, but each of the lessons in this book has been designed so that you can read the entire lesson in just a few hours on a single day.

In just 21 days, you'll learn about such fundamentals as managing input and output, loops and arrays, object-oriented programming, templates, and creating C++ applications—all in well-structured and easy-to-follow lessons. Lessons provide sample listings—complete with sample output and an analysis of the code—to illustrate the topics of the day.

To help you become more proficient, each lesson ends with a set of common questions and answers, a quiz, and exercises. You can check your progress by examining the quiz and exercise answers provided in Appendix D, "Answers."

Who Should Read This Book

You don't need any previous experience in programming to learn C++ with this book. This book starts you from the beginning and teaches you both the language and the concepts involved with programming C++. You'll find the numerous examples of syntax and detailed analysis of code an excellent guide as you begin your journey into this rewarding environment. Whether you are just beginning or already have some experience programming, you will find that this book's clear organization makes learning C++ fast and easy.

Conventions Used in This Book

TIP

> These boxes highlight information that can make your C++ programming more efficient and effective.

NOTE

> These boxes provide additional information related to material you just read.

FAQ

What do FAQs do?

Answer: These Frequently Asked Questions provide greater insight into the use of the language and clarify potential areas of confusion.

CAUTION

These focus your attention on problems or side effects that can occur in specific situations.

These boxes provide clear definitions of essential terms.

Do	Don't
DO use the "Do/Don't" boxes to find a quick summary of a fundamental principle in a lesson.	**DON'T** overlook the useful information offered in these boxes.

This book uses various typefaces to help you distinguish C++ code from regular English. Actual C++ code is typeset in a special monospace font. Placeholders—words or characters temporarily used to represent the real words or characters you would type in code—are typeset in *italic monospace*. New or important terms are typeset in *italic*.

In the listings in this book, each real code line is numbered. If you see an unnumbered line in a listing, you'll know that the unnumbered line is really a continuation of the preceding numbered code line (some code lines are too long for the width of the book). In this case, you should type the two lines as one; do not divide them.

Sample Code for This Book

The sample code described throughout this book and Appendix D, "Answers," are available on the Sams website at http://www.samspublishing.com. Enter this book's ISBN (without the hyphens) in the Search box and click Search. When the book's title is displayed, click the title to go to a page where you can download the code and Appendix D.

Week 1

At a Glance

As you prepare for your first week of learning how to program in C++, you will need a few things: a compiler, an editor, and this book. If you don't have a C++ compiler and an editor, you can still use this book, but you won't get as much out of it as you would if you were to do the exercises.

The best way to learn to program is by writing programs! At the end of each day, you will find a workshop containing a quiz and some exercises. Be certain to take the time to answer all the questions, and to evaluate your work as objectively as you can. The later lessons build on what you learn in the earlier days, so be certain you fully understand the material before moving on.

A Note to C Programmers

The material in the first five days will be familiar to you; however, there are a few minor differences if you want to follow the C++ standards. Be certain to skim the material and to do the exercises, to ensure you are fully up to speed before going on to Day 6, "Understanding Object-Oriented Programming."

Where You Are Going

The first week covers the material you need to get started with programming in general, and with C++ in particular. On Day 1, "Getting Started," and Day 2, "The Anatomy of a C++ Program," you will be introduced to the basic concepts of programming and program flow. On Day 3, "Working with Variables and Constants," you will learn about variables and

1

2

3

4

5

6

7

constants and how to use data in your programs. On Day 4, "Creating Expressions and Statements," you will learn how programs branch based on the data provided and the conditions encountered when the program is running. On Day 5, "Organizing into Functions," you will learn what functions are and how to use them, and on Day 6 you will learn about classes and objects. On Day 7, "More on Program Flow," you will learn more about program flow, and by the end of the first week, you will be writing real object-oriented programs.

WEEK 1

DAY 1

Getting Started

Welcome to *Sams Teach Yourself C++ in 21 Days*! Today, you will get started on your way to becoming a proficient C++ programmer.

Today, you will learn

- Why C++ is a standard in software development
- The steps to develop a C++ program
- How to enter, compile, and link your first working C++ program

A Brief History of C++

Computer languages have undergone dramatic evolution since the first electronic computers were built to assist in artillery trajectory calculations during World War II. Early on, programmers worked with the most primitive computer instructions: machine language. These instructions were represented by long strings of ones and zeros. Soon, assemblers were invented to map machine instructions to human-readable and -manageable mnemonics, such as ADD and MOV.

In time, higher-level languages evolved, such as BASIC and COBOL. These languages let people work with something approximating words and sentences (referred to as source code), such as Let I = 100. These instructions were then translated into machine language by interpreters and compilers.

An *interpreter* translates and executes a program as it reads it, turning the program instructions, or source code, directly into actions.

A *compiler* translates source code into an intermediary form. This step is called compiling, and it produces an object file. The compiler then invokes a linker, which combines the object file into an executable program.

Because interpreters read the source code as it is written and execute the code on the spot, interpreters can be easier for the programmer to work with. Today, most interpreted programs are referred to as scripts, and the interpreter itself is often called a "script engine."

Some languages, such as Visual Basic 6, call the interpreter the runtime library. Other languages, such as the Visual Basic .NET and Java have another component, referred to as a "Virtual Machine" (VM) or a runtime. The VM or runtime is also an interpreter. However, it is not a source code interpreter that translates human-readable language into computer-dependent machine code. Rather, it interprets and executes a compiled computer-independent "virtual machine language" or intermediary language.

Compilers introduce the extra steps of compiling the source code (which is readable by humans) into object code (which is readable by machines). This extra step might seem inconvenient, but compiled programs run very fast because the time-consuming task of translating the source code into machine language has already been done once, at compile time. Because the translation is already done, it is not required when you execute the program.

Another advantage of compiled languages such as C++ is that you can distribute the executable program to people who don't have the compiler. With an interpreted language, you must have the interpreter to run the program.

C++ is typically a compiled language, though there are some C++ interpreters. Like many compiled languages, C++ has a reputation for producing fast but powerful programs.

In fact, for many years, the principal goal of computer programmers was to write short pieces of code that would execute quickly. Programs needed to be small because memory was expensive, and needed to be fast because processing power was also expensive. As computers have become smaller, cheaper, and faster, and as the cost of memory has fallen, these priorities have changed. Today, the cost of a programmer's time far outweighs the cost of most of the computers in use by businesses. Well-written, easy-to-maintain code is at a premium. Easy to maintain means that as requirements change for what the program needs to do, the program can be extended and enhanced without great expense.

NOTE

> The word *program* is used in two ways: to describe individual instructions (or source code) created by the programmer, and to describe an entire piece of executable software. This distinction can cause enormous confusion, so this book tries to distinguish between the source code, on one hand, and the executable, on the other.

The Need for Solving Problems

The problems programmers are asked to solve today are totally different from the problems they were solving twenty years ago. In the 1980s, programs were created to manage and process large amounts of raw data. The people writing the code and the people using the program were computer professionals. Today, computers are in use by far more people, and most know very little about how computers and programs really work. Computers are tools used by people who are more interested in solving their business problems than struggling with the computer.

Ironically, as programs are made easier for this new audience to use, the programs themselves become far more sophisticated and complex. Gone are the days when users typed in cryptic commands at esoteric prompts, only to see a stream of raw data. Today's programs use sophisticated "user-friendly interfaces" involving multiple windows, menus, dialog boxes, and the myriad of metaphors with which we've all become familiar.

With the development of the Web, computers entered a new era of market penetration; more people are using computers than ever before, and their expectations are very high. The ease at which people can use the Web has also increased the expectations. It is not uncommon for people to expect that programs take advantage of the Web and what it has to offer.

In the past few years, applications have expanded to different devices as well. No longer is a desktop PC the only serious target for applications. Rather, mobile phones, personal digital assistants (PDAs), Tablet PCs, and other devices are valid targets for modern applications.

In the few years since the first edition of this book, programmers have responded to the demands of users, and, thus, their programs have become larger and more complex. The need for programming techniques to help manage this complexity has become manifest.

As programming requirements change, both languages and the techniques used for writing programs evolve to help programmers manage complexity. Although the complete history is fascinating, this book only focuses briefly on the key part of this evolution: the transformation from procedural programming to object-oriented programming.

Procedural, Structured, and Object-Oriented Programming

Until recently, computer programs were thought of as a series of procedures that acted upon data. A *procedure*, also called a function or a method, is a set of specific instructions executed one after the other. The data was quite separate from the procedures, and the trick in programming was to keep track of which functions called which other functions, and what data was changed. To make sense of this potentially confusing situation, *structured programming* was created.

The principal idea behind structured programming is the idea of divide and conquer. A computer program can be thought of as consisting of a set of tasks. Any task that is too complex to be described simply is broken down into a set of smaller component tasks, until the tasks are sufficiently small and self-contained enough that they are each easily understood.

As an example, computing the average salary of every employee of a company is a rather complex task. You can, however, break it down into the following subtasks:

1. Count how many employees you have.

2. Find out what each employee earns.

3. Total all the salaries.

4. Divide the total by the number of employees you have.

Totaling the salaries can be broken down into the following steps:

1. Get each employee's record.

2. Access the salary.

3. Add the salary to the running total.

4. Get the next employee's record.

In turn, obtaining each employee's record can be broken down into the following:

1. Open the file of employees.
2. Go to the correct record.
3. Read the data.

Structured programming remains an enormously successful approach for dealing with complex problems. By the late 1980s, however, some of the deficiencies of structured programming had become all too clear.

First, a natural desire is to think of data (employee records, for example) and what you can do with that data (sort, edit, and so on) as a single idea. Unfortunately, structured programs separate data structures from the functions that manipulate them, and there is no natural way to group data with its associated functions within structured programming. Structured programming is often called *procedural programming* because of its focus on procedures (rather than on "objects").

Second, programmers often found themselves needing to reuse functions. But functions that worked with one type of data often could not be used with other types of data, limiting the benefits gained.

Object-Oriented Programming (OOP)

Object-oriented programming responds to these programming requirements, providing techniques for managing enormous complexity, achieving reuse of software components, and coupling data with the tasks that manipulate that data.

The essence of *object-oriented programming* is to model "objects" (that is, things or concepts) rather than "data." The objects you model might be onscreen widgets, such as buttons and list boxes, or they might be real-world objects, such as customers, bicycles, airplanes, cats, and water.

Objects have characteristics, also called properties or attributes, such as age, fast, spacious, black, or wet. They also have capabilities, also called operations or functions, such as purchase, accelerate, fly, purr, or bubble. It is the job of object-oriented programming to represent these objects in the programming language.

C++ and Object-Oriented Programming

C++ fully supports object-oriented programming, including the three pillars of object-oriented development: encapsulation, inheritance, and polymorphism.

Encapsulation

When an engineer needs to add a resistor to the device she is creating, she doesn't typically build a new one from scratch. She walks over to a bin of resistors, examines the colored bands that indicate the properties, and picks the one she needs. The resistor is a "black box" as far as the engineer is concerned—she doesn't much care how it does its work, as long as it conforms to her specifications. She doesn't need to look inside the box to use it in her design.

The property of being a self-contained unit is called *encapsulation*. With encapsulation, you can accomplish data hiding. Data hiding is the highly valued characteristic that an object can be used without the user knowing or caring how it works internally. Just as you can use a refrigerator without knowing how the compressor works, you can use a well-designed object without knowing about its internal workings. Changes can be made to those workings without affecting the operation of the program, as long as the specifications are met; just as the compressor in a refrigerator can be replaced with another one of similar design.

Similarly, when the engineer uses the resistor, she need not know anything about the internal state of the resistor. All the properties of the resistor are encapsulated in the resistor object; they are not spread out through the circuitry. It is not necessary to understand how the resistor works to use it effectively. Its workings are hidden inside the resistor's casing.

C++ supports encapsulation through the creation of user-defined types, called classes. You'll see how to create classes on Day 6, "Understanding Object-Oriented Programming." After being created, a well-defined class acts as a fully encapsulated entity—it is used as a whole unit. The actual inner workings of the class can be hidden. Users of a well-defined class do not need to know how the class works; they just need to know how to use it.

Inheritance and Reuse

When the engineers at Acme Motors want to build a new car, they have two choices: They can start from scratch, or they can modify an existing model. Perhaps their Star model is nearly perfect, but they want to add a turbocharger and a six-speed transmission. The chief engineer prefers not to start from the ground up, but rather to say, "Let's build another Star, but let's add these additional capabilities. We'll call the new model a Quasar." A Quasar is a kind of Star, but a specialized one with new features. (According to NASA, quasars are extremely luminous bodies that emit an astonishing amount of energy.)

C++ supports inheritance. With inheritance, you can declare a new type that is an extension of an existing type. This new subclass is said to derive from the existing type and is sometimes called a derived type. If the Quasar is derived from the Star and, thus, inherits all of the Star's qualities, then the engineers can add to them or modify them as needed. Inheritance and its application in C++ are discussed on Day 12, "Implementing Inheritance," and Day 16, "Advanced Inheritance."

Polymorphism

A new Quasar might respond differently than a Star does when you press down on the accelerator. The Quasar might engage fuel injection and a turbocharger, whereas the Star simply lets gasoline into its carburetor. A user, however, does not have to know about these differences. He can just "floor it," and the right thing happens, depending on which car he's driving.

C++ supports the idea that different objects do "the right thing" through what is called function polymorphism and class polymorphism. Poly means many, and morph means form. Polymorphism refers to the same name taking many forms, and it is discussed on Day 10, "Working with Advanced Functions," and Day 14, "Polymorphism."

How C++ Evolved

As object-oriented analysis, design, and programming began to catch on, Bjarne Stroustrup took the most popular language for commercial software development, C, and extended it to provide the features needed to facilitate object-oriented programming.

Although it is true that C++ is a superset of C and that virtually any legal C program is a legal C++ program, the leap from C to C++ is very significant. C++ benefited from its relationship to C for many years because C programmers could ease into their use of C++. To really get the full benefit of C++, however, many programmers found they had to unlearn much of what they knew and learn a new way of conceptualizing and solving programming problems.

Should I Learn C First?

The question inevitably arises: "Because C++ is a superset of C, should you learn C first?" Stroustrup and most other C++ programmers agree that not only is it unnecessary to learn C first, it might be advantageous not to do so.

C programming is based on structured programming concepts; C++ is based on object-oriented programming. If you learn C first, you'll have to "unlearn" the bad habits fostered by C.

This book does not assume you have any prior programming experience. If you are a C programmer, however, the first few days of this book will largely be review. Starting on Day 6, you will begin the real work of object-oriented software development.

C++, Java, and C#

C++ is one of the predominant languages for the development of commercial software. In recent years, Java has challenged that dominance; however, many of the programmers who left C++ for Java have recently begun to return. In any case, the two languages are so similar that to learn one is to learn 90 percent of the other.

C# is a newer language developed by Microsoft for the .NET platform. C# uses essentially the same syntax as C++, and although the languages are different in a few important ways, learning C++ provides a majority of what you need to know about C#. Should you later decide to learn C#, the work you do on C++ will be an excellent investment.

Microsoft's Managed Extensions to C++

With .NET, Microsoft introduced Managed Extensions to C++ ("Managed C++"). This is an extension of the C++ language to allow it to use Microsoft's new platform and libraries. More importantly, Managed C++ allows a C++ programmer to take advantage of the advanced features of the .NET environment. Should you decide to develop specifically for the .NET platform, you will need to extend your knowledge of standard C++ to include these extensions to the language.

The ANSI Standard

The Accredited Standards Committee, operating under the procedures of the American National Standards Institute (ANSI), has created an international standard for C++.

The C++ Standard is also referred to as the ISO (International Organization for Standardization) Standard, the NCITS (National Committee for Information Technology Standards) Standard, the X3 (the old name for NCITS) Standard, and the ANSI/ISO Standard. This book continues to refer to ANSI standard code because that is the more commonly used term.

NOTE   ANSI is usually pronounced "antsy" with a silent "t."

The ANSI standard is an attempt to ensure that C++ is portable—ensuring, for example, that ANSI-standard-compliant code you write for Microsoft's compiler will compile without errors using a compiler from any other vendor. Further, because the code in this book is ANSI compliant, it should compile without errors on a Macintosh, a Windows box, or an Alpha.

For most students of C++, the ANSI standard is invisible. The most recent version of the standard is ISO/IEC 14882-2003. The previous version, ISO/IEC 14882-1998, was stable and all the major manufacturers support it. All of the code in this edition of this book has been compared to the standard to ensure that it is compliant.

Keep in mind that not all compilers are fully compliant with the standard. In addition, some areas of the standard have been left open to the compiler vendor, which cannot be trusted to compile or operate in the same fashion when compiled with various brands of compilers.

NOTE

> Because the Managed Extensions to C++ only apply to the .NET platform and are not ANSI standard, they are not covered in this book.

Preparing to Program

C++, perhaps more than other languages, demands that the programmer design the program before writing it. Trivial problems, such as the ones discussed in the first few days of this book, don't require much design. Complex problems, however, such as the ones professional programmers are challenged with every day, do require design, and the more thorough the design, the more likely it is that the program will solve the problems it is designed to solve, on time and on budget. A good design also makes for a program that is relatively bug-free and easy to maintain. It has been estimated that fully 90 percent of the cost of software is the combined cost of debugging and maintenance. To the extent that good design can reduce those costs, it can have a significant impact on the bottom-line cost of the project.

The first question you need to ask when preparing to design any program is, "What is the problem I'm trying to solve?" Every program should have a clear, well-articulated goal, and you'll find that even the simplest programs in this book do so.

The second question every good programmer asks is, "Can this be accomplished without resorting to writing custom software?" Reusing an old program, using pen and paper, or buying software off the shelf is often a better solution to a problem than writing something new. The programmer who can offer these alternatives will never suffer from lack of work; finding less-expensive solutions to today's problems always generates new opportunities later.

Assuming you understand the problem and it requires writing a new program, you are ready to begin your design.

The process of fully understanding the problem (analysis) and creating a plan for a solution (design) is the necessary foundation for writing a world-class commercial application.

Your Development Environment

This book makes the assumption that your compiler has a mode in which you can write directly to a "console" (for instance, an MS-DOS/Command prompt or a shell window), without worrying about a graphical environment, such as the ones in Windows or on the Macintosh. Look for an option such as *console* or *easy window* or check your compiler's documentation.

Your compiler might be part of an Integrated Development Environment (IDE) or might have its own built-in source code text editor, or you might be using a commercial text editor or word processor that can produce text files. The important thing is that whatever you write your program in, it must save simple, plain-text files, with no word processing commands embedded in the text. Examples of safe editors include Windows Notepad, the DOS Edit command, Brief, Epsilon, Emacs, and vi. Many commercial word processors, such as WordPerfect, Word, and dozens of others, also offer a method for saving simple text files.

The files you create with your editor are called source files, and for C++ they typically are named with the extension .cpp, .cp, or .c. This book names all the source code files with the .cpp extension, but check your compiler for what it needs.

NOTE	Most C++ compilers don't care what extension you give your source code, but if you don't specify otherwise, many use .cpp by default. Be careful, however; some compilers treat .c files as C code and .cpp files as C++ code. Again, please check your compiler's documentation. In any event, it is easier for other programmers who need to understand your programs if you consistently use .cpp for C++ source code files.

Do	**DON'T**
DO use a simple text editor to create your source code, or use the built-in editor that comes with your compiler.	**DON'T** use a word processor that saves special formatting characters. If you do use a word processor, save the file as ASCII text.
DO save your files with the .c, .cp, or .cpp extension. The .cpp extension is recommended.	**DON'T** use a .c extension if your compiler treats such files as C code instead of C++ code.
DO check your documentation for specifics about your compiler and linker to ensure that you know how to compile and link your programs.	

The Process of Creating the Program

The first step in creating a new program is to write the appropriate commands (statements) into a source file. Although the source code in your file is somewhat cryptic, and anyone who doesn't know C++ will struggle to understand what it is for, it is still in what we call human-readable form. Your source code file is not a program and it can't be executed, or run, as an executable program file can.

Creating an Object File with the Compiler

To turn your source code into a program, you use a compiler. How you invoke your compiler and how you tell it where to find your source code varies from compiler to compiler; check your documentation.

After your source code is compiled, an object file is produced. This file is often named with the extension .obj or .o. This is still not an executable program, however. To turn this into an executable program, you must run your linker.

Creating an Executable File with the Linker

C++ programs are typically created by linking one or more object files (.obj or .o files) with one or more libraries. A library is a collection of linkable files that were supplied with your compiler, that you purchased separately, or that you created and compiled. All C++ compilers come with a library of useful functions and classes that you can include in your program. You'll learn more about functions and classes in great detail in the next few days.

The steps to create an executable file are

1. Create a source code file with a .cpp extension.
2. Compile the source code into an object file with the .obj or .o extension.
3. Link your object file with any needed libraries to produce an executable program.

The Development Cycle

If every program worked the first time you tried it, this would be the complete development cycle: Write the program, compile the source code, link the program, and run it. Unfortunately, almost every program, no matter how trivial, can and will have errors. Some errors cause the compile to fail, some cause the link to fail, and some show up only when you run the program (these are often called "bugs").

Whatever type of error you find, you must fix it, and that involves editing your source code, recompiling and relinking, and then rerunning the program. This cycle is represented in Figure 1.1, which diagrams the steps in the development cycle.

FIGURE 1.1

The steps in the development of a C++ program.

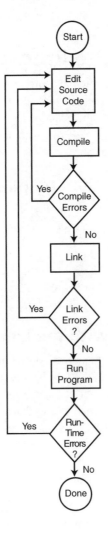

HELLO.cpp—Your First C++ Program

Traditional programming books begin by writing the words "Hello World" to the screen, or a variation on that statement. This time-honored tradition is carried on here.

Type the source code shown in Listing 1.1 directly into your editor, exactly as shown (excluding the line numbering). After you are certain you have entered it correctly, save the file, compile it, link it, and run it. If everything was done correctly, it prints the words Hello World to your screen. Don't worry too much about how it works; this is really just to get you comfortable with the development cycle. Every aspect of this program is covered over the next couple of days.

CAUTION

> The following listing contains line numbers on the left. These numbers are for reference within the book. They should not be typed into your editor. For example, on line 1 of Listing 1.1, you should enter:
>
> #include <iostream>

LISTING 1.1   HELLO.cpp, the Hello World Program

```
1:  #include <iostream>
2:
3:  int main()
4:  {
5:      std::cout << "Hello World!\n";
6:      return 0;
7:  }
```

Be certain you enter this exactly as shown. Pay careful attention to the punctuation. The << on line 5 is the redirection symbol, produced on most keyboards by holding the Shift key and pressing the comma key twice. Between the letters std and cout on line 5 are two colons (:). Lines 5 and 6 each end with semicolon (;).

Also check to ensure you are following your compiler directions properly. Most compilers link automatically, but check your documentation to see whether you need to provide a special option or execute a command to cause the link to occur.

If you receive errors, look over your code carefully and determine how it is different from the preceding listing. If you see an error on line 1, such as cannot find file iostream, you might need to check your compiler documentation for directions on setting up your include path or environment variables.

If you receive an error that there is no prototype for main, add the line int main(); just before line 3 (this is one of those pesky compiler variations). In that case, you need to add this line before the beginning of the main function in every program in this book. Most compilers don't require this, but a few do. If yours does, your finished program needs to look like this:

```
#include <iostream>
int main();              // most compilers don't need this line
int main()
{
    std::cout <<"Hello World!\n";
    return 0;
}
```

NOTE

> It is difficult to read a program to yourself if you don't know how to pro-
> nounce the special characters and keywords. You read the first line "Pound
> include (some say hash-include, others say sharp-include) eye-oh-stream."
> You read the fifth line "ess-tee-dee-see-out Hello World."

On a Windows system, try running HELLO.exe (or whatever the name of an executable is on your operating system; for instance, on a Unix system, you run HELLO, because executable programs do not have extensions in Unix). The program should write

```
Hello World!
```

directly to your screen. If so, congratulations! You've just entered, compiled, and run your first C++ program. It might not look like much, but almost every professional C++ programmer started out with this exact program.

Some programmers using IDEs (such as Visual Studio or Borland C++ Builder) will find that running the program flashes up a window that promptly disappears with no chance to see what result the program produces. If this happens, add these lines to your source code just prior to the "return" statement:

```
char response;
std::cin >> response;
```

These lines cause the program to pause until you type a character (you might also need to press the Enter key). They ensure you have a chance to see the results of your test run. If you need to do this for hello.cpp, you will probably need to do it for most of the programs in this book.

Using the Standard Libraries

If you have a very old compiler, the program shown previously will not work—the new ANSI standard libraries will not be found. In that case, please change your program to look like this:

```
1:  #include <iostream.h>
2:
3:  int main()
4:  {
5:          cout << "Hello World!\n";
6:          return 0;
7:  }
```

Notice that the library name now ends in .h (dot-h) and that we no longer use std:: in front of cout on line 5. This is the old, pre-ANSI style of header files. If your compiler works with this and not with the earlier version, you have an antiquated compiler. Your compiler will be fine for the early days of this book, but when you get to templates and exceptions, your compiler might not work.

Getting Started with Your Compiler

This book is *not* compiler specific. This means that the programs in this book should work with *any* ANSI-compliant C++ compiler on any platform (Windows, Macintosh, Unix, Linux, and so on).

That said, the vast majority of programmers are working in the Windows environment, and the vast majority of professional programmers use the Microsoft compilers. The details of compiling and linking with every possible compiler is too much to show here; however, we can show you how to get started with Microsoft Visual C++ 6, and that ought to be similar enough to whatever compiler you are using to be a good head start.

Compilers differ, however, so be certain to check your documentation.

Building the Hello World Project

To create and test the Hello World program, follow these steps:

1. Start the compiler.
2. Choose File, New from the menus.
3. Choose Win32 Console Application and enter a project name, such as hello, and click OK.
4. Choose An Empty Project from the menu of choices and click Finish. A dialog box is displayed with new project information.

5. Click OK. You are taken back to the main editor window.

6. Choose File, New from the menus.

7. Choose C++ Source File and give it a name, such as `hello`. You enter this name into the File Name text box.

8. Click OK. You are taken back to the main editor window.

9. Enter the code as indicated previously.

10. Choose Build, Build `hello.exe` from the menus.

11. Check that you have no build errors. You can find this information near the bottom of the editor.

12. Run the program by pressing Ctrl+F5 or by selecting Build, Execute hello from the menus.

13. Press the spacebar to end the program.

FAQ

I can run the program but it flashes by so quickly I can't read it. What is wrong?

Answer: Check your compiler documentation; there ought to be a way to cause your program to pause after execution. With the Microsoft compilers, the trick is to use Ctrl+F5.

With any compiler, you can also add the following lines immediately before the return statement (that is, between lines 5 and 6 in Listing 1.1):

```
char response;
std::cin >> response;
```

This causes the program to pause, waiting for you to enter a value. To end the program, type any letter or number (for example, 1) and then press Enter (if necessary).

The meaning of `std::cin` and `std::cout` will be discussed in coming days; for now, just use it as if it were a magical incantation.

Compile Errors

Compile-time errors can occur for any number of reasons. Usually, they are a result of a typo or other inadvertent minor error. Good compilers not only tell you what you did wrong, they point you to the exact place in your code where you made the mistake. The great ones even suggest a remedy!

You can see this by intentionally putting an error into your program. If HELLO.cpp ran smoothly, edit it now and remove the closing brace on line 7 of Listing 1.1. Your program now looks like Listing 1.2.

LISTING 1.2 Demonstration of Compiler Error

```
1:   #include <iostream>
2:
3:   int main()
4:   {
5:       std::cout << "Hello World!\n";
6:       return 0;
```

Recompile your program and you should see an error that looks similar to the following:

```
Hello.cpp(7) : fatal error C1004: unexpected end of file found
```

This error tells you the file and line number of the problem and what the problem is (although I admit it is somewhat cryptic). In this case, the compiler is telling you that it ran out of source lines and hit the end of the source file without finding the closing brace.

Sometimes, the error messages just get you to the general vicinity of the problem. If a compiler could perfectly identify every problem, it would fix the code itself.

Summary

After reading today's lesson, you should have a good understanding of how C++ evolved and what problems it was designed to solve. You should feel confident that learning C++ is the right choice for anyone interested in programming. C++ provides the tools of object-oriented programming and the performance of a systems-level language, which makes C++ the development language of choice.

Today, you learned how to enter, compile, link, and run your first C++ program, and what the normal development cycle is. You also learned a little of what object-oriented programming is all about. You will return to these topics during the next three weeks.

Q&A

Q **What is the difference between a text editor and a word processor?**

A A text editor produces files with plain text in them. No formatting commands or other special symbols are used that might be required by a particular word processor. Simple text editors do not have automatic word wrap, bold print, italic, and so forth.

Q If my compiler has a built-in editor, must I use it?

A Almost all compilers will compile code produced by any text editor. The advantages of using the built-in text editor, however, might include the capability to quickly move back and forth between the edit and compile steps of the development cycle. Sophisticated compilers include a fully integrated development environment, enabling the programmer to access help files, edit, and compile the code in place, and to resolve compile and link errors without ever leaving the environment.

Q Can I ignore warning messages from my compiler?

A Compilers generally give warnings and errors. If there are errors, the program will not be completely built. If there are just warnings, the compiler will generally go ahead and still create the program.

Many books hedge on this question. The appropriate answer is: No! Get into the habit, from day one, of treating warning messages as errors. C++ uses the compiler to warn you when you are doing something you might not intend. Heed those warnings and do what is required to make them go away. Some compilers even have a setting that causes all warnings to be treated like errors, and thus stop the program from building an executable.

Q What is compile time?

A Compile time is the time when you run your compiler, in contrast to link time (when you run the linker) or runtime (when running the program). This is just programmer shorthand to identify the three times when errors usually surface.

Workshop

The Workshop provides quiz questions to help you solidify your understanding of the material covered and exercises to provide you with experience in using what you've learned. Try to answer the quiz and exercise questions before checking the answers in Appendix D, and be certain you understand the answers before continuing to tomorrow's lesson.

Quiz

1. What is the difference between an interpreter and a compiler?
2. How do you compile the source code with your compiler?
3. What does the linker do?
4. What are the steps in the normal development cycle?

Exercises

1. Look at the following program and try to guess what it does without running it.

```
1: #include <iostream>
2: int main()
3: {
4:    int x = 5;
5:    int y = 7;
6:    std::cout << endl;
7:    std::cout << x + y << " " << x * y;
8:    std::cout << end;
9:    return 0;
10:}
```

2. Type in the program from Exercise 1, and then compile and link it. What does it do? Does it do what you guessed?

3. Type in the following program and compile it. What error do you receive?

```
1: include <iostream>
2: int main()
3: {
4:     std::cout << "Hello World \n";
5:     return 0;
6: }
```

4. Fix the error in the program in Exercise 3 and recompile, link, and run it. What does it do?

DAY 2

The Anatomy of a C++ Program

C++ programs consist of classes, functions, variables, and other component parts. Most of this book is devoted to explaining these parts in depth, but to get a sense of how a program fits together, you must see a complete working program.

Today, you will learn

- The parts of a C++ program
- How the parts work together
- What a function is and what it does

A Simple Program

Even the simple program HELLO.cpp from Day 1, "Getting Started," had many interesting parts. This section reviews this program in more detail. Listing 2.1 reproduces the original version of HELLO.cpp for your convenience.

LISTING 2.1   HELLO.cpp Demonstrates the Parts of a C++ Program

```
1:  #include <iostream>
2:
3:  int main()
4:  {
5:      std::cout << "Hello World!\n";
6:      return 0;
7:  }
```

OUTPUT   Hello World!

ANALYSIS   On line 1, the file iostream is included into the current file.

Here's how that works: The first character is the # symbol, which is a signal to a program called the preprocessor. Each time you start your compiler, the preprocessor is run first. The preprocessor reads through your source code, looking for lines that begin with the pound symbol (#) and acts on those lines before the compiler runs. The preprocessor is discussed in detail on Day 21, "What's Next."

The command #include is a preprocessor instruction that says, "What follows is a file-name. Find that file, read it, and place it right here." The angle brackets around the file-name tell the preprocessor to look in all the usual places for this file. If your compiler is set up correctly, the angle brackets cause the preprocessor to look for the file iostream in the directory that holds all the include files for your compiler. The file iostream (Input-Output-Stream) is used by cout, which assists with writing to the console. The effect of line 1 is to include the file iostream into this program as if you had typed it in yourself.

NOTE   The preprocessor runs before your compiler each time the compiler is invoked. The preprocessor translates any line that begins with a pound symbol (#) into a special command, getting your code file ready for the compiler.

NOTE   Not all compilers are consistent in their support for #includes that omit the file extension. If you get error messages, you might need to change the include search path for your compiler, or add the extension to the #include.

Line 3 begins the actual program with a function named `main()`. Every C++ program has a `main()` function. A function is a block of code that performs one or more actions. Usually, functions are invoked or called by other functions, but `main()` is special. When your program starts, `main()` is called automatically.

`main()`, like all functions, must state what kind of value it returns. The return value type for `main()` in `HELLO.cpp` is `int`, which means that this function returns an integer to the operating system when it completes. In this case, it returns the integer value 0, as shown on line 6. Returning a value to the operating system is a relatively unimportant and little used feature, but the C++ standard does require that `main()` be declared as shown.

CAUTION

Some compilers let you declare `main()` to return void. This is no longer legal C++, and you should not get into bad habits. Have `main()` return int, and simply return 0 as the last line in `main()`.

NOTE

Some operating systems enable you to test the value returned by a program. The convention is to return 0 to indicate that the program ended normally.

All functions begin with an opening brace (`{`) and end with a closing brace (`}`). The braces for the `main()` function are on lines 4 and 7. Everything between the opening and closing braces is considered a part of the function.

The meat and potatoes of this program is on line 5.

The object `cout` is used to print a message to the screen. You'll learn about objects in general on Day 6, "Understanding Object-Oriented Programming," and `cout` and its related object `cin` in detail on Day 17, "Working with Streams." These two objects, `cin` and `cout`, are used in C++ to handle input (for example, from the keyboard) and output (for example, to the console), respectively.

`cout` is an object provided by the standard library. A library is a collection of classes. The standard library is the standard collection that comes with every ANSI-compliant compiler.

You designate to the compiler that the `cout` object you want to use is part of the standard library by using the namespace specifier `std`. Because you might have objects with the same name from more than one vendor, C++ divides the world into "namespaces." A namespace is a way to say "when I say `cout`, I mean the `cout` that is part of the standard namespace, not some other namespace." You say that to the compiler by putting the characters std followed by two colons before the cout. You'll learn more about namespaces in coming days.

Here's how cout is used: Type the word cout, followed by the output redirection operator (<<). Whatever follows the output redirection operator is written to the console. If you want a string of characters written, be certain to enclose them in double quotes ("), as shown on line 5.

> **NOTE**   You should note that the redirection operator is two "greater-than" signs with no spaces between them.

A text string is a series of printable characters.

The final two characters, \n, tell cout to put a new line after the words Hello World! This special code is explained in detail when cout is discussed on Day 18, "Creating and Using Namespaces."

The main() function ends on line 7 with the closing brace.

A Brief Look at cout

On Day 17, you will see how to use cout to print data to the screen. For now, you can use cout without fully understanding how it works. To print a value to the screen, write the word cout, followed by the insertion operator (<<), which you create by typing the less-than character (<) twice. Even though this is two characters, C++ treats it as one.

Follow the insertion character with your data. Listing 2.2 illustrates how this is used. Type in the example exactly as written, except substitute your own name where you see Jesse Liberty (unless your name *is* Jesse Liberty).

LISTING 2.2   Using cout

```
1:  // Listing 2.2 using std::cout
2:  #include <iostream>
3:  int main()
4:  {
5:      std::cout << "Hello there.\n";
6:      std::cout << "Here is 5: " << 5 << "\n";
7:      std::cout << "The manipulator std::endl ";
8:      std::cout << "writes a new line to the screen.";
9:      std::cout <<  std::endl;
```

LISTING 2.2   continued

```
10:     std::cout << "Here is a very big number:\t" << 70000;
11:     std::cout << std::endl;
12:     std::cout << "Here is the sum of 8 and 5:\t";
13:     std::cout << 8+5 << std::endl;
14:     std::cout << "Here's a fraction:\t\t";
15:     std::cout << (float) 5/8 << std::endl;
16:     std::cout << "And a very very big number:\t";
17:     std::cout << (double) 7000 * 7000 << std::endl;
18:     std::cout << "Don't forget to replace Jesse Liberty ";
19:     std::cout << "with your name...\n";
20:     std::cout << "Jesse Liberty is a C++ programmer!\n";
21:     return 0;
22: }
```

OUTPUT

```
Hello there.
Here is 5: 5
The manipulator endl writes a new line to the screen.
Here is a very big number:      70000
Here is the sum of 8 and 5:     13
Here's a fraction:              0.625
And a very very big number:     4.9e+007
Don't forget to replace Jesse Liberty with your name...
Jesse Liberty is a C++ programmer!
```

CAUTION

> Some compilers have a bug that requires that you put parentheses around the addition before passing it to cout. Thus, line 13 would change to
>
> ```
> 13:     cout << (8+5) << std::endl;
> ```

ANALYSIS   On line 2, the statement #include <iostream> causes the iostream file to be added to your source code. This is required if you use cout and its related functions.

On line 5 is the simplest use of cout, printing a string or series of characters. The symbol \n is a special formatting character. It tells cout to print a newline character to the screen; it is pronounced "slash-n" or "new line."

Three values are passed to cout on line 6, and each value is separated by the insertion operator. The first value is the string "Here is 5: ". Note the space after the colon. The space is part of the string. Next, the value 5 is passed to the insertion operator and then the newline character (always in double quotes or single quotes) is passed. This causes the line

```
Here is 5: 5
```

to be printed to the console. Because no newline character is present after the first string, the next value is printed immediately afterward. This is called concatenating the two values.

On line 7, an informative message is printed, and then the manipulator `std::endl` is used. The purpose of `endl` is to write a new line to the console. (Other uses for `endl` are discussed on Day 16, "Advanced Inheritance.") Note that `endl` is also provided by the standard library; thus, `std::` is added in front of it just as `std::` was added for `cout`.

NOTE

`endl` stands for *end l*ine and is end-ell rather than end-one. It is commonly pronounced "end-ell."

Use of `endl` is preferable to the use of '\n', because `endl` is adapted to the operating system in use, whereas '\n' might not be the complete newline character required on a particular OS or platform.

On line 10, a new formatting character, `\t`, is introduced. This inserts a tab character and is used on lines 10 to 16 to line up the output. Line 10 shows that not only integers, but long integers as well, can be printed. Lines 13 and 14 demonstrate that `cout` will do simple addition. The value of 8+5 is passed to `cout` on line 14, but the value of 13 is printed.

On line 15, the value 5/8 is inserted into `cout`. The term (`float`) tells `cout` that you want this value evaluated as a decimal equivalent, and so a fraction is printed. On line 17, the value 7000 * 7000 is given to `cout`, and the term (`double`) is used to tell `cout` that this is a floating-point value. All this will be explained on Day 3, "Working with Variables and Constants," when data types are discussed.

On lines 18 and 20, you should have substituted your name for `Jesse Liberty`. If you do this, the output should confirm that you are indeed a C++ programmer. It must be true, because the computer said so!

Using the Standard Namespace

You'll notice that the use of `std::` in front of both `cout` and `endl` becomes rather distracting after a while. Although using the namespace designation is good form, it is tedious to type. The ANSI standard allows two solutions to this minor problem.

The first is to tell the compiler, at the beginning of the code listing, that you'll be using the standard library `cout` and `endl`, as shown on lines 5 and 6 of Listing 2.3.

LISTING 2.3   Using the using Keyword

```
1:   // Listing 2.3 - using the using keyword
2:   #include <iostream>
3:   int main()
4:   {
5:       using std::cout;
6:       using std::endl;
7:
8:       cout << "Hello there.\n";
9:       cout << "Here is 5: " << 5 << "\n";
10:      cout << "The manipulator endl ";
11:      cout << "writes a new line to the screen.";
12:      cout <<  endl;
13:      cout << "Here is a very big number:\t" << 70000;
14:      cout <<  endl;
15:      cout << "Here is the sum of 8 and 5:\t";
16:      cout << 8+5 << endl;
17:      cout << "Here's a fraction:\t\t";
18:      cout << (float) 5/8 << endl;
19:      cout << "And a very very big number:\t";
20:      cout << (double) 7000 * 7000 << endl;
21:      cout << "Don't forget to replace Jesse Liberty ";
22:      cout << "with your name...\n";
23:      cout << "Jesse Liberty is a C++ programmer!\n";
24:      return 0;
25:  }
```

OUTPUT

```
Hello there.
Here is 5: 5
The manipulator endl writes a new line to the screen.
Here is a very big number:      70000
Here is the sum of 8 and 5:     13
Here's a fraction:              0.625
And a very very big number:     4.9e+007
Don't forget to replace Jesse Liberty with your name...
Jesse Liberty is a C++ programmer!
```

ANALYSIS   You will note that the output is identical to the previous listing. The only difference between Listing 2.3 and Listing 2.2 is that on lines 5 and 6, additional statements inform the compiler that two objects from the standard library will be used. This is
done with the keyword using. After this has been done, you no longer need to qualify
the cout and endl objects.

The second way to avoid the inconvenience of writing std:: in front of cout and endl is
to simply tell the compiler that your listing will be using the entire standard namespace;
that is, any object not otherwise designated can be assumed to be from the standard

namespace. In this case, rather than writing using std::cout;, you would simply write using namespace std;, as shown in Listing 2.4.

LISTING 2.4   Using the namespace Keyword

```
 1:  // Listing 2.4 - using namespace std
 2:  #include <iostream>
 3:  int main()
 4:  {
 5:      using namespace std;
 6:
 7:      cout << "Hello there.\n";
 8:      cout << "Here is 5: " << 5 << "\n";
 9:      cout << "The manipulator endl ";
10:      cout << "writes a new line to the screen.";
11:      cout <<  endl;
12:      cout << "Here is a very big number:\t" << 70000;
13:      cout <<  endl;
14:      cout << "Here is the sum of 8 and 5:\t";
15:      cout << 8+5 << endl;
16:      cout << "Here's a fraction:\t\t";
17:      cout << (float) 5/8 << endl;
18:      cout << "And a very very big number:\t";
19:      cout << (double) 7000 * 7000 << endl;
20:      cout << "Don't forget to replace Jesse Liberty ";
21:      cout << "with your name...\n";
22:      cout << "Jesse Liberty is a C++ programmer!\n";
23:      return 0;
24:  }
```

ANALYSIS   Again, the output is identical to the earlier versions of this program. The advantage to writing using namespace std; is that you do not have to specifically designate the objects you're actually using (for example, cout and endl;). The disadvantage is that you run the risk of inadvertently using objects from the wrong library.

Purists prefer to write std:: in front of each instance of cout or endl. The lazy prefer to write using namespace std; and be done with it. In this book, most often the individual items being used are declared, but from time to time each of the other styles are presented just for fun.

Commenting Your Programs

When you are writing a program, your intent is always clear and self-evident to you. Funny thing, though—a month later, when you return to the program, it can be quite confusing and unclear. No one is ever certain how the confusion creeps into a program, but it nearly always does.

To fight the onset of bafflement, and to help others understand your code, you need to use comments. Comments are text that is ignored by the compiler, but that can inform the reader of what you are doing at any particular point in your program.

Types of Comments

C++ comments come in two flavors: single-line comments and multiline comments.

Single-line comments are accomplished using a double slash (//). The double slash tells the compiler to ignore everything that follows, until the end of the line.

Multiline comments are started by using a forward slash followed by an asterisk (/*). This "slash-star" comment mark tells the compiler to ignore everything that follows until it finds a star-slash (*/) comment mark. These marks can be on the same line or they can have one or more lines between them; however, every /* must be matched with a closing */.

Many C++ programmers use the double-slash, single-line comments most of the time and reserve multiline comments for blocking out large blocks of a program. You can include single-line comments within a block "commented out" by the multiline comment marks; everything, including the double-slash comments, are ignored between the multiline comment marks.

NOTE

> The multiline comment style has been referred to as C-style because it was introduced and used in the C programming language. The single-line comments were originally a part of C++ and not a part of C; thus, they have been referred to as C++-style. The current standards for both C and C++ now include both styles of comments.

Using Comments

Some people recommend writing comments at the top of each function, explaining what the function does and what values it returns.

Functions should be named so that little ambiguity exists about what they do, and confusing and obscure bits of code should be redesigned and rewritten so as to be self-evident. Comments should not be used as an excuse for obscurity in your code.

This is not to suggest that comments ought never be used, only that they should not be relied upon to clarify obscure code; instead, fix the code. In short, you should write your code well, and use comments to supplement understanding.

Listing 2.5 demonstrates the use of comments, showing that they do not affect the processing of the program or its output.

LISTING 2.5   HELP.cpp Demonstrates Comments

```
1:   #include <iostream>
2:
3:   int main()
4:   {
5:       using std::cout;
6:
7:       /* this is a comment
8:       and it extends until the closing
9:       star-slash comment mark */
10:      cout << "Hello World!\n";
11:      // this comment ends at the end of the line
12:      cout << "That comment ended!\n";
13:
14:      // double-slash comments can be alone on a line
15:      /* as can slash-star comments */
16:      return 0;
17:  }
```

OUTPUT
```
Hello World!
That comment ended!
```

ANALYSIS   The comment on lines 7–9 is completely ignored by the compiler, as are the comments on lines 11, 14, and 15. The comment on line 11 ended with the end of the line. The comments on lines 7 and 15 required a closing comment mark.

NOTE

> There is a third style of comment that is supported by some C++ compilers. These comments are referred to as document comments and are indicated using three forward slashes (///). The compilers that support this style of comment allow you to generate documentation about the program from these comments. Because these are not currently a part of the C++ standard, they are not covered here.

A Final Word of Caution About Comments

Comments that state the obvious are less than useful. In fact, they can be counterproductive because the code might change and the programmer might neglect to update the comment. What is obvious to one person might be obscure to another, however, so judgment is required when adding comments.

The bottom line is that comments should not say *what* is happening, they should say *why* it is happening.

Functions

Although `main()` is a function, it is an unusual one. To be useful, a function must be called, or invoked, during the course of your program. `main()` is invoked by the operating system.

A program is executed line-by-line in the order it appears in your source code until a function is reached. Then, the program branches off to execute the function. When the function finishes, it returns control to the line of code immediately following the call to the function.

A good analogy for this is sharpening your pencil. If you are drawing a picture and your pencil point breaks, you might stop drawing, go sharpen the pencil, and then return to what you were doing. When a program needs a service performed, it can call a function to perform the service and then pick up where it left off when the function is finished running. Listing 2.6 demonstrates this idea.

NOTE	Functions are covered in more detail on Day 5, "Organizing into Functions." The types that can be returned from a function are covered in more detail on Day 3, "Working with Variables and Constants." The information provided today is to present you with an overview because functions will be used in almost all of your C++ programs.

LISTING 2.6   Demonstrating a Call to a Function

```
1:  #include <iostream>
2:
3:  // function Demonstration Function
4:  // prints out a useful message
5:  void DemonstrationFunction()
6:  {
7:      std::cout << "In Demonstration Function\n";
8:  }
9:
10: // function main - prints out a message, then
11: // calls DemonstrationFunction, then prints out
12: // a second message.
13: int main()
14: {
15:     std::cout << "In main\n" ;
16:     DemonstrationFunction();
17:     std::cout << "Back in main\n";
18:     return 0;
19: }
```

```
In main
In Demonstration Function
Back in main
```

ANALYSIS The function `DemonstrationFunction()` is defined on lines 6–8. When it is called, it prints a message to the console screen and then returns.

Line 13 is the beginning of the actual program. On line 15, `main()` prints out a message saying it is in `main()`. After printing the message, line 16 calls `DemonstrationFunction()`. This call causes the flow of the program to go to the `DemonstrationFunction()` function on line 5. Any commands in `DemonstrationFunction()` are then executed. In this case, the entire function consists of the code on line 7, which prints another message. When `DemonstrationFunction()` completes (line 8), the program flow returns to from where it was called. In this case, the program returns to line 17, where `main()` prints its final line.

Using Functions

Functions either return a value or they return void, meaning they do not return anything. A function that adds two integers might return the sum, and thus would be defined to return an integer value. A function that just prints a message has nothing to return and would be declared to return void.

Functions consist of a header and a body. The header consists, in turn, of the return type, the function name, and the parameters to that function. The parameters to a function enable values to be passed into the function. Thus, if the function were to add two numbers, the numbers would be the parameters to the function. Here's an example of a typical function header that declares a function named `Sum` that receives two integer values (`first` and `second`) and also returns an integer value:

```
int Sum( int first, int second)
```

A parameter is a declaration of what type of value will be passed in; the actual value passed in when the function is called is referred to as an argument. Many programmers use the terms parameters and arguments as synonyms. Others are careful about the technical distinction. The distinction between these two terms is not critical to your programming C++, so you shouldn't worry if the words get interchanged.

The body of a function consists of an opening brace, zero or more statements, and a closing brace. The statements constitute the workings of the function.

A function might return a value using a `return` statement. The value returned must be of the type declared in the function header. In addition, this statement causes the function to exit. If you don't put a `return` statement into your function, it automatically returns void (nothing) at the end of the function. If a function is supposed to return a value but does not contain a `return` statement, some compilers produce a warning or error message.

Listing 2.7 demonstrates a function that takes two integer parameters and returns an integer value. Don't worry about the syntax or the specifics of how to work with integer values (for example, `int first`) for now; that is covered in detail on Day 3.

LISTING 2.7 FUNC.cpp Demonstrates a Simple Function

```
1:  #include <iostream>
2:  int Add (int first, int second)
3:  {
4:      std::cout << "In Add(), received " << first << " and
        ➥ " << second << "\n";
5:      return (first + second);
6:  }
7:
8:  int main()
9:  {
10:     using std::cout;
11:     using std::cin;
12:
13:
14:     cout << "I'm in main()!\n";
15:     int a, b, c;
16:     cout << "Enter two numbers: ";
17:     cin >> a;
18:     cin >> b;
19:     cout << "\nCalling Add()\n";
20:     c=Add(a,b);
21:     cout << "\nBack in main().\n";
22:     cout << "c was set to " << c;
23:     cout << "\nExiting...\n\n";
24:     return 0;
25: }
```

OUTPUT

```
I'm in main()!
Enter two numbers: 3 5

Calling Add()
In Add(), received 3 and 5

Back in main().
c was set to 8
Exiting...
```

ANALYSIS   The function Add() is defined on line 2. It takes two integer parameters and returns an integer value. The program itself begins on line 8. The program prompts the user for two numbers (line 16). The user types each number, separated by a space, and then presses the Enter key. The numbers the user enters are placed in the variables a and b on lines 17 and 18. On line 20, the main() function passes the two numbers typed in by the user as arguments to the Add() function.

Processing branches to the Add() function, which starts on line 2. The values from a and b are received as parameters first and second, respectively. These values are printed and then added. The result of adding the two numbers is returned on line 5, at which point the function returns to the function that called it—main(), in this case.

On lines 17 and 18, the cin object is used to obtain a number for the variables a and b. Throughout the rest of the program, cout is used to write to the console. Variables and other aspects of this program are explored in depth in the next few days.

Methods Versus Functions

A function by any other name is still just a function. It is worth noting here that different programming languages and different programming methodologies might refer to functions using a different term. One of the more common terms used is the term *method*. Method is simply another term for functions that are part of a class.

Summary

The difficulty in learning a complex subject, such as programming, is that so much of what you learn depends on everything else there is to learn. Today's lesson introduced the basic parts of a simple C++ program.

Q&A

Q What does #include do?

A This is a directive to the preprocessor, which runs when you call your compiler. This specific directive causes the file in the "<>" named after the word #include to be read in, as if it were typed in at that location in your source code.

Q What is the difference between // comments and /* style comments?

A The double-slash comments (//) "expire" at the end of the line. Slash-star (/*) comments are in effect until a closing comment mark (*/). The double-slash comments are also referred to as single-line comments, and the slash-star comments are often referred to as multiline comments. Remember, not even the end of the function terminates a slash-star comment; you must put in the closing comment mark, or you will receive a compile-time error.

Q What differentiates a good comment from a bad comment?

A A good comment tells the reader *why* this particular code is doing whatever it is doing or explains what a section of code is about to do. A bad comment restates what a particular line of code is doing. Lines of code should be written so that they speak for themselves. A well-written line of code should tell you what it is doing without needing a comment.

Workshop

The Workshop provides quiz questions to help you solidify your understanding of the material covered and exercises to provide you with experience in using what you've learned. Try to answer the quiz and exercise questions before checking the answers in Appendix D, and be certain you understand the answers before continuing to tomorrow's lesson.

Quiz

1. What is the difference between the compiler and the preprocessor?
2. Why is the function `main()` special?
3. What are the two types of comments, and how do they differ?
4. Can comments be nested?
5. Can comments be longer than one line?

Exercises

1. Write a program that writes "I love C++" to the console.
2. Write the smallest program that can be compiled, linked, and run.
3. **BUG BUSTERS:** Enter this program and compile it. Why does it fail? How can you fix it?

```
1: #include <iostream>
2: main()
3: {
4:     std::cout << Is there a bug here?";
5: }
```

4. Fix the bug in Exercise 3 and recompile, link, and run it.
5. Modify Listing 2.7 to include a subtract function. Name this function `Subtract()` and use it in the same way that the `Add()` function was called. You should also pass the same values that were passed to the `Add()` function.

DAY 3

Working with Variables and Constants

Programs need a way to store the data they use or create so it can be used later in the program's execution. Variables and constants offer various ways to represent, store, and manipulate that data.

Today, you will learn

- How to declare and define variables and constants
- How to assign values to variables and manipulate those values
- How to write the value of a variable to the screen

What Is a Variable?

In C++, a *variable* is a place to store information. A variable is a location in your computer's memory in which you can store a value and from which you can later retrieve that value.

Notice that variables are used for temporary storage. When you exit a program or turn the computer off, the information in variables is lost. Permanent storage is a different matter. Typically, the values from variables are permanently stored either to a database or to a file on disk. Storing to a file on disk is discussed on Day 16, "Advanced Inheritance."

Storing Data in Memory

Your computer's memory can be viewed as a series of cubbyholes. Each cubbyhole is one of many, many such holes all lined up. Each cubbyhole—or memory location—is numbered sequentially. These numbers are known as *memory addresses*. A variable reserves one or more cubbyholes in which you can store a value.

Your variable's name (for example, myVariable) is a label on one of these cubbyholes so that you can find it easily without knowing its actual memory address. Figure 3.1 is a schematic representation of this idea. As you can see from the figure, myVariable starts at memory address 103. Depending on the size of myVariable, it can take up one or more memory addresses.

FIGURE 3.1

A schematic representation of memory.

NOTE

RAM stands for random access memory. When you run your program, it is loaded into RAM from the disk file. All variables are also created in RAM. When programmers talk about memory, it is usually RAM to which they are referring.

Setting Aside Memory

When you define a variable in C++, you must tell the compiler what kind of variable it is (this is usually referred to as the variable's "type"): an integer, a floating-point number, a character, and so forth. This information tells the compiler how much room to set aside and what kind of value you want to store in your variable. It also allows the compiler to warn you or produce an error message if you accidentally attempt to store a value of the wrong type in your variable (this characteristic of a programming language is called "*strong typing*").

Each cubbyhole is one byte in size. If the type of variable you create is four bytes in size, it needs four bytes of memory, or four cubbyholes. The type of the variable (for example, integer) tells the compiler how much memory (how many cubbyholes) to set aside for the variable.

There was a time when it was imperative that programmers understood bits and bytes; after all, these are the fundamental units of storage. Computer programs have gotten better at abstracting away these details, but it is still helpful to understand how data is stored. For a quick review of the underlying concepts in binary math, please take a look at Appendix A, "Working with Numbers: Binary and Hexadecimal."

NOTE   If mathematics makes you want to run from the room screaming, don't bother with Appendix A; you won't really need it. The truth is that programmers no longer need to be mathematicians; though it is important to be comfortable with logic and rational thinking.

Size of Integers

On any one computer, each variable type takes up a single, unchanging amount of room. That is, an integer might be two bytes on one machine and four on another, but on either computer it is always the same, day in and day out.

Single characters—including letters, numbers, and symbols—are stored in a variable of type char. A char variable is most often one byte long.

NOTE   There is endless debate about how to pronounce char. Some say it as "car," some say it as "char"(coal), others say it as "care." Clearly, car is correct because that is how *I* say it, but feel free to say it however you like.

For smaller integer numbers, a variable can be created using the short type. A short integer is two bytes on most computers, a long integer is usually four bytes, and an integer (without the keyword short or long) is usually two or four bytes.

You'd think the language would specify the exact size that each of its types should be; however, C++ doesn't. All it says is that a short must be less than or equal to the size of an int, which, in turn, must be less than or equal to the size of a long.

That said, you're probably working on a computer with a two-byte short and a four-byte int, with a four-byte long.

The size of an integer is determined by the processor (16 bit, 32 bit, or 64 bit) and the compiler you use. On a 32-bit computer with an Intel Pentium processor, using modern compilers, integers are *four* bytes.

CAUTION | When creating programs, you should never assume the amount of memory that is being used for any particular type.

Compile and run Listing 3.1 and it will tell you the exact size of each of these types on your computer.

LISTING 3.1   Determining the Size of Variable Types on Your Computer

```cpp
1:  #include <iostream>
2:
3:  int main()
4:  {
5:      using std::cout;
6:
7:      cout << "The size of an int is:\t\t"
8:          << sizeof(int)    << " bytes.\n";
9:      cout << "The size of a short int is:\t"
10:          << sizeof(short)  << " bytes.\n";
11:     cout << "The size of a long int is:\t"
12:          << sizeof(long)   << " bytes.\n";
13:     cout << "The size of a char is:\t\t"
14:          << sizeof(char)   << " bytes.\n";
15:     cout << "The size of a float is:\t\t"
16:          << sizeof(float)  << " bytes.\n";
17:     cout << "The size of a double is:\t"
18:          << sizeof(double) << " bytes.\n";
19:     cout << "The size of a bool is:\t"
20:          << sizeof(bool)   << " bytes.\n";
21:
22:     return 0;
23: }
```

OUTPUT

```
The size of an int is:          4 bytes.
The size of a short int is:     2 bytes.
The size of a long int is:      4 bytes.
The size of a char is:          1 bytes.
The size of a float is:         4 bytes.
The size of a double is:        8 bytes.
The size of a bool is:          1 bytes.
```

> **NOTE**   On your computer, the number of bytes presented might be different.

Most of Listing 3.1 should be pretty familiar. The lines have been split to make them fit for the book, so for example, lines 7 and 8 could really be on a single line. The compiler ignores whitespace (spaces, tabs, line returns) and so you can treat these as a single line. That's why you need a ";" at the end of most lines.

The new feature in this program to notice is the use of the `sizeof` operator on lines 7–20. The `sizeof` is used like a function. When called, it tells you the size of the item you pass to it as a parameter. On line 8, for example, the keyword `int` is passed to `sizeof`. You'll learn later in today's lesson that `int` is used to describe a standard integer variable. Using `sizeof` on a Pentium 4, Windows XP machine, an `int` is four bytes, which coincidentally also is the size of a `long int` on the same computer.

The other lines of Listing 3.1 show the sizes of other data types. You'll learn about the values these data types can store and the differences between each in a few minutes.

signed and unsigned

All integer types come in two varieties: `signed` and `unsigned`. Sometimes, you need negative numbers, and sometimes you don't. Any integer without the word "unsigned" is assumed to be `signed`. `signed` integers can be negative or positive. `unsigned` integers are always positive.

Integers, whether `signed` or `unsigned` are stored in the same amount of space. Because of this, part of the storage room for a `signed` integer must be used to hold information on whether the number is negative or positive. The result is that the largest number you can store in an `unsigned` integer is twice as big as the largest positive number you can store in a `signed` integer.

For example, if a `short` integer is stored in two bytes, then an `unsigned` `short` integer can handle numbers from 0 to 65,535. Alternatively, for a `signed` `short`, half the numbers that can be stored are negative; thus, a `signed` `short` can only represent positive numbers up to 32,767. The `signed` `short` can also, however, represent negative numbers giving it a total range from –32,768 to 32,767.

For more information on the precedence of operators, read Appendix C, "Operator Precedence."

Fundamental Variable Types

Several variable types are built in to C++. They can be conveniently divided into integer variables (the type discussed so far), floating-point variables, and character variables.

Floating-point variables have values that can be expressed as fractions—that is, they are real numbers. Character variables hold a single byte and are generally used for holding the 256 characters and symbols of the ASCII and extended ASCII character sets.

The types of variables used in C++ programs are described in Table 3.1. This table shows the variable type, how much room the type generally takes in memory, and what kinds of values can be stored in these variables. The values that can be stored are determined by the size of the variable types, so check your output from Listing 3.1 to see if your variable types are the same size. It is most likely that they are the same size unless you are using a computer with a 64-bit processor.

TABLE 3.1 Variable Types

Type	Size	Values
bool	1 byte	true or false
unsigned short int	2 bytes	0 to 65,535
short int	2 bytes	–32,768 to 32,767
unsigned long int	4 bytes	0 to 4,294,967,295
long int	4 bytes	–2,147,483,648 to 2,147,483,647
int (16 bit)	2 bytes	–32,768 to 32,767
int (32 bit)	4 bytes	–2,147,483,648 to 2,147,483,647
unsigned int (16 bit)	2 bytes	0 to 65,535
unsigned int (32 bit)	4 bytes	0 to 4,294,967,295
char	1 byte	256 character values
float	4 bytes	1.2e–38 to 3.4e38
double	8 bytes	2.2e–308 to 1.8e308

apply to your compiler. If your output from Listing 3.1 was different, you should consult your compiler's manual for the values that your variable types can hold.

Defining a Variable

Up to this point, you have seen a number of variables created and used. Now, it is time to learn how to create your own.

You create or *define* a variable by stating its type, followed by one or more spaces, followed by the variable name and a semicolon. The variable name can be virtually any combination of letters, but it cannot contain spaces. Legal variable names include x, J23qrsnf, and myAge. Good variable names tell you what the variables are for; using good names makes it easier to understand the flow of your program. The following statement defines an integer variable called myAge:

```
int myAge;
```

NOTE When you declare a variable, memory is allocated (set aside) for that variable. The *value* of the variable will be whatever happened to be in that memory at that time. You will see in a moment how to assign a new value to that memory.

As a general programming practice, avoid such horrific names as J23qrsnf, and restrict single-letter variable names (such as x or i) to variables that are used only very briefly. Try to use expressive names such as myAge or howMany. Such names are easier to understand three weeks later when you are scratching your head trying to figure out what you meant when you wrote that line of code.

Try this experiment: Guess what these programs do, based on the first few lines of code:

Example 1

```
int main()
{
    unsigned short x;
    unsigned short y;
    unsigned short z;
    z = x * y;
    return 0;
}
```

Example 2

```
int main()
{
    unsigned short Width;
    unsigned short Length;
    unsigned short Area;
    Area = Width * Length;
    return 0;
}
```

> **NOTE** If you compile these programs, your compiler will warn that the values are
> not initialized. You'll see how to solve this problem shortly.

Clearly, the purpose of the second program is easier to guess, and the inconvenience of
having to type the longer variable names is more than made up for by how much easier it
is to understand, and thus maintain, the second program.

Case Sensitivity

C++ is case sensitive. In other words, uppercase and lowercase letters are considered to
be different. A variable named age is different from Age, which is different from AGE.

> **CAUTION** Some compilers allow you to turn case sensitivity off. Don't be tempted to
> do this; your programs won't work with other compilers, and other C++ pro-
> grammers will be very confused by your code.

Naming Conventions

Various conventions exist for how to name variables, and although it doesn't much matter which method you adopt, it is important to be consistent throughout your program.
Inconsistent naming will confuse other programmers when they read your code.

Many programmers prefer to use all lowercase letters for their variable names. If the
name requires two words (for example, my car), two popular conventions are used:
my_car or myCar. The latter form is called camel notation because the capitalization
looks something like a camel's hump.

Some people find the underscore character (my_car) to be easier to read, but others prefer
to avoid the underscore because it is more difficult to type. This book uses camel notation, in which the second and all subsequent words are capitalized: myCar,
theQuickBrownFox, and so forth.

Many advanced programmers employ a notation style referred to as Hungarian notation. The idea behind Hungarian notation is to prefix every variable with a set of characters that describes its type. Integer variables might begin with a lowercase letter i. Variables of type long might begin with a lowercase l. Other notations indicate different constructs within C++ that you will learn about later, such as constants, globals, pointers, and so forth.

NOTE   It is called Hungarian notation because the man who invented it, Charles Simonyi of Microsoft, is Hungarian. You can find his original monograph at http://www.strangecreations.com//library/c/naming.txt.

Microsoft has moved away from Hungarian notation recently, and the design recommendations for C# strongly recommend *not* using Hungarian notation. Their reasoning for C# applies equally well to C++.

Keywords

Some words are reserved by C++, and you cannot use them as variable names. These keywords have special meaning to the C++ compiler. Keywords include if, while, for, and main. A list of keywords defined by C++ is presented in Table 3.2 as well as in Appendix B, "C++ Keywords." Your compiler might have additional reserved words, so you should check its manual for a complete list.

TABLE 3.2   The C++ Keywords

asm	else	new	this
auto	enum	operator	throw
bool	explicit	private	true
break	export	protected	try
case	extern	public	typedef
catch	false	register	typeid
char	float	reinterpret_cast	typename
class	for	return	union
const	friend	short	unsigned
const_cast	goto	signed	using
continue	if	sizeof	virtual
default	inline	static	void

TABLE 3.2   continued

delete	int	static_cast	volatile
do	long	struct	wchar_t
double	mutable	switch	while
dynamic_cast	namespace	template	

In addition, the following words are reserved:

And	bitor	not_eq	xor
and_eq	compl	or	xor_eq
bitand	not	or_eq	

Do	**Don't**
DO define a variable by writing the type, then the variable name.	**DON'T** use C++ keywords as variable names.
DO use meaningful variable names.	**DON'T** make assumptions about how many bytes are used to store a variable.
DO remember that C++ is case sensitive.	**DON'T** use unsigned variables for negative numbers.
DO understand the number of bytes each variable type consumes in memory and what values can be stored in variables of that type.	

Creating More Than One Variable at a Time

You can create more than one variable of the same type in one statement by writing the type and then the variable names, separated by commas. For example:

```
unsigned int myAge, myWeight;     // two unsigned int variables
long int area, width, length;     // three long integers
```

As you can see, myAge and myWeight are each declared as unsigned integer variables. The second line declares three individual long variables named area, width, and length. The type (long) is assigned to all the variables, so you cannot mix types in one definition statement.

Assigning Values to Your Variables

You assign a value to a variable by using the assignment operator (=). Thus, you would assign 5 to width by writing

```
unsigned short width;
width = 5;
```

> **NOTE** long is a shorthand version of long int, and short is a shorthand version of short int.

You can combine the steps of creating a variable and assigning a value to it. For example, you can combine these two steps for the width variable by writing:

```
unsigned short width = 5;
```

This initialization looks very much like the earlier assignment, and when using integer variables like width, the difference is minor. Later, when const is covered, you will see that some variables must be initialized because they cannot be assigned a value at a later time.

Just as you can define more than one variable at a time, you can initialize more than one variable at creation. For example, the following creates two variables of type long and initializes them:

```
long width = 5, length = 7;
```

This example initializes the long integer variable width to the value 5 and the long integer variable length to the value 7. You can even mix definitions and initializations:

```
int myAge = 39, yourAge, hisAge = 40;
```

This example creates three type int variables, and it initializes the first (myAge) and third (hisAge).

Listing 3.2 shows a complete program, ready to compile, that computes the area of a rectangle and writes the answer to the screen.

LISTING 3.2 A Demonstration of the Use of Variables

```
1:  // Demonstration of variables
2:  #include <iostream>
3:
4:  int main()
5:  {
6:      using std::cout;
7:      using std::endl;
8:
9:      unsigned short int Width = 5, Length;
10:     Length = 10;
11:
12:     // create  an unsigned short and initialize with result
13:     // of multiplying Width by Length
14:     unsigned short int Area  = (Width * Length);
```

LISTING 3.2 continued

```
15:
16:     cout << "Width:" << Width << endl;
17:     cout << "Length: " << Length << endl;
18:     cout << "Area: " << Area << endl;
19:     return 0;
20:  }
```

OUTPUT
```
Width:5
Length: 10
Area: 50
```

ANALYSIS As you have seen in the previous listing, line 2 includes the required `include` statement for the `iostream`'s library so that `cout` will work. Line 4 begins the program with the `main()` function. Lines 6 and 7 define `cout` and `endl` as being part of the standard (`std`) namespace.

On line 9, the first variables are defined. `Width` is defined as an `unsigned short` integer, and its value is initialized to 5. Another `unsigned short` integer, `Length`, is also defined, but it is not initialized. On line 10, the value 10 is assigned to `Length`.

On line 14, an `unsigned short` integer, `Area`, is defined, and it is initialized with the value obtained by multiplying `Width` times `Length`. On lines 16–18, the values of the variables are printed to the screen. Note that the special word `endl` creates a new line.

Creating Aliases with `typedef`

It can become tedious, repetitious, and, most important, error-prone to keep writing `unsigned short int`. C++ enables you to create an alias for this phrase by using the keyword `typedef`, which stands for type definition.

In effect, you are creating a synonym, and it is important to distinguish this from creating a new type (which you will do on Day 6, "Understanding Object-Oriented Programming"). `typedef` is used by writing the keyword `typedef`, followed by the existing type, then the new name, and ending with a semicolon. For example,

```
typedef unsigned short int USHORT;
```

creates the new name `USHORT` that you can use anywhere you might have written `unsigned short int`. Listing 3.3 is a replay of Listing 3.2, using the type definition `USHORT` rather than `unsigned short int`.

LISTING 3.3 A Demonstration of *typedef*

```
1:   // Demonstrates typedef keyword
2:   #include <iostream>
3:
4:   typedef unsigned short int USHORT;    //typedef defined
5:
6:   int main()
7:   {
8:
9:       using std::cout;
10:      using std::endl;
11:
12:      USHORT  Width = 5;
13:      USHORT Length;
14:      Length = 10;
15:      USHORT Area  = Width * Length;
16:      cout << "Width:" << Width << endl;
17:      cout << "Length: "  << Length << endl;
18:      cout << "Area: " << Area <<endl;
19:      return 0;
20:  }
```

3

OUTPUT
```
Width:5
Length: 10
Area: 50
```

NOTE

> An asterisk (*) indicates multiplication.

ANALYSIS On line 4, USHORT is typedefined (some programmers say "typedef'ed") as a synonym for unsigned short int. The program is very much like Listing 3.2, and the output is the same.

When to Use short and When to Use long

One source of confusion for new C++ programmers is when to declare a variable to be type long and when to declare it to be type short. The rule, when understood, is fairly straightforward: If any chance exists that the value you'll want to put into your variable will be too big for its type, use a larger type.

As shown in Table 3.1, unsigned short integers, assuming that they are two bytes, can hold a value only up to 65,535. signed short integers split their values between positive and negative numbers, and thus their maximum value is only half that of the unsigned.

Although unsigned long integers can hold an extremely large number (4,294,967,295), that is still quite finite. If you need a larger number, you'll have to go to float or double, and then you lose some precision. Floats and doubles can hold extremely large numbers, but only the first seven or nine digits are significant on most computers. This means that the number is rounded off after that many digits.

Shorter variables use up less memory. These days, memory is cheap and life is short. Feel free to use int, which is probably four bytes on your machine.

Wrapping Around an unsigned Integer

That unsigned long integers have a limit to the values they can hold is only rarely a problem, but what happens if you do run out of room?

When an unsigned integer reaches its maximum value, it wraps around and starts over, much as a car odometer might. Listing 3.4 shows what happens if you try to put too large a value into a short integer.

LISTING 3.4 A Demonstration of Putting Too Large a Value in an unsigned short Integer

```
 1:  #include <iostream>
 2:  int main()
 3:  {
 4:     using std::cout;
 5:     using std::endl;
 6:
 7:     unsigned short int smallNumber;
 8:     smallNumber = 65535;
 9:     cout << "small number:" << smallNumber << endl;
10:     smallNumber++;
11:     cout << "small number:" << smallNumber << endl;
12:     smallNumber++;
13:     cout << "small number:" << smallNumber << endl;
14:     return 0;
15:  }
```

OUTPUT

```
small number:65535
small number:0
small number:1
```

ANALYSIS On line 7, smallNumber is declared to be an unsigned short int, which on a Pentium 4 computer running Windows XP is a two-byte variable, able to hold a value between 0 and 65,535. On line 8, the maximum value is assigned to smallNumber, and it is printed on line 9.

On line 10, `smallNumber` is incremented; that is, 1 is added to it. The symbol for incrementing is ++ (as in the name C++—an incremental increase from C). Thus, the value in `smallNumber` would be 65,536. However, `unsigned short` integers can't hold a number larger than 65,535, so the value is wrapped around to 0, which is printed on line 11.

On line 12 `smallNumber` is incremented again, and then its new value, 1, is printed.

Wrapping Around a `signed` Integer

A `signed` integer is different from an `unsigned` integer, in that half of the values you can represent are negative. Instead of picturing a traditional car odometer, you might picture a clock much like the one shown in Figure 3.2, in which the numbers count upward moving clockwise and downward moving counterclockwise. They cross at the bottom of the clock face (traditional 6 o'clock).

FIGURE 3.2

If clocks used `signed` *numbers.*

One number from 0 is either 1 (clockwise) or –1 (counterclockwise). When you run out of positive numbers, you run right into the largest negative numbers and then count back down to 0. Listing 3.5 shows what happens when you add 1 to the maximum positive number in a `short` integer.

LISTING 3.5 A Demonstration of Adding Too Large a Number to a `signed` `short` Integer

```
1:  #include <iostream>
2:  int main()
3:  {
4:      short int smallNumber;
```

LISTING 3.5 continued

```
 5:     smallNumber = 32767;
 6:     std::cout << "small number:" << smallNumber << std::endl;
 7:     smallNumber++;
 8:     std::cout << "small number:" << smallNumber << std::endl;
 9:     smallNumber++;
10:     std::cout << "small number:" << smallNumber << std::endl;
11:     return 0;
12: }
```

OUTPUT
```
small number:32767
small number:-32768
small number:-32767
```

ANALYSIS On line 4, smallNumber is declared this time to be a signed short integer (if you don't explicitly say that it is unsigned, an integer variable is assumed to be signed). The program proceeds much as the preceding one, but the output is quite different. To fully understand this output, you must be comfortable with how signed numbers are represented as bits in a two-byte integer.

The bottom line, however, is that just like an unsigned integer, the signed integer wraps around from its highest positive value to its highest negative value.

Working with Characters

Character variables (type char) are typically 1 byte, enough to hold 256 values (see Appendix C). A char can be interpreted as a small number (0–255) or as a member of the ASCII set. The ASCII character set and its ISO equivalent are a way to encode all the letters, numerals, and punctuation marks.

NOTE
> Computers do not know about letters, punctuation, or sentences. All they understand are numbers. In fact, all they really know about is whether a sufficient amount of electricity is at a particular junction of wires. These two states are represented symbolically as a 1 and 0. By grouping ones and zeros, the computer is able to generate patterns that can be interpreted as numbers, and these, in turn, can be assigned to letters and punctuation.

In the ASCII code, the lowercase letter "a" is assigned the value 97. All the lower- and uppercase letters, all the numerals, and all the punctuation marks are assigned values between 1 and 128. An additional 128 marks and symbols are reserved for use by the computer maker, although the IBM extended character set has become something of a standard.

NOTE ASCII is usually pronounced "Ask-ee."

Characters and Numbers

When you put a character, for example, "a," into a char variable, what really is there is a number between 0 and 255. The compiler knows, however, how to translate back and forth between characters (represented by a single quotation mark and then a letter, numeral, or punctuation mark, followed by a closing single quotation mark) and the corresponding ASCII values.

The value/letter relationship is arbitrary; there is no particular reason that the lowercase "a" is assigned the value 97. As long as everyone (your keyboard, compiler, and screen) agrees, no problem occurs. It is important to realize, however, that a big difference exists between the value 5 and the character '5'. The character '5' actually has an ASCII value of 53, much as the letter "a" is valued at 97. This is illustrated in Listing 3.6.

LISTING 3.6 Printing Characters Based on Numbers

```
1:  #include <iostream>
2:  int main()
3:  {
4:      for (int i = 32; i<128; i++)
5:          std::cout << (char) i;
6:      return 0;
7:  }
```

OUTPUT
```
!"#$%&'()*+,-./0123456789:;<=>?@ABCDEFGHIJKLMNOPQRSTUVWXYZ[\]^_`abcde-
fghijklmno
pqrstuvwxyz{|}~?
```

ANALYSIS This simple program prints the character values for the integers 32 through 127. This listing uses an integer variable, i, on line 4 to accomplish this task. On line 5, the number in the variable i is forced to display as a character.

A character variable could also have been used as shown in Listing 3.7, which has the same output.

LISTING **3.7**   Printing Characters Based on Numbers, Take 2

```
1:  #include <iostream>
2:  int main()
2:  {
4:      for (unsigned char i = 32; i<128; i++)
5:          std::cout <<  i;
6:      return 0;
7:  }
```

As you can see, an `unsigned` character is used on line 4. Because a character variable is being used instead of a numeric variable, the `cout` on line 5 knows to display the character value.

Special Printing Characters

The C++ compiler recognizes some special characters for formatting. Table 3.3 shows the most common ones. You put these into your code by typing the backslash (called the escape character), followed by the character. Thus, to put a tab character into your code, you enter a single quotation mark, the slash, the letter t, and then a closing single quotation mark:

```
char tabCharacter = '\t';
```

This example declares a `char` variable (`tabCharacter`) and initializes it with the character value `\t`, which is recognized as a tab. The special printing characters are used when printing either to the screen or to a file or other output device.

The escape character (`\`) changes the meaning of the character that follows it. For example, normally the character n means the letter n, but when it is preceded by the escape character, it means new line.

TABLE 3.3   The Escape Characters

Character	What It Means
\a	Bell (alert)
\b	Backspace
\f	Form feed
\n	New line
\r	Carriage return
\t	Tab
\v	Vertical tab
\'	Single quote

TABLE 3.3 continued

Character	
\"	Double quote
\?	Question mark
\\	Backslash
\000	Octal notation
\xhhh	Hexadecimal notation

Constants

Like variables, *constants* are data storage locations. Unlike variables, and as the name implies, constants don't change—they remain constant. You must initialize a constant when you create it, and you cannot assign a new value later.

C++ has two types of constants: literal and symbolic.

Literal Constants

A *literal constant* is a value typed directly into your program wherever it is needed. For example:

```
int myAge = 39;
```

myAge is a variable of type int; 39 is a literal constant. You can't assign a value to 39, and its value can't be changed.

Symbolic Constants

A *symbolic constant* is a constant that is represented by a name, just as a variable is represented. Unlike a variable, however, after a constant is initialized, its value can't be changed.

If your program has an integer variable named students and another named classes, you could compute how many students you have, given a known number of classes, if you knew each class consisted of 15 students:

```
students = classes * 15;
```

In this example, 15 is a literal constant. Your code would be easier to read, and easier to maintain, if you substituted a symbolic constant for this value:

```
students = classes * studentsPerClass
```

3

If you later decided to change the number of students in each class, you could do so where you define the constant `studentsPerClass` without having to make a change every place you used that value.

Two ways exist to declare a symbolic constant in C++. The old, traditional, and now obsolete way is with a preprocessor directive, `#define`. The second, and appropriate way to create them is using the `const` keyword.

Defining Constants with `#define`

Because a number of existing programs use the preprocessor `#define` directive, it is important for you to understand how it has been used. To define a constant in this obsolete manner, you would enter this:

```
#define studentsPerClass 15
```

Note that `studentsPerClass` is of no particular type (`int`, `char`, and so on). The preprocessor does a simple text substitution. In this case, every time the preprocessor sees the word `studentsPerClass`, it puts in the text `15`.

Because the preprocessor runs before the compiler, your compiler never sees your constant; it sees the number 15.

CAUTION

Although `#define` looks very easy to use, it should be avoided as it has been declared obsolete in the C++ standard.

Defining Constants with `const`

Although #define works, a much better way exists to define constants in C++:

```
const unsigned short int studentsPerClass = 15;
```

This example also declares a symbolic constant named `studentsPerClass`, but this time `studentsPerClass` is typed as an `unsigned short int`.

This method of declaring constants has several advantages in making your code easier to maintain and in preventing bugs. The biggest difference is that this constant has a type, and the compiler can enforce that it is used according to its type.

NOTE

Constants cannot be changed while the program is running. If you need to change `studentsPerClass`, for example, you need to change the code and recompile.

Do	Don't
DO watch for numbers overrunning the size of the integer and wrapping around incorrect values. **DO** give your variables meaningful names that reflect their use.	**DON'T** use keywords as variable names. **DON'T** use the #define preprocessor directive to declare constants. Use const.

Enumerated Constants

Enumerated constants enable you to create new types and then to define variables of those types whose values are restricted to a set of possible values. For example, you could create an enumeration to store colors. Specifically, you could declare COLOR to be an enumeration, and then you could define five values for COLOR: RED, BLUE, GREEN, WHITE, and BLACK.

The syntax for creating enumerated constants is to write the keyword enum, followed by the new type name, an opening brace, each of the legal values separated by a comma, and finally, a closing brace and a semicolon. Here's an example:

```
enum COLOR { RED, BLUE, GREEN, WHITE, BLACK };
```

This statement performs two tasks:

1. It makes COLOR the name of an enumeration; that is, a new type.
2. It makes RED a symbolic constant with the value 0, BLUE a symbolic constant with the value 1, GREEN a symbolic constant with the value 2, and so forth.

Every enumerated constant has an integer value. If you don't specify otherwise, the first constant has the value 0, and the rest count up from there. Any one of the constants can be initialized with a particular value, however, and those that are not initialized count upward from the ones before them. Thus, if you write

```
enum Color { RED=100, BLUE, GREEN=500, WHITE, BLACK=700 };
```

then RED has the value 100; BLUE, the value 101; GREEN, the value 500; WHITE, the value 501; and BLACK, the value 700.

You can define variables of type COLOR, but they can be assigned only one of the enumerated values (in this case, RED, BLUE, GREEN, WHITE, or BLACK. You can assign any color value to your COLOR variable.

3

It is important to realize that enumerator variables are generally of type unsigned int, and that the enumerated constants equate to integer variables. It is, however, very convenient to be able to name these values when working with information such as colors, days of the week, or similar sets of values. Listing 3.8 presents a program that uses an enumerated type.

LISTING 3.8   A Demonstration of Enumerated Constants

```
1:   #include <iostream>
2:   int main()
3:   {
4:       enum Days { Sunday, Monday, Tuesday,
5:                   Wednesday, Thursday, Friday, Saturday };
6:
7:       Days today;
8:       today = Monday;
9:
10:      if (today == Sunday || today == Saturday)
11:          std::cout << "\nGotta' love the weekends!\n";
12:      else
13:          std::cout << "\nBack to work.\n";
14:
15:      return 0;
16:  }
```

OUTPUT   Back to work.

ANALYSIS   On lines 4 and 5, the enumerated constant Days is defined, with seven values. Each of these evaluates to an integer, counting upward from 0; thus, Monday's value is 1 (Sunday was 0).

On line 7, a variable of type Days is created—that is, the variable contains a valid value from the list of enumerated constants defined on lines 4 and 5. The value Monday is assigned to the variable on line 8. On line 10, a test is done against the value.

The enumerated constant shown on line 8 could be replaced with a series of constant integers, as shown in Listing 3.9.

LISTING 3.9   Same Program Using Constant Integers

```
1:   #include <iostream>
2:   int main()
3:   {
4:       const int Sunday = 0;
5:       const int Monday = 1;
```

LISTING 3.9 continued

```
 6:     const int Tuesday = 2;
 7:     const int Wednesday = 3;
 8:     const int Thursday = 4;
 9:     const int Friday = 5;
10:     const int Saturday = 6;
11:
12:     int today;
13:     today = Monday;
14:
15:     if (today == Sunday || today == Saturday)
16:         std::cout << "\nGotta' love the weekends!\n";
17:     else
18:         std::cout << "\nBack to work.\n";
19:
20:     return 0;
21: }
```

OUTPUT   Back to work.

CAUTION   A number of the variables you declare in this program are not used. As such, your compiler might give you warnings when you compile this listing.

ANALYSIS   The output of this listing is identical to Listing 3.8. Here, each of the constants (Sunday, Monday, and so on) was explicitly defined, and no enumerated Days type exists. Enumerated constants have the advantage of being self-documenting—the intent of the Days enumerated type is immediately clear.

Summary

Today's lesson discussed numeric and character variables and constants, which are used by C++ to store data during the execution of your program. Numeric variables are either integral (char, short, int, and long int) or they are floating point (float, double, and long double). Numeric variables can also be signed or unsigned. Although all the types can be of various sizes among different computers, the type specifies an exact size on any given computer.

You must declare a variable before it can be used, and then you must store the type of data that you've declared as correct for that variable. If you put a number that is too large into an integral variable, it wraps around and produces an incorrect result.

Today's lesson also presented literal and symbolic constants as well as enumerated constants. You learned two ways to declare a symbolic constant: using #define and using the keyword const; however, you learned that using const is the appropriate way.

Q&A

Q If a short int can run out of room and wrap around, why not always use long integers?

A All integer types can run out of room and wrap around, but a long integer does so with a much larger number. For example, a two-byte unsigned short int wraps around after 65,535, whereas a four-byte unsigned long int does not wrap around until 4,294,967,295. However, on most machines, a long integer takes up twice as much memory every time you declare one (such as four bytes versus two bytes), and a program with 100 such variables consumes an extra 200 bytes of RAM. Frankly, this is less of a problem than it used to be because most personal computers now come with millions (if not billions) of bytes of memory.

Using larger types than you need might also require additional time for your computer's processor to processes.

Q What happens if I assign a number with a decimal point to an integer rather than to a float? Consider the following line of code:

```
int aNumber = 5.4;
```

A A good compiler issues a warning, but the assignment is completely legal. The number you've assigned is truncated into an integer. Thus, if you assign 5.4 to an integer variable, that variable will have the value 5. Information will be lost, however, and if you then try to assign the value in that integer variable to a float variable, the float variable will have only 5.

Q Why not use literal constants; why go to the bother of using symbolic constants?

A If you use a value in many places throughout your program, a symbolic constant allows all the values to change just by changing the one definition of the constant. Symbolic constants also speak for themselves. It might be hard to understand why a number is being multiplied by 360, but it's much easier to understand what's going on if the number is being multiplied by degreesInACircle.

Q What happens if I assign a negative number to an unsigned variable? Consider the following line of code:

```
unsigned int aPositiveNumber = -1;
```

A A good compiler issues a warning, but the assignment is legal. The negative number is assessed as a bit pattern and is assigned to the variable. The value of that variable is then interpreted as an `unsigned` number. Thus, –1, whose bit pattern is 11111111 11111111 (0xFF in hex), is assessed as the `unsigned` value 65,535.

Q Can I work with C++ without understanding bit patterns, binary arithmetic, and hexadecimal?

A Yes, but not as effectively as if you do understand these topics. C++ does not do as good a job as some languages at "protecting" you from what the computer is really doing. This is actually a benefit because it provides you with tremendous power that other languages don't. As with any power tool, however, to get the most out of C++, you must understand how it works. Programmers who try to program in C++ without understanding the fundamentals of the binary system often are confused by their results.

Workshop

The Workshop provides quiz questions to help you solidify your understanding of the material covered and exercises to provide you with experience in using what you've learned. Try to answer the quiz and exercise questions before checking the answers in Appendix D, and be certain that you understand the answers before continuing to tomorrow's lesson.

Quiz

1. What is the difference between an integer variable and a floating-point variable?

2. What are the differences between an `unsigned short int` and a `long int`?

3. What are the advantages of using a symbolic constant rather than a literal constant?

4. What are the advantages of using the `const` keyword rather than `#define`?

5. What makes for a good or bad variable name?

6. Given this enum, what is the value of BLUE?

   ```
   enum COLOR { WHITE, BLACK = 100, RED, BLUE, GREEN = 300 };
   ```

7. Which of the following variable names are good, which are bad, and which are invalid?

   a. `Age`

   b. `!ex`

   c. `R79J`

   d. `TotalIncome`

   e. `__Invalid`

Exercises

1. What would be the correct variable type in which to store the following
   information?

   a. Your age

   b. The area of your backyard

   c. The number of stars in the galaxy

   d. The average rainfall for the month of January

2. Create good variable names for this information.

3. Declare a constant for pi as 3.14159.

4. Declare a `float` variable and initialize it using your pi constant.

WEEK 1

DAY 4

Creating Expressions
and Statements

At its heart, a program is a set of commands executed in sequence. The power
in a program comes from its capability to execute one or another set of commands, based on whether a particular condition is true or false.

Today, you will learn

- What statements are
- What blocks are
- What expressions are
- How to branch your code based on conditions
- What truth is, and how to act on it

Starting with Statements

In C++, a statement controls the sequence of execution, evaluates an expression, or does nothing (the null statement). All C++ statements end with a semicolon and nothing else. One of the most common statements is the following assignment statement:

```
x = a + b;
```

Unlike in algebra, this statement does not mean that x is equal to a+b. Rather, this is read, "Assign the value of the sum of a and b to x," or "Assign to x, a+b," or "Set x equal to a plus b."

This statement is doing two things. It is adding a and b together, and it is assigning the result to x using the assignment operator (=). Even though this statement is doing two things, it is one statement, and thus has one semicolon.

> **NOTE** The assignment operator assigns whatever is on the right side of the equal sign to whatever is on the left side.

Using Whitespace

Whitespace is the invisible characters such as tabs, spaces, and new lines. These are called "whitespace characters" because if they are printed on a piece of white paper, you only see the white of the paper.

Whitespace is generally ignored in statements. For example, the assignment statement previously discussed could be written as

```
x=a+b;
```

or as

```
x                              =a
+              b        ;
```

Although this last variation is perfectly legal, it is also perfectly foolish. Whitespace can be used to make your programs more readable and easier to maintain, or it can be used to create horrific and indecipherable code. In this, as in all things, C++ provides the power; you supply the judgment.

Blocks and Compound Statements

Any place you can put a single statement, you can put a compound statement, also called a block. A block begins with an opening brace ({) and ends with a closing brace (}).

Although every statement in the block must end with a semicolon, the block itself does not end with a semicolon, as shown in the following example:

```
{
    temp = a;
    a = b;
    b = temp;
}
```

This block of code acts as one statement and swaps the values in the variables a and b.

Do	Don't
DO end your statements with a semicolon.	**DON'T** forget to use a closing brace any time you have an opening brace.
DO use whitespace judiciously to make your code clearer.	

Expressions

Anything that evaluates to a value is an expression in C++. An expression is said to *return* a value. Thus, the statement 3+2; returns the value 5, so it is an expression. All expressions are statements.

The myriad pieces of code that qualify as expressions might surprise you. Here are three examples:

```
3.2                 // returns the value 3.2

PI                  // float constant that returns the value 3.14

SecondsPerMinute    // int constant that returns 60
```

Assuming that PI is a constant created that is initialized to 3.14 and SecondsPerMinute is a constant equal to 60, all three of these statements are expressions.

The slightly more complicated expression

```
x = a + b;
```

not only adds a and b and assigns the result to x, but returns the value of that assignment (the value of x) as well. Thus, this assignment statement is also an expression.

As a note, any expression can be used on the right side of an assignment operator. This includes the assignment statement just shown. The following is perfectly legal in C++:

```
y = x = a + b;
```

This line is evaluated in the following order:

Add a to b.

Assign the result of the expression a + b to x.

Assign the result of the assignment expression x = a + b to y.

If a, b, x, and y are all integers, and if a has the value 9 and b has the value 7, both x and y will be assigned the value 16. This is illustrated in Listing 4.1.

LISTING 4.1   Evaluating Complex Expressions

```
 1:  #include <iostream>
 2:  int main()
 3:  {
 4:      using std::cout;
 5:      using std::endl;
 6:
 7:      int a=0, b=0, x=0, y=35;
 8:      cout << "a: " << a << " b: " << b;
 9:      cout << " x: " << x << " y: " << y << endl;
10:      a = 9;
11:      b = 7;
12:      y = x = a+b;
13:      cout << "a: " << a << " b: " << b;
14:      cout << " x: " << x << " y: " << y << endl;
15:      return 0;
16:  }
```

OUTPUT
```
a: 0 b: 0 x: 0 y: 35
a: 9 b: 7 x: 16 y: 16
```

ANALYSIS   On line 7, the four variables are declared and initialized. Their values are printed on lines 8 and 9. On line 10, a is assigned the value 9. On line 11, b is assigned the value 7. On line 12, the values of a and b are summed and the result is assigned to x. This expression (x = a+b) evaluates to a value (the sum of a + b), and that value is, in turn, assigned to y. On lines 13 and 14, these results are confirmed by printing out the values of the four variables.

Working with Operators

An operator is a symbol that causes the compiler to take an action. Operators act on operands, and in C++ any expression can be an operand. In C++, several categories of operators exist. The first two categories of operators that you will learn about are

- Assignment operators
- Mathematical operators

Assignment Operators

You saw the assignment operator (=) earlier. This operator causes the operand on the left side of the assignment operator to have its value changed to the value of the expression on the right side of the assignment operator. The expression

```
x = a + b;
```

assigns the value that is the result of adding a and b to the operand x.

---

l-values and r-values

An operand that legally can be on the left side of an assignment operator is called an l-value. That which can be on the right side is called (you guessed it) an r-value.

You should note that all l-values are r-values, but not all r-values are l-values. An example of an r-value that is not an l-value is a literal. Thus, you can write

```
x = 5;
```

but you cannot write

```
5 = x;
```

x can be an l-value or an r-value, 5 can only be an r-value.

4

NOTE

Constants are r-values. Because they cannot have their values changed, they are not allowed to be on the left side of the assignment operator, which means they can't be l-values.

Mathematical Operators

A second category of operators is the mathematical operators. Five mathematical operators are addition (+), subtraction (–), multiplication (*), division (/), and modulus (%).

Addition and subtraction work as you would expect: Two numbers separated by the plus or minus sign are added or subtracted. Multiplication works in the same manner; however, the operator you use to do multiplication is an asterisk (*). Division is done using a forward slash operator. The following are examples of expressions using each of these operators. In each case, the result is assigned to the variable result. The comments to the right show what the value of result would be

```
result = 56 + 32    // result = 88
result = 12 - 10    // result = 2
result = 21 / 7     // result = 3
result = 12 * 4     // result = 48
```

Subtraction Troubles

Subtraction with unsigned integers can lead to surprising results if the result is a negative number. You saw something much like this yesterday, when variable overflow was described. Listing 4.2 shows what happens when you subtract a large unsigned number from a small unsigned number.

LISTING 4.2   A Demonstration of Subtraction and Integer Overflow

```
 1:  // Listing 4.2 - demonstrates subtraction and
 2:  // integer overflow
 3:  #include <iostream>
 4:
 5:  int main()
 6:  {
 7:      using std::cout;
 8:      using std::endl;
 9:
10:      unsigned int difference;
11:      unsigned int bigNumber = 100;
12:      unsigned int smallNumber = 50;
13:
14:      difference = bigNumber - smallNumber;
15:      cout << "Difference is: " << difference;
16:
17:      difference = smallNumber - bigNumber;
18:      cout << "\nNow difference is: " << difference <<endl;
19:      return 0;
20:  }
```

OUTPUT
```
Difference is: 50
Now difference is: 4294967246
```

ANALYSIS   The subtraction operator is invoked for the first time on line 14, and the result is printed on line 15, much as you might expect. The subtraction operator is called again on line 17, but this time a large unsigned number is subtracted from a small unsigned number. The result would be negative, but because it is evaluated (and printed) as an unsigned number, the result is an overflow, as described yesterday. This topic is reviewed in detail in Appendix C, "Operator Precedence."

Integer Division and Modulus

Integer division is the division you learned when you were in elementary school. When you divide 21 by 4 (21 / 4), and you are doing integer division, the answer is 5 (with a remainder).

The fifth mathematical operator might be new to you. The modulus operator (%) tells you the remainder after an integer division. To get the remainder of 21 divided by 4, you take 21 modulus 4 (21 % 4). In this case, the result is 1.

Finding the modulus can be very useful. For example, you might want to print a statement on every 10th action. Any number whose value is 0 when you modulus 10 with that number is an exact multiple of 10. Thus 1 % 10 is 1, 2 % 10 is 2, and so forth, until 10 % 10, whose result is 0. 11 % 10 is back to 1, and this pattern continues until the next multiple of 10, which is 20. 20%10 = 0 again. You'll use this technique when looping is discussed on Day 7, "More on Program Flow."

FAQ

When I divide 5/3, I get 1. What is going wrong?

Answer: If you divide one integer by another, you get an integer as a result.

Thus, 5/3 is 1. (The actual answer is 1 with a remainder of 2. To get the remainder, try 5%3, whose value is 2.)

To get a fractional return value, you must use floating-point numbers (type `float`, `double`, or `long double`).

5.0 / 3.0 gives you a fractional answer: 1.66667.

If either the divisor or the dividend is a floating point, the compiler generates a floating-point quotient. However, if this is assigned to an I-value that is an integer, the value is once again truncated.

Combining the Assignment and Mathematical Operators

It is not uncommon to want to add a value to a variable and then to assign the result back into the same variable. If you have a variable `myAge` and you want to increase the value stored in it by two, you can write

```
int myAge = 5;
int temp;
temp = myAge + 2;    // add 5 + 2 and put it in temp
myAge = temp;        // put it back in myAge
```

The first two lines create the myAge variable and a temporary variable. As you can see in the third line, the value in myAge has two added to it. The resulting value is assigned to temp. In the next line, this value is then placed back into myAge, thus updating it.

This method, however, is terribly convoluted and wasteful. In C++, you can put the same variable on both sides of the assignment operator; thus, the preceding becomes

```
myAge = myAge + 2;
```

which is much clearer and much better. In algebra, this expression would be meaningless, but in C++ it is read as "add two to the value in myAge and assign the result to myAge."

Even simpler to write, but perhaps a bit harder to read is

```
myAge += 2;
```

This line is using the self-assigned addition operator (+=). The self-assigned addition operator adds the r-value to the l-value and then reassigns the result into the l-value. This operator is pronounced "plus-equals." The statement is read "myAge plus-equals two." If myAge had the value 24 to start, it would have 26 after this statement.

Self-assigned subtraction (-=), division (/=), multiplication (*=), and modulus (%=) operators exist as well.

Incrementing and Decrementing

The most common value to add (or subtract) and then reassign into a variable is 1. In C++, increasing a value by 1 is called *incrementing*, and decreasing by 1 is called *decrementing*. Special operators are provided in C++ to perform these actions.

The increment operator (++) increases the value of the variable by 1, and the decrement operator (--) decreases it by 1. Thus, if you have a variable, Counter, and you want to increment it, you would use the following statement:

```
Counter++;                 // Start with Counter and increment it.
```

This statement is equivalent to the more verbose statement

```
Counter = Counter + 1;
```

which is also equivalent to the moderately verbose statement

```
Counter += 1;
```

NOTE   As you might have guessed, C++ got its name by applying the increment operator to the name of its predecessor language: C. The idea is that C++ is an incremental improvement over C.

Prefixing Versus Postfixing

Both the increment operator (++) and the decrement operator(--) come in two varieties: prefix and postfix. The prefix variety is written before the variable name (++myAge); the postfix variety is written after the variable name (myAge++).

In a simple statement, it doesn't matter which you use, but in a complex statement when you are incrementing (or decrementing) a variable and then assigning the result to another variable, it matters very much.

The prefix operator is evaluated before the assignment; the postfix is evaluated after the assignment. The semantics of prefix is this: Increment the value in the variable and then fetch or use it. The semantics of postfix is different: Fetch or use the value and then increment the original variable.

This can be confusing at first, but if x is an integer whose value is 5 and using a prefix increment operator you write

```
int a = ++x;
```

you have told the compiler to increment x (making it 6) and then fetch that value and assign it to a. Thus, a is now 6 and x is now 6.

If, after doing this, you use the postfix operator to write

```
int b = x++;
```

you have now told the compiler to fetch the value in x (6) and assign it to b, and then go back and increment x. Thus, b is now 6, but x is now 7. Listing 4.3 shows the use and implications of both types.

LISTING 4.3   A Demonstration of Prefix and Postfix Operators

```
1:  // Listing 4.3 - demonstrates use of
2:  // prefix and postfix increment and
3:  // decrement operators
4:  #include <iostream>
5:  int main()
6:  {
7:      using std::cout;
```

LISTING 4.3   continued

```
 8:
 9:     int myAge = 39;      // initialize two integers
10:     int yourAge = 39;
11:     cout << "I am: " << myAge << " years old.\n";
12:     cout << "You are: " << yourAge << " years old\n";
13:     myAge++;             // postfix increment
14:     ++yourAge;           // prefix increment
15:     cout << "One year passes...\n";
16:     cout << "I am: " << myAge << " years old.\n";
17:     cout << "You are: " << yourAge << " years old\n";
18:     cout << "Another year passes\n";
19:     cout << "I am: " << myAge++ << " years old.\n";
20:     cout << "You are: " << ++yourAge << " years old\n";
21:     cout << "Let's print it again.\n";
22:     cout << "I am: " << myAge << " years old.\n";
23:     cout << "You are: " << yourAge << " years old\n";
24:     return 0;
25: }
```

OUTPUT

```
I am        39 years old
You are     39 years old
One year passes
I am        40 years old
You are     40 years old
Another year passes
I am        40 years old
You are     41 years old
Let's print it again
I am        41 years old
You are     41 years old
```

ANALYSIS On lines 9 and 10, two integer variables are declared, and each is initialized with the value 39. Their values are printed on lines 11 and 12.

On line 13, myAge is incremented using the postfix increment operator, and on line 14, yourAge is incremented using the prefix increment operator. The results are printed on lines 16 and 17, and they are identical (both 40).

On line 19, myAge is incremented as part of the printing statement, using the postfix increment operator. Because it is postfix, the increment happens after the printing, and so the value 40 is printed again, and then the myAge variable is incremented. In contrast, on line 20, yourAge is incremented using the prefix increment operator. Thus, it is incremented before being printed, and the value displays as 41.

Finally, on lines 22 and 23, the values are printed again. Because the increment statement has completed, the value in myAge is now 41, as is the value in yourAge.

Understanding Operator Precedence

In the complex statement

```
x = 5 + 3 * 8;
```

which is performed first, the addition or the multiplication? If the addition is performed first, the answer is 8 * 8, or 64. If the multiplication is performed first, the answer is 5 + 24, or 29.

The C++ standard does not leave the order random. Rather, every operator has a precedence value, and the complete list is shown in Appendix C. Multiplication has higher precedence than addition; thus, the value of the expression is 29.

When two mathematical operators have the same precedence, they are performed in left-to-right order. Thus,

```
x = 5 + 3 + 8 * 9 + 6 * 4;
```

is evaluated multiplication first, left to right. Thus, 8*9 = 72, and 6*4 = 24. Now the expression is essentially

```
x = 5 + 3 + 72 + 24;
```

Now, the addition, left to right, is 5 + 3 = 8; 8 + 72 = 80; 80 + 24 = 104.

Be careful with this. Some operators, such as assignment, are evaluated in right-to-left order!

In any case, what if the precedence order doesn't meet your needs? Consider the expression

```
TotalSeconds = NumMinutesToThink + NumMinutesToType * 60
```

In this expression, you do not want to multiply the NumMinutesToType variable by 60 and then add it to NumMinutesToThink. You want to add the two variables to get the total number of minutes, and then you want to multiply that number by 60 to get the total seconds.

You use parentheses to change the precedence order. Items in parentheses are evaluated at a higher precedence than any of the mathematical operators. Thus, the preceding example should be written as:

```
TotalSeconds = (NumMinutesToThink + NumMinutesToType) * 60
```

Nesting Parentheses

For complex expressions, you might need to nest parentheses one within another. For example, you might need to compute the total seconds and then compute the total number of people who are involved before multiplying seconds times people:

```
TotalPersonSeconds = ( ( (NumMinutesToThink + NumMinutesToType) * 60) *
(PeopleInTheOffice + PeopleOnVacation) )
```

This complicated expression is read from the inside out. First, NumMinutesToThink is added to NumMinutesToType because these are in the innermost parentheses. Then, this sum is multiplied by 60. Next, PeopleInTheOffice is added to PeopleOnVacation. Finally, the total number of people found is multiplied by the total number of seconds.

This example raises an important related issue. This expression is easy for a computer to understand, but very difficult for a human to read, understand, or modify. Here is the same expression rewritten, using some temporary integer variables:

```
TotalMinutes = NumMinutesToThink + NumMinutesToType;
TotalSeconds = TotalMinutes * 60;
TotalPeople = PeopleInTheOffice + PeopleOnVacation;
TotalPersonSeconds = TotalPeople * TotalSeconds;
```

This example takes longer to write and uses more temporary variables than the preceding example, but it is far easier to understand. If you add a comment at the top to explain what this code does and change the 60 to a symbolic constant, you will have code that is easy to understand and maintain.

Do	Don't
DO remember that expressions have a value.	**DON'T** nest too deeply because the expression becomes hard to understand and maintain.
DO use the prefix operator (++variable) to increment or decrement the variable before it is used in the expression.	**DON'T** confuse the postfix operator with the prefix operator.
DO use the postfix operator (variable++) to increment or decrement the variable after it is used.	
DO use parentheses to change the order of precedence.	

The Nature of Truth

Every expression can be evaluated for its truth or falsity. Expressions that evaluate mathematically to zero return `false`; all others return `true`.

In previous versions of C++, all truth and falsity was represented by integers, but the ANSI standard introduced the type `bool`. A `bool` can only have one of two values: `false` or `true`.

NOTE

> Many compilers previously offered a `bool` type, which was represented internally as a `long int` and, thus, had a size of four bytes. Now, ANSI-compliant compilers often provide a one-byte `bool`.

Evaluating with the Relational Operators

The relational operators are used to compare two numbers to determine whether they are equal or if one is greater or less than the other. Every relational statement evaluates to either `true` or `false`. The relational operators are presented later, in Table 4.1.

NOTE

> All relational operators return a value of type `bool`, that is either `true` or `false`. In previous versions of C++, these operators returned either 0 for false or a nonzero value (usually 1) for true.

If the integer variable `myAge` has the value `45`, and the integer variable `yourAge` has the value `50`, you can determine whether they are equal by using the relational "equals" operator (==):

```
myAge == yourAge;   // is the value in myAge the same as in yourAge?
```

This expression evaluates to `false` because the variables are not equal. You can check to see if `myAge` is less than `yourAge` using the expression,

```
myAge < yourAge;   // is myAge less than yourAge?
```

which evaluates to `true` because 45 is less than 50.

CAUTION

> Many novice C++ programmers confuse the assignment operator (=) with the equals operator (==). This can create a nasty bug in your program.

The six relational operators are equals (==), less than (<), greater than (>), less than or equal to (<=), greater than or equal to (>=), and not equals (!=). Table 4.1 shows each relational operator and a sample code use.

TABLE 4.1 The Relational Operators

Name	Operator	Sample	Evaluates
Equals	==	100 == 50;	false
		50 == 50;	true
Not equals	!=	100 != 50;	true
		50 != 50;	false
Greater than	>	100 > 50;	true
		50 > 50;	false
Greater than or equal to	>=	100 >= 50;	true
		50 >= 50;	true
Less than	<	100 < 50;	false
		50 < 50;	false
Less than or equal to	<=	100 <= 50;	false
		50 <= 50;	true

Do	Don't
DO remember that relational operators return the value `true` or `false`.	**DON'T** confuse the assignment operator (=) with the equals relational operator (==). This is one of the most common C++ programming mistakes—be on guard for it.

The `if` Statement

Normally, your program flows along line-by-line in the order in which it appears in your source code. The `if` statement enables you to test for a condition (such as whether two variables are equal) and branch to different parts of your code, depending on the result.

The simplest form of an `if` statement is the following:

```
if (expression)
    statement;
```

The expression in the parentheses can be any expression, but it usually contains one of the relational expressions. If the expression has the value `false`, the statement is skipped. If it evaluates `true`, the statement is executed. Consider the following example:

```
if (bigNumber > smallNumber)
    bigNumber = smallNumber;
```

This code compares `bigNumber` and `smallNumber`. If `bigNumber` is larger, the second line sets its value to the value of `smallNumber`. If `bigNumber` is not larger than `smallNumber`, the statement is skipped.

Because a block of statements surrounded by braces is equivalent to a single statement, the branch can be quite large and powerful:

```
if (expression)
{
    statement1;
    statement2;
    statement3;
}
```

Here's a simple example of this usage:

```
if (bigNumber > smallNumber)
{
    bigNumber = smallNumber;
    std::cout << "bigNumber: " << bigNumber << "\n";
    std::cout << "smallNumber: " << smallNumber << "\n";
}
```

This time, if `bigNumber` is larger than `smallNumber`, not only is it set to the value of `smallNumber`, but an informational message is printed. Listing 4.4 shows a more detailed example of branching based on relational operators.

LISTING 4.4 A Demonstration of Branching Based on Relational Operators

```
 1:  // Listing 4.4 - demonstrates if statement
 2:  // used with relational operators
 3:  #include <iostream>
 4:  int main()
 5:  {
 6:      using std::cout;
 7:      using std::cin;
 8:
 9:      int MetsScore, YankeesScore;
10:      cout << "Enter the score for the Mets: ";
11:      cin >> MetsScore;
12:
13:      cout << "\nEnter the score for the Yankees: ";
```

LISTING 4.4 continued

```
14:        cin >> YankeesScore;
15:
16:        cout << "\n";
17:
18:        if (MetsScore > YankeesScore)
19:            cout << "Let's Go Mets!\n";
20:
21:        if (MetsScore < YankeesScore)
22:        {
23:            cout << "Go Yankees!\n";
24:        }
25:
26:        if (MetsScore == YankeesScore)
27:        {
28:            cout << "A tie? Naah, can't be.\n";
29:            cout << "Give me the real score for the Yanks: ";
30:            cin >> YankeesScore;
31:
32:            if (MetsScore > YankeesScore)
33:                cout << "Knew it! Let's Go Mets!";
34:
35:            if (YankeesScore > MetsScore)
36:                cout << "Knew it! Go Yanks!";
37:
38:            if (YankeesScore == MetsScore)
39:                cout << "Wow, it really was a tie!";
40:        }
41:
42:      cout << "\nThanks for telling me.\n";
43:      return 0;
44: }
```

OUTPUT

```
Enter the score for the Mets: 10

Enter the score for the Yankees: 10

A tie? Naah, can't be
Give me the real score for the Yanks: 8
Knew it! Let's Go Mets!
Thanks for telling me.
```

ANALYSIS This program asks for the user to input scores for two baseball teams; the scores are stored in integer variables, MetsScore and YankeesScore. The variables are compared in the if statement on lines 18, 21, and 26.

If one score is higher than the other, an informational message is printed. If the scores are equal, the block of code that begins on line 27 and ends on line 40 is entered. The second score is requested again, and then the scores are compared again.

Note that if the initial Yankees' score is higher than the Mets score, the `if` statement on line 18 evaluates as `false`, and line 19 is not invoked. The test on line 21 evaluates as `true`, and the statement on line 23 is invoked. Then, the `if` statement on line 26 is tested and this is `false` (if line 18 is `true`). Thus, the program skips the entire block, falling through to line 41.

This example illustrates that getting a true result in one `if` statement does not stop other `if` statements from being tested.

Note that the action for the first two `if` statements is one line (printing "Let's Go Mets!" or "Go Yankees!"). In the first example (on line 19), this line is not in braces; a single line block doesn't need them. The braces are legal, however, and are used on lines 22–24.

Avoiding Common Errors with `if` Statements

Many novice C++ programmers inadvertently put a semicolon after their `if` statements:

```
if(SomeValue < 10);    // Oops! Notice the semicolon!
    SomeValue = 10;
```

What was intended here was to test whether `SomeValue` is less than 10, and if so, to set it to 10, making 10 the minimum value for `SomeValue`. Running this code snippet shows that `SomeValue` is always set to 10! Why? The `if` statement terminates with the semicolon (the do-nothing operator).

Remember that indentation has no meaning to the compiler. This snippet could more accurately have been written as

```
if (SomeValue < 10)  // test
; // do nothing
SomeValue = 10;  // assign
```

Removing the semicolon makes the final line part of the `if` statement and makes this code do what was intended.

To minimize the chances of this problem, you can always write your `if` statements with braces, even when the body of the `if` statement is only one line:

```
if (SomeValue < 10)
{
    SomeValue = 10;
};
```

Indentation Styles

Listing 4.4 shows one style of indenting `if` statements. Nothing is more likely to create a religious war, however, than to ask a group of programmers what is the best style for brace alignment. Although dozens of variations are possible, the following appear to be the most popular three:

- Putting the initial brace after the condition and aligning the closing brace under the `if` to close the statement block:

```
if (expression){
    statements
}
```

- Aligning the braces under the `if` and indenting the statements:

```
if (expression)
{
    statements
}
```

- Indenting the braces and statements:

```
if (expression)
    {
    statements
    }
```

This book uses the middle alternative because it is easy to understand where blocks of statements begin and end if the braces line up with each other and with the condition being tested. Again, it doesn't matter which style you choose, so long as you are consistent with it.

The `else` Statement

Often, your program needs to take one branch if your condition is true, or another if it is false. In Listing 4.4, you wanted to print one message (`Let's Go Mets!`) if the first test (`MetsScore > YankeesScore`) evaluated true, and another message (`Go Yankees!`) if it evaluated false.

The method shown so far—testing first one condition and then the other—works fine but is a bit cumbersome. The keyword `else` can make for far more readable code:

```
if (expression)
    statement;
else
    statement;
```

Listing 4.5 demonstrates the use of the keyword `else`.

LISTING 4.5   Demonstrating the `else` Keyword

```
1:  // Listing 4.5 - demonstrates if statement
2:  // with else clause
3:  #include <iostream>
4:  int main()
5:  {
```

LISTING 4.5 continued

```
6:     using std::cout;
7:     using std::cin;
8:
9:     int firstNumber, secondNumber;
10:    cout << "Please enter a big number: ";
11:    cin >> firstNumber;
12:    cout << "\nPlease enter a smaller number: ";
13:    cin >> secondNumber;
14:    if (firstNumber > secondNumber)
15:        cout << "\nThanks!\n";
16:    else
17:        cout << "\nOops. The first number is not bigger!";
18:
19:    return 0;
20: }
```

OUTPUT

```
Please enter a big number: 10

Please enter a smaller number: 12
Oops. The first number is not bigger!
```

ANALYSIS The `if` statement on line 14 is evaluated. If the condition is true, the statement on line 15 is run and then program flow goes to line 18 (after the `else` statement). If the condition on line 14 evaluates to false, control goes to the `else` clause and so the statement on line 17 is run. If the `else` clause on line 16 was removed, the statement on line 17 would run regardless of whether the `if` statement was true.

Remember, the `if` statement ends after line 15. If the `else` was not there, line 17 would just be the next line in the program. You should also note that either or both of the `if` and the `else` statements could be replaced with a block of code in braces.

The `if` Statement

The syntax for the `if` statement is as follows:

Form 1

```
if (expression)
    statement;
next_statement;
```

If the *expression* is evaluated as true, the *statement* is executed and the program continues with the *next_statement*. If the *expression* is not true, the *statement* is ignored and the program jumps to the *next_statement*.

Remember that the statement can be a single statement ending with a semicolon or a block enclosed in braces.

Form 2
```
if (expression)
    statement1;
else
    statement2;
next_statement;
```

If the *expression* evaluates true, *statement1* is executed; otherwise, *statement2* is executed. Afterward, the program continues with the *next_statement*.

Example 1
```
Example
if (SomeValue < 10)
  cout << "SomeValue is less than 10");
else
  cout << "SomeValue is not less than 10!");
cout << "Done." << endl;
```

Advanced `if` Statements

It is worth noting that any statement can be used in an `if` or `else` clause, even another `if` or `else` statement. Thus, you might see complex `if` statements in the following form:

```
if (expression1)
{
    if (expression2)
        statement1;
    else
    {
        if (expression3)
            statement2;
        else
            statement3;
    }
}
else
    statement4;
```

This cumbersome `if` statement says, "If expression1 is true and expression2 is true, execute statement1. If expression1 is true but expression2 is not true, then if expression3 is true execute statement2. If expression1 is true but expression2 and expression3 are false, then execute statement3. Finally, if expression1 is not true, execute statement4." As you can see, complex `if` statements can be confusing!

Listing 4.6 gives an example of one such complex `if` statement.

LISTING 4.6 A Complex, Nested if Statement

```
1:  // Listing 4.6 - a complex nested
2:  // if statement
3:  #include <iostream>
4:  int main()
5:  {
6:      // Ask for two numbers
7:      // Assign the numbers to bigNumber and littleNumber
8:      // If bigNumber is bigger than littleNumber,
9:      // see if they are evenly divisible
10:     // If they are, see if they are the same number
11:
12:     using namespace std;
13:
14:     int firstNumber, secondNumber;
15:     cout << "Enter two numbers.\nFirst: ";
16:     cin >> firstNumber;
17:     cout << "\nSecond: ";
18:     cin >> secondNumber;
19:     cout << "\n\n";
20:
21:     if (firstNumber >= secondNumber)
22:     {
23:         if ( (firstNumber % secondNumber) == 0) // evenly divisible?
24:         {
25:             if (firstNumber == secondNumber)
26:                 cout << "They are the same!\n";
27:             else
28:                 cout << "They are evenly divisible!\n";
29:         }
30:         else
31:             cout << "They are not evenly divisible!\n";
32:     }
33:     else
34:         cout << "Hey! The second one is larger!\n";
35:     return 0;
36: }
```

OUTPUT

```
Enter two numbers.
First: 10

Second: 2
They are evenly divisible!
```

ANALYSIS Two numbers are prompted for one at a time, and then compared. The first if statement, on line 21, checks to ensure that the first number is greater than or equal to the second. If not, the else clause on line 33 is executed.

If the first `if` is true, the block of code beginning on line 22 is executed, and a second `if` statement is tested on line 23. This checks to see whether the first number divided by the second number yields no remainder. If so, the numbers are either evenly divisible or equal. The `if` statement on line 25 checks for equality and displays the appropriate message either way.

If the `if` statement on line 23 fails (evaluates to false), then the `else` statement on line 30 is executed.

Using Braces in Nested `if` Statements

Although it is legal to leave out the braces on `if` statements that are only a single statement, and it is legal to nest `if` statements, doing so can cause enormous confusion. The following is perfectly legal in C++, although it looks somewhat confusing:

```
if (x > y)              // if x is bigger than y
    if (x < z)          // and if x is smaller than z
        x = y;          // set x to the value in y
    else                // otherwise, if x isn't less than z
        x = z;          // set x to the value in z
else                    // otherwise if x isn't greater than y
    y = x;              // set y to the value in x
```

Remember, whitespace and indentation are a convenience for the programmer; they make no difference to the compiler. It is easy to confuse the logic and inadvertently assign an `else` statement to the wrong `if` statement. Listing 4.7 illustrates this problem.

LISTING 4.7   A Demonstration of Why Braces Help Clarify Which `else` Statement Goes with Which `if` Statement

```
1:   // Listing 4.7 - demonstrates why braces
2:   // are important in nested if statements
3:   #include <iostream>
4:   int main()
5:   {
6:       int x;
7:       std::cout << "Enter a number less than 10 or greater than 100: ";
8:       std::cin >> x;
9:       std::cout << "\n";
10:
11:      if (x >= 10)
12:          if (x > 100)
13:              std::cout << "More than 100, Thanks!\n";
14:      else                            // not the else intended!
15:          std::cout << "Less than 10, Thanks!\n";
16:
17:      return 0;
18:  }
```

```
Enter a number less than 10 or greater than 100: 20

Less than 10, Thanks!
```

The programmer intended to ask for a number less than 10 or greater than 100, check for the correct value, and then print a thank-you note.

When the if statement on line 11 evaluates true, the following statement (line 12) is executed. In this case, line 12 executes when the number entered is greater than 10. Line 12 contains an if statement also. This if statement evaluates true if the number entered is greater than 100. If the number is greater than 100, the statement on line 13 is executed, thus printing out an appropriate message.

If the number entered is less than 10, the if statement on line 11 evaluates false. Program control goes to the next line following the if statement, in this case line 16. If you enter a number less than 10, the output is as follows:

```
Enter a number less than 10 or greater than 100: 9
```

As you can see, there was no message printed. The else clause on line 14 was clearly intended to be attached to the if statement on line 11, and thus is indented accordingly. Unfortunately, the else statement is really attached to the if statement on line 12, and thus this program has a subtle bug.

It is a subtle bug because the compiler will not complain. This is a legal C++ program, but it just doesn't do what was intended. Further, most of the times the programmer tests this program, it will appear to work. As long as a number that is greater than 100 is entered, the program will seem to work just fine. However, if you enter a number from 11 to 99, you'll see that there is obviously a problem!

Listing 4.8 fixes the problem by putting in the necessary braces.

LISTING 4.8   A Demonstration of the Proper Use of Braces with an if Statement

```
1:  // Listing 4.8 - demonstrates proper use of braces
2:  // in nested if statements
3:  #include <iostream>
4:  int main()
5:  {
6:      int x;
7:      std::cout << "Enter a number less than 10 or greater than 100: ";
8:      std::cin >> x;
9:      std::cout << "\n";
10:
11:     if (x >= 10)
12:     {
13:         if (x > 100)
```

LISTING 4.8 continued

```
14:              std::cout << "More than 100, Thanks!\n";
15:      }
16:      else                        // fixed!
17:          std::cout << "Less than 10, Thanks!\n";
18:      return 0;
19:  }
```

OUTPUT

Enter a number less than 10 or greater than 100: 9
Less than 10, Thanks!

ANALYSIS

The braces on lines 12 and 15 make everything between them into one statement, and now the else on line 16 applies to the if on line 11, as intended.

If the user types 9, the if statement on line 11 is true; however, the if statement on line 13 is false, so nothing would be printed. It would be better if the programmer put another else clause after line 14 so that errors would be caught and a message printed.

TIP

You can minimize many of the problems that come with if...else statements by always using braces for the statements in the if and else clauses, even when only one statement follows the condition.

```
if (SomeValue < 10)
{
    SomeValue = 10;
}
else
{
    SomeValue = 25;
};
```

NOTE

The programs shown in this book are written to demonstrate the particular issues being discussed. They are kept intentionally simple; no attempt is made to "bulletproof" the code to protect against user error. Ideally, in professional-quality code, every possible user error is anticipated and handled gracefully.

Using the Logical Operators

Often, you want to ask more than one relational question at a time. "Is it true that x is greater than y, and also true that y is greater than z?" A program might need to determine that both of these conditions are true—or that some other set of conditions is true—in order to take an action.

Imagine a sophisticated alarm system that has this logic: "If the door alarm sounds AND it is after 6:00 p.m. AND it is NOT a holiday, OR if it is a weekend, then call the police." C++'s three logical operators are used to make this kind of evaluation. These operators are listed in Table 4.2.

TABLE 4.2 The Logical Operators

Operator	Symbol	Example
AND	&&	*expression1* && *expression2*
OR	||	*expression1* || *expression2*
NOT	!	*!expression*

The Logical AND Operator

A logical AND statement uses the AND operator to connect and evaluates two expressions. If both expressions are true, the logical AND statement is true as well. If it is true that you are hungry, AND it is true that you have money, THEN it is true that you can buy lunch. Thus,

```
if ( (x == 5) && (y == 5) )
```

evaluates true if both x and y are equal to 5, and it evaluates false if either one is not equal to 5. Note that both sides must be true for the entire expression to be true.

Note that the logical AND is two && symbols. A single & symbol is a different operator, which is discussed on Day 21, "What's Next."

The Logical OR Operator

A logical OR statement evaluates two expressions. If either one is true, the expression is true. If you have money OR you have a credit card, you can pay the bill. You don't need both money and a credit card; you need only one, although having both is fine as well. Thus,

```
if ( (x == 5) || (y == 5) )
```

evaluates true if either x or y is equal to 5, or if both are equal to 5.

Note that the logical OR is two || symbols. A single | symbol is a different operator, which is discussed on Day 21.

The Logical NOT Operator

A logical NOT statement evaluates true if the expression being tested is false. Again, if the expression being tested is false, the value of the test is true! Thus,

```
if ( !(x == 5) )
```

is true only if x is not equal to 5. This is the same as writing

```
if (x != 5)
```

Short Circuit Evaluation

When the compiler is evaluating an AND statement, such as

```
if ( (x == 5) && (y == 5) )
```

the compiler evaluates the truth of the first statement (x==5), and if this fails (that is, if x is not equal to 5), the compiler does *NOT* go on to evaluate the truth or falsity of the second statement (y == 5) because AND requires both to be true.

Similarly, if the compiler is evaluating an OR statement, such as

```
if ( (x == 5) || (y == 5) )
```

if the first statement is true (x == 5), the compiler never evaluates the second statement (y == 5) because the truth of *either* is sufficient in an OR statement.

Although this might not seem important, consider the following example:

```
if ( (x == 5 )|| (++y == 3) )
```

If x is not equal to 5, then (++y == 3) is not evaluated. If you are counting on y to be incremented regardless, it might not happen.

Relational Precedence

Like all C++ expressions, the use of relational operators and logical operators each return a value: true or false. Like all expressions, they also have a precedence order (see Appendix C) that determines which relations are evaluated first. This fact is important when determining the value of statements such as the following:

```
if ( x > 5 && y > 5  || z > 5)
```

It might be that the programmer wanted this expression to evaluate true if both x and y are greater than 5 or if z is greater than 5. On the other hand, the programmer might have wanted this expression to evaluate true only if x is greater than 5 and if it is also true that either y is greater than 5 or z is greater than 5.

If x is 3, and y and z are both 10, the first interpretation is true (z is greater than 5, so ignore x and y), but the second is false (it isn't true that x is greater than 5, and thus it doesn't matter what is on the right side of the && symbol because both sides must be true).

Although precedence determines which relation is evaluated first, parentheses can both change the order and make the statement clearer:

```
if (  (x > 5)  && (y > 5 ||  z > 5) )
```

Using the values from earlier, this statement is false. Because it is not true that x is greater than 5, the left side of the AND statement fails, and thus the entire statement is false. Remember that an AND statement requires that both sides be true—something isn't both "good tasting" AND "good for you" if it isn't good tasting.

TIP

It is often a good idea to use extra parentheses to clarify what you want to group. Remember, the goal is to write programs that work and that are easy to read and to understand. Using parentheses help to clarify your intent and avoid errors that come from misunderstanding operator precedence.

4

More About Truth and Falsehood

In C++, zero evaluates to false, and all other values evaluate to true. Because an expression always has a value, many C++ programmers take advantage of this feature in their if statements. A statement such as

```
if (x)          // if x is true (nonzero)
    x = 0;
```

can be read as "If x has a nonzero value, set it to 0." This is a bit of a cheat; it would be clearer if written

```
if (x != 0)     // if x is not zero
    x = 0;
```

Both statements are legal, but the latter is clearer. It is good programming practice to reserve the former method for true tests of logic, rather than for testing for nonzero values.

These two statements also are equivalent:

```
if (!x)          // if x is false (zero)
if (x == 0)      // if x is zero
```

The second statement, however, is somewhat easier to understand and is more explicit if you are testing for the mathematical value of x rather than for its logical state.

Do	Don't
DO put parentheses around your logical tests to make them clearer and to make the precedence explicit.	**DON'T** use if(x) as a synonym for if(x != 0); the latter is clearer.
DO use braces in nested if statements to make the else statements clearer and to avoid bugs.	**DON'T** use if(!x) as a synonym for if(x == 0); the latter is clearer.

The Conditional (Ternary) Operator

The conditional operator (?:) is C++'s only ternary operator; that is, it is the only operator to take three terms.

The conditional operator takes three expressions and returns a value:

```
(expression1) ? (expression2) : (expression3)
```

This line is read as "If *expression1* is true, return the value of *expression2*; otherwise, return the value of *expression3*." Typically, this value is assigned to a variable. Listing 4.9 shows an if statement rewritten using the conditional operator.

LISTING 4.9   A Demonstration of the Conditional Operator

```
1:  // Listing 4.9 - demonstrates the conditional operator
2:  //
3:  #include <iostream>
4:  int main()
5:  {
6:      using namespace std;
7:
8:      int x, y, z;
9:      cout << "Enter two numbers.\n";
10:     cout << "First: ";
11:     cin >> x;
12:     cout << "\nSecond: ";
13:     cin >> y;
14:     cout << "\n";
```

LISTING 4.9 continued

```
15:
16:     if (x > y)
17:         z = x;
18:     else
19:         z = y;
20:
21:     cout << "After if test, z: " << z;
22:     cout << "\n";
23:
24:     z = (x > y) ? x : y;
25:
26:     cout << "After conditional test, z: " << z;
27:     cout << "\n";
28:     return 0;
29: }
```

OUTPUT

```
Enter two numbers.
First: 5

Second: 8

After if test, z: 8
After conditional test, z: 8
```

ANALYSIS Three integer variables are created: x, y, and z. The first two are given values by the user. The if statement on line 16 tests to see which is larger and assigns the larger value to z. This value is printed on line 21.

The conditional operator on line 24 makes the same test and assigns z the larger value. It is read like this: "If x is greater than y, return the value of x; otherwise, return the value of y." The value returned is assigned to z. That value is printed on line 26. As you can see, the conditional statement is a shorter equivalent to the if...else statement.

Summary

In today's lesson, you have learned what C++ statements and expressions are, what C++ operators do, and how C++ if statements work.

You have seen that a block of statements enclosed by a pair of braces can be used anywhere a single statement can be used.

You have learned that every expression evaluates to a value, and that value can be tested in an if statement or by using the conditional operator. You've also seen how to evaluate multiple statements using the logical operator, how to compare values using the relational operators, and how to assign values using the assignment operator.

You have explored operator precedence. And you have seen how parentheses can be used to change the precedence and to make precedence explicit, and thus easier to manage.

Q&A

Q Why use unnecessary parentheses when precedence will determine which operators are acted on first?

A It is true that the compiler will know the precedence and that a programmer can look up the precedence order. Using parentheses, however, makes your code easier to understand, and therefore easier to maintain.

Q If the relational operators always return true or false, why is any nonzero value considered true?

A This convention was inherited from the C language, which was frequently used for writing low-level software, such as operating systems and real-time control software. It is likely that this usage evolved as a shortcut for testing if all of the bits in a mask or variable are 0.

The relational operators return true or false, but every expression returns a value, and those values can also be evaluated in an `if` statement. Here's an example:

```
if ( (x = a + b) == 35 )
```

This is a perfectly legal C++ statement. It evaluates to a value even if the sum of a and b is not equal to 35. Also note that x is assigned the value that is the sum of a and b in any case.

Q What effect do tabs, spaces, and new lines have on the program?

A Tabs, spaces, and new lines (known as whitespace) have no effect on the program, although judicious use of whitespace can make the program easier to read.

Q Are negative numbers true or false?

A All nonzero numbers, positive and negative, are true.

Workshop

The Workshop provides quiz questions to help you solidify your understanding of the material covered and exercises to provide you with experience in using what you've learned. Try to answer the quiz and exercise questions before checking the answers in Appendix D, and be certain that you understand the answers before continuing to tomorrow's lesson on functions.

Quiz

1. What is an expression?

2. Is x = 5 + 7 an expression? What is its value?

3. What is the value of 201 / 4?

4. What is the value of 201 % 4?

5. If myAge, a, and b are all `int` variables, what are their values after

   ```
   myAge = 39;
   a = myAge++;
   b = ++myAge;
   ```

6. What is the value of 8+2*3?

7. What is the difference between `if(x = 3)` and `if(x == 3)`?

8. Do the following values evaluate true or false?

   a. `0`

   b. `1`

   c. `-1`

   d. `x = 0`

   e. `x == 0 // assume that x has the value of 0`

Exercises

1. Write a single `if` statement that examines two integer variables and changes the larger to the smaller, using only one `else` clause.

2. Examine the following program. Imagine entering three numbers, and write what output you expect.

   ```
   1:    #include <iostream>
   2:    using namespace std;
   3:    int main()
   4:    {
   5:         int a, b, c;
   6:         cout << "Please enter three numbers\n";
   7:         cout << "a: ";
   8:         cin >> a;
   9:         cout << "\nb: ";
   10:        cin >> b;
   11:        cout << "\nc: ";
   12:        cin >> c;
   13:
   14:        if (c = (a-b))
   15:             cout << "a: " << a << " minus b: " << b <<
   16:                       _" equals c: " << c;
   ```

```
17:        else
18:             cout << "a-b does not equal c: ";
19:     return 0;
20:  }
```

3. Enter the program from Exercise 2; compile, link, and run it. Enter the numbers 20, 10, and 50. Did you get the output you expected? Why not?

4. Examine this program and anticipate the output:

```
1:     #include <iostream>
2:     using namespace std;
3:     int main()
4:     {
5:          int a = 2, b = 2, c;
6:          if (c = (a-b))
7:               cout << "The value of c is: " << c;
8:          return 0;
9:     }
```

Enter, compile, link, and run the program from Exercise 4. What was the output? Why?

DAY 5

Organizing into Functions

Although object-oriented programming has shifted attention from functions and toward objects, functions nonetheless remain a central component of any program. Global functions can exist outside of objects and classes, and member functions (sometimes called member methods) exist within a class and do its work.

Today, you will learn

- What a function is and what its parts are
- How to declare and define functions
- How to pass parameters into functions
- How to return a value from a function

You'll start with global functions today, and tomorrow you'll see how functions work from within classes and objects as well.

What Is a Function?

A function is, in effect, a subprogram that can act on data and return a value. Every C++ program has at least one function, `main()`. When your program starts, the `main()` function is called automatically. `main()` might call other functions, some of which might call still others.

Because these functions are not part of an object, they are called "global"—that is, they can be accessed from anywhere in your program. For today, you will learn about global functions unless it is otherwise noted.

Each function has its own name, and when that name is encountered, the execution of the program branches to the body of that function. This is referred to as *calling* the function. When the function finishes (through encountering a `return` statement or the final brace of the function), execution resumes on the next line of the calling function. This flow is illustrated in Figure 5.1.

FIGURE 5.1

When a program calls a function, execution switches to the function and then resumes at the line after the function call.

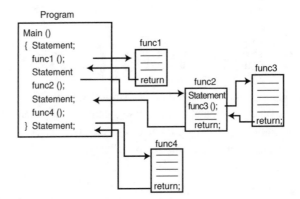

Well-designed functions perform a single, specific, and easily understood task, identified by the function name. Complicated tasks should be broken down into multiple functions, and then each can be called in turn.

Functions come in two varieties: user-defined and built-in. Built-in functions are part of your compiler package—they are supplied by the manufacturer for your use. User-defined functions are the functions you write yourself.

Return Values, Parameters, and Arguments

As you learned on Day 2, "The Anatomy of a C++ Program," functions can receive values and can *return* a value.

When you call a function, it can do work and then send back a value as a result of that work. This is called its *return value*, and the type of that return value must be declared. Thus, if you write

```
int myFunction();
```

you are declaring a function called myFunction that will return an integer value. Now consider the following declaration:

```
int myFunction(int someValue, float someFloat);
```

This declaration indicates that myFunction will still return an integer, but it will also take two values.

When you send values *into* a function, these values act as variables that you can manipulate from within the function. The description of the values you send is called a parameter list. In the previous example, the parameter list contains someValue that is a variable of type integer and someFloat that is a variable of type float.

As you can see, a parameter describes the *type* of the value that will be passed into the function when the function is called. The actual values you pass into the function are called the *arguments*. Consider the following:

```
int theValueReturned = myFunction(5,6.7);
```

Here, you see that an integer variable theValueReturned is initialized with the value returned by myFunction, and that the values 5 and 6.7 are passed in as arguments. The type of the arguments must match the declared parameter types. In this case, the 5 goes to an integer and the 6.7 goes to a float variable, so the values match.

Declaring and Defining Functions

Using functions in your program requires that you first declare the function and that you then define the function. The declaration tells the compiler the name, return type, and parameters of the function. The definition tells the compiler how the function works.

No function can be called from any other function if it hasn't first been declared. A declaration of a function is called a *prototype*.

Three ways exist to declare a function:

- Write your prototype into a file, and then use the #include directive to include it in your program.
- Write the prototype into the file in which your function is used.
- Define the function before it is called by any other function. When you do this, the definition acts as its own prototype.

5

Although you can define the function before using it, and thus avoid the necessity of creating a function prototype, this is not good programming practice for three reasons.

First, it is a bad idea to require that functions appear in a file in a particular order. Doing so makes it hard to maintain the program when requirements change.

Second, it is possible that function A() needs to be able to call function B(), but function B() also needs to be able to call function A() under some circumstances. It is not possible to define function A() before you define function B() and also to define function B() before you define function A(), so at least one of them must be declared in any case.

Third, function prototypes are a good and powerful debugging technique. If your prototype declares that your function takes a particular set of parameters or that it returns a particular type of value, and then your function does not match the prototype, the compiler can flag your error instead of waiting for it to show itself when you run the program. This is like double-entry bookkeeping. The prototype and the definition check each other, reducing the likelihood that a simple typo will lead to a bug in your program.

Despite this, the vast majority of programmers select the third option. This is because of the reduction in the number of lines of code, the simplification of maintenance (changes to the function header also require changes to the prototype), and the order of functions in a file is usually fairly stable. At the same time, prototypes are required in some situations.

Function Prototypes

Many of the built-in functions you use will have their function prototypes already written for you. These appear in the files you include in your program by using #include. For functions you write yourself, you must include the prototype.

The function prototype is a statement, which means it ends with a semicolon. It consists of the function's return type and signature. A function signature is its name and parameter list.

The parameter list is a list of all the parameters and their types, separated by commas. Figure 5.2 illustrates the parts of the function prototype.

FIGURE 5.2

Parts of a function prototype.

The function prototype and the function definition must agree exactly about the return type and signature. If they do not agree, you receive a compile-time error. Note, however, that the function prototype does not need to contain the names of the parameters, just their types. A prototype that looks like this is perfectly legal:

```
long Area(int, int);
```

This prototype declares a function named Area() that returns a long and that has two parameters, both integers. Although this is legal, it is not a good idea. Adding parameter names makes your prototype clearer. The same function with named parameters might be

```
long Area(int length, int width);
```

It is now much more obvious what this function does and what the parameters are.

Note that all functions have a return type. If none is explicitly stated, the return type defaults to int. Your programs will be easier to understand, however, if you explicitly declare the return type of every function, including main().

If your function does not actually return a value, you declare its return type to be void, as shown here:

```
void printNumber( int myNumber);
```

This declares a function called printNumber that has one integer parameter. Because void is used as the return time, nothing is returned.

Defining the Function

The definition of a function consists of the function header and its body. The header is like the function prototype except that the parameters must be named, and no terminating semicolon is used.

The body of the function is a set of statements enclosed in braces. Figure 5.3 shows the header and body of a function.

5

FIGURE 5.3

The header and body of a function.

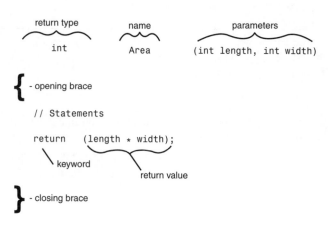

Listing 5.1 demonstrates a program that includes a function prototype for the Area()
function.

LISTING **5.1**   A Function Declaration and the Definition and Use of That Function

```
1:  // Listing 5.1 - demonstrates the use of function prototypes
2:
3:  #include <iostream>
4:  int Area(int length, int width); //function prototype
5:
6:  int main()
7:  {
8:      using std::cout;
9:      using std::cin;
10:
11:     int lengthOfYard;
12:     int widthOfYard;
13:     int areaOfYard;
14:
15:     cout << "\nHow wide is your yard? ";
16:     cin >> widthOfYard;
17:     cout << "\nHow long is your yard? ";
18:     cin >> lengthOfYard;
19:
20:     areaOfYard= Area(lengthOfYard, widthOfYard);
21:
22:     cout << "\nYour yard is ";
23:     cout << areaOfYard;
24:     cout << " square feet\n\n";
25:     return 0;
26: }
27:
28: int Area(int len, int wid)
29: {
30:     return len * wid;
31: }
```

OUTPUT
```
How wide is your yard? 100
How long is your yard? 200

Your yard is 20000 square feet
```

ANALYSIS   The prototype for the Area() function is on line 4. Compare the prototype with
the definition of the function on line 28. Note that the name, the return type, and
the parameter types are the same. If they were different, a compiler error would have
been generated. In fact, the only required difference is that the function prototype ends
with a semicolon and has no body.

Also note that the parameter names in the prototype are `length` and `width`, but the parameter names in the definition are `len` and `wid`. As discussed, the names in the prototype are not used; they are there as information to the programmer. It is good programming practice to match the prototype parameter names to the implementation parameter names, but as this listing shows, this is not required.

The arguments are passed in to the function in the order in which the parameters are declared and defined, but no matching of the names occurs. Had you passed in `widthOfYard`, followed by `lengthOfYard`, the `FindArea()` function would have used the value in `widthOfYard` for length and `lengthOfYard` for width.

NOTE

> The body of the function is always enclosed in braces, even when it consists of only one statement, as in this case.

Execution of Functions

When you call a function, execution begins with the first statement after the opening brace ({). Branching can be accomplished by using the `if` statement. (The `if` and other related statements will be discussed on Day 7, "More on Program Flow.") Functions can also call other functions and can even call themselves (see the section "Recursion," later today).

When a function is done executing, control is returned to the calling function. When the `main()` function finishes, control is returned to the operating system.

5

Determining Variable Scope

A variable has scope, which determines how long it is available to your program and where it can be accessed. Variables declared within a block are scoped to that block; they can be accessed only within that block's braces and "go out of existence" when that block ends. Global variables have global scope and are available anywhere within your program.

Local Variables

Not only can you pass in variables to the function, but you also can declare variables within the body of the function. Variables you declare within the body of the function are called "local" because they exist only locally within the function itself. When the function returns, the local variables are no longer available; they are marked for destruction by the compiler.

Local variables are defined the same as any other variables. The parameters passed in to the function are also considered local variables and can be used exactly as if they had been defined within the body of the function. Listing 5.2 is an example of using parameters and locally defined variables within a function.

LISTING 5.2   The Use of Local Variables and Parameters

```
1:  #include <iostream>
2:
3:  float Convert(float);
4:  int main()
5:  {
6:      using namespace std;
7:
8:      float TempFer;
9:      float TempCel;
10:
11:     cout << "Please enter the temperature in Fahrenheit: ";
12:     cin >> TempFer;
13:     TempCel = Convert(TempFer);
14:     cout << "\nHere's the temperature in Celsius: ";
15:     cout << TempCel << endl;
16:     return 0;
17: }
18:
19: float Convert(float TempFer)
20: {
21:     float TempCel;
22:     TempCel = ((TempFer - 32) * 5) / 9;
23:     return TempCel;
24: }
```

OUTPUT

```
Please enter the temperature in Fahrenheit: 212

Here's the temperature in Celsius: 100

Please enter the temperature in Fahrenheit: 32

Here's the temperature in Celsius: 0

Please enter the temperature in Fahrenheit: 85

Here's the temperature in Celsius: 29.4444
```

ANALYSIS   On lines 8 and 9, two `float` variables are declared, one to hold the temperature in Fahrenheit and one to hold the temperature in degrees Celsius. The user is prompted to enter a Fahrenheit temperature on line 11, and that value is passed to the function `Convert()` on line 13.

With the call of Convert() on line 13, execution jumps to the first line of the Convert() function on line 21, where a local variable, also named TempCel, is declared. Note that this local variable is not the same as the variable TempCel on line 9. This variable exists only within the function Convert(). The value passed as a parameter, TempFer, is also just a local copy of the variable passed in by main().

This function could have named the parameter and local variable anything else and the program would have worked equally well. FerTemp instead of TempFer or CelTemp instead of TempCel would be just as valid and the function would have worked the same. You can enter these different names and recompile the program to see this work.

The local function variable TempCel is assigned the value that results from subtracting 32 from the parameter TempFer, multiplying by 5, and then dividing by 9. This value is then returned as the return value of the function. On line 13, this return value is assigned to the variable TempCel in the main() function. The value is printed on line 15.

The preceding output shows that the program was ran three times. The first time, the value 212 is passed in to ensure that the boiling point of water in degrees Fahrenheit (212) generates the correct answer in degrees Celsius (100). The second test is the freezing point of water. The third test is a random number chosen to generate a fractional result.

Local Variables Within Blocks

You can define variables anywhere within the function, not just at its top. The scope of the variable is the block in which it is defined. Thus, if you define a variable inside a set of braces within the function, that variable is available only within that block. Listing 5.3 illustrates this idea.

LISTING 5.3 Variables Scoped Within a Block

```
1:  // Listing 5.3 - demonstrates variables
2:  // scoped within a block
3:
4:  #include <iostream>
5:
6:  void myFunc();
7:
8:  int main()
9:  {
10:     int x = 5;
11:     std::cout << "\nIn main x is: " << x;
12:
13:     myFunc();
14:
```

LISTING 5.3 continued

```
15:     std::cout << "\nBack in main, x is: " << x;
16:     return 0;
17:  }
18:
19:  void myFunc()
20:  {
21:     int x = 8;
22:     std::cout << "\nIn myFunc, local x: " << x << std::endl;
23:
24:     {
25:        std::cout << "\nIn block in myFunc, x is: " << x;
26:
27:        int x = 9;
28:
29:        std::cout << "\nVery local x: " << x;
30:     }
31:
32:     std::cout << "\nOut of block, in myFunc, x: " << x << std::endl;
33:  }
```

OUTPUT

```
In main x is: 5
In myFunc, local x: 8

In block in myFunc, x is: 8
Very local x: 9
Out of block, in myFunc, x: 8
Back in main, x is: 5
```

ANALYSIS This program begins with the initialization of a local variable, x, on line 10, in main(). The printout on line 11 verifies that x was initialized with the value 5. On line 13, MyFunc() is called.

On line 21 within MyFunc(), a local variable, also named x, is initialized with the value 8. Its value is printed on line 22.

The opening brace on line 24 starts a block. The variable x from the function is printed again on line 25. A new variable also named x, but local to the block, is created on line 27 and initialized with the value 9. The value of this newest variable x is printed on line 29.

The local block ends on line 30, and the variable created on line 27 goes "out of scope" and is no longer visible.

When x is printed on line 32, it is the x that was declared on line 21 within myFunc(). This x was unaffected by the x that was defined on line 27 in the block; its value is still 8.

On line 33, `MyFunc()` goes out of scope, and its local variable x becomes unavailable. Execution returns to line 14. On line 15, the value of the local variable x, which was created on line 10, is printed. It was unaffected by either of the variables defined in `MyFunc()`.

Needless to say, this program would be far less confusing if these three variables were given unique names!

Parameters Are Local Variables

The arguments passed in to the function are local to the function. Changes made to the arguments do not affect the values in the calling function. This is known as passing *by value*, which means a local copy of each argument is made in the function. These local copies are treated the same as any other local variables. Listing 5.4 once again illustrates this important point.

LISTING 5.4 A Demonstration of Passing by Value

```
1:   // Listing 5.4 - demonstrates passing by value
2:   #include <iostream>
3:
4:   using namespace std;
5:   void swap(int x, int y);
6:
7:   int main()
8:   {
9:       int x = 5, y = 10;
10:
11:      cout << "Main. Before swap, x: " << x << " y: " << y << endl;
12:      swap(x,y);
13:      cout << "Main. After swap, x: " << x << " y: " << y << endl;
14:      return 0;
15:  }
16:
17:  void swap (int x, int y)
18:  {
19:      int temp;
20:
21:      cout << "Swap. Before swap, x: " << x << " y: " << y << endl;
22:
23:      temp = x;
24:      x = y;
25:      y = temp;
26:
27:      cout << "Swap. After swap, x: " << x << " y: " << y << endl;
28:  }
```

5

OUTPUT
```
Main. Before swap, x: 5 y: 10
Swap. Before swap, x: 5 y: 10
Swap. After swap, x: 10 y: 5
Main. After swap, x: 5 y: 10
```

ANALYSIS This program initializes two variables in `main()` and then passes them to the `swap()` function, which appears to swap them. When they are examined again in `main()`, however, they are unchanged!

The variables are initialized on line 9, and their values are displayed on line 11. The `swap()` function is called on line 12, and the variables are passed in.

Execution of the program switches to the `swap()` function, where on line 21 the values are printed again. They are in the same order as they were in `main()`, as expected. On lines 23 to 25, the values are swapped, and this action is confirmed by the printout on line 27. Indeed, while in the `swap()` function, the values are swapped.

Execution then returns to line 13, back in `main()`, where the values are no longer swapped.

As you've figured out, the values passed in to the `swap()` function are passed by value, meaning that copies of the values are made that are local to `swap()`. These local variables are swapped on lines 23 to 25, but the variables back in `main()` are unaffected.

On Day 8, "Understanding Pointers," and Day 10, "Working with Advanced Functions," you'll see alternatives to passing by value that will allow the values in `main()` to be changed.

Global Variables

Variables defined outside of any function have global scope, and thus are available from any function in the program, including `main()`.

Local variables with the same name as global variables do not change the global variables. A local variable with the same name as a global variable *hides* the global variable, however. If a function has a variable with the same name as a global variable, the name refers to the local variable—not the global—when used within the function. Listing 5.5 illustrates these points.

LISTING 5.5 Demonstrating Global and Local Variables

```
1: #include <iostream>
2: void myFunction();          // prototype
3:
4: int x = 5, y = 7;           // global variables
5: int main()
```

LISTING 5.5   continued

```
 6:  {
 7:     using namespacestd;
 8:
 9:     cout << "x from main: " << x << endl;
10:     cout << "y from main: " << y << endl << endl;
11:     myFunction();
12:     cout << "Back from myFunction!" << endl << endl;
13:     cout << "x from main: " << x << endl;
14:     cout << "y from main: " << y << endl;
15:     return 0;
16:  }
17:
18:  void myFunction()
19:  {
20:     using std::cout;
21:
22:     int y = 10;
23:
24:     cout << "x from myFunction: " << x << endl;
25:     cout << "y from myFunction: " << y << endl << endl;
26:  }
```

OUTPUT
```
x from main: 5
y from main: 7

x from myFunction: 5
y from myFunction: 10

Back from myFunction!

x from main: 5
y from main: 7
```

5

ANALYSIS This simple program illustrates a few key, and potentially confusing, points about local and global variables. On line 4, two global variables, x and y, are declared. The global variable x is initialized with the value 5, and the global variable y is initialized with the value 7.

On lines 9 and 10 in the function main(), these values are printed to the console. Note that the function main() defines neither variable; because they are global, they are already available to main().

When myFunction() is called on line 11, program execution passes to line 18, and on line 22 a local variable, y, is defined and initialized with the value 10. On line 24, myFunction() prints the value of the variable x, and the global variable x is used, just as it was in `main()`. On line 25, however, when the variable name y is used, the local variable y is used, hiding the global variable with the same name.

The function call ends, and control returns to `main()`, which again prints the values in the global variables. Note that the global variable y was totally unaffected by the value assigned to `myFunction()`'s local y variable.

Global Variables: A Word of Caution

In C++, global variables are legal, but they are almost never used. C++ grew out of C, and in C global variables are a dangerous but necessary tool. They are necessary because at times the programmer needs to make data available to many functions, and it is cumbersome to pass that data as a parameter from function to function, especially when many of the functions in the calling sequence only receive the parameter to pass it on to other functions.

Globals are dangerous because they are shared data, and one function can change a global variable in a way that is invisible to another function. This can and does create bugs that are very difficult to find.

On Day 15, "Special Classes and Functions," you'll see a powerful alternative to global variables called static member variables.

Considerations for Creating Function Statements

Virtually no limit exists to the number or types of statements that can be placed in the body of a function. Although you can't define another function from within a function, you can *call* a function, and of course, `main()` does just that in nearly every C++ program. Functions can even call themselves, which is discussed soon in the section on recursion.

Although no limit exists to the size of a function in C++, well-designed functions tend to be small. Many programmers advise keeping your functions short enough to fit on a single screen so that you can see the entire function at one time. This is a rule of thumb, often broken by very good programmers, but it is true that a smaller function is easier to understand and maintain.

Each function should carry out a single, easily understood task. If your functions start getting large, look for places where you can divide them into component tasks.

More About Function Arguments

Any valid C++ expression can be a function argument, including constants, mathematical and logical expressions, and other functions that return a value. The important thing is that the result of the expression match the argument type that is expected by the function.

It is even valid for a function to be passed as an argument. After all, the function will evaluate to its return type. Using a function as an argument, however, can make for code that is hard to read and hard to debug.

As an example, suppose you have the functions `myDouble()`, `triple()`, `square()`, and `cube()`, each of which returns a value. You could write

```
Answer = (myDouble(triple(square(cube(myValue)))));
```

You can look at this statement in two ways. First, you can see that the function `myDouble()` takes the function `triple()` as an argument. In turn, `triple()` takes the function `square()`, which takes the function `cube()` as its argument. The `cube()` function takes the variable, `myValue`, as its argument.

Looking at this from the other direction, you can see that this statement takes a variable, `myValue`, and passes it as an argument to the function `cube()`, whose return value is passed as an argument to the function `square()`, whose return value is in turn passed to `triple()`, and that return value is passed to `myDouble()`. The return value of this doubled, tripled, squared, and cubed number is now assigned to `Answer`.

It is difficult to be certain what this code does (was the value tripled before or after it was squared?), and if the answer is wrong, it will be hard to figure out which function failed.

An alternative is to assign each step to its own intermediate variable:

```
unsigned long myValue = 2;
unsigned long cubed   = cube(myValue);      // cubed = 8
unsigned long squared = square(cubed);      // squared = 64
unsigned long tripled = triple(squared);    // tripled = 192
unsigned long Answer  = myDouble(tripled);  // Answer = 384
```

Now, each intermediate result can be examined, and the order of execution is explicit.

5

CAUTION

C++ makes it really easy to write compact code like the preceding example used to combine the `cube()`, `square()`, `triple()`, and `myDouble()` functions. Just because you can make compact code does not mean you should. It is better to make your code easier to read, and thus more maintainable, than to make it as compact as you can.

More About Return Values

Functions return a value or return void. Void is a signal to the compiler that no value will be returned.

To return a value from a function, write the keyword `return` followed by the value you want to return. The value might itself be an expression that returns a value. For example:

```
return 5;
return (x > 5);
return (MyFunction());
```

These are all legal `return` statements, assuming that the function `MyFunction()` itself returns a value. The value in the second statement, `return (x > 5)`, will be `false` if x is not greater than 5, or it will be `true`. What is returned is the value of the expression, `false` or `true`, not the value of x.

When the `return` keyword is encountered, the expression following `return` is returned as the value of the function. Program execution returns immediately to the calling function, and any statements following the return are not executed.

It is legal to have more than one return statement in a single function. Listing 5.6 illustrates this idea.

LISTING 5.6 A Demonstration of Multiple Return Statements

```
1:  // Listing 5.6 - demonstrates multiple return
2:  // statements
3:  #include <iostream>
4:
5:  int Doubler(int AmountToDouble);
6:
7:  int main()
8:  {
9:      using std::cout;
10:
11:     int result = 0;
12:     int input;
13:
14:     cout << "Enter a number between 0 and 10,000 to double: ";
15:     std::cin >> input;
16:
17:     cout << "\nBefore doubler is called... ";
18:     cout << "\ninput: " << input << " doubled: " << result << "\n";
19:
20:     result = Doubler(input);
21:
22:     cout << "\nBack from Doubler...\n";
```

Listing 5.6 continued

```
23:     cout << "\ninput: " << input << "   doubled: " << result << "\n";
24:
25:     return 0;
26: }
27:
28: int Doubler(int original)
29: {
30:     if (original <= 10000)
31:         return original * 2;
32:     else
33:         return -1;
34:     std::cout << "You can't get here!\n";
35: }
```

OUTPUT

```
Enter a number between 0 and 10,000 to double: 9000

Before doubler is called...
input: 9000 doubled: 0

Back from doubler...

input: 9000   doubled: 18000

Enter a number between 0 and 10,000 to double: 11000

Before doubler is called...
input: 11000 doubled: 0

Back from doubler...
input: 11000   doubled: -1
```

5

ANALYSIS A number is requested on lines 14 and 15 and printed on lines 17 and 18, along with the local variable result. The function Doubler() is called on line 20, and the input value is passed as a parameter. The result will be assigned to the local variable, result, and the values will be reprinted on line 23.

On line 30, in the function Doubler(), the parameter is tested to see whether it is less than or equal to 10,000. If it is, then the function returns twice the original number. If the value of original is greater than 10,000, the function returns –1 as an error value.

The statement on line 34 is never reached because regardless of whether the value is less than or equal to 10,000 or greater than 10,000, the function returns on either line 31 or line 33—before it gets to line 34. A good compiler warns that this statement cannot be executed, and a good programmer takes it out!

FAQ

What is the difference between `int main()` and `void main()`; which one should I use? I have used both and they both worked fine, so why do we need to use `int main(){ return 0;}`?

Answer: Both will work on most compilers, but only `int main()` is ANSI compliant, and thus only `int main()` is guaranteed to continue working.

Here's the difference: `int main()` returns a value to the operating system. When your program completes, that value can be captured by, for example, batch programs.

You won't be using the return value in programs in this book (it is rare that you will otherwise), but the ANSI standard requires it.

Default Parameters

For every parameter you declare in a function prototype and definition, the calling function must pass in a value. The value passed in must be of the declared type. Thus, if you have a function declared as

```
long myFunction(int);
```

the function must, in fact, take an integer variable. If the function definition differs, or if you fail to pass in an integer, you receive a compiler error.

The one exception to this rule is if the function prototype declares a default value for the parameter. A *default value* is a value to use if none is supplied. The preceding declaration could be rewritten as

```
long myFunction (int x = 50);
```

This prototype says, "myFunction() returns a long and takes an integer parameter. If an argument is not supplied, use the default value of 50." Because parameter names are not required in function prototypes, this declaration could have been written as

```
long myFunction (int = 50);
```

The function definition is not changed by declaring a default parameter. The function definition header for this function would be

```
long myFunction (int x)
```

If the calling function did not include a parameter, the compiler would fill x with the default value of 50. The name of the default parameter in the prototype need not be the same as the name in the function header; the default value is assigned by position, not name.

Any or all of the function's parameters can be assigned default values. The one restriction is this: If any of the parameters does not have a default value, no previous parameter can have a default value.

If the function prototype looks like

```
long myFunction (int Param1, int Param2, int Param3);
```

you can assign a default value to Param2 only if you have assigned a default value to Param3. You can assign a default value to Param1 only if you've assigned default values to both Param2 and Param3. Listing 5.7 demonstrates the use of default values.

LISTING 5.7   A Demonstration of Default Parameter Values

```
 1:  // Listing 5.7 - demonstrates use
 2:  // of default parameter values
 3:  #include <iostream>
 4:
 5:  int AreaCube(int length, int width = 25, int height = 1);
 6:
 7:  int main()
 8:  {
 9:     int length = 100;
10:     int width = 50;
11:     int height = 2;
12:     int area;
13:
14:     area = AreaCube(length, width, height);
15:     std::cout << "First area equals: " << area << "\n";
16:
17:     area = AreaCube(length, width);
18:     std::cout << "Second time area equals: " << area << "\n";
19:
20:     area = AreaCube(length);
21:     std::cout << "Third time area equals: " << area << "\n";
22:     return 0;
23:  }
24:
25:  AreaCube(int length, int width, int height)
26:  {
27:
28:     return (length * width * height);
29:  }
```

5

OUTPUT
```
First area equals: 10000
Second time area equals: 5000
Third time area equals: 2500
```

ANALYSIS On line 5, the AreaCube() prototype specifies that the AreaCube() function takes three integer parameters. The last two have default values.

This function computes the area of the cube whose dimensions are passed in. If no width is passed in, a width of 25 is used and a height of 1 is used. If the width but not the height is passed in, a height of 1 is used. It is not possible to pass in the height without passing in a width.

On lines 9–11, the dimension's length, height, and width are initialized, and they are passed to the AreaCube() function on line 14. The values are computed, and the result is printed on line 15.

Execution continues to line 17, where AreaCube() is called again, but with no value for height. The default value is used, and again the dimensions are computed and printed.

Execution then continues to line 20, and this time neither the width nor the height is passed in. With this call to AreaCube(), execution branches for a third time to line 25. The default values are used and the area is computed. Control returns to the main() function where the final value is then printed.

Do	**Don't**
DO remember that function parameters act as local variables within the function. **DO** remember that changes to a global variable in one function change that variable for all functions.	**DON'T** try to create a default value for a first parameter if no default value exists for the second. **DON'T** forget that arguments passed by value cannot affect the variables in the calling function.

Overloading Functions

C++ enables you to create more than one function with the same name. This is called *function overloading*. The functions must differ in their parameter list with a different type of parameter, a different number of parameters, or both. Here's an example:

```
int myFunction (int, int);
int myFunction (long, long);
int myFunction (long);
```

myFunction() is overloaded with three parameter lists. The first and second versions differ in the types of the parameters, and the third differs in the number of parameters.

The return types can be the same or different on overloaded functions.

NOTE Two functions with the same name and parameter list, but different return types, generate a compiler error. To change the return type, you must also change the signature (name and/or parameter list).

Function overloading is also called *function polymorphism*. Poly means many, and morph means form: A polymorphic function is many-formed.

Function polymorphism refers to the capability to "overload" a function with more than one meaning. By changing the number or type of the parameters, you can give two or more functions the same function name, and the right one will be called automatically by matching the parameters used. This enables you to create a function that can average integers, `doubles`, and other values without having to create individual names for each function, such as `AverageInts()`, `AverageDoubles()`, and so on.

Suppose you write a function that doubles whatever input you give it. You would like to be able to pass in an `int`, a `long`, a `float`, or a `double`. Without function overloading, you would have to create four function names:

```
int DoubleInt(int);
long DoubleLong(long);
float DoubleFloat(float);
double DoubleDouble(double);
```

With function overloading, you make this declaration:

```
int Double(int);
long Double(long);
float Double(float);
double Double(double);
```

This is easier to read and easier to use. You don't have to worry about which one to call; you just pass in a variable, and the right function is called automatically. Listing 5.8 illustrates the use of function overloading.

LISTING 5.8 A Demonstration of Function Polymorphism

```
1:   // Listing 5.8 - demonstrates
2:   // function polymorphism
3:   #include <iostream>
4:
5:   int Double(int);
6:   long Double(long);
7:   float Double(float);
8:   double Double(double);
9:
```

5

LISTING 5.8 continued

```
10:  using namespace std;
11:
12:  int main()
13:  {
14:     int        myInt = 6500;
15:     long       myLong = 65000;
16:     float      myFloat = 6.5F;
17:     double     myDouble = 6.5e20;
18:
19:     int        doubledInt;
20:     long       doubledLong;
21:     float      doubledFloat;
22:     double     doubledDouble;
23:
24:     cout << "myInt: " << myInt << "\n";
25:     cout << "myLong: " << myLong << "\n";
26:     cout << "myFloat: " << myFloat << "\n";
27:     cout << "myDouble: " << myDouble << "\n";
28:
29:     doubledInt = Double(myInt);
30:     doubledLong = Double(myLong);
31:     doubledFloat = Double(myFloat);
32:     doubledDouble = Double(myDouble);
33:
34:     cout << "doubledInt: " << doubledInt << "\n";
35:     cout << "doubledLong: " << doubledLong << "\n";
36:     cout << "doubledFloat: " << doubledFloat << "\n";
37:     cout << "doubledDouble: " << doubledDouble << "\n";
38:
39:     return 0;
40:  }
41:
42:  int Double(int original)
43:  {
44:     cout << "In Double(int)\n";
45:     return 2 * original;
46:  }
47:
48:  long Double(long original)
49:  {
50:     cout << "In Double(long)\n";
51:     return 2 * original;
52:  }
53:
54:  float Double(float original)
55:  {
56:     cout << "In Double(float)\n";
57:     return 2 * original;
58:  }
```

LISTING 5.8   continued

```
59:
60:   double Double(double original)
61:   {
62:       cout << "In Double(double)\n";
63:       return 2 * original;
64:   }
```

OUTPUT
```
myInt: 6500
myLong: 65000
myFloat: 6.5
myDouble: 6.5e+20
In Double(int)
In Double(long)
In Double(float)
In Double(double)
DoubledInt: 13000
DoubledLong: 130000
DoubledFloat: 13
DoubledDouble: 1.3e+21
```

ANALYSIS The Double() function is overloaded with int, long, float, and double. The prototypes are on lines 5–8, and the definitions are on lines 42–64.

Note that in this example, the statement using namespace std; has been added on line 10, outside of any particular function. This makes the statement global to this file, and thus the namespace is used in all the functions declared within this file.

In the body of the main program, eight local variables are declared. On lines 14–17, four of the values are initialized, and on lines 29–32, the other four are assigned the results of passing the first four to the Double() function. Note that when Double() is called, the calling function does not distinguish which one to call; it just passes in an argument, and the correct one is invoked.

The compiler examines the arguments and chooses which of the four Double() functions to call. The output reveals that each of the four was called in turn, as you would expect.

Special Topics About Functions

Because functions are so central to programming, a few special topics arise that might be of interest when you confront unusual problems. Used wisely, inline functions can help you squeak out that last bit of performance. Function recursion is one of those wonderful, esoteric bits of programming, which, every once in a while, can cut through a thorny problem otherwise not easily solved.

Inline Functions

When you define a function, normally the compiler creates just one set of instructions in memory. When you call the function, execution of the program jumps to those instructions, and when the function returns, execution jumps back to the next line in the calling function. If you call the function 10 times, your program jumps to the same set of instructions each time. This means only one copy of the function exists, not 10.

A small performance overhead occurs in jumping in and out of functions. It turns out that some functions are very small, just a line or two of code, and an efficiency might be gained if the program can avoid making these jumps just to execute one or two instructions. When programmers speak of efficiency, they usually mean speed; the program runs faster if the function call can be avoided.

If a function is declared with the keyword inline, the compiler does not create a real function; it copies the code from the inline function directly into the calling function. No jump is made; it is just as if you had written the statements of the function right into the calling function.

Note that inline functions can bring a heavy cost. If the function is called 10 times, the inline code is copied into the calling functions each of those 10 times. The tiny improvement in speed you might achieve might be more than swamped by the increase in size of the executable program, which might in fact actually slow the program!

The reality is that today's optimizing compilers can almost certainly do a better job of making this decision than you can; and so it is generally a good idea not to declare a function inline unless it is only one or at most two statements in length. When in doubt, though, leave inline out.

NOTE

> Performance optimization is a difficult challenge, and most programmers are not good at identifying the location of performance problems in their programs without help. Help, in this case, involves specialized programs like debuggers and profilers.
>
> Also, it is always better to write code that is clear and understandable than to write code that contains your guess about what will run fast or slow, but is harder to understand. This is because it is easier to make understandable code run faster.

Listing 5.9 demonstrates an inline function.

LISTING 5.9 A Demonstration of an Inline Function

```
1:   // Listing 5.9 - demonstrates inline functions
2:   #include <iostream>
3:
4:   inline int Double(int);
5:
6:   int main()
7:   {
8:       int target;
9:       using std::cout;
10:      using std::cin;
11:      using std::endl;
12:
13:      cout << "Enter a number to work with: ";
14:      cin >> target;
15:      cout << "\n";
16:
17:      target = Double(target);
18:      cout << "Target: " << target << endl;
19:
20:      target = Double(target);
21:      cout << "Target: " << target << endl;
22:
23:      target = Double(target);
24:      cout << "Target: " << target << endl;
25:      return 0;
26:   }
27:
28:   int Double(int target)
29:   {
30:       return 2*target;
31:   }
```

5

OUTPUT

```
Enter a number to work with: 20

Target: 40
Target: 80
Target: 160
```

ANALYSIS   On line 4, Double() is declared to be an inline function taking an int parameter and returning an int. The declaration is just like any other prototype except that the keyword inline is prepended just before the return value.

This compiles into code that is the same as if you had written the following:

target = 2 * target;

everywhere you entered

target = Double(target);

By the time your program executes, the instructions are already in place, compiled into the `.obj` file. This saves a jump and return in the execution of the code at the cost of a larger program.

Recursion

A function can call itself. This is called *recursion*, and recursion can be direct or indirect. It is direct when a function calls itself; it is indirect recursion when a function calls another function that then calls the first function.

Some problems are most easily solved by recursion, usually those in which you act on data and then act in the same way on the result. Both types of recursion, direct and indirect, come in two varieties: those that eventually end and produce an answer, and those that never end and produce a runtime failure. Programmers think that the latter is quite funny (when it happens to someone else).

It is important to note that when a function calls itself, a new copy of that function is run. The local variables in the second version are independent of the local variables in the first, and they cannot affect one another directly, any more than the local variables in `main()` can affect the local variables in any function it calls, as was illustrated in Listing 5.3.

To illustrate solving a problem using recursion, consider the Fibonacci series:

1,1,2,3,5,8,13,21,34...

Each number, after the second, is the sum of the two numbers before it. A Fibonacci problem might be to determine what the 12th number in the series is.

To solve this problem, you must examine the series carefully. The first two numbers are 1. Each subsequent number is the sum of the previous two numbers. Thus, the seventh number is the sum of the sixth and fifth numbers. More generally, the nth number is the sum of $n-2$ and $n-1$, as long as $n > 2$.

Recursive functions need a stop condition. Something must happen to cause the program to stop recursing, or it will never end. In the Fibonacci series, $n < 3$ is a stop condition (that is, when n is less than 3 the program can stop working on the problem).

An algorithm is a set of steps you follow to solve a problem. One algorithm for the Fibonacci series is the following:

1. Ask the user for a position in the series.

2. Call the fib() function with that position, passing in the value the user entered.

3. The fib() function examines the argument (*n*). If n < 3 it returns 1; otherwise, fib() calls itself (recursively) passing in n-2. It then calls itself again passing in n-1, and returns the sum of the first call and the second.

If you call fib(1), it returns 1. If you call fib(2), it returns 1. If you call fib(3), it returns the sum of calling fib(2) and fib(1). Because fib(2) returns 1 and fib(1) returns 1, fib(3) returns 2 (the sum of 1 + 1).

If you call fib(4), it returns the sum of calling fib(3) and fib(2). You just saw that fib(3) returns 2 (by calling fib(2) and fib(1)) and that fib(2) returns 1, so fib(4) sums these numbers and returns 3, which is the fourth number in the series.

Taking this one more step, if you call fib(5), it returns the sum of fib(4) and fib(3). You've seen that fib(4) returns 3 and fib(3) returns 2, so the sum returned is 5.

This method is not the most efficient way to solve this problem (in fib(20) the fib() function is called 13,529 times!), but it does work. Be careful—if you feed in too large a number, you'll run out of memory. Every time fib() is called, memory is set aside. When it returns, memory is freed. With recursion, memory continues to be set aside before it is freed, and this system can eat memory very quickly. Listing 5.10 implements the fib() function.

5

CAUTION   When you run Listing 5.10, use a small number (less than 15). Because this uses recursion, it can consume a lot of memory.

LISTING 5.10   A Demonstration of Recursion Using the Fibonacci Series

```
1:  // Fibonacci series using recursion
2:  #include <iostream>
3:  int fib (int n);
4:
5:  int main()
6:  {
7:
8:      int n, answer;
9:      std::cout << "Enter number to find: ";
10:     std::cin >> n;
11:
```

LISTING 5.10   continued

```
12:     std::cout << "\n\n";
13:
14:     answer = fib(n);
15:
16:     std::cout << answer << " is the " << n;
17:         std::cout << "th Fibonacci number\n";
18:     return 0;
19: }
20:
21: int fib (int n)
22: {
23:     std::cout << "Processing fib(" << n << ")... ";
24:
25:     if (n < 3 )
26:     {
27:         std::cout << "Return 1!\n";
28:         return (1);
29:     }
30:     else
31:     {
32:         std::cout << "Call fib(" << n-2 << ") ";
33:             std::cout << "and fib(" << n-1 << ").\n";
34:         return( fib(n-2) + fib(n-1));
35:     }
36: }
```

OUTPUT

```
Enter number to find: 6

Processing fib(6)... Call fib(4) and fib(5).
Processing fib(4)... Call fib(2) and fib(3).
Processing fib(2)... Return 1!
Processing fib(3)... Call fib(1) and fib(2).
Processing fib(1)... Return 1!
Processing fib(2)... Return 1!
Processing fib(5)... Call fib(3) and fib(4).
Processing fib(3)... Call fib(1) and fib(2).
Processing fib(1)... Return 1!
Processing fib(2)... Return 1!
Processing fib(4)... Call fib(2) and fib(3).
Processing fib(2)... Return 1!
Processing fib(3)... Call fib(1) and fib(2).
Processing fib(1)... Return 1!
Processing fib(2)... Return 1!
8 is the 6th Fibonacci number
```

NOTE

Some compilers have difficulty with the use of operators in a cout statement. If you receive a warning on line 32, place parentheses around the subtraction operation so that lines 32 and 33 become:

```
std::cout << "Call fib(" << (n-2) << ") ";
    std::cout << "and fib(" << (n-1) << ").\n";
```

ANALYSIS   The program asks for a number to find on line 9 and assigns that number to n. It
then calls fib() with n. Execution branches to the fib() function, where, on line
23, it prints its argument.

The argument n is tested to see whether it is less than 3 on line 25; if so, fib() returns
the value 1. Otherwise, it returns the sum of the values returned by calling fib() on n-2
and n-1.

It cannot return these values until the call (to fib()) is resolved. Thus, you can picture
the program diving into fib repeatedly until it hits a call to fib that returns a value. The
only calls that return a value are the calls to fib(2) and fib(1). These values are then
passed up to the waiting callers, which, in turn, add the return value to their own, and
then they return. Figures 5.4 and 5.5 illustrate this recursion into fib().

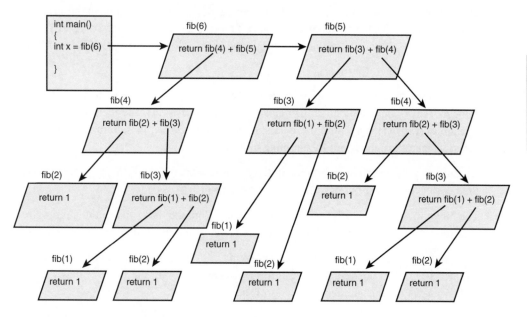

FIGURE 5.4 *Using recursion.*

5

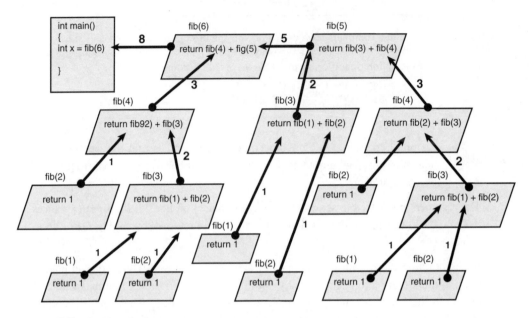

FIGURE 5.5 *Returning from recursion.*

In the example, n is 6 so fib(6) is called from main(). Execution jumps to the fib() function, and n is tested for a value less than 3 on line 25. The test fails, so fib(6) returns on line 34 the sum of the values returned by fib(4) and fib(5). Look at line 34:

```
return( fib(n-2) + fib(n-1));
```

From this return statement a call is made to fib(4) (because n == 6, fib(n-2) is the same as fib(4)) and another call is made to fib(5) (fib(n-1)), and then the function you are in (fib(6)) *waits* until these calls return a value. When these return a value, this function can return the result of summing those two values.

Because fib(5) passes in an argument that is not less than 3, fib() is called again, this time with 4 and 3. fib(4) in turn calls fib(3) and fib(2).

The output traces these calls and the return values. Compile, link, and run this program, entering first 1, then 2, then 3, building up to 6, and watch the output carefully.

This would be a great time to start experimenting with your debugger. Put a break point on line 21 and then trace *into* each call to fib, keeping track of the value of *n* as you work your way into each recursive call to fib.

Recursion is not used often in C++ programming, but it can be a powerful and elegant tool for certain needs.

NOTE   Recursion is a tricky part of advanced programming. It is presented here because it can be useful to understand the fundamentals of how it works, but don't worry too much if you don't fully understand all the details.

How Functions Work—A Peek Under the Hood

When you call a function, the code branches to the called function, parameters are passed in, and the body of the function is executed. When the function completes, a value is returned (unless the function returns void), and control returns to the calling function.

How is this task accomplished? How does the code know where to branch? Where are the variables kept when they are passed in? What happens to variables that are declared in the body of the function? How is the return value passed back out? How does the code know where to resume?

Most introductory books don't try to answer these questions, but without understanding this information, you'll find that programming remains a fuzzy mystery. The explanation requires a brief tangent into a discussion of computer memory.

Levels of Abstraction

One of the principal hurdles for new programmers is grappling with the many layers of intellectual abstraction. Computers, of course, are only electronic machines. They don't know about windows and menus, they don't know about programs or instructions, and they don't even know about ones and zeros. All that is really going on is that voltage is being measured at various places on an integrated circuit. Even this is an abstraction: Electricity itself is just an intellectual concept representing the behavior of subatomic particles, which arguably are themselves intellectual abstractions(!).

Few programmers bother with any level of detail below the idea of values in RAM. After all, you don't need to understand particle physics to drive a car, make toast, or hit a baseball, and you don't need to understand the electronics of a computer to program one.

You do need to understand how memory is organized, however. Without a reasonably strong mental picture of where your variables are when they are created and how values are passed among functions, it will all remain an unmanageable mystery.

5

Partitioning RAM

When you begin your program, your operating system (such as DOS, Linux/Unix, or Microsoft Windows) sets up various areas of memory based on the requirements of your compiler. As a C++ programmer, you'll often be concerned with the global namespace, the free store, the registers, the code space, and the stack.

Global variables are in global namespace. You'll learn more about global namespace and the free store in coming days, but here, the focus is on the registers, code space, and stack.

Registers are a special area of memory built right into the central processing unit (or CPU). They take care of internal housekeeping. A lot of what goes on in the registers is beyond the scope of this book, but what you should be concerned with is the set of registers responsible for pointing, at any given moment, to the next line of code. These registers, together, can be called the instruction pointer. It is the job of the instruction pointer to keep track of which line of code is to be executed next.

The code itself is in the code space, which is that part of memory set aside to hold the binary form of the instructions you created in your program. Each line of source code is translated into a series of instructions, and each of these instructions is at a particular address in memory. The instruction pointer has the address of the next instruction to execute. Figure 5.6 illustrates this idea.

FIGURE 5.6

The instruction pointer.

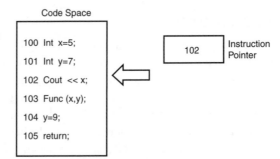

The stack is a special area of memory allocated for your program to hold the data required by each of the functions in your program. It is called a stack because it is a last-in, first-out queue, much like a stack of dishes at a cafeteria, as shown in Figure 5.7.

Last-in, first-out means that whatever is added to the stack last is the first thing taken off. This differs from most queues in which the first in is the first out (like a line at a theater: The first one in line is the first one off). A stack is more like a stack of coins: If you stack 10 pennies on a tabletop and then take some back, the last three you put on top are the first three you take off.

FIGURE 5.7

A stack.

When data is *pushed* onto the stack, the stack grows; as data is *popped* off the stack, the stack shrinks. It isn't possible to pop a dish off the stack without first popping off all the dishes placed on after that dish.

A stack of dishes is the common analogy. It is fine as far as it goes, but it is wrong in a fundamental way. A more accurate mental picture is of a series of cubbyholes aligned top to bottom. The top of the stack is whatever cubby the stack pointer (which is another register) happens to be pointing to.

Each of the cubbies has a sequential address, and one of those addresses is kept in the stack pointer register. Everything below that magic address, known as the top of the stack, is considered to be on the stack. Everything above the top of the stack is considered to be off the stack and invalid. Figure 5.8 illustrates this idea.

FIGURE 5.8

The stack pointer.

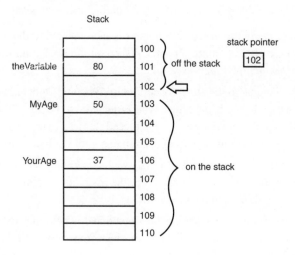

When data is put on the stack, it is placed into a cubby above the stack pointer, and then the stack pointer is moved to the new data. When data is popped off the stack, all that really happens is that the address of the stack pointer is changed by moving it down the stack. Figure 5.9 makes this rule clear.

The data *above* the stack pointer (off the stack) might or might not be changed at any time. These values are referred to as "garbage" because their value is no longer reliable.

FIGURE 5.9

Moving the stack pointer.

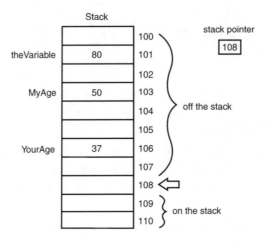

The Stack and Functions

The following is an approximation of what happens when your program branches to a function. (The details will differ depending on the operating system and compiler.)

1. The address in the instruction pointer is incremented to the next instruction past the function call. That address is then placed on the stack, and it will be the return address when the function returns.

2. Room is made on the stack for the return type you've declared. On a system with two-byte integers, if the return type is declared to be int, another two bytes are added to the stack, but no value is placed in these bytes (that means that whatever "garbage" was in those two bytes remains until the local variable is initialized).

3. The address of the called function, which is kept in a special area of memory set aside for that purpose, is loaded into the instruction pointer, so the next instruction executed will be in the called function.

4. The current top of the stack is now noted and is held in a special pointer called the stack frame. Everything added to the stack from now until the function returns will be considered "local" to the function.

5. All the arguments to the function are placed on the stack.

6. The instruction now in the instruction pointer is executed, thus executing the first instruction in the function.

7. Local variables are pushed onto the stack as they are defined.

When the function is ready to return, the return value is placed in the area of the stack reserved at step 2. The stack is then popped all the way up to the stack frame pointer, which effectively throws away all the local variables and the arguments to the function.

The return value is popped off the stack and assigned as the value of the function call itself, and the address stashed away in step 1 is retrieved and put into the instruction pointer. The program thus resumes immediately after the function call, with the value of the function retrieved.

Some of the details of this process change from compiler to compiler, or between computer operating system or processors, but the essential ideas are consistent across environments. In general, when you call a function, the return address and the parameters are put on the stack. During the life of the function, local variables are added to the stack. When the function returns, these are all removed by popping the stack.

In coming days, you will learn about other places in memory that are used to hold data that must persist beyond the life of the function.

Summary

Today's lesson introduced functions. A function is, in effect, a subprogram into which you can pass parameters and from which you can return a value. Every C++ program starts in the `main()` function, and `main()`, in turn, can call other functions.

A function is declared with a function prototype, which describes the return value, the function name, and its parameter types. A function can optionally be declared inline. A function prototype can also declare default values for one or more of the parameters.

The function definition must match the function prototype in return type, name, and parameter list. Function names can be overloaded by changing the number or type of parameters; the compiler finds the right function based on the argument list.

Local function variables, and the arguments passed in to the function, are local to the block in which they are declared. Parameters passed by value are copies and cannot affect the value of variables in the calling function.

5

Q&A

Q Why not make all variables global?

A At one time, this was exactly how programming was done. As programs became more complex, however, it became very difficult to find bugs in programs because data could be corrupted by any of the functions—global data can be changed anywhere in the program. Years of experience have convinced programmers that data should be kept as local as possible, and access to changing that data should be narrowly defined.

Q When should the keyword `inline` be used in a function prototype?

A If the function is very small, no more than a line or two, and won't be called from many places in your program, it is a candidate for inlining.

Q Why aren't changes to the value of function arguments reflected in the calling function?

A Arguments passed to a function are passed by value. That means that the argument in the function is actually a copy of the original value. This concept is explained in depth in the section "How Functions Work—A Peek Under the Hood."

Q If arguments are passed by value, what do I do if I need to reflect the changes back in the calling function?

A On Day 8, pointers will be discussed and on Day 9, you'll learn about references. Use of pointers or references will solve this problem, as well as provide a way around the limitation of returning only a single value from a function.

Q What happens if I have the following two functions?

```
int Area (int width, int length = 1); int Area (int size);
```

Will these overload? A different number of parameters exist, but the first one has a default value.

A The declarations will compile, but if you invoke `Area` with one parameter, you will receive an error: ambiguity between `Area(int, int)` and `Area(int)`.

Workshop

The Workshop provides quiz questions to help you solidify your understanding of the material covered and exercises to provide you with experience in using what you've learned. Try to answer the quiz and exercise questions before checking the answers in Appendix D, and be certain that you understand the answers before continuing to tomorrow's lesson.

Quiz

1. What are the differences between the function prototype and the function definition?

2. Do the names of parameters have to agree in the prototype, definition, and call to the function?

3. If a function doesn't return a value, how do you declare the function?

4. If you don't declare a return value, what type of return value is assumed?

5. What is a local variable?

6. What is scope?

7. What is recursion?

8. When should you use global variables?

9. What is function overloading?

Exercises

1. Write the prototype for a function named `Perimeter()`, which returns an unsigned long int and takes two parameters, both unsigned short ints.

2. Write the definition of the function `Perimeter()` as described in Exercise 1. The two parameters represent the length and width of a rectangle. Have the function return the perimeter (twice the length plus twice the width).

3. **BUG BUSTERS:** What is wrong with the function in the following code?

```
#include <iostream>
void myFunc(unsigned short int x);
int main()
{
    unsigned short int x, y;
    y = myFunc(int);
    std::cout << "x: " << x << " y: " << y << "\n";
    return 0;
}

void myFunc(unsigned short int x)
{
    return (4*x);
}
```

4. **BUG BUSTERS:** What is wrong with the function in the following code?

```
#include <iostream>
int myFunc(unsigned short int x);
int main()
```

5

```
{
    unsigned short int x, y;
    x = 7;
    y = myFunc(x);
    std::cout << "x: " << x << " y: " << y << "\n";
    return 0;
}

int myFunc(unsigned short int x);
{
    return (4*x);
}
```

5. Write a function that takes two unsigned short integer arguments and returns the result of dividing the first by the second. Do not do the division if the second number is zero, but do return –1.

6. Write a program that asks the user for two numbers and calls the function you wrote in Exercise 5. Print the answer, or print an error message if you get –1.

7. Write a program that asks for a number and a power. Write a recursive function that takes the number to the power. Thus, if the number is 2 and the power is 4, the function will return 16.

DAY **6**

Understanding Object-Oriented Programming

Classes extend the built-in capabilities of C++ to assist you in representing and solving complex, real-world problems.

Today, you will learn

- What classes and objects are
- How to define a new class and create objects of that class
- What member functions and member data are
- What constructors are and how to use them

Is C++ Object-Oriented?

At one point, C, the predecessor to C++, was the world's most popular programming language for commercial software development. It was used for creating operating systems (such as the Unix operating system), for real-time programming (machine, device, and electronics control), and only later began to be used as a language for programming conventional languages. Its intent was to provide an easier and safer way to program down close to the hardware.

C was developed as a middle ground between high-level business application languages such as COBOL and the pedal-to-the-metal, high-performance, but difficult-to-use Assembler language. C was to enforce "structured" programming, in which problems were "decomposed" into smaller units of repeatable activities called *procedures* and data was assembled into packages called *structures*.

But research languages such as Smalltalk and CLU had begun to pave a new direction—object-orientation—which combined the data locked away in assemblies like structures with the capabilities of procedures into a single unit: the object.

The world is filled with objects: cars, dogs, trees, clouds, flowers. Objects. Each *object* has characteristics (fast, friendly, brown, puffy, pretty). Most objects have behavior (move, bark, grow, rain, wilt). You don't generally think about a car's specifications and how those specifications might be manipulated. Rather, a car is thought about as an object that looks and acts a certain way. And the same should be true with any real-world object that is brought into the domain of the computer.

The programs being written early in the twenty-first century are much more complex than those written at the end of the twentieth century. Programs created in procedural languages tend to be difficult to manage, hard to maintain, and expensive to extend. Graphical user interfaces, the Internet, digital and wireless telephony, and a host of new technologies have dramatically increased the complexity of our projects at the same time that consumer expectations for the quality of the user interface are rising.

Object-oriented software development offers a tool to help with the challenges of software development. Though there are no silver bullets for complex software development, object-oriented programming languages build a strong link between the data structures and the methods that manipulate that data and have a closer fit to the way humans (programmers and clients) think, improving communication and improving the quality of delivered software. In object-oriented programming, you no longer think about data structures and manipulating functions; you think instead about objects as if they were their real-world counterparts: as things that look and act a certain way.

C++ was created as a bridge between object-oriented programming and C. The goal was to provide object-oriented design to a fast, commercial software development platform, with a special focus on high performance. Next, you'll see more about how C++ meets its objectives.

Creating New Types

Programs are usually written to solve real-world problems, such as keeping track of employee records or simulating the workings of a heating system. Although it is possible to solve complex problems by using programs written with only numbers and characters, it is far easier to grapple with large, complex problems if you can create representations of the objects that you are talking about. In other words, simulating the workings of a heating system is easier if you can create variables that represent rooms, heat sensors, thermostats, and boilers. The closer these variables correspond to reality, the easier it is to write the program.

You've already learned about a number of variable types, including unsigned integers and characters. The type of a variable tells you quite a bit about it. For example, if you declare Height and Width to be unsigned short integers, you know that each one can hold a number between 0 and 65,535, assuming an unsigned short integer is two bytes. That is the meaning of saying they are unsigned integers; trying to hold anything else in these variables causes an error. You can't store your name in an unsigned short integer, and you shouldn't try.

Just by declaring these variables to be unsigned short integers, you know that it is possible to add Height to Width and to assign the result to another number.

The type of these variables tells you

- Their size in memory
- What information they can hold
- What actions can be performed on them

In traditional languages such as C, types were built in to the language. In C++, the programmer can extend the language by creating any type needed, and each of these new types can have all the functionality and power of the built-in types.

6

Downsides of Creating Types with struct

Some capabilities to extend the C language with new types were provided by the ability to combine related variables into structs, which could be made available as a new data type through the typedef statement.

There were things lacking in this capability, however:

- structs and the functions that operate on them aren't cohesive wholes; functions can only be found by reading the header files for the libraries available and looking for those with the new type as a parameter.

- Coordinating the activities of groups of related functions on the struct is harder because anything in the struct can be changed at any time by any piece of program logic. There is no way to protect struct data from interference.
- The built-in operators don't work on structs—it does not work to add two structs with a plus sign (+), even when that might be the most natural way to represent the solution to a problem (for instance, when each struct represents a complex piece of text to be joined together).

Introducing Classes and Members

You make a new type in C++ by declaring a class. A class is just a collection of variables—often of different types—combined with a set of related functions.

One way to think about a car is as a collection of wheels, doors, seats, windows, and so forth. Another way is to think about what a car can do: It can move, speed up, slow down, stop, park, and so on. A class enables you to encapsulate, or bundle, these various parts and various functions into one collection, which is called an object.

Encapsulating everything you know about a car into one class has a number of advantages for a programmer. Everything is in one place, which makes it easy to refer to, copy, and call on functions that manipulate the data. Likewise, clients of your class—that is, the parts of the program that use your class—can use your object without worrying about what is in it or how it works.

A class can consist of any combination of the variable types and also other class types. The variables in the class are referred to as the member variables or data members. A Car class might have member variables representing the seats, radio type, tires, and so forth.

Member variables, also known as data members, are the variables in your class. Member variables are part of your class, just as the wheels and engine are part of your car.

A class can also contain functions called member functions or methods. Member functions are as much a part of your class as the member variables. They determine what your class can do.

The member functions in the class typically manipulate the member variables. For example, methods of the Car class might include Start() and Brake(). A Cat class might have data members that represent age and weight; its methods might include Sleep(), Meow(), and ChaseMice().

Declaring a Class

Declaring a class tells the compiler about the class. To declare a class, use the `class` keyword followed by the class name, an opening brace, and then a list of the data members and methods of that class. End the declaration with a closing brace and a semicolon. Here's the declaration of a class called `Cat`:

```
class Cat
{
    unsigned int  itsAge;
    unsigned int  itsWeight;
    void Meow();
};
```

Declaring this class doesn't allocate memory for a `Cat`. It just tells the compiler what a `Cat` is, what data members it contains (`itsAge` and `itsWeight`), and what it can do (`Meow()`). Although memory isn't allocated, it does let the compiler know how big a `Cat` is—that is, how much room the compiler must set aside for each `Cat` that you will create. In this example, if an integer is four bytes, a `Cat` is eight bytes big: `itsAge` is four bytes, and `itsWeight` is another four bytes. `Meow()` takes up only the room required for storing information on the location of `Meow()`. This is a pointer to a function that can take four bytes on a 32-bit platform.

A Word on Naming Conventions

As a programmer, you must name all your member variables, member functions, and classes. As you learned on Day 3, "Working with Variables and Constants," these should be easily understood and meaningful names. `Cat`, `Rectangle`, and `Employee` are good class names. `Meow()`, `ChaseMice()`, and `StopEngine()` are good function names because they tell you what the functions do. Many programmers name the member variables with the prefix "its," as in `itsAge`, `itsWeight`, and `itsSpeed`. This helps to distinguish member variables from nonmember variables.

Other programmers use different prefixes. Some prefer `myAge`, `myWeight`, and `mySpeed`. Still others simply use the letter `m` (for member), possibly with an underscore (_) such as `mAge` or `m_age`, `mWeight` or `m_weight`, or `mSpeed` or `m_speed`.

Some programmers like to prefix every class name with a particular letter—for example, `cCat` or `cPerson`—whereas others put the name in all uppercase or all lowercase. The convention that this book uses is to name all classes with initial capitalization, as in `Cat` and `Person`.

Similarly, many programmers begin all functions with capital letters and all variables with lowercase. Words are usually separated with an underscore—as in `Chase_Mice`—or by capitalizing each word—for example, `ChaseMice` or `DrawCircle`.

6

The important idea is that you should pick one style and stay with it through each program. Over time, your style will evolve to include not only naming conventions, but also indentation, alignment of braces, and commenting style.

> **NOTE**
> It's common for development companies to have house standards for many style issues. This ensures that all developers can easily read one another's code. Unfortunately, this extends to the companies that develop operating systems and libraries of reusable classes, which usually means that C++ programs must work with several different naming conventions at once.

> **CAUTION**
> As stated before, C++ is case sensitive, so all class, function, and variable names should follow the same pattern so that you never have to check how to spell them—was it Rectangle, rectangle, or RECTANGLE?

Defining an Object

After you declare a class, you can then use it as a new type to declare variables of that type. You declare an object of your new type the same as you declare an integer variable:

```
unsigned int GrossWeight;      // define an unsigned integer
Cat Frisky;                    // define a Cat
```

This code defines a variable called GrossWeight, whose type is an unsigned integer. It also defines Frisky, which is an object whose class (or type) is Cat.

Classes Versus Objects

You never pet the definition of a cat; you pet individual cats. You draw a distinction between the idea of a cat and the particular cat that right now is shedding all over your living room. In the same way, C++ differentiates between the class Cat, which is the idea of a cat, and each individual Cat object. Thus, Frisky is an object of type Cat in the same way that GrossWeight is a variable of type unsigned int.

An object is an individual instance of a class.

Accessing Class Members

After you define an actual Cat object—for example,

```
Cat Frisky;
```

you use the dot operator (.) to access the members of that object. Therefore, to assign 50 to Frisky's Weight member variable, you would write

```
Frisky.itsWeight = 50;
```

In the same way, to call the Meow() function, you would write

```
Frisky.Meow();
```

When you use a class method, you call the method. In this example, you are calling Meow() on Frisky.

Assigning to Objects, Not to Classes

In C++, you don't assign values to types; you assign values to variables. For example, you would never write

```
int = 5;              // wrong
```

The compiler would flag this as an error because you can't assign 5 to an integer. Rather, you must define an integer variable and assign 5 to that variable. For example,

```
int  x;           // define x to be an int
x = 5;            // set x's value to 5
```

This is a shorthand way of saying, "Assign 5 to the variable x, which is of type int." In the same way, you wouldn't write

```
Cat.itsAge=5;             // wrong
```

The compiler would flag this as an error because you can't assign 5 to the age part of a class called Cat. Rather, you must define a specific Cat object and assign 5 to that object. For example,

```
Cat Frisky;           // just like  int x;
Frisky.itsAge = 5;    // just like  x = 5;
```

If You Don't Declare It, Your Class Won't Have It

Try this experiment: Walk up to a three-year-old and show her a cat. Then say, "This is Frisky. Frisky knows a trick. Frisky, bark." The child will giggle and say, "No, silly, cats can't bark."

If you wrote

```
Cat  Frisky;          // make a Cat named Frisky
Frisky.Bark()         // tell Frisky to bark
```

the compiler would say, "No, silly, Cats can't bark." (Your compiler's wording will probably look more like "[531] Error: Member function Bark not found in class Cat".) The

6

compiler knows that Frisky can't bark because the Cat class doesn't have a Bark() method. The compiler wouldn't even let Frisky meow if you didn't define a Meow() function.

Do	Don't
DO use the keyword class to declare a class. DO use the dot operator (.) to access class members and functions.	DON'T confuse a declaration with a definition. A declaration says what a class is. A definition sets aside memory for an object. DON'T confuse a class with an object. DON'T assign values to a class. Assign values to the data members of an object.

Private Versus Public Access

Additional keywords are often used in the declaration of a class. Two of the most important are public and private.

The private and public keywords are used with members of a class—both data members and member methods. Private members can be accessed only within methods of the class itself. Public members can be accessed through any object of the class. This distinction is both important and confusing. All members of a class are private, by default.

To make this a bit clearer, consider an example from earlier:

```
class Cat
{
  unsigned int  itsAge;
  unsigned int  itsWeight;
  void Meow();
};
```

In this declaration, itsAge, itsWeight, and Meow() are all private because all members of a class are private by default. Unless you specify otherwise, they are private. If you create a program and try to write the following within main (for example):

```
int main()
{
  Cat  Boots;
  Boots.itsAge=5;          // error! can't access private data!
  ...
```

the compiler flags this as an error. In effect, by leaving these members as private, you've said to the compiler, "I'll access itsAge, itsWeight, and Meow() only from within member functions of the Cat class." Yet, here, you've accessed the itsAge member variable of the Boots object from outside a Cat method. Just because Boots is an object of class Cat, that doesn't mean that you can access the parts of Boots that are private (even though they are visible in the declaration).

This is a source of endless confusion to new C++ programmers. I can almost hear you yelling, "Hey! I just said Boots is a Cat. Why can't Boots access his own age?" The answer is that Boots can, but you can't. Boots, in his own methods, can access all his parts—public and private. Even though you've created a Cat, that doesn't mean that you can see or change the parts of it that are private.

The way to use Cat so that you can access the data members is to make some of the members public:

```cpp
class Cat
{
  public:
    unsigned int  itsAge;
    unsigned int  itsWeight;
    void Meow();
};
```

In this declaration, itsAge, itsWeight, and Meow() are all public. Boots.itsAge=5 from the previous example will compile without problems.

NOTE

> The keyword public applies to all members in the declaration until the keyword private is encountered—and vice versa. This lets you easily declare sections of your class as public or private.

Listing 6.1 shows the declaration of a Cat class with public member variables.

LISTING 6.1   Accessing the Public Members of a Simple Class

```cpp
1:  // Demonstrates declaration of a class and
2:  // definition of an object of the class
3:
4:  #include <iostream>
5:
6:  class Cat                 // declare the Cat class
7:  {
8:    public:                 // members that follow are public
9:      int itsAge;           // member variable
10:     int itsWeight;        // member variable
11:  };              // note the semicolon
```

LISTING 6.1 continued

```
12:
13:  int main()
14:  {
15:     Cat Frisky;
16:     Frisky.itsAge = 5;     // assign to the member variable
17:     std::cout << "Frisky is a cat who is " ;
18:     std::cout << Frisky.itsAge << " years old.\n";
19:     return 0;
20:  }
```

OUTPUT Frisky is a cat who is 5 years old.

ANALYSIS Line 6 contains the keyword class. This tells the compiler that what follows is a declaration. The name of the new class comes after the keyword class. In this case, the name is Cat.

The body of the declaration begins with the opening brace on line 7 and ends with a closing brace and a semicolon on line 11. Line 8 contains the keyword public followed by a colon, which indicates that everything that follows is public until the keyword private or the end of the class declaration.

Lines 9 and 10 contain the declarations of the class members itsAge and itsWeight.

Line 13 begins the main() function of the program. Frisky is defined on line 15 as an instance of a Cat—that is, as a Cat object. On line 16, Frisky's age is set to 5. On lines 17 and 18, the itsAge member variable is used to print out a message about Frisky. You should notice on lines 16 and 18 how the member of the Frisky object is accessed. itsAge is accessed by using the object name (Frisky in this case) followed by period and then the member name (itsAge in this case).

NOTE Try commenting out line 8 and try to recompile. You will receive an error on line 16 because itsAge will no longer have public access. Rather, itsAge and the other members go to the default access, which is private access.

Making Member Data Private

As a general rule of design, you should keep the data members of a class private. Of course, if you make all of the data members private, you might wonder how you access information about the class. For example, if itsAge is private, how would you be able to set or get a Cat object's age?

To access private data in a class, you must create public functions known as accessor methods. Use these methods to set and get the private member variables. These accessor methods are the member functions that other parts of your program call to get and set your private member variables.

A public accessor method is a class member function used either to read (get) the value of a private class member variable or to set its value.

Why bother with this extra level of indirect access? Why add extra functions when it is simpler and easier to use the data directly? Why work through accessor functions?

The answer to these questions is that accessor functions enable you to separate the details of how the data is *stored* from how it is *used*. By using accessor functions, you can later change how the data is stored without having to rewrite any of the other functions in your programs that use the data.

If a function that needs to know a `Cat`'s age accesses `itsAge` directly, that function would need to be rewritten if you, as the author of the `Cat` class, decided to change how that data is stored. By having the function call `GetAge()`, your `Cat` class can easily return the right value no matter how you arrive at the age. The calling function doesn't need to know whether you are storing it as an `unsigned` integer or a `long`, or whether you are computing it as needed.

This technique makes your program easier to maintain. It gives your code a longer life because design changes don't make your program obsolete.

In addition, accessor functions can include additional logic, for instance, if a `Cat`'s age is unlikely to be more than 100, or its weight is unlikely to be 1000. These values should probably not be allowed. An accessor function can enforce these types of restrictions as well as do other tasks.

Listing 6.2 shows the `Cat` class modified to include private member data and public accessor methods. Note that this is not a listing that can be run if it is compiled.

6

LISTING 6.2 A Class with Accessor Methods

```
1:   // Cat class declaration
2:   // Data members are private, public accessor methods
3:   // mediate setting and getting the values of the private data
4:
4:   class Cat
5:   {
6:     public:
7:       // public accessors
8:       unsigned int GetAge();
```

LISTING **6.2**   continued

```
 9:        void SetAge(unsigned int Age);
10:
11:        unsigned int GetWeight();
12:        void SetWeight(unsigned int Weight);
13:
14:        // public member functions
15:        void Meow();
16:
17:        // private member data
18:     private:
19:        unsigned int  itsAge;
20:        unsigned int  itsWeight;
21:  };
```

ANALYSIS   This class has five public methods. Lines 8 and 9 contain the accessor methods
for itsAge. You can see that on line 8 there is a method for getting the age and
on line 9 there is one for setting it. Lines 11 and 12 contain similar accessor methods for
itsWeight. These accessor functions set the member variables and return their values.

The public member function Meow() is declared on line 15. Meow() is not an accessor
function. It doesn't get or set a member variable; it performs another service for the
class, printing the word "Meow."

The member variables themselves are declared on lines 19 and 20.

To set Frisky's age, you would pass the value to the SetAge() method, as in

```
Cat  Frisky;
Frisky.SetAge(5);    // set Frisky's age using the public accessor
```

Later today, you'll see the specific code for making the SetAge and the other methods
work.

Declaring methods or data private enables the compiler to find programming mistakes
before they become bugs. Any programmer worth his consulting fees can find a way
around privacy if he wants to. Stroustrup, the inventor of C++, said, "The C++ access
control mechanisms provide protection against accident—not against fraud" (ARM,
1990).

The class Keyword

Syntax for the class keyword is as follows:

```
class class_name
{
```

```
    // access control keywords here
    // class variables and methods declared here
};
```

You use the `class` keyword to declare new types. A class is a collection of class member data, which are variables of various types, including other classes. The class also contains class functions—or methods—which are functions used to manipulate the data in the class and to perform other services for the class.

You define objects of the new type in much the same way in which you define any variable. State the type (`class`) and then the variable name (the object). You access the class members and functions by using the dot (.) operator.

You use access control keywords to declare sections of the class as public or private. The default for access control is private. Each keyword changes the access control from that point on to the end of the class or until the next access control keyword. Class declarations end with a closing brace and a semicolon.

Example 1

```
class Cat
{
  public:
    unsigned int Age;
    unsigned int Weight;
    void Meow();
};

Cat  Frisky;
Frisky.Age = 8;
Frisky.Weight = 18;
Frisky.Meow();
```

Example 2

```
class Car
{
  public:                          // the next five are public

    void Start();
    void Accelerate();
    void Brake();
    void SetYear(int year);
    int GetYear();

  private:                         // the rest is private

    int Year;
    Char Model [255];
};                                 // end of class declaration

Car OldFaithful;                   // make an instance of car
int bought;                        // a local variable of type int
OldFaithful.SetYear(84) ;          // assign 84 to the year
bought = OldFaithful.GetYear();    // set bought to 84
OldFaithful.Start();               // call the start method
```

6

Do	Don't
DO use public accessor methods. **DO** access private member variables from within class member functions.	**DON'T** declare member variables public if you don't need to. **DON'T** try to use private member variables from outside the class.

Implementing Class Methods

As you've seen, an accessor function provides a public interface to the private member data of the class. Each accessor function, along with any other class methods that you declare, must have an implementation. The implementation is called the function definition.

A member function definition begins similarly to the definition of a regular function. First, you state the return type that will come from the function, or void if nothing will be returned. This is followed by the name of the class, two colons, the name of the function, and then the function's parameters. Listing 6.3 shows the complete declaration of a simple Cat class and the implementation of its accessor function and one general class member function.

LISTING 6.3 Implementing the Methods of a Simple Class

```
1:  // Demonstrates declaration of a class and
2:  // definition of class methods
3:  #include <iostream>          // for cout
4:
5:  class Cat                    // begin declaration of the class
6:  {
7:    public:                    // begin public section
8:      int GetAge();            // accessor function
9:      void SetAge (int age);   // accessor function
10:     void Meow();             // general function
11:   private:                   // begin private section
12:     int itsAge;              // member variable
13: };
14:
15: // GetAge, Public accessor function
16: // returns value of itsAge member
17: int Cat::GetAge()
18: {
19:    return itsAge;
20: }
21:
```

LISTING 6.3 continued

```
22:    // definition of SetAge, public
23:    // accessor function
24:    // sets itsAge member
25:    void Cat::SetAge(int age)
26:    {
27:        // set member variable itsAge to
28:        // value passed in by parameter age
29:        itsAge = age;
30:    }
31:
32:    // definition of Meow method
33:    // returns: void
34:    // parameters: None
35:    // action: Prints "meow" to screen
36:    void Cat::Meow()
37:    {
38:        std::cout << "Meow.\n";
39:    }
40:
41:    // create a cat, set its age, have it
42:    // meow, tell us its age, then meow again.
43:    int main()
44:    {
45:        Cat Frisky;
46:        Frisky.SetAge(5);
47:        Frisky.Meow();
48:        std::cout << "Frisky is a cat who is " ;
49:        std::cout << Frisky.GetAge() << " years old.\n";
50:        Frisky.Meow();
51:        return 0;
52:    }
```

OUTPUT
```
Meow.
Frisky is a cat who is 5 years old.
Meow.
```

ANALYSIS
Lines 5–13 contain the definition of the Cat class. Line 7 contains the keyword public, which tells the compiler that what follows is a set of public members. Line 8 has the declaration of the public accessor method GetAge(). GetAge() provides access to the private member variable itsAge, which is declared on line 12. Line 9 has the public accessor function SetAge(). SetAge() takes an integer as an argument and sets itsAge to the value of that argument.

Line 10 has the declaration of the class method Meow(). Meow() is not an accessor function. Here it is a general method that prints the word "Meow" to the screen.

6

Line 11 begins the private section, which includes only the declaration on line 12 of the private member variable itsAge. The class declaration ends with a closing brace and semicolon on line 13.

Lines 17–20 contain the definition of the member function GetAge(). This method takes no parameters, and it returns an integer. Note on line 17 that class methods include the class name followed by two colons and the function name. This syntax tells the compiler that the GetAge() function you are defining here is the one that you declared in the Cat class. With the exception of this header line, the GetAge() function is created the same as any other function.

The GetAge() function takes only one line; it returns the value in itsAge. Note that the main() function cannot access itsAge because itsAge is private to the Cat class. The main() function has access to the public method GetAge().

Because GetAge() is a member function of the Cat class, it has full access to the itsAge variable. This access enables GetAge() to return the value of itsAge to main().

Line 25 contains the definition of the SetAge() member function. You can see that this function takes one integer value, called age, and doesn't return any values, as indicated by void. SetAge() takes the value of the age parameter and assigns it to itsAge on line 29. Because SetAge() is a member of the Cat class, it has direct access to the private member variable itsAge.

Line 36 begins the definition, or implementation, of the Meow() method of the Cat class. It is a one-line function that prints the word "Meow" to the screen, followed by a new line. Remember that the \n character prints a new line to the screen. You can see that Meow is set up just like the accessor functions in that it begins with the return type, the class name, the function name, and the parameters (none in this case).

Line 43 begins the body of the program with the familiar main() function. On line 45, main() declares an object called Frisky of type Cat. Read a different way, you could say that main() declares a Cat named Frisky.

On line 46, the value 5 is assigned to the itsAge member variable by way of the SetAge() accessor method. Note that the method is called by using the object name (Frisky) followed by the member operator (.) and the method name (SetAge()). In this same way, you can call any of the other methods in a class.

NOTE | The terms *member function* and *method* can be used interchangeably.

Line 47 calls the `Meow()` member function, and line 48 prints a message using the `GetAge()` accessor. Line 50 calls `Meow()` again. Although these methods are a part of a class (`Cat`) and are being used through an object (`Frisky`), they operate just like the functions you have seen before.

Adding Constructors and Destructors

Two ways exist to define an integer variable. You can define the variable and then assign a value to it later in the program. For example:

```
int Weight;            // define a variable
...                    // other code here
Weight = 7;            // assign it a value
```

Or, you can define the integer and immediately initialize it. For example,

```
int Weight = 7;        // define and initialize to 7
```

Initialization combines the definition of the variable with its initial assignment. Nothing stops you from changing that value later. Initialization ensures that your variable is never without a meaningful value.

How do you initialize the member data of a class? You can initialize the member data of a class using a special member function called a constructor. The constructor can take parameters as needed, but it cannot have a return value—not even `void`. The constructor is a class method with the same name as the class itself.

Whenever you declare a constructor, you'll also want to declare a destructor. Just as constructors create and initialize objects of your class, destructors clean up after your object and free any resources or memory that you might have allocated (either in the constructor, or throughout the lifespan of the object). A destructor always has the name of the class, preceded by a tilde (~). Destructors take no arguments and have no return value. If you were to declare a destructor for the `Cat` class, its declaration would look like the following:

```
~Cat();
```

Getting a Default Constructor and Destructor

Many types of constructors are available; some take arguments, others do not. The one that takes no arguments is called the default constructor. There is only one destructor. Like the default constructor, it takes no arguments.

It turns out that if you don't create a constructor or a destructor, the compiler provides one for you. The constructor that is provided by the compiler is the default constructor.

6

The default constructor and destructor created by the compiler don't have arguments. In addition, they don't appear to do anything! If you want them to do something, you must create your own default constructor or destructor.

Using the Default Constructor

What good is a constructor that does nothing? In part, it is a matter of form. All objects must be "constructed" and "destructed," and these do-nothing functions are called as a part of the process of constructing and destructing.

To declare an object without passing in parameters, such as

```
Cat Rags;            // Rags gets no parameters
```

you must have a constructor in the form

```
Cat();
```

When you define an object of a class, the constructor is called. If the Cat constructor took two parameters, you might define a Cat object by writing

```
Cat Frisky (5,7);
```

In this example, the first parameter might be its age and the second might be its weight. If the constructor took one parameter, you would write

```
Cat Frisky (3);
```

In the event that the constructor takes no parameters at all (that is, that it is a *default* constructor), you leave off the parentheses and write

```
Cat Frisky;
```

This is an exception to the rule that states all functions require parentheses, even if they take no parameters. This is why you are able to write

```
Cat Frisky;
```

This is interpreted as a call to the default constructor. It provides no parameters, and it leaves off the parentheses.

Note that you don't have to use the compiler-provided default constructor. You are always free to write your own default constructor—that is, a constructor with no parameters. You are free to give your default constructor a function body in which you might initialize the object. As a matter of form, it is always recommended that you define a constructor, and set the member variables to appropriate defaults, to ensure that the object will always behave correctly.

Also as a matter of form, if you declare a constructor, be certain to declare a destructor, even if your destructor does nothing. Although it is true that the default destructor would work correctly, it doesn't hurt to declare your own. It makes your code clearer.

Listing 6.4 rewrites the Cat class to use a nondefault constructor to initialize the Cat object, setting its age to whatever initial age you provide, and it demonstrates where the destructor is called.

LISTING 6.4   Using Constructors and Destructors

```
1:   // Demonstrates declaration of  constructors and
2:   // destructor for the Cat class
3:   // Programmer created default constructor
4:   #include <iostream>          // for cout
5:
6:   class Cat                    // begin declaration of the class
7:   {
8:     public:                    // begin public section
9:       Cat(int initialAge);     // constructor
10:      ~Cat();                  // destructor
11:      int GetAge();            // accessor function
12:      void SetAge(int age);    // accessor function
13:      void Meow();
14:    private:                   // begin private section
15:      int itsAge;              // member variable
16:   };
17:
18:   // constructor of Cat,
19:   Cat::Cat(int initialAge)
20:   {
21:       itsAge = initialAge;
22:   }
23:
24:   Cat::~Cat()                 // destructor, takes no action
25:   {
26:   }
27:
28:   // GetAge, Public accessor function
29:   // returns value of itsAge member
30:   int Cat::GetAge()
31:   {
32:       return itsAge;
33:   }
34:
35:   // Definition of SetAge, public
36:   // accessor function
37:   void Cat::SetAge(int age)
38:   {
39:       // set member variable itsAge to
```

6

LISTING 6.4   continued

```
40:     // value passed in by parameter age
41:     itsAge = age;
42:  }
43:
44:  // definition of Meow method
45:  // returns: void
46:  // parameters: None
47:  // action: Prints "meow" to screen
48:  void Cat::Meow()
49:  {
50:     std::cout << "Meow.\n";
51:  }
52:
53:  // create a cat, set its age, have it
54:  // meow, tell us its age, then meow again.
55:  int main()
56:  {
57:     Cat Frisky(5);
58:     Frisky.Meow();
59:     std::cout << "Frisky is a cat who is " ;
60:     std::cout << Frisky.GetAge() << " years old.\n";
61:     Frisky.Meow();
62:     Frisky.SetAge(7);
63:     std::cout << "Now Frisky is " ;
64:     std::cout << Frisky.GetAge() << " years old.\n";
65:     return 0;
66:  }
```

OUTPUT
```
Meow.
Frisky is a cat who is 5 years old.
Meow.
Now Frisky is 7 years old.
```

ANALYSIS   Listing 6.4 is similar to Listing 6.3, except that line 9 adds a constructor that takes an integer. Line 10 declares the destructor, which takes no parameters. Destructors never take parameters, and neither constructors nor destructors return a value—not even void.

Lines 19–22 show the implementation of the constructor. It is similar to the implementation of the SetAge() accessor function. As you can see, the class name precedes the constructor name. As mentioned before, this identifies the method, Cat() in this case as a part of the Cat class. This is a constructor, so there is no return value—not even void. This constructor does, however, take an initial value that is assigned to the data member, itsAge, on line 21.

Lines 24–26 show the implementation of the destructor ~Cat(). For now, this function does nothing, but you must include the definition of the function if you declare it in the class declaration. Like the constructor and other methods, this is also preceded by the class name. Like the constructor, but differing from other methods, no return time or parameters are included. This is standard for a destructor.

Line 57 contains the definition of a Cat object, Frisky. The value 5 is passed in to Frisky's constructor. No need exists to call SetAge() because Frisky was created with the value 5 in its member variable itsAge, as shown on line 60. On line 62, Frisky's itsAge variable is reassigned to 7. Line 64 prints the new value.

Do	Don't
DO use constructors to initialize your objects.	DON'T give constructors or destructors a return value.
DO add a destructor if you add a constructor.	DON'T give destructors parameters.

Including const Member Functions

You have used the const keyword to declare variables that would not change. You can also use the const keyword with member functions within a class. If you declare a class method const, you are promising that the method won't change the value of any of the members of the class.

To declare a class method constant, put the keyword const after the parentheses enclosing any parameters, but before the semicolon ending the method declaration. For example,

```
void SomeFunction() const;
```

This declares a constant member method called SomeFunction() that takes no arguments and returns void. You know this will not change any of the data members within the same class because it has been declared const.

Accessor functions that only get values are often declared as constant functions by using the const modifier. Earlier, you saw that the Cat class has two accessor functions:

```
void SetAge(int anAge);
int GetAge();
```

SetAge() cannot be const because it changes the member variable itsAge. GetAge(), on the other hand, can and should be const because it doesn't change the class at all.

6

`GetAge()` simply returns the current value of the member variable `itsAge`. Therefore, the declaration of these functions should be written like this:

```
void SetAge(int anAge);
int GetAge() const;
```

If you declare a function to be `const`, and the implementation of that function changes the object by changing the value of any of its members, the compiler flags it as an error. For example, if you wrote `GetAge()` in such a way that it kept count of the number of times that the `Cat` was asked its age, it would generate a compiler error. This is because you would be changing the `Cat` object when the method was called.

It is good programming practice to declare as many methods to be `const` as possible. Each time you do, you enable the compiler to catch your errors instead of letting your errors become bugs that will show up when your program is running.

Interface Versus Implementation

Clients are the parts of the program that create and use objects of your class. You can think of the public interface to your class—the class declaration—as a contract with these clients. The contract tells how your class will behave.

In the `Cat` class declaration, for example, you create a contract that every `Cat`'s age can be initialized in its constructor, assigned to by its `SetAge()` accessor function, and read by its `GetAge()` accessor. You also promise that every `Cat` will know how to `Meow()`. Note that you say nothing in the public interface about the member variable `itsAge`; that is an implementation detail that is not part of your contract. You will provide an age (`GetAge()`) and you will set an age (`SetAge()`), but the mechanism (`itsAge`) is invisible.

If you make `GetAge()` a `const` function—as you should—the contract also promises that `GetAge()` won't change the `Cat` on which it is called.

C++ is strongly typed, which means that the compiler enforces these contracts by giving you a compiler error when you violate them. Listing 6.5 demonstrates a program that doesn't compile because of violations of these contracts.

CAUTION

> Listing 6.5 does not compile!

LISTING 6.5   A Demonstration of Violations of the Interface

```
1:  // Demonstrates compiler errors
2:  // This program does not compile!
3:  #include <iostream>          // for cout
4:
5:  class Cat
6:  {
7:    public:
8:      Cat(int initialAge);
9:      ~Cat();
10:     int GetAge() const;        // const accessor function
11:     void SetAge (int age);
12:     void Meow();
13:   private:
14:     int itsAge;
15: };
16:
17: // constructor of Cat,
18: Cat::Cat(int initialAge)
19: {
20:     itsAge = initialAge;
21:     std::cout << "Cat Constructor\n";
22: }
23:
24: Cat::~Cat()                    // destructor, takes no action
25: {
26:     std::cout << "Cat Destructor\n";
27: }
28: // GetAge, const function
29: // but we violate const!
30: int Cat::GetAge() const
31: {
32:     return (itsAge++);         // violates const!
33: }
34:
35: // definition of SetAge, public
36: // accessor function
37:
38: void Cat::SetAge(int age)
39: {
40:     // set member variable its age to
41:     // value passed in by parameter age
42:     itsAge = age;
43: }
44:
45: // definition of Meow method
46: // returns: void
47: // parameters: None
48: // action: Prints "meow" to screen
```

6

LISTING 6.5   continued

```
49:   void Cat::Meow()
50:   {
51:       std::cout << "Meow.\n";
52:   }
53:
54:   // demonstrate various violations of the
55:   // interface, and resulting compiler errors
56:   int main()
57:   {
58:       Cat Frisky;                 // doesn't match declaration
59:       Frisky.Meow();
60:       Frisky.Bark();              // No, silly, cat's can't bark.
61:       Frisky.itsAge = 7;          // itsAge is private
62:       return 0;
63:   }
```

ANALYSIS   As it is written, this program doesn't compile. Therefore, there is no output.

This program was fun to write because so many errors are in it.

Line 10 declares GetAge() to be a const accessor function—as it should be. In the body of GetAge(), however, on line 32, the member variable itsAge is incremented. Because this method is declared to be const, it must not change the value of itsAge. Therefore, it is flagged as an error when the program is compiled.

On line 12, Meow() is not declared const. Although this is not an error, it is poor programming practice. A better design takes into account that this method doesn't change the member variables of Cat. Therefore, Meow() should be const.

Line 58 shows the creation of a Cat object, Frisky. Cat now has a constructor, which takes an integer as a parameter. This means that you must pass in a parameter. Because no parameter exists on line 58, it is flagged as an error.

NOTE   If you provide *any* constructor, the compiler will not provide one at all. Thus, if you create a constructor that takes a parameter, you then have no default constructor unless you write your own.

Line 60 shows a call to a class method, Bark(). Bark() was never declared. Therefore, it is illegal.

Line 61 shows itsAge being assigned the value 7. Because itsAge is a private data member, it is flagged as an error when the program is compiled.

Why Use the Compiler to Catch Errors?

Although it would be wonderful to write 100 percent bug-free code, few programmers have been able to do so. However, many programmers have developed a system to help minimize bugs by catching and fixing them early in the process.

Although compiler errors are infuriating and are the bane of a programmer's existence, they are far better than the alternative. A weakly typed language enables you to violate your contracts without a peep from the compiler, but your program crashes at runtime—when, for example, your boss is watching. Worse yet, testing is of comparatively little help in catching errors, because there are too many paths through real programs to have any hope of testing them all.

Compile-time errors—that is, errors found while you are compiling—are far better than runtime errors—that is, errors found while you are executing the program. This is because compile-time errors can be found much more reliably. It is possible to run a program many times without going down every possible code path. Thus, a runtime error can hide for quite a while. Compile-time errors are found every time you compile. Thus, they are easier to identify and fix. It is the goal of quality programming to ensure that the code has no runtime bugs. One tried-and-true technique to accomplish this is to use the compiler to catch your mistakes early in the development process.

Where to Put Class Declarations and Method Definitions

Each function that you declare for your class must have a definition. The definition is also called the function implementation. Like other functions, the definition of a class method has a function header and a function body.

The definition must be in a file that the compiler can find. Most C++ compilers want that file to end with .c or .cpp. This book uses .cpp, but check your compiler to see what it prefers.

6

NOTE

Many compilers assume that files ending with .c are C programs, and that C++ program files end with .cpp. You can use any extension, but .cpp minimizes confusion.

You are free to put the declaration in this file as well, but that is not good programming practice. The convention that most programmers adopt is to put the declaration into what is called a header file, usually with the same name but ending in .h, .hp, or .hpp. This book names the header files with .hpp, but check your compiler to see what it prefers.

For example, you put the declaration of the Cat class into a file named Cat.hpp, and you put the definition of the class methods into a file called Cat.cpp. You then attach the header file to the .cpp file by putting the following code at the top of Cat.cpp:

```
#include "Cat.hpp"
```

This tells the compiler to read Cat.hpp into the file, the same as if you had typed in its contents at this point. Be aware that some compilers insist that the capitalization agree between your #include statement and your file system.

Why bother separating the contents of your .hpp file and your .cpp file if you're just going to read the .hpp file back into the .cpp file? Most of the time, clients of your class don't care about the implementation specifics. Reading the header file tells them everything they need to know; they can ignore the implementation files. In addition, you might very well end up including the .hpp file into more than one .cpp file.

NOTE

> The declaration of a class tells the compiler what the class is, what data it holds, and what functions it has. The declaration of the class is called its interface because it tells the user how to interact with the class. The interface is usually stored in an .hpp file, which is referred to as a header file.
>
> The function definition tells the compiler how the function works. The function definition is called the implementation of the class method, and it is kept in a .cpp file. The implementation details of the class are of concern only to the author of the class. Clients of the class—that is, the parts of the program that use the class—don't need to know, and don't care, how the functions are implemented.

Inline Implementation

Just as you can ask the compiler to make a regular function inline, you can make class methods inline. The keyword inline appears before the return type. The inline implementation of the GetWeight() function, for example, looks like this:

```
inline int Cat::GetWeight()
{
    return itsWeight;     // return the Weight data member
}
```

You can also put the definition of a function into the declaration of the class, which automatically makes that function inline. For example,

```
class Cat
{
  public:
    int GetWeight() { return itsWeight; }  // inline
    void SetWeight(int aWeight);
};
```

Note the syntax of the `GetWeight()` definition. The body of the `inline` function begins immediately after the declaration of the class method; no semicolon is used after the parentheses. Like any function, the definition begins with an opening brace and ends with a closing brace. As usual, whitespace doesn't matter; you could have written the declaration as

```
class Cat
{
  public:
    int GetWeight() const
    {
        return itsWeight;
    }                       // inline
    void SetWeight(int aWeight);
};
```

Listings 6.6 and 6.7 re-create the `Cat` class, but they put the declaration in `Cat.hpp` and the implementation of the functions in `Cat.cpp`. Listing 6.7 also changes the accessor functions and the `Meow()` function to inline.

LISTING 6.6   Cat Class Declaration in `Cat.hpp`

```
 1:  #include <iostream>
 2:  class Cat
 3:  {
 4:    public:
 5:      Cat (int initialAge);
 6:      ~Cat();
 7:      int GetAge() const { return itsAge;}        // inline!
 8:      void SetAge (int age) { itsAge = age;}      // inline!
 9:      void Meow() const  { std::cout << "Meow.\n";}  // inline!
10:    private:
11:      int itsAge;
12:  };
```

6

LISTING 6.7   Cat Implementation in `Cat.cpp`

```
1:  // Demonstrates inline functions
2:  // and inclusion of header files
3:  // be sure to include the header files!
4:  #include "Cat.hpp"
5:
6:
7:  Cat::Cat(int initialAge)    //constructor
8:  {
9:      itsAge = initialAge;
10: }
11:
12: Cat::~Cat()               //destructor, takes no action
13: {
14: }
15:
16: // Create a cat, set its age, have it
17: // meow, tell us its age, then meow again.
18: int main()
19: {
20:     Cat Frisky(5);
21:     Frisky.Meow();
22:     std::cout << "Frisky is a cat who is " ;
23:     std::cout << Frisky.GetAge() << " years old.\n";
24:     Frisky.Meow();
25:     Frisky.SetAge(7);
26:     std::cout << "Now Frisky is " ;
27:     std::cout << Frisky.GetAge() << " years old.\n";
28:     return 0;
29: }
```

OUTPUT

```
Meow.
Frisky is a cat who is 5 years old.
Meow.
Now Frisky is 7 years old.
```

ANALYSIS   The code presented in Listing 6.6 and Listing 6.7 is similar to the code in Listing 6.4, except that three of the methods are written inline in the declaration file and the declaration has been separated into `Cat.hpp` (Listing 6.6).

`GetAge()` is declared on line 6 of `Cat.hpp`, and its inline implementation is provided. Lines 7 and 8 provide more inline functions, but the functionality of these functions is unchanged from the previous "outline" implementations.

Line 4 of `Cat.cpp` (Listing 6.7) shows #include `"Cat.hpp"`, which brings in the listings from `Cat.hpp`. By including `Cat.hpp`, you have told the precompiler to read `Cat.hpp` into the file as if it had been typed there, starting on line 5.

This technique enables you to put your declarations into a different file from your implementation, yet have that declaration available when the compiler needs it. This is a very common technique in C++ programming. Typically, class declarations are in an `.hpp` file that is then `#include`d into the associated `.cpp` file.

Lines 18–29 repeat the `main` function from Listing 6.4. This shows that making these functions inline doesn't change their performance.

Classes with Other Classes as Member Data

It is not uncommon to build up a complex class by declaring simpler classes and including them in the declaration of the more complicated class. For example, you might declare a wheel class, a motor class, a transmission class, and so forth, and then combine them into a car class. This declares a has-a relationship. A car has a motor, it has wheels, and it has a transmission.

Consider a second example. A rectangle is composed of lines. A line is defined by two points. A point is defined by an x-coordinate and a y-coordinate. Listing 6.8 shows a complete declaration of a `Rectangle` class, as might appear in `Rectangle.hpp`. Because a rectangle is defined as four lines connecting four points, and each point refers to a coordinate on a graph, you first declare a `Point` class to hold the x- and y-coordinates of each point. Listing 6.9 provides the implementation for both classes.

LISTING 6.8 Declaring a Complete Class

```
1:  // Begin Rectangle.hpp
2:  #include <iostream>
3:  class Point      // holds x,y coordinates
4:  {
5:    // no constructor, use default
6:    public:
7:      void SetX(int x) { itsX = x; }
8:      void SetY(int y) { itsY = y; }
9:      int GetX()const { return itsX;}
10:     int GetY()const { return itsY;}
11:   private:
12:     int itsX;
13:     int itsY;
14: };   // end of Point class declaration
15:
16:
17: class  Rectangle
18: {
19:   public:
20:     Rectangle (int top, int left, int bottom, int right);
```

6

LISTING 6.8 continued

```
21:        ~Rectangle () {}
22:
23:        int GetTop() const { return itsTop; }
24:        int GetLeft() const { return itsLeft; }
25:        int GetBottom() const { return itsBottom; }
26:        int GetRight() const { return itsRight; }
27:
28:        Point  GetUpperLeft() const { return itsUpperLeft; }
29:        Point  GetLowerLeft() const { return itsLowerLeft; }
30:        Point  GetUpperRight() const { return itsUpperRight; }
31:        Point  GetLowerRight() const { return itsLowerRight; }
32:
33:        void SetUpperLeft(Point Location)   {itsUpperLeft = Location;}
34:        void SetLowerLeft(Point Location)   {itsLowerLeft = Location;}
35:        void SetUpperRight(Point Location)  {itsUpperRight = Location;}
36:        void SetLowerRight(Point Location)  {itsLowerRight = Location;}
37:
38:        void SetTop(int top) { itsTop = top; }
39:        void SetLeft (int left) { itsLeft = left; }
40:        void SetBottom (int bottom) { itsBottom = bottom; }
41:        void SetRight (int right) { itsRight = right; }
42:
43:        int GetArea() const;
44:
45:     private:
46:        Point   itsUpperLeft;
47:        Point   itsUpperRight;
48:        Point   itsLowerLeft;
49:        Point   itsLowerRight;
50:        int     itsTop;
51:        int     itsLeft;
52:        int     itsBottom;
53:        int     itsRight;
54:     };
55:     // end Rectangle.hpp
```

LISTING 6.9 Rect.cpp

```
1:  // Begin Rect.cpp
2:  #include "Rectangle.hpp"
3:  Rectangle::Rectangle(int top, int left, int bottom, int right)
4:  {
5:     itsTop = top;
6:     itsLeft = left;
7:     itsBottom = bottom;
8:     itsRight = right;
```

LISTING 6.9 continued

```
 9:
10:        itsUpperLeft.SetX(left);
11:        itsUpperLeft.SetY(top);
12:
13:        itsUpperRight.SetX(right);
14:        itsUpperRight.SetY(top);
15:
16:        itsLowerLeft.SetX(left);
17:        itsLowerLeft.SetY(bottom);
18:
19:        itsLowerRight.SetX(right);
20:        itsLowerRight.SetY(bottom);
21:    }
22:
23:
24:    // compute area of the rectangle by finding sides,
25:    // establish width and height and then multiply
26:    int Rectangle::GetArea() const
27:    {
28:        int Width = itsRight-itsLeft;
29:        int Height = itsTop - itsBottom;
30:        return (Width * Height);
31:    }
32:
33:    int main()
34:    {
35:        //initialize a local Rectangle variable
36:        Rectangle MyRectangle (100, 20, 50, 80 );
37:
38:        int Area = MyRectangle.GetArea();
39:
40:        std::cout << "Area: " << Area << "\n";
41:        std::cout << "Upper Left X Coordinate: ";
42:        std::cout << MyRectangle.GetUpperLeft().GetX();
43:        return 0;
44:    }
```

OUTPUT
```
Area: 3000
Upper Left X Coordinate: 20
```

ANALYSIS Lines 3–14 in Rectangle.hpp (Listing 6.8) declare the class Point, which is used to hold a specific x- and y-coordinate on a graph. As written, this program doesn't use Points much; however, other drawing methods require Points.

6

NOTE Some compilers report an error if you declare a class named Rectangle. This is usually because of the existence of an internal class named Rectangle. If you have this problem, simply rename your class to myRectangle.

Within the declaration of the class Point, you declare two member variables (itsX and itsY) on lines 12 and 13. These variables hold the values of the coordinates. As the x-coordinate increases, you move to the right on the graph. As the y-coordinate increases, you move upward on the graph. Other graphs use different systems. Some windowing programs, for example, increase the y-coordinate as you move down in the window.

The Point class uses inline accessor functions declared on lines 7–10 to get and set the x and y points. The Points class uses the default constructor and destructor. Therefore, you must set their coordinates explicitly.

Line 17 begins the declaration of a Rectangle class. A Rectangle consists of four points that represent the corners of the Rectangle.

The constructor for the Rectangle (line 20) takes four integers, known as top, left, bottom, and right. The four parameters to the constructor are copied into four member variables (Listing 6.9), and then the four Points are established.

In addition to the usual accessor functions, Rectangle has a function GetArea() declared on line 43. Instead of storing the area as a variable, the GetArea() function computes the area on lines 28 and 29 of Listing 6.9. To do this, it computes the width and the height of the rectangle, and then it multiplies these two values.

Getting the x-coordinate of the upper-left corner of the rectangle requires that you access the UpperLeft point and ask that point for its x value. Because GetUpperLeft() is a method of Rectangle, it can directly access the private data of Rectangle, including itsUpperLeft. Because itsUpperLeft is a Point and Point's itsX value is private, GetUpperLeft() cannot directly access this data. Rather, it must use the public accessor function GetX() to obtain that value.

Line 33 of Listing 6.9 is the beginning of the body of the actual program. Until line 36, no memory has been allocated, and nothing has really happened. The only thing you've done is tell the compiler how to make a point and how to make a rectangle, in case one is ever needed.

On line 36, you define a Rectangle by passing in values for top, left, bottom, and right.

On line 38, you make a local variable, Area, of type int. This variable holds the area of the Rectangle that you've created. You initialize Area with the value returned by Rectangle's GetArea() function. A client of Rectangle could create a Rectangle object and get its area without ever looking at the implementation of GetArea().

Rectangle.hpp is shown in Listing 6.8. Just by looking at the header file, which contains the declaration of the Rectangle class, the programmer knows that GetArea() returns an int. How GetArea() does its magic is not of concern to the user of class Rectangle. In fact, the author of Rectangle could change GetArea() without affecting the programs that use the Rectangle class as long as it still returned an integer.

Line 42 of Listing 6.9 might look a little strange, but if you think about what is happening, it should be clear. In this line of code, you are getting the x-coordinate from the upper-left point of your rectangle. In this line of code, you are calling the GetUpperLeft() method of your rectangle, which returns to you a Point. From this Point, you want to get the x-coordinate. You saw that the accessor for an x-coordinate in the Point class is GetX(). Line 42 simply puts the GetUpperLeft() and GetX() accessors together:

```
MyRectangle.GetUpperLeft().GetX();
```

This gets the x-coordinate from the upper-left point coordinate that is accessed from the MyRectangle object.

FAQ

What is the difference between declaring and defining?

Answer: A declaration introduces a name of something but does not allocate memory. A definition allocates memory.

With a few exceptions, all declarations are also definitions. The most important exceptions are the declaration of a global function (a prototype) and the declaration of a class (usually in a header file).

6

Exploring Structures

A very close cousin to the keyword class is the keyword struct, which is used to declare a structure. In C++, a struct is the same as a class, except that its members are public by default. You can declare a structure exactly as you declare a class, and you can give it the same data members and functions. In fact, if you follow the good programming practice of always explicitly declaring the private and public sections of your class, no difference will exist whatsoever.

Try re-entering Listing 6.8 with these changes:

- On line 3, change `class Point` to `struct Point`.
- On line 17, change `class Rectangle` to `struct Rectangle`.

Now run the program again and compare the output. No change should have occurred.

You're probably wondering why two keywords do the same thing. This is an accident of history. When C++ was developed, it was built as an extension of the C language. C has structures, although C structures don't have class methods. Bjarne Stroustrup, the creator of C++, built upon `struct`s, but he changed the name to `class` to represent the new, expanded functionality, and the change in the default visibility of members. This also allowed the continued use of a vast library of C functions in C++ programs.

Do	Don't
DO put your class declaration in an `.hpp` (header) file and your member functions in a `.cpp` file. DO use const whenever you can.	DON'T move on until you understand classes.

Summary

Today, you learned how to create new data types using classes. You learned how to define variables of these new types, which are called objects.

A class can have data members, which are variables of various types, including other classes. A class can also include member functions—also known as methods. You use these member functions to manipulate the member data and to perform other services.

Class members, both data and functions, can be public or private. Public members are accessible to any part of your program. Private members are accessible only to the member functions of the class. Members of a class are private by default.

It is good programming practice to isolate the interface, or declaration, of the class in a header file. You usually do this in a file with an `.hpp` extension and then use it in your code files (`.cpp`) using an `include` statement. The implementation of the class methods is written in a file with a `.cpp` extension.

Class constructors can be used to initialize object data members. Class destructors are executed when an object is destroyed and are often used to free memory and other resources that might be allocated by methods of the class.

Q&A

Q How big is a class object?

A A class object's size in memory is determined by the sum of the sizes of its member variables. Class methods take up just a small amount of memory, which is used to store information on the location of the method (a pointer).

Some compilers align variables in memory in such a way that two-byte variables actually consume somewhat more than two bytes. Check your compiler manual to be certain, but at this point you do not need to be concerned with these details.

Q If I declare a class Cat with a private member itsAge and then define two Cat objects, Frisky and Boots, can Boots access Frisky's itsAge member variable?

A No. Different instances of a class can access each other's nonpublic data. In other words, if Frisky and Boots are both instances of Cat, Frisky's member functions can access Frisky's data and but not Boots's data.

Q Why shouldn't I make all the member data public?

A Making member data private enables the client of the class to use the data without being dependent on how it is stored or computed. For example, if the Cat class has a method GetAge(), clients of the Cat class can ask for the Cat's age without knowing or caring if the Cat stores its age in a member variable or computes its age on-the-fly. This means the programmer of the Cat class can change the design of the Cat class in the future without requiring all of the users of Cat to change their programs as well.

Q If using a const function to change the class causes a compiler error, why shouldn't I just leave out the word const and be certain to avoid errors?

A If your member function logically shouldn't change the class, using the keyword const is a good way to enlist the compiler in helping you find mistakes. For example, GetAge() might have no reason to change the Cat class, but your implementation has this line:

```
if (itsAge = 100) cout << "Hey! You're 100 years old\n";
```

Declaring GetAge() to be const causes this code to be flagged as an error. You meant to check whether itsAge is equal to 100, but instead you inadvertently assigned 100 to itsAge. Because this assignment changes the class—and you said this method would not change the class—the compiler is able to find the error.

This kind of mistake can be hard to find just by scanning the code. The eye often sees only what it expects to see. More importantly, the program might appear to run correctly, but itsAge has now been set to a bogus number. This causes problems sooner or later.

6

Q Is there ever a reason to use a structure in a C++ program?

A Many C++ programmers reserve the `struct` keyword for classes that have no functions. This is a throwback to the old C structures, which could not have functions. Frankly, it is confusing and poor programming practice. Today's methodless structure might need methods tomorrow. Then, you'll be forced either to change the type to `class` or to break your rule and end up with a structure with methods. If you need to call a legacy C function that requires a particular struct, then you would have the only good reason to use one.

Q Some people working with object-oriented programming use the term "instantiation." What is this?

A Instantiation is simply a fancy word for the process of creating an object from a class. A specific object defined as being of the type of a class is a single *instance* of a class.

Workshop

The Workshop provides quiz questions to help you solidify your understanding of the material covered and exercises to provide you with experience in using what you've learned. Try to answer the quiz and exercise questions before checking the answers in Appendix D, and be certain you understand the answers before continuing to tomorrow's lesson, where you will learn more about controlling the flow of your program.

Quiz

1. What is the dot operator, and what is it used for?
2. Which sets aside memory—a declaration or a definition?
3. Is the declaration of a class its interface or its implementation?
4. What is the difference between public and private data members?
5. Can member functions be private?
6. Can member data be public?
7. If you declare two `Cat` objects, can they have different values in their `itsAge` member data?
8. Do class declarations end with a semicolon? Do class method definitions?
9. What would the header be for a `Cat` function, `Meow`, that takes no parameters and returns void?
10. What function is called to initialize a class?

Exercises

1. Write the code that declares a class called `Employee` with these data members: `itsAge`, `itsYearsOfService`, and `itsSalary`.

2. Rewrite the `Employee` class declaration to make the data members private, and provide public accessor methods to get and set each of the data members.

3. Write a program with the `Employee` class that makes two employees; sets their `itsAge`, `itsYearsOfService`, and `itsSalary`; and prints their values. You'll need to add the code for the accessor methods as well.

4. Continuing from Exercise 3, write the code for a method of `Employee` that reports how many thousands of dollars the employee earns, rounded to the nearest 1,000.

5. Change the `Employee` class so that you can initialize `itsAge`, `itsYearsOfService`, and `itsSalary` when you create the employee.

6. **BUG BUSTERS:** What is wrong with the following declaration?

```
class Square
{
  public:
    int Side;
}
```

7. **BUG BUSTERS:** Why isn't the following class declaration very useful?

```
class Cat
{
    int GetAge() const;
  private:
    int itsAge;
};
```

8. **BUG BUSTERS:** What three bugs in this code should the compiler find?

```
class  TV
{
  public:
    void SetStation(int Station);
    int GetStation() const;
  private:
    int itsStation;
};

int main()
{
    TV myTV;
    myTV.itsStation = 9;
    TV.SetStation(10);
    TV myOtherTv(2);
}
```

6

DAY 7

More on Program Flow

Programs accomplish most of their work by branching and looping. On Day 4, "Creating Expressions and Statements," you learned how to branch your program using the `if` statement.

Today, you will learn

- What loops are and how they are used
- How to build various loops
- An alternative to deeply nested `if...else` statements

Looping

Many programming problems are solved by repeatedly acting on the same data. Two ways to do this are recursion (discussed on Day 5, "Organizing into Functions") and iteration. Iteration means doing the same thing again and again. The principal method of iteration is the loop.

The Roots of Looping: `goto`

In the primitive days of early computer science, programs were nasty, brutish, and short. Loops consisted of a label, some statements, and a jump that went to the label.

In C++, a label is just a name followed by a colon (:). The label is placed to the left of a legal C++ statement. A jump is accomplished by writing `goto` followed by the name of a label. Listing 7.1 illustrates this primitive way of looping.

LISTING 7.1 Looping with the Keyword `goto`

```
1:  // Listing 7.1
2:  // Looping with goto
3:  #include <iostream>
4:
5:  int main()
6:  {
7:      using namespace std;
8:      int counter = 0;        // initialize counter
9:  loop:
10:      counter ++;            // top of the loop
11:      cout << "counter: " << counter << endl;
12:      if (counter < 5)       // test the value
13:         goto loop;          // jump to the top
14:
15:      cout << "Complete. Counter: " << counter << endl;
16:      return 0;
17:  }
```

OUTPUT
```
counter: 1
counter: 2
counter: 3
counter: 4
counter: 5
Complete. Counter: 5.
```

ANALYSIS On line 8, counter is initialized to zero. A label called `loop` is on line 9, marking the top of the loop. counter is incremented and its new value is printed on line 11. The value of counter is tested on line 12. If the value is less than 5, the `if` statement is true and the `goto` statement is executed. This causes program execution to jump back to the `loop` label on line 9. The program continues looping until counter is equal to 5, at which time it "falls through" the loop and the final output is printed.

Why `goto` Is Shunned

As a rule, programmers avoid `goto`, and with good reason. `goto` statements can cause a jump to any location in your source code, backward or forward. The indiscriminate use of goto statements has caused tangled, miserable, impossible-to-read programs known as "spaghetti code."

The goto Statement

To use the goto statement, you write goto followed by a label name. This causes an unconditioned jump to the label.

Example

```
if (value > 10)
    goto end;
if (value < 10)
    goto end;
cout << "value is 10!";
end:
    cout << "done";
```

To avoid the use of goto, more sophisticated, tightly controlled looping commands have been introduced: for, while, and do...while.

Using while Loops

A while loop causes your program to repeat a sequence of statements as long as the starting condition remains true. In the goto example in Listing 7.1, the counter was incremented until it was equal to 5. Listing 7.2 shows the same program rewritten to take advantage of a while loop.

LISTING 7.2 while Loops

```
1:  // Listing 7.2
2:  // Looping with while
3:  #include <iostream>
4:
5:  int main()
6:  {
7:      using namespace std;
8:      int counter = 0;        // initialize the condition
9:
10:     while(counter < 5)      // test condition still true
11:     {
12:         counter++;          // body of the loop
13:         cout << "counter: " << counter << endl;
14:     }
15:
16:     cout << "Complete. Counter: " << counter << endl;
17:     return 0;
18: }
```

7

OUTPUT
```
counter: 1
counter: 2
counter: 3
counter: 4
counter: 5
Complete. Counter: 5.
```

ANALYSIS This simple program demonstrates the fundamentals of the while loop. On line 8, an integer variable called counter is created and initialized to zero. This is then used as a part of a condition. The condition is tested, and if it is true, the body of the while loop is executed. In this case, the condition tested on line 10 is whether counter is less than 5. If the condition is true, the body of the loop is executed; on line 12, the counter is incremented, and on line 13, the value is printed. When the conditional statement on line 10 fails (when counter is no longer less than 5), the entire body of the while loop (lines 11–14) is skipped. Program execution falls through to line 15.

It is worth noting here that it is a good idea to always use braces around the block executed by a loop, even when it is just a single line of code. This avoids the common error of inadvertently putting a semicolon at the end of a loop and causing it to endlessly repeat—for instance,

```
int counter = 0;
while ( counter < 5 );
    counter++;
```

In this example, the counter++ is never executed.

The while Statement

The syntax for the while statement is as follows:

```
while ( condition )
    statement;
```

condition is any C++ expression, and statement is any valid C++ statement or block of statements. When condition evaluates true, statement is executed, and then condition is tested again. This continues until condition tests false, at which time the while loop terminates and execution continues on the first line below statement.

Example

```
// count to 10
int x = 0;
while (x < 10)
    cout << "X: " << x++;
```

Exploring More Complicated `while` Statements

The condition tested by a `while` loop can be as complex as any legal C++ expression. This can include expressions produced using the logical && (AND), || (OR), and ! (NOT) operators. Listing 7.3 is a somewhat more complicated `while` statement.

LISTING 7.3 Complex `while` Loops

```
1:  // Listing 7.3
2:  // Complex while statements
3:  #include <iostream>
4:
5:  int main()
6:  {
7:      using namespace std;
8:      unsigned short small;
9:      unsigned long  large;
10:     const unsigned short MAXSMALL=65535;
11:
12:     cout << "Enter a small number: ";
13:     cin >> small;
14:     cout << "Enter a large number: ";
15:     cin >> large;
16:
17:     cout << "small: " << small << "...";
18:
19:     // for each iteration, test two conditions
20:     while (small < large  && small < MAXSMALL)
21:     {
22:         if (small % 5000 == 0)  // write a dot every 5k lines
23:             cout << ".";
24:
25:         small++;
26:         large-=2;
27:     }
28:
29:     cout << "\nSmall: " << small << " Large: " << large << endl;
30:     return 0;
31: }
```

OUTPUT

```
Enter a small number: 2
Enter a large number: 100000
small: 2.........
Small: 33335 Large: 33334
```

ANALYSIS This program is a game. Enter two numbers, one small and one large. The smaller number will count up by ones, and the larger number will count down by twos. The goal of the game is to guess when they'll meet.

7

On lines 12–15, the numbers are entered. Line 20 sets up a `while` loop, which will continue only as long as two conditions are met:

1. Small is not bigger than large.

2. Small doesn't overrun the size of a small integer (`MAXSMALL`).

On line 22, the value in `small` is calculated modulo 5,000. This does not change the value in `small`; however, it only returns the value 0 when `small` is an exact multiple of 5,000. Each time it is, a dot (`.`) is printed to the screen to show progress. On line 25, `small` is incremented, and on line 26, `large` is decremented by 2.

When either of the two conditions in the `while` loop fails, the loop ends and execution of the program continues after the `while` loop's closing brace on line 27.

NOTE

> The modulus operator (%) and compound conditions were covered on Day 3, "Working with Variables and Constants."

Introducing `continue` and `break`

At times, you'll want to return to the top of a `while` loop before the entire set of statements in the `while` loop is executed. The `continue` statement jumps back to the top of the loop.

At other times, you might want to exit the loop before the exit conditions are met. The `break` statement immediately exits the `while` loop, and program execution resumes after the closing brace.

Listing 7.4 demonstrates the use of these statements. This time, the game has become more complicated. The user is invited to enter a small number and a large number, a skip number, and a target number. The small number will be incremented by one, and the large number will be decremented by 2. The decrement will be skipped each time the small number is a multiple of the skip. The game ends if `small` becomes larger than `large`. If the large number reaches the target exactly, a statement is printed and the game stops.

The user's goal is to put in a target number for the large number that will stop the game.

LISTING 7.4   break and continue

```
1:  // Listing 7.4 -  Demonstrates break and continue
2:  #include <iostream>
3:
4:  int main()
5:  {
6:      using namespace std;
7:
8:      unsigned short small;
9:      unsigned long  large;
10:     unsigned long  skip;
11:     unsigned long target;
12:     const unsigned short MAXSMALL=65535;
13:
14:     cout << "Enter a small number: ";
15:     cin >> small;
16:     cout << "Enter a large number: ";
17:     cin >> large;
18:     cout << "Enter a skip number: ";
19:     cin >> skip;
20:     cout << "Enter a target number: ";
21:     cin >> target;
22:
23:     cout << "\n";
24:
25:     // set up 2 stop conditions for the loop
26:     while (small < large && small < MAXSMALL)
27:     {
28:         small++;
29:
30:         if (small % skip == 0)  // skip the decrement?
31:         {
32:             cout << "skipping on " << small << endl;
33:             continue;
34:         }
35:
36:         if (large == target)    // exact match for the target?
37:         {
38:             cout << "Target reached!";
39:             break;
40:         }
41:
42:         large-=2;
43:     }                       // end of while loop
44:
45:     cout << "\nSmall: " << small << " Large: " << large << endl;
46:     return 0;
47:  }
```

7

OUTPUT

```
Enter a small number: 2
Enter a large number: 20
Enter a skip number: 4
Enter a target number: 6

skipping on 4
skipping on 8

Small: 10 Large: 8
```

ANALYSIS In this play, the user lost; small became larger than large before the target number of 6 was reached.

On line 26, the while conditions are tested. If small continues to be smaller than large and if small hasn't overrun the maximum value for a small int, the body of the while loop is entered.

On line 30, the small value is taken modulo the skip value. If small is a multiple of skip, the continue statement is reached and program execution jumps to the top of the loop back at line 26. This effectively skips over the test for the target and the decrement of large.

On line 36, target is tested against the value for large. If they are the same, the user has won. A message is printed and the break statement is reached and executed. This causes an immediate break out of the while loop, and program execution resumes on line 44.

NOTE

Both continue and break should be used with caution. They are the next most dangerous commands after goto, for much the same reason. Programs that suddenly change direction are harder to understand, and liberal use of continue and break can render even a small while loop unreadable.

A need for breaking within a loop often indicates that the terminating condition of the loop has not been set up with the appropriate Boolean expression. It is often better to use an if statement within a loop to skip some lines than to use a breaking statement.

The continue Statement

continue; causes a while, do...while, or for loop to begin again at the top of the loop.

See Listing 7.4 for an example of using continue.

The break Statement

break; causes the immediate end of a while, do...while, or for loop. Execution jumps to the closing brace.

Example

```
while (condition)
{
    if (condition2)
        break;
    // statements;
}
```

Examining while (true) Loops

The condition tested in a while loop can be any valid C++ expression. As long as that condition remains true, the while loop continues. You can create a loop that never ends by using the value true for the condition to be tested. Listing 7.5 demonstrates counting to 10 using this construct.

LISTING 7.5 while Loops

```
 1:  // Listing 7.5
 2:  // Demonstrates a while true loop
 3:  #include <iostream>
 4:
 5:  int main()
 6:  {
 7:      int counter = 0;
 8:
 9:      while (true)
10:      {
11:          counter ++;
12:          if (counter > 10)
13:              break;
14:      }
15:      std::cout << "Counter: " << counter << std::endl;
16:      return 0;
17:  }
```

OUTPUT

```
Counter: 11
```

ANALYSIS   On line 9, a while loop is set up with a condition that can never be false. The loop increments the counter variable on line 11, and then on line 12 it tests to see

7

whether counter has gone past 10. If it hasn't, the while loop iterates. If counter is greater than 10, the break on line 13 ends the while loop, and program execution falls through to line 15, where the results are printed.

This program works, but it isn't pretty. This is a good example of using the wrong tool for the job. The same thing can be accomplished by putting the test of counter's value where it belongs—in the while condition.

CAUTION | Eternal loops such as while (true) can cause your computer to hang if the exit condition is never reached. Use these with caution and test them thoroughly.

C++ gives you many ways to accomplish the same task. The real trick is picking the right tool for the particular job.

Do	**Don't**
DO use while loops to iterate while a condition is true.	**DON'T** use the goto statement.
DO exercise caution when using continue and break statements.	**DON'T** forget the difference between continue and break. continue goes to the top; break goes to the bottom.
DO be certain your loop will eventually end.	

Implementing do...while Loops

It is possible that the body of a while loop will never execute. The while statement checks its condition before executing any of its statements, and if the condition evaluates false, the entire body of the while loop is skipped. Listing 7.6 illustrates this.

LISTING 7.6   Skipping the Body of the while Loop

```
1:  // Listing 7.6
2:  // Demonstrates skipping the body of
3:  // the while loop when the condition is false.
4:
5:  #include <iostream>
6:
```

LISTING 7.6   continued

```
 7:   int main()
 8:   {
 9:       int counter;
10:       std::cout << "How many hellos?: ";
11:       std::cin >> counter;
12:       while (counter > 0)
13:       {
14:           std::cout << "Hello!\n";
15:           counter--;
16:       }
17:       std::cout << "Counter is OutPut: " << counter;
18:       return 0;
19:   }
```

OUTPUT

```
How many hellos?: 2
Hello!
Hello!
Counter is OutPut: 0

How many hellos?: 0
Counter is OutPut: 0
```

ANALYSIS   The user is prompted for a starting value on line 10. This starting value is stored in the integer variable counter. The value of counter is tested on line 12 and decremented in the body of the while loop. In the output, you can see that the first time through, counter was set to 2, and so the body of the while loop ran twice. The second time through, however, the 0 was entered. The value of counter was tested on line 12 and the condition was false; counter was not greater than 0. The entire body of the while loop was skipped, and Hello was never printed.

What if you want to ensure that Hello is always printed at least once? The while loop can't accomplish this because the if condition is tested before any printing is done. You can force the issue with an if statement just before entering the while loop

```
if (counter < 1)  // force a minimum value
    counter = 1;
```

but that is what programmers call a "kludge" (pronounced klooj to rhyme with stooge), an ugly and inelegant solution.

7

Using do...while

The do...while loop executes the body of the loop before its condition is tested, thus ensuring that the body always executes at least one time. Listing 7.7 rewrites Listing 7.6, this time using a do...while loop.

LISTING 7.7   Demonstrates do...while Loop

```
1:  // Listing 7.7
2:  // Demonstrates do while
3:
4:  #include <iostream>
5:
6:  int main()
7:  {
8:     using namespace std;
9:     int counter;
10:    cout << "How many hellos? ";
11:    cin >> counter;
12:    do
13:    {
14:       cout << "Hello\n";
15:       counter--;
16:    } while (counter >0 );
17:    cout << "Counter is: " << counter << endl;
18:    return 0;
19: }
```

OUTPUT

```
How many hellos? 2
Hello
Hello
Counter is: 0
```

ANALYSIS   Like the previous program, Listing 7.7 prints the word "Hello" to the console a specified number of times. Unlike the preceding program, however, this program will always print at least once.

The user is prompted for a starting value on line 10, which is stored in the integer variable counter. In the do...while loop, the body of the loop is entered before the condition is tested, and, therefore, the body of the loop is guaranteed to run at least once. On line 14, the hello message is printed, on line 15 the counter is decremented, and then finally, on line 16 the condition is tested. If the condition evaluates true, execution jumps to the top of the loop on line 13; otherwise, it falls through to line 17.

The continue and break statements work in the do...while loop exactly as they do in the while loop. The only difference between a while loop and a do...while loop is when the condition is tested.

The do...while Statement

The syntax for the do...while statement is as follows:

```
do
   statement
while (condition);
```

statement is executed, and then *condition* is evaluated. If *condition* is true, the loop is repeated; otherwise, the loop ends. The statements and conditions are otherwise identical to the while loop.

Example 1

```
// count to 10
int x = 0;
do
   cout << "X: " << x++;
while (x < 10)
```

Example 2

```
// print lowercase alphabet.
char ch = 'a';
do
{
   cout << ch << ' ';
   ch++;
} while ( ch <= 'z' );
```

Do	Don't
DO use do...while when you want to ensure the loop is executed at least once.	**DON'T** use break and continue with loops unless it is clear what your code is doing. There are often clearer ways to accomplish the same tasks.
DO use while loops when you want to skip the loop if the condition is false.	**DON'T** use the goto statement.
DO test all loops to be certain they do what you expect.	

Looping with the for Statement

When programming while loops, you'll often find yourself going through three steps: setting up a starting condition, testing to see whether the condition is true, and incrementing or otherwise changing a variable each time through the loop. Listing 7.8 demonstrates this.

7

LISTING 7.8 while Reexamined

```
 1:  // Listing 7.8
 2:  // Looping with while
 3:
 4:  #include <iostream>
 5:
 6:  int main()
 7:  {
 8:      int counter = 0;
 9:
10:      while(counter < 5)
11:      {
12:          counter++;
13:          std::cout << "Looping!  ";
14:      }
15:
16:      std::cout << "\nCounter: " << counter << std::endl;
17:      return 0;
18:  }
```

OUTPUT   Looping! Looping! Looping! Looping! Looping!
             Counter: 5.

ANALYSIS   In this listing, you can see that three steps are occurring. First, the starting condition is set on line 8: counter is initialized to 0. On line 10, the test of the condition occurs when counter is tested to see if it is less than 5. Finally, the counter variable is incremented on line 12. This loop prints a simple message at line 13. As you can imagine, more important work could be done for each increment of the counter.

A for loop combines the three steps into one statement. The three steps are initializing, testing, and incrementing. A for statement consists of the keyword for followed by a pair of parentheses. Within the parentheses are three statements separated by semicolons:

```
for( initialization; test ; action )
{
    ...
}
```

The first expression, initialization, is the starting conditions or initialization. Any legal C++ statement can be put here, but typically this is used to create and initialize a counting variable. The second expression, test, is the test, and any legal C++ expression can be used here. This test serves the same role as the condition in the while loop. The third expression, action, is the action that will take place. This action is typically the increment or decrement of a value, though any legal C++ statement can be put here. Listing 7.9 demonstrates a for loop by rewriting Listing 7.8.

LISTING 7.9 Demonstrating the for Loop

```
1:  // Listing 7.9
2:  // Looping with for
3:
4:  #include <iostream>
5:
6:  int main()
7:  {
8:      int counter;
9:      for (counter = 0; counter < 5; counter++)
10:         std::cout << "Looping! ";
11:
12:     std::cout << "\nCounter: " << counter << std::endl;
13:     return 0;
14: }
```

OUTPUT

```
Looping!  Looping!  Looping!  Looping!  Looping!
Counter: 5.
```

ANALYSIS The for statement on line 9 combines the initialization of counter, the test that counter is less than 5, and the increment of counter all into one line. The body of the for statement is on line 10. Of course, a block could be used here as well.

The for Statement

The syntax for the for statement is as follows:

```
for (initialization; test; action )
    statement;
```

The *initialization* statement is used to initialize the state of a counter, or to otherwise prepare for the loop. *test* is any C++ expression and is evaluated each time through the loop. If *test* is true, the body of the for loop is executed and then the action in the header is executed (typically the counter is incremented).

Example 1

```
// print Hello ten times
for (int i = 0; i<10; i++)
    cout << "Hello! ";
```

Example 2

```
for (int i = 0; i < 10; i++)
{
    cout << "Hello!" << endl;
    cout << "the value of i is: " << i << endl;
}
```

7

Advanced for Loops

for statements are powerful and flexible. The three independent statements (*initial-ization*, *test*, and *action*) lend themselves to a number of variations.

Multiple Initialization and Increments

It is not uncommon to initialize more than one variable, to test a compound logical expression, and to execute more than one statement. The initialization and the action can be replaced by multiple C++ statements, each separated by a comma. Listing 7.10 demonstrates the initialization and increment of two variables.

LISTING **7.10**   Demonstrating Multiple Statements in for Loops

```
 1:   //Listing 7.10
 2:   // Demonstrates multiple statements in
 3:   // for loops
 4:   #include <iostream>
 5:
 6:   int main()
 7:   {
 8:
 9:       for (int i=0, j=0; i<3; i++, j++)
10:           std::cout << "i: " << i << " j: " << j << std::endl;
11:       return 0;
12:   }
```

OUTPUT
```
i: 0   j: 0
i: 1   j: 1
i: 2   j: 2
```

ANALYSIS   On line 9, two variables, i and j, are each initialized with the value 0. A comma is used to separate the two separate expressions. You can also see that these initializations are separated from the test condition by the expected semicolon.

When this program executes, the test (i<3) is evaluated, and because it is true, the body of the for statement is executed, where the values are printed. Finally, the third clause in the for statement is executed. As you can see, two expressions are here as well. In this case, both i and j are incremented.

After line 10 completes, the condition is evaluated again, and if it remains true, the actions are repeated (i and j are again incremented), and the body of the loop is executed again. This continues until the test fails, in which case the action statement is not executed, and control falls out of the loop.

Null Statements in `for` Loops

Any or all the statements in a `for` loop can be left out. To accomplish this, you use a null statement. A null statement is simply the use of a semicolon (;) to mark where the statement would have been. Using a null statement, you can create a `for` loop that acts exactly like a `while` loop by leaving out the first and third statements. Listing 7.11 illustrates this idea.

LISTING **7.11**   Null Statements in `for` Loops

```
1:  // Listing 7.11
2:  // For loops with null statements
3:
4:  #include <iostream>
5:
6:  int main()
7:  {
8:      int counter = 0;
9:
10:     for( ; counter < 5; )
11:     {
12:         counter++;
13:         std::cout << "Looping!   ";
14:     }
15:
16:     std::cout << "\nCounter: " << counter << std::endl;
17:     return 0;
18: }
```

OUTPUT

```
Looping!  Looping!  Looping!  Looping!  Looping!
Counter: 5.
```

ANALYSIS   You might recognize this as exactly like the `while` loop illustrated in Listing 7.8. On line 8, the `counter` variable is initialized. The `for` statement on line 10 does not initialize any values, but it does include a test for `counter < 5`. No increment statement exists, so this loop behaves exactly as if it had been written:

```
while (counter < 5)
```

You can once again see that C++ gives you several ways to accomplish the same thing. No experienced C++ programmer would use a `for` loop in this way shown in Listing 7.11, but it does illustrate the flexibility of the `for` statement. In fact, it is possible, using `break` and `continue`, to create a `for` loop with none of the three statements. Listing 7.12 illustrates how.

7

LISTING 7.12   Illustrating an Empty for Loop Statement

```
 1:   //Listing 7.12 illustrating
 2:   //empty for loop statement
 3:
 4:   #include <iostream>
 5:
 6:   int main()
 7:   {
 8:       int counter=0;        // initialization
 9:       int max;
10:       std::cout << "How many hellos? ";
11:       std::cin >> max;
12:       for (;;)              // a for loop that doesn't end
13:       {
14:           if (counter < max)      // test
15:           {
16:               std::cout << "Hello! " << std::endl;
17:               counter++;          // increment
18:           }
19:           else
20:               break;
21:       }
22:       return 0;
23:   }
```

OUTPUT

```
How many hellos? 3
Hello!
Hello!
Hello!
```

ANALYSIS   The for loop has now been pushed to its absolute limit. Initialization, test, and action have all been taken out of the for statement on line 12. The initialization is done on line 8, before the for loop begins. The test is done in a separate if statement on line 14, and if the test succeeds, the action, an increment to counter, is performed on line 17. If the test fails, breaking out of the loop occurs on line 20.

Although this particular program is somewhat absurd, sometimes a for(;;) loop or a while (true) loop is just what you'll want. You'll see an example of a more reasonable use of such loops when switch statements are discussed later today.

Empty for Loops

Because so much can be done in the header of a for statement, at times you won't need the body to do anything at all. In that case, be certain to put a null statement (;) as the body of the loop. The semicolon can be on the same line as the header, but this is easy to overlook. Listing 7.13 illustrates an appropriate way to use a null body in a for loop.

LISTING **7.13**   Illustrates the Null Statement in a for Loop

```
1:   //Listing 7.13
2:   //Demonstrates null statement
3:   // as body of for loop
4:
5:   #include <iostream>
6:   int main()
7:   {
8:       for (int i = 0; i<5; std::cout << "i: " << i++ << std::endl)
9:           ;
10:      return 0;
11:  }
```

OUTPUT
```
i: 0
i: 1
i: 2
i: 3
i: 4
```

ANALYSIS The for loop on line 8 includes three statements: The *initialization* statement establishes the counter i and initializes it to 0. The *condition* statement tests for i<5, and the *action* statement prints the value in i and increments it.

Nothing is left to do in the body of the for loop, so the null statement (;) is used. Note that this is not a well-designed for loop: The action statement is doing far too much. This would be better rewritten as

```
8:          for (int i = 0; i<5; i++)
9:              cout << "i: " << i << endl;
```

Although both do the same thing, this example is easier to understand.

Nesting Loops

Any of the loop can be nested within the body of another. The inner loop will be executed in full for every execution of the outer loop. Listing 7.14 illustrates writing marks into a matrix using nested for loops.

LISTING **7.14**   Illustrates Nested for Loops

```
1:   //Listing 7.14
2:   //Illustrates nested for loops
3:   #include <iostream>
4:
5:   int main()
6:   {
7:       using namespace std;
```

7

LISTING **7.14**   continued

```
 8:     int rows, columns;
 9:     char theChar;
10:     cout << "How many rows? ";
11:     cin >> rows;
12:     cout << "How many columns? ";
13:     cin >> columns;
14:     cout << "What character? ";
15:     cin >> theChar;
16:     for (int i = 0; i<rows; i++)
17:     {
18:        for (int j = 0; j<columns; j++)
19:            cout << theChar;
20:        cout << endl;
21:     }
22:     return 0;
23: }
```

OUTPUT

```
How many rows? 4
How many columns? 12
What character? X
XXXXXXXXXXXX
XXXXXXXXXXXX
XXXXXXXXXXXX
XXXXXXXXXXXX
```

ANALYSIS   In this listing, the user is prompted for the number of rows and columns and for a character to print. The first for loop, on line 16, initializes a counter (i) to 0, and then the body of the outer for loop is run.

On line 18, the first line of the body of the outer for loop, another for loop is established. A second counter (j) is initialized to 0, and the body of the inner for loop is executed. On line 19, the chosen character is printed, and control returns to the header of the inner for loop. Note that the inner for loop is only one statement (the printing of the character). The condition is tested (j < columns) and if it evaluates true, j is incremented and the next character is printed. This continues until j equals the number of columns.

When the inner for loop fails its test, in this case after 12 Xs are printed, execution falls through to line 20, and a new line is printed. The outer for loop now returns to its header, where its condition (i < rows) is tested. If this evaluates true, i is incremented and the body of the loop is executed.

In the second iteration of the outer for loop, the inner for loop is started over. Thus, j is reinitialized to 0 and the entire inner loop is run again.

The important idea here is that by using a nested loop, the inner loop is executed for each iteration of the outer loop. Thus, the character is printed `columns` times for each row.

> **NOTE**
>
> As an aside, many C++ programmers use the letters i and j as counting variables. This tradition goes all the way back to FORTRAN, in which the letters i, j, k, l, m, and n were the only counting variables.
>
> Although this might seem innocuous, readers of your program can become confused by the purpose of the counter, and might use it improperly. You can even become confused in a complex program with nested loops. It is better to indicate the use of the index variable in its name—for instance, `CustomerIndex` or `InputCounter`.

Scoping in `for` Loops

In the past, variables declared in the `for` loop were scoped to the outer block. The American National Standards Institute (ANSI) standard changes this to scope these variables only to the block of the `for` loop itself; however, not every compiler supports this change. You can test your compiler with the following code:

```
#include <iostream>
int main()
{
    // i scoped to the for loop?
    for (int i = 0; i<5; i++)
    {
        std::cout << "i: " << i << std::endl;
    }

    i = 7;  // should not be in scope!
    return 0;
}
```

If this compiles without complaint, your compiler does not yet support this aspect of the ANSI standard.

If your compiler complains that i is not yet defined (in the line i=7), your compiler does support the new standard. You can write code that will compile on either compiler by declaring *i* outside of the loop, as shown here:

```
#include <iostream>
int main()
{
```

7

```
int i; //declare outside the for loop
for (i = 0; i<5; i++)
{
    std::cout << "i: " << i << std::endl;
}

i = 7;  // now this is in scope for all compilers
return 0;
}
```

Summing Up Loops

On Day 5, you learned how to solve the Fibonacci series problem using recursion. To review briefly, a Fibonacci series starts with 1, 1, 2, 3, and all subsequent numbers are the sum of the previous two:

1,1,2,3,5,8,13,21,34...

The nth Fibonacci number is the sum of the n-1 and the n-2 Fibonacci numbers. The problem solved on Day 5 was finding the value of the nth Fibonacci number. This was done with recursion. Listing 7.15 offers a solution using iteration.

LISTING 7.15   Solving the nth Fibonacci Number Using Iteration

```
 1: // Listing 7.15 - Demonstrates solving the nth
 2: // Fibonacci number using iteration
 3:
 4: #include <iostream>
 5:
 6: unsigned int fib(unsigned int position );
 7: int main()
 8: {
 9:     using namespace std;
10:     unsigned int answer, position;
11:     cout << "Which position? ";
12:     cin >> position;
13:     cout << endl;
14:
15:     answer = fib(position);
16:     cout << answer << " is the ";
17:     cout << position << "th Fibonacci number. " << endl;
18:     return 0;
19: }
20:
21: unsigned int fib(unsigned int n)
22: {
23:     unsigned int minusTwo=1, minusOne=1, answer=2;
24:
```

LISTING 7.15 continued

```
25:     if (n < 3)
26:         return 1;
27:
28:     for (n -= 3; n != 0; n--)
29:     {
30:         minusTwo = minusOne;
31:         minusOne = answer;
32:         answer = minusOne + minusTwo;
33:     }
34:
35:     return answer;
36: }
```

OUTPUT

```
Which position? 4
3 is the 4th Fibonacci number.
Which position? 5
5 is the 5th Fibonacci number.
Which position? 20
6765 is the 20th Fibonacci number.
Which position? 100
3314859971 is the 100th Fibonacci number.
```

ANALYSIS Listing 7.15 solves the Fibonacci series using iteration rather than recursion. This approach is faster and uses less memory than the recursive solution.

On line 11, the user is asked for the position to check. The function `fib()` is called, which evaluates the position. If the position is less than 3, the function returns the value 1. Starting with position 3, the function iterates using the following algorithm:

1. Establish the starting position: Fill variable answer with 2, minusTwo with 1, and minusOne with 1. Decrement the position by 3 because the first two numbers are handled by the starting position.

2. For every number, count up the Fibonacci series. This is done by

    a. Putting the value currently in minusOne into minusTwo

    b. Putting the value currently in answer into minusOne

    c. Adding minusOne and minusTwo and putting the sum in answer

    d. Decrementing n

3. When n reaches 0, return the answer.

This is exactly how you would solve this problem with pencil and paper. If you were asked for the fifth Fibonacci number, you would write

1, 1, 2,

7

and think, "two more to do." You would then add 2+1 and write 3, and think, "one more to find." Finally, you would write 3+2 and the answer would be 5. In effect, you are shifting your attention right one number each time through and decrementing the number remaining to be found.

Note the condition tested on line 28 (n != 0). Many C++ programmers use the following for line 28:

```
for ( n-=3; n; n-- )
```

You can see that instead of using a relational condition, just the value of n is used for the condition in the for statement. This is a C++ idiom, and n is considered equivalent to n != 0. Using just n relies on the fact that when n reaches 0, it will evaluate false, because 0 has been considered as false in C++. In keeping with the current C++ standards, it is better to rely on a condition to evaluate to the value of false than to use a numeric value.

Compile, link, and run this program, along with the recursive solution offered on Day 5. Try finding position 25 and compare the time it takes each program. Recursion is elegant, but because the function call brings a performance overhead, and because it is called so many times, its performance is noticeably slower than iteration. Microcomputers tend to be optimized for the arithmetic operations, so the iterative solution should be blazingly fast.

Be careful how large a number you enter. fib grows quickly, and even unsigned long integers will overflow after a while.

Controlling Flow with switch Statements

On Day 4, you saw how to write if and if...else statements. These can become quite confusing when nested too deeply, and C++ offers an alternative. Unlike if, which evaluates one value, switch statements enable you to branch on any of several values. The general form of the switch statement is

```
switch (expression)
{
    case valueOne:  statement;
                    break;
    case valueTwo:  statement;
                    break;
    ....
    case valueN:    statement;
                    break;
    default:        statement;
}
```

expression is any legal C++ expression, and the statements are any legal C++ statements or block of statements that evaluate (or can be unambiguously converted to) an integer value. Note, however, that the evaluation is for equality only; relational operators cannot be used here, nor can Boolean operations.

If one of the `case` values matches the expression, program execution jumps to those statements and continues to the end of the `switch` block unless a `break` statement is encountered. If nothing matches, execution branches to the optional `default` statement. If no `default` and no matching `case` value exist, execution falls through the `switch` statement and the statement ends.

TIP

It is almost always a good idea to have a `default` case in `switch` statements. If you have no other need for the default, use it to test for the supposedly impossible case, and print out an error message; this can be a tremendous aid in debugging.

It is important to note that if no `break` statement is at the end of a `case` statement, execution falls through to the next `case` statement. This is sometimes necessary, but usually is an error. If you decide to let execution fall through, be certain to put a comment indicating that you didn't just forget the `break`.

Listing 7.16 illustrates use of the `switch` statement.

LISTING 7.16 Demonstrating the `switch` Statement

```
1:  //Listing 7.16
2:  // Demonstrates switch statement
3:  #include <iostream>
4:
5:  int main()
6:  {
7:      using namespace std;
8:      unsigned short int number;
9:      cout << "Enter a number between 1 and 5: ";
10:     cin >> number;
11:     switch (number)
12:     {
13:       case 0:   cout << "Too small, sorry!";
14:                 break;
15:       case 5:   cout << "Good job! " << endl; // fall through
16:       case 4:   cout << "Nice Pick!" << endl; // fall through
17:       case 3:   cout << "Excellent!" << endl; // fall through
18:       case 2:   cout << "Masterful!" << endl; // fall through
```

7

LISTING 7.16   continued

```
19:        case 1:   cout << "Incredible!" << endl;
20:                  break;
21:        default:  cout << "Too large!" << endl;
22:                  break;
23:     }
24:     cout << endl << endl;
25:     return 0;
26:  }
```

OUTPUT

```
Enter a number between 1 and 5: 3
Excellent!
Masterful!
Incredible!

Enter a number between 1 and 5: 8
Too large!
```

ANALYSIS   The user is prompted for a number on lines 9 and 10. That number is given to the
switch statement on line 11. If the number is 0, the case statement on line 13
matches, the message Too small, sorry! is printed, and the break statement on line 14
ends the switch. If the value is 5, execution switches to line 15 where a message is
printed, and then falls through to line 16, another message is printed, and so forth until
hitting the break on line 20, at which time the switch ends.

The net effect of these statements is that for a number between 1 and 5, that many messages are printed. If the value of number is not 0 to 5, it is assumed to be too large, and
the default statement is invoked on line 21.

The switch Statement

The syntax for the switch statement is as follows:

```
switch (expression)
{
    case    valueOne: statement;
    case    valueTwo: statement;
    ....
    case    valueN: statement;
    default: statement;
}
```

The switch statement allows for branching on multiple values of expression. The expression is evaluated, and if it matches any of the case values, execution jumps to that line.
Execution continues until either the end of the switch statement or a break statement is
encountered.

If *expression* does not match any of the `case` statements, and if there is a `default` statement, execution switches to the `default` statement, otherwise the `switch` statement ends.

Example 1

```
switch (choice)
{
    case 0:
        cout << "Zero!" << endl;
        break;
    case 1:
        cout << "One!" << endl;
        break;
    case 2:
        cout << "Two!" << endl;
    default:
        cout << "Default!" << endl;
}
```

Example 2

```
switch (choice)
{
    case 0:
    case 1:
    case 2:
        cout << "Less than 3!";
        break;
    case 3:
        cout << "Equals 3!";
        break;
    default:
        cout << "greater than 3!";
}
```

Using a `switch` Statement with a Menu

Listing 7.17 returns to the `for(;;)` loop discussed earlier. These loops are also called forever loops, as they will loop forever if a break is not encountered. In Listing 7.17, the forever loop is used to put up a menu, solicit a choice from the user, act on the choice, and then return to the menu. This continues until the user chooses to exit.

7

NOTE

Some programmers like to write:

```
#define EVER ;;
for (EVER)
{
    // statements...
}
```

A forever loop is a loop that does not have an exit condition. To exit the loop, a `break` statement must be used. Forever loops are also known as eternal or infinite loops.

LISTING 7.17 Demonstrating a Forever Loop

```
 1: //Listing 7.17
 2: //Using a forever loop to manage user interaction
 3: #include <iostream>
 4:
 5: // prototypes
 6: int menu();
 7: void DoTaskOne();
 8: void DoTaskMany(int);
 9:
10: using namespace std;
11:
12: int main()
13: {
14:     bool exit = false;
15:     for (;;)
16:     {
17:         int choice = menu();
18:         switch(choice)
19:         {
20:           case (1):
21:               DoTaskOne();
22:               break;
23:           case (2):
24:               DoTaskMany(2);
25:               break;
26:           case (3):
27:               DoTaskMany(3);
28:               break;
29:           case (4):
30:               continue;   // redundant!
31:               break;
32:           case (5):
33:               exit=true;
34:               break;
```

LISTING 7.17   continued

```
35:            default:
36:                cout << "Please select again! " << endl;
37:                break;
38:        }                 // end switch
39:
40:        if (exit == true)
41:            break;
42:    }                     // end forever
43:    return 0;
44: }                        // end main()
45:
46: int menu()
47: {
48:     int choice;
49:
50:     cout << " **** Menu **** "   << endl << endl;
51:     cout << "(1) Choice one. "   << endl;
52:     cout << "(2) Choice two. "   << endl;
53:     cout << "(3) Choice three. " << endl;
54:     cout << "(4) Redisplay menu. " << endl;
55:     cout << "(5) Quit. "     << endl << endl;
56:     cout << ": ";
57:     cin >> choice;
58:     return choice;
59: }
60:
61: void DoTaskOne()
62: {
63:     cout << "Task One! " << endl;
64: }
65:
66: void DoTaskMany(int which)
67: {
68:     if (which == 2)
69:         cout << "Task Two! " << endl;
70:     else
71:         cout << "Task Three! " << endl;
72: }
```

OUTPUT

```
**** Menu ****

(1) Choice one.
(2) Choice two.
(3) Choice three.
(4) Redisplay menu.
(5) Quit.
```

7

```
: 1
Task One!
 **** Menu ****
(1) Choice one.
(2) Choice two.
(3) Choice three.
(4) Redisplay menu.
(5) Quit.

: 3
Task Three!
 **** Menu ****
(1) Choice one.
(2) Choice two.
(3) Choice three.
(4) Redisplay menu.
(5) Quit.

: 5
```

ANALYSIS   This program brings together a number of concepts from today and previous days. It also shows a common use of the switch statement.

The forever loop begins on line 15. The menu() function is called, which prints the menu to the screen and returns the user's selection. The switch statement, which begins on line 18 and ends on line 38, switches on the user's choice.

If the user enters 1, execution jumps to the case (1): statement on line 20. Line 21 switches execution to the DoTaskOne() function, which prints a message and returns. On its return, execution resumes on line 22, where the break ends the switch statement, and execution falls through to line 39. On line 40, the variable exit is evaluated to see whether it is true. If it evaluates true, the break on line 41 is executed and the for(;;) loop ends; but if it evaluates false, execution resumes at the top of the loop on line 15.

Note that the continue statement on line 30 is redundant. If it were left out and the break statement were encountered, the switch would end, exit would evaluate false, the loop would reiterate, and the menu would be reprinted. The continue does, however, bypass the test of exit.

Do	**Don't**
DO carefully document all intentional fall-through cases.	**DON'T** use complex if...else statements if a clearer switch statement will work.
DO put a default case in switch statements, if only to detect seemingly impossible situations.	**DON'T** forget break at the end of each case unless you want to fall through.

Summary

Today's lesson started with a look at the goto command that you were told to avoid using. You were then shown different methods to cause a C++ program to loop that don't require a goto.

The while statement loops check a condition, and if it is true, execute the statements in the body of the loop. do...while loops execute the body of the loop and then test the condition. for loops initialize a value, then test an expression. If the expression is true, the body of the loop is executed. The final expression in the for header is then executed and the condition is then checked again. This process of checking the condition, executing the statements in the body, and executing the final expression in the for statement continues until the conditional expression evaluates to false.

You also learned about continue, which causes while, do...while, and for loops to start over, and break, which causes while, do...while, for, and switch statements to end.

Q&A

Q How do I choose between if...else and switch?

A If more than just one or two else clauses are used, and all are testing the same value, consider using a switch statement.

Q How do I choose between while and do...while?

A If the body of the loop should always execute at least once, consider a do...while loop; otherwise, try to use the while loop.

Q How do I choose between while and for?

A If you are initializing a counting variable, testing that variable, and incrementing it each time through the loop, consider the for loop. If your variable is already initialized and is not incremented on each loop, a while loop might be the better choice. Experienced programmers look for this usage and will find your program harder to understand if you violate this expectation.

Q Is it better to use while (true) or for (;;)?

A No significant difference exists; however, it is best to avoid both.

Q Why shouldn't a variable be used as a condition, such as while(n)?

A In the current C++ standard, an expression is evaluated to a Boolean value of true or false. Although you can equate false to 0 and true to any other value, it is

7

better—and more in line with the current standards—to use an expression that evaluates to a Boolean value of true or false. However, a variable of type `bool` can be used in a condition without any potential problems.

Workshop

The Workshop provides quiz questions to help you solidify your understanding of the material covered as well as exercises to provide you with experience in using what you've learned. Try to answer the quiz and exercise questions before checking the answers in Appendix D, and be certain you understand the answers before continuing to tomorrow's lesson.

Quiz

1. How do you initialize more than one variable in a `for` loop?
2. Why is `goto` avoided?
3. Is it possible to write a `for` loop with a body that is never executed?
4. What is the value of x when the `for` loop completes?

   ```
   for (int x = 0; x < 100; x++)
   ```
5. Is it possible to nest `while` loops within `for` loops?
6. Is it possible to create a loop that never ends? Give an example.
7. What happens if you create a loop that never ends?

Exercises

1. Write a nested `for` loop that prints a 10×10 pattern of 0s.
2. Write a `for` statement to count from 100 to 200 by twos.
3. Write a `while` loop to count from 100 to 200 by twos.
4. Write a do...while loop to count from 100 to 200 by twos.
5. **BUG BUSTERS:** What is wrong with this code?

   ```
   int counter = 0;
   while (counter < 10)
   {
       cout << "counter: " << counter;
   }
   ```
6. **BUG BUSTERS:** What is wrong with this code?

   ```
   for (int counter = 0; counter < 10; counter++);
       cout << counter << " ";
   ```

7. **BUG BUSTERS:** What is wrong with this code?

```cpp
int counter = 100;
while (counter < 10)
{
    cout << "counter now: " << counter;
    counter--;
}
```

8. **BUG BUSTERS:** What is wrong with this code?

```cpp
cout << "Enter a number between 0 and 5: ";
cin >> theNumber;
switch (theNumber)
{
    case 0:
        doZero();
    case 1:              // fall through
    case 2:              // fall through
    case 3:              // fall through
    case 4:              // fall through
    case 5:
        doOneToFive();
        break;
    default:
        doDefault();
        break;
}
```

7

WEEK 1

In Review

You have finished your first week of learning how to program in C++. You should feel comfortable entering programs and using your editor and compiler. Now that you have some experience using C++, it is time for a more robust program. The following program pulls together many of the topics you have learned over the previous seven days' lessons.

After you look through Listing R1.1, you will see that analysis has been included. You will find that every topic in this listing has been covered in the preceding week's lessons. You will see similar Weeks in Review after Weeks 2 and 3.

1

2

3

4

5

6

7

LISTING R1.1 Week 1 in Review Listing

DAY 2

```
1: /* Listing: WR01.cpp
2:  * Description: Week in Review listing for week 1
3:  *=================================================*/
```

DAY 1

```
4: #include <iostream>
```

DAY 2

```
5: using namespace std;
6:
```

DAY 3

```
7: enum CHOICE {
8:      DrawRect = 1,
9:      GetArea,
10:     GetPerim,
11:     ChangeDimensions,
12:     Quit  };
13:
```

DAY 2

```
14: // Rectangle class declaration
```

DAY 6

```
15: class Rectangle
16: {
```

DAY 6

```
17:   public:
18:       // constructors
19:       Rectangle(int width, int height);
20:       ~Rectangle();
21:
22:       // accessors
23:       int GetHeight() const { return itsHeight; }
24:       int GetWidth() const { return itsWidth; }
25:       int GetArea() const { return itsHeight * itsWidth; }
26:       int GetPerim() const { return 2*itsHeight + 2*itsWidth; }
27:       void SetSize(int newWidth, int newHeight);
28:
29:       // Misc. methods
30:
```

LISTING R1.1 continued

DAY 6

```
31:   private:
```

DAY 3

```
32:       int itsWidth;
33:       int itsHeight;
34: };
35:
36: // Class method implementations
37: void Rectangle::SetSize(int newWidth, int newHeight)
38: {
39:     itsWidth = newWidth;
40:     itsHeight = newHeight;
41: }
42:
43: Rectangle::Rectangle(int width, int height)
44: {
45:     itsWidth = width;
46:     itsHeight = height;
47: }
48:
```

DAY 6

```
49: Rectangle::~Rectangle() {}
50:
```

DAY 2

```
51: int DoMenu();
52: void DoDrawRect(Rectangle);
53: void DoGetArea(Rectangle);
54: void DoGetPerim(Rectangle);
55:
```

DAY 2

```
56: /*===============================================*/
57: int main()
58: {
59:     // initialize a rectangle to 30,5
```

DAY 6

```
60:     Rectangle theRect(30,5);
61:
62:     int choice = DrawRect;
```

DAY 3

```
63:     int fQuit = false;
64:
```

LISTING R1.1 continued

DAY 7

```
65:    while (!fQuit)
66:    {
```

DAY 5

```
67:      choice = DoMenu();
```

DAY 4

```
68:      if (choice < DrawRect || choice >  Quit)
69:      {
70:        cout << "\nInvalid Choice, try again. ";
71:        cout << endl << endl;
```

DAY 4

```
72:        continue;
73:      }
```

DAY 7

```
74:      switch (choice)
75:      {
```

DAY 7

```
76:        case  DrawRect:
77:          DoDrawRect(theRect);
78:          break;
79:        case GetArea:
```

DAY 5

```
80:          DoGetArea(theRect);
81:          break;
82:        case GetPerim:
83:          DoGetPerim(theRect);
84:          break;
85:        case ChangeDimensions:
```

DAY 3

```
86:          int newLength, newWidth;
87:          cout << "\nNew width: ";
88:          cin >> newWidth;
89:          cout << "New height: ";
90:          cin >> newLength;
```

DAY 6

```
91:          theRect.SetSize(newWidth, newLength);
92:          DoDrawRect(theRect);
```

LISTING R1.1   continued

```
93:           break;
94:        case Quit:
```

DAY 3

```
95:           fQuit = true;
96:           cout << "\nExiting... " << endl << endl;
97:           break;
```

DAY 7

```
98:        default:
99:          cout << "Error in choice!" << endl;
100:          fQuit = true;
101:          break;
102:    }   // end switch
103:    }      // end while
```

DAY 5

```
104:    return 0;
105: }       // end main
106:
```

DAY 7

```
107: int DoMenu()
108: {
```

DAY 3

```
109:    int choice;
```

DAY 2

```
110:    cout << endl << endl;    // create two new lines
111:    cout << "    *** Menu *** "    << endl;
112:    cout << "(1) Draw Rectangle" << endl;
113:    cout << "(2) Area"           << endl;
114:    cout << "(3) Perimeter"      << endl;
115:    cout << "(4) Resize"         << endl;
116:    cout << "(5) Quit"           << endl;
117:
```

DAY 3

```
118:  cin >> choice;
119:    return choice;
120: }
121:
122:  void DoDrawRect(Rectangle theRect)
123:  {
```

LISTING R1.1   continued

DAY 6

```
124:    int height = theRect.GetHeight();
125:    int width = theRect.GetWidth();
126:
```

DAY 7

```
127:    for (int i = 0; i<height; i++)
128:    {
129:      for (int j = 0; j< width; j++)
130:          cout << "*";
131:      cout << endl;
132:    }
133: }
134:
135:
```

DAY 5

```
136: void DoGetArea(Rectangle theRect)
137: {
```

DAY 3

```
138:    cout << "Area: " <<  theRect.GetArea() << endl;
139: }
140:
```

DAY 5

```
141: void DoGetPerim(Rectangle theRect)
142: {
143:    cout << "Perimeter: " <<  theRect.GetPerim() << endl;
144: }
145: // ==========   End of Listing   ==========
```

OUTPUT

```
*** Menu ***
(1) Draw Rectangle
(2) Area
(3) Perimeter
(4) Resize
(5) Quit
1
*****************************
*****************************
*****************************
*****************************
*****************************
```

```
    *** Menu ***
(1) Draw Rectangle
(2) Area
(3) Perimeter
(4) Resize
(5) Quit
2
Area: 150

    *** Menu ***
(1) Draw Rectangle
(2) Area
(3) Perimeter
(4) Resize
(5) Quit
3
Perimeter: 70

    *** Menu ***
(1) Draw Rectangle
(2) Area
(3) Perimeter
(4) Resize
(5) Quit
4

New Width: 10
New height: 8
*********
*********
*********
*********
*********
*********
*********
*********

    *** Menu ***
(1) Draw Rectangle
(2) Area
(3) Perimeter
(4) Resize
(5) Quit
2
Area: 80

    *** Menu ***
(1) Draw Rectangle
(2) Area
(3) Perimeter
```

```
(4) Resize
(5) Quit
3
Perimeter: 36

    *** Menu ***
(1) Draw Rectangle
(2) Area
(3) Perimeter
(4) Resize
(5) Quit
5

Exiting...
```

ANALYSIS This program utilizes most of the skills you learned this week. You should not only be able to enter, compile, link, and run this program, but also understand what it does and how it works, based on the work you've done this week. If you are confused by any of the lines in this listing, you should go back and review the previous week's material. To the left of many of the lines are references to which day that line's primary function is covered.

This program presents a text menu and waits for you to make a selection. The menu works with a rectangle. You have options to print out a representation of the rectangle as well as options to get its area and perimeter. You can also change the default values for the rectangle. The menu does not do all of the error checking that a full-fledged program should do; however, it does do some checking.

On lines 7–12, the program listing sets up the new types and definitions that will be used throughout the program.

Lines 15–34 declare the Rectangle class. There are public accessor methods for obtaining and setting the width and height of the rectangle, as well as for computing the area and perimeter. Lines 37–47 contain the class function definitions that were not declared inline. Because a constructor was created on lines 43–47, a destructor is also created on line 49.

The function prototypes, for the nonclass member functions, are on lines 51–54, and the entry point of the program begins on line 57. As stated, the essence of this program is to generate a rectangle, and then to print out a menu offering five options: Draw the rectangle, determine its area, determine its perimeter, resize the rectangle, or quit.

A flag is set on line 63, and as long as the flag is set to false, the menu loop continues. The flag is only set to true if the user chooses Quit from the menu.

Each of the other choices, with the exception of ChangeDimensions, calls a function. This makes the switch statement on lines 74–102 cleaner. ChangeDimensions cannot call out to a function because it must change the dimensions of the rectangle. If the rectangle were passed (by value) to a function such as DoChangeDimensions(), the dimensions would be changed on the local copy of the rectangle in DoChangeDimensions() and not on the rectangle in main(). On Day 8, "Understanding Pointers," and Day 10, "Working with Advanced Functions," you'll learn how to overcome this restriction, but for now the change is made in the main() function.

Note how the use of an enumeration makes the switch statement much cleaner and easier to understand. Had the switch depended on the numeric choices (1–5) of the user, you would have to constantly refer to the description of the menu to see which pick was which.

On line 68, the user's choice is checked to be certain it is in range. If not, an error message is printed and the menu is reprinted. Note that the switch statement includes an "impossible" default condition. This is an aid in debugging. If the program is working, that statement can never be reached.

Congratulations! You've completed the first week! Now, you can create and understand sophisticated C++ programs. Of course, there's much more to do, and next week starts with one of the most difficult concepts in C++: pointers. Don't give up now, you're about to delve deeply into the meaning and use of object-oriented programming, virtual functions, and many of the advanced features of this powerful language.

Take a break, bask in the glory of your accomplishment, and then turn the page to start Week 2.

WEEK 2

At a Glance

You have finished the first week of learning how to program in C++. By now, you should feel comfortable entering programs, using your compiler, and thinking about objects, classes, and program flow.

Where You Are Going

Week 2 begins with pointers. Pointers are traditionally a difficult subject for new C++ programmers, but you will find them explained fully and clearly, and they should not be a stumbling block. On Day 9, "Exploiting References," you will learn about references, which are a close cousin to pointers. On Day 10, "Working with Advanced Functions," you will see how to overload functions.

Day 11, "Object-Oriented Analysis and Design," is a departure: Rather than focusing on the syntax of the language, you will take a day out to learn about object-oriented analysis and design. On Day 12, "Implementing Inheritance," you will be introduced to inheritance, a fundamental concept in object-oriented programming. On Day 13, "Managing Arrays and Strings," you will learn how to work with arrays and collections. Day 14, "Polymorphism," extends the lessons of Day 12 to discuss polymorphism.

8

9

10

11

12

13

14

WEEK 2

DAY 8

Understanding Pointers

One of the powerful but low-level tools available to a C++ programmer is the capability to manipulate computer memory directly by using pointers. This is an advantage that C++ has over some other languages, such as C# and Visual Basic.

Today, you will learn

- What pointers are
- How to declare and use pointers
- What the free store is and how to manipulate memory

Pointers present two special challenges when you're learning C++: They can be somewhat confusing, and it isn't immediately obvious why they are needed. Today's lesson explains how pointers work, step-by-step. You will fully understand the need for pointers, however, only as the book progresses.

> The ability to use pointers and manipulate memory at a low level is one of
> the factors that makes C++ the language of choice for embedded and real-
> time applications.

What Is a Pointer?

A pointer is a variable that holds a memory address. That's it. If you understand this simple sentence, then you know the core of what there is to know about pointers.

A Bit About Memory

To understand pointers, you must know a little about computer memory. Computer memory is divided into sequentially numbered memory locations. Each variable is located at a
unique location in memory, known as its address. Figure 8.1 shows a schematic representation of the storage of an unsigned long integer variable named theAge.

FIGURE 8.1

*A schematic
representation
of theAge.*

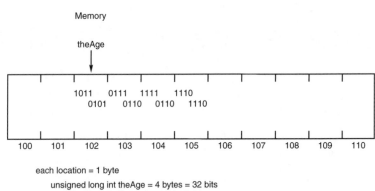

each location = 1 byte

unsigned long int theAge = 4 bytes = 32 bits
variable name theAge points to 1st byte
the address of theAge is 102

Getting a Variable's Memory Address

Different computers number this memory using different complex schemes. Usually, as a
programmer, you don't need to know the particular address of any given variable because
the compiler handles the details. If you want this information, though, you can use the
address-of operator (&), which returns the address of an object in memory. Listing 8.1 is
used to illustrate the use of this operator.

LISTING 8.1   Demonstrating the Address-of Operator

```
1:  // Listing 8.1 Demonstrates address-of operator
2:  // and addresses of local variables
3:  #include <iostream>
4:
5:  int main()
6:  {
7:      using namespace std;
8:      unsigned short shortVar=5;
9:      unsigned long  longVar=65535;
10:     long sVar = -65535;
11:
12:     cout << "shortVar:\t" << shortVar;
13:     cout << "\tAddress of shortVar:\t";
14:     cout <<   &shortVar  << endl;
15:
16:     cout << "longVar:\t"  << longVar;
17:     cout  << "\tAddress of longVar:\t" ;
18:     cout <<   &longVar  << endl;
19:
20:     cout << "sVar:\t\t"      << sVar;
21:     cout << "\tAddress of sVar:\t" ;
22:     cout <<   &sVar       << endl;
23:
24:     return 0;
25:  }
```

OUTPUT

```
shortVar:      5       Address of shortVar:   0012FF7C
longVar:       65535   Address of longVar:    0012FF78
sVar:          -65535  Address of sVar:       0012FF74
```

(Your printout might look different, especially the last column.)

ANALYSIS   Three variables are declared and initialized: an `unsigned short` on line 8, an `unsigned long` on line 9, and a `long` on line 10. Their values and addresses are printed on lines 12–22. You can see on lines 14, 18, and 22 that the address-of operator (&) is used to get the address of the variable. This operator is simply placed on the front of the variable name in order to have the address returned.

Line 12 prints the value of *shortVar* as 5, which is expected. In the first line of the output, you can see that its address is 0012FF7C when run on a Pentium (32-bit) computer. This address is computer-specific and might change slightly each time the program is run. Your results will be different.

When you declare a variable, the compiler determines how much memory to allow based on the variable type. The compiler takes care of allocating memory and automatically assigns an address for it. For a `long` integer that is typically four bytes, for example, an address to four bytes of memory is used.

NOTE

> Note that your compiler might insist on assigning new variables on four-byte boundaries. (Thus, `longVar` was assigned an address four bytes after `shortVar` even though `shortVar` only needed two bytes!)

Storing a Variable's Address in a Pointer

Every variable has an address. Even without knowing the specific address, you can store a variable's address in a pointer.

Suppose, for example, that `howOld` is an integer. To declare a pointer called `pAge` to hold its address, you write

```
int *pAge = 0;
```

This declares `pAge` to be a pointer to an `int`. That is, `pAge` is declared to hold the address of an integer.

Note that `pAge` is a variable. When you declare an integer variable (type `int`), the compiler sets aside enough memory to hold an integer. When you declare a pointer variable such as `pAge`, the compiler sets aside enough memory to hold an address (on most computers, four bytes). A pointer, and thus `pAge`, is just a different type of variable.

Pointer Names

Because pointers are just another variable, you can use any name that is legal for other variables. The same naming rules and suggestions apply. Many programmers follow the convention of naming all pointers with an initial p, as in `pAge` or `pNumber`.

In the example,

```
int *pAge = 0;
```

`pAge` is initialized to zero. A pointer whose value is zero is called a *null* pointer. All pointers, when they are created, should be initialized to something. If you don't know what you want to assign to the pointer, assign 0. A pointer that is not initialized is called a *wild* pointer because you have no idea what it is pointing to—and it could be pointing to anything! Wild pointers are very dangerous.

8

NOTE   Practice safe computing: Initialize all of your pointers!

For a pointer to hold an address, the address must be assigned to it. For the previous example, you must specifically assign the address of howOld to pAge, as shown in the following example:

```
unsigned short int howOld = 50;     // make a variable
unsigned short int * pAge = 0;      // make a pointer
pAge = &howOld;                     // put howOld's address in pAge
```

The first line creates a variable named howOld—whose type is unsigned short int—and initializes it with the value 50. The second line declares pAge to be a pointer to type unsigned short int and initializes it to zero. You know that pAge is a pointer because of the asterisk (*) after the variable type and before the variable name.

The third and final line assigns the address of howOld to the pointer pAge. You can tell that the address of howOld is being assigned because of the address-of operator (&). If the address-of operator had not been used, the value of howOld would have been assigned. That might, or might not, have been a valid address.

At this point, pAge has as its value the address of howOld. howOld, in turn, has the value 50. You could have accomplished this with one fewer step, as in

```
unsigned short int howOld = 50;        // make a variable
unsigned short int * pAge = &howOld;   // make pointer to howOld
```

pAge is a pointer that now contains the address of the howOld variable.

Getting the Value from a Variable

Using pAge, you can actually determine the value of howOld, which in this case is 50. Accessing the value stored in a variable by using a pointer is called indirection because you are indirectly accessing the variable by means of the pointer. For example, you can use indirection with the pAge pointer to access the value in howOld.

Indirection means accessing the value at the address held by a pointer. The pointer provides an indirect way to get the value held at that address.

NOTE   With a normal variable, the type tells the compiler how much memory is needed to hold the value. With a pointer, the type does not do this; all pointers are the same size—usually four bytes on a machine with a 32-bit processor and eight bytes on a machine with a 64-bit processor.

The type tells the compiler how much memory is needed for the object at the address, which the pointer holds!

In the declaration

```
unsigned short int * pAge = 0;        // make a pointer
```

pAge is declared to be a pointer to an unsigned short integer. This tells the compiler that the pointer (which needs four bytes to hold an address) will hold the address of an object of type unsigned short int, which itself requires two bytes.

Dereferencing with the Indirection Operator

The indirection operator (*) is also called the *dereference* operator. When a pointer is dereferenced, the value at the address stored by the pointer is retrieved.

Normal variables provide direct access to their own values. If you create a new variable of type unsigned short int called yourAge, and you want to assign the value in howOld to that new variable, you write

```
unsigned short int yourAge;
yourAge = howOld;
```

A pointer provides *indirect* access to the value of the variable whose address it stores. To assign the value in howOld to the new variable yourAge by way of the pointer pAge, you write

```
unsigned short int yourAge;
yourAge = *pAge;
```

The indirection operator (*) in front of the pointer variable pAge means "the value stored at." This assignment says, "Take *the value stored at* the address in pAge and assign it to yourAge." If you didn't include the indirection operator:

```
yourAge = pAge;   // bad!!
```

you would be attempting to assign the value in pAge, a memory address, to YourAge. Your compiler would most likely give you a warning that you are making a mistake.

Different Uses of the Asterisk

The asterisk (*) is used in two distinct ways with pointers: as part of the pointer declaration and also as the dereference operator.

When you declare a pointer, the * is part of the declaration and it follows the type of the object pointed to. For example,

```
// make a pointer to an unsigned short
unsigned short * pAge = 0;
```

When the pointer is dereferenced, the dereference (or indirection) operator indicates that the value at the memory location stored in the pointer is to be accessed, rather than the address itself.

```
// assign 5 to the value at pAge
*pAge = 5;
```

Also note that this same character (*) is used as the multiplication operator. The compiler knows which operator to call based on how you are using it (context).

Pointers, Addresses, and Variables

It is important to distinguish between a pointer, the address that the pointer holds, and the value at the address held by the pointer. This is the source of much of the confusion about pointers.

Consider the following code fragment:

```
int theVariable = 5;
int * pPointer = &theVariable ;
```

theVariable is declared to be an integer variable initialized with the value 5. pPointer is declared to be a pointer to an integer; it is initialized with the address of theVariable. pPointer is the pointer. The address that pPointer holds is the address of theVariable. The value at the address that pPointer holds is 5. Figure 8.2 shows a schematic representation of theVariable and pPointer.

FIGURE 8.2

A schematic representation of memory.

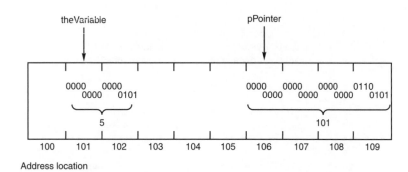

In Figure 8.2, the value 5 is stored at address location 101. This is shown in the binary number

```
0000 0000 0000 0101
```

This is two bytes (16 bits) whose decimal value is 5.

The pointer variable is at location 106. Its value is

000 0000 0000 0000 0000 0000 0110 0101

This is the binary representation of the value 101, which is the address of theVariable, whose value is 5.

The memory layout here is schematic, but it illustrates the idea of how pointers store an address.

Manipulating Data by Using Pointers

In addition to using the indirection operator to see what data is stored at a location pointed to by a variable, you can also manipulate that data. After the pointer is assigned the address, you can use that pointer to access the data in the variable being pointed to.

Listing 8.2 pulls together what you have just learned about pointers. In this listing, you see how the address of a local variable is assigned to a pointer and how the pointer can be used along with the indirection operator to manipulate the values in that variable.

LISTING 8.2   Manipulating Data by Using Pointers

```
1:  // Listing 8.2 Using pointers
2:  #include <iostream>
3:
4:  typedef unsigned short int USHORT;
5:
6:  int main()
7:  {
8:
9:      using namespace std;
10:
11:     USHORT myAge;           // a variable
12:     USHORT * pAge = 0;      // a pointer
13:
14:     myAge = 5;
15:
16:     cout << "myAge: " << myAge << endl;
17:     pAge = &myAge;       // assign address of myAge to pAge
18:     cout << "*pAge: " << *pAge << endl << endl;
19:
20:     cout << "Setting *pAge = 7... " << endl;
21:     *pAge = 7;           // sets myAge to 7
22:
23:     cout << "*pAge: " << *pAge << endl;
24:     cout << "myAge: " << myAge << endl << endl;
25:
```

LISTING 8.2 continued

```
26:     cout << "Setting myAge = 9… " << endl;
27:     myAge = 9;
28:
29:     cout << "myAge: " << myAge << endl;
30:     cout << "*pAge: " << *pAge << endl;
31:
32:     return 0;
33: }
```

OUTPUT

```
myAge: 5
*pAge: 5

Setting *pAge = 7...
*pAge: 7
myAge: 7

Setting myAge = 9...
myAge: 9
*pAge: 9
```

ANALYSIS This program declares two variables: an unsigned short, myAge, and a pointer to an unsigned short, pAge. myAge is assigned the value 5 on line 14; this is verified by the printout on line 16.

On line 17, pAge is assigned the address of myAge. On line 18, pAge is dereferenced—using the indirection operator (*)—and printed, showing that the value at the address that pAge stores is the 5 stored in myAge.

On line 21, the value 7 is assigned to the variable at the address stored in pAge. This sets myAge to 7, and the printouts on lines 23 and 24 confirm this. Again, you should notice that the indirect access to the variable was obtained by using an asterisk—the indirection operator in this context.

On line 27, the value 9 is assigned to the variable myAge. This value is obtained directly on line 29 and indirectly (by dereferencing pAge) on line 30.

Examining the Address

Pointers enable you to manipulate addresses without ever knowing their real value. After today, you'll take it on faith that when you assign the address of a variable to a pointer, it really has the address of that variable as its value. But just this once, why not check to be certain? Listing 8.3 illustrates this idea.

LISTING 8.3   Finding Out What Is Stored in Pointers

```
1:   // Listing 8.3
2:   // What is stored in a pointer.
3:   #include <iostream>
4:
5:   int main()
6:   {
7:      using namespace std;
8:
9:      unsigned short int myAge = 5, yourAge = 10;
10:
11:      // a pointer
12:      unsigned short int * pAge = &myAge;
13:
14:      cout << "myAge:\t" << myAge
15:         <<  "\t\tyourAge:\t" << yourAge << endl;
16:
17:      cout << "&myAge:\t" << &myAge
18:         << "\t&yourAge:\t" << &yourAge << endl;
19:
20:      cout << "pAge:\t" << pAge << endl;
21:      cout << "*pAge:\t" << *pAge << endl;
22:
23:
24:      cout << "\nReassigning: pAge = &yourAge..." << endl << endl;
25:      pAge = &yourAge;        // reassign the pointer
26:
27:      cout << "myAge:\t" << myAge <<
28:         "\t\tyourAge:\t" << yourAge << endl;
29:
30:      cout << "&myAge:\t" << &myAge
31:         << "\t&yourAge:\t" << &yourAge << endl;
32:
33:      cout << "pAge:\t" << pAge << endl;
34:      cout << "*pAge:\t" << *pAge << endl;
35:
36:      cout << "\n&pAge:\t" << &pAge << endl;
37:
38:      return 0;
39:   }
```

OUTPUT

```
myAge:   5              yourAge:        10
&myAge: 0012FF7C        &yourAge:       0012FF78
pAge:   0012FF7C
*pAge:  5

Reassigning: pAge = &yourAge...
```

8

```
myAge:   5              yourAge:      10
&myAge:  0012FF7C       &yourAge:     0012FF78
pAge:    0012FF78
*pAge:   10

&pAge:   0012FF74
```

(Your output might look different.)

ANALYSIS On line 9, myAge and yourAge are declared to be variables of type unsigned short integer. On line 12, pAge is declared to be a pointer to an unsigned short integer, and it is initialized with the address of the variable myAge.

Lines 14–18 print the values and the addresses of myAge and yourAge. Line 20 prints the *contents* of pAge, which is the address of myAge. You should notice that the output confirms that the value of pAge matches the value of myAge's address. Line 21 prints the result of dereferencing pAge, which prints the value at pAge—the value in myAge, or 5.

This is the essence of pointers. Line 20 shows that pAge stores the address of myAge, and line 21 shows how to get the value stored in myAge by dereferencing the pointer pAge. Be certain that you understand this fully before you go on. Study the code and look at the output.

On line 25, pAge is reassigned to point to the address of yourAge. The values and addresses are printed again. The output shows that pAge now has the address of the variable yourAge and that dereferencing obtains the value in yourAge.

Line 36 prints the address of pAge itself. Like any variable, it has an address, and that address can be stored in a pointer. (Assigning the address of a pointer to another pointer will be discussed shortly.)

Do	**DON'T**
DO use the indirection operator (*) to access the data stored at the address in a pointer.	**DON'T** confuse the address in a pointer with the value at that address.
DO initialize all pointers either to a valid address or to null (0).	

Using Pointers

To declare a pointer, write the type of the variable or object whose address will be stored in the pointer, followed by the pointer operator (*) and the name of the pointer. For example,

```
unsigned short int * pPointer = 0;
```
To assign or initialize a pointer, prepend the name of the variable whose address is being assigned with the address-of operator (&). For example,
```
unsigned short int theVariable = 5;
unsigned short int * pPointer = &theVariable;
```
To dereference a pointer, prepend the pointer name with the dereference operator (*). For example:
```
unsigned short int theValue = *pPointer
```

Why Would You Use Pointers?

So far, you've seen step-by-step details of assigning a variable's address to a pointer. In practice, though, you would never do this. After all, why bother with a pointer when you already have a variable with access to that value? The only reason for this kind of pointer manipulation of an automatic variable is to demonstrate how pointers work. Now that you are comfortable with the syntax of pointers, you can put them to good use. Pointers are used, most often, for three tasks:

- Managing data on the free store
- Accessing class member data and functions
- Passing variables by reference to functions

The remainder of today's lesson focuses on managing data on the free store and accessing class member data and functions. Tomorrow, you will learn about passing variables using pointers, which is called passing by reference.

The Stack and the Free Store (Heap)

In the section "How Functions Work—A Peek Under the Hood" on Day 5, "Organizing into Functions," five areas of memory are mentioned:

- Global namespace
- The free store
- Registers
- Code space
- The stack

Local variables are on the stack, along with function parameters. Code is in code space, of course, and global variables are in the global namespace. The registers are used for internal housekeeping functions, such as keeping track of the top of the stack and the instruction pointer. Just about all of the remaining memory is given to the free store, which is often referred to as the heap.

Local variables don't persist; when a function returns, its local variables are destroyed. This is good, because it means the programmer doesn't have to do anything to manage this memory space, but is bad because it makes it hard for functions to create objects for use by other objects or functions without generating the extra overhead of copying objects from stack to return value to destination object in the caller. Global variables solve that problem at the cost of providing unrestricted access to those variables through-out the program, which leads to the creation of code that is difficult to understand and maintain. Putting data in the free store can solve both of these problems if that data is managed properly.

You can think of the free store as a massive section of memory in which thousands of sequentially numbered cubbyholes lie waiting for your data. You can't label these cubby-holes, though, as you can with the stack. You must ask for the address of the cubbyhole that you reserve and then stash that address away in a pointer.

One way to think about this is with an analogy: A friend gives you the 800 number for Acme Mail Order. You go home and program your telephone with that number, and then you throw away the piece of paper with the number on it. If you push the button, a tele-phone rings somewhere, and Acme Mail Order answers. You don't remember the num-ber, and you don't know where the other telephone is located, but the button gives you access to Acme Mail Order. Acme Mail Order is your data on the free store. You don't know where it is, but you know how to get to it. You access it by using its address—in this case, the telephone number. You don't have to know that number; you just have to put it into a pointer (the button). The pointer gives you access to your data without both-ering you with the details.

The stack is cleaned automatically when a function returns. All the local variables go out of scope, and they are removed from the stack. The free store is not cleaned until your program ends, and it is your responsibility to free any memory that you've reserved when you are done with it. This is where destructors are absolutely critical, because they provide a place where any heap memory allocated in a class can be reclaimed.

The advantage to the free store is that the memory you reserve remains available until you explicitly state you are done with it by freeing it. If you reserve memory on the free store while in a function, the memory is still available when the function returns.

The disadvantage of the free store is also that the memory you reserve remains available until you explicitly state you are done with it by freeing it. If you neglect to free that memory, it can build up over time and cause the system to crash.

The advantage of accessing memory in this way, rather than using global variables, is that only functions with access to the pointer (which has the appropriate address) have access to the data. This requires the object containing the pointer to the data, or the pointer itself, to be explicitly passed to any function making changes, thus reducing the chances that a function can change the data without that change being traceable.

For this to work, you must be able to create a pointer to an area on the free store and to pass that pointer among functions. The following sections describe how to do this.

Allocating Space with the new Keyword

You allocate memory on the free store in C++ by using the new keyword. new is followed by the type of the object that you want to allocate, so that the compiler knows how much memory is required. Therefore, new unsigned short int allocates two bytes in the free store, and new long allocates four, assuming your system uses a two-byte unsigned short int and a four-byte long.

The return value from new is a memory address. Because you now know that memory addresses are stored in pointers, it should be no surprise to you that the return value from new should be assigned to a pointer. To create an unsigned short on the free store, you might write

```
unsigned short int * pPointer;
pPointer = new unsigned short int;
```

You can, of course, do this all on one line by initializing the pointer at the same time you declare it:

```
unsigned short int * pPointer = new unsigned short int;
```

In either case, pPointer now points to an unsigned short int on the free store. You can use this like any other pointer to a variable and assign a value into that area of memory by writing

```
*pPointer = 72;
```

This means "Put 72 at the value in pPointer," or "Assign the value 72 to the area on the free store to which pPointer points."

NOTE

> If new cannot create memory on the free store (memory is, after all, a limited resource), it throws an exception (see Day 20, "Handling Errors and Exceptions").

Putting Memory Back: The delete Keyword

When you are finished with an area of memory, you must free it back to the system. You do this by calling delete on the pointer. delete returns the memory to the free store.

It is critical to remember that memory allocated with new is not freed automatically. If a pointer variable is pointing to memory on the free store and the pointer goes out of scope, the memory is not automatically returned to the free store. Rather, it is considered allocated and because the pointer is no longer available, you can no longer access the memory. This happens, for instance, if a pointer is a local variable. When the function in which that pointer is declared returns, that pointer goes out of scope and is lost. The memory allocated with new is not freed—instead, it becomes unavailable.

This situation is called a *memory leak*. It's called a memory leak because that memory can't be recovered until the program ends. It is as though the memory has leaked out of your computer.

To prevent memory leaks, you should restore any memory you allocate back to the free store. You do this by using the keyword delete. For example:

```
delete pPointer;
```

When you delete the pointer, you are really freeing up the memory whose address is stored in the pointer. You are saying, "Return to the free store the memory that this pointer points to." The pointer is still a pointer, and it can be reassigned. Listing 8.4 demonstrates allocating a variable on the heap, using that variable, and deleting it.

Most commonly, you will allocate items from the heap in a constructor, and deallocate them in the destructor. In other cases, you will initialize pointers in the constructor, allocate memory for those pointers as the object is used, and, in the destructor, test the pointers for null and deallocate them if they are not null.

CAUTION

> When you call delete on a pointer, the memory it points to is freed. Calling delete on that pointer again crashes your program! When you delete a pointer, set it to zero (null). Calling delete on a null pointer is guaranteed to be safe. For example:

```
Animal *pDog = new Animal; // allocate memory
delete pDog;   //frees the memory
   pDog = 0;   //sets pointer to null
   //...
delete pDog;   //harmless
```

LISTING 8.4 Allocating, Using, and Deleting Pointers

```
 1:  // Listing 8.4
 2:  // Allocating and deleting a pointer
 3:  #include <iostream>
 4:  int main()
 5:  {
 6:      using namespace std;
 7:      int localVariable = 5;
 8:      int * pLocal= &localVariable;
 9:      int * pHeap = new int;
10:      *pHeap = 7;
11:      cout << "localVariable: " << localVariable << endl;
12:      cout << "*pLocal: " << *pLocal << endl;
13:      cout << "*pHeap: " << *pHeap << endl;
14:      delete pHeap;
15:      pHeap = new int;
16:      *pHeap = 9;
17:      cout << "*pHeap: " << *pHeap << endl;
18:      delete pHeap;
19:      return 0;
20:  }
```

OUTPUT

```
localVariable: 5
*pLocal: 5
*pHeap: 7
*pHeap: 9
```

ANALYSIS Line 7 declares and initializes a local variable ironically called `localVariable`. Line 8 declares a pointer called `pLocal` and initializes it with the address of the local variable. On line 9, a second pointer called `pHeap` is declared; however, it is initialized with the result obtained from calling `new int`. This allocates space on the free store for an `int`, which can be accessed using the `pHeap` pointer. This allocated memory is assigned the value 7 on line 10.

Lines 11–13 print a few values. Line 11 prints the value of the local variable (`localVariable`), line 12 prints the value pointed to by the `pLocal` pointer, and line 13 prints the value pointed to by the `pHeap` pointer. You should notice that, as expected, the values printed on lines 11 and 12 match. In addition, line 13 confirms that the value assigned on line 10 is, in fact, accessible.

On line 14, the memory allocated on line 9 is returned to the free store by a call to delete. This frees the memory and disassociates the pointer from that memory. pHeap is now free to be used to point to other memory. It is reassigned on lines 15 and 16, and line 17 prints the result. Line 18 restores that memory to the free store.

Although line 18 is redundant (the end of the program would have returned that memory), it is a good idea to free this memory explicitly. If the program changes or is extended, having already taken care of this step is beneficial.

Another Look at Memory Leaks

Memory leaks are one of the most serious issues and complaints about pointers. You have seen one way that memory leaks can occur. Another way you might inadvertently create a memory leak is by reassigning your pointer before deleting the memory to which it points. Consider this code fragment:

```
1:    unsigned short int * pPointer = new unsigned short int;
2:    *pPointer = 72;
3:    pPointer = new unsigned short int;
4:    *pPointer = 84;
```

Line 1 creates pPointer and assigns it the address of an area on the free store. Line 2 stores the value 72 in that area of memory. Line 3 reassigns pPointer to another area of memory. Line 4 places the value 84 in that area. The original area—in which the value 72 is now held—is unavailable because the pointer to that area of memory has been reassigned. No way exists to access that original area of memory, nor is there any way to free it before the program ends.

The code should have been written like this:

```
1: unsigned short int * pPointer = new unsigned short int;
2: *pPointer = 72;
3: delete pPointer;
4: pPointer = new unsigned short int;
5: *pPointer = 84;
```

Now, the memory originally pointed to by pPointer is deleted, and thus freed, on line 3.

NOTE
> For every time in your program that you call new, there should be a call to delete. It is important to keep track of which pointer owns an area of memory and to ensure that the memory is returned to the free store when you are done with it.

Creating Objects on the Free Store

Just as you can create a pointer to an integer, you can create a pointer to any data type, including classes. If you have declared an object of type Cat, you can declare a pointer to that class and instantiate a Cat object on the free store, just as you can make one on the stack. The syntax is the same as for integers:

```
Cat *pCat = new Cat;
```

This calls the default constructor—the constructor that takes no parameters. The constructor is called whenever an object is created (on the stack or on the free store). Be aware, however, that you are not limited to using only the default constructor when creating an object with new—any constructor can be used.

Deleting Objects from the Free Store

When you call delete on a pointer to an object on the free store, that object's destructor is called before the memory is released. This gives your class a chance to clean up (generally deallocating heap allocated memory), just as it does for objects destroyed on the stack. Listing 8.5 illustrates creating and deleting objects on the free store.

LISTING 8.5   Creating and Deleting Objects on the Free Store

```
 1:  // Listing 8.5 - Creating objects on the free store
 2:  // using new and delete
 3:
 4:  #include <iostream>
 5:
 6:  using namespace std;
 7:
 8:  class SimpleCat
 9:  {
10:  public:
11:      SimpleCat();
12:      ~SimpleCat();
13:  private:
14:      int itsAge;
15:  };
16:
17:  SimpleCat::SimpleCat()
18:  {
19:      cout << "Constructor called. " << endl;
20:      itsAge = 1;
21:  }
22:
23:  SimpleCat::~SimpleCat()
24:  {
```

LISTING 8.5 continued

```
25:    cout << "Destructor called. " << endl;
26: }
27:
28: int main()
29: {
30:    cout << "SimpleCat Frisky... " << endl;
31:    SimpleCat Frisky;
32:    cout << "SimpleCat *pRags = new SimpleCat..." << endl;
33:    SimpleCat * pRags = new SimpleCat;
34:    cout << "delete pRags... " << endl;
35:    delete pRags;
36:    cout << "Exiting, watch Frisky go... " << endl;
37:    return 0;
38: }
```

OUTPUT

```
SimpleCat Frisky...
Constructor called.
SimpleCat *pRags = new SimpleCat..
Constructor called.
delete pRags...
Destructor called.
Exiting, watch Frisky go...
Destructor called.
```

ANALYSIS Lines 8–15 declare the stripped-down class SimpleCat. Line 11 declares SimpleCat's constructor, and lines 17–21 contain its definition. Line 12 declares SimpleCat's destructor, and lines 23–26 contain its definition. As you can see, both the constructor and destructor simply print a simple message to let you know they have been called.

On line 31, Frisky is created as a regular local variable, thus it is created on the stack. This creation causes the constructor to be called. On line 33, the SimpleCat pointed to by pRags is also created; however, because a pointer is being used, it is created on the heap. Once again, the constructor is called.

On line 35, delete is called on the pointer, pRags. This causes the destructor to be called and the memory that had been allocated to hold this SimpleCat object to be returned. When the function ends on line 38, Frisky goes out of scope, and its destructor is called.

Accessing Data Members

You learned on Day 6, "Understanding Object-Oriented Programming," that you accessed data members and functions by using the dot (.) operator. As you should be aware, this works for Cat objects created locally.

Accessing the members of an object when using a pointer is a little more complex. To access the Cat object on the free store, you must dereference the pointer and call the dot operator on the object pointed to by the pointer. It is worth repeating this. You must first dereference the pointer. You then use the dereferenced value—the value being pointed to—along with the dot operator to access the members of the object. Therefore, to access the GetAge member function of an object pointed to by pRags, you write

```
(*pRags).GetAge();
```

As you can see, parentheses are used to ensure that pRags is dereferenced first—before GetAge() is accessed. Remember, parentheses have a higher precedence than other operators.

Because this is cumbersome, C++ provides a shorthand operator for indirect access: the *class member access* operator (->), which is created by typing the dash (-) immediately followed by the greater-than symbol (>). C++ treats this as a single symbol. Listing 8.6 demonstrates accessing member variables and functions of objects created on the free store.

NOTE

Because the class member access operator (->) can also be used for indirect access to members of an object (through a pointer), it can also be referred to as an indirection operator. Some people also refer to it as the *points-to* operator because that is what it does.

LISTING 8.6   Accessing Member Data of Objects on the Free Store

```
 1:  // Listing 8.6 - Accessing data members of objects on the heap
 2:  // using the -> operator
 3:
 4:  #include <iostream>
 5:
 6:  class SimpleCat
 7:  {
 8:    public:
 9:       SimpleCat() {itsAge = 2; }
10:       ~SimpleCat() {}
11:       int GetAge() const { return itsAge; }
12:       void SetAge(int age) { itsAge = age; }
13:    private:
14:       int itsAge;
15:  };
16:
17:  int main()
18:  {
```

LISTING 8.6 continued

```
19:     using namespace std;
20:     SimpleCat * Frisky = new SimpleCat;
21:     cout << "Frisky is " << Frisky->GetAge() << " years old " << endl;
22:     Frisky->SetAge(5);
23:     cout << "Frisky is " << Frisky->GetAge() << " years old " << endl;
24:     delete Frisky;
25:     return 0;
26:  }
```

OUTPUT
Frisky is 2 years old
Frisky is 5 years old

ANALYSIS On line 20, a SimpleCat object that is pointed to by the pointer Frisky is instantiated (created) on the free store. The default constructor of the object sets its age to 2, and the GetAge() method is called on line 21. Because Frisky is a pointer, the indirection operator (->) is used to access the member data and functions. On line 22, the SetAge() method is called, and GetAge() is accessed again on line 23.

Creating Member Data on the Free Store

In addition to creating objects on the free store, you can also create data members within an object on the free store. One or more of the data members of a class can be a pointer to an object on the free store. Using what you have already learned, you can allocate memory on the free store for these pointers to use. The memory can be allocated in the class constructor or in one of the class' methods. When you are done using the member, you can—and should—delete it in one of the methods or in the destructor, as Listing 8.7 illustrates.

LISTING 8.7 Pointers as Member Data

```
1:  // Listing 8.7 - Pointers as data members
2:  // accessed with -> operator
3:
4:  #include <iostream>
5:
6:  class SimpleCat
7:  {
8:    public:
9:      SimpleCat();
10:     ~SimpleCat();
11:     int GetAge() const { return *itsAge; }
12:     void SetAge(int age) { *itsAge = age; }
13:
```

LISTING 8.7   continued

```
14:        int GetWeight() const { return *itsWeight; }
15:        void setWeight (int weight) { *itsWeight = weight; }
16:
17:     private:
18:        int * itsAge;
19:        int * itsWeight;
20:  };
21:
22:  SimpleCat::SimpleCat()
23:  {
24:      itsAge = new int(2);
25:      itsWeight = new int(5);
26:  }
27:
28:  SimpleCat::~SimpleCat()
29:  {
30:      delete itsAge;
31:      delete itsWeight;
32:  }
33:
34:  int main()
35:  {
36:      using namespace std;
37:      SimpleCat *Frisky = new SimpleCat;
38:      cout << "Frisky is " << Frisky->GetAge()
39:                << " years old " << endl;
40:      Frisky->SetAge(5);
41:      cout << "Frisky is " << Frisky->GetAge()
42:                << " years old " << endl;
43:      delete Frisky;
44:      return 0;
45:  }
```

OUTPUT
```
Frisky is 2 years old
Frisky is 5 years old
```

ANALYSIS   The class SimpleCat is declared to have two member variables—both of which are pointers to integers—on lines 18 and 19. The constructor (lines 22–26) initializes the pointers to memory on the free store and to the default values.

Notice on lines 24 and 25 that a pseudoconstructor is called on the new integer, passing in the value for the integer. This creates an integer on the heap and initializes its value (on line 24 to the value 2 and on line 25 to the value 5).

The destructor (lines 28–32) cleans up the allocated memory. Because this is the destructor, there is no point in assigning these pointers to null because they will no longer be accessible. This is one of the safe places to break the rule that deleted pointers should be assigned to null, although following the rule doesn't hurt.

The calling function (in this case, main()) is unaware that itsAge and itsWeight are pointers to memory on the free store. main() continues to call GetAge() and SetAge(), and the details of the memory management are hidden in the implementation of the class—as they should be.

When Frisky is deleted on line 41, its destructor is called. The destructor deletes each of its member pointers. If these, in turn, point to objects of other user-defined classes, their destructors are called as well.

Understanding What You Are Accomplishing

The use of pointers as was done in Listing 8.7 would be pretty silly in a real program unless a good reason existed for the Cat object to hold its members by reference. In this case, there is no good reason to use pointers to access itsAge and itsWeight, but in other cases, this can make a lot of sense.

This brings up the obvious question: What are you trying to accomplish by using pointers as references to variables instead of just using variables? Understand, too, that you must start with design. If what you've designed is an object that refers to another object, but the second object might come into existence before the first object and continue after the first object is gone, then the first object must contain the second by reference.

For example, the first object might be a window and the second object might be a document. The window needs access to the document, but it doesn't control the lifetime of the document. Thus, the window needs to hold the document by reference.

This is implemented in C++ by using pointers or references. References are covered on Day 9, "Exploiting References."

The this Pointer

Every class member function has a hidden parameter: the this pointer. this points to "this" individual object. Therefore, in each call to GetAge() or SetAge(), each function gets this for its object as a hidden parameter.

It is possible to use the pointer to this explicitly, as Listing 8.8 illustrates.

LISTING 8.8 Using the this Pointer

```
1:  // Listing 8.8
2:  // Using the this pointer
3:
4:  #include <iostream>
5:
6:  class Rectangle
7:  {
8:    public:
9:      Rectangle();
10:     ~Rectangle();
11:     void SetLength(int length)
12:       { this->itsLength = length; }
13:     int GetLength() const
14:       { return this->itsLength; }
15:
16:     void SetWidth(int width)
17:       { itsWidth = width; }
18:     int GetWidth() const
19:       { return itsWidth; }
20:
21:   private:
22:     int itsLength;
23:     int itsWidth;
24:  };
25:
26:  Rectangle::Rectangle()
27:  {
28:     itsWidth = 5;
29:     itsLength = 10;
30:  }
31:  Rectangle::~Rectangle()
32:  {}
33:
34:  int main()
35:  {
36:     using namespace std;
37:     Rectangle theRect;
38:     cout << "theRect is " << theRect.GetLength()
39:       << " feet long." << endl;
40:     cout << "theRect is " << theRect.GetWidth()
41:       << " feet wide." << endl;
42:     theRect.SetLength(20);
43:     theRect.SetWidth(10);
44:     cout << "theRect is " << theRect.GetLength()
45:       << " feet long." << endl;
46:     cout << "theRect is " << theRect.GetWidth()
47:       << " feet wide. " << endl;
48:     return 0;
49:  }
```

8

OUTPUT

```
theRect is 10 feet long.
theRect is 5 feet wide.
theRect is 20 feet long.
theRect is 10 feet wide.
```

ANALYSIS The SetLength() accessor function on lines 11–12 and the GetLength() accessor function on lines 13–14, both explicitly use the this pointer to access the member variables of the Rectangle object. The SetWidth() and GetWidth() accessors on lines 16–19 do not. No difference exists in their behavior, although the syntax is easier to understand.

If that were all there was to this, there would be little point in bothering you with it. this, however, is a pointer; it stores the memory address of an object. As such, it can be a powerful tool.

You'll see a practical use for this on Day 10, "Working with Advanced Functions," when operator overloading is discussed. For now, your goal is to know about this and to understand what it is: a pointer to the object that holds the function.

You don't have to worry about creating or deleting the this pointer. The compiler takes care of that.

Stray, Wild, or Dangling Pointers

Yet again, issues with pointers are being brought up. This is because errors you create in your programs with pointers can be among the most difficult to find and among the most problematic. One source of bugs that are especially nasty and difficult to find in C++ is stray pointers. A stray pointer (also called a wild or dangling pointer) is created when you call delete on a pointer—thereby freeing the memory that it points to—and then you don't set it to null. If you then try to use that pointer again without reassigning it, the result is unpredictable and, if you are lucky, your program will crash.

It is as though the Acme Mail Order company moved away, but you still pressed the programmed button on your phone. It is possible that nothing terrible happens—a telephone rings in a deserted warehouse. On the other hand, perhaps the telephone number has been reassigned to a munitions factory, and your call detonates an explosive and blows up your whole city!

In short, be careful not to use a pointer after you have called delete on it. The pointer still points to the old area of memory, but the compiler is free to put other data there; using the pointer without reallocating new memory for it can cause your program to crash. Worse, your program might proceed merrily on its way and crash several minutes later. This is called a time bomb, and it is no fun. To be safe, after you delete a pointer, set it to null (0). This disarms the pointer.

Listing 8.9 illustrates creating a stray pointer.

LISTING 8.9   Creating a Stray Pointer

```
1:  // Listing 8.9 - Demonstrates a stray pointer
2:
3:  typedef unsigned short int USHORT;
4:  #include <iostream>
5:
6:  int main()
7:  {
8:      USHORT * pInt = new USHORT;
9:      *pInt = 10;
10:     std::cout << "*pInt: " << *pInt << std::endl;
11:     delete pInt;
12:
13:     long * pLong = new long;
14:     *pLong = 90000;
15:     std::cout << "*pLong: " << *pLong << std::endl;
16:
17:     *pInt = 20;      // uh oh, this was deleted!
18:
19:     std::cout << "*pInt: " << *pInt  << std::endl;
20:     std::cout << "*pLong: " << *pLong  << std::endl;
21:     delete pLong;
22:     return 0;
23: }
```

OUTPUT
```
*pInt:    10
*pLong:   90000
*pInt:    20
*pLong:   65556
```

(Do not try to re-create this output; yours will differ if you are lucky; or your computer will crash if you are not.)

ANALYSIS This is a listing you should avoid running because it could lock up your machine. On line 8, pInt is declared to be a pointer to USHORT, and is pointed to newly allocated memory. On line 9, the value 10 is put into that memory allocated for pInt. The value pointed to is then printed on line 10. After the value is printed, delete is called on the pointer. After line 11 executes, pInt is a stray, or dangling, pointer.

Line 13 declares a new pointer, pLong, which is pointed at the memory allocated by new. On line 14, the value 90000 is assigned to pLong, and on line 15, this value prints.

It is on line 17 that the troubles begin. On line 17, the value 20 is assigned to the memory that pInt points to, but pInt no longer points anywhere that is valid. The memory that pInt points to was freed by the call to delete on line 11. Assigning a value to that memory is certain disaster.

On line 19, the value at pInt is printed. Sure enough, it is 20. Line 20 prints the value at pLong; it has suddenly been changed to 65556. Two questions arise:

1. How could pLong's value change, given that pLong wasn't touched?
2. Where did the 20 go when pInt was used on line 17?

As you might guess, these are related questions. When a value was placed at pInt on line 17, the compiler happily placed the value 20 at the memory location that pInt previously pointed to. However, because that memory was freed on line 11, the compiler was free to reassign it. When pLong was created on line 13, it was given pInt's old memory location. (On some computers, this might not happen, depending on where in memory these values are stored.) When the value 20 was assigned to the location that pInt previously pointed to, it wrote over the value pointed to by pLong. This is called "stomping on a pointer." It is often the unfortunate outcome of using a stray pointer.

This is a particularly nasty bug because the value that changed wasn't associated with the stray pointer. The change to the value at pLong was a side effect of the misuse of pInt. In a large program, this would be very difficult to track down.

Just for Fun

Here are the details of how 65,556 got into the memory address of pLong in Listing 8.9:

1. pInt was pointed at a particular memory location, and the value 10 was assigned.

2. delete was called on pInt, which told the compiler that it could put something else at that location. Then, pLong was assigned the same memory location.

3. The value 90000 was assigned to *pLong. The particular computer used in this example stored the four-byte value of 90,000 (00 01 5F 90) in byte-swapped order. Therefore, it was stored as 5F 90 00 01.

4. `pInt` was assigned the value `20`—or `00 14` in hexadecimal notation. Because `pInt` still pointed to the same address, the first two bytes of `pLong` were overwritten, leaving `00 14 00 01`.

5. The value at `pLong` was printed, reversing the bytes back to their correct order of `00 01 00 14`, which was translated into the DOS value of `65556`.

FAQ

What is the difference between a null pointer and a stray pointer?

Answer: When you delete a pointer, you tell the compiler to free the memory, but the pointer itself continues to exist. It is now a stray pointer.

When you then write `myPtr = 0;` you change it from being a stray pointer to being a null pointer.

Normally, if you delete a pointer and then delete it again, your program is undefined. That is, anything might happen—if you are lucky, the program will crash. If you delete a null pointer, nothing happens; it is safe.

Using a stray *or* a null pointer (for example, writing `myPtr = 5;`) is illegal, and it might crash. If the pointer is null, it *will* crash, another benefit of null over stray. Predictable crashes are preferred because they are easier to debug.

Using const Pointers

You can use the keyword `const` for pointers before the type, after the type, or in both places. For example, all the following are legal declarations:

```
const int * pOne;
int * const pTwo;
const int * const pThree;
```

Each of these, however, does something different:

- `pOne` is a pointer to a constant integer. The value that is pointed to can't be changed.

- `pTwo` is a constant pointer to an integer. The integer can be changed, but `pTwo` can't point to anything else.

- `pThree` is a constant pointer to a constant integer. The value that is pointed to can't be changed, and `pThree` can't be changed to point to anything else.

The trick to keeping this straight is to look to the right of the keyword const to find out what is being declared constant. If the type is to the right of the keyword, it is the value that is constant. If the variable is to the right of the keyword const, it is the pointer variable itself that is constant. The following helps to illustrate this:

```
const int * p1;   // the int pointed to is constant
int * const p2;   // p2 is constant, it can't point to anything else
```

const Pointers and const Member Functions

On Day 6, you learned that you can apply the keyword const to a member function. When a function is declared const, the compiler flags as an error any attempt to change data in the object from within that function.

If you declare a pointer to a const object, the only methods that you can call with that pointer are const methods. Listing 8.10 illustrates this.

LISTING 8.10 Using Pointers to const Objects

```
1:  // Listing 8.10 - Using pointers with const methods
2:
3:  #include <iostream>
4:  using namespace std;
5:
6:  class Rectangle
7:  {
8:    public:
9:      Rectangle();
10:     ~Rectangle();
11:     void SetLength(int length) { itsLength = length; }
12:     int GetLength() const { return itsLength; }
13:     void SetWidth(int width) { itsWidth = width; }
14:     int GetWidth() const { return itsWidth; }
15:
16:    private:
17:      int itsLength;
18:      int itsWidth;
19:  };
20:
21:  Rectangle::Rectangle()
22:  {
23:      itsWidth = 5;
24:      itsLength = 10;
25:  }
26:
27:  Rectangle::~Rectangle()
28:  {}
29:
```

LISTING **8.10** continued

```
30:  int main()
31:  {
32:      Rectangle* pRect =  new Rectangle;
33:      const Rectangle * pConstRect = new Rectangle;
34:      Rectangle * const pConstPtr = new Rectangle;
35:
36:      cout << "pRect width: " << pRect->GetWidth()
37:          << " feet"  << endl;
38:      cout << "pConstRect width: " << pConstRect->GetWidth()
39:          << " feet" << endl;
40:      cout << "pConstPtr width: " << pConstPtr->GetWidth()
41:          << " feet" << endl;
42:
43:      pRect->SetWidth(10);
44:      // pConstRect->SetWidth(10);
45:      pConstPtr->SetWidth(10);
46:
47:      cout << "pRect width: " << pRect->GetWidth()
48:          << " feet\n";
49:      cout << "pConstRect width: " << pConstRect->GetWidth()
50:          << " feet\n";
51:      cout << "pConstPtr width: " << pConstPtr->GetWidth()
52:          << " feet\n";
53:      return 0;
54:  }
```

OUTPUT

```
pRect width: 5 feet
pConstRect width: 5 feet
pConstPtr width: 5 feet
pRect width: 10 feet
pConstRect width: 5 feet
pConstPtr width: 10 feet
```

ANALYSIS

Lines 6–19 declare the Rectangle class. Line 14 declares the GetWidth() member method const.

Line 32 declares a pointer to Rectangle called pRect. On line 33, a pointer to a constant Rectangle object is declared and named pConstRect. On line 34, pConstPtr is declared as a constant pointer to a Rectangle. Lines 36–41 print the values of these three variables.

On line 43, pRect is used to set the width of the rectangle to 10. On line 44, pConstRect would be used to set the width, but it was declared to point to a constant Rectangle. Therefore, it cannot legally call a non-const member function. Because it is not a valid statement, it is commented out.

On line 45, pConstPtr calls SetWidth(). pConstPtr is declared to be a constant pointer to a rectangle. In other words, the pointer is constant and cannot point to anything else,

8

but the rectangle is not constant, so methods such as GetWidth() and SetWidth() can be used.

Using a const this Pointers

When you declare an object to be const, you are in effect declaring that the object's this pointer is a pointer to a const object. A const this pointer can be used only with const member functions.

Do	Don't
DO protect objects passed by reference with const if they should not be changed. **DO** set pointers to null rather than leaving them uninitialized or dangling.	**DON'T** use a pointer that has been deleted. **DON'T** delete pointers more than once.

Constant objects and constant pointers will be discussed again tomorrow, when references to constant objects are discussed.

Summary

Pointers provide a powerful way to access data by indirection. Every variable has an address, which can be obtained using the address-of operator (&). The address can be stored in a pointer.

Pointers are declared by writing the type of object that they point to, followed by the indirection operator (*) and the name of the pointer. Pointers should be initialized to point to an object or to null (0).

You access the value at the address stored in a pointer by using the indirection operator (*).

You can declare const pointers, which can't be reassigned to point to other objects, and pointers to const objects, which can't be used to change the objects to which they point.

To create new objects on the free store, you use the new keyword and assign the address that is returned to a pointer. You free that memory by calling the delete keyword on the pointer. delete frees the memory, but it doesn't destroy the pointer. Therefore, you must reassign the pointer after its memory has been freed.

Q&A

Q Why are pointers so important?

A Pointers are important for a number of reasons. These include being able to use pointers to hold the address of objects and to use them to pass arguments by reference. On Day 14, "Polymorphism," you'll see how pointers are used in class polymorphism. In addition, many operating systems and class libraries create objects on your behalf and return pointers to them.

Q Why should I bother to declare anything on the free store?

A Objects on the free store persist after the return of a function. In addition, the capability to store objects on the free store enables you to decide at runtime how many objects you need, instead of having to declare this in advance. This is explored in greater depth tomorrow.

Q Why should I declare an object const if it limits what I can do with it?

A As a programmer, you want to enlist the compiler in helping you find bugs. One serious bug that is difficult to find is a function that changes an object in ways that aren't obvious to the calling function. Declaring an object const prevents such changes.

Workshop

The Workshop provides quiz questions to help you solidify your understanding of the material covered and exercises to provide you with experience in using what you've learned. Try to answer the quiz and exercise questions before checking the answers in Appendix D, and be certain you understand the answers before continuing to tomorrow's lesson.

Quiz

1. What operator is used to determine the address of a variable?
2. What operator is used to find the value stored at an address held in a pointer?
3. What is a pointer?
4. What is the difference between the address stored in a pointer and the value at that address?

5. What is the difference between the indirection operator and the address-of operator?

6. What is the difference between const int * ptrOne and int * const ptrTwo?

Exercises

1. What do these declarations do?

    a. int * pOne;

    b. int vTwo;

    c. int * pThree = &vTwo;

2. If you have an unsigned short variable named yourAge, how would you declare a pointer to manipulate yourAge?

3. Assign the value 50 to the variable yourAge by using the pointer that you declared in Exercise 2.

4. Write a small program that declares an integer and a pointer to integer. Assign the address of the integer to the pointer. Use the pointer to set a value in the integer variable.

5. **BUG BUSTERS:** What is wrong with this code?

```
#include <iostream>
using namespace std;
int main()
{
    int *pInt;
    *pInt = 9;
    cout << "The value at pInt: " << *pInt;
    return 0;
}
```

6. **BUG BUSTERS:** What is wrong with this code?

```
#include <iostream>
using namespace std;
int main()
{
    int SomeVariable = 5;
    cout << "SomeVariable: " << SomeVariable << endl;
    int *pVar = & SomeVariable;
    pVar = 9;
    cout << "SomeVariable: " << *pVar << endl;
    return 0;
}
```

DAY 9

Exploiting References

Yesterday, you learned how to use pointers to manipulate objects on the free store and how to refer to those objects indirectly. References, the topic of today's lesson, give you almost all the power of pointers but with a much easier syntax.

Today, you will learn

- What references are
- How references differ from pointers
- How to create references and use them
- What the limitations of references are
- How to pass values and objects into and out of functions by reference

What Is a Reference?

A *reference* is an alias; when you create a reference, you initialize it with the name of another object, the target. From that moment on, the reference acts as an alternative name for the target, and anything you do to the reference is really done to the target.

You create a reference by writing the type of the target object, followed by the reference operator (&), followed by the name of the reference, followed by an equal sign, followed by the name of the target object.

References can have any legal variable name, but some programmers prefer to prefix reference names with the letter "r." Thus, if you have an integer variable named someInt, you can make a reference to that variable by writing the following:

```
int &rSomeRef = someInt;
```

This statement is read as "rSomeRef is a reference to an integer. The reference is initialized to refer to someInt." References differ from other variables that you can declare in that they must be initialized when they are declared. If you try to create a reference variable without assigning, you receive a compiler error. Listing 9.1 shows how references are created and used.

NOTE ──────

> Note that the reference operator (&) is the same symbol as the one used for the address-of operator. These are not the same operators, however, although clearly they are related.
>
> The space before the reference operator is required; the space between the reference operator and the name of the reference variable is optional. Thus
>
> ```
> int &rSomeRef = someInt;  // ok
> int & rSomeRef = someInt; // ok
> ```

LISTING 9.1 Creating and Using References

```
 1:  //Listing 9.1 - Demonstrating the use of references
 2:
 3:  #include <iostream>
 4:
 5:  int main()
 6:  {
 7:      using namespace std;
 8:      int  intOne;
 9:      int &rSomeRef = intOne;
10:
11:      intOne = 5;
12:      cout << "intOne: " << intOne << endl;
13:      cout << "rSomeRef: " << rSomeRef << endl;
14:
15:      rSomeRef = 7;
16:      cout << "intOne: " << intOne << endl;
17:      cout << "rSomeRef: " << rSomeRef << endl;
18:
19:      return 0;
20:  }
```

OUTPUT

```
intOne: 5
rSomeRef: 5
intOne: 7
rSomeRef: 7
```

ANALYSIS On line 8, a local integer variable, intOne, is declared. On line 9, a reference to an integer (int), rSomeRef, is declared and initialized to refer to intOne. As already stated, if you declare a reference but don't initialize it, you receive a compile-time error. References must be initialized.

On line 11, intOne is assigned the value 5. On lines 12 and 13, the values in intOne and rSomeRef are printed, and are, of course, the same.

On line 15, 7 is assigned to rSomeRef. Because this is a reference, it is an alias for intOne, and thus the 7 is really assigned to intOne, as is shown by the printouts on lines 16 and 17.

Using the Address-Of Operator (&) on References

You have now seen that the & symbol is used for both the address of a variable and to declare a reference. But what if you take the address of a reference variable? If you ask a reference for its address, it returns the address of its target. That is the nature of references. They are aliases for the target. Listing 9.2 demonstrates taking the address of a reference variable called rSomeRef.

LISTING 9.2   Taking the Address of a Reference

```
1:  //Listing 9.2 - Demonstrating the use of references
2:
3:  #include <iostream>
4:
5:  int main()
6:  {
7:     using namespace std;
8:     int  intOne;
9:     int &rSomeRef = intOne;
10:
11:    intOne = 5;
12:    cout << "intOne: " << intOne << endl;
13:    cout << "rSomeRef: " << rSomeRef << endl;
14:
15:    cout << "&intOne: "  << &intOne << endl;
16:    cout << "&rSomeRef: " << &rSomeRef << endl;
17:
18:    return 0;
19: }
```

OUTPUT
```
intOne: 5
rSomeRef: 5
&intOne:  0x3500
&rSomeRef: 0x3500
```

CAUTION | Because the final two lines print memory addresses that might be unique to your computer or to a specific run of the program, your output might differ.

ANALYSIS Once again, rSomeRef is initialized as a reference to intOne. This time, the addresses of the two variables are printed in lines 15 and 16, and they are identical.

C++ gives you no way to access the address of the reference itself because it is not meaningful as it would be if you were using a pointer or other variable. References are initialized when created, and they always act as a synonym for their target, even when the address-of operator is applied.

For example, if you have a class called President, you might declare an instance of that class as follows:

```
President George_Washington;
```

You might then declare a reference to President and initialize it with this object:

```
President &FatherOfOurCountry = George_Washington;
```

Only one President exists; both identifiers refer to the same object of the same class. Any action you take on FatherOfOurCountry is taken on George_Washington as well.

Be careful to distinguish between the & symbol on line 9 of Listing 9.2, which declares a reference to an integer named rSomeRef, and the & symbols on lines 15 and 16, which return the addresses of the integer variable intOne and the reference rSomeRef. The compiler knows how to distinguish these two uses by the context in which they are being used.

NOTE | Normally, when you use a reference, you do not use the address-of operator. You simply use the reference as you would use the target variable.

Attempting to Reassign References (Not!)

Reference variables cannot be reassigned. Even experienced C++ programmers can be confused by what happens when you try to reassign a reference. Reference variables are always aliases for their target. What appears to be a reassignment turns out to be the assignment of a new value to the target. Listing 9.3 illustrates this fact.

LISTING 9.3   Assigning to a Reference

```
 1:    //Listing 9.3 - //Reassigning a reference
 2:
 3:    #include <iostream>
 4:
 5:    int main()
 6:    {
 7:       using namespace std;
 8:       int  intOne;
 9:       int &rSomeRef = intOne;
10:
11:       intOne = 5;
12:       cout << "intOne:    " << intOne << endl;
13:       cout << "rSomeRef: " << rSomeRef << endl;
14:       cout << "&intOne:   " << &intOne << endl;
15:       cout << "&rSomeRef: " << &rSomeRef << endl;
16:
17:       int intTwo = 8;
18:       rSomeRef = intTwo;  // not what you think!
19:       cout << "\nintOne:   " << intOne << endl;
20:       cout << "intTwo:   " << intTwo << endl;
21:       cout << "rSomeRef: " << rSomeRef << endl;
22:       cout << "&intOne:   " << &intOne << endl;
23:       cout << "&intTwo:   " << &intTwo << endl;
24:       cout << "&rSomeRef: " << &rSomeRef << endl;
25:       return 0;
26:    }
```

OUTPUT
```
intOne:    5
rSomeRef:  5
&intOne:   0012FEDC
&rSomeRef: 0012FEDC

intOne:    8
intTwo:    8
rSomeRef:  8
&intOne:   0012FEDC
&intTwo:   0012FEE0
&rSomeRef: 0012FEDC
```

ANALYSIS Once again, on lines 8 and 9, an integer variable and a reference to an integer are declared. The integer is assigned the value 5 on line 11, and the values and their addresses are printed on lines 12–15.

On line 17, a new variable, intTwo, is created and initialized with the value 8. On line 18, the programmer tries to reassign rSomeRef to now be an alias to the variable intTwo, but that is not what happens. What actually happens is that rSomeRef continues to act as an alias for intOne, so this assignment is equivalent to the following:

```
intOne = intTwo;
```

Sure enough, when the values of intOne and rSomeRef are printed (lines 19–21), they are the same as intTwo. In fact, when the addresses are printed on lines 22–24, you see that rSomeRef continues to refer to intOne and not intTwo.

Do	Don't
DO use references to create an alias to an object. **DO** initialize all references.	**DON'T** try to reassign a reference. **DON'T** confuse the address-of operator with the reference operator.

Referencing Objects

Any object can be referenced, including user-defined objects. Note that you create a reference to an object, but not to a class. For instance, your compiler will not allow this:

```
int & rIntRef = int;     // wrong
```

You must initialize rIntRef to a particular integer, such as this:

```
int howBig = 200;
int & rIntRef = howBig;
```

In the same way, you don't initialize a reference to a Cat:

```
Cat & rCatRef = Cat;    // wrong
```

You must initialize a reference to a particular Cat object:

```
Cat Frisky;
Cat & rCatRef = Frisky;
```

References to objects are used just like the object itself. Member data and methods are accessed using the normal class member access operator (.), and just as with the built-in types, the reference acts as an alias to the object. Listing 9.4 illustrates this.

LISTING 9.4 References to Objects

```
 1:  // Listing 9.4 - References to class objects
 2:
 3:  #include <iostream>
 4:
 5:  class SimpleCat
 6:  {
 7:    public:
 8:      SimpleCat (int age, int weight);
 9:      ~SimpleCat() {}
10:      int GetAge() { return itsAge; }
11:      int GetWeight() { return itsWeight; }
12:    private:
13:      int itsAge;
14:      int itsWeight;
15:  };
16:
17:  SimpleCat::SimpleCat(int age, int weight)
18:  {
19:      itsAge = age;
20:      itsWeight = weight;
21:  }
22:
23:  int main()
24:  {
25:      SimpleCat Frisky(5,8);
26:      SimpleCat & rCat = Frisky;
27:
28:      std::cout << "Frisky is: ";
29:      std::cout << Frisky.GetAge() << " years old." << std::endl;
30:      std::cout << "And Frisky weighs: ";
31:      std::cout << rCat.GetWeight() << " pounds." << std::endl;
32:      return 0;
33:  }
```

9

OUTPUT Frisky is: 5 years old.
And Frisky weighs 8 pounds.

ANALYSIS On line 25, Frisky is declared to be a SimpleCat object. On line 26, a
SimpleCat reference, rCat, is declared and initialized to refer to Frisky. On
lines 29 and 31, the SimpleCat accessor methods are accessed by using first the
SimpleCat object and then the SimpleCat reference. Note that the access is identical.
Again, the reference is an alias for the actual object.

> **References**
>
> References act as an alias to another variable. Declare a reference by writing the type, followed by the reference operator (&), followed by the reference name. References must be initialized at the time of creation.
>
> **Example 1**
> ```
> int hisAge;
> int &rAge = hisAge;
> ```
>
> **Example 2**
> ```
> Cat Boots;
> Cat &rCatRef = Boots;
> ```

Null Pointers and Null References

When pointers are not initialized or when they are deleted, they ought to be assigned to null (0). This is not true for references because they must be initialized to what they reference when they are declared.

However, because C++ needs to be usable for device drivers, embedded systems, and real-time systems that can reach directly into the hardware, the ability to reference specific addresses is valuable and required. For this reason, most compilers support a null or numeric initialization of a reference without much complaint, crashing only if you try to use the object in some way when that reference would be invalid.

Taking advantage of this in normal programming, however, is still not a good idea. When you move your program to another machine or compiler, mysterious bugs might develop if you have null references.

Passing Function Arguments by Reference

On Day 5, "Organizing into Functions," you learned that functions have two limitations: Arguments are passed by value, and the return statement can return only one value.

Passing values to a function by reference can overcome both of these limitations. In C++, passing a variable by reference is accomplished in two ways: using pointers and using references. Note the difference: You pass *by reference* using a pointer, or you pass *a reference* using a reference.

The syntax of using a pointer is different from that of using a reference, but the net effect is the same. Rather than a copy being created within the scope of the function, the actual original object is (effectively) made directly available to the function.

Passing an object by reference enables the function to change the object being referred to. On Day 5, you learned that functions are passed their parameters on the stack. When a function is passed a value by reference (using either pointers or references), the address of the original object is put on the stack, not the entire object. In fact, on some computers, the address is actually held in a register and nothing is put on the stack. In either case, because an address is being passed, the compiler now knows how to get to the original object, and changes are made there and not in a copy.

Recall that Listing 5.5 on Day 5 demonstrated that a call to the swap() function did not affect the values in the calling function. Listing 5.5 is reproduced here as Listing 9.5, for your convenience.

9

LISTING 9.5   Demonstrating Passing by Value

```
1:  //Listing 9.5 - Demonstrates passing by value
2:  #include <iostream>
3:
4:  using namespace std;
5:  void swap(int x, int y);
6:
7:  int main()
8:  {
9:      int x = 5, y = 10;
10:
11:     cout << "Main. Before swap, x: " << x << " y: " << y << endl;
12:     swap(x,y);
13:     cout << "Main. After swap, x: " << x << " y: " << y << endl;
14:     return 0;
15: }
16:
17: void swap (int x, int y)
18: {
19:     int temp;
20:
21:     cout << "Swap. Before swap, x: " << x << " y: " << y << endl;
22:
23:     temp = x;
24:     x = y;
25:     y = temp;
26:
27:     cout << "Swap. After swap, x: " << x << " y: " << y << endl;
28: }
```

OUTPUT
```
Main. Before swap, x: 5 y: 10
Swap. Before swap, x: 5 y: 10
Swap. After swap, x: 10 y: 5
Main. After swap, x: 5 y: 10
```

ANALYSIS This program initializes two variables in main() and then passes them to the swap() function, which appears to swap them. When they are examined again in main(), they are unchanged!

The problem here is that x and y are being passed to swap() by value. That is, local copies were made in the function. These local copies were changed and then thrown away when the function returned and its local storage was deallocated. What is preferable is to pass x and y by reference, which changes the source values of the variable rather than a local copy.

Two ways to solve this problem are possible in C++: You can make the parameters of swap() pointers to the original values, or you can pass in references to the original values.

Making swap() Work with Pointers

When you pass in a pointer, you pass in the address of the object, and thus the function can manipulate the value at that address. To make swap() change the actual values of x and y by using pointers, the function, swap(), should be declared to accept two int pointers. Then, by dereferencing the pointers, the values of x and y will actually be accessed and, in fact, be swapped. Listing 9.6 demonstrates this idea.

LISTING 9.6   Passing by Reference Using Pointers

```
1:  //Listing 9.6 Demonstrates passing by reference
2:  #include <iostream>
3:
4:  using namespace std;
5:  void swap(int *x, int *y);
6:
7:  int main()
8:  {
9:      int x = 5, y = 10;
10:
11:     cout << "Main. Before swap, x: " << x << " y: " << y << endl;
12:     swap(&x,&y);
13:     cout << "Main. After swap, x: " << x << " y: " << y << endl;
14:     return 0;
15:  }
16:
17:  void swap (int *px, int *py)
18:  {
19:      int temp;
20:
21:      cout << "Swap. Before swap, *px: " << *px <<
22:          " *py: " << *py << endl;
```

LISTING 9.6   continued

```
23:
24:       temp = *px;
25:       *px = *py;
26:       *py = temp;
27:
28:       cout << "Swap. After swap, *px: " << *px <<
29:           " *py: " << *py << endl;
30:
31:   }
```

OUTPUT

```
Main. Before swap, x: 5 y: 10
Swap. Before swap, *px: 5 *py: 10
Swap. After swap, *px: 10 *py: 5
Main. After swap, x: 10 y: 5
```

ANALYSIS   Success! On line 5, the prototype of swap() is changed to indicate that its two parameters will be pointers to int rather than int variables. When swap() is called on line 12, the addresses of x and y are passed as the arguments. You can see that the addresses are passed because the address-of operator (&) is being used.

On line 19, a local variable, temp, is declared in the swap() function. temp need not be a pointer; it will just hold the value of *px (that is, the value of x in the calling function) for the life of the function. After the function returns, temp is no longer needed.

On line 24, temp is assigned the value at px. On line 25, the value at px is assigned to the value at py. On line 26, the value stashed in temp (that is, the original value at px) is put into py.

The net effect of this is that the values in the calling function, whose address was passed to swap(), are, in fact, swapped.

Implementing swap() with References

The preceding program works, but the syntax of the swap() function is cumbersome in two ways. First, the repeated need to dereference the pointers within the swap() function makes it error-prone—for instance, if you fail to dereference the pointer, the compiler still lets you assign an integer to the pointer, and a subsequent user experiences an addressing error. This is also hard to read. Finally, the need to pass the address of the variables in the calling function makes the inner workings of swap() overly apparent to its users.

It is a goal of an object-oriented language such as C++ to prevent the user of a function from worrying about how it works. Passing by pointers puts the burden on the calling function rather than where it belongs—on the function being called. Listing 9.7 rewrites the swap() function, using references.

LISTING 9.7   swap() Rewritten with References

```
1:   //Listing 9.7 Demonstrates passing by reference
2:   // using references!
3:   #include <iostream>
4:
5:   using namespace std;
6:   void swap(int &x, int &y);
7:
8:   int main()
9:   {
10:      int x = 5, y = 10;
11:
12:      cout << "Main. Before swap, x: " << x << " y: "
13:         << y << endl;
14:
15:      swap(x,y);
16:
17:      cout << "Main. After swap, x: " << x << " y: "
18:         << y << endl;
19:
20:      return 0;
21:   }
22:
23:   void swap (int &rx, int &ry)
24:   {
25:      int temp;
26:
27:      cout << "Swap. Before swap, rx: " << rx << " ry: "
28:         << ry << endl;
29:
30:      temp = rx;
31:      rx = ry;
32:      ry = temp;
33:
34:
35:      cout << "Swap. After swap, rx: " << rx << " ry: "
36:         << ry << endl;
37:
38:   }
```

OUTPUT
```
Main. Before swap, x:5 y: 10
Swap. Before swap, rx:5 ry:10
Swap. After swap, rx:10 ry:5
Main. After swap, x:10, y:5
```

ANALYSIS Just as in the example with pointers, two variables are declared on line 10, and their values are printed on line 12. On line 15, the function swap() is called, but note that x and y, not their addresses, are passed. The calling function simply passes the variables.

When swap() is called, program execution jumps to line 23, where the variables are identified as references. The values from the variables are printed on line 27, but note that no special operators are required. These variables are aliases for the original variables and can be used as such.

On lines 30–32, the values are swapped, and then they're printed on line 35. Program execution jumps back to the calling function, and on line 17, the values are printed in main(). Because the parameters to swap() are declared to be references, the variables from main() are passed by reference, and thus their changed values are what is seen in main() as well.

As you can see from this listing, references provide the convenience and ease of use of normal variables, with the power and pass-by-reference capability of pointers!

Understanding Function Headers and Prototypes

Listing 9.6 shows swap() using pointers, and Listing 9.7 shows it using references. Using the function that takes references is easier, and the code is easier to read, but how does the calling function know if the values are passed by reference or by value? As a client (or user) of swap(), the programmer must ensure that swap() will, in fact, change the parameters.

This is another use for the function prototype. By examining the parameters declared in the prototype, which is typically in a header file along with all the other prototypes, the programmer knows that the values passed into swap() are passed by reference, and thus will be swapped properly. On line 6 of Listing 9.7, you can see the prototype for swap()—you can see that the two parameters are passed as references.

If swap() had been a member function of a class, the class declaration, also available in a header file, would have supplied this information.

In C++, clients of classes and functions can rely on the header file to tell all that is needed; it acts as the interface to the class or function. The actual implementation is hidden from the client. This enables the programmer to focus on the problem at hand and to use the class or function without concern for how it works.

When Colonel John Roebling designed the Brooklyn Bridge, he worried in detail about how the concrete was poured and how the wire for the bridge was manufactured. He was intimately involved in the mechanical and chemical processes required to create his materials. Today, however, engineers make more efficient use of their time by using well-understood building materials, without regard to how their manufacturer produced them.

It is the goal of C++ to enable programmers to rely on well-understood classes and functions without regard to their internal workings. These "component parts" can be assembled to produce a program, much the same way wires, pipes, clamps, and other parts are assembled to produce buildings and bridges.

In much the same way that an engineer examines the spec sheet for a pipe to determine its load-bearing capacity, volume, fitting size, and so forth, a C++ programmer reads the declaration of a function or class to determine what services it provides, what parameters it takes, and what values it returns.

Returning Multiple Values

As discussed, functions can only return one value. What if you need to get two values back from a function? One way to solve this problem is to pass two objects into the function, by reference. The function can then fill the objects with the correct values. Because passing by reference allows a function to change the original objects, this effectively enables the function to return two pieces of information. This approach bypasses the return value of the function, which can then be reserved for reporting errors.

Once again, this can be done with references or pointers. Listing 9.8 demonstrates a function that returns three values: two as pointer parameters and one as the return value of the function.

LISTING 9.8   Returning Values with Pointers

```
 1:  //Listing 9.8 - Returning multiple values from a function
 2:
 3:  #include <iostream>
 4:
 5:  using namespace std;
 6:  short Factor(int n, int* pSquared, int* pCubed);
 7:
 8:  int main()
 9:  {
10:     int number, squared, cubed;
11:     short error;
12:
```

LISTING 9.8 continued

```
13:    cout << "Enter a number (0 - 20): ";
14:    cin >> number;
15:
16:    error = Factor(number, &squared, &cubed);
17:
18:    if (!error)
19:    {
20:       cout << "number: " << number << endl;
21:       cout << "square: " << squared << endl;
22:       cout << "cubed: " << cubed   << endl;
23:    }
24:    else
25:       cout << "Error encountered!!" << endl;
26:    return 0;
27: }
28:
29: short Factor(int n, int *pSquared, int *pCubed)
30: {
31:    short Value = 0;
32:    if (n > 20)
33:       Value = 1;
34:    else
35:    {
36:       *pSquared = n*n;
37:       *pCubed = n*n*n;
38:       Value = 0;
39:    }
40:    return Value;
41: }
```

OUTPUT

```
Enter a number (0-20): 3
number: 3
square: 9
cubed: 27
```

ANALYSIS On line 10, number, squared, and cubed are defined as short integers. number is assigned a value based on user input on line 14. On line 16, this number and the addresses of squared and cubed are passed to the function Factor().

On line 32, Factor() examines the first parameter, which is passed by value. If it is greater than 20 (the maximum value this function can handle), it sets the return value, Value, to a simple error value. Note that the return value from Function() is reserved for either this error value or the value 0, indicating all went well, and note that the function returns this value on line 40.

The actual values needed, the square and cube of number, are not returned by using the return mechanism; rather, they are returned by changing the pointers that were passed into the function.

On lines 36 and 37, the pointers are assigned their return values. These values are assigned to the original variables by the use of indirection. You know this by the use of the dereference operator (*) with the pointer names. On line 38, Value is assigned a success value and then on line 40 it is returned.

TIP

> Because passing by reference or by pointer allows uncontrolled access to object attributes and methods, you should pass the minimum required for the function to do its job. This helps to ensure that the function is safer to use and more easily understandable.

Returning Values by Reference

Although Listing 9.8 works, it can be made easier to read and maintain by using references rather than pointers. Listing 9.9 shows the same program rewritten to use references.

Listing 9.9 also includes a second improvement. An enum has been added to make the return value easier to understand. Rather than returning 0 or 1, using an enum, the program can return SUCCESS or FAILURE.

LISTING 9.9 Rewritten Using References

```
 1:  //Listing 9.9
 2:  // Returning multiple values from a function
 3:  // using references
 4:  #include <iostream>
 5:
 6:  using namespace std;
 7:
 8:  enum ERR_CODE { SUCCESS, ERROR };
 9:
10:  ERR_CODE Factor(int, int&, int&);
11:
12:  int main()
13:  {
14:      int number, squared, cubed;
15:      ERR_CODE result;
16:
17:      cout << "Enter a number (0 - 20): ";
```

LISTING 9.9 continued

```
18:    cin >> number;
19:
20:    result = Factor(number, squared, cubed);
21:
22:    if (result == SUCCESS)
23:    {
24:       cout << "number: " << number << endl;
25:       cout << "square: " << squared << endl;
26:       cout << "cubed: "  << cubed   << endl;
27:    }
28:    else
29:       cout << "Error encountered!!" << endl;
30:    return 0;
31: }
32:
33: ERR_CODE Factor(int n, int &rSquared, int &rCubed)
34: {
35:    if (n > 20)
36:       return ERROR;   // simple error code
37:    else
38:    {
39:       rSquared = n*n;
40:       rCubed = n*n*n;
41:       return SUCCESS;
42:    }
43: }
```

OUTPUT

```
Enter a number (0 - 20): 3
number: 3
square: 9
cubed: 27
```

ANALYSIS Listing 9.9 is identical to 9.8, with two exceptions. The ERR_CODE enumeration makes the error reporting a bit more explicit on lines 36 and 41, as well as the error handling on line 22.

The larger change, however, is that Factor() is now declared to take references to squared and cubed rather than to pointers. This makes the manipulation of these parameters far simpler and easier to understand.

Passing by Reference for Efficiency

Each time you pass an object into a function by value, a copy of the object is made. Each time you return an object from a function by value, another copy is made.

On Day 5, you learned that these objects are copied onto the stack. Doing so takes time and memory. For small objects, such as the built-in integer values, this is a trivial cost.

However, with larger, user-created objects, the cost is greater. The size of a user-created object on the stack is the sum of each of its member variables. These, in turn, can each be user-created objects, and passing such a massive structure by copying it onto the stack can be very expensive in performance and memory consumption.

Another cost occurs as well. With the classes you create, each of these temporary copies is created when the compiler calls a special constructor: the copy constructor. Tomorrow, you will learn how copy constructors work and how you can make your own, but for now it is enough to know that the copy constructor is called each time a temporary copy of the object is put on the stack.

When the temporary object is destroyed, which happens when the function returns, the object's destructor is called. If an object is returned by the function by value, a copy of that object must be made and destroyed as well.

With large objects, these constructor and destructor calls can be expensive in speed and use of memory. To illustrate this idea, Listing 9.10 creates a stripped-down, user-created object: SimpleCat. A real object would be larger and more expensive, but this is suffi-cient to show how often the copy constructor and destructor are called.

LISTING 9.10   Passing Objects by Reference

```
1:  //Listing 9.10 - Passing pointers to objects
2:
3:  #include <iostream>
4:
5:  using namespace std;
6:  class SimpleCat
7:  {
8:    public:
9:      SimpleCat ();            // constructor
10:     SimpleCat(SimpleCat&);   // copy constructor
11:     ~SimpleCat();            // destructor
12:  };
13:
14:  SimpleCat::SimpleCat()
15:  {
16:     cout << "Simple Cat Constructor..." << endl;
17:  }
18:
19:  SimpleCat::SimpleCat(SimpleCat&)
20:  {
21:     cout << "Simple Cat Copy Constructor..." << endl;
```

LISTING 9.10 continued

```
22:   }
23:
24:   SimpleCat::~SimpleCat()
25:   {
26:       cout << "Simple Cat Destructor..." << endl;
27:   }
28:
29:   SimpleCat FunctionOne (SimpleCat theCat);
30:   SimpleCat* FunctionTwo (SimpleCat *theCat);
31:
32:   int main()
33:   {
34:       cout << "Making a cat..." << endl;
35:       SimpleCat Frisky;
36:       cout << "Calling FunctionOne..." << endl;
37:       FunctionOne(Frisky);
38:       cout << "Calling FunctionTwo..." << endl;
39:       FunctionTwo(&Frisky);
40:       return 0;
41:   }
42:
43:   // FunctionOne, passes by value
44:   SimpleCat FunctionOne(SimpleCat theCat)
45:   {
46:       cout << "Function One. Returning... " << endl;
47:       return theCat;
48:   }
49:
50:   // functionTwo, passes by reference
51:   SimpleCat* FunctionTwo (SimpleCat   *theCat)
52:   {
53:       cout << "Function Two. Returning... " << endl;
54:       return theCat;
55:   }
```

OUTPUT

```
Making a cat...
Simple Cat Constructor...
Calling FunctionOne...
Simple Cat Copy Constructor...
Function One. Returning...
Simple Cat Copy Constructor...
Simple Cat Destructor...
Simple Cat Destructor...
Calling FunctionTwo...
Function Two. Returning...
Simple Cat Destructor...
```

ANALYSIS   Listing 9.10 creates the SimpleCat object and then calls two functions. The first function receives the Cat by value and then returns it by value. The second one receives a pointer to the object, rather than the object itself, and returns a pointer to the object.

The very simplified SimpleCat class is declared on lines 6–12. The constructor, copy constructor, and destructor all print an informative message so that you can tell when they've been called.

On line 34, main() prints out a message, and that is seen on the first line of the output. On line 35, a SimpleCat object is instantiated. This causes the constructor to be called, and the output from the constructor is seen on the second line of output.

On line 36, main() reports that it is calling FunctionOne, which creates the third line of output. Because FunctionOne() is called passing the SimpleCat object by value, a copy of the SimpleCat object is made on the stack as an object local to the called function. This causes the copy constructor to be called, which creates the fourth line of output.

Program execution jumps to line 46 in the called function, which prints an informative message, the fifth line of output. The function then returns, and returns the SimpleCat object by value. This creates yet another copy of the object, calling the copy constructor and producing the sixth line of output.

The return value from FunctionOne() is not assigned to any object, and so the temporary object created for the return is thrown away, calling the destructor, which produces the seventh line of output. Because FunctionOne() has ended, its local copy goes out of scope and is destroyed, calling the destructor and producing the eighth line of output.

Program execution returns to main(), and FunctionTwo() is called, but the parameter is passed by reference. No copy is produced, so there's no output. FunctionTwo() prints the message that appears as the tenth line of output and then returns the SimpleCat object, again by reference, and so again produces no calls to the constructor or destructor.

Finally, the program ends and Frisky goes out of scope, causing one final call to the destructor and printing the final line of output.

The net effect of this is that the call to FunctionOne(), because it passed the Frisky by value, produced two calls to the copy constructor and two to the destructor, while the call to FunctionTwo() produced none.

Passing a const Pointer

Although passing a pointer to FunctionTwo() is more efficient, it is dangerous. FunctionTwo() is not meant to be allowed to change the SimpleCat object it is passed, yet it is given the address of the SimpleCat. This seriously exposes the original object to change and defeats the protection offered in passing by value.

Passing by value is like giving a museum a photograph of your masterpiece instead of the real thing. If vandals mark it up, there is no harm done to the original. Passing by reference is like sending your home address to the museum and inviting guests to come over and look at the real thing.

The solution is to pass a pointer to a constant SimpleCat. Doing so prevents calling any non-const method on SimpleCat, and thus protects the object from change.

Passing a constant reference allows your guests to see the original painting, but not to alter it in any way. Listing 9.11 demonstrates this idea.

LISTING 9.11 Passing Pointer to a Constant Object

```
1:  //Listing 9.11 - Passing pointers to objects
2:
3:  #include <iostream>
4:
5:  using namespace std;
6:  class SimpleCat
7:  {
8:    public:
9:      SimpleCat();
10:      SimpleCat(SimpleCat&);
11:      ~SimpleCat();
12:
13:      int GetAge() const { return itsAge; }
14:      void SetAge(int age) { itsAge = age; }
15:
16:    private:
17:      int itsAge;
18:  };
19:
20:  SimpleCat::SimpleCat()
21:  {
22:    cout << "Simple Cat Constructor..." << endl;
23:    itsAge = 1;
24:  }
25:
26:  SimpleCat::SimpleCat(SimpleCat&)
27:  {
28:    cout << "Simple Cat Copy Constructor..." << endl;
29:  }
30:
31:  SimpleCat::~SimpleCat()
32:  {
```

9

LISTING 9.11 continued

```
33:       cout << "Simple Cat Destructor..." << endl;
34:    }
35:
36:    const SimpleCat * const FunctionTwo
37:       (const SimpleCat * const theCat);
38:
39:    int main()
40:    {
41:       cout << "Making a cat..." << endl;
42:       SimpleCat Frisky;
43:       cout << "Frisky is " ;
44:       cout << Frisky.GetAge();
45:       cout << " years old" << endl;
46:       int age = 5;
47:       Frisky.SetAge(age);
48:       cout << "Frisky is " ;
49:       cout << Frisky.GetAge();
50:       cout << " years old" << endl;
51:       cout << "Calling FunctionTwo..." << endl;
52:       FunctionTwo(&Frisky);
53:       cout << "Frisky is " ;
54:       cout << Frisky.GetAge();
55:       cout << " years old" << endl;
56:       return 0;
57:    }
58:
59:    // functionTwo, passes a const pointer
60:    const SimpleCat * const FunctionTwo
61:       (const SimpleCat * const theCat)
62:    {
63:       cout << "Function Two. Returning..." << endl;
64:       cout << "Frisky is now " << theCat->GetAge();
65:       cout << " years old " << endl;
66:       // theCat->SetAge(8);    const!
67:       return theCat;
68:    }
```

OUTPUT

```
Making a cat...
Simple Cat constructor...
Frisky is 1 years old
Frisky is 5 years old
Calling FunctionTwo...
FunctionTwo. Returning...
Frisky is now 5 years old
Frisky is 5 years old
Simple Cat Destructor...
```

9

ANALYSIS SimpleCat has added two accessor functions, GetAge() on line 13, which is a const function, and SetAge() on line 14, which is not a const function. It has also added the member variable itsAge on line 17.

The constructor, copy constructor, and destructor are still defined to print their messages. The copy constructor is never called, however, because the object is passed by reference and so no copies are made. On line 42, an object is created, and its default age is printed, starting on line 43.

On line 47, itsAge is set using the accessor SetAge, and the result is printed on line 48. FunctionOne is not used in this program, but FunctionTwo() is called. FunctionTwo() has changed slightly; the parameter and return value are now declared, on line 36, to take a constant pointer to a constant object and to return a constant pointer to a constant object.

Because the parameter and return value are still passed by reference, no copies are made and the copy constructor is not called. The object being pointed to in FunctionTwo(), however, is now constant, and thus cannot call the non-const method, SetAge(). If the call to SetAge() on line 66 was not commented out, the program would not compile.

Note that the object created in main() is not constant, and Frisky can call SetAge(). The address of this nonconstant object is passed to FunctionTwo(), but because FunctionTwo()'s declaration declares the pointer to be a constant pointer to a constant object, the object is treated as if it were constant!

References as an Alternative

Listing 9.11 solves the problem of making extra copies, and thus saves the calls to the copy constructor and destructor. It uses constant pointers to constant objects, and thereby solves the problem of the function changing the object. It is still somewhat cumbersome, however, because the objects passed to the function are pointers.

Because you know the object will never be null, it would be easier to work within the function if a reference were passed in, rather than a pointer. Listing 9.12 illustrates this.

LISTING 9.12 Passing References to Objects

```
1:   //Listing 9.12 - Passing references to objects
2:
3:   #include <iostream>
4:
5:   using namespace std;
6:   class SimpleCat
7:   {
8:     public:
9:       SimpleCat();
10:      SimpleCat(SimpleCat&);
```

LISTING 9.12   continued

```
11:       ~SimpleCat();
12:
13:       int GetAge() const { return itsAge; }
14:       void SetAge(int age) { itsAge = age; }
15:
16:   private:
17:      int itsAge;
18:   };
19:
20:   SimpleCat::SimpleCat()
21:   {
22:      cout << "Simple Cat Constructor..." << endl;
23:      itsAge = 1;
24:   }
25:
26:   SimpleCat::SimpleCat(SimpleCat&)
27:   {
28:      cout << "Simple Cat Copy Constructor..." << endl;
29:   }
30:
31:   SimpleCat::~SimpleCat()
32:   {
33:      cout << "Simple Cat Destructor..." << endl;
34:   }
35:
36:   const     SimpleCat & FunctionTwo (const SimpleCat & theCat);
37:
38:   int main()
39:   {
40:      cout << "Making a cat..." << endl;
41:      SimpleCat Frisky;
42:      cout << "Frisky is " << Frisky.GetAge() << " years old" << endl;
43:      int age = 5;
44:      Frisky.SetAge(age);
45:      cout << "Frisky is " << Frisky.GetAge() << " years old" << endl;
46:      cout << "Calling FunctionTwo..." << endl;
47:      FunctionTwo(Frisky);
48:      cout << "Frisky is " << Frisky.GetAge() << " years old" << endl;
49:      return 0;
50:   }
51:
52:   // functionTwo, passes a ref to a const object
53:   const SimpleCat & FunctionTwo (const SimpleCat & theCat)
54:   {
55:      cout << "Function Two. Returning..." << endl;
56:      cout << "Frisky is now " << theCat.GetAge();
57:      cout << " years old " << endl;
58:      // theCat.SetAge(8);    const!
59:      return theCat;
60:   }
```

OUTPUT
```
Making a cat...
Simple Cat constructor...
Frisky is 1 years old
Frisky is 5 years old
Calling FunctionTwo...
FunctionTwo. Returning...
Frisky is now 5 years old
Frisky is 5 years old
Simple Cat Destructor...
```

9

ANALYSIS The output is identical to that produced by Listing 9.11. The only significant change is that `FunctionTwo()` now takes and returns a reference to a constant object. Once again, working with references is somewhat simpler than working with pointers, and the same savings and efficiency are achieved, as well as the safety provided by using `const`.

---

const References

C++ programmers do not usually differentiate between "constant reference to a `SimpleCat` object" and "reference to a constant `SimpleCat` object." References themselves can never be reassigned to refer to another object, and so they are always constant. If the keyword `const` is applied to a reference, it is to make the object referred to constant.

Knowing When to Use References Versus Pointers

Experienced C++ programmers strongly prefer references to pointers. References are cleaner and easier to use, and they do a better job of hiding information, as you saw in the previous example.

References cannot be reassigned, however. If you need to point first to one object and then to another, you must use a pointer. References cannot be null, so if any chance exists that the object in question might be null, you must not use a reference. You must use a pointer.

An example of the latter concern is the operator new. If new cannot allocate memory on the free store, it returns a null pointer. Because a reference shouldn't be null, you must not initialize a reference to this memory until you've checked that it is not null. The following example shows how to handle this:

```
int *pInt = new int;
if (pInt != NULL)
int &rInt = *pInt;
```

In this example, a pointer to int, pInt, is declared and initialized with the memory returned by the operator new. The address in pInt is tested, and if it is not null, pInt is dereferenced. The result of dereferencing an int variable is an int object, and rInt is initialized to refer to that object. Thus, rInt becomes an alias to the int returned by the operator new.

Do	**Don't**
DO pass parameters by reference whenever possible.	**DON'T** use pointers if references will work.
DO use const to protect references and pointers whenever possible.	**DON'T** try to reassign a reference to a different variable. You can't.

Mixing References and Pointers

It is perfectly legal to declare both pointers and references in the same function parameter list, along with objects passed by value. Here's an example:

```
Cat * SomeFunction (Person &theOwner, House *theHouse, int age);
```

This declaration says that SomeFunction takes three parameters. The first is a reference to a Person object, the second is a pointer to a House object, and the third is an integer. It returns a pointer to a Cat object.

The question of where to put the reference (&) or the indirection operator (*) when declaring these variables is a great controversy. When declaring a reference, you can legally write any of the following:

```
1:   Cat&  rFrisky;
2:   Cat & rFrisky;
3:   Cat  &rFrisky;
```

Whitespace is completely ignored, so anywhere you see a space here you can put as many spaces, tabs, and new lines as you want.

Setting aside freedom of expression issues, which is best? Here are the arguments for all three:

The argument for case 1 is that rFrisky is a variable whose name is rFrisky and whose type can be thought of as "reference to Cat object." Thus, this argument goes, the & should be with the type.

The counterargument is that the type is Cat. The & is part of the "declarator," which includes the variable name and the ampersand. More important, having the & near the Cat can lead to the following bug:

```
Cat&   rFrisky, rBoots;
```

Casual examination of this line would lead you to think that both rFrisky and rBoots are references to Cat objects, but you'd be wrong. This really says that rFrisky is a reference to a Cat, and rBoots (despite its name) is not a reference but a plain old Cat variable. This should be rewritten as follows:

```
Cat    &rFrisky, rBoots;
```

The answer to this objection is that declarations of references and variables should never be combined like this. Here's the right way to declare the reference and nonreference variable:

```
Cat& rFrisky;
Cat  boots;
```

Finally, many programmers opt out of the argument and go with the middle position, that of putting the & in the middle of the two, as illustrated in case 2.

Of course, everything said so far about the reference operator (&) applies equally well to the indirection operator (*). The important thing is to recognize that reasonable people differ in their perceptions of the one true way. Choose a style that works for you, and be consistent within any one program; clarity is, and remains, the goal.

NOTE

Many programmers like the following conventions for declaring references and pointers:

- Put the ampersand and asterisk in the middle, with a space on either side.
- Never declare references, pointers, and variables all on the same line.

Returning Out-of-Scope Object References

After C++ programmers learn to pass by reference, they have a tendency to go hog-wild. It is possible, however, to overdo it. Remember that a reference is always an alias to some other object. If you pass a reference into or out of a function, be certain to ask yourself, "What is the object I'm aliasing, and will it still exist every time it's used?"

Listing 9.13 illustrates the danger of returning a reference to an object that no longer exists.

LISTING 9.13   Returning a Reference to a Nonexistent Object

```
1:  // Listing 9.13
2:  // Returning a reference to an object
3:  // which no longer exists
4:
5:  #include <iostream>
6:
7:  class SimpleCat
8:  {
9:    public:
10:      SimpleCat (int age, int weight);
11:      ~SimpleCat() {}
12:      int GetAge() { return itsAge; }
13:      int GetWeight() { return itsWeight; }
14:    private:
15:      int itsAge;
16:      int itsWeight;
17:  };
18:
19:  SimpleCat::SimpleCat(int age, int weight)
20:  {
21:      itsAge = age;
22:      itsWeight = weight;
23:  }
24:
25:  SimpleCat &TheFunction();
26:
27:  int main()
28:  {
29:      SimpleCat &rCat = TheFunction();
30:      int age = rCat.GetAge();
31:      std::cout << "rCat is " << age << " years old!" << std::endl;
32:      return 0;
33:  }
34:
35:  SimpleCat &TheFunction()
36:  {
37:      SimpleCat Frisky(5,9);
38:      return Frisky;
39:  }
```

OUTPUT   Compile error: Attempting to return a reference to a local object!

CAUTION   This program won't compile on the Borland compiler. It will compile on Microsoft compilers; however, it should be noted that it is a poor coding practice.

ANALYSIS On lines 7–17, SimpleCat is declared. On line 29, a reference to a SimpleCat is initialized with the results of calling TheFunction(), which is declared on line 25 to return a reference to a SimpleCat.

The body of TheFunction() in lines 35–39 declares a local object of type SimpleCat and initializes its age and weight. It then returns that local object by reference on line 38. Some compilers are smart enough to catch this error and don't let you run the program. Others let you run the program, with unpredictable results.

When TheFunction() returns, the local object, Frisky, is destroyed (painlessly, I assure you). The reference returned by this function is an alias to a nonexistent object, and this is a bad thing.

Returning a Reference to an Object on the Heap

You might be tempted to solve the problem in Listing 9.13 by having TheFunction() create Frisky on the heap. That way, when you return from TheFunction(), Frisky still exists.

The problem with this approach is: What do you do with the memory allocated for Frisky when you are done with it? Listing 9.14 illustrates this problem.

LISTING 9.14 Memory Leaks

```
1:  // Listing 9.14 - Resolving memory leaks
2:
3:  #include <iostream>
4:
5:  class SimpleCat
6:  {
7:    public:
8:      SimpleCat (int age, int weight);
9:      ~SimpleCat() {}
10:     int GetAge() { return itsAge; }
11:     int GetWeight() { return itsWeight; }
12:
13:   private:
14:     int itsAge;
15:     int itsWeight;
16: };
17:
18: SimpleCat::SimpleCat(int age, int weight)
19: {
20:   itsAge = age;
21:   itsWeight = weight;
22: }
23:
```

LISTING 9.14 continued

```
24:  SimpleCat & TheFunction();
25:
26:  int main()
27:  {
28:      SimpleCat & rCat = TheFunction();
29:      int age = rCat.GetAge();
30:      std::cout << "rCat is " << age << " years old!" << std::endl;
31:      std::cout << "&rCat: " << &rCat << std::endl;
32:      // How do you get rid of that memory?
33:      SimpleCat * pCat = &rCat;
34:      delete pCat;
35:      // Uh oh, rCat now refers to ??
36:      return 0;
37:  }
38:
39:  SimpleCat &TheFunction()
40:  {
41:      SimpleCat * pFrisky = new SimpleCat(5,9);
42:      std::cout << "pFrisky: " << pFrisky << std::endl;
43:      return *pFrisky;
44:  }
```

OUTPUT

```
pFrisky: 0x00431C60
rCat is 5 years old!
&rCat: 0x00431C60
```

CAUTION | This compiles, links, and appears to work. But it is a time bomb waiting to go off.

ANALYSIS TheFunction() in lines 39–44 has been changed so that it no longer returns a reference to a local variable. Memory is allocated on the free store and assigned to a pointer on line 41. The address that pointer holds is printed, and then the pointer is dereferenced and the SimpleCat object is returned by reference.

On line 28, the return of TheFunction() is assigned to a reference to SimpleCat, and that object is used to obtain the cat's age, which is printed on line 30.

To prove that the reference declared in main() is referring to the object put on the free store in TheFunction(), the address-of operator is applied to rCat. Sure enough, it displays the address of the object it refers to, and this matches the address of the object on the free store.

So far, so good. But how will that memory be freed? You can't call delete on the reference. One clever solution is to create another pointer and initialize it with the address obtained from rCat. This does delete the memory, and it plugs the memory leak. One small problem, though: What is rCat referring to after line 34? As stated earlier, a reference must always alias an actual object; if it references a null object (as this does now), the program is invalid.

9

Three solutions exist to this problem. The first is to declare a SimpleCat object on line 28 and to return that cat from TheFunction() by value. The second is to go ahead and declare the SimpleCat on the free store in TheFunction(), but have TheFunction() return a pointer to that memory. Then, the calling function can delete the pointer when it is done.

The third workable solution, and the right one, is to declare the object in the calling function and then to pass it to TheFunction() by reference.

Pointer, Pointer, Who Has the Pointer?

When your program allocates memory on the free store, a pointer is returned. It is imperative that you keep a pointer to that memory because after the pointer is lost, the memory cannot be deleted and becomes a memory leak.

As you pass this block of memory between functions, someone will "own" the pointer. Typically, the value in the block is passed using references, and the function that created the memory is the one that deletes it. But this is a general rule, not an ironclad one.

It is dangerous for one function to create memory and another to free it, however. Ambiguity about who owns the pointer can lead to one of two problems: forgetting to delete a pointer or deleting it twice. Either one can cause serious problems in your program. It is safer to build your functions so that they delete the memory they create.

If you are writing a function that needs to create memory and then pass it back to the calling function, consider changing your interface. Have the calling function allocate the memory and then pass it into your function by reference. This moves all memory management out of your program and back to the function that is prepared to delete it.

Do	**Don't**
DO pass parameters by value when you must.	**DON'T** pass by reference if the item referred to might go out of scope.
DO return by value when you must.	**DON'T** lose track of when and where memory is allocated so you can be certain it is also freed.

Summary

Today, you learned what references are and how they compare to pointers. You saw that references must be initialized to refer to an existing object and cannot be reassigned to refer to anything else. Any action taken on a reference is in fact taken on the reference's target object. Proof of this is that taking the address of a reference returns the address of the target.

You saw that passing objects by reference can be more efficient than passing by value. Passing by reference also allows the called function to change the value in the arguments back in the calling function.

You saw that arguments to functions and values returned from functions can be passed by reference, and that this can be implemented with pointers or with references.

You saw how to use pointers to constant objects and constant references to pass values between functions safely while achieving the efficiency of passing by reference.

Q&A

Q Why have references if pointers can do everything references can?

A References are easier to use and to understand. The indirection is hidden, and no need exists to repeatedly dereference the variable.

Q Why have pointers if references are easier?

A References cannot be null, and they cannot be reassigned. Pointers offer greater flexibility but are slightly more difficult to use.

Q Why would you ever return by value from a function?

A If the object being returned is local, you must return by value or you will be returning a reference to a nonexistent object.

Q Given the danger in returning by reference, why not always return by value?

A Far greater efficiency is achieved in returning by reference. Memory is saved and the program runs faster.

Workshop

The Workshop contains quiz questions to help solidify your understanding of the material covered and exercises to provide you with experience in using what you've learned. Try to answer the quiz and exercise questions before checking the answers in Appendix D, and be certain you understand the answers before going to tomorrow's lesson.

Quiz

9

1. What is the difference between a reference and a pointer?
2. When must you use a pointer rather than a reference?
3. What does `new` return if there is insufficient memory to make your new object?
4. What is a constant reference?
5. What is the difference between passing by reference and passing a reference?
6. When declaring a reference, which is correct:

    a. `int& myRef = myInt;`

    b. `int & myRef = myInt;`

    c. `int  &myRef = myInt;`

Exercises

1. Write a program that declares an `int`, a reference to an `int`, and a pointer to an `int`. Use the pointer and the reference to manipulate the value in the `int`.
2. Write a program that declares a constant pointer to a constant integer. Initialize the pointer to an integer variable, `varOne`. Assign 6 to `varOne`. Use the pointer to assign 7 to `varOne`. Create a second integer variable, `varTwo`. Reassign the pointer to `varTwo`. Do not compile this exercise yet.
3. Now compile the program in Exercise 2. What produces errors? What produces warnings?
4. Write a program that produces a stray pointer.
5. Fix the program from Exercise 4.
6. Write a program that produces a memory leak.
7. Fix the program from Exercise 6.
8. **BUG BUSTERS:** What is wrong with this program?

```
1:     #include <iostream>
2:     using namespace std;
3:     class CAT
4:     {
5:         public:
```

```
6:          CAT(int age) { itsAge = age; }
7:          ~CAT(){}
8:          int GetAge() const { return itsAge;}
9:      private:
10:         int itsAge;
11:     };
12:
13:     CAT & MakeCat(int age);
14:     int main()
15:     {
16:        int age = 7;
17:        CAT Boots = MakeCat(age);
18:        cout << "Boots is " << Boots.GetAge()
19:             << " years old" << endl;
20:      return 0;
21:     }
22:
23:     CAT & MakeCat(int age)
24:     {
25:        CAT * pCat = new CAT(age);
26:        return *pCat;
27:     }
```

9. Fix the program from Exercise 8.

DAY 10

Working with Advanced Functions

On Day 5, "Organizing into Functions," you learned the fundamentals of working with functions. Now that you know how pointers and references work, you can do more with functions.

Today, you will learn

- How to overload member functions
- How to overload operators
- How to write functions to support classes with dynamically allocated variables

Overloaded Member Functions

On Day 5, you learned how to implement function polymorphism, or function overloading, by writing two or more functions with the same name but with different parameters. Class member functions can be overloaded as well, in much the same way.

The `Rectangle` class, demonstrated in Listing 10.1, has two `DrawShape()` functions. One, which takes no parameters, draws the rectangle based on the class's current values. The other takes two values, width and length, and draws the rectangle based on those values, ignoring the current class values.

LISTING 10.1 Overloading Member Functions

```
1:   //Listing 10.1 Overloading class member functions
2:   #include <iostream>
3:
4:   // Rectangle class declaration
5:   class Rectangle
6:   {
7:     public:
8:        // constructors
9:        Rectangle(int width, int height);
10:       ~Rectangle(){}
11:
12:       // overloaded class function DrawShape
13:       void DrawShape() const;
14:       void DrawShape(int aWidth, int aHeight) const;
15:
16:     private:
17:        int itsWidth;
18:        int itsHeight;
19:   };
20:
21:   //Constructor implementation
22:   Rectangle::Rectangle(int width, int height)
23:   {
24:       itsWidth = width;
25:       itsHeight = height;
26:   }
27:
28:
29:   // Overloaded DrawShape - takes no values
30:   // Draws based on current class member values
31:   void Rectangle::DrawShape() const
32:   {
33:       DrawShape( itsWidth, itsHeight);
34:   }
35:
36:
37:   // overloaded DrawShape - takes two values
38:   // draws shape based on the parameters
39:   void Rectangle::DrawShape(int width, int height) const
40:   {
41:       for (int i = 0; i<height; i++)
42:       {
```

LISTING 10.1 continued

```
43:        for (int j = 0; j< width; j++)
44:        {
45:            std::cout << "*";
46:        }
47:        std::cout << std::endl;
48:    }
49: }
50:
51: // Driver program to demonstrate overloaded functions
52: int main()
53: {
54:     // initialize a rectangle to 30,5
55:     Rectangle theRect(30,5);
56:     std::cout << "DrawShape():" << std::endl;
57:     theRect.DrawShape();
58:     std::cout << "\nDrawShape(40,2):" << std::endl;
59:     theRect.DrawShape(40,2);
60:     return 0;
61: }
```

OUTPUT

```
DrawShape():
******************************
******************************
******************************
******************************
******************************

DrawShape(40,2):
****************************************************************
****************************************************************
```

ANALYSIS Listing 10.1 represents a stripped-down version of the Week in Review project from Week 1. The test for illegal values has been taken out to save room, as have some of the accessor functions. The main program has been stripped down to a simple driver program, rather than a menu.

The important code, however, is on lines 13 and 14, where DrawShape() is overloaded. The implementation for these overloaded class methods is on lines 31–49. Note that the version of DrawShape() that takes no parameters simply calls the version that takes two parameters, passing in the current member variables. Try very hard to avoid duplicating code in two functions. Otherwise, keeping them in sync when changes are made to one or the other will be difficult and error-prone.

The driver program on lines 52–61 creates a rectangle object and then calls DrawShape(), first passing in no parameters and then passing in two unsigned short integers.

The compiler decides which method to call based on the number and type of parameters entered. You can imagine a third overloaded function named DrawShape() that takes one dimension and an enumeration for whether it is the width or height, at the user's choice.

Using Default Values

Just as global functions can have one or more default values, so can each member function of a class. The same rules apply for declaring the default values, as illustrated in Listing 10.2.

LISTING 10.2   Using Default Values

```
1:  //Listing 10.2 Default values in member functions
2:  #include <iostream>
3:
4:  using namespace std;
5:
6:  // Rectangle class declaration
7:  class Rectangle
8:  {
9:    public:
10:      // constructors
11:      Rectangle(int width, int height);
12:      ~Rectangle(){}
13:      void DrawShape(int aWidth, int aHeight,
14:          bool UseCurrentVals = false) const;
15:
16:    private:
17:      int itsWidth;
18:      int itsHeight;
19:  };
20:
21:  //Constructor implementation
22:  Rectangle::Rectangle(int width, int height):
23:  itsWidth(width),         // initializations
24:  itsHeight(height)
25:  {}                       // empty body
26:
27:
28:  // default values used for third parameter
29:  void Rectangle::DrawShape(
30:  int width,
31:  int height,
32:  bool UseCurrentValue
33:  ) const
34:  {
```

LISTING 10.2   continued

```
35:     int printWidth;
36:     int printHeight;
37:
38:     if (UseCurrentValue == true)
39:     {
40:        printWidth = itsWidth;        // use current class values
41:        printHeight = itsHeight;
42:     }
43:     else
44:     {
45:        printWidth = width;           // use parameter values
46:        printHeight = height;
47:     }
48:
49:
50:     for (int i = 0; i<printHeight; i++)
51:     {
52:        for (int j = 0; j< printWidth; j++)
53:        {
54:           cout << "*";
55:        }
56:        cout << endl;
57:     }
58:  }
59:
60:  // Driver program to demonstrate overloaded functions
61:  int main()
62:  {
63:     // initialize a rectangle to 30,5
64:     Rectangle theRect(30,5);
65:     cout << "DrawShape(0,0,true)..." << endl;
66:     theRect.DrawShape(0,0,true);
67:     cout <<"DrawShape(40,2)..." << endl;
68:     theRect.DrawShape(40,2);
69:     return 0;
70:  }
```

10

OUTPUT

```
DrawShape(0,0,true)...
******************************
******************************
******************************
******************************
******************************
DrawShape(40,2)...
************************************************************
************************************************************
```

ANALYSIS Listing 10.2 replaces the overloaded `DrawShape()` function with a single function with default parameters. The function is declared on line 13 to take three parameters. The first two, `aWidth` and `aHeight`, are integers, and the third, `UseCurrentVals`, is a `bool` that defaults to `false`.

The implementation for this somewhat awkward function begins on line 29. Remember that whitespace doesn't matter in C++, so the function header is actually on lines 29–33.

Within the method, the third parameter, `UseCurrentValue`, is evaluated on line 38. If it is `true`, the member variables `itsWidth` and `itsHeight` are used to set the local variables `printWidth` and `printHeight`, respectively.

If `UseCurrentValue` is false, either because it has defaulted false or was set by the user, the first two parameters are used for setting `printWidth` and `printHeight`.

Note that if `UseCurrentValue` is true, the values of the other two parameters are completely ignored.

Choosing Between Default Values and Overloaded Functions

Listings 10.1 and 10.2 accomplish the same thing, but the overloaded functions in Listing 10.1 are easier to understand and more natural to use. Also, if a third variation is needed—perhaps the user wants to supply either the width or the height, but not both—it is easy to extend the overloaded functions. The default value, however, will quickly become unusably complex as new variations are added.

How do you decide whether to use function overloading or default values? Here's a rule of thumb:

Use function overloading when

- No reasonable default value exists.
- You need different algorithms.
- You need to support different types in your parameter list.

The Default Constructor

The point of a constructor is to establish the object; for example, the point of a `Rectangle` constructor is to make a valid rectangle object. Before the constructor runs, no rectangle exists, only an area of memory. After the constructor finishes, there is a complete, ready-to-use rectangle object. This is a key benefit of object-oriented programming—the calling program does not have to do anything to ensure that the object starts in a self-consistent state.

As discussed on Day 6, "Understanding Object-Oriented Programming," if you do not explicitly declare a constructor for your class, a default constructor is created that takes no parameters and does nothing. You are free to make your own default constructor, however, that takes no arguments but that "sets up" your object as required.

The constructor provided for you is called the "default" constructor, but by convention so is any constructor that takes no parameters. This can be a bit confusing, but it is usually clear which one is meant from the context.

Take note that if you make any constructors at all, the default constructor is not provided by the compiler. So if you want a constructor that takes no parameters and you've created any other constructors, you must add the default constructor yourself!

Overloading Constructors

Constructors, like all member functions, can be overloaded. The capability to overload constructors is very powerful and very flexible.

For example, you might have a rectangle object that has two constructors: The first takes a length and a width and makes a rectangle of that size. The second takes no values and makes a default-sized rectangle. Listing 10.3 implements this idea.

LISTING 10.3 Overloading the Constructor

```
1:   // Listing 10.3 - Overloading constructors
2:
3:   #include <iostream>
4:   using namespace std;
5:
6:   class Rectangle
7:   {
8:     public:
9:       Rectangle();
10:      Rectangle(int width, int length);
11:      ~Rectangle() {}
12:      int GetWidth() const { return itsWidth; }
13:      int GetLength() const { return itsLength; }
14:    private:
15:      int itsWidth;
16:      int itsLength;
17:   };
18:
19:   Rectangle::Rectangle()
20:   {
```

LISTING **10.3** continued

```
21:        itsWidth = 5;
22:        itsLength = 10;
23:    }
24:
25:    Rectangle::Rectangle (int width, int length)
26:    {
27:        itsWidth = width;
28:        itsLength = length;
29:    }
30:
31:    int main()
32:    {
33:        Rectangle Rect1;
34:        cout << "Rect1 width: " << Rect1.GetWidth() << endl;
35:        cout << "Rect1 length: " << Rect1.GetLength() << endl;
36:
37:        int aWidth, aLength;
38:        cout << "Enter a width: ";
39:        cin >> aWidth;
40:        cout << "\nEnter a length: ";
41:        cin >> aLength;
42:
43:        Rectangle Rect2(aWidth, aLength);
44:        cout << "\nRect2 width: " << Rect2.GetWidth() << endl;
45:        cout << "Rect2 length: " << Rect2.GetLength() << endl;
46:        return 0;
47:    }
```

OUTPUT
```
Rect1 width: 5
Rect1 length: 10
Enter a width: 20

Enter a length: 50

Rect2 width: 20
Rect2 length: 50
```

ANALYSIS The Rectangle class is declared on lines 6–17. Two constructors are declared: the "default constructor" on line 9 and a second constructor on line 10, which takes two integer variables.

On line 33, a rectangle is created using the default constructor, and its values are printed on lines 34 and 35. On lines 38–41, the user is prompted for a width and length, and the constructor taking two parameters is called on line 43. Finally, the width and height for this rectangle are printed on lines 44 and 45.

Just as it does any overloaded function, the compiler chooses the right constructor, based on the number and type of the parameters.

Initializing Objects

Up to now, you've been setting the member variables of objects in the body of the constructor. Constructors, however, are invoked in two stages: the initialization stage and the body.

Most variables can be set in either stage, either by initializing in the initialization stage or by assigning in the body of the constructor. It is cleaner, and often more efficient, to initialize member variables at the initialization stage. The following example shows how to initialize member variables:

```
Cat():              // constructor name and parameters
itsAge(5),          // initialization list
itsWeight(8)
{ }                 // body of constructor
```

After the closing parentheses on the constructor's parameter list, write a colon. Then write the name of the member variable and a pair of parentheses. Inside the parentheses, write the expression to be used to initialize that member variable. If more than one initialization exists, separate each one with a comma.

Listing 10.4 shows the definition of the constructors from Listing 10.3 with initialization of the member variables in the initialization portion of the constructor rather than by doing assignments in the body.

LISTING 10.4 A Code Snippet Showing Initialization of Member Variables

```
 1:    // Listing 10.4 - Initializing Member Variables
 2:    Rectangle::Rectangle():
 3:         itsWidth(5),
 4:         itsLength(10)
 5:    {
 6:    }
 7:
 8:    Rectangle::Rectangle (int width, int length):
 9:         itsWidth(width),
10:         itsLength(length)
11:    {
12:    }
```

ANALYSIS Listing 10.4 is just a snippet of code, so there isn't output. Looking at the code, line 2 starts the default constructor. As was mentioned previously, after the standard header, a colon was added. This is followed by setting default values of 5 and 10 for itsWidth and itsLength on lines 3 and 4.

Line 8 contains the second constructor definition. In this overloaded version, two parameters are passed. These parameters are then set to the class's members on lines 9 and 10.

Some variables must be initialized and cannot be assigned to, such as references and constants. It is common to have other assignments or action statements in the body of the constructor; however, it is best to use initialization as much as possible.

The Copy Constructor

In addition to providing a default constructor and destructor, the compiler provides a default copy constructor. The copy constructor is called every time a copy of an object is made.

As you learned on Day 9, "Exploiting References," when you pass an object by value, either into a function or as a function's return value, a temporary copy of that object is made. If the object is a user-defined object, the class's copy constructor is called. You saw this yesterday in Listing 9.6.

All copy constructors take one parameter, a reference to an object of the same class. It is a good idea to make it a constant reference because the constructor will not have to alter the object passed in. For example,

```
Cat(const Cat & theCat);
```

Here, the Cat constructor takes a constant reference to an existing Cat object. The goal of this copy constructor is to make a copy of theCat.

The default copy constructor simply copies each member variable from the object passed as a parameter to the member variables of the new object. This is called a member-wise (or shallow) copy, and although this is fine for most member variables, it breaks pretty quickly for member variables that are pointers to objects on the free store.

A shallow or member-wise copy copies the exact values of one object's member variables into another object. Pointers in both objects end up pointing to the same memory. A deep copy copies the values allocated on the heap to newly allocated memory.

If the Cat class includes a member variable, itsAge, that is a pointer to an integer on the free store, the default copy constructor copies the passed-in Cat's itsAge member variable to the new Cat's itsAge member variable. The two objects now point to the same memory, as illustrated in Figure 10.1.

This leads to a disaster when either Cat goes out of scope. If the original Cat's destructor frees this memory and the new Cat is still pointing to the memory, a stray pointer has been created, and the program is in mortal danger. Figure 10.2 illustrates this problem.

FIGURE 10.1

Using the default copy constructor.

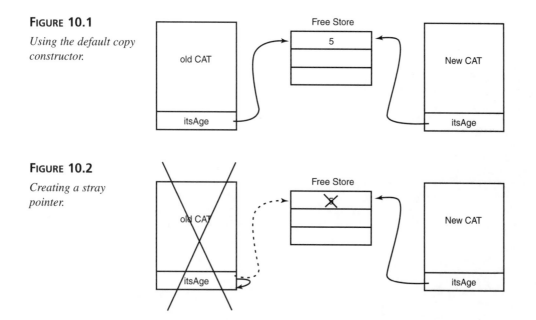

FIGURE 10.2

Creating a stray pointer.

10

The solution to this is to create your own copy constructor and to allocate the memory as required. After the memory is allocated, the old values can be copied into the new memory. This is called a deep copy. Listing 10.5 illustrates how to do this.

LISTING 10.5   Copy Constructors

```
 1:  // Listing 10.5 - Copy constructors
 2:
 3:  #include <iostream>
 4:  using namespace std;
 5:
 6:  class Cat
 7:  {
 8:    public:
 9:      Cat();                   // default constructor
10:      Cat (const Cat &);  // copy constructor
11:      ~Cat();                  // destructor
12:      int GetAge()    const   { return *itsAge; }
13:      int GetWeight() const   { return *itsWeight; }
14:      void SetAge(int age)    { *itsAge = age; }
15:
16:    private:
17:      int *itsAge;
18:      int *itsWeight;
19:  };
20:
```

LISTING 10.5 continued

```
21:  Cat::Cat()
22:  {
23:      itsAge = new int;
24:      itsWeight = new int;
25:      *itsAge = 5;
26:      *itsWeight = 9;
27:  }
28:
29:  Cat::Cat(const Cat & rhs)
30:  {
31:      itsAge = new int;
32:      itsWeight = new int;
33:      *itsAge = rhs.GetAge();   // public access
34:      *itsWeight = *(rhs.itsWeight); // private access
35:  }
36:
37:  Cat::~Cat()
38:  {
39:      delete itsAge;
40:      itsAge = 0;
41:      delete itsWeight;
42:      itsWeight = 0;
43:  }
44:
45:  int main()
46:  {
47:      Cat Frisky;
48:      cout << "Frisky's age: " << Frisky.GetAge() << endl;
49:      cout << "Setting Frisky to 6...\n";
50:      Frisky.SetAge(6);
51:      cout << "Creating Boots from Frisky\n";
52:      Cat Boots(Frisky);
53:      cout << "Frisky's age: " <<      Frisky.GetAge() << endl;
54:      cout << "Boots' age: " << Boots.GetAge() << endl;
55:      cout << "setting Frisky to 7...\n";
56:      Frisky.SetAge(7);
57:      cout << "Frisky's age: " <<      Frisky.GetAge() << endl;
58:      cout << "boot's age: " << Boots.GetAge() << endl;
59:      return 0;
60:  }
```

OUTPUT

```
Frisky's age: 5
Setting Frisky to 6...
Creating Boots from Frisky
Frisky's age: 6
Boots' age:  6
setting Frisky to 7...
Frisky's age: 7
Boots' age: 6
```

ANALYSIS On lines 6–19, the Cat class is declared. Note that on line 9 a default constructor is declared, and on line 10 a copy constructor is declared. You know this is a copy constructor on line 10 because the constructor is receiving a reference—a constant reference in this case—to an object of its same type.

On lines 17 and 18, two member variables are declared, each as a pointer to an integer. Typically, there is little reason for a class to store int member variables as pointers, but this was done to illustrate how to manage member variables on the free store.

The default constructor on lines 21–27 allocates room on the free store for two int variables and then assigns values to them.

The copy constructor begins on line 29. Note that the parameter is rhs. It is common to refer to the parameter to a copy constructor as rhs, which stands for right-hand side. When you look at the assignments on lines 33 and 34, you'll see that the object passed in as a parameter is on the right-hand side of the equal sign. Here's how it works:

On lines 31 and 32, memory is allocated on the free store. Then, on lines 33 and 34, the value at the new memory location is assigned the values from the existing Cat.

The parameter rhs is a Cat object that is passed into the copy constructor as a constant reference. As a Cat object, rhs has all the member variables of any other Cat.

Any Cat object can access private member variables of any other Cat object; however, it is good programming practice to use public accessor methods when possible. The member function rhs.GetAge() returns the value stored in the memory pointed to by rhs's member variable itsAge. In a real-world application, you should get the value for itsWeight in the same way—using an accessor method. On line 34, however, you see confirmation that different objects of the same class can access each other's members. In this case, a copy is made directly from the rhs object's private itsWeight member.

Figure 10.3 diagrams what is happening here. The values pointed to by the existing Cat's member variables are copied to the memory allocated for the new Cat.

On line 47, a Cat called Frisky is created. Frisky's age is printed, and then his age is set to 6 on line 50. On line 52, a new Cat, Boots, is created, using the copy constructor and passing in Frisky. Had Frisky been passed as a parameter to a function by value (not by reference), this same call to the copy constructor would have been made by the compiler.

On lines 53 and 54, the ages of both Cats are printed. Sure enough, Boots has Frisky's age, 6, not the default age of 5. On line 56, Frisky's age is set to 7, and then the ages are printed again. This time Frisky's age is 7, but Boots's age is still 6, demonstrating that they are stored in separate areas of memory.

10

FIGURE 10.3

Deep copy illustrated.

When the Cats fall out of scope, their destructors are automatically invoked. The implementation of the Cat destructor is shown on lines 37–43. delete is called on both pointers, itsAge and itsWeight, returning the allocated memory to the free store. Also, for safety, the pointers are reassigned to a null value.

Operator Overloading

C++ has a number of built-in types, including int, float, char, and so forth. Each of these has a number of built-in operators, such as addition (+) and multiplication (*). C++ enables you to add these operators to your own classes as well.

To explore operator overloading fully, Listing 10.6 creates a new class, Counter. A Counter object will be used in counting (surprise!) in loops and other applications in which a number must be incremented, decremented, or otherwise tracked.

LISTING 10.6 The Counter Class

```
1:  // Listing 10.6 - The Counter class
2:
3:  #include <iostream>
4:  using namespace std;
5:
6:  class Counter
7:  {
8:    public:
9:      Counter();
10:     ~Counter(){}
11:     int GetItsVal()const { return itsVal; }
12:     void SetItsVal(int x) {itsVal = x; }
13:
14:    private:
```

LISTING 10.6 continued

```
15:      int itsVal;
16:  };
17:
18:  Counter::Counter():
19:  itsVal(0)
20:  {}
21:
22:  int main()
23:  {
24:      Counter i;
25:      cout << "The value of i is " << i.GetItsVal() << endl;
26:      return 0;
27:  }
```

OUTPUT The value of i is 0

ANALYSIS As it stands, this is a pretty useless class. It is defined on lines 6–16. Its only member variable is an `int`. The default constructor, which is declared on line 9 and whose implementation is on line 18, initializes the one member variable, `itsVal`, to zero.

Unlike an honest, red-blooded `int`, the `Counter` object cannot be incremented, decremented, added, assigned, or otherwise manipulated. In exchange for this, it makes printing its value far more difficult!

Writing an Increment Function

Operator overloading restores much of the functionality that has been stripped out of this class. Two ways exist, for example, to add the capability to increment a `Counter` object. The first is to write an increment method, as shown in Listing 10.7.

LISTING 10.7 Adding an Increment Operator

```
1:  // Listing 10.7 - The Counter class
2:
3:  #include <iostream>
4:  using namespace std;
5:
6:  class Counter
7:  {
8:    public:
9:      Counter();
10:     ~Counter(){}
11:     int GetItsVal()const { return itsVal; }
```

LISTING 10.7   continued

```
12:       void SetItsVal(int x) {itsVal = x; }
13:       void Increment() { ++itsVal; }
14:
15:    private:
16:       int itsVal;
17:  };
18:
19:  Counter::Counter():
20:  itsVal(0)
21:  {}
22:
23:  int main()
24:  {
25:     Counter i;
26:     cout << "The value of i is " << i.GetItsVal() << endl;
27:     i.Increment();
28:     cout << "The value of i is " << i.GetItsVal() << endl;
29:     return 0;
30:  }
```

OUTPUT

```
The value of i is 0
The value of i is 1
```

ANALYSIS   Listing 10.7 adds an Increment function, defined on line 13. Although this works, it is cumbersome to use. The program cries out for the capability to add a ++ operator, and, of course, this can be done.

Overloading the Prefix Operator

Prefix operators can be overloaded by declaring functions with the form:

returnType operator *op* ()

Here, *op* is the operator to overload. Thus, the ++ operator can be overloaded with the following syntax:

void operator++ ()

This statement indicates that you are overloading the ++ operator and that it will not result in a return value—thus void is the return type. Listing 10.8 demonstrates this alternative.

LISTING 10.8   Overloading operator++

```
1:  // Listing 10.8 - The Counter class
2:  // prefix increment operator
3:
```

LISTING 10.8   continued

```
4:   #include <iostream>
5:   using namespace std;
6:
7:   class Counter
8:   {
9:     public:
10:       Counter();
11:       ~Counter(){}
12:       int GetItsVal()const { return itsVal; }
13:       void SetItsVal(int x) {itsVal = x; }
14:       void Increment() { ++itsVal; }
15:       void operator++ () { ++itsVal; }
16:
17:     private:
18:       int itsVal;
19:   };
20:
21:   Counter::Counter():
22:   itsVal(0)
23:   {}
24:
25:   int main()
26:   {
27:       Counter i;
28:       cout << "The value of i is " << i.GetItsVal() << endl;
29:       i.Increment();
30:       cout << "The value of i is " << i.GetItsVal() << endl;
31:       ++i;
32:       cout << "The value of i is " << i.GetItsVal() << endl;
33:       return 0;
34:   }
```

OUTPUT

```
The value of i is 0
The value of i is 1
The value of i is 2
```

ANALYSIS   On line 15, operator++ is overloaded. You can see on line 15 that the overloaded operator simply increments the value of the private member, itsVal. This overloaded operator is then used on line 31. This use is much closer to the syntax of a built-in type such as int.

At this point, you might consider putting in the extra capabilities for which Counter was created in the first place, such as detecting when the Counter overruns its maximum size. A significant defect exists in the way the increment operator was written, however. If you want to put the Counter on the right side of an assignment, it will fail. For example,

```
Counter a = ++i;
```

This code intends to create a new `Counter`, a, and then assign to it the value in i after i is incremented. The built-in copy constructor will handle the assignment, but the current increment operator does not return a `Counter` object. It returns void. You can't assign a void to anything, including a `Counter` object. (You can't make something from nothing!)

Returning Types in Overloaded Operator Functions

Clearly, what you want is to return a `Counter` object so that it can be assigned to another `Counter` object. Which object should be returned? One approach is to create a temporary object and return that. Listing 10.9 illustrates this approach.

LISTING 10.9   Returning a Temporary Object

```
1:  // Listing 10.9 - operator++ returns a temporary object
2:
3:  #include <iostream>
4:
5:  using namespace std;
6:
7:  class Counter
8:  {
9:    public:
10:      Counter();
11:      ~Counter(){}
12:      int GetItsVal()const { return itsVal; }
13:      void SetItsVal(int x) {itsVal = x; }
14:      void Increment() { ++itsVal; }
15:      Counter operator++ ();
16:
17:    private:
18:      int itsVal;
19:
20:  };
21:
22:  Counter::Counter():
23:  itsVal(0)
24:  {}
25:
26:  Counter Counter::operator++()
27:  {
28:      ++itsVal;
29:      Counter temp;
30:      temp.SetItsVal(itsVal);
31:      return temp;
32:  }
33:
34:  int main()
35:  {
```

LISTING **10.9**   continued

```
36:     Counter i;
37:     cout << "The value of i is " << i.GetItsVal() << endl;
38:     i.Increment();
39:     cout << "The value of i is " << i.GetItsVal() << endl;
40:     ++i;
41:     cout << "The value of i is " << i.GetItsVal() << endl;
42:     Counter a = ++i;
43:     cout << "The value of a: " << a.GetItsVal();
44:     cout << " and i: " << i.GetItsVal() << endl;
45:     return 0;
46:  }
```

OUTPUT
```
The value of i is 0
The value of i is 1
The value of i is 2
The value of a: 3 and i: 3
```

ANALYSIS   In this version, `operator++` has been declared on line 15 and is defined on lines 26–32. This version has been declared to return a `Counter` object. On line 29, a temporary variable, `temp`, is created, and its value is set to match that in the current object being incremented. When the increment is completed, the temporary variable is returned. You can see on line 42, that the temporary variable that is returned is immediately assigned to a.

Returning Nameless Temporaries

There is really no need to name the temporary object created on line 29. If `Counter` had a constructor that took a value, you could simply return the result of that constructor as the return value of the increment operator. Listing 10.10 illustrates this idea.

LISTING **10.10**   Returning a Nameless Temporary Object

```
1:  // Listing 10.10 - operator++ returns a nameless temporary object
2:
3:  #include <iostream>
4:
5:  using namespace std;
6:
7:  class Counter
8:  {
9:    public:
10:      Counter();
11:      Counter(int val);
12:      ~Counter(){}
13:      int GetItsVal()const { return itsVal; }
```

10

LISTING 10.10 continued

```
14:       void SetItsVal(int x) {itsVal = x; }
15:       void Increment() { ++itsVal; }
16:       Counter operator++ ();
17:
18:   private:
19:       int itsVal;
20:  };
21:
22:  Counter::Counter():
23:  itsVal(0)
24:  {}
25:
26:  Counter::Counter(int val):
27:  itsVal(val)
28:  {}
29:
30:  Counter Counter::operator++()
31:  {
32:       ++itsVal;
33:       return Counter (itsVal);
34:  }
35:
36:  int main()
37:  {
38:      Counter i;
39:      cout << "The value of i is " << i.GetItsVal() << endl;
40:      i.Increment();
41:      cout << "The value of i is " << i.GetItsVal() << endl;
42:      ++i;
43:      cout << "The value of i is " << i.GetItsVal() << endl;
44:      Counter a = ++i;
45:      cout << "The value of a: " << a.GetItsVal();
46:      cout << " and i: " << i.GetItsVal() << endl;
47:      return 0;
48:  }
```

OUTPUT

```
The value of i is 0
The value of i is 1
The value of i is 2
The value of a: 3 and i: 3
```

ANALYSIS On line 11, a new constructor is declared that takes an int. The implementation is on lines 26–28. It initializes itsVal with the passed-in value.

The implementation of operator++ is now simplified. On line 32, itsVal is incremented. Then on line 33, a temporary Counter object is created, initialized to the value in itsVal, and then returned as the result of the operator++.

This is more elegant, but raises the question, "Why create a temporary object at all?" Remember that each temporary object must be constructed and later destroyed—each of these is potentially an expensive operation. Also, the object i already exists and already has the right value, so why not return it? This problem can be solved by using the this pointer.

Using the this Pointer

The this pointer is passed to all member functions, including overloaded operators such as operator++(). In the listings you've been creating, this points to i, and if it is dereferenced it returns the object i, which already has the right value in its member variable itsVal. Listing 10.11 illustrates returning the dereferenced this pointer and avoiding the creation of an unneeded temporary object.

LISTING 10.11 Returning the this Pointer

```
1:   // Listing 10.11 - Returning the dereferenced this pointer
2:
3:   #include <iostream>
4:
5:   using namespace std;
6:
7:   class Counter
8:   {
9:     public:
10:       Counter();
11:       ~Counter(){}
12:       int GetItsVal()const { return itsVal; }
13:       void SetItsVal(int x) {itsVal = x; }
14:       void Increment() { ++itsVal; }
15:       const Counter& operator++ ();
16:
17:     private:
18:       int itsVal;
19:   };
20:
21:   Counter::Counter():
22:   itsVal(0)
23:   {};
24:
25:   const Counter& Counter::operator++()
26:   {
27:       ++itsVal;
28:       return *this;
29:   }
30:
31:   int main()
32:   {
```

10

LISTING 10.11 continued

```
33:      Counter i;
34:      cout << "The value of i is " << i.GetItsVal() << endl;
35:      i.Increment();
36:      cout << "The value of i is " << i.GetItsVal() << endl;
37:      ++i;
38:      cout << "The value of i is " << i.GetItsVal() << endl;
39:      Counter a = ++i;
40:      cout << "The value of a: " << a.GetItsVal();
41:      cout << " and i: " << i.GetItsVal() << endl;
42:      return 0;
43:  }
```

OUTPUT
```
The value of i is 0
The value of i is 1
The value of i is 2
The value of a: 3 and i: 3
```

ANALYSIS The implementation of operator++, on lines 25–29, has been changed to dereference the this pointer and to return the current object. This provides a Counter
object to be assigned to a. As discussed, if the Counter object allocated memory, it
would be important to override the copy constructor. In this case, the default copy constructor works fine.

Note that the value returned is a Counter reference, thereby avoiding the creation of an
extra temporary object. It is a const reference because the value should not be changed
by the function using the returned Counter.

The returned Counter object must be constant. If it were not, it would be possible to perform operations on that returned object that might change its values. For example, if the
returned value were not constant, then you might write line 39 as

```
Counter a = ++++i;
```

What you should expect from this is for the increment operator (++) to be called on the
result of calling ++i. This would actually result in calling the increment operator on the
object, i, twice—which is something you should most likely block.

Try this: Change the return value to nonconstant in both the declaration and the implementation (lines 15 and 25), and change line 39 as shown (++++i). Put a break point in
your debugger on line 39 and step in. You will find that you step into the increment operator twice. The increment is being applied to the (now nonconstant) return value.

It is to prevent this that you declare the return value to be constant. If you change lines
15 and 25 back to constant, and leave line 39 as shown (++++i), the compiler complains
that you can't call the increment operator on a constant object.

Overloading the Postfix Operator

So far, you've overloaded the prefix operator. What if you want to overload the postfix increment operator? Here, the compiler has a problem: How is it to differentiate between prefix and postfix? By convention, an integer variable is supplied as a parameter to the operator declaration. The parameter's value is ignored; it is just a signal that this is the postfix operator.

Difference Between Prefix and Postfix

Before you can write the postfix operator, you must understand how it is different from the prefix operator. You learned about this in detail on Day 4, "Creating Expressions and Statements" (see Listing 4.3).

To review, prefix says "increment, and then fetch," but postfix says "fetch, and then increment."

Thus, although the prefix operator can simply increment the value and then return the object itself, the postfix must return the value that existed before it was incremented. To do this, you must create a temporary object that will hold the original value, increment the value of the original object, and then return the temporary object.

Let's go over that again. Consider the following line of code:

```
a = x++;
```

If x was 5, after this statement a is 5, but x is 6. Thus, the value in x was returned and assigned to a, and then the value of x is increased. If x is an object, its postfix increment operator must stash away the original value (5) in a temporary object, increment x's value to 6, and then return that temporary object to assign its original value to a.

Note that because the temporary is being returned, it must be returned by value and not by reference, because the temporary will go out of scope as soon as the function returns.

Listing 10.12 demonstrates the use of both the prefix and the postfix operators.

LISTING 10.12   Prefix and Postfix Operators

```
1:  // Listing 10.12 - Prefix and Postfix operator overloading
2:
3:  #include <iostream>
4:
5:  using namespace std;
6:
7:  class Counter
8:  {
```

10

LISTING 10.12 continued

```
 9:   public:
10:      Counter();
11:      ~Counter(){}
12:      int GetItsVal()const { return itsVal; }
13:      void SetItsVal(int x) {itsVal = x; }
14:      const Counter& operator++ ();    // prefix
15:      const Counter operator++ (int); // postfix
16:
17:   private:
18:      int itsVal;
19:  };
20:
21:  Counter::Counter():
22:  itsVal(0)
23:  {}
24:
25:  const Counter& Counter::operator++()
26:  {
27:     ++itsVal;
28:     return *this;
29:  }
30:
31:  const Counter Counter::operator++(int theFlag)
32:  {
33:     Counter temp(*this);
34:     ++itsVal;
35:     return temp;
36:  }
37:
38:  int main()
39:  {
40:     Counter i;
41:     cout << "The value of i is " << i.GetItsVal() << endl;
42:     i++;
43:     cout << "The value of i is " << i.GetItsVal() << endl;
44:     ++i;
45:     cout << "The value of i is " << i.GetItsVal() << endl;
46:     Counter a = ++i;
47:     cout << "The value of a: " << a.GetItsVal();
48:     cout << " and i: " << i.GetItsVal() << endl;
49:     a = i++;
50:     cout << "The value of a: " << a.GetItsVal();
51:     cout << " and i: " << i.GetItsVal() << endl;
52:     return 0;
53:  }
```

```
The value of i is 0
The value of i is 1
The value of i is 2
The value of a: 3 and i: 3
The value of a: 3 and i: 4
```

The postfix operator is declared on line 15 and implemented on lines 31–36. The prefix operator is declared on line 14.

The parameter passed into the postfix operator on line 32 (theFlag) serves to signal that it is the postfix operator, but this value is never used.

Overloading Binary Mathematical Operators

The increment operator is a unary operator. It operates on only one object. Many of the mathematical operators are binary operators; they take two objects (one of the current class, and one of any class). Obviously, overloading operators such as the addition (+), subtraction (-), multiplication (*), division (/), and modulus (%) operators is going to be different from overloading the prefix and postfix operators. Consider how you would implement overloading the + operator for Count.

The goal is to be able to declare two Counter variables and then add them, as in the following example:

```
Counter varOne, varTwo, varThree;
VarThree = VarOne + VarTwo;
```

Once again, you could start by writing a function, Add(), which would take a Counter as its argument, add the values, and then return a Counter with the result. Listing 10.13 illustrates this approach.

LISTING 10.13   The Add() Function

```
1:  // Listing 10.13 - Add function
2:
3:  #include <iostream>
4:
5:  using namespace std;
6:
7:  class Counter
8:  {
9:    public:
10:      Counter();
11:      Counter(int initialValue);
12:      ~Counter(){}
13:      int GetItsVal()const { return itsVal; }
14:      void SetItsVal(int x) {itsVal = x; }
```

10

LISTING 10.13 continued

```
15:       Counter Add(const Counter &);
16:
17:    private:
18:       int itsVal;
19:  };
20:
21:  Counter::Counter(int initialValue):
22:  itsVal(initialValue)
23:  {}
24:
25:  Counter::Counter():
26:  itsVal(0)
27:  {}
28:
29:  Counter Counter::Add(const Counter & rhs)
30:  {
31:      return Counter(itsVal+ rhs.GetItsVal());
32:  }
33:
34:  int main()
35:  {
36:      Counter varOne(2), varTwo(4), varThree;
37:      varThree = varOne.Add(varTwo);
38:      cout << "varOne: " << varOne.GetItsVal()<< endl;
39:      cout << "varTwo: " << varTwo.GetItsVal() << endl;
40:      cout << "varThree: " << varThree.GetItsVal() << endl;
41:
42:    return 0;
43:  }
```

OUTPUT

```
varOne: 2
varTwo: 4
varThree: 6
```

ANALYSIS The Add() function is declared on line 15. It takes a constant Counter reference, which is the number to add to the current object. It returns a Counter object, which is the result to be assigned to the left side of the assignment statement, as shown on line 37. That is, VarOne is the object, varTwo is the parameter to the Add() function, and the result is assigned to VarThree.

To create varThree without having to initialize a value for it, a default constructor is required. The default constructor initializes itsVal to 0, as shown on lines 25–27. Because varOne and varTwo need to be initialized to a nonzero value, another constructor was created, as shown on lines 21–23. Another solution to this problem is to provide the default value 0 to the constructor declared on line 11.

The Add() function itself is shown on lines 29–32. It works, but its use is unnatural.

Overloading the Addition Operator (`operator+`)

Overloading the + operator would make for a more natural use of the `Counter` class.
Remember, you saw earlier that to overload an operator, you use the structure:

returnType `operator` *op* `()`

Listing 10.14 illustrates using this to overload the addition operator.

LISTING 10.14 operator+

```
1:  // Listing 10.14 - Overload operator plus (+)
2:
3:  #include <iostream>
4:
5:  using namespace std;
6:
7:  class Counter
8:  {
9:    public:
10:      Counter();
11:      Counter(int initialValue);
12:      ~Counter(){}
13:      int GetItsVal()const { return itsVal; }
14:      void SetItsVal(int x) {itsVal = x; }
15:      Counter operator+ (const Counter &);
16:    private:
17:      int itsVal;
18:  };
19:
20:  Counter::Counter(int initialValue):
21:  itsVal(initialValue)
22:  {}
23:
24:  Counter::Counter():
25:  itsVal(0)
26:  {}
27:
28:  Counter Counter::operator+ (const Counter & rhs)
29:  {
30:     return Counter(itsVal + rhs.GetItsVal());
31:  }
32:
33:  int main()
34:  {
35:     Counter varOne(2), varTwo(4), varThree;
36:     varThree = varOne + varTwo;
37:     cout << "varOne: " << varOne.GetItsVal()<< endl;
38:     cout << "varTwo: " << varTwo.GetItsVal() << endl;
39:     cout << "varThree: " << varThree.GetItsVal() << endl;
40:
41:     return 0;
42:  }
```

10

OUTPUT

```
varOne: 2
varTwo: 4
varThree: 6
```

ANALYSIS operator+ is declared on line 15 and defined on lines 28–31.

Compare these with the declaration and definition of the Add() function in the previous listing; they are nearly identical. The syntax of their use, however, is quite different. It is more natural to say this:

```
varThree = varOne + varTwo;
```

than to say:

```
varThree = varOne.Add(varTwo);
```

Not a big change, but enough to make the program easier to use and understand.

On line 36, the operator is used

```
36:         varThree = varOne + varTwo;
```

This is translated by the compiler into

```
VarThree = varOne.operator+(varTwo);
```

You could, of course, have written it this way yourself, and the compiler would have been equally happy.

The operator+ method is called on the left-hand operand, passing in the right-hand operand.

Issues in Operator Overloading

Overloaded operators can be member functions, as described in today's lesson, or non-member functions. The latter is described on Day 15, "Special Classes and Functions," when you learn about friend functions.

The only operators that must be class members are the assignment (=), subscript([ ]), function call (( )), and indirection (->) operators.

Operator [ ] is discussed on Day 13, "Managing Arrays and Strings," when arrays are covered. Overloading operator -> is discussed on Day 15, when smart pointers are discussed.

Limitations on Operator Overloading

Operators for built-in types (such as int) cannot be overloaded. The precedence order cannot be changed, and the arity of the operator, that is, whether it is unary or binary, cannot be changed. You cannot make up new operators, so you cannot declare ** to be the "power of" operator.

Arity refers to how many terms are used in the operator. Some C++ operators are unary and use only one term (`myValue++`). Some operators are binary and use two terms (`a+b`). Only one operator is ternary and uses three terms. The `?` operator is often called the ternary operator because it is the only ternary operator in C++ (`a > b ? x : y`).

What to Overload

Operator overloading is one of the aspects of C++ most overused and abused by new programmers. It is tempting to create new and interesting uses for some of the more obscure operators, but these invariably lead to code that is confusing and difficult to read.

Of course, making the + operator subtract and the * operator add can be fun, but no professional programmer would do that. The greater danger lies in the well-intentioned but idiosyncratic use of an operator—using + to mean concatenate a series of letters or / to mean split a string. There is good reason to consider these uses, but there is even better reason to proceed with caution. Remember, the goal of overloading operators is to increase usability and understanding.

Do	Don't
DO use operator overloading when it will clarify the program.	**DON'T** create counterintuitive operator behaviors.
DO return an object of the class from overloaded operators.	**DON'T** confuse the prefix and postfix operators, especially when overloading.

The Assignment Operator

The fourth and final function that is supplied by the compiler, if you don't specify one, is the assignment operator (`operator=()`). This operator is called whenever you assign to an object. For example:

```
Cat catOne(5,7);
Cat catTwo(3,4);
// ... other code here
catTwo = catOne;
```

Here, catOne is created and initialized with itsAge equal to 5 and itsWeight equal to 7. catTwo is then created and assigned the values 3 and 4.

After a while, catTwo is assigned the values in catOne. Two issues are raised here: What happens if itsAge is a pointer, and what happens to the original values in catTwo?

Handling member variables that store their values on the free store was discussed earlier during the examination of the copy constructor. The same issues arise here, as you saw illustrated in Figures 10.1 and 10.2.

C++ programmers differentiate between a shallow, or member-wise, copy on the one hand and a deep copy on the other. A shallow copy just copies the members, and both objects end up pointing to the same area on the free store. A deep copy allocates the necessary memory. This was illustrated in Figure 10.3.

An added wrinkle occurs with the assignment operator, however. The object catTwo already exists and has memory already allocated. That memory must be deleted to avoid any memory leaks. But what happens if you assign catTwo to itself?

```
catTwo = catTwo;
```

No one is likely to do this on purpose. It is, however, possible for this to happen by accident when references and dereferenced pointers hide the fact that the assignment is to itself.

If you did not handle this problem carefully, catTwo would delete its memory allocation. Then, when it was ready to copy in the values from memory on the right-hand side of the assignment, there would be a very big problem: The value would be gone!

To protect against this, your assignment operator must check to see if the right-hand side of the assignment operator is the object itself. It does this by examining the value of the this pointer. Listing 10.15 shows a class with an assignment operator overloaded. It also avoids the issue just mentioned.

LISTING 10.15   An Assignment Operator

```
 1:  // Listing 10.15 - Copy constructors
 2:
 3:  #include <iostream>
 4:
 5:  using namespace std;
 6:
 7:  class Cat
 8:  {
 9:    public:
10:      Cat();                  // default constructor
11:      // copy constructor and destructor elided!
12:      int GetAge() const { return *itsAge; }
13:      int GetWeight() const { return *itsWeight; }
```

LISTING **10.15**   continued

```
14:        void SetAge(int age) { *itsAge = age; }
15:        Cat & operator=(const Cat &);
16:
17:     private:
18:        int *itsAge;
19:        int *itsWeight;
20:     };
21:
22:     Cat::Cat()
23:     {
24:        itsAge = new int;
25:        itsWeight = new int;
26:        *itsAge = 5;
27:        *itsWeight = 9;
28:     }
29:
30:
31:     Cat & Cat::operator=(const Cat & rhs)
32:     {
33:        if (this == &rhs)
34:            return *this;
35:        *itsAge = rhs.GetAge();
36:        *itsWeight = rhs.GetWeight();
37:        return *this;
38:     }
39:
40:
41:     int main()
42:     {
43:        Cat Frisky;
44:        cout << "Frisky's age: " << Frisky.GetAge() << endl;
45:        cout << "Setting Frisky to 6...\n";
46:        Frisky.SetAge(6);
47:        Cat Whiskers;
48:        cout << "Whiskers' age: " << Whiskers.GetAge() << endl;
49:        cout << "copying Frisky to Whiskers...\n";
50:        Whiskers = Frisky;
51:        cout << "Whiskers' age: " << Whiskers.GetAge() << endl;
52:        return 0;
53:     }
```

OUTPUT

```
Frisky's age: 5
Setting Frisky to 6...
Whiskers' age: 5
copying Frisky to Whiskers...
Whiskers' age: 6
```

10

ANALYSIS Listing 10.15 brings back the Cat class, but leaves out the copy constructor and destructor to save room. New to the listing on line 15 is the declaration of the assignment operator. This is the method that will be used to overload the assignment operator. On lines 31–38, this overload method is defined.

On line 33, the current object (the Cat being assigned to) is tested to see whether it is the same as the Cat being assigned. This is done by checking whether the address of the Cat object on the right side (rhs) is the same as the address stored in the this pointer. If they are the same, there is no need to do anything because the object on the left is the same object that is on the right. Because of this, line 34 returns the current object.

If the object on the right-hand side is not the same, then the members are copied on lines 35 and 36 before returning.

You see the use of the assignment operator on line 50 of the main program when a Cat object called Frisky is assigned to the Cat object Whiskers. The rest of this listing should be familiar.

This listing assumes that if the two objects are pointing to the same address, then they must be the same. Of course, the equality operator (==) can be overloaded as well, enabling you to determine for yourself what it means for your objects to be equal.

Handling Data Type Conversion

Now that you've seen how to assign an object to another object of the same type, consider another situation. What happens when you try to assign a variable of a built-in type, such as int or unsigned short, to an object of a user-defined class? For example, the Counter class was created earlier. What if you wanted to assign an integer to this class? Listing 10.16 attempts to do this.

CAUTION | Listing 10.16 will not compile!

LISTING 10.16 Attempting to Assign a Counter to an int

```
1:  // Listing 10.16 - This code won't compile!
2:
3:  #include <iostream>
4:
5:  using namespace std;
6:
7:  class Counter
8:  {
```

LISTING **10.16**   continued

```
 9:    public:
10:      Counter();
11:      ~Counter(){}
12:      int GetItsVal()const { return itsVal; }
13:      void SetItsVal(int x) {itsVal = x; }
14:    private:
15:      int itsVal;
16:  };
17:
18:  Counter::Counter():
19:  itsVal(0)
20:  {}
21:
22:  int main()
23:  {
24:      int theInt = 5;
25:      Counter theCtr = theInt;
26:      cout << "theCtr: " << theCtr.GetItsVal() << endl;
27:      return 0;
28:  }
```

10

OUTPUT   Compiler error! Unable to convert int to Counter

ANALYSIS   The Counter class declared on lines 7–16 has only a default constructor. It does
               not declare methods for turning any built-in types into a Counter object. In the
main() function, an integer is declared on line 24. This is then assigned to a Counter
object. This line, however, leads to an error. The compiler cannot figure out, unless you
tell it that, given an int, it should assign that value to the member variable itsVal.

Listing 10.17 corrects this by creating a conversion operator: a constructor that takes an
int and produces a Counter object.

LISTING **10.17**   Converting int to Counter

```
 1:  // Listing 10.17 - Constructor as conversion operator
 2:
 3:  #include <iostream>
 4:
 5:  using namespace std;
 6:
 7:  class Counter
 8:  {
 9:    public:
10:      Counter();
11:      Counter(int val);
```

LISTING **10.17**   continued

```
12:        ~Counter(){}
13:        int GetItsVal()const { return itsVal; }
14:        void SetItsVal(int x) {itsVal = x; }
15:     private:
16:        int itsVal;
17:  };
18:
19:  Counter::Counter():
20:  itsVal(0)
21:  {}
22:
23:  Counter::Counter(int val):
24:  itsVal(val)
25:  {}
26:
27:  int main()
28:  {
29:      int theInt = 5;
30:      Counter theCtr = theInt;
31:      cout << "theCtr: " << theCtr.GetItsVal() << endl;
32:      return 0;
33:  }
```

OUTPUT
theCtr: 5

ANALYSIS
The important change is on line 11, where the constructor is overloaded to take an int, and on lines 23–25, where the constructor is implemented. The effect of this constructor is to create a Counter out of an int.

Given this, the compiler is able to call the constructor that takes an int as its argument. Here's how:

Step 1: Create a Counter *called* theCtr.

This is like saying int x = 5; which creates an integer variable x and then initializes it with the value 5. In this case, a Counter object theCtr is being created and initialized with the integer variable theInt.

Step 2: Assign to theCtr *the value of* theInt.

But theInt is an integer, not a counter! First, you have to convert it into a Counter. The compiler will try to make certain conversions for you automatically, but you have to teach it how. You teach the compiler how to make the conversion by creating a constructor. In this case, you need a constructor for Counter that takes an integer as its only parameter:

```
class Counter
{
    Counter (int x);
    // ..
};
```

This constructor creates `Counter` objects from integers. It does this by creating a temporary and unnamed counter. For illustration purposes, suppose that the temporary `Counter` object created from the integer is called `wasInt`.

Step 3: Assign `wasInt` *to* `theCtr`, *which is equivalent to*

```
theCtr = wasInt;
```

In this step, `wasInt` (the temporary `Counter` created when you ran the constructor) is substituted for what was on the right-hand side of the assignment operator. That is, now that the compiler has made a temporary `Counter` for you, it initializes `theCtr` with that temporary object.

To further understand this, you must understand that *all* operator overloading works the same way—you declare an overloaded operator using the keyword `operator`. With binary operators (such as = or +), the right-hand side variable becomes the parameter. This is done by the constructor. Thus

```
a = b;
```

becomes

```
a.operator=(b);
```

What happens, however, if you try to reverse the assignment with the following?

```
1:   Counter theCtr(5);
2:   int theInt = theCtr;
3:   cout << "theInt : " << theInt  << endl;
```

Again, this generates a compile error. Although the compiler now knows how to create a `Counter` out of an `int`, it does not know how to reverse the process.

Conversion Operators

To solve the conversion back to a different type from objects of your class, C++ provides conversion operators. These conversion operators can be added to your class. This enables your class to specify how to do implicit conversions to built-in types. Listing 10.18 illustrates this. One note, however: Conversion operators do not specify a return value, even though they do return a converted value.

10

LISTING **10.18**   Converting from Counter to unsigned short()

```
1:  // Listing 10.18 - Conversion Operators
2:  #include <iostream>
3:
4:  class Counter
5:  {
6:    public:
7:      Counter();
8:      Counter(int val);
9:      ~Counter(){}
10:     int GetItsVal()const { return itsVal; }
11:     void SetItsVal(int x) {itsVal = x; }
12:     operator unsigned int();
13:   private:
14:     int itsVal;
15: };
16:
17: Counter::Counter():
18: itsVal(0)
19: {}
20:
21: Counter::Counter(int val):
22: itsVal(val)
23: {}
24:
25: Counter::operator unsigned int ()
26: {
27:    return ( int (itsVal) );
28: }
29:
30: int main()
31: {
32:    Counter ctr(5);
33:    int theInt = ctr;
34:    std::cout << "theInt: " << theInt << std::endl;
35:    return 0;
36: }
```

OUTPUT   theShort: 5

ANALYSIS   On line 12, the conversion operator is declared. Note that this declaration starts with the operator keyword, and that it has no return value. The implementation of this function is on lines 25–28. Line 27 returns the value of itsVal, converted to an int.

Now, the compiler knows how to turn ints into Counter objects and vice versa, and they can be assigned to one another freely. You assign and return other data types in the exact same manner.

Summary

Today, you learned how to overload member functions of your classes. You also learned how to supply default values to functions and how to decide when to use default values and when to overload.

Overloading class constructors enables you to create flexible classes that can be created from other objects. Initialization of objects happens at the initialization stage of construction and is more efficient than assigning values in the body of the constructor.

The copy constructor and the assignment operator are supplied by the compiler if you don't create your own, but they do a member-wise copy of the class. In classes in which member data includes pointers to the free store, these methods must be overridden so that you can allocate memory for the target member variable.

Almost all C++ operators can be overloaded, although you want to be cautious not to create operators whose use is counterintuitive. You cannot change the arity of operators, nor can you invent new operators.

`this` refers to the current object and is an invisible parameter to all member functions. The dereferenced `this` pointer is often returned by overloaded operators so that they can participate in expressions.

Conversion operators enable you to create classes that can be used in expressions that expect a different type of object. They are exceptions to the rule that all functions return an explicit value; like constructors and destructors, they have no return type.

Q&A

Q Why would I ever use default values when I can overload a function?

A It is easier to maintain one function than two, and it is often easier to understand a function with default parameters than to study the bodies of two functions. Furthermore, updating one of the functions and neglecting to update the second is a common source of bugs.

Q Given the problems with overloaded functions, why not always use default values instead?

A Overloaded functions supply capabilities not available with default variables, such as varying the list of parameters by type rather than just by number or providing a different implementation for different parameter type combinations.

Q When writing a class constructor, how do I decide what to put in the initialization and what to put in the body of the constructor?

A A simple rule of thumb is to do as much as possible in the initialization phase—that is, initialize all member variables there. Some things, like computations (including those used for initialization) and print statements, must be in the body of the constructor.

Q Can an overloaded function have a default parameter?

A Yes. One or more of the overloaded functions can have its own default values, following the normal rules for default variables in any function.

Q Why are some member functions defined within the class declaration and others are not?

A Defining the implementation of a member function within the declaration makes it inline. Generally, this is done only if the function is extremely simple. Note that you can also make a member function inline by using the keyword `inline`, even if the function is declared outside the class declaration.

Workshop

The Workshop provides quiz questions to help solidify your understanding of the material covered and exercises to provide you with experience in using what you've learned. Try to answer the quiz and exercise questions before checking the answers in Appendix D, and be certain you understand the answers before going to tomorrow's lesson.

Quiz

1. When you overload member functions, in what ways must they differ?
2. What is the difference between a declaration and a definition?
3. When is the copy constructor called?
4. When is the destructor called?
5. How does the copy constructor differ from the assignment operator (=)?
6. What is the `this` pointer?
7. How do you differentiate between overloading the prefix and postfix increment operators?
8. Can you overload the `operator+` for `short` integers?
9. Is it legal in C++ to overload the `operator++` so that it decrements a value in your class?
10. What return value must conversion operators have in their declarations?

Exercises

1. Write a `SimpleCircle` class declaration (only) with one member variable: `itsRadius`. Include a default constructor, a destructor, and accessor methods for radius.

2. Using the class you created in Exercise 1, write the implementation of the default constructor, initializing `itsRadius` with the value 5. Do this within the initialization phase of the constructor and not within the body.

3. Using the same class, add a second constructor that takes a value as its parameter and assigns that value to `itsRadius`.

4. Create a prefix and postfix increment operator for your `SimpleCircle` class that increments `itsRadius`.

5. Change `SimpleCircle` to store `itsRadius` on the free store, and fix the existing methods.

6. Provide a copy constructor for `SimpleCircle`.

7. Provide an assignment operator for `SimpleCircle`.

8. Write a program that creates two `SimpleCircle` objects. Use the default constructor on one and instantiate the other with the value 9. Call the increment operator on each and then print their values. Finally, assign the second to the first and print its values.

9. **BUG BUSTERS:** What is wrong with this implementation of the assignment operator?

```
SQUARE SQUARE ::operator=(const SQUARE & rhs)
{
    itsSide = new int;
    *itsSide = rhs.GetSide();
    return *this;
}
```

10. **BUG BUSTERS:** What is wrong with this implementation of the addition operator?

```
VeryShort  VeryShort::operator+ (const VeryShort& rhs)
{
   itsVal += rhs.GetItsVal();
   return *this;
}
```

10

DAY **11**

Object-Oriented Analysis and Design

It is easy to become focused on the syntax of C++ and to lose sight of how and why you use these techniques to build programs.

Today, you will learn

- How to use object-oriented analysis to understand the problem you are trying to solve
- How to use object-oriented design to create a robust, extensible, and reliable solution
- How to use the Unified Modeling Language (UML) to document your analysis and design

Building Models

If complexity is to be managed, a model of the universe must be created. The goal of the model is to create a meaningful abstraction of the real world. Such an abstraction should be simpler than the real world but should also accurately reflect the real world so that the model can be used to predict the behavior of things in the real world.

A child's globe is a classic model. The model isn't the thing itself; a child's globe would never be confused with the Earth, but one maps the other well enough that you can learn about the Earth by studying the globe.

There are, of course, significant simplifications. My daughter's globe never has rain, floods, globe-quakes, and so forth, but I can use her globe to predict how long it will take me to fly from my home to Indianapolis should I ever need to come in and explain myself to the Sams senior management when they ask me why my manuscript was late ("you see, I was doing great, but then I got lost in a metaphor and it took me hours to get out").

A model that is not simpler than the thing being modeled is not much use. The comedian Steve Wright quips: "I have a map on which one inch equals one inch. I live at E5."

Object-oriented software design is about building good models. It consists of two significant pieces: a modeling language and a process.

Software Design: The Modeling Language

The *modeling language* is the least important aspect of object-oriented analysis and design; unfortunately, it tends to get the most attention. A modeling language is nothing more than a convention for representing a model in some other medium such as paper or a computer system, and in some format such as graphics, text, or symbols. For example, you can easily decide to draw your classes as triangles and draw the inheritance relationship as a dotted line. If so, you might model a geranium as shown in Figure 11.1.

FIGURE 11.1

Generalization/ specialization.

In the figure, you see that a Geranium is a special kind of Flower. If you and I agree to draw our inheritance (generalization/specialization) diagrams like this, we'll understand each other perfectly. Over time, we'll probably want to model lots of complex relationships, and so we'll develop our own complicated set of diagramming conventions and rules.

Of course, we'll need to explain our conventions to everyone else with whom we work, and each new employee or collaborator will have to learn our conventions. We might interact with other companies that have their own conventions, and we'll need to allow time to negotiate a common convention and to compensate for the inevitable misunderstandings.

It would be more convenient if everyone in the industry agreed on a common modeling language. (For that matter, it would be convenient if everyone in the world agreed on a single spoken language, but one thing at a time.)

The *lingua franca* of software analysis and design is UML—the Unified Modeling Language. The job of the UML specification is to answer questions such as, "How should we draw an inheritance relationship?" The geranium drawing shown in Figure 11.1 would be drawn in UML as shown in Figure 11.2.

11

FIGURE 11.2

UML drawing of specialization.

In UML, classes are drawn as rectangles, and inheritance is drawn as a line with an arrowhead. Interestingly, the arrowhead points from the more specialized class to the more general class. The direction of the arrow can be counterintuitive, but it doesn't matter; as long as we all agree, then after we learn the representation, we can communicate.

The details of the UML are rather straightforward. The diagrams generally are not hard to use or to understand, and you'll learn about them as they are presented. Although it is possible to write a whole book on the UML, the truth is that 90 percent of the time, you use only a small subset of the UML notation, and that subset is easily learned.

Software Design: The Process

The *process* of object-oriented analysis and design is much more complex and important than the modeling language. So, of course, it is ironic that you hear much less about it.

That is because the debate about modeling languages is pretty much settled; as an industry, it has been decided that UML is the primary standard to be used. The debate about process, however, rages on.

A *method* is a modeling language and a process. Method is often incorrectly referred to as "methodology," but "methodology" is the study of methods.

A *methodologist* is someone who develops or studies one or more methods. Typically, methodologists develop and publish their own methods. Three of the leading methodologists and their methods are Grady Booch, who developed the Booch method, Ivar Jacobson, who developed object-oriented software engineering, and James Rumbaugh, who developed Object Modeling Technology (OMT). Together, these three men have created what is now called the *Rational Unified Process* (formerly known as Objectory), a method and a commercial product from Rational Software, Inc. All three men have been employed at IBM's Rational Software division, where they are affectionately known as the *Three Amigos*.

Today's lesson loosely follows their process rather than slavishly adhering to academic theory—it is much more important to ship a product than to adhere to a method. Other methods have something to offer, and so you will learn the bits and pieces that are valuable to use when stitching together a workable framework. Not every practitioner agrees with this approach, and you are encouraged to read the extensive literature on software engineering practice to determine what you think is the best practice. If you work for a company that follows a specific method as their official practice, you need to be prepared to follow that method to the level of compliance they require.

The process of software design can be *iterative*. In that case, as software is developed, you can go through the entire process repeatedly as you strive to enhance your understanding of the requirements. The design directs the implementation, but the details uncovered during implementation feed back into the design. In this approach, you should not try to develop any sizable project in a single, orderly, straight line; rather, you should iterate over pieces of the project, constantly improving your design and refining your implementation.

Waterfall Versus Iterative Development

Iterative development can be distinguished from waterfall development. In waterfall development, the output from one stage becomes the input to the next. Just like you can't easily go up a waterfall, with this method of development, there is no going back to previous stages (see Figure 11.3).

FIGURE 11.3

The waterfall method.

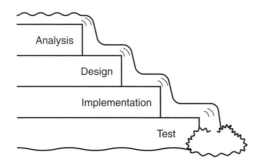

In a waterfall development process, the requirements are detailed, and the clients sign off ("Yes, this is what I want"); the requirements are then passed on to the designer, set in stone. The designer creates the design (and a wonder to behold it is), and passes it off to the programmer who implements the design. The programmer, in turn, hands the code to a QA person who tests the code and then releases it to the customer. Great in theory, however, this is potentially disastrous in practice.

The Process of Iterative Development

In iterative development, you start with a concept; an idea of what you might want to build. As the details are examined, the vision might grow and evolve.

When you have a good start on the requirements, you begin the design, knowing full well that the questions that arise during design might cause modifications back in the requirements. As you work on design, you can also begin prototyping and then implementing the product. The issues that arise in development feed back into design and might even influence your understanding of the requirements. Most important, you design and implement only pieces of the full product, iterating over the design and implementation phases repeatedly.

Although the steps of the process are repeated iteratively, it is nearly impossible to describe them in such a cyclical manner. Therefore, the following list describes them in sequence.

The following are the steps of the iterative development process you'll use for this:

Step 1: Conceptualization

> **Conceptualization** is the "vision thing." It is the single sentence that describes the great idea.

Step 2: Analysis

> **Analysis** is the process of understanding the requirements.

11

Step 3: Design

Design is the process of creating the model of your classes, from which you will generate your code.

Step 4: Implementation

Implementation is writing it in code (for example, in C++).

Step 5: Testing

Testing is making sure that you did it right.

Step 6: Rollout

Rollout is getting it to your customers.

NOTE

These are not the same as the *phases* of the Rational Unified Process, which are

- Inception
- Elaboration
- Construction
- Transition

Or the *workflows* of the Rational Unified Process, which are

- Business Modeling
- Requirements
- Analysis and Design
- Implementation
- Test
- Deployment
- Configuration and Change Management
- Project Management
- Environment

Don't misunderstand—in reality, you run through each of these steps many times during the course of the development of a single product. The iterative development process is just hard to present and understand if you cycle through each step.

This process should sound easy. All the rest of today's lesson is simply the details.

> **Controversies**
>
> Endless controversies exist about what happens in each stage of the iterative design process, and even about what you name those stages.
>
> Here's a secret: *It doesn't matter.*
>
> The essential steps are the same in just about every object-oriented process: Find out what you need to build, design a solution, and implement that design.
>
> Although the newsgroups and object-technology mailing lists thrive on splitting hairs, the essentials of object-oriented analysis and design are fairly straightforward. This lesson lays out a practical approach to the process as the bedrock on which you can build the architecture of your application.
>
> The goal of all this work is to produce code that meets the stated requirements and that is reliable, extensible, and maintainable. Most important, the goal is to produce high-quality code on time and on budget.

Step 1: The Conceptualization Phase: Starting with The Vision

All great software starts with a vision. One individual has an insight into a product he thinks would be good to build. In a business, someone envisions a product or service he wants the business to create or offer. Rarely do committees create compelling visions.

The very first phase of object-oriented analysis and design is to capture this vision in a single sentence (or at most, a short paragraph). The vision becomes the guiding principle of development, and the team that comes together to implement the vision ought to refer back to it—and update it if necessary—as it goes forward.

Even if the vision statement comes out of a committee in the marketing department, one person should be designated as the "visionary." It is her job to be the keeper of the sacred light. As you progress, the requirements will evolve. Scheduling and time-to-market demands might (and should) modify what you try to accomplish in the first iteration of the program, but the visionary must keep an eye on the essential idea, to ensure that whatever is produced reflects the core vision with high fidelity. It is this ruthless dedication—this passionate commitment—that sees the project through to completion. If you lose sight of the vision, your product is doomed.

The conceptualization phase, in which the vision is articulated, is very brief. It might be no longer than a flash of insight followed by the time it takes to write down what the visionary has in mind. In other projects, the vision requires a complex and sometimes challenging "scoping" phase, in which agreement on the components of the vision must be generated between the people or groups involved. In such a process, what's in and what's out can be a key determinant of the success of the project, especially because this effort is usually when initial estimates of costs are set forth.

Often, as the object-oriented expert, you join the project after the vision has been articulated.

Step 2: The Analysis Phase: Gathering Requirements

Some companies confuse the vision statement with the requirements. A strong vision is necessary, but it is not sufficient. To move on to design, you must understand how the product will be used and how it must perform. The goal of the analysis phase is to articulate and capture these requirements. The outcome of the analysis phase is the production of a requirements document. The first section in the requirements document is the use-case analysis.

Use Cases

The driving force in analysis, design, and implementation is the use cases. A *use case* is nothing more than a high-level description of how the product will be used. Use cases drive not only the analysis, but they also drive the design, they help you determine the classes, and they are especially important in testing the product.

Creating a robust and comprehensive set of use cases might be the single most important task in analysis. It is here that you depend most heavily on your domain experts—those experts having the most information about the business requirements you are trying to capture.

Use cases pay little attention to the details of the user interface, and they pay no attention to the internals of the system you are building. Rather, they should be focused on the interactions that need to occur and those people and systems (called *actors*) that will need to be working together to produce the desired results.

To summarize, the following are some definitions:

- **Use case**—A description of how the software will be used
- **Domain experts**—People with expertise in the *domain* (area) of business for which you are creating the product
- **Actor**—Any person or system that interacts with the system you are developing

A use case is a description of the interaction between an actor and the system itself. For purposes of use-case analysis, the system is treated as a "black box." An actor "sends a message" to the system, and something happens: Information is returned; the state of the system is changed; the spaceship changes direction; whatever.

Use cases are not sufficient to capture all of the requirements, but they are a key component and often receive the most attention. Other items might include business rules, data elements, and technical requirements for performance, security, and so on.

Identifying the Actors

It is important to note that not all actors are people. Systems that interact with the system you are building are also actors. Thus, if you are building an automated teller machine (ATM), the customer and the bank clerk can both be actors—as can other systems with which the new system interacts, such as a mortgage-tracking or student-loan system. The essential characteristics of actors are as follows:

- They are external to the system.
- They interact with the system.

TIP

> Getting started is often the hardest part of use-case analysis. Often, the best way to get going is with a "brainstorming" session. Simply write down the list of people and systems that will interact with your new system. Remember that *people* really means *roles*—the bank clerk, the manager, the customer, and so forth. One person can have more than one role.

11

For the ATM example just mentioned, the list of roles would include the following:

- The customer
- The bank personnel
- A back-office system
- The person who fills the ATM with money and supplies

No need exists to go beyond the obvious list at first. Generating even three or four actors might be enough to get you started on generating use cases. Each of these actors interacts with the system in different ways. You need to capture these interactions in the use cases.

Determining the First Use Cases

You have to start somewhere. For the ATM example, start with the customer role. What are the actions for the customer role? Brainstorming could lead to the following use cases for a *customer*:

- Customer checks his balances.
- Customer deposits money to his account.
- Customer withdraws money from his account.
- Customer transfers money between accounts.
- Customer opens an account.
- Customer closes an account.

Should you distinguish between "Customer deposits money in his checking account" and "Customer deposits money in his savings account," or should these actions be combined (as they are in the preceding list) into "Customer deposits money to his account?" The answer to this question lies in whether this distinction is meaningful in the domain (the domain is the real-world environment being modeled—in this case, banking).

To determine whether these actions are one use case or two, you must ask whether the *mechanisms* are different (does the customer do something significantly different with these deposits) and whether the *outcomes* are different (does the system reply in a different way). The answer to both questions for the deposit issue is "no": The customer deposits money to either account in essentially the same way, and the outcome is pretty much the same; the ATM responds by incrementing the balance in the appropriate account.

Given that the actor and the system behave and respond more or less identically, regardless of whether the deposit is made to the checking or to the savings account, these two use cases are actually a single use case. Later, when the use-case scenarios are fleshed out, you can try the two variations to see whether they make any difference at all.

As you think about each actor, you might discover additional use cases by asking these questions:

- Why is the actor using this system?

  The customer is using the system to get cash, to make a deposit, or to check an account balance.
- What outcome does the actor want or expect from each request?

  Add cash to an account or get cash to make a purchase.
- What happened to cause the actor to use this system now?

  She might recently have been paid or might be on the way to make a purchase.
- What must the actor do to use the system?

  Identify herself by putting an ATM card into the slot in the machine.

  Aha! We need a use case for the customer logging in to the system.

- What information must the actor provide to the system?

  Enter a Personal ID number.

  Aha! We need use cases for obtaining and editing the Personal ID number.

- What information does the actor hope to get from the system?

  Balances, and so on.

You can often find additional use cases by focusing on the attributes of the objects in the domain. The customer has a name, a PIN, and an account number; do you have use cases to manage these objects? An account has an account number, a balance, and a transaction history; have these elements been captured in the use cases?

After the customer use cases have been explored in detail, the next step in fleshing out the list of use cases is to develop the use cases for each of the other actors. The following list shows a reasonable first set of use cases for the ATM example:

- Customer checks his balances.
- Customer deposits money to his account.
- Customer withdraws money from his account.
- Customer transfers money between accounts.
- Customer opens an account.
- Customer closes an account.
- Customer logs in to his account.
- Customer checks recent transactions.
- Bank clerk logs in to special management account.
- Bank clerk makes an adjustment to a customer's account.
- A back-office system updates a user's account based on external activity.
- Changes in a user's account are reflected in a back-office system.
- The ATM signals it is out of cash to dispense.
- The bank technician fills the ATM with cash and supplies.

Creating the Domain Model

After you have a first cut at your use cases, the requirements document can be fleshed out with a detailed domain model. The *domain model* is a document that captures all you know about the domain (the field of business you are working in). As part of your domain model, you create domain objects that describe all the objects mentioned in your use cases. So far, the ATM example includes these objects: customer, bank personnel, back-office systems, checking account, savings account, and so forth.

11

For each of these domain objects, you need to capture essential data, such as the name of the object (for example, customer, account, and so on), whether the object is an actor, the object's principal attributes and behavior, and so forth. Many modeling tools support capturing this information in "class" descriptions. Figure 11.4 shows how this information is captured with the Rational Rose modeling tool.

FIGURE 11.4

Rational Rose.

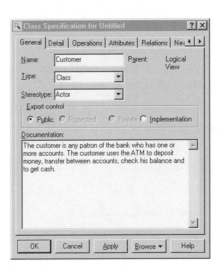

It is important to realize that what is being described here is *not* the class that will be used in the design (even though there will probably be similar classes used in the design), but rather classes of objects in the requirements domain. This is documentation of what the requirements will demand of the system, not documentation of how the system will meet those requirements.

You can diagram the relationship among the objects in the domain of the ATM example using the UML—with the same diagramming conventions that will be used later to describe the relationships among classes in the design. This is one of the great strengths of the UML: You can use the similar representations at every stage of the project.

For example, you can capture that checking accounts and savings accounts are both specializations of the more general concept of bank account by using the UML conventions for classes and generalization relationships, as shown in Figure 11.5.

In the diagram in Figure 11.5, the boxes represent the various domain objects, and the line with an arrowhead indicates generalization. The UML specifies that this line is drawn from the *specialized* class to the more general "base" class. Thus, both Checking Account and Savings Account point up to Bank Account, indicating that each is a specialized form of Bank Account.

FIGURE 11.5

Specialization.

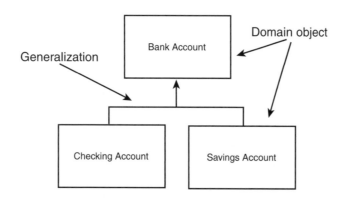

NOTE

> Again, it is important to note that what is being shown at this time are the relationships among classes in the requirements domain. Later, you might decide to have a CheckingAccount object in your design as well as a BankAccount object, and you can implement this relationship using inheritance; but these are design-time decisions. At analysis time, all you are documenting is your understanding of these requirements domain.

The UML is a rich modeling language, and you can capture any number of relationships. The principal relationships captured in analysis, however, are as follows:

- Generalization (or specialization)
- Containment
- Association

Generalization   Generalization is often equated with "inheritance," but a sharp and meaningful distinction exists between the two. Generalization describes the relationship; inheritance is the programming implementation of generalization. Inheritance is *how* generalization is manifested in code. The other side of the generalization coin is specialization. A cat is a specialized form of animal; animal is a generalized concept that unifies cat and dog.

Specialization implies that the derived object *is a* subtype of the base object. Thus, a checking account *is a* bank account. The relationship is symmetrical: Bank account *generalizes* the common behavior and attributes of checking and savings accounts.

During domain analysis, you should seek to capture these relationships *as they exist in the real world*.

Containment   Often, one object is composed of many subobjects. For example, a car is composed of a steering wheel, tires, doors, radio, and so forth. A checking account is composed of a balance, a transaction history, a customer ID, and so on. The checking account *has* these items; containment models the *"has a"* relationship. The UML illustrates the containment relationship by drawing a line with a diamond from the containing object to the contained object, as shown in Figure 11.6.

FIGURE 11.6

Containment.

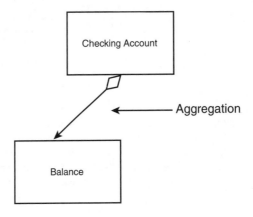

The diagram in Figure 11.6 suggests that the Checking Account *has a* Balance. You can combine these diagrams to show a fairly complex set of relationships (see Figure 11.7).

FIGURE 11.7

Object relationships.

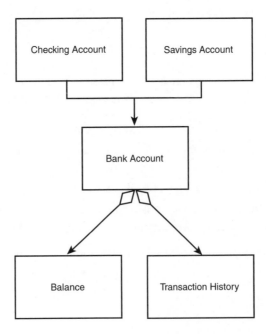

The diagram in Figure 11.7 states that a Checking Account and a Savings Account are both Bank Accounts, and that all Bank Accounts have both a Balance and a Transaction History.

Association   The third relationship commonly captured in the domain analysis is a simple association. An association suggests that two objects interact in some way, without being terribly precise about what that way actually might be. This definition will become much more precise in the design stage, but for analysis, it is only being suggested that Object A and Object B interact, but that neither contains the other and neither is a specialization of the other. This association is shown in the UML with a simple straight line between the objects, as shown in Figure 11.8.

Figure 11.8

Association.

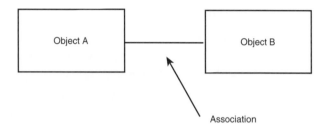

The diagram in Figure 11.8 indicates that Object A associates in some way with Object B.

Establishing Scenarios

Now that you have a preliminary set of use cases and the tools with which to diagram the relationship among the objects in the domain, you are ready to formalize the use cases and give them more depth.

Each use case can be broken into a series of scenarios. A *scenario* is a description of a specific set of circumstances that distinguish among the various elements of the use case. For example, the use case "Customer withdraws money from his account" might have the following scenarios:

- Customer requests a $300 withdrawal from checking, takes the cash from the cash slot, and the system prints a receipt.

- Customer requests a $300 withdrawal from checking, but his balance is $200. Customer is informed that not enough cash is in the checking account to accomplish the withdrawal.

- Customer requests a $300 withdrawal from checking, but he has already withdrawn $100 today and the limit is $300 per day. Customer is informed of the problem, and he chooses to withdraw only $200.

- Customer requests a $300 withdrawal from checking, but the receipt roll is out of paper. Customer is informed of the problem, and he chooses to proceed without a receipt.

And so forth. Each scenario explores a variation on the original use case. Often, these variations are exception conditions (not enough money in account, not enough money in machine, and so on). Sometimes, the variations explore nuances of decisions in the use case itself. (For example, did the customer want to transfer money before making the withdrawal?)

Not every possible scenario must be explored. Rather, you are looking for those scenarios that tease out requirements of the system or details of the interaction with the actor.

Establishing Guidelines

As part of your method, you need to create guidelines for documenting each scenario. You capture these guidelines in your requirements document. Typically, you need to ensure that each scenario includes the following:

- Preconditions—What must be true for the scenario to begin
- Triggers—What event causes the scenario to begin
- What actions the actors take
- What results or changes are caused by the system
- What feedback the actors receive
- Whether repeating activities occur, and what causes them to conclude
- A description of the logical flow of the scenario
- What causes the scenario to end
- Postconditions—What must be true when the scenario is complete

In addition, you need to name each use case and each scenario. Thus, you might have the following situation:

Use Case:	Customer withdraws cash.
Scenario:	Successful cash withdrawal from checking.
Preconditions:	Customer is already logged in to system.
Trigger:	Customer requests "withdrawal."
Description:	Customer chooses to withdraw cash from a checking account. Sufficient cash is in the account, sufficient cash and receipt paper are in the ATM, and the network is up and running. The ATM asks the customer to indicate the amount of the withdrawal, and

the customer asks for $300, a legal amount to withdraw at this time. The machine dispenses $300 and prints a receipt, and the customer takes the money and the receipt.

Postconditions: Customer account is debited $300, and customer has $300 cash.

This use case can be shown with the incredibly simple diagram given in Figure 11.9.

FIGURE 11.9

Use-case diagram.

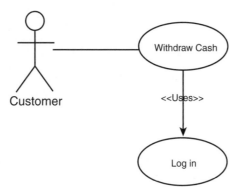

Little information is captured here except a high-level abstraction of an interaction between an actor (the customer) and the system. This diagram becomes slightly more useful when you show the interaction among use cases. I say only *slightly* more useful because only two interactions are possible: <<uses>> and <<extends>>. The <<uses>> stereotype indicates that one use case is a superset of another. For example, it isn't possible to *withdraw cash* without first *logging in*. This relationship can be shown with the diagram in Figure 11.10.

11

FIGURE 11.10

The <<uses>> stereotype.

Figure 11.10 indicates that the Withdraw Cash use case "uses" the Log In use case, and, thus, Log In is a part of Withdraw Cash.

The <<extends>> use case was intended to indicate conditional relationships and some-thing akin to inheritance, but so much confusion exists in the object-modeling commu-nity about the distinction between <<uses>> and <<extends>> that many developers have simply set aside <<extends>>, feeling that its meaning is not sufficiently well under-stood. Personally, I use <<uses>> when I would otherwise copy and paste the entire use case in place, and I use <<extends>> when I only *use* the use case under certain defin-able conditions.

Interaction Diagrams   Although the diagram of the use case itself might be of lim-ited value, you can associate diagrams with the use case that can dramatically improve the documentation and understanding of the interactions. For example, you know that the Withdraw Cash scenario represents the interactions among the following domain objects: customer, checking account, and the user interface. You can document this interaction with an interaction diagram (also called a collaboration diagram), as shown in Figure 11.11.

FIGURE 11.11

UML interaction diagram.

The interaction diagram in Figure 11.11 captures details of the scenario that might not be evident by reading the text. The objects that are interacting are *domain* objects, and the entire ATM/UI is treated as a single object, with only the specific bank account called out in any detail.

This rather simple ATM example shows only a fanciful set of interactions, but nailing down the specifics of these interactions can be a powerful tool in understanding both the problem domain and the requirements of your new system.

Creating Packages

Because you generate many use cases for any problem of significant complexity, the UML enables you to group your use cases in packages.

A *package* is like a directory or a folder—it is a collection of modeling objects (classes, actors, and so forth). To manage the complexity of use cases, you can create packages aggregated by whatever characteristics make sense for your problem. Thus, you can aggregate your use cases by account type (everything affecting checking or savings), by credit or debit, by customer type, or by whatever characteristics make sense to you. More important, a single use case can appear in different packages, allowing you great flexibility.

Application Analysis

In addition to creating use cases, the requirements document must capture your customer's assumptions, and any constraints or requirements concerning hardware and operating systems, security, performance, and so forth. These requirements are your *particular* customer's prerequisites—those things that you would normally determine during design and implementation but that your client has decided for you.

The application requirements (sometimes called "technical requirements") are often driven by the need to interface with existing systems. In this case, understanding what the existing systems do and how they work is an essential component of your analysis.

Ideally, you analyze the problem, design the solution, and then decide which platform and operating system best fits your design. That scenario is as ideal as it is rare. More often, the client has a standing investment in a particular operating system or hardware platform. The client's business plan depends on your software running on the existing system, and you must capture these requirements early and design accordingly.

Systems Analysis

Some software is written to stand alone, interacting only with the end user. Often, however, you will be called on to interface to an existing system. *Systems analysis* is the process of collecting all the details of the systems with which you will interact. Will your new system be a server, providing services to the existing system, or will it be a client? Will you be able to negotiate an interface between the systems, or must you adapt to an existing standard? Will the other system be stable, or must you continually hit a moving target?

These and related questions must be answered in the analysis phase, before you begin to design your new system. In addition, you need to try to capture the constraints and limitations implicit in interacting with the other systems. Will they slow down the responsiveness of your system? Will they put high demands on your new system, consuming resources and computing time?

Planning Documents

After you understand what your system must do and how it must behave, it is time to take a first stab at creating a time and budget document. Often, the client dictates the timeline: "You have 18 months to get this done." Ideally, you examine the requirements and estimate the time it will take to design and implement the solution. That is the ideal; the practical reality is that most systems come with an imposed time limit and cost limit, and the real trick is to figure out how much of the required functionality you can build in the allotted time—and at the allotted cost.

Here are a couple guidelines to keep in mind when you are creating a project budget and timeline:

- If you are given a range, the outer number is probably optimistic.
- Liberty's Law states that everything takes longer than you expect—even if you take into account Liberty's Law.

Given these realities, it is imperative that you prioritize your work so that the most important tasks are done first. *You should not expect to have time to finish*—it is that simple. It is important that when you run out of time, what you have works and is adequate for a first release. If you are building a bridge and run out of time, if you didn't get a chance to put in the bicycle path, that is too bad; but you can still open the bridge and start collecting tolls. If you run out of time and you're only halfway across the river, that is not as good.

An essential thing to know about planning documents is that they are generally wrong. This early in the process, it is virtually impossible to offer a reliable estimate of the duration of the project. After you have the requirements, you can get a good handle on how long the design will take, a fair estimate of how long the implementation will take, and a reasonable guesstimate of the testing time. Then, you must allow yourself at least 20 to 25 percent "wiggle room," which you can tighten as you move forward through the iterations and learn more.

11

NOTE

> The inclusion of "wiggle room" in your planning document is not an excuse to avoid planning documents. It is merely a warning not to rely on them too much early on. As the project goes forward, you'll strengthen your understanding of how the system works, and your estimates will become increasingly precise.

Visualizations

The final piece of the requirements document is the visualization. The visualization is a fancy name for the diagrams, pictures, screen shots, prototypes, and any other visual representations created to help you think through and design the graphical user interface of your product.

For many large projects, you can develop a full prototype to help you (and your customers) understand how the system will behave. On some teams, the prototype becomes the living requirements document; the "real" system is designed to implement the functionality demonstrated in the prototype.

Artifacts

At the end of each phase of analysis and design, you will create a series of documents (often called "artifacts" or "deliverables"). Table 11.1 shows some of the artifacts of the analysis phase. Several groups use these documents. The customer will use the documents to be certain that you understand what they need. End users will use them to give feedback and guidance to the project. The project team will use them to design and implement the code. Many of these documents also provide material crucial both to your documentation team and to Quality Assurance to tell them how the system *ought* to behave.

TABLE 11.1 Artifacts Created During the Analysis Stage of Project Development

Artifact	Description
Use-case report	Document detailing the use cases, scenarios, stereotypes, preconditions, postconditions, and visualizations
Domain analysis	Document and diagrams describing the relationships among the domain objects
Analysis collaboration diagrams	Collaboration diagrams describing interactions among objects in the problem domain

TABLE 11.1   continued

Artifact	Description
Analysis activity diagrams	Activity diagrams describing interactions among objects in the problem domain
Systems analysis	Report and diagrams describing low-level and hardware systems on which the project will be built
Application analysis document	Report and diagrams describing the customer's requirements specific to this particular project
Operational constraints report	Report describing performance characteristics and constraints imposed by this client
Cost and planning document	Report with charts and graphs indicating projected scheduling, milestones, and costs

Step 3: The Design Phase

Analysis focuses on understanding the problem domain, whereas the next step of the processes, design, focuses on creating the solution. *Design* is the process of transforming your understanding of the requirements into a model that can be implemented in software. The result of this process is the production of a design document.

A design document can be divided into two sections: Class Design and Architectural Mechanisms. The Class Design section, in turn, is divided into static design (which details the various classes and their relationships and characteristics) and dynamic design (which details how the classes interact).

The Architectural Mechanisms section of the design document provides details about how you will implement object persistence, concurrency, a distributed object system, and so forth. The rest of today's lesson focuses on the class design aspect of the design document; other lessons in the rest of this book explain elements of how to implement various architectural mechanisms.

What Are the Classes?

As a C++ programmer, you are now used to creating classes. Formal design methods require you to separate the concept of the C++ class from the concept of the design class, although they are intimately related. The C++ class you write in code is the implementation of the class you designed. There is a one-to-one relationship: Each class in your design corresponds to a class in your code, but don't confuse one for the other. It is certainly possible to implement your design classes in another language, and the *syntax* of the class definitions might be changed.

That said, most of the time these classes are discussed without distinguishing them because the differences are highly abstract. When you say that in your model the Cat class will have a Meow() method, understand that this means that you will put a Meow() method into your C++ class as well.

You capture the design model's classes in UML diagrams, and you capture the implementation's C++ classes in code that can be compiled. The distinction is meaningful, yet subtle.

In any case, the biggest stumbling block for many novices is finding the initial set of classes and understanding what makes a well-designed class. One simplistic technique suggests writing out the use-case scenarios and then creating a class for every noun. Consider the following use-case scenario:

Customer chooses to withdraw **cash** from **checking**. Sufficient cash is in the **account**, sufficient cash and **receipts** are in the **ATM**, and the **network** is up and running. The ATM asks the customer to indicate an **amount** for the **withdrawal**, and the customer asks for $300, a legal amount to withdraw at this time. The **machine** dispenses $300 and prints a receipt, and the customer takes the **money** and the receipt.

You might pull out of this scenario the following classes:

- Customer
- Cash
- Checking
- Account
- Receipts
- ATM
- Network
- Amount
- Withdrawal
- Machine
- Money

You might then aggregate the synonyms to create this list, and then create classes for each of these nouns:

- Customer
- Cash (money, amount, withdrawal)
- Checking

- Account
- Receipts
- ATM (machine)
- Network

This is not a bad way to start, as far as it goes. You might then go on to diagram the obvious relationships among some of these classes, as shown in Figure 11.12.

FIGURE 11.12

Preliminary classes.

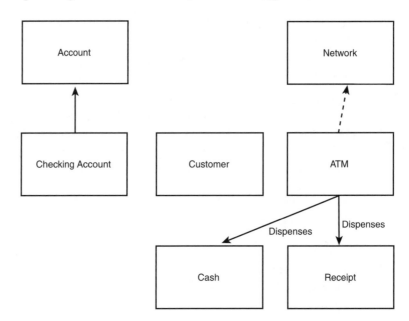

Transformations

What you began to do in the preceding section was not so much extract the nouns from the scenario as to begin transforming objects from the domain analysis into objects in the design. That is a fine first step. Often, many of the objects in the domain have *surrogates* in the design. An object is called a surrogate to distinguish between the actual physical receipt dispensed by an ATM and the object in your design that is merely an intellectual abstraction implemented in code.

You will likely find that *most* of the domain objects have a representation in the design—that is, a one-to-one correspondence exists between the domain object and the design object. Other times, however, a single domain object is represented in the design by an entire series of design objects. And at times, a series of domain objects might be represented by a single design object.

Note that in Figure 11.12, `CheckingAccount` has already been captured as a specialization of `Account`. You didn't set out to find the generalization relationship, but this one was self-evident, so it has been captured. Similarly, from the domain analysis, you know that the `ATM` dispenses both `Cash` and `Receipts`, so that information has been captured immediately into the design.

The relationship between `Customer` and `CheckingAccount` is less obvious. Such a relationship exists, but the details are not obvious, so you should hold off.

Other Transformations

After you have transformed the domain objects, you can begin to look for other useful design-time objects. Often, each actor has a class. A good starting place is with the interface between your new system and any existing systems—this should be encapsulated in an interface class. However, be careful when considering databases and other external storage media. It is generally better to make it a responsibility of each class to manage its own "persistence"—that is, how it is stored and retrieved between user sessions. Those design classes, of course, can use common classes for accessing files or databases, but most commonly, the operating system or the database vendor provides these to you.

These interface classes allow you to encapsulate your system's interactions with the other system, and, thus, shield your code from changes in the other system. Interface classes allow you to change your own design, or to accommodate changes in the design of other systems, without breaking the rest of the code. As long as the two systems continue to support the agreed-on interface, they can change independently of one another.

Data Manipulation

Similarly, you might need to create classes for data manipulation. If you have to transform data from one format into another format (for example, from Fahrenheit to Celsius or from English to Metric), you might want to encapsulate these transformations behind a special class. You can use this technique when converting data into required formats for other systems or for transmission over the Internet—in short, any time you must manipulate data into a specified format, you encapsulate the protocol behind a data manipulation class.

Views and Reports

Every "view" or "report" your system generates (or, if you generate many reports, every set of reports) is a candidate for a class. The rules behind the report—both how the information is gathered and how it is to be displayed—can be productively encapsulated inside a view class.

Devices

If your system interacts with or manipulates devices (such as printers, cameras, modems, scanners, and so forth), the specifics of the device protocol ought to be encapsulated in a class. Again, by creating classes for the interface to the device, you can plug in new devices with new protocols and not break any of the rest of your code; just create a new interface class that supports the same interface (or a derived interface), and off you go.

Building the Static Model

When you have established your preliminary set of classes, it is time to begin modeling their relationships and interactions. For purposes of clarity, the static model is explained first, and then the dynamic model. In the actual design process, you will move freely between the static and dynamic models, filling in details of both—and, in fact, adding new classes and sketching them in as you learn from each.

The static model focuses on three areas of concern: responsibilities, attributes, and relationships. The most important of these—and the one you focus on first—is the set of responsibilities for each class. The most important guiding principle is this: *Each class should be responsible for one thing*.

That is not to say that each class has only one method. Far from it; many classes will have dozens of methods. But all these methods must be coherent and cohesive; that is, they must all relate to one another and contribute to the class's capability to accomplish a single area of responsibility.

In a well-designed system, each object is an instance of a well-defined and well-understood class that is responsible for one area of concern. Classes typically delegate extraneous responsibilities to other, related classes. By creating classes that have only a single area of concern, you promote the creation of highly maintainable code.

To get a handle on the responsibilities of your classes, you might find it beneficial to begin your design work with the use of CRC cards.

Using CRC Cards

CRC stands for Class, Responsibility, and Collaboration. A CRC card is nothing more than a 4×6 index card. This simple, low-tech device enables you to work with other people in understanding the primary responsibilities of your initial set of classes. You assemble a stack of blank 4×6 index cards and meet around a conference table for a series of CRC card sessions.

How to Conduct a CRC Session　　For a large project or component, each CRC session should be attended, ideally, by a group of three to six people; any more becomes unwieldy. You should have a *facilitator*, whose job it is to keep the session on track and to help the participants capture what they learn. At least one senior software architect should be present, ideally someone with significant experience in object-oriented analysis and design. In addition, you need to include at least one or two "domain experts" who understand the system requirements and who can provide expert advice in how things ought to work.

The most essential ingredient in a CRC session is the conspicuous absence of managers. This is a creative, free-wheeling session that must be unencumbered by the need to impress one's boss. The goal here is to explore, to take risks, to tease out the responsibilities of the classes, and to understand how they might interact with one another.

You begin the CRC session by assembling your group around a conference table, with a small stack of 4×6 index cards. At the top of each CRC card, you write the name of a single class. Draw a line down the center of the card and write *Responsibilities* on the left and *Collaborations* on the right.

Begin by filling out cards for the most important classes you've identified. For each card, write a one-sentence or two-sentence definition on the back. You can also capture what other class this class specializes if that is obvious at the time you're working with the CRC card. Just write *Superclass:* below the class name and fill in the name of the class from which this class derives.

Focusing on Responsibilities   The point of the CRC session is to identify the *responsibilities* of each class. Pay little attention to the attributes, capturing only the most essential and obvious attributes as you go. The important work is to identify the responsibilities. If, in fulfilling a responsibility, the class must delegate work to another class, you capture that information under *collaborations*.

As you progress, keep an eye on your list of responsibilities. If you run out of room on your 4×6 card, it might make sense to wonder whether you're asking this class to do too much. Remember, each class should be responsible for one general area of work, and the various responsibilities listed should be cohesive and coherent—that is, they should work together to accomplish the overall responsibility of the class.

At this point, you do *not* want to focus on relationships, nor do you want to worry about the class interface or which methods will be public and which will be private. The focus is only on understanding what each class *does*.

Anthropomorphic and Use-Case Driven   The key feature of CRC cards is to make them anthropomorphic—that is, you attribute humanlike qualities to each class. Here's how it works: After you have a preliminary set of classes, return to your CRC scenarios. Divide the cards around the table arbitrarily, and walk through the scenario together. For example, return to the following scenario:

Customer chooses to withdraw cash from checking. Sufficient cash is in the account, sufficient cash and receipts are in the ATM, and the network is up and running. The ATM asks the customer to indicate an amount for the withdrawal, and the customer asks for $300, a legal amount to withdraw at this time. The machine dispenses $300 and prints a receipt, and the customer takes the money and the receipt.

Assume there are five participants in the CRC session: Amy, the facilitator and object-oriented designer; Barry, the lead programmer; Charlie, the client; Dorris, the domain expert; and Ed, a programmer.

Amy holds up a CRC card representing `CheckingAccount` and says "I tell the customer how much money is available. He asks me to give him $300. I send a message to the dispenser telling him to give out $300 cash." Barry holds up his card and says "I'm the dispenser; I spit out $300 and send Amy a message telling her to decrement her balance by $300. Who do I tell that the machine now has $300 less? Do I keep track of that?" Charlie says, "I think we need an object to keep track of cash in the machine." Ed says, "No, the dispenser should know how much cash it has; that's part of being a dispenser." Amy disagrees: "No, someone has to coordinate the dispensing of cash. The dispenser needs to know whether cash is available and whether the customer has enough in the account, and it has to count out the money and know when to close the drawer. It should delegate responsibility for keeping track of cash on hand—some kind of internal account. Whoever knows about cash on hand can also notify the back office when it is time to be refilled. Otherwise, that's asking the dispenser to do too much."

The discussion continues. By holding up cards and interacting with one another, the requirements and opportunities to delegate are teased out; each class comes alive, and its responsibilities are clarified. When the group becomes bogged down in design questions, the facilitator can make a decision and help the group move on.

Limitations of CRC Cards   Although CRC cards can be a powerful tool for getting started with design, they have inherent limitations. The first problem is that they don't scale well. In a very complex project, you can be overwhelmed with CRC cards; just keeping track of them all can be difficult.

CRC cards also don't capture the interrelationship among classes. Although it is true that collaborations are noted, the nature of the collaboration is not modeled well. Looking at the CRC cards, you can't tell whether classes aggregate one another, who creates whom, and so forth. CRC cards also don't capture attributes, so it is difficult to go from CRC cards to code. Most important, CRC cards are static; although you can act out the interactions among the classes, the CRC cards themselves do not capture this information.

In short, CRC cards are a good start, but you need to move the classes into the UML if you are to build a robust and complete model of your design. Although the transition *into* the UML is not terribly difficult, it is a one-way street. After you move your classes into UML diagrams, there is no turning back; you set aside the CRC cards and don't come back to them. It is simply too difficult to keep the two models synchronized with one another.

Transforming CRC Cards to UML   Each CRC card can be translated directly into a class modeled with the UML. Responsibilities are translated into class methods, and whatever attributes you have captured are added as well. The class definition from the back of the card is put into the class documentation. Figure 11.13 shows the relationship between the CheckingAccount CRC card and the UML class created from that card.

Class: CheckingAccount

SuperClass: Account

Responsibilities:

> Track current balance

> Accept deposits and transfers in

> Write checks

> Transfer cash out

> Keep current day's ATM withdrawal balance

Collaborations:

> Other accounts

> Back-office systems

> Cash dispenser

FIGURE 11.13

CRC card.

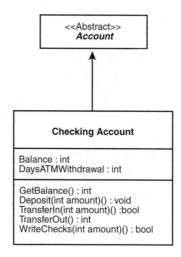

11

Class Relationships

After the classes are in the UML, you can begin to turn your attention to the relationships among the various classes. The principal relationships you'll model are the following:

- Generalization
- Association
- Aggregation
- Composition

The generalization relationship is implemented in C++ through public inheritance. From a design perspective, however, you focus less on the mechanism and more on the semantics: what it is that this relationship implies.

You examined the generalization relationship in the analysis phase, but now turn your attention to the objects in your design rather than to just the objects in the domain. Your efforts should now be to "factor out" common functionality in related classes into base classes that can encapsulate the shared responsibilities.

When you "factor out" common functionality, you move that functionality out of the specialized classes and up into the more general class. Thus, if you notice that both your checking and your savings account need methods for transferring money in and out, you'll move the TransferFunds() method up into the account base class. The more you factor out of the derived classes, the more polymorphic your design will be.

One of the capabilities available in C++, which is not available in Java, is *multiple inheritance* (although Java has a similar, if limited, capability with its multiple *interfaces*). Multiple inheritance allows a class to inherit from more than one base class, bringing in the members and methods of two or more classes.

Experience has shown that you should use multiple inheritance judiciously because it can complicate both your design and the implementation. Many problems initially solved with multiple inheritance are today solved using aggregation. That said, multiple inheritance is a powerful tool, and your design might require that a single class specializes the behavior of two or more other classes.

Multiple Inheritance Versus Containment   Is an object the sum of its parts? Does it make sense to model a Car object as a specialization of SteeringWheel, Door, and Tire, as shown in Figure 11.14?

FIGURE 11.14

False inheritance.

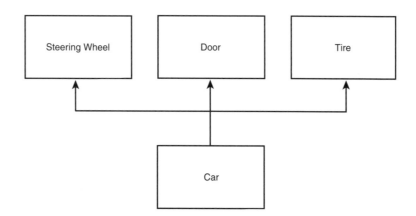

It is important to come back to the fundamentals: Public inheritance should always model generalization. The common expression for this is that inheritance should model *is-a* relationships. If you want to model the has-a relationship (for example, a car *has-a* steering wheel), you do so with aggregation, as shown in Figure 11.15.

FIGURE 11.15

Aggregation.

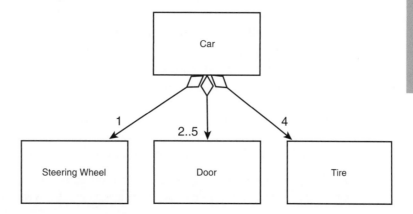

The diagram in Figure 11.15 indicates that a car has a steering wheel, four wheels, and two to five doors. This is a more accurate model of the relationship among a car and its parts. Notice that the diamond in the diagram is not filled in; this is so because this relationship is being modeled as an aggregation, not as a composition. Composition implies control for the lifetime of the object. Although the car *has* tires and a door, the tires and door can exist before they are part of the car and can continue to exist after they are no longer part of the car.

Figure 11.16 models composition. This model says that the body is not only an aggregation of a head, two arms, and two legs, but that these objects (head, arms, legs) are created when the body is created and disappear when the body disappears. That is, they have no independent existence; the body is composed of these things and their lifetimes are intertwined.

FIGURE 11.16

Composition.

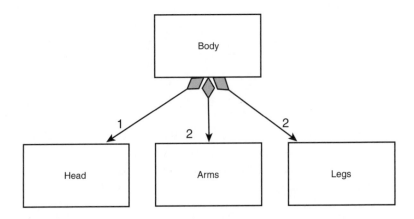

Discriminators and Powertypes   How might you design the classes required to reflect the various model lines of a typical car manufacturer? Suppose that you've been hired to design a system for Acme Motors, which currently manufactures five cars: the Pluto (a slow, compact car with a small engine), the Venus (a four-door sedan with a middle-sized engine), the Mars (a sport coupe with the company's biggest engine, engineered for maximum performance), the Jupiter (a minivan with the same engine as the sports coupe but designed to shift at a lower RPM and to use its power to move its greater weight), and the Earth (a station wagon with a small engine but high RPM).

You might start by creating subtypes of car that reflect the various models, and then create instances of each model as it rolls off the assembly line, as shown in Figure 11.17.

FIGURE 11.17

Modeling subtypes.

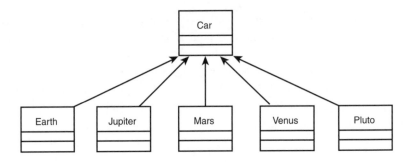

How are these models differentiated? As was stated, they are differentiated by the engine size, body type, and performance characteristics. These various discriminating characteristics can be mixed and matched to create various models. This can be modeled in the UML with the *discriminator* stereotype, as shown in Figure 11.18.

FIGURE 11.18

Modeling the discriminator.

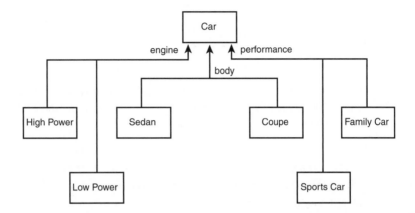

The diagram in Figure 11.18 indicates that classes can be derived from Car based on mixing and matching three discriminating attributes. The size of the engine dictates how powerful the car is, and the performance characteristics indicate how sporty the car is. Thus, you can have a powerful and sporty station wagon, a low-power family sedan, and so forth.

Each attribute can be implemented with a simple enumerator. Thus, in code, the body type might be implemented with the following statement:

```
enum BodyType = { sedan, coupe, minivan, stationwagon };
```

It might turn out, however, that a simple value is insufficient to model a particular discriminator. For example, the performance characteristic might be rather complex. In this case, the discriminator can be modeled as a class, and the discrimination can be encapsulated in an instance of that type.

Thus, the car might model the performance characteristics in a *performance* type, which contains information about where the engine shifts and how fast it can turn. The UML stereotype for a class that encapsulates a discriminator, and that can be used to create *instances* of a class (Car) that are logically of different types (for example, SportsCar versus LuxuryCar) is <<powertype>>. In this case, the Performance class is a powertype for Car. When you instantiate Car, you also instantiate a Performance object, and you associate a given Performance object with a given Car, as shown in Figure 11.19.

11

FIGURE **11.19**

A discriminator as a powertype.

Powertypes enable you to create a variety of *logical* types without using inheritance. You can thus manage a large and complex set of types without the combinatorial explosion you might encounter with inheritance.

Typically, you *implement* the powertype in C++ with pointers. In this case, the Car class holds a pointer to an instance of PerformanceCharacteristics class (see Figure 11.20). I'll leave it as an exercise to the ambitious reader to convert the body and engine discriminators into powertypes.

CAUTION

Keep in mind that the practice of creating new types in this way at runtime can reduce the benefits of C++ strong typing, in which the compiler can enforce the correctness of interclass relationships. Therefore, use it carefully.

FIGURE **11.20**

The relationship between a Car object and its powertype.

```
Class Car : public Vehicle
{
  public:
    Car();
```

```
      ~Car();
      // other public methods elided
  private:
      PerformanceCharacteristics * pPerformance;
};
```

As a final note, powertypes enable you to create new *types* (not just instances) at runtime. Because each logical type is differentiated only by the attributes of the associated powertype, these attributes can be parameters to the powertype's constructor. This means that you can, at runtime, create new *types* of cars on the fly. That is, by passing different engine sizes and shift points to the powertype, you can effectively create new performance characteristics. By assigning those characteristics to various cars, you can effectively enlarge the set of types of cars *at runtime*.

Dynamic Model

In addition to modeling the relationships among the classes, it is critical to model how they interact. For example, the CheckingAccount, ATM, and Receipt classes can interact with the Customer in fulfilling the "Withdraw Cash" use case. You now return to the kinds of sequence diagrams first used in analysis, but now flesh out the details based on the methods developed in the classes, as shown in Figure 11.21.

11

FIGURE 11.21

Sequence diagram.

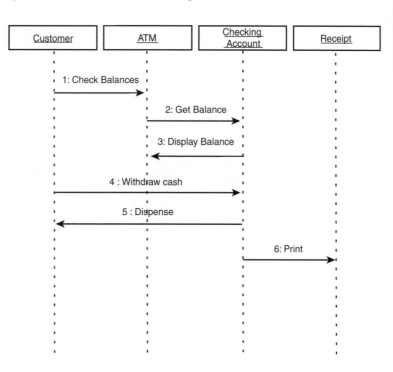

This simple interaction diagram shows the interaction among a number of design classes over time. It suggests that the ATM class delegates to the CheckingAccount class all responsibility for managing the balance, while the CheckingAccount calls on the ATM to manage display to the user.

Interaction diagrams comes in two flavors. The one in Figure 11.21 is called a *sequence diagram*. Another view on the same information is provided by the *collaboration diagram*. The sequence diagram emphasizes the sequence of events over time; the collaboration diagram emphasizes the "timeless" interactions among the classes. You can generate a collaboration diagram directly from a sequence diagram; tools such as Rational Rose automate this task at the click of a button (see Figure 11.22).

FIGURE 11.22

Collaboration diagram.

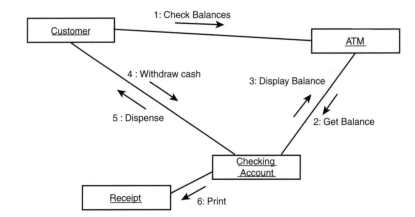

State Transition Diagrams

As you come to understand the interactions among the objects, you also have to understand the various possible *states* of each individual object. You can model the transitions among the various states in a state diagram (or state transition diagram). Figure 11.23 shows the various states of the CustomerAccount class as the customer logs in to the system.

Every state diagram begins with a single start state and ends with zero or more end states. The individual states are named, and the transitions might be labeled. The guard indicates a condition that must be satisfied for an object to move from one state to another.

FIGURE 11.23

*Customer account
state.*

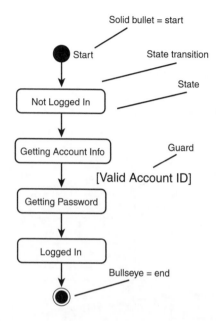

Super States   The customer can change her mind at any time and decide not to log in. She can do this after she swipes her card to identify her account or after she enters her password. In either case, the system must accept her request to cancel and return to the "not logged in state" (see Figure 11.24).

FIGURE 11.24

User can cancel.

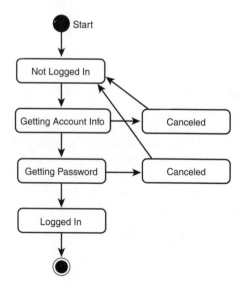

As you can see, in a more complicated diagram, the Canceled state quickly becomes a distraction. This is particularly annoying because canceling is an exceptional condition that should not be given prominence in the diagram. You can simplify this diagram by using a *super state*, as shown in Figure 11.25.

FIGURE 11.25

Super state.

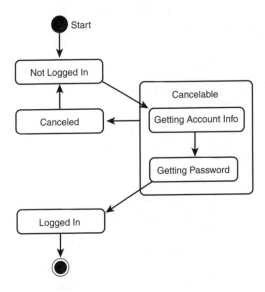

The diagram in Figure 11.25 provides the same information in Figure 11.24 but is much cleaner and easier to read. From the time you start logging in until the system finalizes your login, you can cancel the process. If you do cancel, you return to the state "not logged in."

Steps 4–6: Implementation, Testing, and Rollout?

The remaining three stages of the processes are important, but not covered here. In regard to implementation, if you are using C++, the rest of this book covers the details. Testing and rollout are each their own complex discipline with their own demands; however, detailed coverage of them is beyond the scope of this book. Nevertheless, don't forget that carefully testing your classes in isolation and together is key to determining that you have successfully implemented the design.

Iterations

In the Rational Unified Process, the activities listed previously are "workflows" that proceed at different levels across the phases of inception, elaboration, construction, and transition. For instance, business modeling peaks during inception but can still be occurring during construction as the review of the developed system fleshes out the requirements, whereas implementation peaks during construction, but can be occurring when prototypes are created for the elaboration phase.

Within each phase, such as construction, there can be several iterations. In the first iteration of construction, for instance, the core functions of the system can be developed; in the second iteration, those capabilities can be deepened and others added, In the third iteration, yet more deepening and addition might occur, until an iteration is reached in which the system is complete.

Summary

Today's lesson provided an introduction to the issues involved in object-oriented analysis and design. The essence of this approach is to analyze how your system will be used (use cases) and how it must perform, and then to design the classes and model their relationships and interactions.

In the old days, ideas for what should be accomplished were sketched out and the writing of the code began quickly. The problem is that complex projects are never finished; and if they are, they are unreliable and brittle. By investing up front in understanding the requirements and modeling the design, you ensure a finished product that is correct (that is, it meets the design) and that is robust, reliable, and extensible.

Much of the rest of this book focuses on the details of implementation. Issues relating to testing and rollout are beyond the scope of this book, except to mention that you want to plan your unit testing as you implement, and that you will use your requirements document as the foundation of your test plan prior to rollout.

Q&A

Q I didn't learn any C++ programming in today's lesson. Why was this lesson included?

A To be effective in writing C++ programs, you have to know how to structure them. By planning and designing before you start coding, you will build better, more effective C++ programs.

Q **In what way is object-oriented analysis and design fundamentally different from other approaches?**

A Prior to the development of these object-oriented techniques, analysts and programmers tended to think of programs as groups of functions that acted on data. Object-oriented programming focuses on the integrated data and functionality as discrete units that have both knowledge (data) and capabilities (functions). Procedural programs, on the other hand, focus on functions and how they act on data. It has been said that Pascal and C programs are collections of procedures, and C++ programs are collections of classes.

Q **Is object-oriented programming finally the silver bullet that will solve all programming problems?**

A No, it was never intended to be. For large, complex problems, however, object-oriented analysis, design, and programming can provide the programmer with tools to manage enormous complexity in ways that were previously impossible.

Q **Is C++ the perfect object-oriented language?**

A C++ has a number of advantages and disadvantages when compared with alternative object-oriented programming languages, but it has one killer advantage above and beyond all others: It is the single most popular object-oriented programming language for writing fully executable applications. This book exists—and I'd wager you are reading it—because C++ is the development language of choice at so many corporations.

Workshop

The Workshop provides quiz questions to help you solidify your understanding of the material covered and exercises to provide you with experience in using what you've learned. Try to answer the quiz and exercise questions before checking the answers in Appendix D, and be certain you understand the answers before continuing to tomorrow's lesson.

Quiz

1. What is the difference between object-oriented programming and procedural programming?

2. What are the phases of object-oriented analysis and design?

3. What is encapsulation?

4. In regard to analysis, what is a domain?

5. In regard to analysis, what is an actor?

6. What is a use case?

7. Which of the following is true?

   a. A cat is a specialized form of animal.

   b. Animal is a specialized form of cat and dog.

Exercises

1. A computer system is made up of a number of pieces. These include a keyboard, a mouse, a monitor, and a CPU. Draw a composition diagram to illustrate the relationship between the computer and its pieces. *Hint:* This is an aggregation.

2. Suppose you had to simulate the intersection of Massachusetts Avenue and Vassar Street—two typical two-lane roads, with traffic lights and crosswalks. The purpose of the simulation is to determine whether the timing of the traffic signal allows for a smooth flow of traffic.

   What kinds of objects should be modeled in the simulation? What would the classes be for the simulation?

3. You are asked to design a group scheduler. The software enables you to arrange meetings among individuals or groups and to reserve a limited number of conference rooms. Identify the principal subsystems.

4. Design and show the interfaces to the classes in the room reservation portion of the program discussed in Exercise 3.

11

DAY **12**

Implementing Inheritance

Yesterday, you learned about a number of object-oriented relationships, including specialization/generalization. C++ implements this relationship through inheritance.

Today, you will learn

- The nature of what inheritance is
- How to use inheritance to derive one class from another
- What protected access is and how to use it
- What virtual functions are

What Is Inheritance?

What is a dog? When you look at your pet, what do you see? I see four legs in service to a mouth. A biologist sees a network of interacting organs, a physicist sees atoms and forces at work, and a taxonomist sees a representative of the species *canine domesticus*.

It is that last assessment that is of interest at the moment. A dog is a kind of canine, a canine is a kind of mammal, and so forth. Taxonomists divide the world of living things into Kingdom, Phylum, Class, Order, Family, Genus, and Species.

This specialization/generalization hierarchy establishes an *is-a* relationship. A Homo sapiens (human) is a kind of primate. This relationship can be seen everywhere: A station wagon is a kind of car, which is a kind of vehicle. A sundae is a kind of dessert, which is a kind of food.

When something is said to be a kind of something else, it is implied that it is a specialization of that thing. That is, a car is a special kind of vehicle.

Inheritance and Derivation

The concept dog inherits—that is, it automatically gets—all the features of a mammal. Because it is a mammal, you know that it moves and that it breathes air. All mammals, by definition, move and breathe air. The concept of a dog adds the idea of barking, wagging its tail, eating my revisions to this chapter just when I was finally done, barking when I'm trying to sleep... Sorry. Where was I? Oh yes:

You can divide dogs into working dogs, sporting dogs, and terriers, and you can divide sporting dogs into retrievers, spaniels, and so forth. Finally, each of these can be specialized further; for example, retrievers can be subdivided into Labradors and Goldens.

A Golden is a kind of retriever, which is a sporting dog, which is a dog, and thus a kind of mammal, which is a kind of animal, and, therefore, a kind of living thing. This hierarchy is represented in Figure 12.1.

C++ attempts to represent these relationships by enabling you to define classes that derive from one another. Derivation is a way of expressing the *is-a* relationship. You derive a new class, Dog, from the class Mammal. You don't have to state explicitly that dogs move because they inherit that from Mammal.

A class that adds new functionality to an existing class is said to derive from that original class. The original class is said to be the new class's base class.

If the Dog class derives from the Mammal class, then Mammal is a base class of Dog. Derived classes are supersets of their base classes. Just as dog adds certain features to the idea of mammal, the Dog class adds certain methods or data to the Mammal class.

Typically, a base class has more than one derived class. Because dogs, cats, and horses are all types of mammals, their classes would all derive from the Mammal class.

Figure 12.1

Hierarchy of animals.

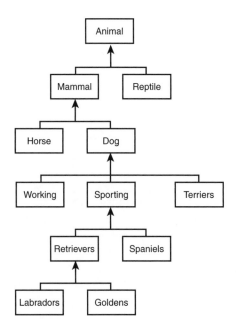

The Animal Kingdom

To facilitate the discussion of derivation and inheritance, this chapter focuses on the relationships among a number of classes representing animals. You can imagine that you have been asked to design a children's game—a simulation of a farm.

In time, you will develop a whole set of farm animals, including horses, cows, dogs, cats, sheep, and so forth. You will create methods for these classes so that they can act in the ways the child might expect, but for now you'll stub-out each method with a simple print statement.

Stubbing-out a function means you'll write only enough to show that the function was called, leaving the details for later when you have more time. Please feel free to extend the minimal code provided in today's lesson to enable the animals to act more realistically.

You should find that the examples using animals are easy to follow. You also find it easy to apply the concepts to other areas. For example, if you were building an ATM bank machine program, then you might have a checking account, which is a type of bank account, which is a type of account. This parallels the idea of a dog being an mammal, which in turn is an animal.

12

The Syntax of Derivation

When you declare a class, you can indicate what class it derives from by writing a colon after the class name, the type of derivation (public or otherwise), and the class from which it derives. The format of this is:

```
class derivedClass : accessType baseClass
```

As an example, if you create a new class called Dog that inherits from the existing class Mammal:

```
class Dog : public Mammal
```

The type of derivation (*accessType*) is discussed later in today's lesson. For now, always use public. The class from which you derive must have been declared earlier, or you receive a compiler error. Listing 12.1 illustrates how to declare a Dog class that is derived from a Mammal class.

LISTING 12.1   Simple Inheritance

```
 1:  //Listing 12.1 Simple inheritance
 2:  #include <iostream>
 3:  using namespace std;
 4:
 5:  enum BREED { GOLDEN, CAIRN, DANDIE, SHETLAND, DOBERMAN, LAB };
 6:
 7:  class Mammal
 8:  {
 9:    public:
10:       // constructors
11:       Mammal();
12:       ~Mammal();
13:
14:       //accessors
15:       int GetAge()         const;
16:       void SetAge(int);
17:       int GetWeight() const;
18:       void SetWeight();
19:
20:       //Other methods
21:       void Speak() const;
22:       void Sleep() const;
23:
24:
25:    protected:
26:       int itsAge;
27:       int itsWeight;
28:  };
```

LISTING 12.1 continued

```
29:
30:   class Dog : public Mammal
31:   {
32:     public:
33:
34:        // Constructors
35:        Dog();
36:        ~Dog();
37:
38:        // Accessors
39:        BREED GetBreed() const;
40:        void  SetBreed(BREED);
41:
42:        // Other methods
43:        WagTail();
44:        BegForFood();
45:
46:     protected:
47:        BREED itsBreed;
48:   };
```

This program has no output because it is only a set of class declarations without their implementations. Nonetheless, there is much to see here.

ANALYSIS On lines 7–28, the Mammal class is declared. Note that in this example, Mammal does not derive from any other class. In the real world, mammals do derive—that is, mammals are kinds of animals. In a C++ program, you can represent only a fraction of the information you have about any given object. Reality is far too complex to capture all of it, so every C++ hierarchy is a carefully limited representation of the data available. The trick of good design is to represent the areas that you care about in a way that maps back to reality in a reasonably faithful manner without adding unnecessary complication.

The hierarchy has to begin somewhere; this program begins with Mammal. Because of this decision, some member variables that might properly belong in a higher base class are now represented here. Certainly all animals have an age and weight, for example, so if Mammal is derived from Animal, you would expect to inherit those attributes. As it is, the attributes appear in the Mammal class.

In the future, if another animal sharing some of these features were added (for instance, Insect), the relevant attributes could be hoisted to a newly created Animal class that would become the base class of Mammal and Insect. This is how class hierarchies evolve over time.

12

To keep the program reasonably simple and manageable, only six methods have been put in the Mammal class—four accessor methods, Speak(), and Sleep().

The Dog class inherits from Mammal, as indicated on line 30. You know Dog inherits from Mammal because of the colon following the class name (Dog), which is then followed by the base class name (Mammal).

Every Dog object will have three member variables: itsAge, itsWeight, and itsBreed. Note that the class declaration for Dog does not include the member variables itsAge and itsWeight. Dog objects inherit these variables from the Mammal class, along with all Mammal's methods except the copy operator and the constructors and destructor.

Private Versus Protected

You might have noticed that a new access keyword, protected, has been introduced on lines 25 and 46 of Listing 12.1. Previously, class data had been declared private. However, private members are not available outside of the existing class. This privacy even applies to prevent access from derived classes. You could make itsAge and itsWeight public, but that is not desirable. You don't want other classes accessing these data members directly.

NOTE

> There is an argument to be made that you ought to make all member data private and never protected. Stroustrup (the creator of C++) makes this argument in *The Design and Evolution of C++*, ISBN 0-201-543330-3, Addison Wesley, 1994. Protected methods, however, are not generally regarded as problematic, and can be very useful.

What you want is a designation that says, "Make these visible to this class and to classes that derive from this class." That designation is protected. Protected data members and functions are fully visible to derived classes, but are otherwise private.

In total, three access specifiers exist: public, protected, and private. If a function has an object of your class, it can access all the public member data and functions. The member functions, in turn, can access all private data members and functions of their own class and all protected data members and functions of any class from which they derive.

Thus, the function Dog::WagTail() can access the private data itsBreed and can access the protected data of itsAge and itsWeight in the Mammal class.

Even if other classes are layered between Mammal and Dog (for example, DomesticAnimals), the Dog class will still be able to access the protected members of

Mammal, assuming that these other classes all use public inheritance. Private inheritance is discussed on Day 16, "Advanced Inheritance."

Listing 12.2 demonstrates how to create objects of type Dog and then how to access the data and methods of that type.

LISTING 12.2   Using a Derived Object

```
1:  //Listing 12.2 Using a derived object
2:  #include <iostream>
3:  using std::cout;
4:  using std::endl;
5:
6:  enum BREED { GOLDEN, CAIRN, DANDIE, SHETLAND, DOBERMAN, LAB };
7:
8:  class Mammal
9:  {
10:   public:
11:      // constructors
12:      Mammal():itsAge(2), itsWeight(5){}
13:      ~Mammal(){}
14:
15:      //accessors
16:      int GetAge() const    { return itsAge; }
17:      void SetAge(int age) { itsAge = age; }
18:      int GetWeight() const { return itsWeight; }
19:      void SetWeight(int weight) { itsWeight = weight; }
20:
21:      //Other methods
22:      void Speak()const { cout << "Mammal sound!\n"; }
23:      void Sleep()const { cout << "shhh. I'm sleeping.\n"; }
24:
25:   protected:
26:      int itsAge;
27:      int itsWeight;
28:  };
29:
30:  class Dog : public Mammal
31:  {
32:   public:
33:
34:      // Constructors
35:      Dog():itsBreed(GOLDEN){}
36:      ~Dog(){}
37:
38:      // Accessors
39:      BREED GetBreed() const { return itsBreed; }
40:      void SetBreed(BREED breed) { itsBreed = breed; }
41:
42:      // Other methods
```

12

LISTING 12.2   continued

```
43:          void WagTail() const { cout << "Tail wagging...\n"; }
44:          void BegForFood() const { cout << "Begging for food...\n"; }
45:
46:      private:
47:          BREED itsBreed;
48:     };
49:
50:     int main()
51:     {
52:          Dog Fido;
53:          Fido.Speak();
54:          Fido.WagTail();
55:          cout << "Fido is " << Fido.GetAge() << " years old" << endl;
56:          return 0;
57:     }
```

OUTPUT

```
Mammal sound!
Tail wagging...
Fido is 2 years old
```

ANALYSIS   On lines 8–28, the Mammal class is declared (all its functions are inline to save space here). On lines 30–48, the Dog class is declared as a derived class of Mammal. Thus, by these declarations, all Dogs have an age, a weight, and a breed. As stated before, the age and weight come from the base class, Mammal.

On line 52, a Dog is declared: Fido. Fido inherits all the attributes of a Mammal, as well as all the attributes of a Dog. Thus, Fido knows how to WagTail(), but he also knows how to Speak() and Sleep(). On lines 53 and 54, Fido calls two of these methods from the Mammal base class. On line 55, the GetAge() accessor method from the base class is also called successfully.

Inheritance with Constructors and Destructors

Dog objects are Mammal objects. This is the essence of the is-a relationship.

When Fido is created, his base constructor is called first, creating a Mammal. Then, the Dog constructor is called, completing the construction of the Dog object. Because Fido is given no parameters, the default constructor was called in each case. Fido doesn't exist until he is completely constructed, which means that both his Mammal part and his Dog part must be constructed. Thus, both constructors must be called.

When Fido is destroyed, first the Dog destructor is called and then the destructor for the Mammal part of Fido is called. Each destructor is given an opportunity to clean up after its own part of Fido. Remember to clean up after your Dog! Listing 12.3 demonstrates the calling of the constructors and destructors.

LISTING 12.3 Constructors and Destructors Called

```
 1:  //Listing 12.3 Constructors and destructors called.
 2:  #include <iostream>
 3:  using namespace std;
 4:  enum BREED { GOLDEN, CAIRN, DANDIE, SHETLAND, DOBERMAN, LAB };
 5:
 6:  class Mammal
 7:  {
 8:    public:
 9:        // constructors
10:        Mammal();
11:        ~Mammal();
12:
13:        //accessors
14:        int GetAge() const { return itsAge; }
15:        void SetAge(int age) { itsAge = age; }
16:        int GetWeight() const { return itsWeight; }
17:        void SetWeight(int weight) { itsWeight = weight; }
18:
19:        //Other methods
20:        void Speak() const { cout << "Mammal sound!\n"; }
21:        void Sleep() const { cout << "shhh. I'm sleeping.\n"; }
22:
23:    protected:
24:        int itsAge;
25:        int itsWeight;
26:  };
27:
28:  class Dog : public Mammal
29:  {
30:    public:
31:
32:        // Constructors
33:        Dog();
34:        ~Dog();
35:
36:        // Accessors
37:        BREED GetBreed() const { return itsBreed; }
38:        void SetBreed(BREED breed) { itsBreed = breed; }
39:
40:        // Other methods
41:        void WagTail() const { cout << "Tail wagging...\n"; }
42:        void BegForFood() const { cout << "Begging for food...\n"; }
```

12

LISTING 12.3   continued

```
43:
44:    private:
45:      BREED itsBreed;
46:  };
47:
48:  Mammal::Mammal():
49:  itsAge(3),
50:  itsWeight(5)
51:  {
52:     std::cout << "Mammal constructor... " << endl;
53:  }
54:
55:  Mammal::~Mammal()
56:  {
57:     std::cout << "Mammal destructor... " << endl;
58:  }
59:
60:  Dog::Dog():
61:  itsBreed(GOLDEN)
62:  {
63:     std::cout << "Dog constructor... " << endl;
64:  }
65:
66:  Dog::~Dog()
67:  {
68:     std::cout << "Dog destructor... " << endl;
69:  }
70:  int main()
71:  {
72:     Dog Fido;
73:     Fido.Speak();
74:     Fido.WagTail();
75:     std::cout << "Fido is " << Fido.GetAge() << " years old" << endl;
76:     return 0;
77:  }
```

OUTPUT

```
Mammal constructor...
Dog constructor...
Mammal sound!
Tail wagging...
Fido is 3 years old
Dog destructor...
Mammal destructor...
```

ANALYSIS   Listing 12.3 is like Listing 12.2, except that on lines 48 to 69 the constructors and destructors now print to the screen when called. Mammal's constructor is called, then Dog's. At that point, the Dog fully exists, and its methods can be called.

When Fido goes out of scope, Dog's destructor is called, followed by a call to Mammal's destructor. You see that this is confirmed in the output from the listing.

Passing Arguments to Base Constructors

It is possible that you will want to initialize values in a base constructor. For example, you might want to overload the constructor of Mammal to take a specific age, and want to overload the Dog constructor to take a breed. How do you get the age and weight parameters passed up to the right constructor in Mammal? What if Dogs want to initialize weight but Mammals don't?

Base class initialization can be performed during class initialization by writing the base class name, followed by the parameters expected by the base class. Listing 12.4 demonstrates this.

LISTING 12.4   Overloading Constructors in Derived Classes

```
1:   //Listing 12.4 Overloading constructors in derived classes
2:   #include <iostream>
3:   using namespace std;
4:
5:   enum BREED { GOLDEN, CAIRN, DANDIE, SHETLAND, DOBERMAN, LAB };
6:
7:   class Mammal
8:   {
9:     public:
10:       // constructors
11:       Mammal();
12:       Mammal(int age);
13:       ~Mammal();
14:
15:       //accessors
16:       int GetAge() const { return itsAge; }
17:       void SetAge(int age) { itsAge = age; }
18:       int GetWeight() const { return itsWeight; }
19:       void SetWeight(int weight) { itsWeight = weight; }
20:
21:       //Other methods
22:       void Speak() const { cout << "Mammal sound!\n"; }
23:       void Sleep() const { cout << "shhh. I'm sleeping.\n"; }
24:
25:
26:     protected:
27:        int itsAge;
28:        int itsWeight;
29:   };
30:
31:   class Dog : public Mammal
```

12

LISTING 12.4 continued

```
32:  {
33:    public:
34:
35:      // Constructors
36:      Dog();
37:      Dog(int age);
38:      Dog(int age, int weight);
39:      Dog(int age, BREED breed);
40:      Dog(int age, int weight, BREED breed);
41:      ~Dog();
42:
43:      // Accessors
44:      BREED GetBreed() const { return itsBreed; }
45:      void SetBreed(BREED breed) { itsBreed = breed; }
46:
47:      // Other methods
48:      void WagTail() const { cout << "Tail wagging...\n"; }
49:      void BegForFood() const { cout << "Begging for food...\n"; }
50:
51:    private:
52:      BREED itsBreed;
53:  };
54:
55:  Mammal::Mammal():
56:  itsAge(1),
57:  itsWeight(5)
58:  {
59:      cout << "Mammal constructor..." << endl;
60:  }
61:
62:  Mammal::Mammal(int age):
63:  itsAge(age),
64:  itsWeight(5)
65:  {
66:      cout << "Mammal(int) constructor..." << endl;
67:  }
68:
69:  Mammal::~Mammal()
70:  {
71:      cout << "Mammal destructor..." << endl;
72:  }
73:
74:  Dog::Dog():
75:  Mammal(),
76:  itsBreed(GOLDEN)
77:  {
78:      cout << "Dog constructor..." << endl;
79:  }
80:
```

LISTING 12.4   continued

```
81:   Dog::Dog(int age):
82:   Mammal(age),
83:   itsBreed(GOLDEN)
84:   {
85:       cout << "Dog(int) constructor..." << endl;
86:   }
87:
88:   Dog::Dog(int age, int weight):
89:   Mammal(age),
90:   itsBreed(GOLDEN)
91:   {
92:       itsWeight = weight;
93:       cout << "Dog(int, int) constructor..." << endl;
94:   }
95:
96:   Dog::Dog(int age, int weight, BREED breed):
97:   Mammal(age),
98:   itsBreed(breed)
99:   {
100:      itsWeight = weight;
101:      cout << "Dog(int, int, BREED) constructor..." << endl;
102:  }
103:
104:  Dog::Dog(int age, BREED breed):
105:  Mammal(age),
106:  itsBreed(breed)
107:  {
108:      cout << "Dog(int, BREED) constructor..." << endl;
109:  }
110:
111:  Dog::~Dog()
112:  {
113:      cout << "Dog destructor..." << endl;
114:  }
115:  int main()
116:  {
117:      Dog Fido;
118:      Dog rover(5);
119:      Dog buster(6,8);
120:      Dog yorkie (3,GOLDEN);
121:      Dog dobbie (4,20,DOBERMAN);
122:      Fido.Speak();
123:      rover.WagTail();
124:      cout << "Yorkie is " << yorkie.GetAge()
125:          << " years old" << endl;
126:      cout << "Dobbie weighs ";
127:      cout << dobbie.GetWeight() << " pounds" << endl;
128:      return 0;
129:  }
```

12

NOTE The output has been numbered here so that each line can be referred to in the analysis.

OUTPUT

```
 1:  Mammal constructor...
 2:  Dog constructor...
 3:  Mammal(int) constructor...
 4:  Dog(int) constructor...
 5:  Mammal(int) constructor...
 6:  Dog(int, int) constructor...
 7:  Mammal(int) constructor...
 8:  Dog(int, BREED) constructor....
 9:  Mammal(int) constructor...
10:  Dog(int, int, BREED) constructor...
11:  Mammal sound!
12:  Tail wagging...
13:  Yorkie is 3 years old.
14:  Dobbie weighs 20 pounds.
15:  Dog destructor. . .
16:  Mammal destructor...
17:  Dog destructor...
18:  Mammal destructor...
19:  Dog destructor...
20:  Mammal destructor...
21:  Dog destructor...
22:  Mammal destructor...
23:  Dog destructor...
24:  Mammal destructor...
```

ANALYSIS In Listing 12.4, Mammal's constructor has been overloaded on line 12 to take an integer, the Mammal's age. The implementation on lines 62–67 initializes itsAge with the value passed into the constructor and initializes itsWeight with the value 5.

Dog has overloaded five constructors on lines 36–40. The first is the default constructor. On line 37, the second constructor takes the age, which is the same parameter that the Mammal constructor takes. The third constructor takes both the age and the weight, the fourth takes the age and the breed, and the fifth takes the age, the weight, and the breed.

On line 74 is the code for Dog's default constructor. You can see that this has something new. When this constructor is called, it in turn calls Mammal's default constructor as you can see on line 75. Although it is not strictly necessary to do this, it serves as documentation that you intended to call the base constructor, which takes no parameters. The base constructor would be called in any case, but actually doing so makes your intentions explicit.

The implementation for the Dog constructor, which takes an integer, is on lines 81–86. In its initialization phase (lines 82 and 83), Dog initializes its base class, passing in the parameter, and then it initializes its breed.

Another Dog constructor is on lines 88–94. This constructor takes two parameters. Once again, it initializes its base class by calling the appropriate constructor on line 89, but this time it also assigns weight to its base class's variable itsWeight. Note that you cannot assign to the base class variable in the initialization phase. Because Mammal does not have a constructor that takes this parameter, you must do this within the body of the Dog's constructor.

Walk through the remaining constructors to be certain you are comfortable with how they work. Note what is initialized and what must wait for the body of the constructor.

The output has been numbered so that each line can be referred to in this analysis. The first two lines of output represent the instantiation of Fido, using the default constructor.

In the output, lines 3 and 4 represent the creation of rover. Lines 5 and 6 represent buster. Note that the Mammal constructor that was called is the constructor that takes one integer, but the Dog constructor is the constructor that takes two integers.

After all the objects are created, they are used and then go out of scope. As each object is destroyed, first the Dog destructor and then the Mammal destructor is called, five of each in total.

Overriding Base Class Functions

A Dog object has access to all the data members and functions in class Mammal, as well as to any of its own data members and functions, such as WagTail(), that the declaration of the Dog class might add. A derived class can also override a base class function. Overriding a function means changing the implementation of a base class function in a derived class.

When a derived class creates a function with the same return type and signature as a member function in the base class, but with a new implementation, it is said to be overriding that function. When you make an object of the derived class, the correct function is called.

When you override a function, its signature must agree with the signature of the function in the base class. The signature is the function prototype other than the return type; that is, the name of the function, the parameter list, and the keyword const, if used. The return types might differ.

12

Listing 12.5 illustrates what happens if the Dog class overrides the Speak() method in Mammal. To save room, the accessor functions have been left out of these classes.

LISTING 12.5   Overriding a Base Class Method in a Derived Class

```
1:   //Listing 12.5 Overriding a base class method in a derived class
2:   #include <iostream>
3:   using std::cout;
4:
5:   enum BREED { GOLDEN, CAIRN, DANDIE, SHETLAND, DOBERMAN, LAB };
6:
7:   class Mammal
8:   {
9:     public:
10:       // constructors
11:       Mammal() { cout << "Mammal constructor...\n"; }
12:       ~Mammal() { cout << "Mammal destructor...\n"; }
13:
14:       //Other methods
15:       void Speak()const { cout << "Mammal sound!\n"; }
16:       void Sleep()const { cout << "shhh. I'm sleeping.\n"; }
17:
18:     protected:
19:       int itsAge;
20:       int itsWeight;
21:   };
22:
23:   class Dog : public Mammal
24:   {
25:     public:
26       // Constructors
27:       Dog(){ cout << "Dog constructor...\n"; }
28:       ~Dog(){ cout << "Dog destructor...\n"; }
29:
30:       // Other methods
31:       void WagTail() const  { cout << "Tail wagging...\n"; }
32:       void BegForFood() const  { cout << "Begging for food...\n"; }
33:       void Speak() const { cout << "Woof!\n"; }
34:
35:     private:
36:       BREED itsBreed;
37:   };
38:
39:   int main()
40:   {
41:      Mammal bigAnimal;
42:      Dog Fido;
43:      bigAnimal.Speak();
44:      Fido.Speak();
45:      return 0;
46:   }
```

OUTPUT
```
Mammal constructor...
Mammal constructor...
Dog constructor...
Mammal sound!
Woof!
Dog destructor...
Mammal destructor...
Mammal destructor...
```

ANALYSIS   Looking at the Mammal class, you can see a method called Speak() defined on line 15. The Dog class declared on lines 23–37 inherits from Mammal (line 23), and, therefore, has access to this Speak() method. The Dog class, however, overrides this method on line 33, causing Dog objects to say Woof! when the Speak() method is called.

In the main() function, a Mammal object, bigAnimal, is created on line 41, causing the first line of output when the Mammal constructor is called. On line 42, a Dog object, Fido, is created, causing the next two lines of output, where the Mammal constructor and then the Dog constructor are called.

On line 43, the Mammal object calls its Speak() method; then on line 44, the Dog object calls its Speak() method. The output reflects that the correct methods were called. The bigAnimal made a mammal sound and Fido woofed. Finally, the two objects go out of scope and the destructors are called.

Overloading Versus Overriding

These terms are similar, and they do similar things. When you overload a method, you create more than one method with the same name, but with a different signature. When you override a method, you create a method in a derived class with the same name as a method in the base class and the same signature.

12

Hiding the Base Class Method

In the previous listing, the Dog class's Speak() method hides the base class's method. This is what is wanted, but it can have unexpected results. If Mammal has a method, Move(), which is overloaded, and Dog overrides that method, the Dog method hides all the Mammal methods with that name.

If Mammal overloads Move() as three methods—one that takes no parameters, one that takes an integer, and one that takes an integer and a direction—and Dog overrides just the Move() method that takes no parameters, it will not be easy to access the other two methods using a Dog object. Listing 12.6 illustrates this problem.

LISTING 12.6   Hiding Methods

```
1:  //Listing 12.6 Hiding methods
2:  #include <iostream>
3:  using std::cout;
4:
5:  class Mammal
6:  {
7:    public:
8:      void Move() const { cout << "Mammal move one step.\n"; }
9:      void Move(int distance) const
10:     {
11:       cout << "Mammal move ";
12:       cout << distance <<" steps.\n";
13:     }
14:   protected:
15:     int itsAge;
16:     int itsWeight;
17: };
18:
19: class Dog : public Mammal
20: {
21:   public:
22:     // You might receive a warning that you are hiding a function!
23:     void Move() const { cout << "Dog move 5 steps.\n"; }
24: };
25:
26: int main()
27: {
28:    Mammal bigAnimal;
29:    Dog Fido;
30:    bigAnimal.Move();
31:    bigAnimal.Move(2);
32:    Fido.Move();
33:    // Fido.Move(10);
34:    return 0;
35: }
```

OUTPUT
```
Mammal move one step.
Mammal move 2 steps.
Dog move 5 steps.
```

ANALYSIS   All the extra methods and data have been removed from these classes. On lines 8 and 9, the Mammal class declares the overloaded Move() methods. On line 23, Dog overrides the version of Move() with no parameters. These methods are invoked on lines 30–32, and the output reflects this as executed.

Line 33, however, is commented out because it causes a compile-time error. After you override one of the methods, you can no longer use any of the base methods of the same name. So, although the Dog class could have called the Move(int) method if it had not overridden the version of Move() without parameters, now that it has done so, it must override both if it wants to use both. Otherwise, it *hides* the method that it doesn't override. This is reminiscent of the rule that if you supply any constructor, the compiler no longer supplies a default constructor.

The rule is this: After you override any overloaded method, all the other overrides of that method are hidden. If you want them not to be hidden, you must override them all.

It is a common mistake to hide a base class method when you intend to override it, by forgetting to include the keyword const. const is part of the signature, and leaving it off changes the signature, and thus hides the method rather than overrides it.

Overriding Versus Hiding

In the next section, virtual methods are described. Overriding a virtual method supports polymorphism—hiding it undermines polymorphism. You'll see more on this very soon.

Calling the Base Method

If you have overridden the base method, it is still possible to call it by fully qualifying the name of the method. You do this by writing the base name, followed by two colons and then the method name:

baseClass::*Method*()

You can call the Move() method of the Mammal class as follows:

Mammal::Move().

You can use these qualified names just as you would any other method name. It would have been possible to rewrite line 33 in Listing 12.6 so that it would compile, by writing

Fido.Mammal::Move(10);

This calls the Mammal method explicitly. Listing 12.7 fully illustrates this idea.

LISTING 12.7   Calling a Base Method from a Overridden Method

```
1:  //Listing 12.7 Calling a base method from a overridden method.
2:  #include <iostream>
3:  using namespace std;
4:
5:  class Mammal
6:  {
```

LISTING 12.7 continued

```
7:    public:
8:       void Move() const { cout << "Mammal move one step\n"; }
9:       void Move(int distance) const
10:      {
11:         cout << "Mammal move " << distance;
12:         cout << " steps." << endl;
13:      }
14:
15:   protected:
16:      int itsAge;
17:      int itsWeight;
18:  };
19:
20:  class Dog : public Mammal
21:  {
22:    public:
23:       void Move() const;
24:  };
25:
26:  void Dog::Move() const
27:  {
28:     cout << "In dog move...\n";
29:     Mammal::Move(3);
30:  }
31:
32:  int main()
33:  {
34:     Mammal bigAnimal;
35:     Dog Fido;
36:     bigAnimal.Move(2);
37:     Fido.Mammal::Move(6);
38:     return 0;
39:  }
```

OUTPUT

```
Mammal move 2 steps.
Mammal move 6 steps.
```

ANALYSIS On line 34, a Mammal, bigAnimal, is created, and on line 35, a Dog, Fido, is created. The method call on line 36 invokes the Move() method of Mammal, which takes an integer.

The programmer wanted to invoke Move(int) on the Dog object, but had a problem. Dog overrides the Move() method (with no parameters), but does not overload the method that takes an integer—it does not provide a version that takes an integer. This is solved by the explicit call to the base class Move(int) method on line 37.

TIP

When calling overridden ancestor class functions using ": :", keep in mind that if a new class is inserted in the inheritance hierarchy between the descendant and its ancestor, the descendant will be now making a call that skips past the intermediate class and, therefore, might miss invoking some key capability implemented by the intermediate ancestor.

Do	Don't
DO extend the functionality of existing, tested classes by deriving. **DO** change the behavior of certain functions in the derived class by overriding the base class methods.	**DON'T** hide a base class function by changing the function signature. **DON'T** forget that const is a part of the signature. **DON'T** forget that the return type is not part of the signature.

Virtual Methods

This lesson has emphasized the fact that a Dog object is a Mammal object. So far that has meant only that the Dog object has inherited the attributes (data) and capabilities (methods) of its base class. In C++, the is-a relationship runs deeper than that, however.

C++ extends its polymorphism to allow pointers to base classes to be assigned to derived class objects. Thus, you can write

```
Mammal* pMammal = new Dog;
```

This creates a new Dog object on the heap and returns a pointer to that object, which it assigns to a pointer to Mammal. This is fine because a dog is a mammal.

12

NOTE

This is the essence of polymorphism. For example, you could create many types of windows, including dialog boxes, scrollable windows, and list boxes, and give them each a virtual draw() method. By creating a pointer to a window and assigning dialog boxes and other derived types to that pointer, you can call draw() without regard to the actual runtime type of the object pointed to. The correct draw() function will be called.

You can then use this pointer to invoke any method on Mammal. What you would like is for those methods that are overridden in Dog() to call the correct function. Virtual functions enable you to do that. To create a virtual function, you add the keyword vir-tual in front of the function declaration. Listing 12.8 illustrates how this works, and what happens with nonvirtual methods.

LISTING 12.8   Using Virtual Methods

```
 1:  //Listing 12.8 Using virtual methods
 2:  #include <iostream>
 3:  using std::cout;
 4:
 5:  class Mammal
 6:  {
 7:    public:
 8:        Mammal():itsAge(1) { cout << "Mammal constructor...\n"; }
 9:        virtual ~Mammal() { cout << "Mammal destructor...\n"; }
10:        void Move() const { cout << "Mammal move one step\n"; }
11:        virtual void Speak() const { cout << "Mammal speak!\n"; }
12:
13:    protected:
14:        int itsAge;
15:  };
16:
17:  class Dog : public Mammal
18:  {
19:    public:
20:      Dog() { cout << "Dog Constructor...\n"; }
21:      virtual ~Dog() { cout << "Dog destructor...\n"; }
22:      void WagTail() { cout << "Wagging Tail...\n"; }
23:      void Speak()const { cout << "Woof!\n"; }
24:      void Move()const { cout << "Dog moves 5 steps...\n"; }
25:  };
26:
27:  int main()
28:  {
29:     Mammal *pDog = new Dog;
30:     pDog->Move();
31:     pDog->Speak();
32:
33:     return 0;
34:  }
```

OUTPUT

```
Mammal constructor...
Dog Constructor...
Mammal move one step
Woof!
```

ANALYSIS   On line 11, Mammal is provided a virtual method—Speak(). The designer of this class thereby signals that she expects this class eventually to be another class's base type. The derived class will probably want to override this function.

On line 29, a pointer to Mammal is created (pDog), but it is assigned the address of a new Dog object. Because a dog is a mammal, this is a legal assignment. The pointer is then used on line 30 to call the Move() function. Because the compiler knows pDog only to be a Mammal, it looks to the Mammal object to find the Move() method. On line 10, you can see that this is a standard, nonvirtual method, so the Mammal's version is called.

On line 31, the pointer then calls the Speak() method. Because Speak() is virtual (see line 11), the Speak() method overridden in Dog is invoked.

This is almost magical. As far as the calling function knew, it had a Mammal pointer, but here a method on Dog was called. In fact, if you had an array of pointers to Mammal, each of which pointed to a different subclass of Mammal, you could call each in turn, and the correct function would be called. Listing 12.9 illustrates this idea.

LISTING 12.9 Multiple Virtual Functions Called in Turn

```
1:  //Listing 12.9 Multiple virtual functions called in turn
2:  #include <iostream>
3:  using namespace std;
4:
5:  class Mammal
6:  {
7:    public:
8:        Mammal():itsAge(1) {  }
9:        virtual ~Mammal() { }
10:       virtual void Speak() const { cout << "Mammal speak!\n"; }
11:
12:   protected:
13:       int itsAge;
14:  };
15:
16:  class Dog : public Mammal
17:  {
18:    public:
19:       void Speak()const { cout << "Woof!\n"; }
20:  };
21:
22:  class Cat : public Mammal
23:  {
24:    public:
25:       void Speak()const { cout << "Meow!\n"; }
26:  };
27:
28:
29:  class Horse : public Mammal
30:  {
31:    public:
32:       void Speak()const { cout << "Winnie!\n"; }
```

12

LISTING 12.9   continued

```
33:   };
34:
35:   class Pig : public Mammal
36:   {
37:     public:
38:       void Speak()const { cout << "Oink!\n"; }
39:   };
40:
41:   int main()
42:   {
43:     Mammal* theArray[5];
44:     Mammal* ptr;
45:     int choice, i;
46:     for ( i = 0; i<5; i++)
47:     {
48:       cout << "(1)dog (2)cat (3)horse (4)pig: ";
49:       cin >> choice;
50:       switch (choice)
51:       {
52:         case 1: ptr = new Dog;
53:                 break;
54:         case 2: ptr = new Cat;
55:                 break;
56:         case 3: ptr = new Horse;
57:                 break;
58:         case 4: ptr = new Pig;
59:                 break;
60:         default: ptr = new Mammal;
61:                  break;
62:       }
63:       theArray[i] = ptr;
64:     }
65:     for (i=0;i<5;i++)
66:       theArray[i]->Speak();
67:     return 0;
68:   }
```

OUTPUT

```
(1)dog (2)cat (3)horse (4)pig: 1
(1)dog (2)cat (3)horse (4)pig: 2
(1)dog (2)cat (3)horse (4)pig: 3
(1)dog (2)cat (3)horse (4)pig: 4
(1)dog (2)cat (3)horse (4)pig: 5
Woof!
Meow!
Whinny!
Oink!
Mammal speak!
```

ANALYSIS This stripped-down program, which provides only the barest functionality to each class, illustrates virtual functions in their purest form. Four classes are declared: Dog, Cat, Horse, and Pig. All four are derived from Mammal.

On line 10, Mammal's Speak() function is declared to be virtual. On lines 19, 25, 32, and 38, the four derived classes override the implementation of Speak().

On lines 46–64, the program loops five times. Each time, the user is prompted to pick which object to create, and a new pointer to that object type is added to the array from within the switch statement on lines 50–62.

At the time this program is compiled, it is impossible to know which object types will be created, and thus which Speak() methods will be invoked. The pointer ptr is bound to its object at runtime. This is called dynamic binding, or runtime binding, as opposed to static binding, or compile-time binding.

On lines 65 and 66, the program loops through the array again. This time, each object in the array has its Speak() method called. Because Speak() was virtual in the base class, the appropriate Speak() methods are called for each type. You can see in the output that if you choose each different type, that the corresponding method is indeed called.

FAQ

If I mark a member method as virtual in the base class, do I need to also mark it as virtual in derived classes?

Answer: No, once a method is virtual, if you override it in derived classes, it remains virtual. It is a good idea (though not required) to continue to mark it virtual—this makes the code easier to understand.

12

How Virtual Functions Work

When a derived object, such as a Dog object, is created, first the constructor for the base class is called, and then the constructor for the derived class is called. Figure 12.2 shows what the Dog object looks like after it is created. Note that the Mammal part of the object is contiguous in memory with the Dog part.

FIGURE 12.2

The Dog object after it is created.

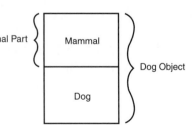

When a virtual function is created in an object, the object must keep track of that function. Many compilers build a virtual function table, called a v-table. One of these is kept for each type, and each object of that type keeps a virtual table pointer (called a vptr or v-pointer), which points to that table.

Although implementations vary, all compilers must accomplish the same thing.

Each object's vptr points to the v-table that, in turn, has a pointer to each of the virtual functions. (Note: Pointers to functions are discussed in depth on Day 15, "Special Classes and Functions.") When the Mammal part of the Dog is created, the vptr is initialized to point to the correct part of the v-table, as shown in Figure 12.3.

FIGURE 12.3

The v-table of a
Mammal.

When the Dog constructor is called, and the Dog part of this object is added, the vptr is adjusted to point to the virtual function overrides (if any) in the Dog object (see Figure 12.4).

FIGURE 12.4

The v-table of a Dog.

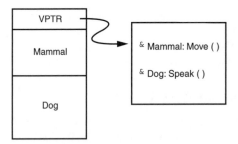

When a pointer to a Mammal is used, the vptr continues to point to the correct function, depending on the "real" type of the object. Thus, when Speak() is invoked, the correct function is invoked.

Trying to Access Methods from a Base Class

You have seen methods accessed in a derived class from a base class using virtual functions. What if there is a method in the derived class that isn't in the base class? Can you access it in the same way you have been using the base class to access the virtual methods? There shouldn't be a name conflict because only the derived class has the method.

If the Dog object had a method, WagTail(), which is not in Mammal, you could not use the pointer to Mammal to access that method. Because WagTail() is not a virtual function, and because it is not in a Mammal object, you can't get there without either a Dog object or a Dog pointer.

You could cast the Mammal to act as a Dog; however, this is not safe if the Mammal is not a Dog. Although this would transform the Mammal pointer into a Dog pointer, a much better and safer way exists to call the WagTail() method. Besides, C++ frowns on explicit casts because they are error-prone. This subject is addressed in depth when multiple inheritance is covered on Day 15, and again when templates are covered on Day 20, "Handling Errors and Exceptions."

Slicing

Note that the virtual function magic operates only on pointers and references. Passing an object by value does not enable the virtual functions to be invoked. Listing 12.10 illustrates this problem.

LISTING 12.10   Data Slicing When Passing by Value

```
1:   //Listing 12.10 Data slicing with passing by value
2:   #include <iostream>
3:   using namespace std;
4:
5:   class Mammal
6:   {
7:     public:
8:         Mammal():itsAge(1) { }
9:         virtual ~Mammal() { }
10:        virtual void Speak() const { cout << "Mammal speak!\n"; }
11:
12:    protected:
13:        int itsAge;
14:  };
15:
16:  class Dog : public Mammal
17:  {
18:    public:
19:        void Speak()const { cout << "Woof!\n"; }
20:  };
21:
22:  class Cat : public Mammal
23:  {
24:    public:
```

12

LISTING 12.10   continued

```
25:         void Speak()const { cout << "Meow!\n"; }
26:    };
27:
28:    void ValueFunction (Mammal);
29:    void PtrFunction (Mammal*);
30:    void RefFunction (Mammal&);
31:    int main()
32:    {
33:       Mammal* ptr=0;
34:       int choice;
35:       while (1)
36:       {
37:          bool fQuit = false;
38:          cout << "(1)dog (2)cat (0)Quit: ";
39:          cin >> choice;
40:          switch (choice)
41:          {
42:             case 0: fQuit = true;
43:                     break;
44:             case 1: ptr = new Dog;
45:                     break;
46:             case 2: ptr = new Cat;
47:                     break;
48:             default: ptr = new Mammal;
49:                      break;
50:          }
51:          if (fQuit == true)
52:             break;
53:          PtrFunction(ptr);
54:          RefFunction(*ptr);
55:          ValueFunction(*ptr);
56:       }
57:       return 0;
58:    }
59:
60:    void ValueFunction (Mammal MammalValue)
61:    {
62:       MammalValue.Speak();
63:    }
64:
65:    void PtrFunction (Mammal * pMammal)
66:    {
67:       pMammal->Speak();
68:    }
69:
70:    void RefFunction (Mammal & rMammal)
71:    {
72:       rMammal.Speak();
73:    }
```

OUTPUT

```
(1)dog (2)cat (0)Quit: 1
Woof
Woof
Mammal Speak!
(1)dog (2)cat (0)Quit: 2
Meow!
Meow!
Mammal Speak!
(1)dog (2)cat (0)Quit: 0
```

ANALYSIS On lines 4–26, stripped-down versions of the Mammal, Dog, and Cat classes are declared. Three functions are declared—PtrFunction(), RefFunction(), and ValueFunction(). They take a pointer to a Mammal, a Mammal reference, and a Mammal object, respectively. As you can see on lines 60–73, all three functions do the same thing—they call the Speak() method.

The user is prompted to choose a Dog or a Cat, and based on the choice that is made, a pointer to the correct type is created on lines 44 or 46.

In the first line of the output, the user chooses Dog. The Dog object is created on the free store on line 44. The Dog is then passed to a function as a pointer on line 53, as a reference on line 54, and by value on line 55.

The pointer and reference calls invoke the virtual functions, and the Dog->Speak() member function is invoked. This is shown on the first two lines of output after the user's choice.

The dereferenced pointer, however, is passed by value on line 55 to the function on lines 60–63. The function expects a Mammal object, and so the compiler slices down the Dog object to just the Mammal part. When the Mammal Speak() method is called on line 72, only Mammal information is available. The Dog pieces are gone. This is reflected in the third line of output after the user's choice. This effect is called slicing because the Dog portions (your derived class portions) of your object were sliced off when converting to just a Mammal (the base class).

This experiment is then repeated for the Cat object, with similar results.

Creating Virtual Destructors

It is legal and common to pass a pointer to a derived object when a pointer to a base object is expected. What happens when that pointer to a derived subject is deleted? If the destructor is virtual, as it should be, the right thing happens—the derived class's destructor is called. Because the derived class's destructor automatically invokes the base class's destructor, the entire object is properly destroyed.

12

The rule of thumb is this: If any of the functions in your class are virtual, the destructor should be as well.

Virtual Copy Constructors

Constructors cannot be virtual, and so, technically, no such thing exists as a virtual copy constructor. Nonetheless, at times, your program desperately needs to be able to pass in a pointer to a base object and have a copy of the correct derived object that is created. A common solution to this problem is to create a Clone() method in the base class and to make that be virtual. The Clone() method creates a new object copy of the current class and returns that object.

Because each derived class overrides the Clone() method, a copy of the derived class is created. Listing 12.11 illustrates how the Clone() method is used.

LISTING 12.11   Virtual Copy Constructor

```
1:   //Listing 12.11 Virtual copy constructor
2:   #include <iostream>
3:   using namespace std;
4:
5:   class Mammal
6:   {
7:     public:
8:         Mammal():itsAge(1) { cout << "Mammal constructor...\n"; }
9:         virtual ~Mammal() { cout << "Mammal destructor...\n"; }
10:        Mammal (const Mammal & rhs);
11:        virtual void Speak() const { cout << "Mammal speak!\n"; }
12:        virtual Mammal* Clone() { return new Mammal(*this); }
13:        int GetAge()const { return itsAge; }
14:     protected:
15:         int itsAge;
16:   };
17:
18:   Mammal::Mammal (const Mammal & rhs):itsAge(rhs.GetAge())
19:   {
20:      cout << "Mammal Copy Constructor...\n";
21:   }
22:
23:   class Dog : public Mammal
```

LISTING **12.11** continued

```
24:  {
25:    public:
26:      Dog() { cout << "Dog constructor...\n"; }
27:      virtual ~Dog() { cout << "Dog destructor...\n"; }
28:      Dog (const Dog & rhs);
29:      void Speak()const { cout << "Woof!\n"; }
30:      virtual Mammal* Clone() { return new Dog(*this); }
31:  };
32:
33:  Dog::Dog(const Dog & rhs):
34:  Mammal(rhs)
35:  {
36:     cout << "Dog copy constructor...\n";
37:  }
38:
39:  class Cat : public Mammal
40:  {
41:    public:
42:      Cat() { cout << "Cat constructor...\n"; }
43:      ~Cat() { cout << "Cat destructor...\n"; }
44:      Cat (const Cat &);
45:      void Speak()const { cout << "Meow!\n"; }
46:      virtual Mammal* Clone() { return new Cat(*this); }
47:  };
48:
49:  Cat::Cat(const Cat & rhs):
50:  Mammal(rhs)
51:  {
52:     cout << "Cat copy constructor...\n";
53:  }
54:
55:  enum ANIMALS { MAMMAL, DOG, CAT};
56:  const int NumAnimalTypes = 3;
57:  int main()
58:  {
59:     Mammal *theArray[NumAnimalTypes];
60:     Mammal* ptr;
61:     int choice, i;
62:     for ( i = 0; i<NumAnimalTypes; i++)
63:     {
64:        cout << "(1)dog (2)cat (3)Mammal: ";
65:        cin >> choice;
66:        switch (choice)
67:        {
68:          case DOG:  ptr = new Dog;
69:                     break;
70:          case CAT:  ptr = new Cat;
71:                     break;
72:          default:   ptr = new Mammal;
```

12

LISTING 12.11   continued

```
73:                         break;
74:             }
75:         theArray[i] = ptr;
76:     }
77:     Mammal *OtherArray[NumAnimalTypes];
78:     for (i=0;i<NumAnimalTypes;i++)
79:     {
80:         theArray[i]->Speak();
81:         OtherArray[i] = theArray[i]->Clone();
82:     }
83:     for (i=0;i<NumAnimalTypes;i++)
84:         OtherArray[i]->Speak();
85:     return 0;
86: }
```

OUTPUT

```
 1:  (1)dog (2)cat (3)Mammal: 1
 2:  Mammal constructor...
 3:  Dog constructor...
 4:  (1)dog (2)cat (3)Mammal: 2
 5:  Mammal constructor...
 6:  Cat constructor...
 7:  (1)dog (2)cat (3)Mammal: 3
 8:  Mammal constructor...
 9:  Woof!
10:  Mammal Copy Constructor...
11:  Dog copy constructor...
12:  Meow!
13:  Mammal Copy Constructor...
14:  Cat copy constructor...
15:  Mammal speak!
16:  Mammal Copy Constructor...
17:  Woof!
18:  Meow!
19:  Mammal speak!
```

ANALYSIS   Listing 12.11 is very similar to the previous two listings, except that on line 12 a new virtual method has been added to the Mammal class: Clone(). This method returns a pointer to a new Mammal object by calling the copy constructor, passing in itself (*this) as a const reference.

Dog and Cat both override the Clone() method, initializing their data and passing in copies of themselves to their own copy constructors. Because Clone() is virtual, this effectively creates a virtual copy constructor. You see this when line 81 executes.

Similar to the last listing, the user is prompted to choose dogs, cats, or mammals, and these are created on lines 68–73. A pointer to each choice is stored in an array on line 75.

As the program iterates over the array on lines 78 to 82, each object has its `Speak()` and its `Clone()` methods called, in turn. The result of the `Clone()` call on line 81 is a pointer to a copy of the object, which is then stored in a second array.

On line 1 of the output, the user is prompted and responds with 1, choosing to create a dog. The `Mammal` and `Dog` constructors are invoked. This is repeated for `Cat` on line 4 and for `Mammal` on line 8 of the constructor.

Line 9 of the output represents the call to `Speak()` on the first object, the `Dog`. The virtual `Speak()` method is called, and the correct version of `Speak()` is invoked. The `Clone()` function is then called, and because this is also virtual, `Dog`'s `Clone()` method is invoked, causing the `Mammal` constructor and the `Dog` copy constructor to be called.

The same is repeated for `Cat` on lines 12–14, and then for `Mammal` on lines 15 and 16. Finally, the new array is iterated on lines 83 and 84 of the listing, and each of the new objects has `Speak()` invoked, as can be seen by output lines 17 to 19.

The Cost of Virtual Methods

Because objects with virtual methods must maintain a v-table, some overhead occurs in having virtual methods. If you have a very small class from which you do not expect to derive other classes, there might not be a reason to have any virtual methods at all.

After you declare any methods virtual, you've paid most of the price of the v-table (although each entry does add a small memory overhead). At that point, you want the destructor to be virtual, and the assumption is that all other methods probably are virtual as well. Take a long, hard look at any nonvirtual methods, and be certain you understand why they are not virtual.

Do	Don't
DO use virtual methods when you expect to derive from a class.	**DON'T** mark the constructor as virtual.
DO use a virtual destructor if any methods are virtual.	**DON'T** try to access private data in a base class from a derived class.

Summary

Today, you learned how derived classes inherit from base classes. Today's class discussed public inheritance and virtual functions. Classes inherit all the public and protected data and functions from their base classes.

Protected access is public to derived classes and private to all other classes. Even derived classes cannot access private data or functions in their base classes.

Constructors can be initialized before the body of the constructor. At that time, the base constructors are invoked and parameters can be passed to the base class.

Functions in the base class can be overridden in the derived class. If the base class functions are virtual, and if the object is accessed by pointer or reference, the derived class's functions will be invoked, based on the runtime type of the object pointed to.

Methods in the base class can be invoked by explicitly naming the function with the prefix of the base class name and two colons. For example, if Dog inherits from Mammal, Mammal's walk() method can be called with Mammal::walk().

In classes with virtual methods, the destructor should almost always be made virtual. A virtual destructor ensures that the derived part of the object will be freed when delete is called on the pointer. Constructors cannot be virtual. Virtual copy constructors can be effectively created by making a virtual member function that calls the copy constructor.

Q&A

Q Are inherited members and functions passed along to subsequent generations? If Dog derives from Mammal, and Mammal derives from Animal, does Dog inherit Animal's functions and data?

A Yes. As derivation continues, derived classes inherit the sum of all the functions and data in all their base classes, but can only access those that are public or protected.

Q If, in the preceding example, Mammal overrides a function in Animal, which does Dog get, the original or the overridden function?

A If Dog inherits from Mammal, it gets the overridden function.

Q Can a derived class make a public base function private?

A Yes, the derived class can override the method and make it private. It then remains private for all subsequent derivation. However, this should be avoided when possible, because users of your class will expect it to contain the sum of the methods provided by its ancestors.

Q Why not make all class functions virtual?

A Overhead occurs with the first virtual function in the creation of a v-table. After that, the overhead is trivial. Many C++ programmers feel that if one function is virtual, all others should be. Other programmers disagree, feeling that there should always be a reason for what you do.

Q If a function (`SomeFunc()`) is virtual in a base class and is also overloaded, so as to take either an integer or two integers, and the derived class overrides the form taking one integer, what is called when a pointer to a derived object calls the two-integer form?

A As you learned in today's lesson, the overriding of the one-integer form hides the entire base class function, and thus you receive a compile error complaining that that function requires only one `int`.

Workshop

The Workshop provides quiz questions to help you solidify your understanding of the material that was covered and exercises to provide you with experience in using what you've learned. Try to answer the quiz and exercise questions before checking the answers in Appendix D, and be certain you understand the answers before continuing to tomorrow's lesson.

Quiz

1. What is a v-table?

2. What is a virtual destructor?

3. How do you show the declaration of a virtual constructor?

4. How can you create a virtual copy constructor?

5. How do you invoke a base member function from a derived class in which you've overridden that function?

6. How do you invoke a base member function from a derived class in which you have not overridden that function?

7. If a base class declares a function to be virtual, and a derived class does not use the term `virtual` when overriding that class, is it still virtual when inherited by a third-generation class?

8. What is the `protected` keyword used for?

Exercises

1. Show the declaration of a virtual function that takes an integer parameter and returns `void`.

2. Show the declaration of a class `Square`, which derives from `Rectangle`, which in turn derives from `Shape`.

12

3. If, in Exercise 2, Shape takes no parameters, Rectangle takes two (length and width), but Square takes only one (length), show the constructor initialization for Square.

4. Write a virtual copy constructor for the class Square (in Exercise 3).

5. **BUG BUSTERS:** What is wrong with this code snippet?

```
void SomeFunction (Shape);
Shape * pRect = new Rectangle;
SomeFunction(*pRect);
```

6. **BUG BUSTERS:** What is wrong with this code snippet?

```
class Shape()
{
  public:
      Shape();
      virtual ~Shape();
      virtual Shape(const Shape&);
};
```

DAY 13

Managing Arrays and Strings

In lessons on previous days, you declared a single `int`, `char`, or other object. You often want to declare a collection of objects, such as 20 `int`s or a litter of `Cat`s.

Today, you will learn

- What arrays are and how to declare them
- What strings are and how to use character arrays to make them
- The relationship between arrays and pointers
- How to use pointer arithmetic
- What linked lists are

What Is an Array?

An array is a sequential collection of data storage locations, each of which holds the same type of data. Each storage location is called an *element* of the array.

You declare an array by writing the type, followed by the array name and the subscript. The subscript is the number of elements in the array, surrounded by square brackets. For example,

```
long LongArray[25];
```

declares an array of 25 `long` integers, named `LongArray`. When the compiler sees this declaration, it sets aside enough memory to hold all 25 elements. If each `long` integer requires four bytes, this declaration sets aside 100 contiguous bytes of memory, as illustrated in Figure 13.1.

FIGURE 13.1

Declaring an array.

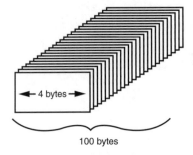

← 4 bytes →

100 bytes

Accessing Array Elements

You access an array element by referring to its offset from the beginning of the array. Array element offsets are counted from zero. Therefore, the first array element is referred to as `arrayName[0]`. In the `LongArray` example, `LongArray[0]` is the first array element, `LongArray[1]` the second, and so forth.

This can be somewhat confusing. The array `SomeArray[3]` has three elements. They are `SomeArray[0]`, `SomeArray[1]`, and `SomeArray[2]`. More generally, `SomeArray[n]` has n elements that are numbered `SomeArray[0]` through `SomeArray[n-1]`. Again, remember that this is because the index is an offset, so the first array element is 0 storage locations from the beginning of the array, the second is 1 storage location, and so on.

Therefore, `LongArray[25]` is numbered from `LongArray[0]` through `LongArray[24]`. Listing 13.1 shows how to declare an array of five integers and fill each with a value.

NOTE

Starting with today's listings, the line numbers will start with zero. This is to help you remember that arrays in C++ start from zero!

LISTING 13.1   Using an Integer Array

```
0:   //Listing 13.1 - Arrays
1:   #include <iostream>
2:
3:   int main()
4:   {
5:      int myArray[5];      // Array of 5 integers
6:      int i;
7:      for ( i=0; i<5; i++)  // 0-4
8:      {
9:         std::cout << "Value for myArray[" << i << "]: ";
10:        std::cin >> myArray[i];
11:     }
12:     for (i = 0; i<5; i++)
13:        std::cout << i << ": " << myArray[i] << std::endl;
14:     return 0;
15:  }
```

OUTPUT
```
Value for myArray[0]:   3
Value for myArray[1]:   6
Value for myArray[2]:   9
Value for myArray[3]:   12
Value for myArray[4]:   15
0: 3
1: 6
2: 9
3: 12
4: 15
```

ANALYSIS   Listing 13.1 creates an array, has you enter values for each element, and then prints the values to the console. In line 5, the array, called myArray, is declared and is of type integer. You can see that it is declared with five in the square brackets. This means that myArray can hold five integers. Each of these elements can be treated like an integer variable.

In line 7, a for loop is started that counts from zero through four. This is the proper set of offsets for a five-element array. The user is prompted for a value on line 9, and on line 10 the value is saved at the correct offset into the array.

Looking closer at line 10, you see that each element is accessed using the name of the array followed by square brackets with the offset in between. Each of these elements can then be treated like a variable of the array's type.

The first value is saved at myArray[0], the second at myArray[1], and so forth. On lines 12 and 13, a second for loop prints each value to the console.

13

Writing Past the End of an Array

When you write a value to an element in an array, the compiler computes where to store the value based on the size of each element and the subscript. Suppose that you ask to write over the value at `LongArray[5]`, which is the sixth element. The compiler multiplies the offset (5) by the size of each element—in this case, 4 bytes. It then moves that many bytes (20) from the beginning of the array and writes the new value at that location.

If you ask to write at `LongArray[50]`, most compilers ignore the fact that no such element exists. Rather, the compiler computes how far past the first element it should look (200 bytes) and then writes over whatever is at that location. This can be virtually any data, and writing your new value there might have unpredictable results. If you're lucky, your program will crash immediately. If you're unlucky, you'll get strange results much later in your program, and you'll have a difficult time figuring out what went wrong.

The compiler is like a blind man pacing off the distance from a house. He starts out at the first house, `MainStreet[0]`. When you ask him to go to the sixth house on Main Street, he says to himself, "I must go five more houses. Each house is four big paces. I must go an additional 20 steps." If you ask him to go to `MainStreet[100]` and Main Street is only 25 houses long, he paces off 400 steps. Long before he gets there, he will, no doubt, step in front of a truck. So be careful where you send him.

Listing 13.2 writes past the end of an array. You should compile this listing to see what error and warning messages you get. If you don't get any, you should be extra careful when working with arrays!

CAUTION

Do not run this program; it might crash your system!

LISTING 13.2 Writing Past the End of an Array

```
0:   //Listing 13.2 -  Demonstrates what happens when you write
1:   // past the end of an array
2:   #include <iostream>
3:   using namespace std;
4:
5:   int main()
6:   {
7:       // sentinels
8:       long sentinelOne[3];
9:       long TargetArray[25]; // array to fill
10:      long sentinelTwo[3];
11:      int i;
12:      for (i=0; i<3; i++)
13:         {
14:            sentinelOne[i] = 0;
15:            sentinelTwo[i] = 0;
16:         }
17:      for (i=0; i<25; i++)
18:         TargetArray[i] = 10;
19:
20:      cout << "Test 1: \n";  // test current values (should be 0)
21:      cout << "TargetArray[0]: " << TargetArray[0] << endl;
22:      cout << "TargetArray[24]: " << TargetArray[24] << endl << endl;
23:
24:      for (i = 0; i<3; i++)
25:         {
26:            cout << "sentinelOne[" << i << "]: ";
27:            cout << sentinelOne[i] << endl;
28:            cout << "sentinelTwo[" << i << "]: ";
29:            cout << sentinelTwo[i]<< endl;
30:         }
31:
32:      cout << "\nAssigning...";
33:      for (i = 0; i<=25; i++)      // Going a little too far!
34:         TargetArray[i] = 20;
35:
36:      cout << "\nTest 2: \n";
37:      cout << "TargetArray[0]: " << TargetArray[0] << endl;
38:      cout << "TargetArray[24]: " << TargetArray[24] << endl;
39:      cout << "TargetArray[25]: " << TargetArray[25] << endl << endl;
40:      for (i = 0; i<3; i++)
41:         {
42:            cout << "sentinelOne[" << i << "]: ";
43:            cout << sentinelOne[i]<< endl;
44:            cout << "sentinelTwo[" << i << "]: ";
45:            cout << sentinelTwo[i]<< endl;
46:         }
47:
48:      return 0;
49:   }
```

13

```
Test 1:
TargetArray[0]: 10
TargetArray[24]: 10

SentinelOne[0]: 0
SentinelTwo[0]: 0
SentinelOne[1]: 0
SentinelTwo[1]: 0
SentinelOne[2]: 0
SentinelTwo[2]: 0

Assigning...
Test 2:
TargetArray[0]: 20
TargetArray[24]: 20
TargetArray[25]: 20

SentinelOne[0]: 20
SentinelTwo[0]: 0
SentinelOne[1]: 0
SentinelTwo[1]: 0
SentinelOne[2]: 0
SentinelTwo[2]: 0
```

ANALYSIS Lines 8 and 10 declare two arrays of three long integers that act as sentinels around TargetArray. These sentinel arrays are initialized with the value 0 on lines 12–16. Because these are declared before and after TargetArray, there is a good chance that they will be placed in memory just before and just after it. If memory is written to beyond the end of TargetArray, it is the sentinels that are likely to be changed rather than some unknown area of data. Some compilers count down in memory; others count up. For this reason, the sentinels are placed both before and after TargetArray.

Lines 20–30 confirm the sentinel values are okay by printing them as well as the first and last elements of TargetArray. On line 34, TargetArray's members are all reassigned from the initial value of 10 to the new value of 20. Line 34, however, counts to TargetArray offset 25, which doesn't exist in TargetArray.

Lines 37–39 print TargetArray's values again as a second test to see what the values are. Note that on line 39 TargetArray[25] is perfectly happy to print the value 20. However, when SentinelOne and SentinelTwo are printed, SentinelOne[0] reveals that its value has changed. This is because the memory that is 25 elements after TargetArray[0] is the same memory that is at SentinelOne[0]. When the nonexistent TargetArray[25] was accessed, what was actually accessed was SentinelOne[0].

Note that because all compilers use memory differently, your results might vary. You might find that the sentinels did not get overwritten. If this is the case, try changing line 33 to assign yet another value—change the 25 to 26. This increases the likelihood that you'll overwrite a sentinel. Of course, you might overwrite something else or crash your system instead.

This nasty bug can be very hard to find, because SentinelOne [0]'s value was changed in a part of the code that was not writing to SentinelOne at all.

Fence Post Errors

It is so common to write to one past the end of an array that this bug has its own name. It is called a fence post error. This refers to the problem in counting how many fence posts you need for a 10-foot fence if you need one post for every foot. Most people answer 10, but of course you need 11. Figure 13.2 makes this clear.

FIGURE 13.2

Fence post errors.

This type of "off by one" counting can be the bane of any C++ programmer's life. Over time, however, you'll get used to the idea that a 25-element array counts only to element 24, and that everything counts from 0.

NOTE Some programmers refer to ArrayName[0] as the zeroth element. Getting into this habit is a mistake. If ArrayName[0] is the zeroth element, what is ArrayName[1]? The oneth? If so, when you see ArrayName[24], will you realize that it is not the 24th element in the array, but rather the 25th? It is far less confusing to say that ArrayName[0] is at offset zero and is the first element.

13

Initializing Arrays

You can initialize a simple array of built-in types, such as integers and characters, when you first declare the array. After the array name, you put an equal sign (=) and a list of comma-separated values enclosed in braces. For example,

```
int IntegerArray[5] = { 10, 20, 30, 40, 50 };
```

declares `IntegerArray` to be an array of five integers. It assigns `IntegerArray[0]` the value `10`, `IntegerArray[1]` the value `20`, and so forth.

If you omit the size of the array, an array just big enough to hold the initialization is created. Therefore, if you write

```
int IntegerArray[] = { 10, 20, 30, 40, 50 };
```

you will create the same array as you did in the previous example, an array that holds five elements.

You cannot initialize more elements than you've declared for the array. Therefore,

```
int IntegerArray[5] = { 10, 20, 30, 40, 50, 60};
```

generates a compiler error because you've declared a five-member array and initialized six values. It is legal, however, to write

```
int IntegerArray[5] = {10, 20};
```

In this case, you have declared a five-element array and only initialized the first two elements, `IntegerArray[0]` and `IntegerArray[1]`.

Do	Don't
DO let the compiler set the size of initialized arrays. **DO** remember that the first member of the array is at offset 0.	**DON'T** write past the end of the array. **DON'T** get goofy with naming arrays. They should have meaningful names just as any other variable would have.

Declaring Arrays

This code uses "magic numbers" such as 3 for the size of the sentinel arrays and 25 for the size of `TargetArray`. It is safer to use constants so that you can change all these values in one place.

Arrays can have any legal variable name, but they cannot have the same name as another variable or array within their scope. Therefore, you cannot have an array named `myCats[5]` and a variable named `myCats` at the same time.

In addition, when declaring the number of elements, in addition to using literals, you can use a constant or enumeration. It is actually better to use these rather than a literal number because it gives you a single location to control the number of elements. In Listing 13.2, literal numbers were used. If you want to change the `TargetArray` so it holds only

20 elements instead of 25, you have to change several lines of code. If you used a constant, you only have to change the value of your constant.

Creating the number of elements, or dimension size, with an enumeration is a little different. Listing 13.3 illustrates this by creating an array that holds values—one for each day of the week.

LISTING 13.3 Using consts and enums in Arrays

```
0:  // Listing 13.3
1:  // Dimensioning arrays with consts and enumerations
2:
3:  #include <iostream>
4:  int main()
5:  {
6:      enum WeekDays { Sun, Mon, Tue,
7:              Wed, Thu, Fri, Sat, DaysInWeek };
8:      int ArrayWeek[DaysInWeek] = { 10, 20, 30, 40, 50, 60, 70 };
9:
10:     std::cout << "The value at Tuesday is: " << ArrayWeek[Tue];
11:     return 0;
12: }
```

OUTPUT

The value at Tuesday is: 30

ANALYSIS
Line 6 creates an enumeration called WeekDays. It has eight members. Sunday is equal to 0, and DaysInWeek is equal to 7. On line 8, an array called ArrayWeek is declared to have DaysInWeek elements, which is 7.

Line 10 uses the enumerated constant Tue as an offset into the array. Because Tue evaluates to 2, the third element of the array, ArrayWeek[2], is returned and printed on line 10.

Arrays

To declare an array, write the type of object stored, followed by the name of the array and a subscript with the number of objects to be held in the array.

Example 1

```
int MyIntegerArray[90];
```

Example 2

```
long * ArrayOfPointersToLongs[100];
```

To access members of the array, use the subscript operator.

13

> **Example 1**
> ```
> // assign ninth member of MyIntegerArray to theNinethInteger
> int theNinethInteger = MyIntegerArray[8];
> ```
>
> **Example 2**
> ```
> // assign ninth member of ArrayOfPointersToLongs to pLong.
> long * pLong = ArrayOfPointersToLongs[8];
> ```
>
> Arrays count from zero. An array of *n* items is numbered from 0 to *n–1*.

Using Arrays of Objects

Any object, whether built-in or user defined, can be stored in an array. When you declare the array to hold objects, you tell the compiler the type of object to store and the number for which to allocate room. The compiler knows how much room is needed for each object based on the class declaration. The class must have a default constructor that takes no arguments so that the objects can be created when the array is defined.

Accessing member data in an array of objects is a two-step process. You identify the member of the array by using the index operator ([ ]), and then you add the member operator (.) to access the particular member variable. Listing 13.4 demonstrates how you would create and access an array of five Cats.

LISTING 13.4   Creating an Array of Objects

```
0:  // Listing 13.4 - An array of objects
1:
2:  #include <iostream>
3:  using namespace std;
4:
5:  class Cat
6:  {
7:    public:
8:       Cat() { itsAge = 1; itsWeight=5; }
9:       ~Cat() {}
10:       int GetAge() const { return itsAge; }
11:       int GetWeight() const { return itsWeight; }
12:       void SetAge(int age) { itsAge = age; }
13:
14:    private:
15:       int itsAge;
16:       int itsWeight;
17:  };
18:
```

LISTING 13.4 continued

```
19:  int main()
20:  {
21:      Cat Litter[5];
22:      int i;
23:      for (i = 0; i < 5; i++)
24:          Litter[i].SetAge(2*i +1);
25:
26:      for (i = 0; i < 5; i++)
27:      {
28:          cout << "Cat #" << i+1<< ": ";
29:          cout << Litter[i].GetAge() << endl;
30:      }
31:      return 0;
32:  }
```

OUTPUT

```
cat #1: 1
cat #2: 3
cat #3: 5
cat #4: 7
cat #5: 9
```

ANALYSIS Lines 5–17 declare the Cat class. The Cat class must have a default constructor so that Cat objects can be created in an array. In this case, the default constructor is declared and defined on line 8. For each Cat, a default age of 1 is set as well as a default weight of 5. Remember that if you create any other constructor, the compiler-supplied default constructor is not created; you must create your own.

The first for loop (lines 23 and 24) sets values for the age of each of the five Cat objects in the array. The second for loop (lines 26–30) accesses each member of the array and calls GetAge() to display the age of each Cat object.

Each individual Cat's GetAge() method is called by accessing the member in the array, Litter, followed by the dot operator (.), and the member function. You can access other members and methods in the exact same way.

Declaring Multidimensional Arrays

It is possible to have arrays of more than one dimension. Each dimension is represented as a subscript in the array. Therefore, a two-dimensional array has two subscripts; a three-dimensional array has three subscripts; and so on. Arrays can have any number of dimensions, although it is likely that most of the arrays you create will be of one or two dimensions.

13

A good example of a two-dimensional array is a chess board. One dimension represents the eight rows; the other dimension represents the eight columns. Figure 13.3 illustrates this idea.

FIGURE 13.3

A chess board and a two-dimensional array.

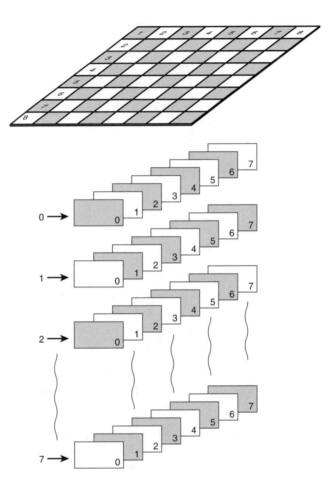

Suppose that you have a class named SQUARE. The declaration of an array named Board that represents it would be

```
SQUARE Board[8][8];
```

You could also represent the same data with a one-dimensional, 64-square array. For example:

```
SQUARE Board[64];
```

This, however, doesn't correspond as closely to the real-world object as the two-dimension. When the game begins, the king is located in the fourth position in the first row; that position corresponds to

```
Board[0][3];
```

assuming that the first subscript corresponds to row and the second to column.

Initializing Multidimensional Arrays

You can initialize multidimensional arrays. You assign the list of values to array elements in order, with the last array subscript (the one farthest to the right) changing while each of the former holds steady. Therefore, if you have an array

```
int theArray[5][3];
```

the first three elements go into `theArray[0]`; the next three into `theArray[1]`; and so forth.

You initialize this array by writing

```
int theArray[5][3] = { 1,2,3,4,5,6,7,8,9,10,11,12,13,14,15 };
```

For the sake of clarity, you could group the initializations with braces. For example:

```
int theArray[5][3] = {  {1,2,3},
    {4,5,6},
    {7,8,9},
    {10,11,12},
    {13,14,15} };
```

The compiler ignores the inner braces, but they do make it easier to understand how the numbers are distributed.

When initializing elements of an array, each value must be separated by a comma, without regard to the braces. The entire initialization set must be within braces, and it must end with a semicolon.

Listing 13.5 creates a two-dimensional array. The first dimension is the set of numbers from zero to four. The second dimension consists of the double of each value in the first dimension.

13

LISTING 13.5 Creating a Multidimensional Array

```
0:  // Listing 13.5 - Creating a Multidimensional Array
1:  #include <iostream>
2:  using namespace std;
3:
4:  int main()
```

LISTING 13.5   continued

```
5:  {
6:      int SomeArray[2][5] = { {0,1,2,3,4}, {0,2,4,6,8}};
7:      for (int i = 0; i<2; i++)
8:      {
9:          for (int j=0; j<5; j++)
10:          {
11:            cout << "SomeArray[" << i << "][" << j << "]: ";
12:            cout << SomeArray[i][j]<< endl;
13:          }
14:      }
15:      return 0;
16:  }
```

OUTPUT
```
SomeArray[0][0]: 0
SomeArray[0][1]: 1
SomeArray[0][2]: 2
SomeArray[0][3]: 3
SomeArray[0][4]: 4
SomeArray[1][0]: 0
SomeArray[1][1]: 2
SomeArray[1][2]: 4
SomeArray[1][3]: 6
SomeArray[1][4]: 8
```

ANALYSIS   Line 6 declares SomeArray to be a two-dimensional array. The first dimension indicates that there will be two sets; the second dimension consists of five integers. This creates a 2×5 grid, as Figure 13.4 shows.

FIGURE 13.4

A 2×5 array.

Some Array [5] [2]

The values are based on the two sets of numbers. The first set is the original numbers; the second set is the doubled numbers. In this listing, the values are simply set, although they could be computed as well. Lines 7 and 9 create a nested for loop. The outer for loop (starting on line 7) ticks through each member of the first dimension, which is each of the two sets of integers. For every member in that dimension, the inner for loop (starting on line 9) ticks through each member of the second dimension. This is consistent with the printout. SomeArray[0][0] is followed by SomeArray[0][1]. The first dimension is incremented only after the second dimension has gone through all of its increments. Then counting for the second dimension starts over.

A Word About Memory

When you declare an array, you tell the compiler exactly how many objects you expect to store in it. The compiler sets aside memory for all the objects, even if you never use it. This isn't a problem with arrays for which you have a good idea of how many objects you'll need. For example, a chessboard has 64 squares, and cats have between 1 and 10 kittens. When you have no idea of how many objects you'll need, however, you must use more advanced data structures.

This book looks at arrays of pointers, arrays built on the free store, and various other collections. You'll see a few advanced data structures, but you can learn more in the book *C++ Unleashed* from Sams Publishing. You can also check out Appendix E, "A Look at Linked Lists."

Two of the great things about programming are that there are always more things to learn and that there are always more books from which to learn them.

Building Arrays of Pointers

The arrays discussed so far store all their members on the stack. Usually, stack memory is more limited, whereas free store memory is much larger. It is possible to declare each object on the free store and then to store only a pointer to the object in the array. This dramatically reduces the amount of stack memory used. Listing 13.6 rewrites the array from Listing 13.4, but it stores all the objects on the free store. As an indication of the greater memory that this enables, the array is expanded from 5 to 500, and the name is changed from `Litter` to `Family`.

LISTING 13.6 Storing an Array on the Free Store

13

```
0:   // Listing 13.6 - An array of pointers to objects
1:
2:   #include <iostream>
3:   using namespace std;
4:
5:   class Cat
6:   {
7:     public:
8:       Cat() { itsAge = 1; itsWeight=5; }
9:       ~Cat() {}                          // destructor
10:      int GetAge() const { return itsAge; }
11:      int GetWeight() const { return itsWeight; }
12:      void SetAge(int age) { itsAge = age; }
```

LISTING 13.6   continued

```
13:
14:    private:
15:       int itsAge;
16:       int itsWeight;
17: };
18:
19: int main()
20: {
21:    Cat * Family[500];
22:    int i;
23:    Cat * pCat;
24:    for (i = 0; i < 500; i++)
25:    {
26:       pCat = new Cat;
27:       pCat->SetAge(2*i +1);
28:       Family[i] = pCat;
29:    }
30:
31:    for (i = 0; i < 500; i++)
32:    {
33:       cout << "Cat #" << i+1 << ": ";
34:       cout << Family[i]->GetAge() << endl;
35:    }
36:    return 0;
37: }
```

OUTPUT

```
Cat #1: 1
Cat #2: 3
Cat #3: 5
...
Cat #499: 997
Cat #500: 999
```

ANALYSIS The Cat object declared on lines 5–17 is identical to the Cat object declared in Listing 13.4. This time, however, the array declared on line 21 is named Family, and it is declared to hold 500 elements. More importantly, these 500 elements are pointers to Cat objects.

In the initial loop (lines 24–29), 500 new Cat objects are created on the free store, and each one has its age set to twice the index plus one. Therefore, the first Cat is set to 1, the second Cat to 3, the third Cat to 5, and so on. After the pointer is created, line 28 assigns the pointer to the array. Because the array has been declared to hold pointers, the pointer—rather than the dereferenced value in the pointer—is added to the array.

The second loop in lines 31–35 prints each of the values. On line 33, a number is printed to show which object is being printed. Because index offsets start at zero, line 33 adds 1 to display a count starting at 1 instead. On line 34, the pointer is accessed by using the index, `Family[i]`. That address is then used to access the `GetAge()` method.

In this example, the array `Family` and all its pointers are stored on the stack, but the 500 `Cat` objects that are created are stored on the free store.

A Look at Pointer Arithmetic—An Advanced Topic

On Day 8, "Understanding Pointers," you initially learned about pointers. Before continuing with arrays, it is worth coming back to pointers to cover an advanced topic—pointer arithmetic.

There are a few things that can be done mathematically with pointers. Pointers can be subtracted, one from another. One powerful technique is to point two pointers at different elements in an array and to take their difference to see how many elements separate the two members. This can be very useful when parsing arrays of characters, as illustrated in Listing 13.7.

LISTING 13.7   Illustrates How to Parse Out Words from a Character String

```
 0:   #include <iostream>
 1:   #include <ctype.h>
 2:   #include <string.h>
 3:
 4:   bool GetWord(char* theString,
 5:              char* word, int& wordOffset);
 6:
 7:   // driver program
 8:   int main()
 9:   {
10:      const int bufferSize = 255;
11:      char buffer[bufferSize+1];    // hold the entire string
12:      char word[bufferSize+1];      // hold the word
13:      int wordOffset = 0;           // start at the beginning
14:
15:      std::cout << "Enter a string: ";
16:      std::cin.getline(buffer,bufferSize);
17:
18:      while (GetWord(buffer, word, wordOffset))
19:      {
20:          std::cout << "Got this word: " << word << std::endl;
21:      }
22:      return 0;
23:   }
24:
```

13

LISTING 13.7   continued

```
25:   // function to parse words from a string.
26:   bool GetWord(char* theString, char* word, int& wordOffset)
27:   {
28:       if (theString[wordOffset] == 0)  // end of string?
29:           return false;
30:
31:       char *p1, *p2;
32:       p1 = p2 = theString+wordOffset;  // point to the next word
33:
34:       // eat leading spaces
35:       for (int i = 0; i<(int)strlen(p1) && !isalnum(p1[0]); i++)
36:           p1++;
37:
38:       // see if you have a word
39:       if (!isalnum(p1[0]))
40:           return false;
41:
42:       // p1 now points to start of next word
43:       // point p2 there as well
44:       p2 = p1;
45:
46:       // march p2 to end of word
47:       while (isalnum(p2[0]))
48:           p2++;
49:
50:       // p2 is now at end of word
51:       // p1 is at beginning of word
52:       // length of word is the difference
53:       int len = int (p2 - p1);
54:
55:       // copy the word into the buffer
56:       strncpy (word,p1,len);
57:
58:       // null terminate it
59:       word[len]='\0';
60:
61:       // now find the beginning of the next word
62:       for (int j = int(p2-theString); j<(int)strlen(theString)
63:           && !isalnum(p2[0]); j++)
64:       {
65:           p2++;
66:       }
67:
68:       wordOffset = int(p2-theString);
69:
70:       return true;
71:   }
```

OUTPUT

```
Enter a string: this code first appeared in C++ Report
Got this word: this
Got this word: code
Got this word: first
Got this word: appeared
Got this word: in
Got this word: C
Got this word: Report
```

ANALYSIS This program allows the user to enter in a sentence. The program then breaks out each word (each set of alphanumeric characters) of the sentence. On line 15 is the prompt asking the user to enter a string—basically a sentence. This is fed to a method called GetWord() on line 18, along with a buffer to hold the first word and an integer variable called WordOffset, which is initialized on line 13 to zero.

GetWord() returns each word from the string until the end of the string is reached. As words are returned from GetWord(), they are printed on line 20 until GetWord() returns false.

Each call to GetWord() causes a jump to line 26. On line 28, a check is done to see if the value of string[wordOffset]) is zero. This will be true if you are at or past the end of the string, at which time GetWord() will return false. cin.GetLine() makes sure the string entered is terminated with a null—that is, that it ends with a zero valued character '\0';.

On line 31, two character pointers, p1 and p2, are declared, and on line 32, they are set to point into string offset by wordOffset. Initially, wordOffset is zero, so they point to the beginning of the string.

Lines 35 and 36 tick through the string, pushing p1 to the first alphanumeric character. Lines 39 and 40 ensure that an alphanumeric character is found. If not, false is returned.

p1 now points to the start of the next word, and line 44 sets p2 to point to the same position.

Lines 47 and 48 then cause p2 to march through the word, stopping at the first nonalphanumeric character. p2 is now pointing to the end of the word that p1 points to the beginning of. By subtracting p1 from p2 on line 53 and casting the result to an integer, you are able to establish the length of the word. That word is then copied into the buffer word using a string-copying method from the Standard Library, passing in as the starting point p1 and as the length the difference that you've established.

On line 59, a null value is appended to mark the end of the word. p2 is then incremented to point to the beginning of the next word, and the offset of that word is pushed into the integer reference wordOffset. Finally, true is returned to indicate that a word has been found.

13

This is a classic example of code that is best understood by putting it into a debugger and stepping through its execution.

Pointer arithmetic is used in a number of places in this listing. In this listing, you can see that by subtracting one pointer from another (as on line 53), you determine the number of elements between the two pointers. In addition, you saw on line 55 that incrementing a pointer shifts it to the next element within an array rather than just adding one. Using pointer arithmetic is very common when working with pointers and arrays, but it is also a dangerous activity and needs to be approached with respect.

Declaring Arrays on the Free Store

It is possible to put the entire array on the free store, also known as the heap. You do this by creating a pointer to the array. Create the pointer by calling new and using the subscript operator. The result is a pointer to an area on the free store that holds the array. For example,

```
Cat *Family = new Cat[500];
```

declares Family to be a pointer to the first element in an array of 500 Cats. In other words, Family points to—or has the address of—Family[0].

The advantage of using Family in this way is that you can use pointer arithmetic to access each member of Family. For example, you can write

```
Cat *Family = new Cat[500];
Cat *pCat = Family;          //pCat points to Family[0]
pCat->SetAge(10);            // set Family[0] to 10
pCat++;                      // advance to Family[1]
pCat->SetAge(20);            // set Family[1] to 20
```

This declares a new array of 500 Cats and a pointer to point to the start of the array. Using that pointer, the first Cat's SetAge() function is called with a value of 10. The pointer is then incremented. This causes the pointer to be incremented to point to the next Cat object in the array. The second Cat's SetAge() method is then called with a value of 20.

A Pointer to an Array Versus an Array of Pointers

Examine the following three declarations:

```
1:  Cat   FamilyOne[500];
2:  Cat * FamilyTwo[500];
3:  Cat * FamilyThree = new Cat[500];
```

FamilyOne is an array of 500 Cat objects. FamilyTwo is an array of 500 pointers to Cat objects. FamilyThree is a pointer to an array of 500 Cat objects.

The differences among these three code lines dramatically affect how these arrays operate. What is perhaps even more surprising is that FamilyThree is a variant of FamilyOne, but it is very different from FamilyTwo.

This raises the thorny issue of how pointers relate to arrays. In the third case, FamilyThree is a pointer to an array. That is, the address in FamilyThree is the address of the first item in that array. This is exactly the case for FamilyOne.

Pointers and Array Names

In C++, an array name is a constant pointer to the first element of the array. Therefore, in the declaration

```
Cat Family[500];
```

Family is a pointer to &Family[0], which is the address of the first element of the array Family.

It is legal to use array names as constant pointers, and vice versa. Therefore, Family + 4 is a legitimate way of accessing the data at Family[4].

The compiler does all the arithmetic when you add to, increment, and decrement pointers. The address accessed when you write Family + 4 isn't four bytes past the address of Family—it is four objects. If each object is four bytes long, Family + 4 is 16 bytes past the start of the array. If each object is a Cat that has four long member variables of four bytes each and two short member variables of two bytes each, each Cat is 20 bytes, and Family + 4 is 80 bytes past the start of the array.

Listing 13.8 illustrates declaring and using an array on the free store.

LISTING 13.8   Creating an Array by Using new

13

```
 0:   // Listing 13.8 - An array on the free store
 1:
 2:   #include <iostream>
 3:
 4:   class Cat
 5:   {
 6:     public:
 7:       Cat() { itsAge = 1; itsWeight=5; }
 8:       ~Cat();
 9:       int GetAge() const { return itsAge; }
10:       int GetWeight() const { return itsWeight; }
```

LISTING 13.8 continued

```
11:        void SetAge(int age) { itsAge = age; }
12:
13:    private:
14:        int itsAge;
15:        int itsWeight;
16:    };
17:
18:    Cat :: ~Cat()
19:    {
20:       // std::cout << "Destructor called!\n";
21:    }
22:
23:    int main()
24:    {
25:        Cat * Family = new Cat[500];
26:        int i;
27:
28:        for (i = 0; i < 500; i++)
29:        {
30:            Family[i].SetAge(2*i +1);
31:        }
32:
33:        for (i = 0; i < 500; i++)
34:        {
35:            std::cout << "Cat #" << i+1 << ": ";
36:            std::cout << Family[i].GetAge() << std::endl;
37:        }
38:
39:        delete [] Family;
40:
41:        return 0;
42:    }
```

OUTPUT

```
Cat #1: 1
Cat #2: 3
Cat #3: 5
...
Cat #499: 997
Cat #500: 999
```

ANALYSIS Line 25 declares Family, which is a pointer to an array of 500 Cat objects. The entire array is created on the free store with the call to new Cat[500].

On line 30, you can see that the pointer you declared can be used with the index operator [], and thus be treated just like a regular array. On line 36, you see that it is once again used to call the GetAge() method. For all practical purposes, you can treat this pointer to the `Family` array as an array name. The one thing you will need to do, however, is to free the memory you allocated in setting up the array. This is done on line 39 with a call to `delete`.

Deleting Arrays on the Free Store

What happens to the memory allocated for these `Cat` objects when the array is destroyed? Is there a chance of a memory leak?

Deleting `Family` automatically returns all the memory set aside for the array if you use the `delete` with the `[ ]` operator. By including the square brackets, the compiler is smart enough to destroy each object in the array and to return its memory to the free store.

To see this, change the size of the array from 500 to 10 on lines 25, 28, and 33. Then uncomment the `cout` statement on line 20. When line 39 is reached and the array is destroyed, each `Cat` object destructor is called.

When you create an item on the heap by using `new`, you always delete that item and free its memory with `delete`. Similarly, when you create an array by using `new` `<class>[size]`, you delete that array and free all its memory with `delete[]`. The brackets signal the compiler that this array is being deleted.

If you leave the brackets off, only the first object in the array is deleted. You can prove this to yourself by removing the bracket on line 39. If you edited line 20 so that the destructor prints, you should now see only one `Cat` object destroyed. Congratulations! You just created a memory leak.

Resizing Arrays at Runtime

The biggest advantage of being able to allocate arrays on the heap is that you determine the size of the array at runtime and then allocate it. For instance, if you asked the user to enter the size of a family into a variable called `SizeOfFamily`, you could then declare a `Cat` array as follows:

```
Cat *pFamily = new Cat[SizeOfFamily];
```

With that, you now have a pointer to an array of `Cat` objects. You can then create a pointer to the first element and loop through this array using a pointer and pointer arithmetic:

```
Cat *pCurrentCat = Family[0];
for ( int Index = 0; Index < SizeOfFamily; Index++, pCurrentCat++ )
{
        pCurrentCat->SetAge(Index);
};
```

13

Because C++ views arrays as no more than special cases of pointers, you can skip the second pointer and simply use standard array indexing:

```
for (int Index = 0; Index < SizeOfFamily; Index++)
{
        pFamily[Index].SetAge(Index);
};
```

The use of the subscript brackets automatically dereferences the resulting pointer and the compiler causes the appropriate pointer arithmetic to be performed.

A further advantage is that you can use a similar technique to resize an array at runtime when you run out of room. Listing 13.9 illustrates this reallocation.

LISTING **13.9**   Reallocating an Array at Runtime

```
0:   //Listing 13.9
1:
2:   #include <iostream>
3:   using namespace std;
4:   int main()
5:   {
6:       int  AllocationSize = 5;
7:       int *pArrayOfNumbers = new int[AllocationSize];
8:       int  ElementsUsedSoFar = 0;
9:       int  MaximumElementsAllowed = AllocationSize;
10:      int InputNumber = -1;
11:
12:      cout << endl << "Next number = ";
13:      cin >> InputNumber;
14:
15:      while ( InputNumber > 0 )
16:      {
17:         pArrayOfNumbers[ElementsUsedSoFar++] = InputNumber;
18:
19:         if ( ElementsUsedSoFar == MaximumElementsAllowed )
20:         {
21:             int *pLargerArray =
22:                 new int[MaximumElementsAllowed+AllocationSize];
23:
24:             for ( int CopyIndex = 0;
25:                   CopyIndex < MaximumElementsAllowed;
26:                   CopyIndex++ )
27 :             {
28:                 pLargerArray[CopyIndex] = pArrayOfNumbers[CopyIndex];
29:             };
30:
31:             delete [] pArrayOfNumbers;
32:             pArrayOfNumbers = pLargerArray;
33:             MaximumElementsAllowed+= AllocationSize;
```

LISTING 13.9   continued

```
34:        };
35:        cout << endl << "Next number = ";
36:        cin >> InputNumber;
37:     }
38:
39:     for (int Index = 0; Index < ElementsUsedSoFar; Index++)
40:     {
41:       cout << pArrayOfNumbers[Index] << endl;
42:     }
43:     return 0;
44:   }
```

OUTPUT

```
Next number = 10

Next number = 20

Next number = 30

Next number = 40

Next number = 50

Next number = 60

Next number = 70

Next number = 0
10
20
30
40
50
60
70
```

ANALYSIS   In this example, numbers are entered one after the other and stored in an array. When a number less or equal to 0 is entered, the array of numbers that has been gathered is printed.

Looking closer, you can see on lines 6–9 that a number of variables are declared. More specifically, the initial size of the array is set at 5 on line 6 and then the array is allocated on line 7 and its address is assigned to pArrayOfNumbers.

Lines 12–13 get the first number from the user and place it into the variable, InputNumber. On line 15, if the number entered is greater than zero, processing occurs. If not, the program jumps to line 38.

13

On line 17, `InputNumber` is put into the array. This is safe the first time in because you know you have room at this point. On line 19, a check is done to see if this is the last element that the array has room for. If there is room, control passes to line 35; otherwise, the body of the `if` statement is processed in order to increase the size of the array (lines 20–34).

A new array is created on line 21. This array is created to hold five more elements (`AllocationSize`) than the current array. Lines 24–29 then copy the old array to the new array using array notation (you could also use pointer arithmetic).

Line 31 deletes the old array and line 32 then replaces the old pointer with the pointer to the larger array. Line 33 increases the `MaximumElementsAllowed` to match the new larger size.

Lines 39–42 display the resulting array.

Do	Don't
DO remember that an array of *n* items is numbered from zero through *n–1*.	**DON'T** write or read past the end of an array.
DO use array indexing with pointers that point to arrays.	**DON'T** confuse an array of pointers with a pointer to an array.
DO use `delete[]` to remove an entire array created on the free store. Using just `delete` without the `[]` only deletes the first element.	**DON'T** forget to delete any memory you allocate using new.

char Arrays and Strings

There is a type of array that gets special attention. This is an array of characters that is terminated by a null. This array is considered a "C-style string." The only C-style strings you've seen until now have been unnamed C-style string constants used in `cout` statements, such as

```
cout << "hello world";
```

You can declare and initialize a C-style string the same as you would any other array. For example:

```
char Greeting[] =
{ 'H', 'e', 'l', 'l', 'o', ' ', 'W','o','r','l','d','\0' };
```

In this case, `Greeting` is declared as an array of characters and it is initialized with a number of characters. The last character, `'\0'`, is the null character, which many C++

functions recognize as the terminator for a C-style string. Although this character-by-character approach works, it is difficult to type and admits too many opportunities for error. C++ enables you to use a shorthand form of the previous line of code. It is

```
char Greeting[] = "Hello World";
```

You should note two things about this syntax:

- Instead of single-quoted characters separated by commas and surrounded by braces, you have a double-quoted C-style string, no commas, and no braces.
- You don't need to add the null character because the compiler adds it for you.

When you declare a string, you need to ensure that you make it as large as you will need. The length of a C-style string includes the number of characters including the null character. For example, Hello World is 12 bytes. Hello is 5 bytes, the space is 1 byte, World is 5 bytes, and the null character is 1 byte.

You can also create uninitialized character arrays. As with all arrays, it is important to ensure that you don't put more into it than there is room for. Listing 13.10 demonstrates the use of an uninitialized buffer.

Listing 13.10 Filling an Array

```
0:  //Listing 13.10 char array buffers
1:
2:  #include <iostream>
3:
4:  int main()
5:  {
6:      char buffer[80];
7:      std::cout << "Enter the string: ";
8:      std::cin >> buffer;
9:      std::cout << "Here's the buffer: " << buffer << std::endl;
10:     return 0;
11: }
```

13

OUTPUT
```
Enter the string: Hello World
Here's the buffer: Hello
```

ANALYSIS On line 6, a character array is created to act as a buffer to hold 80 characters. This is large enough to hold a 79-character C-style string and a terminating null character.

On line 7, the user is prompted to enter a C-style string, which is entered into the buffer on line 8. cin writes a terminating null to the buffer after it writes the string.

Two problems occur with the program in Listing 13.10. First, if the user enters more than 79 characters, cin writes past the end of the buffer. Second, if the user enters a space, cin thinks that it is the end of the string, and it stops writing to the buffer.

To solve these problems, you must call a special method on cin called get(). cin.get() takes three parameters:

- The buffer to fill
- The maximum number of characters to get
- The delimiter that terminates input

The delimiter defaults to a newline character. Listing 13.11 illustrates the use of get().

LISTING **13.11**   Filling an Array With a Maximum Number of Characters.

```
0:   //Listing 13.11 using cin.get()
1:
2:   #include <iostream>
3:   using namespace std;
4:
5:   int main()
6:   {
7:       char buffer[80];
8:       cout << "Enter the string: ";
9:       cin.get(buffer, 79);        // get up to 79 or newline
10:      cout << "Here's the buffer:  " << buffer << endl;
11:      return 0;
12:  }
```

OUTPUT

Enter the string: **Hello World**
Here's the buffer: Hello World

ANALYSIS   Line 9 calls the method get() of cin. The buffer declared on line 7 is passed in as the first argument. The second argument is the maximum number of characters to get. In this case, it must be no greater than 79 to allow for the terminating null. No need exists to provide a terminating character because the default value of newline is sufficient.

If you enter spaces, tabs, or other whitespace characters, they are assigned to the string. A newline character ends the input. Entering 79 characters also results in the end of the input. You can verify this by rerunning the listing and trying to enter a string longer than 79 characters.

Using the `strcpy()` and `strncpy()` Methods

A number of existing functions are available in the C++ library for dealing with strings. C++ inherits many of these functions for dealing with C-style strings from the C language. Among the many functions provided are two for copying one string into another: `strcpy()` and `strncpy()`. `strcpy()` copies the entire contents of one string into a designated buffer. The other, `strncpy()` copies a number of characters from one string to another. Listing 13.12 demonstrates the use of `strcpy()`.

LISTING 13.12 Using `strcpy()`

```
 0:   //Listing 13.12 Using strcpy()
 1:
 2:   #include <iostream>
 3:   #include <string.h>
 4:   using namespace std;
 5:
 6:   int main()
 7:   {
 8:      char String1[] = "No man is an island";
 9:      char String2[80];
10:
11:      strcpy(String2,String1);
12:
13:      cout << "String1: " << String1 << endl;
14:      cout << "String2: " << String2 << endl;
15:      return 0;
16:   }
```

OUTPUT
```
String1: No man is an island
String2: No man is an island
```

ANALYSIS This listing is relatively simple. It copies data from one string into another. The header file `string.h` is included on line 3. This file contains the prototype of the `strcpy()` function. `strcpy()` takes two character arrays—a destination followed by a source. On line 11, this function is used to copy `String1` into `String2`.

You have to be careful using the `strcpy()` function. If the source is larger than the destination, `strcpy()` overwrites past the end of the buffer. To protect against this, the Standard Library also includes `strncpy()`. This variation takes a maximum number of characters to copy. `strncpy()` copies up to the first null character or the maximum number of characters specified into the destination buffer. Listing 13.13 illustrates the use of `strncpy()`.

13

LISTING 13.13 Using strncpy()

```
0:   //Listing 13.13 Using strncpy()
1:
2:   #include <iostream>
3:   #include <string.h>
4:
5:   int main()
6:   {
7:       const int MaxLength = 80;
8:       char String1[] = "No man is an island";
9:       char String2[MaxLength+1];
10:
11:      strncpy(String2,String1,MaxLength);
12:
13:      std::cout << "String1: " << String1 << std::endl;
14:      std::cout << "String2: " << String2 << std::endl;
15:      return 0;
16:  }
```

OUTPUT
```
String1: No man is an island
String2: No man is an island
```

ANALYSIS Once again, a simple listing is presented. Like the preceding listing, this one simply copies data from one string into another. On line 11, the call to strcpy() has been changed to a call to strncpy(), which takes a third parameter: the maximum number of characters to copy. The buffer String2 is declared to take MaxLength+1 characters. The extra character is for the null, which both strcpy() and strncpy() automatically add to the end of the string.

NOTE

> As with the integer array shown in Listing 13.9, character arrays can be resized using heap allocation techniques and element-by-element copying. Most flexible string classes provided to C++ programmers use some variation on that technique to allow strings to grow and shrink or to insert or delete elements from the middle of the string.

String Classes

C++ inherited the null-terminated C-style string and the library of functions that includes strcpy() from C, but these functions aren't integrated into an object-oriented framework. The Standard Library includes a String class that provides an encapsulated set of data and functions for manipulating that data, as well as accessor functions so that the data itself is hidden from the clients of the String class.

Before using this class, you will create a custom String class as an exercise in understanding the issues involved. At a minimum, your String class should overcome the basic limitations of character arrays.

Like all arrays, character arrays are static. You define how large they are. They always take up that much room in memory, even if you don't need it all. Writing past the end of the array is disastrous.

A good String class allocates only as much memory as it needs and always enough to hold whatever it is given. If it can't allocate enough memory, it should fail gracefully.

Listing 13.14 provides a first approximation of a String class.

NOTE
This custom String class is quite limited and is by no means complete, robust, or ready for commercial use. That is fine, however, as the Standard Library does provide a complete and robust String class.

LISTING 13.14 Using a String class

```
0:  //Listing 13.14 Using a String class
1:
2:  #include <iostream>
3:  #include <string.h>
4:  using namespace std;
5:
6:  // Rudimentary string class
7:  class String
8:  {
9:    public:
10:       // constructors
11:       String();
12:       String(const char *const);
13:       String(const String &);
14:       ~String();
15:
16:       // overloaded operators
17:       char & operator[](unsigned short offset);
18:       char operator[](unsigned short offset) const;
19:       String operator+(const String&);
20:       void operator+=(const String&);
21:       String & operator= (const String &);
22:
23:       // General accessors
24:       unsigned short GetLen()const { return itsLen; }
25:       const char * GetString() const { return itsString; }
26:
27:    private:
```

13

LISTING **13.14**   continued

```
28:        String (unsigned short);           // private constructor
29:        char * itsString;
30:        unsigned short itsLen;
31:    };
32:
33:    // default constructor creates string of 0 bytes
34:    String::String()
35:    {
36:        itsString = new char[1];
37:        itsString[0] = '\0';
38:        itsLen=0;
39:    }
40:
41:    // private (helper) constructor, used only by
42:    // class methods for creating a new string of
43:    // required size. Null filled.
44:    String::String(unsigned short len)
45:    {
46:        itsString = new char[len+1];
47:        for (unsigned short i = 0; i<=len; i++)
48:            itsString[i] = '\0';
49:        itsLen=len;
50:    }
51:
52:    // Converts a character array to a String
53:    String::String(const char * const cString)
54:    {
55:        itsLen = strlen(cString);
56:        itsString = new char[itsLen+1];
57:        for (unsigned short i = 0; i<itsLen; i++)
58:            itsString[i] = cString[i];
59:        itsString[itsLen]='\0';
60:    }
61:
62:    // copy constructor
63:    String::String (const String & rhs)
64:    {
65:        itsLen=rhs.GetLen();
66:        itsString = new char[itsLen+1];
67:        for (unsigned short i = 0; i<itsLen;i++)
68:            itsString[i] = rhs[i];
69:        itsString[itsLen] = '\0';
70:    }
71:
72:    // destructor, frees allocated memory
73:    String::~String ()
74:    {
75:        delete [] itsString;
76:        itsLen = 0;
77:    }
```

LISTING 13.14   continued

```
78:
79:    // operator equals, frees existing memory
80:    // then copies string and size
81:    String& String::operator=(const String & rhs)
82:    {
83:       if (this == &rhs)
84:          return *this;
85:       delete [] itsString;
86:       itsLen=rhs.GetLen();
87:       itsString = new char[itsLen+1];
88:       for (unsigned short i = 0; i<itsLen;i++)
89:          itsString[i] = rhs[i];
90:       itsString[itsLen] = '\0';
91:       return *this;
92:    }
93:
94:    //nonconstant offset operator, returns
95:    // reference to character so it can be
96:    // changed!
97:    char & String::operator[](unsigned short offset)
98:    {
99:       if (offset > itsLen)
100:         return itsString[itsLen-1];
101:      else
102:         return itsString[offset];
103:   }
104:
105:   // constant offset operator for use
106:   // on const objects (see copy constructor!)
107:   char String::operator[](unsigned short offset) const
108:   {
109:      if (offset > itsLen)
110:         return itsString[itsLen-1];
111:      else
112:         return itsString[offset];
113:   }
114:
115:   // creates a new string by adding current
116:   // string to rhs
117:   String String::operator+(const String& rhs)
118:   {
119:      unsigned short  totalLen = itsLen + rhs.GetLen();
120:      String temp(totalLen);
121:      unsigned short i;
122:      for ( i= 0; i<itsLen; i++)
123:         temp[i] = itsString[i];
124:      for (unsigned short j = 0; j<rhs.GetLen(); j++, i++)
125:         temp[i] = rhs[j];
126:      temp[totalLen]='\0';
127:      return temp;
```

LISTING **13.14**   continued

```
128:  }
129:
130:  // changes current string, returns nothing
131:  void String::operator+=(const String& rhs)
132:  {
133:     unsigned short rhsLen = rhs.GetLen();
134:     unsigned short totalLen = itsLen + rhsLen;
135:     String  temp(totalLen);
136:     unsigned short i;
137:     for (i = 0; i<itsLen; i++)
138:         temp[i] = itsString[i];
139:     for (unsigned short j = 0; j<rhs.GetLen(); j++, i++)
140:         temp[i] = rhs[i-itsLen];
141:     temp[totalLen]='\0';
142:     *this = temp;
143:  }
144:
145:  int main()
146:  {
147:     String s1("initial test");
148:     cout << "S1:\t" << s1.GetString() << endl;
149:
150:     char * temp = "Hello World";
151:     s1 = temp;
152:     cout << "S1:\t" << s1.GetString() << endl;
153:
154:     char tempTwo[20];
155:     strcpy(tempTwo,"; nice to be here!");
156:     s1 += tempTwo;
157:     cout << "tempTwo:\t" << tempTwo << endl;
158:     cout << "S1:\t" << s1.GetString() << endl;
159:
160:     cout << "S1[4]:\t" << s1[4] << endl;
161:     s1[4]='x';
162:     cout << "S1:\t" << s1.GetString() << endl;
163:
164:     cout << "S1[999]:\t" << s1[999] << endl;
165:
166:     String s2(" Another string");
167:     String s3;
168:     s3 = s1+s2;
169:     cout << "S3:\t" << s3.GetString() << endl;
170:
171:     String s4;
172:     s4 = "Why does this work?";
173:     cout << "S4:\t" << s4.GetString() << endl;
174:     return 0;
175:  }
```

OUTPUT
```
S1:      initial test
S1:      Hello World
tempTwo:         ; nice to be here!
S1:      Hello World; nice to be here!
S1[4]:   o
S1:      Hellx World; nice to be here!
S1[999]:         !
S3:      Hellx World; nice to be here! Another string
S4:      Why does this work?
```

ANALYSIS Your `String` class's declaration is on lines 7–31. To add flexibility to the class, there are three constructors in lines 11–13: the default constructor, the copy constructor, and a constructor that takes an existing null-terminated (C-style) string.

To allow the your users to manipulate strings easily, this `String` class overloads several operators including the offset operator (`[ ]`), operator plus (+), and operator plus-equals (+=). The offset operator is overloaded twice: once as a constant function returning a `char` and again as a nonconstant function returning a reference to a `char`.

The nonconstant version is used in statements such as

`S1[4]='x';`

as seen on line 161. This enables direct access to each of the characters in the string. A reference to the character is returned so that the calling function can manipulate it.

The constant version is used when a constant `String` object is being accessed, such as in the implementation of the copy constructor starting on line 63. Note that `rhs[i]` is accessed, yet `rhs` is declared as a `const String &`. It isn't legal to access this object by using a nonconstant member function. Therefore, the offset operator must be overloaded with a constant accessor. If the object being returned were large, you might want to declare the return value to be a constant reference. However, because a `char` is only one byte, there would be no point in doing that.

The default constructor is implemented on lines 34–39. It creates a string whose length is 0. It is the convention of this `String` class to report its length not counting the terminating null. This default string contains only a terminating null.

The copy constructor is implemented on lines 63–70. This constructor sets the new string's length to that of the existing string—plus one for the terminating null. It copies each character from the existing string to the new string, and it null-terminates the new string. Remember that, unlike assignment operators, copy constructors do not need to test if the string being copied into this new object is itself—that can never happen.

Stepping back, you see in lines 53–60 the implementation of the constructor that takes an existing C-style string. This constructor is similar to the copy constructor. The length of

13

the existing string is established by a call to the standard `String` library function `strlen()`.

On line 28, another constructor, `String(unsigned short)`, is declared to be a private member function. It is the intent of the designer of this class that no client class ever create a `String` of arbitrary length. This constructor exists only to help in the internal creation of Strings as required, for example, by `operator+=`, on line 131. This is discussed in depth when `operator+=` is described later.

On lines 44–50, you can see that the `String(unsigned short)` constructor fills every member of its array with a null character (`'\0'`). Therefore, the `for` loop checks for `i<=len` rather than `i<len`.

The destructor, implemented on lines 73–77, deletes the character string maintained by the class. Be certain to include the brackets in the call to the `delete` operator so that every member of the array is deleted, instead of only the first.

The assignment operator is overloaded on lines 81–92. This method first checks to see whether the right-hand side of the assignment is the same as the left-hand side. If it isn't, the current string is deleted, and the new string is created and copied into place. A reference is returned to facilitate stacked assignments such as

```
String1 = String2 = String3;
```

Another overloaded operator is the offset operator. This operator is overloaded twice, first on lines 97–103 and again on lines 107–113. Rudimentary bounds checking is performed both times. If the user attempts to access a character at a location beyond the end of the array, the last character—that is, `len-1`—is returned.

Lines 117–127 implement the overloading of the operator plus (+) as a concatenation operator. It is convenient to be able to write

```
String3 = String1 + String2;
```

and have `String3` be the concatenation of the other two strings. To accomplish this, the operator plus function computes the combined length of the two strings and creates a temporary string `temp`. This invokes the private constructor, which takes an integer, and creates a string filled with nulls. The nulls are then replaced by the contents of the two strings. The left-hand side string (`*this`) is copied first, followed by the right-hand side string (`rhs`). The first `for` loop counts through the string on the left-hand side and adds each character to the new string. The second `for` loop counts through the right-hand side. Note that `i` continues to count the place for the new string, even as `j` counts into the `rhs` string.

On line 127, operator plus returns the string, temp, by value, which is assigned to the string on the left-hand side of the assignment (string1). On lines 131–143, operator += operates on the existing string—that is, the left-hand side of the statement string1 += string2. It works the same as operator plus, except that the temporary value, temp, is assigned to the current string (*this = temp) on line 142.

The main() function (lines 145–175) acts as a test driver program for this class. Line 147 creates a String object by using the constructor that takes a null-terminated C-style string. Line 148 prints its contents by using the accessor function GetString(). Line 150 creates a second C-style string, which is assigned on line 151 to the original string, s1. Line 152 prints the result of this assignment, thus showing that the overloading of the assignment operator truly does work.

Line 154 creates a third C-style string called tempTwo. Line 155 invokes strcpy() to fill the buffer with the characters ; nice to be here! Line 156 invokes the overloaded operator += in order to concatenate tempTwo onto the existing string s1. Line 158 prints the results.

On line 160, the fifth character in s1 is accessed using the overloaded offset operator. This value is printed. On line 161, a new value of 'x' is assigned to this character within the string. This invokes the nonconstant offset operator ([ ]). Line 162 prints the result, which shows that the actual value has, in fact, been changed.

Line 164 attempts to access a character beyond the end of the array. From the information printed, you can see that the last character of the array is returned, as designed.

Lines 166 and 167 create two more String objects, and line 168 calls the addition operator. Line 169 prints the results.

Line 171 creates a new String object, s4. Line 172 uses the overloaded assignment operator to assign a literal C-style string to s4. Line 173 prints the results. You might be thinking, "The assignment operator is defined to take a constant String reference on line 21, but here the program passes in a C-style string. Why is this legal?"

The answer is that the compiler expects a String, but it is given a character array. Therefore, it checks whether it can create a String from what it is given. On line 12, you declared a constructor that creates Strings from character arrays. The compiler creates a temporary String from the character array and passes it to the assignment operator. This is known as implicit casting, or promotion. If you had not declared—and provided the implementation for—the constructor that takes a character array, this assignment would have generated a compiler error.

13

In looking through Listing 13.14, you see that the String class that you've built is beginning to become pretty robust. You'll also realize that it is a longer listing than what you've seen. Fortunately, the Standard C++ Library provides an even more robust String class that you'll be able to use by including the <string> library.

Linked Lists and Other Structures

Arrays are much like Tupperware. They are great containers, but they are of a fixed size. If you pick a container that is too large, you waste space in your storage area. If you pick one that is too small, its contents spill all over and you have a big mess.

One way to solve this problem is shown in Listing 13.9. However, when you start using large arrays or when you want to move, delete, or insert entries in the array, the number of allocations and deallocations can be expensive.

One way to solve such a problem is with a linked list. A linked list is a data structure that consists of small containers that are designed to link together as needed. The idea is to write a class that holds one object of your data—such as one Cat or one Rectangle—and that can point at the next container. You create one container for each object that you need to store, and you chain them together as needed.

Linked lists are considered an advanced level topic. More information can be found on them in Appendix E, "A Look at Linked Lists."

Creating Array Classes

Writing your own array class has many advantages over using the built-in arrays. For starters, you can prevent array overruns. You might also consider making your array class dynamically sized: At creation, it might have only one member, growing as needed during the course of the program.

You might also want to sort or otherwise order the members of the array. You might have a need for one or more of these powerful array variants:

- **Ordered collection**—Each member is in sorted order.
- **Set**—No member appears more than once.
- **Dictionary**—This uses matched pairs in which one value acts as a key to retrieve the other value.
- **Sparse array**—Indices are permitted for a large set, but only those values actually added to the array consume memory. Thus, you can ask for SparseArray[5] or SparseArray[200], but it is possible that memory is allocated only for a small number of entries.

• **Bag**—An unordered collection that is added to and retrieved in indeterminate order.

By overloading the index operator ([ ]), you can turn a linked list into an ordered collection. By excluding duplicates, you can turn a collection into a set. If each object in the list has a pair of matched values, you can use a linked list to build a dictionary or a sparse array.

> **NOTE**
>
> Writing your own array class has many advantages over using the built-in arrays. Using the Standard Library implementations of similar classes usually has advantages over writing your own classes.

Summary

Today, you learned how to create arrays in C++. An array is a fixed-size collection of objects that are all the same type.

Arrays don't do bounds checking. Therefore, it is legal—even if disastrous—to read or write past the end of an array. Arrays count from 0. A common mistake is to write to offset *n* of an array of *n* members.

Arrays can be one dimensional or multidimensional. In either case, the members of the array can be initialized, as long as the array contains either built-in types, such as int, or objects of a class that has a default constructor.

Arrays and their contents can be on the free store or on the stack. If you delete an array on the free store, remember to use the brackets in the call to delete.

Array names are constant pointers to the first elements of the array. Pointers and arrays use pointer arithmetic to find the next element of an array.

Strings are arrays of characters, or chars. C++ provides special features for managing char arrays, including the capability to initialize them with quoted strings.

13

Q&A

Q **What is in an uninitialized array element?**

A Whatever happens to be in memory at a given time. The results of using an uninitialized array member without assigning a value can be unpredictable. If the compiler is following the C++ standards, array elements that are static, nonlocal objects will be zero initialized.

Q Can I combine arrays?

A Yes. With simple arrays, you can use pointers to combine them into a new, larger array. With strings, you can use some of the built-in functions, such as `strcat`, to combine strings.

Q Why should I create a linked list if an array will work?

A An array must have a fixed size, whereas a linked list can be sized dynamically at runtime. Appendix E provides more information on creating linked lists.

Q Why would I ever use built-in arrays if I can make a better array class?

A Built-in arrays are quick and easy to use, and you generally need them to build your better array class.

Q Is there a better construct to use than arrays?

A On Day 19, "Templates," you learn about templates as well as the Standard Template Library. This library contains templates for arrays that contain all the functionality you will generally need. Using these templates is a safer alternative to building your own.

Q Must a string class use a `char *` to hold the contents of the string?

A No. It can use any memory storage the designer thinks is best.

Workshop

The Workshop provides quiz questions to help you solidify your understanding of the material covered and exercises to provide you with experience in using what you've learned. Try to answer the quiz and exercise questions before checking the answers in Appendix D, and be certain you understand the answers before continuing to tomorrow's lesson.

Quiz

1. What are the first and last elements in `SomeArray[25]`?
2. How do you declare a multidimensional array?
3. Initialize the members of an array declared as `SomeArray[2][3][2]`.
4. How many elements are in the array `SomeArray[10][5][20]`?
5. How does a linked list differ from an array?
6. How many characters are stored in the string "Jesse knows C++"?
7. What is the last character in the string "Brad is a nice guy"?

Exercises

1. Declare a two-dimensional array that represents a tic-tac-toe game board.

2. Write the code that initializes all the elements in the array you created in Exercise 1 to the value 0.

3. Write a program that contains four arrays. Three of the arrays should contain your first name, middle initial, and last name. Use the string-copying function presented in today's lesson to copy these strings together into the fourth array, full name.

4. **BUG BUSTERS:** What is wrong with this code fragment?

```
unsigned short SomeArray[5][4];
for (int i = 0; i<4; i++)
    for (int j = 0; j<5; j++)
        SomeArray[i][j] = i+j;
```

5. **BUG BUSTERS:** What is wrong with this code fragment?

```
unsigned short SomeArray[5][4];
for (int i = 0; i<=5; i++)
    for (int j = 0; j<=4; j++)
        SomeArray[i][j] = 0;
```

13

DAY 14

Polymorphism

On Day 12, "Implementing Inheritance," you learned how to write virtual functions in derived classes. This is the fundamental building block of polymorphism: the capability to bind specific, derived class objects to base class pointers at runtime.

Today, you will learn

- What multiple inheritance is and how to use it
- What virtual inheritance is and when to use it
- What abstract classes are and when to use them
- What pure virtual functions are

Problems with Single Inheritance

Suppose you've been working with your animal classes for a while, and you've divided the class hierarchy into Birds and Mammals. The Bird class includes the member function Fly(). The Mammal class has been divided into a number of types of Mammals, including Horse. The Horse class includes the member functions Whinny() and Gallop().

Suddenly, you realize you need a Pegasus object: a cross between a Horse and a Bird. A Pegasus can Fly(), it can Whinny(), and it can Gallop(). With single inheritance, you're in quite a jam.

With single inheritance, you can only pull from one of these existing classes. You can make Pegasus a Bird, but then it won't be able to Whinny() or Gallop(). You can make it a Horse, but then it won't be able to Fly().

Your first solution is to copy the Fly() method into the Pegasus class and derive Pegasus from Horse. This works fine, at the cost of having the Fly() method in two places (Bird and Pegasus). If you change one, you must remember to change the other. Of course, a developer who comes along months or years later to maintain your code must also know to fix both places.

Soon, however, you have a new problem. You want to create a list of Horse objects and a list of Bird objects. You'd like to be able to add your Pegasus objects to either list, but if a Pegasus is a Horse, you can't add it to a list of Birds.

You have a couple of potential solutions. You can rename the Horse method Gallop() to Move(), and then override Move() in your Pegasus object to do the work of Fly(). You would then override Move() in your other horses to do the work of Gallop(). Perhaps Pegasus could be clever enough to gallop short distances and fly longer distances.

```
Pegasus::Move(long distance)
{
   if (distance > veryFar)
      fly(distance);
   else
      gallop(distance);
}
```

This is a bit limiting. Perhaps one day Pegasus will want to fly a short distance or gallop a long distance. Your next solution might be to move Fly() up into Horse, as illustrated in Listing 14.1. The problem is that most horses can't fly, so you have to make this method do nothing unless it is a Pegasus.

LISTING 14.1   If Horses Could Fly...

```
0:  // Listing 14.1. If horses could fly...
1:  // Percolating Fly() up into Horse
2:
3:  #include <iostream>
4:  using namespace std;
5:
6:  class Horse
7:  {
8:     public:
```

LISTING 14.1 continued

```
 9:         void Gallop(){ cout << "Galloping...\n"; }
10:         virtual void Fly() { cout << "Horses can't fly.\n" ; }
11:     private:
12:         int itsAge;
13:     };
14:
15:     class Pegasus : public Horse
16:     {
17:       public:
18:         virtual void Fly()
19:             {cout<<"I can fly! I can fly! I can fly!\n";}
20:     };
21:
22:     const int NumberHorses = 5;
23:     int main()
24:     {
25:         Horse* Ranch[NumberHorses];
26:         Horse* pHorse;
27:         int choice,i;
28:         for (i=0; i<NumberHorses; i++)
29:         {
30:             cout << "(1)Horse (2)Pegasus: ";
31:             cin >> choice;
32:             if (choice == 2)
33:                 pHorse = new Pegasus;
34:             else
35:                 pHorse = new Horse;
36:             Ranch[i] = pHorse;
37:         }
38:         cout << endl;
39:         for (i=0; i<NumberHorses; i++)
40:         {
41:             Ranch[i]->Fly();
42:             delete Ranch[i];
43:         }
44:         return 0;
45:     }
```

OUTPUT
```
(1)Horse (2)Pegasus: 1
(1)Horse (2)Pegasus: 2
(1)Horse (2)Pegasus: 1
(1)Horse (2)Pegasus: 2
(1)Horse (2)Pegasus: 1

Horses can't fly.
I can fly! I can fly! I can fly!
Horses can't fly.
I can fly! I can fly! I can fly!
Horses can't fly.
```

14

ANALYSIS This program certainly works, although at the expense of the Horse class having a Fly() method. On line 10, the method Fly() is provided to Horse. In a real-world class, you might have it issue an error, or fail quietly. On line 18, the Pegasus class overrides the Fly() method to "do the right thing," represented here by printing a happy message.

The array of Horse pointers called Ranch on line 25 is used to demonstrate that the correct Fly() method is called, based on the runtime binding of the Horse or Pegasus object.

In lines 28–37, the user is prompted to select a Horse or a Pegasus. An object of the corresponding type is then created and placed into the Ranch array.

In lines 38–43, the program loops again through the Ranch array. This time, each object in the array has its Fly() method called. Depending on whether the object is a Horse or a Pegasus, the correct Fly() method is called. You can see this in the output. Because this program will no longer use the objects in Ranch, in line 42 a call to delete is made to free the memory used by each object.

NOTE
These examples have been stripped down to their bare essentials to illustrate the points under consideration. Constructors, virtual destructors, and so on have been removed to keep the code simple. This is not recommended for your programs.

Percolating Upward

Putting the required function higher in the class hierarchy is a common solution to this problem and results in many functions "percolating up" into the base class. The base class is then in grave danger of becoming a global namespace for all the functions that might be used by any of the derived classes. This can seriously undermine the class typing of C++, and can create a large and cumbersome base class.

In general, you want to percolate shared functionality up the hierarchy, without migrating the interface of each class. This means that if two classes that share a common base class (for example, Horse and Bird both share Animal) and have a function in common (both birds and horses eat, for example), you'll want to move that functionality up into the base class and create a virtual function.

What you'll want to avoid, however, is percolating a function (such as Fly) up where it doesn't belong just so you can call that function only on some derived classes, when it doesn't fit the meaning of that base class.

Casting Down

An alternative to this approach, still within single inheritance, is to keep the `Fly()` method within `Pegasus` and only call it if the pointer is actually pointing to a `Pegasus` object. To make this work, you need to be able to ask your pointer what type it is really pointing to. This is known as Run Time Type Identification (RTTI).

Because RTTI is a newer feature of the C++ specification, not all compilers support it. If your compiler does not support RTTI, you can mimic it by putting a method that returns an enumerated type in each of the classes. You can then test that type at runtime and call `Fly()` if it returns `Pegasus`.

CAUTION

> Beware of using RTTI in your programs. Needing to use it might be an indication of poor inheritance hierarchy design. Consider using virtual functions, templates, or multiple inheritance instead.

In the previous example, you declared both `Horse` and `Pegasus` objects and placed them in an array of `Horse` objects. Everything was placed as a `Horse`. With RTTI, you would check each of these `Horses` to see if it was just a horse or if indeed a `Pegasus` had actually been created.

To call `Fly()`, however, you must cast the pointer, telling it that the object it is pointing to is a `Pegasus` object, not a `Horse`. This is called casting down because you are casting the `Horse` object down to a more derived type.

C++ now officially, though perhaps reluctantly, supports casting down using the new `dynamic_cast` operator. Here's how it works.

If you have a pointer to a base class such as `Horse`, and you assign to it a pointer to a derived class, such as `Pegasus`, you can use the `Horse` pointer polymorphically. If you then need to get at the `Pegasus` object, you create a `Pegasus` pointer and use the `dynamic_cast` operator to make the conversion.

At runtime, the base pointer is examined. If the conversion is proper, your new `Pegasus` pointer is fine. If the conversion is improper, if you didn't really have a `Pegasus` object after all, then your new pointer is null. Listing 14.2 illustrates this point.

LISTING 14.2 Casting Down

```
0:  // Listing 14.2 Using dynamic_cast.
1:  // Using rtti
2:
```

14

LISTING 14.2   continued

```
3:  #include <iostream>
4:  using namespace std;
5:
6:  enum TYPE { HORSE, PEGASUS };
7:
8:  class Horse
9:  {
10:    public:
11:       virtual void Gallop(){ cout << "Galloping...\n"; }
12:
13:    private:
14:       int itsAge;
15:  };
16:
17:  class Pegasus : public Horse
18:  {
19:    public:
20:       virtual void Fly()
21:          {cout<<"I can fly! I can fly! I can fly!\n";}
22:  };
23:
24:  const int NumberHorses = 5;
25:  int main()
26:  {
27:     Horse* Ranch[NumberHorses];
28:     Horse* pHorse;
29:     int choice,i;
30:     for (i=0; i<NumberHorses; i++)
31:     {
32:        cout << "(1)Horse (2)Pegasus: ";
33:        cin >> choice;
34:        if (choice == 2)
35:           pHorse = new Pegasus;
36:        else
37:           pHorse = new Horse;
38:        Ranch[i] = pHorse;
39:     }
40:     cout << endl;
41:     for (i=0; i<NumberHorses; i++)
42:     {
43:        Pegasus *pPeg = dynamic_cast< Pegasus *> (Ranch[i]);
44:        if (pPeg != NULL)
45:           pPeg->Fly();
46:        else
47:           cout << "Just a horse\n";
48:
49:        delete Ranch[i];
50:     }
51:     return 0;
52:  }
```

OUTPUT
```
(1)Horse (2)Pegasus: 1
(1)Horse (2)Pegasus: 2
(1)Horse (2)Pegasus: 1
(1)Horse (2)Pegasus: 2
(1)Horse (2)Pegasus: 1

Just a horse
I can fly! I can fly! I can fly!
Just a horse
I can fly! I can fly! I can fly!
Just a horse
```

FAQ

When compiling, I got a warning from Microsoft Visual C++: "warning C4541: 'dynamic_cast' used on polymorphic type 'class Horse' with /GR-; unpredictable behavior may result." What should I do? When running this program, I get a message:

"This application has requested the Runtime to terminate it in an unusual way. Please contact the application's support team for more information."

Answer: These are some of this compiler's most confusing error messages. To fix these, do the following:

1. In your project, choose Project, Settings.

2. Go to the C++ tab.

3. Change the drop-down to C++ Language.

4. Click Enable Runtime Type Information (RTTI).

5. Rebuild your entire project.

Alternatively, if you are using the command-line compiler for Visual C++, add the /GR flag:

```
cl /GR List1402.cpp
```

ANALYSIS   This solution also works; however, it is not recommended.

The desired results are achieved. Fly() is kept out of Horse, and it is not called on Horse objects. When it is called on Pegasus objects (line 45), however, the objects must be explicitly cast (line 43); Horse objects don't have the method Fly(), so the pointer must be told it is pointing to a Pegasus object before being used.

The need for you to cast the Pegasus object is a warning that something might be wrong with your design. This program effectively undermines the virtual function polymorphism because it depends on casting the object to its real runtime type.

14

Adding to Two Lists

The other problem with these solutions is that you've declared Pegasus to be a type of Horse, so you cannot add a Pegasus object to a list of Birds. You've paid the price of either moving Fly() up into Horse or casting down the pointer, and yet you still don't have the full functionality you need.

One final, single inheritance solution presents itself. You can push Fly(), Whinny(), and Gallop() all up into a common base class of both Bird and Horse: Animal. Now, instead of having a list of Birds and a list of Horses, you can have one unified list of Animals. This works, but eventually leads to a base class that has all of the characteristics of all of its descendant classes. So who needs descendant classes then?

Alternatively, you can leave the methods where they are and cast down Horses and Birds and Pegasus objects, but that is even worse!

Do	Don't
DO move functionality up the inheritance hierarchy when it is conceptually cohesive with the meaning of the ancestor class.	DON'T clutter ancestor classes with capabilities that are only added to support a need for polymorphism in descendant classes.
DO avoid performing actions based on the runtime type of the object—use virtual methods, templates, and multiple inheritance.	DON'T cast pointers to base objects down to derived objects.

Multiple Inheritance

It is possible to derive a new class from more than one base class. This is called multiple inheritance. To derive from more than the base class, you separate each base class by commas in the class designation, as shown here:

```
class DerivedClass : public BaseClass1, public BaseClass2 {}
```

This is exactly like declaring single inheritance with an additional base class, BaseClass2, added.

Listing 14.3 illustrates how to declare Pegasus so that it derives from both Horses and Birds. The program then adds Pegasus objects to both types of lists.

LISTING 14.3   Multiple Inheritance

```
0:   // Listing 14.3. Multiple inheritance.
1:
2:   #include <iostream>
3:   using std::cout;
4:   using std::cin;
5:   using std::endl;
6:
7:   class Horse
8:   {
9:     public:
10:        Horse() { cout << "Horse constructor... "; }
11:        virtual ~Horse() { cout << "Horse destructor... "; }
12:        virtual void Whinny() const { cout << "Whinny!... "; }
13:     private:
14:        int itsAge;
15:   };
16:
17:   class Bird
18:   {
19:     public:
20:        Bird() { cout << "Bird constructor... "; }
21:        virtual ~Bird() { cout << "Bird destructor... "; }
22:        virtual void Chirp() const { cout << "Chirp... ";  }
23:        virtual void Fly() const
24:        {
25:           cout << "I can fly! I can fly! I can fly! ";
26:        }
27:     private:
28:        int itsWeight;
29:   };
30:
31:   class Pegasus : public Horse, public Bird
32:   {
33:     public:
34:        void Chirp() const { Whinny(); }
35:        Pegasus() { cout << "Pegasus constructor... "; }
36:        ~Pegasus() { cout << "Pegasus destructor...  "; }
37:   };
38:
39:   const int MagicNumber = 2;
40:   int main()
41:   {
42:      Horse* Ranch[MagicNumber];
43:      Bird* Aviary[MagicNumber];
44:      Horse * pHorse;
45:      Bird * pBird;
46:      int choice,i;
47:      for (i=0; i<MagicNumber; i++)
```

14

LISTING **14.3**   continued

```
48:       {
49:          cout << "\n(1)Horse (2)Pegasus: ";
50:          cin >> choice;
51:          if (choice == 2)
52:             pHorse = new Pegasus;
53:          else
54:             pHorse = new Horse;
55:          Ranch[i] = pHorse;
56:       }
57:       for (i=0; i<MagicNumber; i++)
58:       {
59:          cout << "\n(1)Bird (2)Pegasus: ";
60:          cin >> choice;
61:          if (choice == 2)
62:             pBird = new Pegasus;
63:          else
64:             pBird = new Bird;
65:          Aviary[i] = pBird;
66:       }
67:
68:       cout << endl;
69:       for (i=0; i<MagicNumber; i++)
70:       {
71:          cout << "\nRanch[" << i << "]: " ;
72:          Ranch[i]->Whinny();
73:          delete Ranch[i];
74:       }
75:
76:       for (i=0; i<MagicNumber; i++)
77:       {
78:          cout << "\nAviary[" << i << "]: " ;
79:          Aviary[i]->Chirp();
80:          Aviary[i]->Fly();
81:          delete Aviary[i];
82:       }
83:       return 0;
84:   }
```

OUTPUT

```
(1)Horse (2)Pegasus: 1
Horse constructor...
(1)Horse (2)Pegasus: 2
Horse constructor... Bird constructor... Pegasus constructor...
(1)Bird (2)Pegasus: 1
Bird constructor...
(1)Bird (2)Pegasus: 2
Horse constructor... Bird constructor... Pegasus constructor...
```

```
Ranch[0]: Whinny!... Horse destructor...
Ranch[1]: Whinny!... Pegasus destructor...  Bird destructor...
Horse destructor...
Aviary[0]: Chirp... I can fly! I can fly! I can fly! Bird destructor...
Aviary[1]: Whinny!... I can fly! I can fly! I can fly!
Pegasus destructor... Bird destructor... Horse destructor...
```

ANALYSIS On lines 7–15, a Horse class is declared. The constructor and destructor print out a message, and the Whinny() method prints Whinny!....

On lines 17–29, a Bird class is declared. In addition to its constructor and destructor, this class has two methods: Chirp() and Fly(), both of which print identifying messages. In a real program, these might, for example, activate the speaker or generate animated images.

Finally, on lines 31–37, you see the new code—using multiple inheritance, the class Pegasus is declared. In line 31, you can see that this class is derived from both Horse and Bird. The Pegasus class overrides the Chirp() method in line 34. The Pegasus' Chirp() method simply does a call to the Whinny() method, which it inherits from Horse.

In the main section of this program, two lists are created: a Ranch with pointers to Horse objects on line 42, and an Aviary with pointers to Bird objects on line 43. On lines 47–56, Horse and Pegasus objects are added to the Ranch. On lines 57–66, Bird and Pegasus objects are added to the Aviary.

Invocations of the virtual methods on both the Bird pointers and the Horse pointers do the right things for Pegasus objects. For example, on line 79 the members of the Aviary array are used to call Chirp() on the objects to which they point. The Bird class declares this to be a virtual method, so the right function is called for each object.

Note that each time a Pegasus object is created, the output reflects that both the Bird part and the Horse part of the Pegasus object are also created. When a Pegasus object is destroyed, the Bird and Horse parts are destroyed as well, thanks to the destructors being made virtual.

Declaring Multiple Inheritance

Declare an object to inherit from more than one class by listing the base classes following the colon after the class name. Separate the base classes by commas.

Example 1

```
class Pegasus : public Horse, public Bird
```

Example 2

```
class Schnoodle : public Schnauzer, public Poodle
```

14

The Parts of a Multiply Inherited Object

When the `Pegasus` object is created in memory, both the base classes form part of the `Pegasus` object, as illustrated in Figure 14.1. This figure represents an entire `Pegasus` object. This includes the new features added in the `Pegasus` class and the features picked up from the base classes.

FIGURE 14.1

Multiply inherited objects.

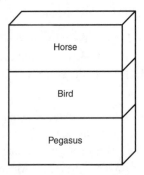

Several issues arise with objects with multiple base classes. For example, what happens if two base classes that happen to have the same name have virtual functions or data? How are multiple base class constructors initialized? What happens if multiple base classes both derive from the same class? The next sections answer these questions and explore how multiple inheritance can be put to work.

Constructors in Multiply Inherited Objects

If `Pegasus` derives from both `Horse` and `Bird`, and each of the base classes has constructors that take parameters, the `Pegasus` class initializes these constructors in turn. Listing 14.4 illustrates how this is done.

LISTING 14.4 Calling Multiple Constructors

```
0:  // Listing 14.4
1:  // Calling multiple constructors
2:
3:  #include <iostream>
4:  using namespace std;
5:
6:  typedef int HANDS;
7:  enum COLOR { Red, Green, Blue, Yellow, White, Black, Brown } ;
8:
9:  class Horse
10: {
11:    public:
```

LISTING 14.4 continued

```
12:     Horse(COLOR color, HANDS height);
13:     virtual ~Horse() { cout << "Horse destructor...\n"; }
14:     virtual void Whinny()const { cout << "Whinny!... "; }
15:     virtual HANDS GetHeight() const { return itsHeight; }
16:     virtual COLOR GetColor() const { return itsColor; }
17:   private:
18:     HANDS itsHeight;
19:     COLOR itsColor;
20: };
21:
22: Horse::Horse(COLOR color, HANDS height):
23: itsColor(color),itsHeight(height)
24: {
25:    cout << "Horse constructor...\n";
26: }
27:
28: class Bird
29: {
30:   public:
31:     Bird(COLOR color, bool migrates);
32:     virtual ~Bird() {cout << "Bird destructor...\n";  }
33:     virtual void Chirp()const { cout << "Chirp... ";  }
34:     virtual void Fly()const
35:     {
36:       cout << "I can fly! I can fly! I can fly! ";
37:     }
38:     virtual COLOR GetColor()const { return itsColor; }
39:     virtual bool GetMigration() const { return itsMigration; }
40:
41:   private:
42:     COLOR itsColor;
43:     bool itsMigration;
44: };
45:
46: Bird::Bird(COLOR color, bool migrates):
47: itsColor(color), itsMigration(migrates)
48: {
49:    cout << "Bird constructor...\n";
50: }
51:
52: class Pegasus : public Horse, public Bird
53: {
54:   public:
55:     void Chirp()const { Whinny(); }
56:     Pegasus(COLOR, HANDS, bool,long);
57:     ~Pegasus() {cout << "Pegasus destructor...\n";}
58:     virtual long GetNumberBelievers() const
59:     {
```

14

LISTING 14.4 continued

```
60:         return itsNumberBelievers;
61:       }
62:
63:   private:
64:      long itsNumberBelievers;
65: };
66:
67: Pegasus::Pegasus(
68:     COLOR aColor,
69:     HANDS height,
70:     bool migrates,
71:     long NumBelieve):
72:     Horse(aColor, height),
73:     Bird(aColor, migrates),
74:     itsNumberBelievers(NumBelieve)
75: {
76:     cout << "Pegasus constructor...\n";
77: }
78:
79: int main()
80: {
81:     Pegasus *pPeg = new Pegasus(Red, 5, true, 10);
82:     pPeg->Fly();
83:     pPeg->Whinny();
84:     cout << "\nYour Pegasus is " << pPeg->GetHeight();
85:     cout << " hands tall and ";
86:     if (pPeg->GetMigration())
87:        cout << "it does migrate.";
88:     else
89:        cout << "it does not migrate.";
90:     cout << "\nA total of " << pPeg->GetNumberBelievers();
91:     cout << " people believe it exists." << endl;
92:     delete pPeg;
93:     return 0;
94: }
```

OUTPUT

```
Horse constructor...
Bird constructor...
Pegasus constructor...
I can fly! I can fly! I can fly! Whinny!...
Your Pegasus is 5 hands tall and it does migrate.
A total of 10 people believe it exists.
Pegasus destructor...
Bird destructor...
Horse destructor...
```

ANALYSIS On lines 9–20, the Horse class is declared. The constructor takes two parameters: One is an enumeration for colors, which is declared on line 7, and the other is a typedef declared on line 6. The implementation of the constructor on lines 22–26 simply initializes the member variables and prints a message.

On lines 28–44, the Bird class is declared, and the implementation of its constructor is on lines 46–50. Again, the Bird class takes two parameters. Interestingly, the Horse constructor takes color (so that you can detect horses of different colors), and the Bird constructor takes the color of the feathers (so those of one feather can stick together). This leads to a problem when you want to ask the Pegasus for its color, which you'll see in the next example.

The Pegasus class itself is declared on lines 52–65, and its constructor is on lines 67–77. The initialization of the Pegasus object includes three statements. First, the Horse constructor is initialized with color and height (line 72). Then, the Bird constructor is initialized with color and the Boolean indicating if it migrates (line 73). Finally, the Pegasus member variable itsNumberBelievers is initialized. After all that is accomplished, the body of the Pegasus constructor is called.

In the main() function, a Pegasus pointer is created in line 81. This object is then used to access the member functions that were derived from the base classes. The access of these methods is straightforward.

Ambiguity Resolution

In Listing 14.4, both the Horse class and the Bird class have a method GetColor(). You'll notice that these methods were not called in Listing 14.4! You might need to ask the Pegasus object to return its color, but you have a problem—the Pegasus class inherits from both Bird and Horse. They both have a color, and their methods for getting that color have the same names and signature. This creates an ambiguity for the compiler, which you must resolve.

If you simply write

```
COLOR currentColor = pPeg->GetColor();
```

you receive a compiler error:

```
Member is ambiguous: 'Horse::GetColor' and 'Bird::GetColor'
```

You can resolve the ambiguity with an explicit call to the function you want to invoke:

```
COLOR currentColor = pPeg->Horse::GetColor();
```

14

Any time you need to resolve which class a member function or member data inherits from, you can fully qualify the call by prepending the class name to the base class data or function.

Note that if Pegasus were to override this function, the problem would be moved, as it should be, into the Pegasus member function:

```
virtual COLOR GetColor()const { return Horse::GetColor(); }
```

This hides the problem from clients of the Pegasus class and encapsulates within Pegasus the knowledge of which base class from which it wants to inherit its color. A client is still free to force the issue by writing

```
COLOR currentColor = pPeg->Bird::GetColor();
```

Inheriting from Shared Base Class

What happens if both Bird and Horse inherit from a common base class, such as Animal? Figure 14.2 illustrates what this looks like.

FIGURE **14.2**

Common base classes.

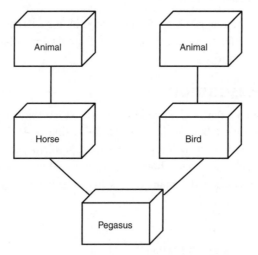

As you can see in Figure 14.2, two base class objects exist. When a function or data member is called in the shared base class, another ambiguity exists. For example, if Animal declares itsAge as a member variable and GetAge() as a member function, and you call pPeg->GetAge(), did you mean to call the GetAge() function you inherit from Animal by way of Horse, or by way of Bird? You must resolve this ambiguity as well, as illustrated in Listing 14.5.

LISTING 14.5 Common Base Classes

```
0:  // Listing 14.5
1:  // Common base classes
2:
3:  #include <iostream>
4:  using namespace std;
5:
6:  typedef int HANDS;
7:  enum COLOR { Red, Green, Blue, Yellow, White, Black, Brown } ;
8:
9:  class Animal          // common base to both horse and bird
10: {
11:   public:
12:     Animal(int);
13:     virtual ~Animal() { cout << "Animal destructor...\n"; }
14:     virtual int GetAge() const { return itsAge; }
15:     virtual void SetAge(int age) { itsAge = age; }
16:   private:
17:     int itsAge;
18: };
19:
20: Animal::Animal(int age):
21: itsAge(age)
22: {
23:    cout << "Animal constructor...\n";
24: }
25:
26: class Horse : public Animal
27: {
28:   public:
29:     Horse(COLOR color, HANDS height, int age);
30:     virtual ~Horse() { cout << "Horse destructor...\n"; }
31:     virtual void Whinny()const { cout << "Whinny!... "; }
32:     virtual HANDS GetHeight() const { return itsHeight; }
33:     virtual COLOR GetColor() const { return itsColor; }
34:   protected:
35:     HANDS itsHeight;
36:     COLOR itsColor;
37: };
38:
39: Horse::Horse(COLOR color, HANDS height, int age):
40: Animal(age),
41: itsColor(color),itsHeight(height)
42: {
43:    cout << "Horse constructor...\n";
44: }
45:
46: class Bird : public Animal
47: {
48:   public:
```

14

LISTING 14.5 continued

```
49:        Bird(COLOR color, bool migrates, int age);
50:        virtual ~Bird() {cout << "Bird destructor...\n";  }
51:        virtual void Chirp()const { cout << "Chirp... ";  }
52:        virtual void Fly()const
53:                { cout << "I can fly! I can fly! I can fly! "; }
54:        virtual COLOR GetColor()const { return itsColor; }
55:        virtual bool GetMigration() const { return itsMigration; }
56:     protected:
57:        COLOR itsColor;
58:        bool itsMigration;
59:     };
60:
61:     Bird::Bird(COLOR color, bool migrates, int age):
62:     Animal(age),
63:     itsColor(color), itsMigration(migrates)
64:     {
65:        cout << "Bird constructor...\n";
66:     }
67:
68:     class Pegasus : public Horse, public Bird
69:     {
70:       public:
71:         void Chirp()const { Whinny(); }
72:         Pegasus(COLOR, HANDS, bool, long, int);
73:         virtual ~Pegasus() {cout << "Pegasus destructor...\n";}
74:         virtual long GetNumberBelievers() const
75:         { return  itsNumberBelievers; }
76:         virtual COLOR GetColor()const { return Horse::itsColor; }
77:         virtual int GetAge() const { return Horse::GetAge(); }
78:       private:
79:         long itsNumberBelievers;
80:     };
81:
82:     Pegasus::Pegasus(
83:        COLOR aColor,
84:        HANDS height,
85:        bool migrates,
86:        long NumBelieve,
87:        int age):
88:        Horse(aColor, height,age),
89:        Bird(aColor, migrates,age),
90:        itsNumberBelievers(NumBelieve)
91:     {
92:        cout << "Pegasus constructor...\n";
93:     }
94:
95:     int main()
96:     {
97:        Pegasus *pPeg = new Pegasus(Red, 5, true, 10, 2);
```

LISTING 14.5 continued

```
98:    int age = pPeg->GetAge();
99:    cout << "This pegasus is " << age << " years old.\n";
100:   delete pPeg;
101:   return 0;
102: }
```

OUTPUT
```
Animal constructor...
Horse constructor...
Animal constructor...
Bird constructor...
Pegasus constructor...
This pegasus is 2 years old.
Pegasus destructor...
Bird destructor...
Animal destructor...
Horse destructor...
Animal destructor...
```

ANALYSIS Several interesting features are in this listing. The Animal class is declared on lines 9–18. Animal adds one member variable, itsAge, and two accessors: GetAge() and SetAge().

On line 26, the Horse class is declared to derive from Animal. The Horse constructor now has a third parameter, age, which it passes to its base class, Animal (see line 40). Note that the Horse class does not override GetAge(), it simply inherits it.

On line 46, the Bird class is declared to derive from Animal. Its constructor also takes an age and uses it to initialize its base class, Animal (see line 62). It also inherits GetAge() without overriding it.

Pegasus inherits from both Bird and Horse in line 68, and so has two Animal classes in its inheritance chain. If you were to call GetAge() on a Pegasus object, you would have to disambiguate, or fully qualify, the method you want if Pegasus did not override the method.

This is solved on line 77 when the Pegasus object overrides GetAge() to do nothing more than to chain up—that is, to call the same method in a base class.

Chaining up is done for two reasons: either to disambiguate which base class to call, as in this case, or to do some work and then let the function in the base class do some more work. At times, you might want to do work and then chain up, or chain up and then do the work when the base class function returns.

The Pegasus constructor, which starts on line 82, takes five parameters: the creature's color, its height (in HANDS), whether it migrates, how many believe in it, and its age.

14

The constructor initializes the Horse part of the Pegasus with the color, height, and age on line 88. It initializes the Bird part with color, whether it migrates, and age on line 89. Finally, it initializes itsNumberBelievers on line 90.

The call to the Horse constructor on line 88 invokes the implementation shown on line 39. The Horse constructor uses the age parameter to initialize the Animal part of the Horse part of the Pegasus. It then goes on to initialize the two member variables of Horse—itsColor and itsHeight.

The call to the Bird constructor on line 89 invokes the implementation shown on line 61. Here, too, the age parameter is used to initialize the Animal part of the Bird.

Note that the color parameter to the Pegasus is used to initialize member variables in each of Bird and Horse. Note also that the age is used to initialize itsAge in the Horse's base Animal and in the Bird's base Animal.

CAUTION

> Keep in mind that whenever you explicitly disambiguate an ancestor class, you create a risk that a new class inserted between your class and its ancestor will cause this class to inadvertently call "past" the new ancestor into the old ancestor, and this can have unexpected effects.

Virtual Inheritance

In Listing 14.5, the Pegasus class went to some lengths to disambiguate which of its Animal base classes it meant to invoke. Most of the time, the decision as to which one to use is arbitrary—after all, the Horse and the Bird have the same base class.

It is possible to tell C++ that you do not want two copies of the shared base class, as shown in Figure 14.2, but rather to have a single shared base class, as shown in Figure 14.3.

You accomplish this by making Animal a virtual base class of both Horse and Bird. The Animal class does not change at all. The Horse and Bird classes change only in their use of the term virtual in their declarations. Pegasus, however, changes substantially.

Normally, a class's constructor initializes only its own variables and its base class. Virtually inherited base classes are an exception, however. They are initialized by their most derived class. Thus, Animal is initialized not by Horse and Bird, but by Pegasus. Horse and Bird have to initialize Animal in their constructors, but these initializations will be ignored when a Pegasus object is created.

FIGURE 14.3

*A diamond
inheritance.*

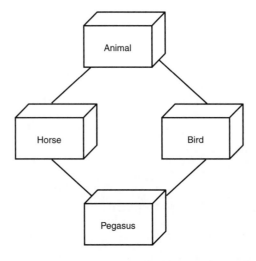

Listing 14.6 rewrites Listing 14.5 to take advantage of virtual derivation.

LISTING 14.6   Illustration of the Use of Virtual Inheritance

```
0:   // Listing 14.6
1:   // Virtual inheritance
2:   #include <iostream>
3:   using namespace std;
4:
5:   typedef int HANDS;
6:   enum COLOR { Red, Green, Blue, Yellow, White, Black, Brown } ;
7:
8:   class Animal        // common base to both horse and bird
9:   {
10:    public:
11:      Animal(int);
12:      virtual ~Animal() { cout << "Animal destructor...\n"; }
13:      virtual int GetAge() const { return itsAge; }
14:      virtual void SetAge(int age) { itsAge = age; }
15:    private:
16:      int itsAge;
17:   };
18:
19:   Animal::Animal(int age):
20:   itsAge(age)
21:   {
22:      cout << "Animal constructor...\n";
23:   }
24:
25:   class Horse : virtual public Animal
```

14

LISTING 14.6 continued

```
26:    {
27:      public:
28:        Horse(COLOR color, HANDS height, int age);
29:        virtual ~Horse() { cout << "Horse destructor...\n"; }
30:        virtual void Whinny()const { cout << "Whinny!... "; }
31:        virtual HANDS GetHeight() const { return itsHeight; }
32:        virtual COLOR GetColor() const { return itsColor; }
33:      protected:
34:        HANDS itsHeight;
35:        COLOR itsColor;
36:    };
37:
38:    Horse::Horse(COLOR color, HANDS height, int age):
39:    Animal(age),
40:    itsColor(color),itsHeight(height)
41:    {
42:        cout << "Horse constructor...\n";
43:    }
44:
45:    class Bird : virtual public Animal
46:    {
47:      public:
48:        Bird(COLOR color, bool migrates, int age);
49:        virtual ~Bird() {cout << "Bird destructor...\n";  }
50:        virtual void Chirp()const { cout << "Chirp... ";  }
51:        virtual void Fly()const
52:                { cout << "I can fly! I can fly! I can fly! "; }
53:        virtual COLOR GetColor()const { return itsColor; }
54:        virtual bool GetMigration() const { return itsMigration; }
55:      protected:
56:        COLOR itsColor;
57:        bool itsMigration;
58:    };
59:
60:    Bird::Bird(COLOR color, bool migrates, int age):
61:    Animal(age),
62:    itsColor(color), itsMigration(migrates)
63:    {
64:        cout << "Bird constructor...\n";
65:    }
66:
67:    class Pegasus : public Horse, public Bird
68:    {
69:      public:
70:        void Chirp()const { Whinny(); }
71:        Pegasus(COLOR, HANDS, bool, long, int);
72:        virtual ~Pegasus() {cout << "Pegasus destructor...\n";}
73:        virtual long GetNumberBelievers() const
74:                { return  itsNumberBelievers; }
```

LISTING 14.6   continued

```
75:        virtual COLOR GetColor()const { return Horse::itsColor; }
76:     private:
77:        long itsNumberBelievers;
78:    };
79:
80:    Pegasus::Pegasus(
81:        COLOR aColor,
82:        HANDS height,
83:        bool migrates,
84:        long NumBelieve,
85:        int age):
86:        Horse(aColor, height,age),
87:        Bird(aColor, migrates,age),
88:        Animal(age*2),
89:        itsNumberBelievers(NumBelieve)
90:    {
91:        cout << "Pegasus constructor...\n";
92:    }
93:
94:    int main()
95:    {
96:        Pegasus *pPeg = new Pegasus(Red, 5, true, 10, 2);
97:        int age = pPeg->GetAge();
98:        cout << "This pegasus is " << age << " years old.\n";
99:        delete pPeg;
100:       return 0;
101: }
```

OUTPUT
```
Animal constructor...
Horse constructor...
Bird constructor...
Pegasus constructor...
This pegasus is 4 years old.
Pegasus destructor...
Bird destructor...
Horse destructor...
Animal destructor...
```

ANALYSIS   On line 25, Horse declares that it inherits virtually from Animal, and on line 45, Bird makes the same declaration. Note that the constructors for both Bird and Animal still initialize the Animal object.

Pegasus inherits from both Bird and Animal, and as the most derived object of Animal, it also initializes Animal. It is Pegasus's initialization which is called, however, and the calls to Animal's constructor in Bird and Horse are ignored. You can see this because the value 2 is passed in, and Horse and Bird pass it along to Animal, but Pegasus doubles it. The result, 4, is reflected in the output generated from line 98.

14

Pegasus no longer has to disambiguate the call to GetAge(), and so is free to simply inherit this function from Animal. Note that Pegasus must still disambiguate the call to GetColor() because this function is in both of its base classes and not in Animal.

Declaring Classes for Virtual Inheritance

To ensure that derived classes have only one instance of common base classes, declare the intermediate classes to inherit virtually from the base class.

Example 1

```
class Horse : virtual public Animal
class Bird : virtual public Animal
class Pegasus : public Horse, public Bird
```

Example 2

```
class Schnauzer : virtual public Dog
class Poodle : virtual public Dog
class Schnoodle : public Schnauzer, public Poodle
```

Problems with Multiple Inheritance

Although multiple inheritance offers several advantages over single inheritance, many C++ programmers are reluctant to use it. The problems they cite are that it makes debugging harder, that evolving multiple inheritance class hierarchies is harder and more risky than evolving single inheritance class hierarchies, and that nearly everything that can be done with multiple inheritance can be done without it. Other languages, such as Java and C#, don't support multiple inheritance of classes for some of these same reasons.

These are valid concerns, and you will want to be on your guard against installing needless complexity into your programs. Some debuggers have a hard time with multiple inheritance, and some designs are needlessly made complex by using multiple inheritance when it is not needed.

Do	Don't
DO use multiple inheritance when a new class needs functions and features from more than one base class.	**DON'T** use multiple inheritance when single inheritance will do.
DO use virtual inheritance when the most derived classes must have only one instance of the shared base class.	
DO initialize the shared base class from the most derived class when using virtual base classes.	

Mixins and Capabilities Classes

One way to strike a middle ground between multiple inheritance and single inheritance is to use what are called mixins. Thus, you might have your Horse class derive from Animal and from Displayable. Displayable would just add a few methods for displaying any object onscreen.

A *mixin*, or capability class, is a class that adds specialized functionality without adding many additional methods or much data.

Capability classes are mixed into a derived class the same as any other class might be, by declaring the derived class to inherit publicly from them. The only difference between a capability class and any other class is that the capability class has little or no data. This is an arbitrary distinction, of course, and is just a shorthand way of noting that at times all you want to do is mix in some additional capabilities without complicating the derived class.

This will, for some debuggers, make it easier to work with mixins than with more complex multiply inherited objects. In addition, less likelihood exists of ambiguity in accessing the data in the other principal base class.

For example, if Horse derives from Animal and from Displayable, Displayable would have no data. Animal would be just as it always was, so all the data in Horse would derive from Animal, but the functions in Horse would derive from both.

NOTE

The term *mixin* comes from an ice cream store in Sommerville, Massachusetts, where candies and cakes were mixed into the basic ice cream flavors. This seemed like a good metaphor to some of the object-oriented programmers who used to take a summer break there, especially while working with the object-oriented programming language SCOOPS.

Abstract Data Types

Often, you will create a hierarchy of classes together. For example, you might create a Shape class, and derive from that Rectangle and Circle. From Rectangle, you might derive Square as a special case of Rectangle.

Each of the derived classes will override the Draw() method, the GetArea() method, and so forth. Listing 14.7 illustrates a bare-bones implementation of the Shape class and its derived Circle and Rectangle classes.

14

LISTING 14.7 Shape Classes

```
0:   //Listing 14.7. Shape classes.
1:
2:   #include <iostream>
3:   using std::cout;
4:   using std::cin;
5:   using std::endl;
6:
7:   class Shape
8:   {
9:     public:
10:       Shape(){}
11:       virtual ~Shape(){}
12:       virtual long GetArea() { return -1; } // error
13:       virtual long GetPerim() { return -1; }
14:       virtual void Draw() {}
15:     private:
16:   };
17:
18:   class Circle : public Shape
19:   {
20:     public:
21:       Circle(int radius):itsRadius(radius){}
22:       ~Circle(){}
23:       long GetArea() { return 3 * itsRadius * itsRadius; }
24:       long GetPerim() { return 6 * itsRadius; }
25:       void Draw();
26:     private:
27:       int itsRadius;
28:       int itsCircumference;
29:   };
30:
31:   void Circle::Draw()
32:   {
33:      cout << "Circle drawing routine here!\n";
34:   }
35:
36:
37:   class Rectangle : public Shape
38:   {
39:     public:
40:       Rectangle(int len, int width):
41:       itsLength(len), itsWidth(width){}
42:       virtual ~Rectangle(){}
43:       virtual long GetArea() { return itsLength * itsWidth; }
44:       virtual long GetPerim() {return 2*itsLength + 2*itsWidth; }
45:       virtual int GetLength() { return itsLength; }
46:       virtual int GetWidth() { return itsWidth; }
47:       virtual void Draw();
48:     private:
```

LISTING 14.7   continued

```
49:        int itsWidth;
50:        int itsLength;
51:    };
52:
53:    void Rectangle::Draw()
54:    {
55:       for (int i = 0; i<itsLength; i++)
56:       {
57:          for (int j = 0; j<itsWidth; j++)
58:             cout << "x ";
59:
60:       cout << "\n";
61:       }
62:    }
63:
64:    class Square : public Rectangle
65:    {
66:      public:
67:         Square(int len);
68:         Square(int len, int width);
69:         ~Square(){}
70:         long GetPerim() {return 4 * GetLength();}
71:    };
72:
73:    Square::Square(int len):
74:    Rectangle(len,len)
75:    {}
76:
77:    Square::Square(int len, int width):
78:    Rectangle(len,width)
79:    {
80:       if (GetLength() != GetWidth())
81:       cout << "Error, not a square... a Rectangle??\n";
82:    }
83:
84:    int main()
85:    {
86:       int choice;
87:       bool fQuit = false;
88:       Shape * sp;
89:
90:       while ( !fQuit )
91:       {
92:          cout << "(1)Circle (2)Rectangle (3)Square (0)Quit: ";
93:          cin >> choice;
94:
95:          switch (choice)
96:          {
97:            case 0:   fQuit = true;
```

14

LISTING 14.7   continued

```
98:                break;
99:            case 1: sp = new Circle(5);
100:               break;
101:           case 2: sp = new Rectangle(4,6);
102:               break;
103:           case 3: sp = new Square(5);
104:               break;
105:          default:
106:             cout <<"Please enter a number between 0 and 3"<<endl;
107:             continue;
108:             break;
109:        }
110:        if( !fQuit )
111:            sp->Draw();
112:        delete sp;
113:        sp = 0;
114:        cout << endl;
115:    }
116:    return 0;
117: }
```

OUTPUT

```
(1)Circle (2)Rectangle (3)Square (0)Quit: 2
x x x x x x
x x x x x x
x x x x x x
x x x x x x

(1)Circle (2)Rectangle (3)Square (0)Quit:3
x x x x x
x x x x x
x x x x x
x x x x x
x x x x x

(1)Circle (2)Rectangle (3)Square (0)Quit:0
```

ANALYSIS   On lines 7–16, the Shape class is declared. The GetArea() and GetPerim() methods return an error value, and Draw() takes no action. After all, what does it mean to draw a Shape? Only types of shapes (circles, rectangles, and so on) can be drawn; Shapes as an abstraction cannot be drawn.

Circle derives from Shape in lines 18–29 and overrides the three virtual methods. Note that no reason exists to add the word "virtual," because that is part of their inheritance. But there is no harm in doing so either, as shown in the Rectangle class on lines 43, 44, and 47. It is a good idea to include the term virtual as a reminder, a form of documentation.

Square derives from Rectangle in lines 64–71, and it, too, overrides the GetPerim() method, inheriting the rest of the methods defined in Rectangle.

It is troubling, though, that a client might try to instantiate a Shape, and it might be desirable to make that impossible. After all, the Shape class exists only to provide an interface for the classes derived from it; as such, it is an abstract data type, or ADT.

In an *abstract* class, the interface represents a concept (such as shape) rather than a specific object (such as circle). In C++, an abstract class is always the base class to other classes, and it is not valid to make an instance of an abstract class.

Pure Virtual Functions

C++ supports the creation of abstract classes by providing the pure virtual function. A virtual function is made pure by initializing it with zero, as in

```
virtual void Draw() = 0;
```

In this example, the class has a Draw() function, but it has a null implementation and cannot be called. It can, however, be overwritten within descendant classes.

Any class with one or more pure virtual functions is an abstract class, and it becomes illegal to instantiate. In fact, it is illegal to instantiate an object of any class that is an abstract class or any class that inherits from an abstract class and doesn't implement all of the pure virtual functions. Trying to do so causes a compile-time error. Putting a pure virtual function in your class signals two things to clients of your class:

- Don't make an object of this class; derive from it.
- Be certain to override the pure virtual functions your class inherits.

Any class that derives from an abstract class inherits the pure virtual function as pure, and so must override every pure virtual function if it wants to instantiate objects. Thus, if Rectangle inherits from Shape, and Shape has three pure virtual functions, Rectangle must override all three or it, too, will be an abstract class. Listing 14.8 rewrites the Shape class to be an abstract data type. To save space, the rest of Listing 14.7 is not reproduced here. Replace the declaration of Shape in Listing 14.7, lines 7–16, with the declaration of Shape in Listing 14.8 and run the program again.

LISTING 14.8 Abstract Class

```
0:  //Listing 14.8 Abstract Classes
1:
2:  class Shape
3:  {
4:    public:
```

14

LISTING 14.8 continued

```
 5:        Shape(){}
 6:        ~Shape(){}
 7:        virtual long GetArea() = 0;
 8:        virtual long GetPerim()= 0;
 9:        virtual void Draw() = 0;
10:    private:
11:  };
```

OUTPUT

```
(1)Circle (2)Rectangle (3)Square (0)Quit: 2
x x x x x x
x x x x x x
x x x x x x
x x x x x x

(1)Circle (2)Rectangle (3)Square (0)Quit: 3
x x x x x
x x x x x
x x x x x
x x x x x
x x x x x

(1)Circle (2)Rectangle (3)Square (0)Quit: 0
```

ANALYSIS As you can see, the workings of the program are totally unaffected. The only difference is that it would now be impossible to make an object of class Shape.

Abstract Data Types

Declare a class to be an abstract class (also called an *abstract data type*) by including one or more pure virtual functions in the class declaration. Declare a pure virtual function by writing = 0 after the function declaration.

Example

```
class Shape
{
    virtual void Draw() = 0;    // pure virtual
};
```

Implementing Pure Virtual Functions

Typically, the pure virtual functions in an abstract base class are never implemented. Because no objects of that type are ever created, no reason exists to provide implementations, and the abstract class works purely as the definition of an interface to objects, which derive from it.

It is possible, however, to provide an implementation to a pure virtual function. The function can then be called by objects derived from the abstract class, perhaps to provide common functionality to all the overridden functions. Listing 14.9 reproduces Listing 14.7, this time with Shape as an abstract class and with an implementation for the pure virtual function Draw(). The Circle class overrides Draw(), as it must, but it then chains up to the base class function for additional functionality.

In this example, the additional functionality is simply an additional message printed, but one can imagine that the base class provides a shared drawing mechanism, perhaps setting up a window that all derived classes will use.

LISTING 14.9   Implementing Pure Virtual Functions

```
0:   //Listing 14.9 Implementing pure virtual functions
1:
2:   #include <iostream>
3:   using namespace std;
4:
5:   class Shape
6:   {
7:     public:
8:       Shape(){}
9:       virtual ~Shape(){}
10:      virtual long GetArea() = 0;
11:      virtual long GetPerim()= 0;
12:      virtual void Draw() = 0;
13:    private:
14:  };
15:
16:  void Shape::Draw()
17:  {
18:     cout << "Abstract drawing mechanism!\n";
19:  }
20:
21:  class Circle : public Shape
22:  {
23:    public:
24:      Circle(int radius):itsRadius(radius){}
25:      virtual ~Circle(){}
26:      long GetArea() { return 3.14 * itsRadius * itsRadius; }
27:      long GetPerim() { return 2 * 3.14 * itsRadius; }
28:      void Draw();
29:    private:
30:      int itsRadius;
31:      int itsCircumference;
32:  };
33:
34:  void Circle::Draw()
```

14

LISTING 14.9   continued

```
35:  {
36:     cout << "Circle drawing routine here!\n";
37:     Shape::Draw();
38:  }
39:
40:
41:  class Rectangle : public Shape
42:  {
43:    public:
44:      Rectangle(int len, int width):
45:      itsLength(len), itsWidth(width){}
46:      virtual ~Rectangle(){}
47:      long GetArea() { return itsLength * itsWidth; }
48:      long GetPerim() {return 2*itsLength + 2*itsWidth; }
49:      virtual int GetLength() { return itsLength; }
50:      virtual int GetWidth() { return itsWidth; }
51:      void Draw();
52:    private:
53:      int itsWidth;
54:      int itsLength;
55:  };
56:
57:  void Rectangle::Draw()
58:  {
59:     for (int i = 0; i<itsLength; i++)
60:     {
61:        for (int j = 0; j<itsWidth; j++)
62:           cout << "x ";
63:
64:     cout << "\n";
65:     }
66:     Shape::Draw();
67:  }
68:
69:
70:  class Square : public Rectangle
71:  {
72:    public:
73:      Square(int len);
74:      Square(int len, int width);
75:      virtual ~Square(){}
76:      long GetPerim() {return 4 * GetLength();}
77:  };
78:
79:  Square::Square(int len):
80:  Rectangle(len,len)
81:  {}
82:
```

LISTING 14.9   continued

```
83:    Square::Square(int len, int width):
84:    Rectangle(len,width)
85:
86:    {
87:       if (GetLength() != GetWidth())
88:       cout << "Error, not a square... a Rectangle??\n";
89:    }
90:
91:    int main()
92:    {
93:       int choice;
94:       bool fQuit = false;
95:       Shape * sp;
96:
97:       while (fQuit == false)
98:       {
99:          cout << "(1)Circle (2)Rectangle (3)Square (0)Quit: ";
100:         cin >> choice;
101:
102:         switch (choice)
103:         {
104:          case 1: sp = new Circle(5);
105:                break;
106:          case 2: sp = new Rectangle(4,6);
107:                break;
108:          case 3: sp = new Square (5);
109:                break;
110:          default: fQuit = true;
111:                break;
112:         }
113:          if (fQuit == false)
114:          {   115:          sp->Draw();
116:             delete sp;
117:             cout << endl;
118:          }
119:       }
120:       return 0;
121:    }
```

OUTPUT

```
(1)Circle (2)Rectangle (3)Square (0)Quit: 2
x x x x x x
x x x x x x
x x x x x x
x x x x x x
Abstract drawing mechanism!
```

14

```
(1)Circle (2)Rectangle (3)Square (0)Quit: 3
x x x x x
x x x x x
x x x x x
x x x x x
x x x x x
Abstract drawing mechanism!

(1)Circle (2)Rectangle (3)Square (0)Quit: 0
```

ANALYSIS On lines 5–14, the abstract class Shape is declared, with all three of its accessor methods declared to be pure virtual. Note that this is not necessary, but is still a good practice. If any one were declared pure virtual, the class would have been an abstract class.

The GetArea() and GetPerim() methods are not implemented, but Draw() is implemented in lines 16–19. Circle and Rectangle both override Draw(), and both chain up to the base method, taking advantage of shared functionality in the base class.

Complex Hierarchies of Abstraction

At times, you will derive abstract classes from other abstract classes. It might be that you will want to make some of the derived pure virtual functions nonpure, and leave others pure.

If you create the Animal class, you can make Eat(), Sleep(), Move(), and Reproduce() all be pure virtual functions. Perhaps from Animal you derive Mammal and Fish.

On examination, you decide that every Mammal will reproduce in the same way, and so you make Mammal::Reproduce() nonpure, but you leave Eat(), Sleep(), and Move() as pure virtual functions.

From Mammal, you derive Dog, and Dog must override and implement the three remaining pure virtual functions so that you can make objects of type Dog.

What you've said, as class designer, is that no Animals or Mammals can be instantiated, but that all Mammals can inherit the provided Reproduce() method without overriding it.

Listing 14.10 illustrates this technique with a bare-bones implementation of these classes.

LISTING 14.10 Deriving Abstract Classes from Other Abstract Classes

```
0:  // Listing 14.10
1:  // Deriving Abstract Classes from other Abstract Classes
2:  #include <iostream>
3:  using namespace std;
```

LISTING **14.10**   continued

```
 4:
 5:  enum COLOR { Red, Green, Blue, Yellow, White, Black, Brown } ;
 6:
 7:  class Animal        // common base to both Mammal and Fish
 8:  {
 9:    public:
10:      Animal(int);
11:      virtual ~Animal() { cout << "Animal destructor...\n"; }
12:      virtual int GetAge() const { return itsAge; }
13:      virtual void SetAge(int age) { itsAge = age; }
14:      virtual void Sleep() const = 0;
15:      virtual void Eat() const = 0;
16:      virtual void Reproduce() const = 0;
17:      virtual void Move() const = 0;
18:      virtual void Speak() const = 0;
19:    private:
20:      int itsAge;
21:  };
22:
23:  Animal::Animal(int age):
24:  itsAge(age)
25:  {
26:     cout << "Animal constructor...\n";
27:  }
28:
29:  class Mammal : public Animal
30:  {
31:    public:
32:      Mammal(int age):Animal(age)
33:        { cout << "Mammal constructor...\n";}
34:      virtual ~Mammal() { cout << "Mammal destructor...\n";}
35:      virtual void Reproduce() const
36:        { cout << "Mammal reproduction depicted...\n"; }
37:  };
38:
39:  class Fish : public Animal
40:  {
41:    public:
42:      Fish(int age):Animal(age)
43:        { cout << "Fish constructor...\n";}
44:      virtual ~Fish() {cout << "Fish destructor...\n";  }
45:      virtual void Sleep() const { cout << "fish snoring...\n"; }
46:      virtual void Eat() const { cout << "fish feeding...\n"; }
47:      virtual void Reproduce() const
48:        { cout << "fish laying eggs...\n"; }
49:      virtual void Move() const
50:        { cout << "fish swimming...\n";    }
51:      virtual void Speak() const { }
52:  };
```

14

LISTING **14.10** continued

```
53:
54:  class Horse : public Mammal
55:  {
56:    public:
57:      Horse(int age, COLOR color ):
58:      Mammal(age), itsColor(color)
59:        { cout << "Horse constructor...\n"; }
60:      virtual ~Horse() { cout << "Horse destructor...\n"; }
61:      virtual void Speak()const { cout << "Whinny!... \n"; }
62:      virtual COLOR GetItsColor() const { return itsColor; }
63:      virtual void Sleep() const
64:        { cout << "Horse snoring...\n"; }
65:      virtual void Eat() const { cout << "Horse feeding...\n"; }
66:      virtual void Move() const { cout << "Horse running...\n";}
67:
68:    protected:
69:      COLOR itsColor;
70:  };
71:
72:  class Dog : public Mammal
73:  {
74:    public:
75:      Dog(int age, COLOR color ):
76:      Mammal(age), itsColor(color)
77:         { cout << "Dog constructor...\n"; }
78:      virtual ~Dog() { cout << "Dog destructor...\n"; }
79:      virtual void Speak()const { cout << "Whoof!... \n"; }
80:      virtual void Sleep() const { cout << "Dog snoring...\n"; }
81:      virtual void Eat() const { cout << "Dog eating...\n"; }
82:      virtual void Move() const  { cout << "Dog running...\n"; }
83:      virtual void Reproduce() const
84:        { cout << "Dogs reproducing...\n"; }
85:
86:    protected:
87:      COLOR itsColor;
88:  };
89:
90:  int main()
91:  {
92:     Animal *pAnimal=0;
93:     int choice;
94:     bool fQuit = false;
95:
96:     while (fQuit == false)
97:     {
98:        cout << "(1)Dog (2)Horse (3)Fish (0)Quit: ";
99:        cin >> choice;
100:
```

LISTING 14.10   continued

```
101:        switch (choice)
102:        {
103:           case 1: pAnimal = new Dog(5,Brown);
104:                   break;
105:           case 2: pAnimal = new Horse(4,Black);
106:                   break;
107:           case 3: pAnimal = new Fish (5);
108:                   break;
109:          default: fQuit = true;
110:                   break;
111:        }
112:        if (fQuit == false)
113:        {
114:           pAnimal->Speak();
115:           pAnimal->Eat();
116:           pAnimal->Reproduce();
117:           pAnimal->Move();
118:           pAnimal->Sleep();
119:           delete pAnimal;
120:           cout << endl;
121:        }
122:     }
123:     return 0;
124:  }
```

OUTPUT

```
(1)Dog (2)Horse (3)Bird (0)Quit: 1
Animal constructor...
Mammal constructor...
Dog constructor...
Whoof!...
Dog eating...
Dog reproducing....
Dog running...
Dog snoring...
Dog destructor...
Mammal destructor...
Animal destructor...

(1)Dog (2)Horse (3)Bird (0)Quit: 0
```

ANALYSIS   On lines 7–21, the abstract class Animal is declared. Animal has nonpure virtual accessors for itsAge, which are shared by all Animal objects. It has five pure virtual functions, Sleep(), Eat(), Reproduce(), Move(), and Speak().

Mammal is derived from Animal on lines 29–37, and adds no data. It overrides Reproduce(), however, providing a common form of reproduction for all mammals. Fish must override Reproduce() because Fish derives directly from Animal and cannot take

14

advantage of Mammalian reproduction (and a good thing, too!). `Fish` does this in lines 47–48.

`Mammal` classes no longer have to override the `Reproduce()` function, but they are free to do so if they choose, as `Dog` does on line 83. `Fish`, `Horse`, and `Dog` all override the remaining pure virtual functions, so that objects of their type can be instantiated.

In the body of the main program, an `Animal` pointer is used to point to the various derived objects in turn. The virtual methods are invoked, and based on the runtime binding of the pointer, the correct method is called in the derived class.

It would be a compile-time error to try to instantiate an `Animal` or a `Mammal`, as both are abstract classes.

Which Classes Are Abstract?

In one program, the class `Animal` is abstract; in another, it is not. What determines whether to make a class abstract?

The answer to this question is decided not by any real-world intrinsic factor, but by what makes sense in your program. If you are writing a program that depicts a farm or a zoo, you might want `Animal` to be an abstract class, but `Dog` to be a class from which you can instantiate objects.

On the other hand, if you are making an animated kennel, you might want to keep `Dog` as an abstract class and only instantiate types of dogs: retrievers, terriers, and so forth. The level of abstraction is a function of how finely you need to distinguish your types.

Do	Don't
DO use abstract classes to provide common description of capabilities provided in a number of related classes.	DON'T try to instantiate an object of an abstract classes.
DO make pure virtual any function that must be overridden.	

Summary

Today, you learned how to overcome some of the limitations in single inheritance. You learned about the danger of percolating functions up the inheritance hierarchy and the risks in casting down the inheritance hierarchy. You also learned how to use multiple inheritance, what problems multiple inheritance can create, and how to solve them using virtual inheritance.

You also learned what abstract classes are and how to create abstract classes using pure virtual functions. You learned how to implement pure virtual functions and when and why you might do so.

Q&A

Q What is the v-ptr?

A The v-ptr, or virtual-function pointer, is an implementation detail of virtual functions. Each object in a class with virtual functions has a v-ptr, which points to the virtual function table for that class. The virtual function table is consulted when the compiler needs to determine which function to call in a particular situation.

Q Is percolating upward always a good thing?

A Yes, if you are percolating shared functionality upward. No, if all you are moving is interface. That is, if all the derived classes can't use the method, it is a mistake to move it up into a common base class. If you do, you'll have to switch on the runtime type of the object before deciding if you can invoke the function.

Q Why is making a decision on the runtime type of an object bad?

A Because this is an indication that the inheritance hierarchy for the class has not been properly constructed, and it is better to go back and fix the design than to use this workaround.

Q Why is casting bad?

A Casting isn't bad if it is done in a way that is type-safe. Casting can, however, be used to undermine the strong type checking in C++, and that is what you want to avoid. If you are switching on the runtime type of the object and then casting a pointer, that might be a warning sign that something is wrong with your design.

In addition, functions should work with the declared type of their arguments and member variables, and not depend on "knowing" what the calling program will provide through some sort of implicit contract. If the assumption turns out to be wrong, strange and unpredictable problems can result.

Q Why not make all functions virtual?

A Virtual functions are supported by a virtual function table, which incurs runtime overhead, both in the size of the program and in the performance of the program. If you have very small classes that you don't expect to subclass, you might not want to make any of the functions virtual. However, when this assumption changes, you need to be careful to go back and make the ancestor class functions virtual, or unexpected problems can result.

14

Q When should the destructor be made virtual?

A The destructor should be made virtual any time you think the class will be sub-classed, and a pointer to the base class will be used to access an object of the sub-class. As a general rule of thumb, if you've made any functions in your class virtual, be certain to make the destructor virtual as well.

Q Why bother making an abstract class—why not just make it nonabstract and avoid creating any objects of that type?

A The purpose of many of the conventions in C++ is to enlist the compiler in finding bugs, so as to avoid runtime bugs in code that you give your customers. Making a class abstract—that is, giving it pure virtual functions—causes the compiler to flag any objects created of that abstract type as errors.

Workshop

The Workshop provides quiz questions to help you solidify your understanding of the material covered and exercises to provide you with experience in using what you've learned. Try to answer the quiz and exercise questions before checking the answers in Appendix D, and be certain you understand the answers before continuing to tomorrow's lesson.

Quiz

1. What is a down cast?

2. What does "percolating functionality upward" mean?

3. If a round-rectangle has straight edges and rounded corners, and your `RoundRect` class inherits both from `Rectangle` and from `Circle`, and they in turn both inherit from `Shape`, how many `Shapes` are created when you create a `RoundRect`?

4. If `Horse` and `Bird` inherit from `Animal` using public virtual inheritance, do their constructors initialize the `Animal` constructor? If `Pegasus` inherits from both `Horse` and `Bird`, how does it initialize `Animal`'s constructor?

5. Declare a class called `Vehicle` and make it an abstract class.

6. If a base class is an abstract class, and it has three pure virtual functions, how many of these must be overridden in its derived classes?

Exercises

1. Show the declaration for a class JetPlane, which inherits from Rocket and Airplane.

2. Show the declaration for Seven47, which inherits from the JetPlane class described in Exercise 1.

3. Write the code that derives Car and Bus from the class Vehicle. Make Vehicle be an abstract class with two pure virtual functions. Make Car and Bus not be abstract classes.

4. Modify the code in Exercise 3 so that Car is an abstract class, and derive SportsCar and Coupe from Car. In the Car class, provide an implementation for one of the pure virtual functions in Vehicle and make it nonpure.

14

WEEK 2

In Review

The Week in Review program for Week 2 brings together many of the skills you've acquired over the past fortnight and produces a powerful program.

This demonstration of linked lists utilizes virtual functions, pure virtual functions, function overriding, polymorphism, public inheritance, function overloading, pointers, references, and more.

On Day 13, "Managing Arrays and Strings," linked lists were mentioned. In addition, Appendix E, "A Look at Linked Lists," provides a robust example of using a linked list. If you haven't looked at Appendix E, don't fret, linked lists are composed of C++ code you have learned about already. Note that this is a different linked list from the one shown in the appendix; in C++, there are many ways to accomplish the same thing.

The goal of Listing R2.1 is to create a linked list. The nodes on the list are designed to hold parts, as might be used in a factory. Although this is not the final form of this program, it does make a good demonstration of a fairly advanced data structure. The code list is 298 lines. Try to analyze the code on your own before reading the analysis that follows the output.

8

9

10

11

12

13

14

LISTING R2.1   Week 2 in Review Listing

```
0:   // ****************************************************
1:   //
2:   // Title:        Week 2 in Review
3:   //
4:   // File:         Week2
5:   //
6:   // Description:   Provide a linked list demonstration program
7:   //
8:   // Classes:       PART - holds part numbers and potentially other
9:   //                        information about parts
10:  //
11:  //                PartNode - acts as a node in a PartsList
12:  //
13:  //                PartsList - provides the mechanisms for
14:  //                        a linked list of parts
15:  //
16:  //
17:  // ****************************************************
18:
19:   #include <iostream>
20:   using namespace std;
21:
22:
23:
24:   // *************** Part ***********
25:
26:   // Abstract base class of parts
27:   class Part
28:   {
29:     public:
30:       Part():itsPartNumber(1) {}
31:       Part(int PartNumber):itsPartNumber(PartNumber){}
32:       virtual ~Part(){};
33:       int GetPartNumber() const { return itsPartNumber; }
34:       virtual void Display() const =0;  // must be overridden
35:     private:
36:       int itsPartNumber;
37:   };
38:
39:   // implementation of pure virtual function so that
40:   // derived classes can chain up
```

DAY 12

```
41:   void Part::Display() const
42:   {
43:       cout << "\nPart Number: " << itsPartNumber << endl;
44:   }
45:
46:   // *************** Car Part ***********
47:
```

LISTING R2.1 continued

DAY 12

```
48:    class CarPart : public Part
49:    {
50:      public:
51:        CarPart():itsModelYear(94){}
52:        CarPart(int year, int partNumber);
```

DAY 14

```
53:        virtual void Display() const
54:        {
```

DAY 12

```
55:          Part::Display(); cout << "Model Year: ";
56:          cout << itsModelYear << endl;
57:        }
58:      private:
59:        int itsModelYear;
60:    };
61:
```

DAY 12

```
62:    CarPart::CarPart(int year, int partNumber):
63:      itsModelYear(year),
64:      Part(partNumber)
65:    {}
66:
67:
68:    // *************** AirPlane Part ************
69:
```

DAY 12

```
70:    class AirPlanePart : public Part
71:    {
72:      public:
```

DAY 12

```
73:        AirPlanePart():itsEngineNumber(1){};
74:        AirPlanePart(int EngineNumber, int PartNumber);
```

DAY 14

```
75:        virtual void Display() const
76:        {
```

DAY 12

```
77:          Part::Display(); cout << "Engine No.: ";
78:          cout << itsEngineNumber << endl;
```

LISTING R2.1 continued

```
79:      }
80:    private:
81:      int itsEngineNumber;
82:  };
83:
```

DAY 12

```
84:  AirPlanePart::AirPlanePart(int EngineNumber, int PartNumber):
85:      itsEngineNumber(EngineNumber),
86:      Part(PartNumber)
87:  {}
88:
89:  // *************** Part Node ************
90:  class PartNode
91:  {
92:    public:
93:      PartNode (Part*);
94:      ~PartNode();
```

DAY 8

```
95:      void SetNext(PartNode * node) { itsNext = node; }
```

DAY 8

```
96:      PartNode * GetNext() const;
97:      Part * GetPart() const;
98:    private:
```

DAY 8

```
99:      Part *itsPart;
100:      PartNode * itsNext;
101:  };
102:
103:  // PartNode Implementations...
104:
105:  PartNode::PartNode(Part* pPart):
106:  itsPart(pPart),
107:  itsNext(0)
108:  {}
109:
110:  PartNode::~PartNode()
111:  {
112:      delete itsPart;
113:      itsPart = 0;
114:      delete itsNext;
115:      itsNext = 0;
116:  }
117:
118:  // Returns NULL if no next PartNode
```

LISTING R2.1 continued

DAY 8

```
119:    PartNode * PartNode::GetNext() const
120:    {
121:        return itsNext;
122:    }
123:
124:    Part * PartNode::GetPart() const
125:    {
126:       if (itsPart)
127:          return itsPart;
128:       else
129:          return NULL; //error
130:    }
131:
132:    // **************** Part List ************
133:    class PartsList
134:    {
135:      public:
136:        PartsList();
137:        ~PartsList();
138:        // needs copy constructor and operator equals!
```

DAY 9

```
139:        Part*      Find(int & position, int PartNumber)  const;
140:        int        GetCount() const { return itsCount; }
141:        Part*      GetFirst() const;
```

DAY 8

```
142:        void       Insert(Part *);
143:        void       Iterate() const;
```

DAY 10

```
144:        Part*      operator[](int) const;
145:      private:
```

DAY 8

```
146:        PartNode * pHead;
147:        int itsCount;
148:    };
149:
150:    // Implementations for Lists...
151:
152:    PartsList::PartsList():
153:       pHead(0),
154:       itsCount(0)
155:       {}
156:
157:    PartsList::~PartsList()
158:    {
```

LISTING R2.1   continued

DAY 8

```
159:        delete pHead;
160:    }
161:
```

DAY 8

```
162:    Part*   PartsList::GetFirst() const
163:    {
164:        if (pHead)
165:            return pHead->GetPart();
166:        else
167:            return NULL;   // error catch here
168:    }
169:
```

DAY 10

```
170:    Part * PartsList::operator[](int offSet) const
171:    {
```

DAY 8

```
172:        PartNode* pNode = pHead;
173:
174:        if (!pHead)
175:            return NULL; // error catch here
176:
177:        if (offSet > itsCount)
178:            return NULL; // error
179:
180:        for (int i=0;i<offSet; i++)
181:            pNode = pNode->GetNext();
182:
183:        return   pNode->GetPart();
184:    }
185:
```

DAY 9

```
186:    Part*   PartsList::Find(int & position, int PartNumber)  const
187:    {
```

DAY 8

```
188:        PartNode * pNode = 0;
189:        for (pNode = pHead, position = 0;
190:               pNode!=NULL;
191:               pNode = pNode->GetNext(), position++)
192:        {
```

```
193:            if (pNode->GetPart()->GetPartNumber() == PartNumber)
194:               break;
195:         }
196:      if (pNode == NULL)
197:         return NULL;
198:      else
199:         return pNode->GetPart();
200:   }
201:
202:   void PartsList::Iterate() const
203:   {
204:      if (!pHead)
205:         return;
```

DAY 8

```
206:      PartNode* pNode = pHead;
207:      do
```

DAY 8

```
208:          pNode->GetPart()->Display();
209:      while (pNode = pNode->GetNext());
210:   }
211:
212:   void PartsList::Insert(Part* pPart)
213:   {
```

DAY 8

```
214:      PartNode * pNode = new PartNode(pPart);
215:      PartNode * pCurrent = pHead;
216:      PartNode * pNext = 0;
217:
218:      int New =  pPart->GetPartNumber();
219:      int Next = 0;
220:      itsCount++;
221:
222:      if (!pHead)
223:      {
224:         pHead = pNode;
225:         return;
226:      }
227:
228:      // if this one is smaller than head
229:      // this one is the new head
230:      if (pHead->GetPart()->GetPartNumber() > New)
231:      {
232:         pNode->SetNext(pHead);
233:         pHead = pNode;
234:         return;
235:      }
236:
```

LISTING R2.1   continued

```
237:        for (;;)
238:        {
239:            // if there is no next, append this new one
240:            if (!pCurrent->GetNext())
241:            {
242:                pCurrent->SetNext(pNode);
243:                return;
244:            }
245:
246:            // if this goes after this one and before the next
247:            // then insert it here, otherwise get the next
248:            pNext = pCurrent->GetNext();
249:            Next = pNext->GetPart()->GetPartNumber();
250:            if (Next > New)
251:            {
252:                pCurrent->SetNext(pNode);
253:                pNode->SetNext(pNext);
254:                return;
255:            }
256:            pCurrent = pNext;
257:        }
258:    }
259:
260:    int main()
261:    {
262:
263:        PartsList pl;
264:
```

DAY 8

```
265:        Part * pPart = 0;
266:        int PartNumber;
267:        int value;
268:        int choice = 99;
269:
270:        while (choice != 0)
271:        {
272:            cout << "(0)Quit (1)Car (2)Plane: ";
273:            cin >> choice;
274:
275:            if (choice != 0 )
276:            {
277:                cout << "New PartNumber?: ";
278:                cin >>  PartNumber;
279:
280:                if (choice == 1)
281:                {
282:                    cout << "Model Year?: ";
283:                    cin >> value;
```

```
284:                    pPart = new CarPart(value,PartNumber);
285:                }
286:                else
287:                {
288:                    cout << "Engine Number?: ";
289:                    cin >> value;
290:                    pPart = new AirPlanePart(value,PartNumber);
291:                }
292:
293:                pl.Insert(pPart);
294:            }
295:        }
296:        pl.Iterate();
297:        return 0;
298:    }
```

OUTPUT

```
(0)Quit (1)Car (2)Plane: 1
New PartNumber?: 2837
Model Year? 90
(0)Quit (1)Car (2)Plane: 2
New PartNumber?: 378
Engine Number?: 4938
(0)Quit (1)Car (2)Plane: 1
New PartNumber?: 4499
Model Year? 94
(0)Quit (1)Car (2)Plane: 1
New PartNumber?: 3000
Model Year? 93
(0)Quit (1)Car (2)Plane: 0

Part Number: 378
Engine No.: 4938

Part Number: 2837
Model Year: 90

Part Number: 3000
Model Year: 93

Part Number: 4499
Model Year: 94
```

ANALYSIS The Week 2 in Review listing provides a linked list implementation for Part objects. A linked list is a dynamic data structure; that is, it is like an array but it is sized to fit as objects are added and deleted. Linked lists also include pointers to objects of the same time in order to link the objects together.

This particular linked list is designed to hold objects of class Part, where Part is an abstract data type serving as a base class to any objects with a part number. In this example, Part has been subclassed into CarPart and AirPlanePart.

Class Part is declared on lines 27–37, and consists of a part number and some accessors. Presumably, this class could be fleshed out to hold other important information about the parts, such as what components they are used in, how many are in stock, and so forth. Part is an abstract data type, enforced by the pure virtual function Display().

Note that Display() does have an implementation, on lines 41–44. It is the designer's intention that derived classes will be forced to create their own Display() method, but can chain up to this method as well.

Two simple derived classes, CarPart and AirPlanePart, are provided on lines 48–60 and 70–82, respectively. Each provides an overridden Display() method, which does, in fact, chain up to the base class Display() method.

The class PartNode on lines 90–101 serves as the interface between the Part class and the PartList class. It contains a pointer to a part and a pointer to the next node in the list. Its only methods are to get and set the next node in the list and to return the Part to which it points.

The intelligence of the list is, appropriately, in the class PartsList, whose declaration is on lines 133–148. PartsList keeps a pointer to the first element in the list (pHead) and uses that to access all other methods by walking the list. Walking the list means asking each node in the list for the next node, until you reach a node whose next pointer is NULL.

This is only a partial implementation; a fully developed list would provide either greater access to its first and last nodes, or would provide an iterator object, which allows clients to easily walk the list.

PartsList nonetheless provides a number of interesting methods, which are listed in alphabetical order. This is often a good idea, as it makes finding the functions easier.

Find() takes a PartNumber and an int (lines 186–200). If the part corresponding to PartNumber is found, it returns a pointer to the Part and fills the int with the position of that part in the list. If PartNumber is not found, it returns NULL, and the position is meaningless.

GetCount() returns the number of elements in the list (line 140). PartsList keeps this number as a member variable, itsCount, though it could, of course, compute this number by walking the list.

GetFirst() returns a pointer to the first Part in the list, or returns NULL if the list is empty (line 162–168).

On lines 212–258, the Insert() method takes a pointer to a Part, creates a PartNode for it, and adds the Part to the list, ordered by PartNumber.

Iterate() on lines 202–210 takes a pointer to a member function of Part, which takes no parameters, returns void, and is const. It calls that function for every Part object in the list. In the sample program, this is called on Display(), which is a virtual function, so the appropriate Display() method is called based on the runtime type of the Part object called.

On lines 170–184, the bracket operator is overloaded. Operator[] allows direct access to the Part at the offset provided. Rudimentary bounds checking is provided; if the list is NULL or if the offset requested is greater than the size of the list, NULL is returned as an error condition.

Note that in a real program, these comments on the functions would be written into the class declaration.

The driver program starts on line 260. The PartList object is created on line 263.

On line 277, the user is repeatedly prompted to choose whether to enter a car part or an airplane part. Depending on the choice, the right value is requested, and the appropriate part is created. After it is created, the part is inserted into the list on line 293.

The implementation for the Insert() method of PartsList is on lines 212–258. When the first part number is entered, 2837, a CarPart with that part number and the model year 90 is created and passed in to LinkedList::Insert().

On line 214, a new PartNode is created with that part, and the variable New is initialized with the part number. The PartsList's itsCount member variable is incremented on line 220.

On line 222, the test that pHead is NULL will evaluate true. Because this is the first node, it is true that the PartsList's pHead pointer has zero. Thus, on line 224, pHead is set to point to the new node and this function returns.

The user is prompted to enter a second part, and this time an AirPlane part with part number 37 and engine number 4938 is entered. Once again, PartsList::Insert() is called, and once again, pNode is initialized with the new node. The static member variable itsCount is incremented to 2, and pHead is tested. Because pHead was assigned last time, it is no longer null and the test fails.

On line 230, the part number held by pHead, 2837, is compared against the current part number, 378. Because the new one is smaller than the one held by pHead, the new one must become the new head pointer, and the test on line 230 is true.

On line 232, the new node is set to point to the node currently pointed to by pHead. Note that this does not point the new node to pHead, but rather to the node to which pHead was pointing! On line 233, pHead is set to point to the new node.

The third time through the loop, the user enters the part number 4499 for a Car with model year 94. The counter is incremented and the number this time is not less than the number pointed to by pHead, so the for loop that begins on line 237 is entered.

The value pointed to by pHead is 378. The value pointed to by the second node is 2837. The current value is 4499. The pointer pCurrent points to the same node as pHead and so has a next value; pCurrent points to the second node, and so the test on line 240 fails.

The pointer pCurrent is set to point to the next node and the loop repeats. This time, the test on line 240 succeeds. There is no next item, so the current node is told to point to the new node on line 242, and the insert is finished.

The fourth time through, the part number 3000 is entered. This proceeds just like the previous iteration, but this time when the current node is pointing to 2837 and the next node has 4499, the test on line 250 returns TRUE and the new node is inserted into position.

When the user finally presses 0, the test on line 275 evaluates true and the while loop breaks. Execution falls to line 296 where Iterate() is called, branching to line 202 where on line 208 the PNode is used to access the Part and the Display() method is called on that Part object.

WEEK 3

15

At a Glance

You have finished the second week of learning C++. By now, you should feel comfortable with some of the more advanced aspects of object-oriented programming, including encapsulation and polymorphism.

16

Where You Are Going

17

The last week begins with a discussion of static functions and friends. Day 16 discusses advanced inheritance. On Day 17, "Working with Streams," you will learn about streams in depth, and on Day 18, "Creating and Using Namespaces," you will learn how to work with this exciting addition to the C++ Standard. On Day 19, "Templates," you will be introduced to templates, and on Day 20, "Handling Errors and Exceptions," you will learn about exceptions. Day 21, "What's Next," the last day of this book, covers some miscellaneous subjects not covered elsewhere, followed by a discussion of the next steps to take in becoming a C++ guru.

18

19

20

21

WEEK 3

DAY 15

Special Classes and Functions

C++ offers several ways to limit the scope and impact of variables and pointers. So far, you've seen how to create global variables, local function variables, pointers to variables, and class member variables.

Today, you will learn

- How to share information across objects of the same type
- What static member variables and static member functions are
- How to use static member variables and static member functions
- How to create and manipulate pointers to functions and pointers to member functions
- How to work with arrays of pointers to functions

Sharing Data Among Objects of the Same Type: Static Member Data

Until now, you have probably thought of the data in each object as unique to that object and not shared among objects in a class. If you have five Cat objects, for example, each has its own age, weight, and other data. The age of one does not affect the age of another.

At times, however, you'll want to keep track of data that applies to all objects of the same type. For example, you might want to know how many objects for a specific class have been created in your program, and how many are still in existence. Static member variables are variables that are shared among all instances of a class. They are a compromise between global data, which is available to all parts of your program, and member data, which is usually available only to each object.

You can think of a static member as belonging to the class rather than to the object. Normal member data is one per object, but static members are one per class. Listing 15.1 declares a Cat object with a static data member, HowManyCats. This variable keeps track of how many Cat objects have been created. This is done by incrementing the static variable, HowManyCats, with each construction and decrementing it with each destruction.

LISTING 15.1   Static Member Data

```
0:   //Listing 15.1 static data members
1:
2:   #include <iostream>
3:   using namespace std;
4:
5:   class Cat
6:   {
7:     public:
8:       Cat(int age):itsAge(age){HowManyCats++; }
9:       virtual ~Cat() { HowManyCats--; }
10:      virtual int GetAge() { return itsAge; }
11:      virtual void SetAge(int age) { itsAge = age; }
12:      static int HowManyCats;
13:
14:    private:
15:        int itsAge;
16:   };
17:
18:   int Cat::HowManyCats = 0;
19:
20:   int main()
21:   {
```

LISTING 15.1 continued

```
22:    const int MaxCats = 5; int i;
23:    Cat *CatHouse[MaxCats];
24:
25:    for (i = 0; i < MaxCats; i++)
26:       CatHouse[i] = new Cat(i);
27:
28:    for (i = 0; i < MaxCats; i++)
29:    {
30:       cout << "There are ";
31:       cout << Cat::HowManyCats;
32:       cout << " cats left!" << endl;
33:       cout << "Deleting the one that is ";
34:       cout << CatHouse[i]->GetAge();
35:       cout << " years old" << endl;
36:       delete CatHouse[i];
37:       CatHouse[i] = 0;
38:    }
39:    return 0;
40: }
```

OUTPUT

```
There are 5 cats left!
Deleting the one that is 0 years old
There are 4 cats left!
Deleting the one that is 1 years old
There are 3 cats left!
Deleting the one that is 2 years old
There are 2 cats left!
Deleting the one that is 3 years old
There are 1 cats left!
Deleting the one that is 4 years old
```

ANALYSIS On lines 5–16, the simplified class Cat is declared. On line 12, HowManyCats is declared to be a static member variable of type int.

The declaration of HowManyCats does not define an integer; no storage space is set aside. Unlike the nonstatic member variables, no storage space is set aside by instantiating a Cat object because the HowManyCats member variable is not in the object. Thus, on line 18, the variable is defined and initialized.

It is a common mistake to forget to declare static member variables and then to forget to define them. Don't let this happen to you! Of course, if it does, the linker will catch it with a pithy error message such as the following:

```
undefined symbol Cat::HowManyCats
```

You don't need to do this for itsAge because it is a nonstatic member variable and is defined each time you make a Cat object, which you do here on line 26.

On line 8, the constructor for Cat increments the static member variable. The destructor decrements it on line 9. Thus, at any moment, HowManyCats has an accurate measure of how many Cat objects were created but not yet destroyed.

The driver program on lines 20–40 instantiates five Cats and puts them in an array. This calls five Cat constructors, and, thus, HowManyCats is incremented five times from its initial value of 0.

The program then loops through each of the five positions in the array and prints out the value of HowManyCats before deleting the current Cat pointer on line 36. The printout reflects that the starting value is 5 (after all, 5 are constructed), and that each time the loop is run, one fewer Cat remains.

Note that HowManyCats is public and is accessed directly by main(). There is no reason for you to expose this member variable in this way. In fact, it is preferable to make it private along with the other member variables and provide a public accessor method, as long as you will always access the data through an instance of Cat. On the other hand, if you want to access this data directly, without necessarily having a Cat object available, you have two options: Keep it public, as shown in Listing 15.2, or provide a static member function, as discussed later in today's lesson.

LISTING 15.2   Accessing Static Members Without an Object

```
0:   //Listing 15.2 static data members
1:
2:   #include <iostream>
3:   using namespace std;
4:
5:   class Cat
6:   {
7:     public:
8:        Cat(int age):itsAge(age){HowManyCats++; }
9:        virtual ~Cat() { HowManyCats--; }
10:       virtual int GetAge() { return itsAge; }
11:       virtual void SetAge(int age) { itsAge = age; }
12:       static int HowManyCats;
13:
14:     private:
15:        int itsAge;
16:   };
17:
18:   int Cat::HowManyCats = 0;
19:
20:   void TelepathicFunction();
21:
```

15

LISTING 15.2   continued

```
22:   int main()
23:   {
24:      const int MaxCats = 5; int i;
25:      Cat *CatHouse[MaxCats];
26:
27:      for (i = 0; i < MaxCats; i++)
28:      {
29:         CatHouse[i] = new Cat(i);
30:         TelepathicFunction();
31:      }
32:
33:      for ( i = 0; i < MaxCats; i++)
34:      {
35:         delete CatHouse[i];
36:         TelepathicFunction();
37:      }
38:      return 0;
39:   }
40:
41:   void TelepathicFunction()
42:   {
43:      cout << "There are ";
44:      cout << Cat::HowManyCats << " cats alive!" << endl;
45:   }
```

OUTPUT

```
There are 1 cats alive!
There are 2 cats alive!
There are 3 cats alive!
There are 4 cats alive!
There are 5 cats alive!
There are 4 cats alive!
There are 3 cats alive!
There are 2 cats alive!
There are 1 cats alive!
There are 0 cats alive!
```

ANALYSIS   Listing 15.2 is very much like Listing 15.1 except for the addition of a new function, TelepathicFunction(). This function, which is defined on lines 41–45, does not create a Cat object, nor does it take a Cat object as a parameter, yet it can access the HowManyCats member variable. Again, it is worth reemphasizing that this member variable is not in any particular object; it is in the class, where it is accessible to any member function. If public, this variable can be accessed by any function in the program, even when that function does not have an instance of a class.

The alternative to making this member variable public is to make it private. If you do, you can access it through a member function, but then you must have an object of that class available. Listing 15.3 shows this approach. You'll learn an alternative to this access—using static member functions—immediately after the analysis of Listing 15.3.

LISTING 15.3 Accessing Static Members Using Nonstatic Member Functions

```
0:   //Listing 15.3 private static data members
1:   #include <iostream>
2:   using std::cout;
3:   using std::endl;
4:
5:   class Cat
6:   {
7:     public:
8:       Cat(int age):itsAge(age){HowManyCats++; }
9:       virtual ~Cat() { HowManyCats--; }
10:      virtual int GetAge() { return itsAge; }
11:      virtual void SetAge(int age) { itsAge = age; }
12:      virtual int GetHowMany() { return HowManyCats; }
13:
14:    private:
15:        int itsAge;
16:        static int HowManyCats;
17:  };
18:
19:  int Cat::HowManyCats = 0;
20:
21:  int main()
22:  {
23:      const int MaxCats = 5; int i;
24:      Cat *CatHouse[MaxCats];
25:
26:      for (i = 0; i < MaxCats; i++)
27:         CatHouse[i] = new Cat(i);
28:
29:      for (i = 0; i < MaxCats; i++)
30:      {
31:          cout << "There are ";
32:          cout << CatHouse[i]->GetHowMany();
33:          cout << " cats left!\n";
34:          cout << "Deleting the one that is ";
35:          cout << CatHouse[i]->GetAge()+2;
36:          cout << " years old" << endl;
37:          delete CatHouse[i];
38:          CatHouse[i] = 0;
39:      }
40:      return 0;
41:  }
```

OUTPUT
```
There are 5 cats left!
Deleting the one that is 2 years old
There are 4 cats left!
Deleting the one that is 3 years old
There are 3 cats left!
Deleting the one that is 4 years old
There are 2 cats left!
Deleting the one that is 5 years old
There are 1 cats left!
Deleting the one that is 6 years old
```

15

ANALYSIS On line 16, the static member variable HowManyCats is declared to have private access. Now, you cannot access this variable from nonmember functions, such as TelepathicFunction() from the previous listing.

Even though HowManyCats is static, it is still within the scope of the class. As such, any class function, such as GetHowMany(), can access it, just as member functions can access any member data. However, for a function outside of a Cat object to call GetHowMany(), it must have a Cat object on which to call the function.

Do	Don't
DO use static member variables to share data among all instances of a class.	**DON'T** use static member variables to store data for one object. Static member data is shared among all objects of its class.
DO make static member variables protected or private if you want to restrict access to them.	

Using Static Member Functions

Static member functions are like static member variables: They exist not in an object but in the scope of the class. Thus, they can be called without having an object of that class, as illustrated in Listing 15.4.

LISTING 15.4 Static Member Functions

```
0:  //Listing 15.4 static data members
1:
2:  #include <iostream>
3:
4:  class Cat
5:  {
6:    public:
7:      Cat(int age):itsAge(age){HowManyCats++; }
```

LISTING 15.4   continued

```
8:        virtual ~Cat() { HowManyCats--; }
9:        virtual int GetAge() { return itsAge; }
10:       virtual void SetAge(int age) { itsAge = age; }
11:       static int GetHowMany() { return HowManyCats; }
12:    private:
13:       int itsAge;
14:       static int HowManyCats;
15:    };
16:
17:    int Cat::HowManyCats = 0;
18:
19:    void TelepathicFunction();
20:
21:    int main()
22:    {
23:       const int MaxCats = 5;
24:       Cat *CatHouse[MaxCats]; int i;
25:       for (i = 0; i < MaxCats; i++)
26:       {
27:          CatHouse[i] = new Cat(i);
28:          TelepathicFunction();
29:       }
30:
31:       for ( i = 0; i < MaxCats; i++)
32:       {
33:          delete CatHouse[i];
34:          TelepathicFunction();
35:       }
36:       return 0;
37:    }
38:
39:    void TelepathicFunction()
40:    {
41:       std::cout <<"There are "  << Cat::GetHowMany()
42:                 <<" cats alive!" << std::endl;
43:    }
```

OUTPUT
```
There are 1 cats alive!
There are 2 cats alive!
There are 3 cats alive!
There are 4 cats alive!
There are 5 cats alive!
There are 4 cats alive!
There are 3 cats alive!
There are 2 cats alive!
There are 1 cats alive!
There are 0 cats alive!
```

15

ANALYSIS The static member variable HowManyCats is declared to have private access on line 14 of the Cat declaration. The public accessor function, GetHowMany(), is declared to be both public and static on line 11.

Because GetHowMany() is public, it can be accessed by any function, and because it is static, no need exists to have an object of type Cat on which to call it. Thus, on line 41, the function TelepathicFunction() is able to access the public static accessor, even though it has no access to a Cat object. You should note, however, that the function is fully qualified when it is called, meaning the function call is prefixed with the class name followed by two colons:

```
Cat::TelepathicFunction()
```

Of course, you could also have called GetHowMany() on the Cat objects available in main(), the same as with any other accessor functions.

NOTE

Static member functions do not have a this pointer. Therefore, they cannot be declared const. Also, because member data variables are accessed in member functions using the this pointer, static member functions cannot access any nonstatic member variables!

Static Member Functions

You can access static member functions by calling them on an object of the class the same as you do any other member function, or you can call them without an object by fully qualifying the class and object name.

Example

```
class Cat
{
  public:
     static int GetHowMany() { return HowManyCats; }
  private:
     static int HowManyCats;
};
int Cat::HowManyCats = 0;
int main()
{
   int howMany;
   Cat theCat;                    // define a cat
   howMany = theCat.GetHowMany(); // access through an object
   howMany = Cat::GetHowMany();   // access without an object
}
```

Pointers to Functions

Just as an array name is a constant pointer to the first element of the array, a function name is a constant pointer to the function. It is possible to declare a pointer variable that points to a function and to invoke the function by using that pointer. This can be very useful; it enables you to create programs that decide which functions to invoke based on user input.

The only tricky part about function pointers is understanding the type of the object being pointed to. A pointer to int points to an integer variable, and a pointer to a function must point to a function of the appropriate return type and signature.

In the declaration

```
long (* funcPtr) (int);
```

funcPtr is declared to be a pointer (note the * in front of the name) that points to a function that takes an integer parameter and returns a long. The parentheses around * funcPtr are necessary because the parentheses around int bind more tightly; that is, they have higher precedence than the indirection operator (*). Without the first parentheses, this would declare a function that takes an integer and returns a pointer to a long. (Remember that spaces are meaningless here.)

Examine these two declarations:

```
long * Function (int);
```

```
long (* funcPtr) (int);
```

The first, Function (), is a function taking an integer and returning a pointer to a variable of type long. The second, funcPtr, is a pointer to a function taking an integer and returning a variable of type long.

The declaration of a function pointer will always include the return type and the parentheses indicating the type of the parameters, if any. Listing 15.5 illustrates the declaration and use of function pointers.

LISTING 15.5   Pointers to Functions

```
0:  // Listing 15.5 Using function pointers
1:
2:  #include <iostream>
3:  using namespace std;
4:
5:  void Square (int&,int&);
6:  void Cube (int&, int&);
```

LISTING 15.5   continued

```
 7:   void Swap (int&, int &);
 8:   void GetVals(int&, int&);
 9:   void PrintVals(int, int);
10:
11:   int main()
12:   {
13:      void (* pFunc) (int &, int &);
14:      bool fQuit = false;
15:
16:      int valOne=1, valTwo=2;
17:      int choice;
18:      while (fQuit == false)
19:      {
20:         cout <<
            ➥"(0)Quit (1)Change Values (2)Square (3)Cube (4)Swap: ";
21:         cin >> choice;
22:         switch (choice)
23:         {
24:            case 1: pFunc = GetVals; break;
25:            case 2: pFunc = Square; break;
26:            case 3: pFunc = Cube; break;
27:            case 4: pFunc = Swap; break;
28:            default: fQuit = true; break;
29:         }
30:
31:         if (fQuit == false)
32:         {
33:            PrintVals(valOne, valTwo);
34:            pFunc(valOne, valTwo);
35:            PrintVals(valOne, valTwo);
36:         }
37:      }
38:      return 0;
39:   }
40:
41:   void PrintVals(int x, int y)
42:   {
43:      cout << "x: " << x << " y: " << y << endl;
44:   }
45:
46:   void Square (int & rX, int & rY)
47:   {
48:      rX *= rX;
49:      rY *= rY;
50:   }
51:
52:   void Cube (int & rX, int & rY)
53:   {
54:      int tmp;
```

LISTING **15.5**   continued

```
55:
56:      tmp = rX;
57:      rX *= rX;
58:      rX = rX * tmp;
59:
60:      tmp = rY;
61:      rY *= rY;
62:      rY = rY * tmp;
63:  }
64:
65:  void Swap(int & rX, int & rY)
66:  {
67:      int temp;
68:      temp = rX;
69:      rX = rY;
70:      rY = temp;
71:  }
72:
73:  void GetVals (int & rValOne, int & rValTwo)
74:  {
75:      cout << "New value for ValOne: ";
76:      cin >> rValOne;
77:      cout << "New value for ValTwo: ";
78:      cin >> rValTwo;
79:  }
```

OUTPUT

```
(0)Quit (1)Change Values (2)Square (3)Cube (4)Swap: 1
x: 1 y: 2
New value for ValOne: 2
New value for ValTwo: 3
x: 2 y: 3
(0)Quit (1)Change Values (2)Square (3)Cube (4)Swap: 3
x: 2 y: 3
x: 8 y: 27
(0)Quit (1)Change Values (2)Square (3)Cube (4)Swap: 2
x: 8 y: 27
x: 64 y: 729
(0)Quit (1)Change Values (2)Square (3)Cube (4)Swap: 4
x: 64 y: 729
x: 729 y: 64
(0)Quit (1)Change Values (2)Square (3)Cube (4)Swap: 0
```

ANALYSIS   On lines 5–8, four functions are declared, each with the same return type and signature, returning void and taking two references to integers.

On line 13, pFunc is declared to be a pointer to a function that returns void and takes two integer reference parameters. Because the signatures match, any of the previous

15

functions can be pointed to by pFunc. The user is repeatedly offered the choice of which functions to invoke, and pFunc is assigned accordingly. On lines 33–35, the current value of the two integers is printed, the currently assigned function is invoked, and then the values are printed again.

Pointer to Function

A pointer to function is invoked the same as the functions it points to, except that the function pointer name is used instead of the function name.

Assign a pointer to function to a specific function by assigning to the function name without the parentheses. The function name is a constant pointer to the function itself. Use the pointer to function the same as you would the function name. The pointer to function must agree in return value and signature with the function to which you assign it.

Example

```
long (*pFuncOne) (int, int);
long SomeFunction (int, int);
pFuncOne = SomeFunction;
pFuncOne(5,7);
```

CAUTION

Be aware that pointers to functions can be highly dangerous. You can accidentally assign to a function pointer when you want to call the function, or you can accidentally call the function when you want to assign to its pointer.

Why Use Function Pointers?

Generally, you shouldn't use function pointers. Function pointers date from the days of C, before object-oriented programming was available. They were provided to allow for a programming style that had some of the virtues of object orientation; however, if you are writing a program that is highly dynamic and needs to operate different functionality based on runtime decisions, this can be a viable solution.

You certainly could write a program like Listing 15.5 without function pointers, but the use of these pointers makes the intent and use of the program explicit: Pick a function from a list, and then invoke it.

Listing 15.6 uses the function prototypes and definitions from Listing 15.5, but the body of the program does not use a function pointer. Examine the differences between these two listings.

LISTING 15.6   Rewriting Listing 15.5 Without the Pointer to Function

```
0:   // Listing 15.6 Without function pointers
1:
2:   #include <iostream>
3:   using namespace std;
4:
5:   void Square (int&,int&);
6:   void Cube (int&, int&);
7:   void Swap (int&, int &);
8:   void GetVals(int&, int&);
9:   void PrintVals(int, int);
10:
11:  int main()
12:  {
13:     bool fQuit = false;
14:     int valOne=1, valTwo=2;
15:     int choice;
16:     while (fQuit == false)
17:     {
18:        cout << "(0)Quit (1)Change Values (2)Square (3)Cube (4)Swap: ";
19:        cin >> choice;
20:        switch (choice)
21:        {
22:          case 1:
23:            PrintVals(valOne, valTwo);
24:            GetVals(valOne, valTwo);
25:            PrintVals(valOne, valTwo);
26:            break;
27:
28:          case 2:
29:            PrintVals(valOne, valTwo);
30:            Square(valOne,valTwo);
31:            PrintVals(valOne, valTwo);
32:            break;
33:
34:          case 3:
35:            PrintVals(valOne, valTwo);
36:            Cube(valOne, valTwo);
37:            PrintVals(valOne, valTwo);
38:            break;
39:
40:          case 4:
41:            PrintVals(valOne, valTwo);
42:            Swap(valOne, valTwo);
43:            PrintVals(valOne, valTwo);
44:            break;
45:
46:          default :
```

15

LISTING 15.6 continued

```
47:             fQuit = true;
48:             break;
49:         }
50:     }
51:     return 0;
52: }
53:
54: void PrintVals(int x, int y)
55: {
56:     cout << "x: " << x << " y: " << y << endl;
57: }
58:
59: void Square (int & rX, int & rY)
60: {
61:     rX *= rX;
62:     rY *= rY;
63: }
64:
65: void Cube (int & rX, int & rY)
66: {
67:     int tmp;
68:
69:     tmp = rX;
70:     rX *= rX;
71:     rX = rX * tmp;
72:
73:     tmp = rY;
74:     rY *= rY;
75:     rY = rY * tmp;
76: }
77:
78: void Swap(int & rX, int & rY)
79: {
80:     int temp;
81:     temp = rX;
82:     rX = rY;
83:     rY = temp;
84: }
85:
86: void GetVals (int & rValOne, int & rValTwo)
87: {
88:     cout << "New value for ValOne: ";
89:     cin >> rValOne;
90:     cout << "New value for ValTwo: ";
91:     cin >> rValTwo;
92: }
```

```
(0)Quit (1)Change Values (2)Square (3)Cube (4)Swap: 1
x: 1 y: 2
New value for ValOne: 2
New value for ValTwo: 3
(0)Quit (1)Change Values (2)Square (3)Cube (4)Swap: 3
x: 2 y: 3
x: 8 y: 27
(0)Quit (1)Change Values (2)Square (3)Cube (4)Swap: 2
x: 8 y: 27
x: 64 y: 729
(0)Quit (1)Change Values (2)Square (3)Cube (4)Swap: 4
x: 64 y: 729
x: 729 y: 64
(0)Quit (1)Change Values (2)Square (3)Cube (4)Swap: 0
```

ANALYSIS   It was tempting to put `PrintVals()` at the top of the `while` loop and again at the bottom, rather than in each `case` statement. This would have called `PrintVals()` even for the exit case, however, and that was not part of the specification.

Setting aside the increased size of the code and the repeated calls to do the same thing, the overall clarity is somewhat diminished. This is an artificial case, however, created to show how pointers to functions work. In real-world conditions, the advantages are even clearer: Pointers to functions can eliminate duplicate code, clarify a program, and enable tables of functions that can be called based on runtime conditions.

TIP

> Object-oriented programming should generally allow you to avoid the need to create or pass pointers to functions. Instead, call the desired function on the desired object or the desired static member function on the class. If you need an array of function pointers, ask yourself whether what you really need is an array of appropriate objects.

Shorthand Invocation

The pointer to function does not need to be dereferenced, although you are free to do so. Therefore, if `pFunc` is a pointer to a function taking an integer and returning a variable of type `long`, and you assign `pFunc` to a matching function, you can invoke that function with either

```
pFunc(x);
```

or

```
(*pFunc)(x);
```

The two forms are identical. The former is just a shorthand version of the latter.

Arrays of Pointers to Functions

Just as you can declare an array of pointers to integers, you can declare an array of pointers to functions returning a specific value type and with a specific signature. Listing 15.7 again rewrites Listing 15.5, this time using an array to invoke all the choices at once.

LISTING 15.7   Demonstrates Use of an Array of Pointers to Functions

```
0:  // Listing 15.7
1:  //demonstrates use of an array of pointers to functions
2:
3:  #include <iostream>
4:  using namespace std;
5:
6:  void Square(int&,int&);
7:  void Cube(int&, int&);
8:  void Swap(int&, int &);
9:  void GetVals(int&, int&);
10: void PrintVals(int, int);
11:
12: int main()
13: {
14:     int valOne=1, valTwo=2;
15:     int choice, i;
16:     const MaxArray = 5;
17:     void (*pFuncArray[MaxArray])(int&, int&);
18:
19:     for (i=0; i < MaxArray; i++)
20:     {
21:         cout << "(1)Change Values (2)Square (3)Cube (4)Swap: ";
22:         cin >> choice;
23:         switch (choice)
24:         {
25:           case 1:   pFuncArray[i] = GetVals; break;
26:           case 2:   pFuncArray[i] = Square; break;
27:           case 3:   pFuncArray[i] = Cube; break;
28:           case 4:   pFuncArray[i] = Swap; break;
29:           default:  pFuncArray[i] = 0;
30:         }
31:     }
32:
33:     for (i=0; i < MaxArray; i++)
34:     {
35:         if ( pFuncArray[i] == 0 )
36:             continue;
37:         pFuncArray[i](valOne,valTwo);
38:         PrintVals(valOne,valTwo);
39:     }
40:     return 0;
```

LISTING 15.7 continued

```
41:   }
42:
43:   void PrintVals(int x, int y)
44:   {
45:      cout << "x: " << x << " y: " << y << endl;
46:   }
47:
48:   void Square (int & rX, int & rY)
49:   {
50:      rX *= rX;
51:      rY *= rY;
52:   }
53:
54:   void Cube (int & rX, int & rY)
55:   {
56:      int tmp;
57:
58:      tmp = rX;
59:      rX *= rX;
60:      rX = rX * tmp;
61:
62:      tmp = rY;
63:      rY *= rY;
64:      rY = rY * tmp;
65:   }
66:
67:   void Swap(int & rX, int & rY)
68:   {
69:      int temp;
70:      temp = rX;
71:      rX = rY;
72:      rY = temp;
73:   }
74:
75:   void GetVals (int & rValOne, int & rValTwo)
76:   {
77:      cout << "New value for ValOne: ";
78:      cin >> rValOne;
79:      cout << "New value for ValTwo: ";
80:      cin >> rValTwo;
81:   }
```

OUTPUT

```
(1)Change Values (2)Square (3)Cube (4)Swap: 1
(1)Change Values (2)Square (3)Cube (4)Swap: 2
(1)Change Values (2)Square (3)Cube (4)Swap: 3
(1)Change Values (2)Square (3)Cube (4)Swap: 4
(1)Change Values (2)Square (3)Cube (4)Swap: 2
New Value for ValOne: 2
New Value for ValTwo: 3
```

```
x: 2 y: 3
x: 4 y: 9
x: 64 y: 729
x: 729 y: 64
x: 531441 y:4096
```

ANALYSIS On line 17, the array pFuncArray is declared to be an array of five pointers to functions that return void and that take two integer references.

On lines 19–31, the user is asked to pick the functions to invoke, and each member of the array is assigned the address of the appropriate function. On lines 33–39, each function is invoked in turn. The result is printed after each invocation.

Passing Pointers to Functions to Other Functions

The pointers to functions (and arrays of pointers to functions, for that matter) can be passed to other functions, which can take action and then call the right function using the pointer.

You might improve Listing 15.5, for example, by passing the chosen function pointer to another function (outside of main()), which prints the values, invokes the function, and then prints the values again. Listing 15.8 illustrates this variation.

LISTING 15.8 Passing Pointers to Functions as Function Arguments

```
0:  // Listing 15.8 Without function pointers
1:
2:  #include <iostream>
3:  using namespace std;
4:
5:  void Square(int&,int&);
6:  void Cube(int&, int&);
7:  void Swap(int&, int &);
8:  void GetVals(int&, int&);
9:  void PrintVals(void (*)(int&, int&),int&, int&);
10:
11: int main()
12: {
13:     int valOne=1, valTwo=2;
14:     int choice;
15:     bool fQuit = false;
16:
17:     void (*pFunc)(int&, int&);
18:
19:     while (fQuit == false)
20:     {
21:        cout << "(0)Quit (1)Change Values (2)Square (3)Cube (4)Swap: ";
22:        cin >> choice;
```

LISTING 15.8   continued

```
23:         switch (choice)
24:         {
25:           case 1:    pFunc = GetVals; break;
26:           case 2:    pFunc = Square; break;
27:           case 3:    pFunc = Cube; break;
28:           case 4:    pFunc = Swap; break;
29:           default:  fQuit = true; break;
30:         }
31:
32:         if (fQuit == false)
33:             PrintVals ( pFunc, valOne, valTwo);
34:     }
35:
36:     return 0;
37: }
38:
39: void PrintVals( void (*pFunc)(int&, int&),int& x, int& y)
40: {
41:     cout << "x: " << x << " y: " << y << endl;
42:     pFunc(x,y);
43:     cout << "x: " << x << " y: " << y << endl;
44: }
45:
46: void Square (int & rX, int & rY)
47: {
48:     rX *= rX;
49:     rY *= rY;
50: }
51:
52: void Cube (int & rX, int & rY)
53: {
54:     int tmp;
55:
56:     tmp = rX;
57:     rX *= rX;
58:     rX = rX * tmp;
59:
60:     tmp = rY;
61:     rY *= rY;
62:     rY = rY * tmp;
63: }
64:
65: void Swap(int & rX, int & rY)
66: {
67:     int temp;
68:     temp = rX;
69:     rX = rY;
70:     rY = temp;
71: }
72:
```

LISTING 15.8 continued

```
73:  void GetVals (int & rValOne, int & rValTwo)
74:  {
75:     cout << "New value for ValOne: ";
76:     cin >> rValOne;
77:     cout << "New value for ValTwo: ";
78:     cin >> rValTwo;
79:  }
```

OUTPUT

```
(0)Quit (1)Change Values (2)Square (3)Cube (4)Swap: 1
x: 1 y: 2
New value for ValOne: 2
New value for ValTwo: 3
x: 2 y: 3
(0)Quit (1)Change Values (2)Square (3)Cube (4)Swap: 3
x: 2 y: 3
x: 8 y: 27
(0)Quit (1)Change Values (2)Square (3)Cube (4)Swap: 2
x: 8 y: 27
x: 64 y: 729
(0)Quit (1)Change Values (2)Square (3)Cube (4)Swap: 4
x: 64 y: 729
x: 729 y:64
(0)Quit (1)Change Values (2)Square (3)Cube (4)Swap: 0
```

ANALYSIS On line 17, pFunc is declared to be a pointer to a function returning void and taking two parameters, both integer references. On line 9, PrintVals is declared to be a function taking three parameters. The first is a pointer to a function that returns void but takes two integer reference parameters, and the second and third arguments to PrintVals are integer references. The user is again prompted on lines 19 and 20 for which functions to call, and then on line 33 PrintVals is called using the function pointer, pFunc, as the first parameter.

Go find a C++ programmer and ask him what this declaration means:

```
void PrintVals(void (*)(int&, int&),int&, int&);
```

This is the kind of declaration that you use infrequently and probably look up in the book each time you need it, but it will save your program on those rare occasions when it is exactly the required construct.

Using `typedef` with Pointers to Functions

The construct `void (*)(int&, int&)` is cumbersome, at best. You can use `typedef` to simplify this, by declaring a type (in Listing 15.9, it is called VPF) as a pointer to a function returning void and taking two integer references. Listing 15.9 rewrites Listing 15.8 using this `typedef` statement.

LISTING 15.9   Using `typedef` to Make Pointers to Functions More Readable

```
0:  // Listing 15.9.
1:  // Using typedef to make pointers to functions more readable
2:
3:  #include <iostream>
4:  using namespace std;
5:
6:  void Square(int&,int&);
7:  void Cube(int&, int&);
8:  void Swap(int&, int &);
9:  void GetVals(int&, int&);
10: typedef  void (*VPF) (int&, int&) ;
11: void PrintVals(VPF,int&, int&);
12:
13: int main()
14: {
15:     int valOne=1, valTwo=2;
16:     int choice;
17:     bool fQuit = false;
18:
19:     VPF pFunc;
20:
21:     while (fQuit == false)
22:     {
23:        cout << "(0)Quit (1)Change Values (2)Square (3)Cube (4)Swap: ";
24:        cin >> choice;
25:        switch (choice)
26:        {
27:          case 1:   pFunc = GetVals; break;
28:          case 2:   pFunc = Square; break;
29:          case 3:   pFunc = Cube; break;
30:          case 4:   pFunc = Swap; break;
31:          default: fQuit = true; break;
32:        }
33:
34:        if (fQuit == false)
35:            PrintVals ( pFunc, valOne, valTwo);
36:     }
37:     return 0;
38: }
39:
40: void PrintVals( VPF pFunc,int& x, int& y)
41: {
42:    cout << "x: " << x << " y: " << y << endl;
43:    pFunc(x,y);
44:    cout << "x: " << x << " y: " << y << endl;
45: }
46:
47: void Square (int & rX, int & rY)
48: {
```

LISTING 15.9 continued

```
49:       rX *= rX;
50:       rY *= rY;
51:    }
52:
53:    void Cube (int & rX, int & rY)
54:    {
55:       int tmp;
56:
57:       tmp = rX;
58:       rX *= rX;
59:       rX = rX * tmp;
60:
61:       tmp = rY;
62:       rY *= rY;
63:       rY = rY * tmp;
64:    }
65:
66:    void Swap(int & rX, int & rY)
67:    {
68:       int temp;
69:       temp = rX;
70:       rX = rY;
71:       rY = temp;
72:    }
73:
74:    void GetVals (int & rValOne, int & rValTwo)
75:    {
76:       cout << "New value for ValOne: ";
77:       cin >> rValOne;
78:       cout << "New value for ValTwo: ";
79:       cin >> rValTwo;
80:    }
```

OUTPUT

```
(0)Quit (1)Change Values (2)Square (3)Cube (4)Swap: 1
x: 1 y: 2
New value for ValOne: 2
New value for ValTwo: 3
x: 2 y: 3
(0)Quit (1)Change Values (2)Square (3)Cube (4)Swap: 3
x: 2 y: 3
x: 8 y: 27
(0)Quit (1)Change Values (2)Square (3)Cube (4)Swap: 2
x: 8 y: 27
x: 64 y: 729
(0)Quit (1)Change Values (2)Square (3)Cube (4)Swap: 4
x: 64 y: 729
x: 729 y: 64
(0)Quit (1)Change Values (2)Square (3)Cube (4)Swap: 0
```

ANALYSIS On line 10, `typedef` is used to declare VPF to be of the type "pointer to function that returns void and takes two parameters, both integer references."

On line 11, the function `PrintVals()` is declared to take three parameters: a VPF and two integer references. On line 19, pFunc is now declared to be of type VPF.

After the type VPF is defined, all subsequent uses to declare pFunc and `PrintVals()` are much cleaner. As you can see, the output is identical. Remember, a `typedef` primarily does a replacement. In this case, using the `typedef` makes your code much easier to follow.

Pointers to Member Functions

Up until this point, all the function pointers you've created have been for general, non-class functions. It is also possible to create pointers to functions that are members of classes. This is a highly advanced and infrequently used technique that should be avoided whenever possible. It is, however, important to understand this technique as some people do choose to use it.

To create a pointer to member function, use the same syntax as with a pointer to function, but include the class name and the scoping operator (`::`). Thus, if pFunc points to a member function of the class Shape, which takes two integers and returns void, the declaration for pFunc is the following:

```
void (Shape::*pFunc) (int, int);
```

Pointers to member functions are used in the same way as pointers to functions, except that they require an object of the correct class on which to invoke them. Listing 15.10 illustrates the use of pointers to member functions.

LISTING 15.10   Pointers to Member Functions

```
0:  //Listing 15.10 Pointers to member functions using virtual methods
1:
2:  #include <iostream>
3:  using namespace std;
4:
5:  class Mammal
6:  {
7:    public:
8:      Mammal():itsAge(1) {  }
9:      virtual ~Mammal() { }
10:     virtual void Speak() const = 0;
11:     virtual void Move() const = 0;
12:   protected:
```

LISTING 15.10   continued

```
13:        int itsAge;
14:  };
15:
16:  class Dog : public Mammal
17:  {
18:    public:
19:      void Speak()const { cout << "Woof!" << endl; }
20:      void Move() const { cout << "Walking to heel..." << endl; }
21:  };
22:
23:
24:  class Cat : public Mammal
25:  {
26:    public:
27:      void Speak()const { cout << "Meow!" << endl; }
28:      void Move() const { cout << "slinking..." << endl; }
29:  };
30:
31:
32:  class Horse : public Mammal
33:  {
34:    public:
35:      void Speak()const { cout << "Winnie!" << endl; }
36:      void Move() const { cout << "Galloping..." << endl; }
37:  };
38:
39:
40:  int main()
41:  {
42:      void (Mammal::*pFunc)() const =0;
43:      Mammal* ptr =0;
44:      int Animal;
45:      int Method;
46:      bool fQuit = false;
47:
48:      while (fQuit == false)
49:      {
50:        cout << "(0)Quit (1)dog (2)cat (3)horse: ";
51:        cin >> Animal;
52:        switch (Animal)
53:        {
54:          case 1:   ptr = new Dog; break;
55:          case 2:   ptr = new Cat; break;
56:          case 3:   ptr = new Horse; break;
57:          default:  fQuit = true; break;
58:        }
59:        if (fQuit == false)
60:        {
61:            cout << "(1)Speak  (2)Move: ";
```

LISTING 15.10   continued

```
62:            cin >> Method;
63:            switch (Method)
64:            {
65:              case 1:  pFunc = Mammal::Speak; break;
66:              default: pFunc = Mammal::Move; break;
67:            }
68:
69:              (ptr->*pFunc)();
70:            delete ptr;
71:        }
72:    }
73:    return 0;
74: }
```

OUTPUT
```
(0)Quit (1)dog (2)cat (3)horse: 1
(1)Speak (2)Move: 1
Woof!
(0)Quit (1)dog (2)cat (3)horse: 2
(1)Speak (2)Move: 1
Meow!
(0)Quit (1)dog (2)cat (3)horse: 3
(1)Speak (2)Move: 2
Galloping
(0)Quit (1)dog (2)cat (3)horse: 0
```

ANALYSIS   On lines 5–14, the abstract class Mammal is declared with two pure virtual methods: Speak() and Move(). Mammal is subclassed into Dog, Cat, and Horse, each of which overrides Speak() and Move().

The driver program in main() starts on line 40. On line 50, the user is asked to choose the type of animal to create. Based on this selection, a new subclass of Animal is created on the free store and assigned to ptr on lines 54–56.

On line 61, the user is given a second prompt asking him to select the method to invoke. The method selected, either Speak or Move, is assigned to the pointer pFunc on lines 65–66. On line 69, the method chosen is invoked by the object created, by using the pointer ptr to access the object and pFunc to access the function.

Finally, on line 70, delete is called on the pointer ptr to return the memory set aside for the object to the free store. Note that no reason exists to call delete on pFunc because this is a pointer to code, not to an object on the free store. In fact, attempting to do so generates a compile-time error.

Arrays of Pointers to Member Functions

As with pointers to functions, pointers to member functions can be stored in an array. The array can be initialized with the addresses of various member functions, and these can be invoked by offsets into the array. Listing 15.11 illustrates this technique.

LISTING 15.11   Array of Pointers to Member Functions

```
0:  //Listing 15.11 Array of pointers to member functions
1:  #include <iostream>
2:  using std::cout;
3:  using std::endl;
4:
5:  class Dog
6:  {
7:    public:
8:      void Speak()const { cout << "Woof!" << endl; }
9:      void Move() const { cout << "Walking to heel..." << endl; }
10:      void Eat() const { cout << "Gobbling food..." << endl; }
11:      void Growl() const { cout << "Grrrrr" << endl; }
12:      void Whimper() const { cout << "Whining noises..." << endl; }
13:      void RollOver() const { cout << "Rolling over..." << endl; }
14:      void PlayDead() const
            { cout << "The end of Little Caesar?" << endl; }
15:  };
16:
17:  typedef void (Dog::*PDF)()const ;
18:  int main()
19:  {
20:      const int MaxFuncs = 7;
21:      PDF DogFunctions[MaxFuncs] =
22:          {Dog::Speak,
23:           Dog::Move,
24:           Dog::Eat,
25:           Dog::Growl,
26:           Dog::Whimper,
27:           Dog::RollOver,
28:           Dog::PlayDead };
29:
30:      Dog* pDog =0;
31:      int Method;
32:      bool fQuit = false;
33:
34:      while (!fQuit)
35:      {
36:          cout << "(0)Quit (1)Speak (2)Move (3)Eat (4)Growl";
37:          cout << " (5)Whimper (6)Roll Over (7)Play Dead: ";
38:          std::cin >> Method;
39:          if (Method <= 0 || Method >= 8)
```

15

LISTING **15.11**   continued

```
40:        {
41:            fQuit = true;
42:        }
43:        else
44:        {
45:            pDog = new Dog;
46:            (pDog->*DogFunctions[Method-1])();
47:            delete pDog;
48:        }
49:    }
50:    return 0;
51: }
```

OUTPUT

```
 (0)Quit (1)Speak (2)Move (3)Eat (4)Growl (5)Whimper (6)Roll Over
➥(7)Play Dead: 1
Woof!
 (0)Quit (1)Speak (2)Move (3)Eat (4)Growl (5)Whimper (6)Roll Over
➥(7)Play Dead: 4
Grrr
 (0)Quit (1)Speak (2)Move (3)Eat (4)Growl (5)Whimper (6)Roll Over
➥(7)Play Dead: 7
The end of Little Caesar?
 (0)Quit (1)Speak (2)Move (3)Eat (4)Growl (5)Whimper (6)Roll Over
➥(7)Play Dead: 0
```

ANALYSIS   On lines 5–15, the class Dog is created, with seven member functions all sharing the same return type and signature. On line 17, a typedef declares PDF to be a pointer to a member function of Dog that takes no parameters and returns no values, and that is const: the signature of the seven member functions of Dog.

On lines 21–28, the array DogFunctions is declared to hold seven such member functions, and it is initialized with the addresses of these functions.

On lines 36 and 37, the user is prompted to pick a method. Unless Quit is picked, a new Dog is created on the heap, and then the correct method is invoked on the array on line 46. Here's another good line to show to the hotshot C++ programmers in your company; ask them what this does:

```
(pDog->*DogFunctions[Method-1])();
```

You'll be able to tell the hotshot that it is a call to a method in an object using a pointer stored to the method that is stored in an array at the offset of Method-1.

Once again, this is a technique that should be avoided whenever possible. If it must be used, document it extensively and try to think of another way to accomplish the desired task.

Do	Don't
DO invoke pointers to member functions on a specific object of a class.	**DON'T** use pointer to member functions when simpler solutions are possible.
DO use `typedef` to make pointer to member function declarations easier to read.	**DON'T** forget the parenthesis when declaring a pointer to a function (versus a function that returns a pointer).

15

Summary

Today, you learned how to create static member variables in your class. Each class, rather than each object, has one instance of the static member variable. It is possible to access this member variable without an object of the class type by fully qualifying the name, assuming you've declared the static member to have public access.

You learned that one use of static member variables is as counters across instances of the class. Because they are not part of the object, the declaration of static member variables does not allocate memory, and static member variables must be defined and initialized outside the declaration of the class.

Static member functions are part of the class in the same way that static member variables are. They can be accessed without a particular object of the class and can be used to access static member data. Static member functions cannot be used to access nonstatic member data because they do not have the `this` pointer.

Because static member functions do not have a `this` pointer, they also cannot be made const. const in a member function indicates that `this` is const.

Today's lesson also included one of the more complex topics in C++. You learned how to declare and use pointers to functions and pointers to member functions. You saw how to create arrays of these pointers and how to pass them to functions, and how to call the functions whose pointers were stored in this way. You learned that this is not really a great idea, and that object-oriented techniques should allow you to avoid this in almost every situation.

Q&A

Q Why use static data when I can use global data?

A Static data is scoped to the class. In this manner, static data is available only through an object of the class, through an explicit call using the class name if they are public, or by using a static member function. Static data is typed to the class type, however, and the restricted access and strong typing makes static data safer than global data.

Q Why use static member functions when I can use global functions?

A Static member functions are scoped to the class and can be called only by using an object of the class or an explicit full specification (such as `ClassName::FunctionName()`).

Q Is it common to use many pointers to functions and pointers to member functions?

A No, these have their special uses, but are not common constructs. Many complex and powerful programs have neither. There might, however, be times when these offer the only solution.

Workshop

The Workshop contains quiz questions to help solidify your understanding of the material covered and exercises to provide you with experience in using what you've learned. Try to answer the quiz and exercise questions before checking the answers in Appendix D, and be certain you understand the answers before going to tomorrow's lesson.

Quiz

1. Can static member variables be private?

2. Show the declaration for a static member variable called `itsStatic` that is of type `int`.

3. Show the declaration for a static function called `SomeFunction` that returns an integer and takes no parameters.

4. Show the declaration for a pointer to function returning `long` and taking an integer parameter.

5. Modify the pointer in Question 4 so it's a pointer to member function of class `Car`.

6. Show the declaration for an array called `theArray` that contains 10 pointers as defined in Question 5.

Exercises

1. Write a short program declaring a class with one member variable and one static member variable. Have the constructor initialize the member variable and increment the static member variable. Have the destructor decrement the member variable.

2. Using the program from Exercise 1, write a short driver program that makes three objects and then displays their member variables and the static member variable. Then destroy each object and show the effect on the static member variable.

3. Modify the program from Exercise 2 to use a static member function to access the static member variable. Make the static member variable private.

4. Write a pointer to member function to access the nonstatic member data in the program in Exercise 3, and use that pointer to print the value of that data.

5. Add two more member variables to the class from the previous exercises. Add accessor functions that get the value of this data and give all the member functions the same return values and signatures. Use the pointer to member function to access these functions.

15

Advanced Inheritance

So far, you have worked with single and multiple inheritance to create *is-a* relationships.

Today, you will learn

- What aggregation is and how to model it (the *has-a* relationship)
- What delegation is and how to model it
- How to implement one class in terms of another
- How to use private inheritance

Aggregation

You have seen in previous examples that it is possible for the member data of a class to contain objects of other class types. This is often called aggregation, or the *has-a* relationship.

As an illustration, consider classes such as a Name class and an Address class:

```
Class Name
{
    // Class information for Name
};
Class Address
{
    // Class information for Address
};
```

As an illustration of aggregation, these two classes could be included as part of an Employee class:

```
Class Employee
{
    Name      EmpName;
    Address EmpAddress;
    // Any other employee class stuff...
}
```

Thus, an Employee class contains member variables for a name and for an address (Employee *has-a* Name and Employee *has-an* Address).

A more complex example is presented in Listing 16.1. This is an incomplete, but still useful, String class, not unlike the String class created on Day 13, "Managing Arrays and Strings." This listing does not produce any output. Instead, Listing 16.1 will be used with later listings.

LISTING **16.1**   The String Class

```
0:  // Listing 16.1 The String Class
1:
2:  #include <iostream>
3:  #include <string.h>
4:  using namespace std;
5:
6:  class String
7:  {
8:    public:
9:        // constructors
10:       String();
11:       String(const char *const);
12:       String(const String &);
13:       ~String();
14:
15:       // overloaded operators
16:       char & operator[](int offset);
17:       char operator[](int offset) const;
```

LISTING 16.1 continued

```
18:        String operator+(const String&);
19:        void operator+=(const String&);
20:        String & operator= (const String &);
21:
22:        // General accessors
23:        int GetLen()const { return itsLen; }
24:        const char * GetString() const { return itsString; }
25:        // static int ConstructorCount;
26:
27:      private:
28:        String (int);          // private constructor
29:        char * itsString;
30:        unsigned short itsLen;
31:
32:    };
33:
34:    // default constructor creates string of 0 bytes
35:    String::String()
36:    {
37:       itsString = new char[1];
38:       itsString[0] = '\0';
39:       itsLen=0;
40:       // cout << "\tDefault string constructor\n";
41:       // ConstructorCount++;
42:    }
43:
44:    // private (helper) constructor, used only by
45:    // class methods for creating a new string of
46:    // required size.  Null filled.
47:    String::String(int len)
48:    {
49:       itsString = new char[len+1];
50:       for (int i = 0; i<=len; i++)
51:          itsString[i] = '\0';
52:       itsLen=len;
53:       // cout << "\tString(int) constructor\n";
54:       // ConstructorCount++;
55:    }
56:
57:    // Converts a character array to a String
58:    String::String(const char * const cString)
59:    {
60:       itsLen = strlen(cString);
61:       itsString = new char[itsLen+1];
62:       for (int i = 0; i<itsLen; i++)
63:          itsString[i] = cString[i];
64:       itsString[itsLen]='\0';
65:       // cout << "\tString(char*) constructor\n";
66:       // ConstructorCount++;
67:    }
68:
```

LISTING **16.1**   continued

```
69:    // copy constructor
70:    String::String (const String & rhs)
71:    {
72:        itsLen=rhs.GetLen();
73:        itsString = new char[itsLen+1];
74:        for (int i = 0; i<itsLen;i++)
75:            itsString[i] = rhs[i];
76:        itsString[itsLen] = '\0';
77:        // cout << "\tString(String&) constructor\n";
78:        // ConstructorCount++;
79:    }
80:
81:    // destructor, frees allocated memory
82:    String::~String ()
83:    {
84:        delete [] itsString;
85:        itsLen = 0;
86:        // cout << "\tString destructor\n";
87:    }
88:
89:    // operator equals, frees existing memory
90:    // then copies string and size
91:    String& String::operator=(const String & rhs)
92:    {
93:        if (this == &rhs)
94:            return *this;
95:        delete [] itsString;
96:        itsLen=rhs.GetLen();
97:        itsString = new char[itsLen+1];
98:        for (int i = 0; i<itsLen;i++)
99:            itsString[i] = rhs[i];
100:        itsString[itsLen] = '\0';
101:        return *this;
102:        // cout << "\tString operator=\n";
103:    }
104:
105:    //non constant offset operator, returns
106:    // reference to character so it can be
107:    // changed!
108:    char & String::operator[](int offset)
109:    {
110:        if (offset > itsLen)
111:            return itsString[itsLen-1];
112:        else
113:            return itsString[offset];
114:    }
115:
116:    // constant offset operator for use
```

LISTING 16.1   continued

```
117:    // on const objects (see copy constructor!)
118:    char String::operator[](int offset) const
119:    {
120:        if (offset > itsLen)
121:            return itsString[itsLen-1];
122:        else
123:            return itsString[offset];
124:    }
125:
126:    // creates a new string by adding current
127:    // string to rhs
128:    String String::operator+(const String& rhs)
129:    {
130:        int  totalLen = itsLen + rhs.GetLen();
131:        String temp(totalLen);
132:        int i, j;
133:        for (i = 0; i<itsLen; i++)
134:            temp[i] = itsString[i];
135:        for (j = 0; j<rhs.GetLen(); j++, i++)
136:            temp[i] = rhs[j];
137:        temp[totalLen]='\0';
138:        return temp;
139:    }
140:
141:    // changes current string, returns nothing
142:    void String::operator+=(const String& rhs)
143:    {
144:        unsigned short rhsLen = rhs.GetLen();
145:        unsigned short totalLen = itsLen + rhsLen;
146:        String  temp(totalLen);
147:        int i, j;
148:        for (i = 0; i<itsLen; i++)
149:            temp[i] = itsString[i];
150:        for (j = 0; j<rhs.GetLen(); j++, i++)
151:            temp[i] = rhs[i-itsLen];
152:        temp[totalLen]='\0';
153:        *this = temp;
154:    }
155:
156:    // int String::ConstructorCount = 0;
```

NOTE   Put the code from Listing 16.1 into a file called `MyString.hpp`. Then, any time you need the `String` class, you can include Listing 16.1 by using `#include "MyString.hpp"`, such as in this listing. You might notice a number of commented lines in this listing. The purpose of these lines are explained throughout today's lesson.

ANALYSIS Listing 16.1 provides a String class much like the one used in Listing 13.12 of Day 13. The significant difference here is that the constructors and a few other functions in Listing 13.12 have print statements to show their use, which are currently commented out in Listing 16.1. These functions will be used in later examples.

On line 25, the static member variable ConstructorCount is declared, and on line 156 it is initialized. This variable is incremented in each string constructor. All this is currently commented out; it will be used in a later listing.

For convenience, the implementation is included with the declaration of the class. In a real-world program, you would save the class declaration in String.hpp and the implementation in String.cpp. You would then add String.cpp into your program (using add files or a make file) and have String.cpp #include String.hpp.

Of course, in a real program, you'd use the C++ Standard Library String class, and not this string class in the first place.

Listing 16.2 describes an Employee class that contains three string objects. These objects are used to hold an employee's first and last names as well as their address.

LISTING 16.2   The Employee Class and Driver Program

```
0:  // Listing 16.2 The Employee Class and Driver Program
1:  #include "MyString.hpp"
2:
3:  class Employee
4:  {
5:    public:
6:      Employee();
7:      Employee(char *, char *, char *, long);
8:      ~Employee();
9:      Employee(const Employee&);
10:     Employee & operator= (const Employee &);
11:
12:     const String & GetFirstName() const
13:       { return itsFirstName; }
14:     const String & GetLastName() const { return itsLastName; }
15:     const String & GetAddress() const { return itsAddress; }
16:     long GetSalary() const { return itsSalary; }
17:
18:     void SetFirstName(const String & fName)
19:       { itsFirstName = fName; }
20:     void SetLastName(const String & lName)
21:       { itsLastName = lName; }
22:     void SetAddress(const String & address)
23:       { itsAddress = address; }
24:     void SetSalary(long salary) { itsSalary = salary; }
```

LISTING 16.2 continued

```
25:    private:
26:       String    itsFirstName;
27:       String    itsLastName;
28:       String    itsAddress;
29:       long      itsSalary;
30:    };
31:
32:    Employee::Employee():
33:        itsFirstName(""),
34:        itsLastName(""),
35:        itsAddress(""),
36:        itsSalary(0)
37:    {}
38:
39:    Employee::Employee(char * firstName, char * lastName,
40:        char * address, long salary):
41:        itsFirstName(firstName),
42:        itsLastName(lastName),
43:        itsAddress(address),
44:        itsSalary(salary)
45:    {}
46:
47:    Employee::Employee(const Employee & rhs):
48:        itsFirstName(rhs.GetFirstName()),
49:        itsLastName(rhs.GetLastName()),
50:        itsAddress(rhs.GetAddress()),
51:        itsSalary(rhs.GetSalary())
52:    {}
53:
54:    Employee::~Employee() {}
55:
56:    Employee & Employee::operator= (const Employee & rhs)
57:    {
58:        if (this == &rhs)
59:           return *this;
60:
61:        itsFirstName = rhs.GetFirstName();
62:        itsLastName = rhs.GetLastName();
63:        itsAddress = rhs.GetAddress();
64:        itsSalary = rhs.GetSalary();
65:
66:        return *this;
67:    }
68:
69:    int main()
70:    {
71:        Employee Edie("Jane","Doe","1461 Shore Parkway", 20000);
72:        Edie.SetSalary(50000);
73:        String LastName("Levine");
74:        Edie.SetLastName(LastName);
75:        Edie.SetFirstName("Edythe");
```

LISTING 16.2   continued

```
76:
77:     cout << "Name: ";
78:     cout << Edie.GetFirstName().GetString();
79:     cout << " " << Edie.GetLastName().GetString();
80:     cout << ".\nAddress: ";
81:     cout << Edie.GetAddress().GetString();
82:     cout << ".\nSalary: " ;
83:     cout << Edie.GetSalary();
84:     return 0;
85:  }
```

OUTPUT   Name: Edythe Levine.
Address: 1461 Shore Parkway.
Salary: 50000

ANALYSIS   Listing 16.2 shows the Employee class, which contains three string objects (see lines 26–28): itsFirstName, itsLastName, and itsAddress.

On line 71, an Employee object called Edie is created, and four values are passed in. On line 72, the Employee access function SetSalary() is called, with the constant value 50000. Note that in a real program, this would be either a dynamic value (set at runtime) or a constant.

On line 73, a string called LastName is created and initialized using a C++ string constant. This string object is then used as an argument to SetLastName() on line 74.

On line 75, the Employee function SetFirstName() is called with yet another string constant. However, if you are paying close attention, you will notice that Employee does not have a function SetFirstName() that takes a character string as its argument; SetFirstName() requires a constant string reference (see line 18).

The compiler resolves this because it knows how to make a string from a constant character string. It knows this because you told it how to do so on line 11 of Listing 16.1.

Looking at lines 78, 79, and 81, you see something that might appear unusual. You might be wondering why GetString() has been tacked onto the different methods from the Employee class:

```
78:     cout << Edie.GetFirstName().GetString();
```

The Edie object's GetFirstName() method returns a String. Unfortunately, the String object created in Listing 16.1 does not yet support the cout << operator. To satisfy cout, you need to return a C-Style string. GetString() is a method on your String object that returns a C-Style string. This problem will be fixed soon.

Accessing Members of the Aggregated Class

A class that aggregates other objects does not have special access to those object's member data and functions. Rather, it has whatever access is normally exposed. For example, `Employee` objects do not have special access to the member variables of `String`. If the `Employee` object `Edie` tries to access the private member variable `itsLen` of its own `itsFirstName` member variable, it receives a compile-time error. This is not much of a burden, however. The accessor functions provide an interface for the `String` class, and the `Employee` class need not worry about the implementation details, any more than it worries about how the integer variable, `itsSalary`, stores its information.

16

NOTE

> Aggregated members don't have any special access to the members of the class within which they are aggregated. The only ability they have to access the instance that aggregates them is to have a copy of the owner class "`this`" pointer passed to them at creation or at some point thereafter. If this is done, they have the same normal access to that object as they would to any other.

Controlling Access to Aggregated Members

Note that the `String` class provides an overloaded plus operator: `operator+`. The designer of the `Employee` class has blocked access to the `operator+` being called on `Employee` objects by declaring that all the string accessors, such as `GetFirstName()`, return a constant reference. Because `operator+` is not (and can't be) a `const` function (it changes the object it is called on), attempting to write the following causes a compile-time error:

```
String buffer = Edie.GetFirstName() + Edie.GetLastName();
```

`GetFirstName()` returns a constant `String`, and you can't call `operator+` on a constant object.

To fix this, overload `GetFirstName()` to be non-const:

```
const String & GetFirstName() const { return itsFirstName; }
String & GetFirstName()  { return itsFirstName; }
```

Note that the return value is no longer `const` and that the member function itself is no longer `const`. Changing just the return value is not sufficient to overload the function name; you must change the "constness" of the function itself.

Cost of Aggregation

When you have aggregated objects, there can be a cost in performance. Each time an
Employee string is constructed or copied, you are also constructing each of its aggregated
string objects.

Uncommenting the cout statements in Listing 16.1 reveals how often the constructors
are called. Listing 16.3 rewrites the driver program to add print statements indicating
where in the program objects are being created. Uncomment the lines in Listing 16.1,
and then compile Listing 16.3.

NOTE _____ | To compile this listing, uncomment lines 40, 53, 65, 77, 86, and 102 in
Listing 16.1.

LISTING 16.3   Aggregated Class Constructors

```
0:  //Listing 16.3 Aggregated Class Constructors
1:  #include "MyString.hpp"
2:
3:  class Employee
4:  {
5:    public:
6:      Employee();
7:      Employee(char *, char *, char *, long);
8:      ~Employee();
9:      Employee(const Employee&);
10:     Employee & operator= (const Employee &);
11:
12:     const String & GetFirstName() const
13:        { return itsFirstName; }
14:     const String & GetLastName() const { return itsLastName; }
15:     const String & GetAddress() const { return itsAddress; }
16:     long GetSalary() const { return itsSalary; }
17:
18:     void SetFirstName(const String & fName)
19:        { itsFirstName = fName; }
20:     void SetLastName(const String & lName)
21:        { itsLastName = lName; }
22:     void SetAddress(const String & address)
23:        { itsAddress = address; }
24:     void SetSalary(long salary) { itsSalary = salary; }
25:    private:
26:     String    itsFirstName;
27:     String    itsLastName;
28:     String    itsAddress;
29:     long      itsSalary;
```

LISTING 16.3   continued

```
30:  };
31:
32:  Employee::Employee():
33:      itsFirstName(""),
34:      itsLastName(""),
35:      itsAddress(""),
36:      itsSalary(0)
37:  {}
38:
39:  Employee::Employee(char * firstName, char * lastName,
40:      char * address, long salary):
41:      itsFirstName(firstName),
42:      itsLastName(lastName),
43:      itsAddress(address),
44:      itsSalary(salary)
45:  {}
46:
47:  Employee::Employee(const Employee & rhs):
48:      itsFirstName(rhs.GetFirstName()),
49:      itsLastName(rhs.GetLastName()),
50:      itsAddress(rhs.GetAddress()),
51:      itsSalary(rhs.GetSalary())
52:  {}
53:
54:  Employee::~Employee() {}
55:
56:  Employee & Employee::operator= (const Employee & rhs)
57:  {
58:      if (this == &rhs)
59:         return *this;
60:
61:      itsFirstName = rhs.GetFirstName();
62:      itsLastName = rhs.GetLastName();
63:      itsAddress = rhs.GetAddress();
64:      itsSalary = rhs.GetSalary();
65:
66:      return *this;
67:  }
68:
69:  int main()
70:  {
71:      cout << "Creating Edie...\n";
72:      Employee Edie("Jane","Doe","1461 Shore Parkway", 20000);
73:      Edie.SetSalary(20000);
74:      cout << "Calling SetFirstName with char *...\n";
75:      Edie.SetFirstName("Edythe");
76:      cout << "Creating temporary string LastName...\n";
77:      String LastName("Levine");
78:      Edie.SetLastName(LastName);
79:
80:      cout << "Name: ";
```

16

LISTING 16.3   continued

```
81:     cout << Edie.GetFirstName().GetString();
82:     cout << " " << Edie.GetLastName().GetString();
83:     cout << "\nAddress: ";
84:     cout << Edie.GetAddress().GetString();
85:     cout << "\nSalary: " ;
86:     cout << Edie.GetSalary();
87:     cout << endl;
88:     return 0;
89:   }
```

OUTPUT

```
 1:  Creating Edie...
 2:          String(char*) constructor
 3:          String(char*) constructor
 4:          String(char*) constructor
 5:  Calling SetFirstName with char *...
 6:          String(char*) constructor
 7:          String destructor
 8:  Creating temporary string LastName...
 9:          String(char*) constructor
10:  Name: Edythe Levine
11:  Address: 1461 Shore Parkway
12:  Salary: 20000
13:          String destructor
14:          String destructor
15:          String destructor
16:          String destructor
```

ANALYSIS Listing 16.3 uses the same class declarations as Listings 16.1 and 16.2. However, the cout statements have been uncommented. The output from Listing 16.3 has been numbered to make analysis easier.

On line 71 of Listing 16.3, the statement Creating Edie... is printed, as reflected on line 1 of the output. On line 72, an Employee object, Edie, is created with four parameters, the first three being strings. The output reflects the constructor for String being called three times, as expected.

Line 74 prints an information statement, and then on line 75 is the statement Edie.SetFirstName("Edythe"). This statement causes a temporary string to be created from the character string "Edythe", as reflected on lines 5 and 6 of the output. Note that the temporary String object is destroyed immediately after it is used in the assignment statement.

On line 77, a String object is created in the body of the program. Here, the programmer is doing explicitly what the compiler did implicitly on the previous statement. This time you see the constructor on line 8 of the output, but no destructor. This object is not destroyed until it goes out of scope at the end of the function.

On lines 81–87, the strings in the Employee object are destroyed as the Employee object falls out of scope, and the string LastName, created on line 77, is destroyed as well when it falls out of scope.

Copying by Value

Listing 16.3 illustrates how the creation of one Employee object caused five string constructor calls. Listing 16.4 again rewrites the driver program. This time, the print statements are not used, but the string static member variable ConstructorCount is uncommented and used.

Examination of Listing 16.1 shows that ConstructorCount is incremented each time a string constructor is called. The driver program in 16.4 calls the print functions, passing in the Employee object, first by reference and then by value. ConstructorCount keeps track of how many string objects are created when the employee is passed as a parameter.

NOTE

> To compile this listing, leave in the lines that you uncommented in Listing 16.1 to run Listing 16.3, and in addition, uncomment lines 25, 41, 54, 66, 78, and 155 from Listing 16.1.

LISTING 16.4   Passing by Value

```
0:  // Listing 16.4 Passing by Value
1:  #include "MyString.hpp"
2:
3:  class Employee
4:  {
5:    public:
6:      Employee();
7:      Employee(char *, char *, char *, long);
8:      ~Employee();
9:      Employee(const Employee&);
10:     Employee & operator= (const Employee &);
11:
12:     const String & GetFirstName() const
13:        { return itsFirstName; }
14:     const String & GetLastName() const { return itsLastName; }
15:     const String & GetAddress() const { return itsAddress; }
16:     long GetSalary() const { return itsSalary; }
17:
18:     void SetFirstName(const String & fName)
19:        { itsFirstName = fName; }
20:     void SetLastName(const String & lName)
21:        { itsLastName = lName; }
```

LISTING **16.4** continued

```
22:        void SetAddress(const String & address)
23:          { itsAddress = address; }
24:        void SetSalary(long salary) { itsSalary = salary; }
25:     private:
26:       String    itsFirstName;
27:       String    itsLastName;
28:       String    itsAddress;
29:       long      itsSalary;
30:   };
31:
32:   Employee::Employee():
33:       itsFirstName(""),
34:       itsLastName(""),
35:       itsAddress(""),
36:       itsSalary(0)
37:   {}
38:
39:   Employee::Employee(char * firstName, char * lastName,
40:      char * address, long salary):
41:       itsFirstName(firstName),
42:       itsLastName(lastName),
43:       itsAddress(address),
44:       itsSalary(salary)
45:   {}
46:
47:   Employee::Employee(const Employee & rhs):
48:       itsFirstName(rhs.GetFirstName()),
49:       itsLastName(rhs.GetLastName()),
50:       itsAddress(rhs.GetAddress()),
51:       itsSalary(rhs.GetSalary())
52:   {}
53:
54:   Employee::~Employee() {}
55:
56:   Employee & Employee::operator= (const Employee & rhs)
57:   {
58:      if (this == &rhs)
59:         return *this;
60:
61:      itsFirstName = rhs.GetFirstName();
62:      itsLastName = rhs.GetLastName();
63:      itsAddress = rhs.GetAddress();
64:      itsSalary = rhs.GetSalary();
65:
66:      return *this;
67:   }
68:
69:   void PrintFunc(Employee);
```

LISTING 16.4   continued

```
70:   void rPrintFunc(const Employee&);
71:
72:   int main()
73:   {
74:       Employee Edie("Jane","Doe","1461 Shore Parkway", 20000);
75:       Edie.SetSalary(20000);
76:       Edie.SetFirstName("Edythe");
77:       String LastName("Levine");
78:       Edie.SetLastName(LastName);
79:
80:       cout << "Constructor count: " ;
81:       cout << String::ConstructorCount << endl;
82:       rPrintFunc(Edie);
83:       cout << "Constructor count: ";
84:       cout << String::ConstructorCount << endl;
85:       PrintFunc(Edie);
86:       cout << "Constructor count: ";
87:       cout << String::ConstructorCount << endl;
88:       return 0;
89:   }
90:   void PrintFunc (Employee Edie)
91:   {
92:       cout << "Name: ";
93:       cout << Edie.GetFirstName().GetString();
94:       cout << " " << Edie.GetLastName().GetString();
95:       cout << ".\nAddress: ";
96:       cout << Edie.GetAddress().GetString();
97:       cout << ".\nSalary: " ;
98:       cout << Edie.GetSalary();
99:       cout << endl;
100:  }
101:
102:  void rPrintFunc (const Employee& Edie)
103:  {
104:      cout << "Name: ";
105:      cout << Edie.GetFirstName().GetString();
106:      cout << " " << Edie.GetLastName().GetString();
107:      cout << "\nAddress: ";
108:      cout << Edie.GetAddress().GetString();
109:      cout << "\nSalary: " ;
110:      cout << Edie.GetSalary();
111:      cout << endl;
112:  }
```

OUTPUT

```
String(char*) constructor
String(char*) constructor
String(char*) constructor
String(char*) constructor
String destructor
String(char*) constructor
```

```
Constructor count: 5
Name: Edythe Levine
Address: 1461 Shore Parkway
Salary: 20000
Constructor count: 5
        String(String&) constructor
        String(String&) constructor
        String(String&) constructor
Name: Edythe Levine.
Address: 1461 Shore Parkway.
Salary: 20000
        String destructor
        String destructor
        String destructor
Constructor count: 8
        String destructor
        String destructor
        String destructor
        String destructor
```

ANALYSIS The output shows that five string objects were created as part of creating one Employee object on line 74. When the Employee object is passed on line 82 to rPrintFunc() by reference, no additional Employee objects are created, and so no additional String objects are created. (They, too, are passed by reference.) You can see this in the early part of the output where the constructure count remains at 5 and no constructures are called.

When, on line 85, the Employee object is passed to PrintFunc() by value, a copy of the Employee is created, and three more string objects are created (by calls to the copy constructor).

Implementation in Terms of Inheritance Versus Aggregation/Delegation

At times, one class wants to draw on some of the capabilities of another class. For example, suppose you need to create a PartsCatalog class. The specification you've been given defines a PartsCatalog as a collection of parts; each part has a unique part number. The PartsCatalog does not allow duplicate entries and does allow access by part number.

The listing for the Week in Review for Week 2 provides a PartsList class. This PartsList is well tested and understood, and you'd like to build on that when making your PartsCatalog, rather than inventing it from scratch.

You could create a new `PartsCatalog` class and have it contain a `PartsList`. The `PartsCatalog` could delegate management of the linked list to its aggregated `PartsList` object.

An alternative would be to make the `PartsCatalog` derive from `PartsList` and, thereby, inherit the properties of a `PartsList`. Remembering, however, that public inheritance provides an *is-a* relationship, you should ask whether a `PartsCatalog` really is a type of `PartsList`.

One way to answer the question of whether `PartsCatalog` is a `PartsList` is to assume that `PartsList` is the base and `PartsCatalog` is the derived class, and then to ask these other questions:

1. Is anything in the base class that should not be in the derived? For example, does the `PartsList` base class have functions that are inappropriate for the `PartsCatalog` class? If so, you probably don't want public inheritance.

2. Might the class you are creating have more than one of the base? For example, might a `PartsCatalog` need two `PartsLists` to do its job? If it might, you almost certainly want to use aggregation.

3. Do you need to inherit from the base class so that you can take advantage of virtual functions or access protected members? If so, you must use inheritance, public or private.

Based on the answers to these questions, you must choose between public inheritance (the *is-a* relationship) and either private inheritance (explained later today) or aggregation (the *has-a* relationship).

Terminology

Several terms are being used here. The following helps to summarize these key terms:

- **Aggregation**—Declaring an object as a member of another class contained by that class. This is also referred to as *has-a*.

- **Delegation**—Using the members of an aggregated class to perform functions for the containing class.

- **Implemented in terms of**—Building one class on the capabilities of another without using public inheritance (for instance, by using protected or private inheritance).

Using Delegation

Why not derive `PartsCatalog` from `PartsList`? The `PartsCatalog` isn't a `PartsList` because `PartsLists` are ordered collections, and each member of the collection can repeat. The PartsCatalog has unique entries that are not ordered. The fifth member of the PartsCatalog is not part number 5.

Certainly, it would have been possible to inherit publicly from PartsList and then override Insert() and the offset operators ([]) to do the right thing, but then you would have changed the essence of the PartsList class. Instead, you'll build a PartsCatalog that has no offset operator, does not allow duplicates, and defines the operator+ to combine two sets.

The first way to accomplish this is with aggregation. The PartsCatalog will delegate list management to an aggregated PartsList. Listing 16.5 illustrates this approach.

LISTING 16.5   Delegating to an Aggregated PartsList

```
0:   // Listing 16.5 Delegating to an Aggregated PartsList
1:
2:   #include <iostream>
3:   using namespace std;
4:
5:   // *************** Part ***********
6:
7:   // Abstract base class of parts
8:   class Part
9:   {
10:    public:
11:       Part():itsPartNumber(1) {}
12:       Part(int PartNumber):
13:       itsPartNumber(PartNumber){}
14:       virtual ~Part(){}
15:       int GetPartNumber() const
16:          { return itsPartNumber; }
17:       virtual void Display() const =0;
18:    private:
19:       int itsPartNumber;
20:   };
21:
22:   // implementation of pure virtual function so that
23:   // derived classes can chain up
24:   void Part::Display() const
25:   {
26:       cout << "\nPart Number: " << itsPartNumber << endl;
27:   }
28:
29:   // *************** Car Part ***********
30:
31:   class CarPart : public Part
32:   {
33:    public:
34:       CarPart():itsModelYear(94){}
35:       CarPart(int year, int partNumber);
```

LISTING 16.5   continued

```
36:     virtual void Display() const
37:     {
38:        Part::Display();
39:        cout << "Model Year: ";
40:        cout << itsModelYear << endl;
41:     }
42:   private:
43:     int itsModelYear;
44: };
45:
46: CarPart::CarPart(int year, int partNumber):
47:    itsModelYear(year),
48:    Part(partNumber)
49: {}
50:
51:
52: // *************** AirPlane Part ************
53:
54: class AirPlanePart : public Part
55: {
56:   public:
57:     AirPlanePart():itsEngineNumber(1){};
58:     AirPlanePart
59:     (int EngineNumber, int PartNumber);
60:     virtual void Display() const
61:     {
62:        Part::Display();
63:        cout << "Engine No.: ";
64:        cout << itsEngineNumber << endl;
65:     }
66:   private:
67:     int itsEngineNumber;
68: };
69:
70: AirPlanePart::AirPlanePart
71: (int EngineNumber, int PartNumber):
72:    itsEngineNumber(EngineNumber),
73:    Part(PartNumber)
74: {}
75:
76: // *************** Part Node ************
77: class PartNode
78: {
79:   public:
80:     PartNode (Part*);
81:     ~PartNode();
82:     void SetNext(PartNode * node)
83:        { itsNext = node; }
84:     PartNode * GetNext() const;
85:     Part * GetPart() const;
86:   private:
87:     Part *itsPart;
```

16

LISTING 16.5 continued

```
88:        PartNode * itsNext;
89:    };
90:    // PartNode Implementations...
91:
92:    PartNode::PartNode(Part* pPart):
93:        itsPart(pPart),
94:        itsNext(0)
95:    {}
96:
97:    PartNode::~PartNode()
98:    {
99:        delete itsPart;
100:       itsPart = 0;
101:       delete itsNext;
102:       itsNext = 0;
103:   }
104:
105:   // Returns NULL if no next PartNode
106:   PartNode * PartNode::GetNext() const
107:   {
108:       return itsNext;
109:   }
110:
111:   Part * PartNode::GetPart() const
112:   {
113:       if (itsPart)
114:           return itsPart;
115:       else
116:           return NULL; //error
117:   }
118:
119:
120:
121:   // *************** Part List ***********
122:   class PartsList
123:   {
124:     public:
125:       PartsList();
126:       ~PartsList();
127:       // needs copy constructor and operator equals!
128:       void    Iterate(void (Part::*f)()const) const;
129:       Part*   Find(int & position, int PartNumber)  const;
130:       Part*   GetFirst() const;
131:       void    Insert(Part *);
132:       Part*   operator[](int) const;
133:       int     GetCount() const { return itsCount; }
134:       static  PartsList& GetGlobalPartsList()
135:       {
136:           return  GlobalPartsList;
137:       }
```

LISTING 16.5 continued

```
138:    private:
139:      PartNode * pHead;
140:      int itsCount;
141:      static PartsList GlobalPartsList;
142:  };
143:
144:  PartsList PartsList::GlobalPartsList;
145:
146:
147:  PartsList::PartsList():
148:    pHead(0),
149:    itsCount(0)
150:  {}
151:
152:  PartsList::~PartsList()
153:  {
154:    delete pHead;
155:  }
156:
157:  Part*   PartsList::GetFirst() const
158:  {
159:    if (pHead)
160:      return pHead->GetPart();
161:    else
162:      return NULL;  // error catch here
163:  }
164:
165:  Part *  PartsList::operator[](int offSet) const
166:  {
167:    PartNode* pNode = pHead;
168:
169:    if (!pHead)
170:      return NULL; // error catch here
171:
172:    if (offSet > itsCount)
173:      return NULL; // error
174:
175:    for (int i=0;i<offSet; i++)
176:      pNode = pNode->GetNext();
177:
178:    return   pNode->GetPart();
179:  }
180:
181:  Part*   PartsList::Find(
182:    int & position,
183:    int PartNumber)  const
184:  {
185:    PartNode * pNode = 0;
186:    for (pNode = pHead, position = 0;
187:         pNode!=NULL;
188:         pNode = pNode->GetNext(), position++)
189:      {
```

LISTING **16.5**   continued

```
190:            if (pNode->GetPart()->GetPartNumber() == PartNumber)
191:                break;
192:        }
193:        if (pNode == NULL)
194:            return NULL;
195:        else
196:            return pNode->GetPart();
197:    }
198:
199:    void PartsList::Iterate(void (Part::*func)()const) const
200:    {
201:        if (!pHead)
202:            return;
203:        PartNode* pNode = pHead;
204:        do
205:            (pNode->GetPart()->*func)();
206:        while ((pNode = pNode->GetNext()) != 0);
207:    }
208:
209:    void PartsList::Insert(Part* pPart)
210:    {
211:        PartNode * pNode = new PartNode(pPart);
212:        PartNode * pCurrent = pHead;
213:        PartNode * pNext = 0;
214:
215:        int New =  pPart->GetPartNumber();
216:        int Next = 0;
217:        itsCount++;
218:
219:        if (!pHead)
220:        {
221:            pHead = pNode;
222:            return;
223:        }
224:
225:        // if this one is smaller than head
226:        // this one is the new head
227:        if (pHead->GetPart()->GetPartNumber() > New)
228:        {
229:            pNode->SetNext(pHead);
230:            pHead = pNode;
231:            return;
232:        }
233:
234:        for (;;)
235:        {
236:            // if there is no next, append this new one
237:            if (!pCurrent->GetNext())
238:            {
239:                pCurrent->SetNext(pNode);
```

LISTING 16.5   continued

```
240:              return;
241:          }
242:
243:          // if this goes after this one and before the next
244:          // then insert it here, otherwise get the next
245:          pNext = pCurrent->GetNext();
246:          Next = pNext->GetPart()->GetPartNumber();
247:          if (Next > New)
248:          {
249:              pCurrent->SetNext(pNode);
250:              pNode->SetNext(pNext);
251:              return;
252:          }
253:          pCurrent = pNext;
254:      }
255:  }
256:
257:  class PartsCatalog
258:  {
259:    public:
260:      void Insert(Part *);
261:      int Exists(int PartNumber);
262:      Part * Get(int PartNumber);
263:      operator+(const PartsCatalog &);
264:      void ShowAll() { thePartsList.Iterate(Part::Display); }
265:    private:
266:      PartsList thePartsList;
267:  };
268:
269:  void PartsCatalog::Insert(Part * newPart)
270:  {
271:      int partNumber =  newPart->GetPartNumber();
272:      int offset;
273:
274:      if (!thePartsList.Find(offset, partNumber))
275:      {
276:          thePartsList.Insert(newPart);
277:      }
278:      else
279:      {
280:          cout << partNumber << " was the ";
281:          switch (offset)
282:          {
283:            case 0:  cout << "first "; break;
284:            case 1:  cout << "second "; break;
285:            case 2:  cout << "third "; break;
286:            default: cout << offset+1 << "th ";
287:          }
288:          cout << "entry. Rejected!" << endl;
289:      }
290:  }
291:
```

16

LISTING 16.5 continued

```
292:  int PartsCatalog::Exists(int PartNumber)
293:  {
294:     int offset;
295:     thePartsList.Find(offset,PartNumber);
296:     return offset;
297:  }
298:
299:  Part * PartsCatalog::Get(int PartNumber)
300:  {
301:     int offset;
302:     Part * thePart = thePartsList.Find(offset, PartNumber);
303:     return thePart;
304:  }
305:
306:
307:  int main()
308:  {
309:     PartsCatalog pc;
310:     Part * pPart = 0;
311:     int PartNumber;
312:     int value;
313:     int choice = 99;
314:
315:     while (choice != 0)
316:     {
317:        cout << "(0)Quit (1)Car (2)Plane: ";
318:        cin >> choice;
319:
320:        if (choice != 0)
321:        {
322:           cout << "New PartNumber?: ";
323:           cin >> PartNumber;
324:
325:           if (choice == 1)
326:           {
327:              cout << "Model Year?: ";
328:              cin >> value;
329:              pPart = new CarPart(value,PartNumber);
330:           }
331:           else
332:           {
333:              cout << "Engine Number?: ";
334:              cin >> value;
335:              pPart = new AirPlanePart(value,PartNumber);
336:           }
337:           pc.Insert(pPart);
338:        }
339:     }
340:     pc.ShowAll();
341:     return 0;
342:  }
```

OUTPUT

```
(0)Quit (1)Car (2)Plane:  1
New PartNumber?: 1234
Model Year?: 94
(0)Quit (1)Car (2)Plane:  1
New PartNumber?: 4434
Model Year?: 93
(0)Quit (1)Car (2)Plane:  1
New PartNumber?: 1234
Model Year?: 94
1234 was the first entry. Rejected!
(0)Quit (1)Car (2)Plane:  1
New PartNumber?: 2345
Model Year?: 93
(0)Quit (1)Car (2)Plane:  0

Part Number: 1234
Model Year: 94

Part Number: 2345
Model Year: 93

Part Number: 4434
Model Year: 93
```

16

NOTE

> Some compilers cannot compile line 264, even though it is legal C++. If your
> compiler complains about this line, change it to
>
> 264:   void ShowAll() { thePartsList.Iterate(&Part::Display); }
>
> (Note the addition of the ampersand in front of Part::Display.) If this fixes
> the problem, immediately call your compiler vendor and complain.

ANALYSIS   Listing 16.5 reproduces the Part, PartNode, and PartsList classes from Week 2 in Review.

A new class, PartsCatalog, is declared on lines 257–267. PartsCatalog has a PartsList as its data member (line 265), to which it delegates list management. Another way to say this is that the PartsCatalog is implemented in terms of this PartsList.

Note that clients of the PartsCatalog do not have access to the PartsList directly. You can see that PartsList is declared as a private member. The interface to this is through the PartsCatalog, and as such, the behavior of the PartsList is dramatically changed. For example, the PartsCatalog::Insert() method does not allow duplicate entries into the PartsList.

The implementation of PartsCatalog::Insert() starts on line 269. The Part that is passed in as a parameter is asked for the value of its itsPartNumber member variable.

On line 274, this value is fed to the PartsList's Find() method, and if no match is found, the number is inserted (line 276); otherwise, an informative error message is printed (starting on line 280).

Note that PartsCatalog does the actual insert by calling Insert() on its member variable, pl, which is a PartsList. The mechanics of the actual insertion and the maintenance of the linked list, as well as searching and retrieving from the linked list, are maintained in the aggregated PartsList member of PartsCatalog. No reason exists for PartsCatalog to reproduce this code; it can take full advantage of the well-defined interface.

This is the essence of reusability within C++: PartsCatalog can reuse the PartsList code, and the designer of PartsCatalog is free to ignore the implementation details of PartsList. The interface to PartsList (that is, the class declaration) provides all the information needed by the designer of the PartsCatalog class.

NOTE	If you want more information about PartsList, review the Week 2 in Review listing and analysis!

Private Inheritance

If PartsCatalog needed access to the protected members of PartsList (in this case, none exist), or needed to override any of the PartsList methods, then PartsCatalog would be forced to inherit from PartsList.

Because a PartsCatalog is not a PartsList object, and because you don't want to expose the entire set of functionality of PartsList to clients of PartsCatalog, you would need to use private inheritance. Private inheritance allows you to inherit from another class and to keep the internals of that class completely private to your derived class.

The first thing to know about private inheritance is that all the base member variables and functions are treated as if they were declared to be private, regardless of their actual access level in the base. Thus, to any function that is not a member function of PartsCatalog, every function inherited from PartsList is inaccessible. This is critical: Private inheritance does not involve inheriting interface, only implementation.

To clients of the PartsCatalog class, the PartsList class is invisible. None of its interface is available to them: They can't call any of its methods. They can call PartsCatalog methods; however, PartsCatalog methods can then access all of PartsList because PartsCatalog is derived from PartsList. The important thing here is that the PartsCatalog isn't a PartsList, as would have been implied by public inheritance. It is implemented in terms of a `PartsList`, just as would have been the case with aggregation. The private inheritance is just a convenience.

Listing 16.6 demonstrates the use of private inheritance by rewriting the `PartsCatalog` class as privately derived from `PartsList`.

LISTING 16.6   Private Inheritance

```
0:  //Listing 16.6 demonstrates private inheritance
1:  #include <iostream>
2:  using namespace std;
3:
4:  // *************** Part ***********
5:
6:  // Abstract base class of parts
7:  class Part
8:  {
9:    public:
10:      Part():itsPartNumber(1) {}
11:      Part(int PartNumber):
12:      itsPartNumber(PartNumber){}
13:      virtual ~Part(){}
14:      int GetPartNumber() const
15:        { return itsPartNumber; }
16:      virtual void Display() const =0;
17:    private:
18:      int itsPartNumber;
19:  };
20:
21:  // implementation of pure virtual function so that
22:  // derived classes can chain up
23:  void Part::Display() const
24:  {
25:    cout << "\nPart Number: " << itsPartNumber << endl;
26:  }
27:
28:  // *************** Car Part ***********
29:
30:  class CarPart : public Part
31:  {
32:    public:
33:      CarPart():itsModelYear(94){}
34:      CarPart(int year, int partNumber);
35:      virtual void Display() const
36:      {
37:        Part::Display();
38:        cout << "Model Year: ";
39:        cout << itsModelYear << endl;
40:      }
41:    private:
42:      int itsModelYear;
```

16

LISTING 16.6 continued

```
43:  };
44:
45:  CarPart::CarPart(int year, int partNumber):
46:      itsModelYear(year),
47:      Part(partNumber)
48:  {}
49:
50:
51:  // **************** AirPlane Part ************
52:
53:  class AirPlanePart : public Part
54:  {
55:    public:
56:      AirPlanePart():itsEngineNumber(1){};
57:      AirPlanePart(int EngineNumber, int PartNumber);
58:      virtual void Display() const
59:      {
60:         Part::Display();
61:         cout << "Engine No.: ";
62:         cout << itsEngineNumber << endl;
63:      }
64:    private:
65:      int itsEngineNumber;
66:  };
67:
68:  AirPlanePart::AirPlanePart
69:  (int EngineNumber, int PartNumber):
70:      itsEngineNumber(EngineNumber),
71:      Part(PartNumber)
72:  {}
73:
74:  // *************** Part Node ************
75:  class PartNode
76:  {
77:    public:
78:      PartNode (Part*);
79:      ~PartNode();
80:      void SetNext(PartNode * node)
81:         { itsNext = node; }
82:      PartNode * GetNext() const;
83:      Part * GetPart() const;
84:    private:
85:      Part *itsPart;
86:      PartNode * itsNext;
87:  };
88:  // PartNode Implementations...
89:
90:  PartNode::PartNode(Part* pPart):
91:      itsPart(pPart),
92:      itsNext(0)
```

LISTING **16.6**   continued

```
 93:  {}
 94:
 95:  PartNode::~PartNode()
 96:  {
 97:     delete itsPart;
 98:     itsPart = 0;
 99:     delete itsNext;
100:     itsNext = 0;
101:  }
102:
103:  // Returns NULL if no next PartNode
104:  PartNode * PartNode::GetNext() const
105:  {
106:     return itsNext;
107:  }
108:
109:  Part * PartNode::GetPart() const
110:  {
111:     if (itsPart)
112:        return itsPart;
113:     else
114:        return NULL; //error
115:  }
116:
117:
118:
119:  // **************** Part List ************
120:  class PartsList
121:  {
122:    public:
123:      PartsList();
124:      ~PartsList();
125:      // needs copy constructor and operator equals!
126:      void     Iterate(void (Part::*f)()const) const;
127:      Part*    Find(int & position, int PartNumber)  const;
128:      Part*    GetFirst() const;
129:      void     Insert(Part *);
130:      Part*    operator[](int) const;
131:      int    GetCount() const { return itsCount; }
132:      static    PartsList& GetGlobalPartsList()
133:      {
134:         return  GlobalPartsList;
135:      }
136:    private:
137:      PartNode * pHead;
138:      int itsCount;
139:      static PartsList GlobalPartsList;
140:  };
141:
142:  PartsList PartsList::GlobalPartsList;
143:
144:
```

16

LISTING 16.6   Continued

```
145:  PartsList::PartsList():
146:     pHead(0),
147:     itsCount(0)
148:  {}
149:
150:  PartsList::~PartsList()
151:  {
152:     delete pHead;
153:  }
154:
155:  Part*   PartsList::GetFirst() const
156:  {
157:     if (pHead)
158:        return pHead->GetPart();
159:     else
160:        return NULL;  // error catch here
161:  }
162:
163:  Part *  PartsList::operator[](int offSet) const
164:  {
165:     PartNode* pNode = pHead;
166:
167:     if (!pHead)
168:        return NULL; // error catch here
169:
170:     if (offSet > itsCount)
171:        return NULL; // error
172:
173:     for (int i=0;i<offSet; i++)
174:        pNode = pNode->GetNext();
175:
176:     return   pNode->GetPart();
177:  }
178:
179:  Part*   PartsList::Find(int & position, int PartNumber)  const
180:  {
181:     PartNode * pNode = 0;
182:     for (pNode = pHead, position = 0;
183:        pNode!=NULL;
184:     pNode = pNode->GetNext(), position++)
185:     {
186:        if (pNode->GetPart()->GetPartNumber() == PartNumber)
187:        break;
188:     }
189:     if (pNode == NULL)
190:        return NULL;
191:     else
192:        return pNode->GetPart();
193:  }
194:
```

LISTING 16.6 continued

```
195:  void PartsList::Iterate(void (Part::*func)()const) const
196:  {
197:      if (!pHead)
198:          return;
199:      PartNode* pNode = pHead;
200:      do
201:          (pNode->GetPart()->*func)();
202:      while ((pNode = pNode->GetNext()) != 0);
203:  }
204:
205:  void PartsList::Insert(Part* pPart)
206:  {
207:      PartNode * pNode = new PartNode(pPart);
208:      PartNode * pCurrent = pHead;
209:      PartNode * pNext = 0;
210:
211:      int New =  pPart->GetPartNumber();
212:      int Next = 0;
213:      itsCount++;
214:
215:      if (!pHead)
216:      {
217:          pHead = pNode;
218:          return;
219:      }
220:
221:      // if this one is smaller than head
222:      // this one is the new head
223:      if (pHead->GetPart()->GetPartNumber() > New)
224:      {
225:          pNode->SetNext(pHead);
226:          pHead = pNode;
227:          return;
228:      }
229:
230:      for (;;)
231:      {
232:          // if there is no next, append this new one
233:          if (!pCurrent->GetNext())
234:          {
235:              pCurrent->SetNext(pNode);
236:              return;
237:          }
238:
239:          // if this goes after this one and before the next
240:          // then insert it here, otherwise get the next
241:          pNext = pCurrent->GetNext();
242:          Next = pNext->GetPart()->GetPartNumber();
243:          if (Next > New)
244:          {
245:              pCurrent->SetNext(pNode);
246:              pNode->SetNext(pNext);
```

16

LISTING 16.6   Continued

```
247:              return;
248:          }
249:          pCurrent = pNext;
250:      }
251:  }
252:
253:  class PartsCatalog : private PartsList
254:  {
255:    public:
256:      void Insert(Part *);
257:      int Exists(int PartNumber);
258:      Part * Get(int PartNumber);
259:      operator+(const PartsCatalog &);
260:      void ShowAll() { Iterate(Part::Display); }
261:    private:
262:  };
263:
264:  void PartsCatalog::Insert(Part * newPart)
265:  {
266:      int partNumber =  newPart->GetPartNumber();
267:      int offset;
268:
269:      if (!Find(offset, partNumber))
270:      {
271:          PartsList::Insert(newPart);
272:      }
273:      else
274:      {
275:          cout << partNumber << " was the ";
276:          switch (offset)
277:          {
278:            case 0:  cout << "first "; break;
279:            case 1:  cout << "second "; break;
280:            case 2:  cout << "third "; break;
281:            default: cout << offset+1 << "th ";
282:          }
283:          cout << "entry. Rejected!" << endl;
284:      }
285:  }
286:
287:  int PartsCatalog::Exists(int PartNumber)
288:  {
289:      int offset;
290:      Find(offset,PartNumber);
291:      return offset;
292:  }
293:
294:  Part * PartsCatalog::Get(int PartNumber)
295:  {
296:      int offset;
```

LISTING 16.6   continued

```
297:        return (Find(offset, PartNumber));
298:
299:    }
300:
301:    int main()
302:    {
303:        PartsCatalog pc;
304:        Part * pPart = 0;
305:        int PartNumber;
306:        int value;
307:        int choice = 99;
308:
309:        while (choice != 0)
310:        {
311:            cout << "(0)Quit (1)Car (2)Plane: ";
312:            cin >> choice;
313:
314:            if (choice != 0)
315:            {
316:                cout << "New PartNumber?: ";
317:                cin >>  PartNumber;
318:
319:                if (choice == 1)
320:                {
321:                    cout << "Model Year?: ";
322:                    cin >> value;
323:                    pPart = new CarPart(value,PartNumber);
324:                }
325:                else
326:                {
327:                    cout << "Engine Number?: ";
328:                    cin >> value;
329:                    pPart = new AirPlanePart(value,PartNumber);
330:                }
331:                pc.Insert(pPart);
332:            }
333:        }
334:        pc.ShowAll();
335:        return 0;
336:    }
```

OUTPUT
```
(0)Quit (1)Car (2)Plane:  1
New PartNumber?: 1234
Model Year?: 94
(0)Quit (1)Car (2)Plane:  1
New PartNumber?: 4434
Model Year?: 93
(0)Quit (1)Car (2)Plane:  1
New PartNumber?: 1234
Model Year?: 94
```

```
1234 was the first entry. Rejected!
(0)Quit (1)Car (2)Plane:  1
New PartNumber?: 2345
Model Year?: 93
(0)Quit (1)Car (2)Plane:  0

Part Number: 1234
Model Year: 94

Part Number: 2345
Model Year: 93

Part Number: 4434
Model Year: 93
```

ANALYSIS Listing 16.6 shows a changed interface to `PartsCatalog` and the rewritten driver program. The interfaces to the other classes are unchanged from Listing 16.5.

On line 253 of Listing 16.6, `PartsCatalog` is declared to derive privately from `PartsList`. The interface to `PartsCatalog` doesn't change from Listing 16.5, although, of course, it no longer needs an object of type `PartsList` as member data.

The `PartsCatalog ShowAll()` function on line 160 calls `PartsList Iterate()` with the appropriate pointer to member function of class `Part`. `ShowAll()` acts as a public interface to `Iterate()`, providing the correct information but preventing client classes from calling `Iterate()` directly. Although `PartsList` might allow other functions to be passed to `Iterate()`, `PartsCatalog` does not.

The `Insert()` function on lines 164–284 has changed as well. Note, on line 269, that `Find()` is now called directly because it is inherited from the base class. The call on line 271 to `Insert()` must be fully qualified, of course, or it would endlessly recurse into itself.

In short, when methods of `PartsCatalog` want to call `PartsList` methods, they can do so directly. The only exception is when `PartsCatalog` has overridden the method and the `PartsList` version is needed, in which case the function name must be qualified fully.

Private inheritance enables the `PartsCatalog` to inherit what it can use, but still provides mediated access to `Insert()` and other methods to which client classes should not have direct access.

Do	Don't
DO inherit publicly when the derived object is a kind of the base class. **DO** use aggregation when you want to delegate functionality to another class, but you don't need access to its protected members. **DO** use private inheritance when you need to implement one class in terms of another, and you need access to the base class's protected members.	**DON'T** use private inheritance when you need to use more than one instance of the base class. You must use aggregation. For example, if `PartsCatalog` needed two `PartsLists`, you could not have used private inheritance. **DON'T** use public inheritance when members of the base class should not be available to clients of the derived class.

16

Adding Friend Classes

Sometimes, you will create classes together, as a set. For example, `PartNode` and `PartsList` were tightly coupled, and it would have been convenient if `PartsList` could have read `PartNode`'s `Part` pointer, `itsPart`, directly.

You wouldn't want to make `itsPart` public, or even protected, because this is an implementation detail of `PartNode` and you want to keep it private. You do want to expose it to `PartsList`, however.

If you want to expose your private member data or functions to another class, you must declare that class to be a friend. This extends the interface of your class to include the friend class.

After a class declares another to be its friend, all of the declaring classes' member data and functions are public to the friend class. For example, if `PartsNode` declares `PartsList` to be a friend, all `PartsNode`'s member data and functions are public as far as `PartsList` is concerned.

It is important to note that friendship cannot be transferred. Although you are my friend and Joe is your friend, that doesn't mean Joe is my friend. Friendship is not inherited, either. Again, although you are my friend and I'm willing to share my secrets with you, that doesn't mean I'm willing to share my secrets with your children.

Finally, friendship is not commutative. Assigning Class One to be a friend of Class Two does not make Class Two a friend of Class One. You might be willing to tell me your secrets, but that doesn't mean I am willing to tell you mine.

To declare a class as a friend, you use the C++ friend keyword:

```
class ClassOne
{
   public:
      friend class BefriendedClass;
      . . .
```

In this example, *ClassOne* has declared *BefriendedClass* as its friend. This means that *BefriendedClass* now has full access to any of *ClassOne*'s members.

Listing 16.7 illustrates friendship by rewriting the example from Listing 16.6, making PartsList a friend of PartNode. Note that this does not make PartNode a friend of PartsList.

LISTING 16.7   Friend Class Illustrated

```
 0:   //Listing 16.7 Friend Class Illustrated
 1:
 2:   #include <iostream>
 3:   using namespace std;
 4:
 5:   // *************** Part ***********
 6:
 7:   // Abstract base class of parts
 8:   class Part
 9:   {
10:    public:
11:      Part():itsPartNumber(1) {}
12:      Part(int PartNumber):
13:      itsPartNumber(PartNumber){}
14:      virtual ~Part(){}
15:      int GetPartNumber() const
16:        { return itsPartNumber; }
17:      virtual void Display() const =0;
18:    private:
19:       int itsPartNumber;
20:   };
21:
22:   // implementation of pure virtual function so that
23:   // derived classes can chain up
24:   void Part::Display() const
25:   {
26:     cout << "\nPart Number: ";
27:     cout << itsPartNumber << endl;
28:   }
29:
30:   // *************** Car Part ***********
31:
32:   class CarPart : public Part
33:   {
```

LISTING 16.7 continued

```
34:    public:
35:      CarPart():itsModelYear(94){}
36:      CarPart(int year, int partNumber);
37:      virtual void Display() const
38:      {
39:         Part::Display();
40:         cout << "Model Year: ";
41:         cout << itsModelYear << endl;
42:      }
43:    private:
44:      int itsModelYear;
45:   };
46:
47: CarPart::CarPart(int year, int partNumber):
48:      itsModelYear(year),
49:      Part(partNumber)
50: {}
51:
52:
53: // *************** AirPlane Part ************
54:
55: class AirPlanePart : public Part
56: {
57:    public:
58:      AirPlanePart():itsEngineNumber(1){};
59:      AirPlanePart(int EngineNumber, int PartNumber);
60:      virtual void Display() const
61:      {
62:         Part::Display();
63:         cout << "Engine No.: ";
64:         cout << itsEngineNumber << endl;
65:      }
66:    private:
67:      int itsEngineNumber;
68:   };
69:
70: AirPlanePart::AirPlanePart(int EngineNumber, int PartNumber):
71:      itsEngineNumber(EngineNumber),
72:      Part(PartNumber)
73: {}
74:
75: // *************** Part Node ************
76: class PartNode
77: {
78:    public:
79:      friend class PartsList;
80:      PartNode (Part*);
81:      ~PartNode();
82:      void SetNext(PartNode * node)
83:         { itsNext = node; }
84:      PartNode * GetNext() const;
85:      Part * GetPart() const;
```

16

LISTING 16.7   continued

```
86:    private:
87:      Part *itsPart;
88:      PartNode * itsNext;
89:  };
90:
91:
92:  PartNode::PartNode(Part* pPart):
93:    itsPart(pPart),
94:    itsNext(0)
95:  {}
96:
97:  PartNode::~PartNode()
98:  {
99:      delete itsPart;
100:     itsPart = 0;
101:     delete itsNext;
102:     itsNext = 0;
103: }
104:
105: // Returns NULL if no next PartNode
106: PartNode * PartNode::GetNext() const
107: {
108:     return itsNext;
109: }
110:
111: Part * PartNode::GetPart() const
112: {
113:     if (itsPart)
114:         return itsPart;
115:     else
116:         return NULL; //error
117: }
118:
119:
120: // *************** Part List ***********
121: class PartsList
122: {
123:   public:
124:     PartsList();
125:     ~PartsList();
126:     // needs copy constructor and operator equals!
127:     void     Iterate(void (Part::*f)()const) const;
128:     Part*    Find(int & position, int PartNumber) const;
129:     Part*    GetFirst() const;
130:     void     Insert(Part *);
131:     Part*    operator[](int) const;
132:     int      GetCount() const { return itsCount; }
133:     static   PartsList& GetGlobalPartsList()
134:     {
135:         return  GlobalPartsList;
```

LISTING 16.7   continued

```
136:      }
137:    private:
138:       PartNode * pHead;
139:       int itsCount;
140:       static PartsList GlobalPartsList;
141:  };
142:
143:  PartsList PartsList::GlobalPartsList;
144:
145:  // Implementations for Lists...
146:
147:  PartsList::PartsList():
148:     pHead(0),
149:     itsCount(0)
150:  {}
151:
152:  PartsList::~PartsList()
153:  {
154:     delete pHead;
155:  }
156:
157:  Part*   PartsList::GetFirst() const
158:  {
159:     if (pHead)
160:        return pHead->itsPart;
161:     else
162:        return NULL;   // error catch here
163:  }
164:
165:  Part * PartsList::operator[](int offSet) const
166:  {
167:     PartNode* pNode = pHead;
168:
169:     if (!pHead)
170:        return NULL; // error catch here
171:
172:     if (offSet > itsCount)
173:        return NULL; // error
174:
175:     for (int i=0;i<offSet; i++)
176:        pNode = pNode->itsNext;
177:
178:     return   pNode->itsPart;
179:  }
180:
181:  Part* PartsList::Find(int & position, int PartNumber) const
182:  {
183:     PartNode * pNode = 0;
184:     for (pNode = pHead, position = 0;
185:        pNode!=NULL;
186:     pNode = pNode->itsNext, position++)
187:        {
```

LISTING 16.7 continued

```
188:           if (pNode->itsPart->GetPartNumber() == PartNumber)
189:              break;
190:        }
191:     if (pNode == NULL)
192:        return NULL;
193:     else
194:        return pNode->itsPart;
195: }
196:
197: void PartsList::Iterate(void (Part::*func)()const) const
198: {
199:     if (!pHead)
200:        return;
201:     PartNode* pNode = pHead;
202:     do
203:        (pNode->itsPart->*func)();
204:     while (pNode = pNode->itsNext);
205: }
206:
207: void PartsList::Insert(Part* pPart)
208: {
209:     PartNode * pNode = new PartNode(pPart);
210:     PartNode * pCurrent = pHead;
211:     PartNode * pNext = 0;
212:
213:     int New = pPart->GetPartNumber();
214:     int Next = 0;
215:     itsCount++;
216:
217:     if (!pHead)
218:     {
219:        pHead = pNode;
220:        return;
221:     }
222:
223:     // if this one is smaller than head
224:     // this one is the new head
225:     if (pHead->itsPart->GetPartNumber() > New)
226:     {
227:        pNode->itsNext = pHead;
228:        pHead = pNode;
229:        return;
230:     }
231:
232:     for (;;)
233:     {
234:        // if there is no next, append this new one
235:        if (!pCurrent->itsNext)
236:        {
237:           pCurrent->itsNext = pNode;
```

LISTING 16.7   continued

16

```
238:              return;
239:          }
240:
241:          // if this goes after this one and before the next
242:          // then insert it here, otherwise get the next
243:          pNext = pCurrent->itsNext;
244:          Next = pNext->itsPart->GetPartNumber();
245:          if (Next > New)
246:          {
247:              pCurrent->itsNext = pNode;
248:              pNode->itsNext = pNext;
249:              return;
250:          }
251:          pCurrent = pNext;
252:      }
253: }
254:
255: class PartsCatalog : private PartsList
256: {
257:   public:
258:      void Insert(Part *);
259:      int Exists(int PartNumber);
260:      Part * Get(int PartNumber);
261:      operator+(const PartsCatalog &);
262:      void ShowAll() { Iterate(Part::Display); }
263:   private:
264: };
265:
266: void PartsCatalog::Insert(Part * newPart)
267: {
268:    int partNumber =  newPart->GetPartNumber();
269:    int offset;
270:
271:    if (!Find(offset, partNumber))
272:        PartsList::Insert(newPart);
273:    else
274:    {
275:       cout << partNumber << " was the ";
276:       switch (offset)
277:       {
278:          case 0:  cout << "first "; break;
279:          case 1:  cout << "second "; break;
280:          case 2:  cout << "third "; break;
281:          default: cout << offset+1 << "th ";
282:       }
283:       cout << "entry. Rejected!" << endl;
284:    }
285: }
286:
287: int PartsCatalog::Exists(int PartNumber)
288: {
289:    int offset;
```

LISTING 16.7   continued

```
290:     Find(offset,PartNumber);
291:     return offset;
292: }
293:
294: Part * PartsCatalog::Get(int PartNumber)
295: {
296:     int offset;
297:     return (Find(offset, PartNumber));
298: }
299:
300: int main()
301: {
302:     PartsCatalog pc;
303:     Part * pPart = 0;
304:     int PartNumber;
305:     int value;
306:     int choice = 99;
307:
308:     while (choice != 0)
309:     {
310:        cout << "(0)Quit (1)Car (2)Plane: ";
311:        cin >> choice;
312:
313:        if (choice != 0)
314:         {
315:           cout << "New PartNumber?: ";
316:           cin >>  PartNumber;
317:
318:           if (choice == 1)
319:           {
320:              cout << "Model Year?: ";
321:              cin >> value;
322:              pPart = new CarPart(value,PartNumber);
323:           }
324:           else
325:           {
326:              cout << "Engine Number?: ";
327:              cin >> value;
328:              pPart = new AirPlanePart(value,PartNumber);
329:            }
330:           pc.Insert(pPart);
331:         }
332:     }
333:     pc.ShowAll();
334:     return 0;
335: }
```

OUTPUT

```
(0)Quit (1)Car (2)Plane:  1
New PartNumber?: 1234
Model Year?: 94
(0)Quit (1)Car (2)Plane:  1
New PartNumber?: 4434
Model Year?: 93
(0)Quit (1)Car (2)Plane:  1
New PartNumber?: 1234
Model Year?: 94
1234 was the first entry. Rejected!
(0)Quit (1)Car (2)Plane:  1
New PartNumber?: 2345
Model Year?: 93
(0)Quit (1)Car (2)Plane:  0

Part Number: 1234
Model Year: 94

Part Number: 2345
Model Year: 93

Part Number: 4434
Model Year: 93
```

16

ANALYSIS On line 79, the class PartsList is declared to be a friend to the PartNode class.

This listing places the friend declaration in the public section, but this is not required; it can be put anywhere in the class declaration without changing the meaning of the statement. Because of this statement, all the private member data and functions are available to any member function of class PartsList.

On line 157, the implementation of the member function GetFirst() reflects this change. Rather than returning pHead->GetPart, this function can now return the otherwise private member data by writing pHead->itsPart. Similarly, the Insert() function can now write pNode->itsNext = pHead, rather than writing pNode->SetNext(pHead).

Admittedly, these are trivial changes, and a good enough reason does not exist to make PartsList a friend of PartNode, but they do serve to illustrate how the keyword friend works.

Declarations of friend classes should be used with extreme caution. If two classes are inextricably entwined, and one must frequently access data in the other, good reason might exist to use this declaration. But use it sparingly; it is often just as easy to use the public accessor methods, and doing so enables you to change one class without having to recompile the other.

NOTE

You will often hear novice C++ programmers complain that friend declarations "undermine" the encapsulation so important to object-oriented programming. This is not necessarily true. The friend declaration makes the declared friend part of the class interface and does not have to undermine encapsulation. Use of a friend implies a commitment to parallel maintenance of both classes, which could reduce modularity.

Friend Class

Declare one class to be a friend of another by putting the word `friend` into the class granting the access rights. That is, I can declare you to be my friend, but you can't declare yourself to be my friend.

Example

```
class PartNode{
public:
friend class PartsList;  // declares PartsList to be a friend of PartNode
};
```

Friend Functions

You just learned that declaring another class a friend gives it total access. At times, you might want to grant this level of access not to an entire class, but only to one or two functions of that class. You can do this by declaring the member functions of the other class to be friends, rather than declaring the entire class to be a friend. In fact, you can declare any function, regardless of whether it is a member function of another class, to be a friend function.

Friend Functions and Operator Overloading

Listing 16.1 provided a `String` class that overrode the `operator+`. It also provided a constructor that took a constant character pointer, so that string objects could be created from C-style strings. This enabled you to create a string and add to it with a C-style string.

NOTE

C-style strings are null-terminated character arrays, such as `char myString[] = "Hello World"`.

What you could not do, however, was create a C-style string (a character string) and add to it using a string object, as shown in this example:

```
char cString[] = {"Hello"};
String sString(" World");
String sStringTwo = cString + sString;  //error!
```

C-style strings don't have an overloaded operator+. As discussed on Day 10, "Working with Advanced Functions," when you say cString + sString; what you are really calling is cString.operator+(sString). Because you can't call operator+() on a C-style string, this causes a compile-time error.

You can solve this problem by declaring a friend function in String, which overloads operator+ but takes two string objects. The C-style string is converted to a string object by the appropriate constructor, and then operator+ is called using the two string objects. To clarify this, take a look at Listing 16.8.

LISTING 16.8   Friendly operator+

```
 0:  //Listing 16.8 - friendly operators
 1:
 2:  #include <iostream>
 3:  #include <string.h>
 4:  using namespace std;
 5:
 6:  // Rudimentary string class
 7:  class String
 8:  {
 9:    public:
10:      // constructors
11:      String();
12:      String(const char *const);
13:      String(const String &);
14:      ~String();
15:
16:      // overloaded operators
17:      char & operator[](int offset);
18:      char operator[](int offset) const;
19:      String operator+(const String&);
20:      friend String operator+(const String&, const String&);
21:      void operator+=(const String&);
22:      String & operator= (const String &);
23:
24:      // General accessors
25:      int GetLen()const { return itsLen; }
26:      const char * GetString() const { return itsString; }
27:
28:    private:
```

16

LISTING 16.8   continued

```
29:       String (int);          // private constructor
30:       char * itsString;
31:       unsigned short itsLen;
32:   };
33:
34:   // default constructor creates string of 0 bytes
35:   String::String()
36:   {
37:       itsString = new char[1];
38:       itsString[0] = '\0';
39:       itsLen=0;
40:       // cout << "\tDefault string constructor" << endl;
41:       // ConstructorCount++;
42:   }
43:
44:   // private (helper) constructor, used only by
45:   // class methods for creating a new string of
46:   // required size.  Null filled.
47:   String::String(int len)
48:   {
49:       itsString = new char[len+1];
50:       for (int i = 0; i<=len; i++)
51:           itsString[i] = '\0';
52:       itsLen=len;
53:       // cout << "\tString(int) constructor" << endl;
54:       // ConstructorCount++;
55:   }
56:
57:   // Converts a character array to a String
58:   String::String(const char * const cString)
59:   {
60:       itsLen = strlen(cString);
61:       itsString = new char[itsLen+1];
62:       for (int i = 0; i<itsLen; i++)
63:           itsString[i] = cString[i];
64:       itsString[itsLen]='\0';
65:       // cout << "\tString(char*) constructor" << endl;
66:       // ConstructorCount++;
67:   }
68:
69:   // copy constructor
70:   String::String (const String & rhs)
71:   {
72:       itsLen=rhs.GetLen();
73:       itsString = new char[itsLen+1];
74:       for (int i = 0; i<itsLen;i++)
75:           itsString[i] = rhs[i];
76:       itsString[itsLen] = '\0';
77:       // cout << "\tString(String&) constructor" << endl;
78:       // ConstructorCount++;
```

LISTING 16.8   continued

```
79:   }
80:
81:   // destructor, frees allocated memory
82:   String::~String ()
83:   {
84:      delete [] itsString;
85:      itsLen = 0;
86:      // cout << "\tString destructor" << endl;
87:   }
88:
89:   // operator equals, frees existing memory
90:   // then copies string and size
91:   String& String::operator=(const String & rhs)
92:   {
93:      if (this == &rhs)
94:         return *this;
95:      delete [] itsString;
96:      itsLen=rhs.GetLen();
97:      itsString = new char[itsLen+1];
98:      for (int i = 0;  i<itsLen;i++)
99:         itsString[i] = rhs[i];
100:     itsString[itsLen] = '\0';
101:     return *this;
102:     // cout << "\tString operator=" << endl;
103:  }
104:
105:  //non constant offset operator, returns
106:  // reference to character so it can be
107:  // changed!
108:  char & String::operator[](int offset)
109:  {
110:     if (offset > itsLen)
111:        return itsString[itsLen-1];
112:     else
113:        return itsString[offset];
114:  }
115:
116:  // constant offset operator for use
117:  // on const objects (see copy constructor!)
118:  char String::operator[](int offset) const
119:  {
120:     if (offset > itsLen)
121:        return itsString[itsLen-1];
122:     else
123:        return itsString[offset];
124:  }
125:
126:  // creates a new string by adding current
127:  // string to rhs
128:  String String::operator+(const String& rhs)
129:  {
130:     int  totalLen = itsLen + rhs.GetLen();
```

LISTING 16.8   continued

```
131:       String temp(totalLen);
132:       int i, j;
133:       for (i = 0; i<itsLen; i++)
134:          temp[i] = itsString[i];
135:       for (j = 0, i = itsLen; j<rhs.GetLen(); j++, i++)
136:          temp[i] = rhs[j];
137:       temp[totalLen]='\0';
138:       return temp;
139:    }
140:
141:    // creates a new string by adding
142:    // one string to another
143:    String operator+(const String& lhs, const String& rhs)
144:    {
145:       int  totalLen = lhs.GetLen() + rhs.GetLen();
146:       String temp(totalLen);
147:       int i, j;
148:       for (i = 0; i<lhs.GetLen(); i++)
149:          temp[i] = lhs[i];
150:       for (j = 0, i = lhs.GetLen(); j<rhs.GetLen(); j++, i++)
151:          temp[i] = rhs[j];
152:       temp[totalLen]='\0';
153:       return temp;
154:    }
155:
156:    int main()
157:    {
158:       String s1("String One ");
159:       String s2("String Two ");
160:       char *c1 = { "C-String One " } ;
161:       String s3;
162:       String s4;
163:       String s5;
164:
165:       cout << "s1: " << s1.GetString() << endl;
166:       cout << "s2: " << s2.GetString() << endl;
167:       cout << "c1: " << c1 << endl;
168:       s3 = s1 + s2;
169:       cout << "s3: " << s3.GetString() << endl;
170:       s4 = s1 + c1;
171:       cout << "s4: " << s4.GetString() << endl;
172:       s5 = c1 + s2;
173:       cout << "s5: " << s5.GetString() << endl;
174:       return 0;
175:    }
```

OUTPUT

```
s1: String One
s2: String Two
c1: C-String One
s3: String One String Two
s4: String One C-String One
s5: C-String One String Two
```

ANALYSIS The implementation of all the string methods except operator+ are unchanged from Listing 16.1. On line 20, a new operator+ is overloaded to take two constant string references and to return a string, and this function is declared to be a friend.

Note that this operator+ is not a member function of this or any other class. It is declared within the declaration of the String class only so that it can be made a friend, but because it is declared, no other function prototype is needed.

The implementation of this operator+ is on lines 143–154. Note that it is similar to the earlier operator+, except that it takes two strings and accesses them both through their public accessor methods.

The driver program demonstrates the use of this function on line 172, where operator+ is now called on a C-style string!

Friend Functions

Declare a function to be a friend by using the keyword friend and then the full specification of the function. Declaring a function to be a friend does not give the friend function access to your this pointer, but it does provide full access to all private and protected member data and functions.

Example

```
class PartNode
{   // ...
    // make another class's member function a _friend
    friend void PartsList::Insert(Part *);
    // make a global function a friend
    friend int SomeFunction();
    // ...
};
```

Overloading the Insertion Operator

You are finally ready to give your String class the capability to use cout the same as any other type. Until now, when you've wanted to print a string, you've been forced to write the following:

```
cout << theString.GetString();
```

What you would like to do is write this:

```
cout << theString;
```

To accomplish this, you must override operator<<(). Day 17, "Working with Streams," presents the ins and outs (cins and couts?) of working with iostreams; for now, Listing 16.9 illustrates how operator<< can be overloaded using a friend function.

LISTING 16.9   Overloading operator<<()

```
0:   // Listing 16.9 Overloading operator<<()
1:
2:   #include <iostream>
3:   #include <string.h>
4:   using namespace std;
5:
6:   class String
7:   {
8:     public:
9:         // constructors
10:        String();
11:        String(const char *const);
12:        String(const String &);
13:        ~String();
14:
15:        // overloaded operators
16:        char & operator[](int offset);
17:        char operator[](int offset) const;
18:        String operator+(const String&);
19:        void operator+=(const String&);
20:        String & operator= (const String &);
21:        friend ostream& operator<<
22:            ( ostream& theStream,String& theString);
23:        // General accessors
24:        int GetLen()const { return itsLen; }
25:        const char * GetString() const { return itsString; }
26:
27:     private:
28:        String (int);         // private constructor
29:        char * itsString;
30:        unsigned short itsLen;
31:   };
32:
33:
34:   // default constructor creates string of 0 bytes
35:   String::String()
36:   {
37:       itsString = new char[1];
38:       itsString[0] = '\0';
39:       itsLen=0;
40:       // cout << "\tDefault string constructor" << endl;
```

LISTING **16.9**   continued

```
41:       // ConstructorCount++;
42:   }
43:
44:   // private (helper) constructor, used only by
45:   // class methods for creating a new string of
46:   // required size.  Null filled.
47:   String::String(int len)
48:   {
49:       itsString = new char[len+1];
50:       for (int i = 0; i<=len; i++)
51:           itsString[i] = '\0';
52:       itsLen=len;
53:       // cout << "\tString(int) constructor" << endl;
54:       // ConstructorCount++;
55:   }
56:
57:   // Converts a character array to a String
58:   String::String(const char * const cString)
59:   {
60:       itsLen = strlen(cString);
61:       itsString = new char[itsLen+1];
62:       for (int i = 0; i<itsLen; i++)
63:           itsString[i] = cString[i];
64:       itsString[itsLen]='\0';
65:       // cout << "\tString(char*) constructor" << endl;
66:       // ConstructorCount++;
67:   }
68:
69:   // copy constructor
70:   String::String (const String & rhs)
71:   {
72:       itsLen=rhs.GetLen();
73:       itsString = new char[itsLen+1];
74:       for (int i = 0; i<itsLen;i++)
75:           itsString[i] = rhs[i];
76:       itsString[itsLen] = '\0';
77:       // cout << "\tString(String&) constructor" << endl;
78:       // ConstructorCount++;
79:   }
80:
81:   // destructor, frees allocated memory
82:   String::~String ()
83:   {
84:       delete [] itsString;
85:       itsLen = 0;
86:       // cout << "\tString destructor" << endl;
87:   }
88:
89:   // operator equals, frees existing memory
90:   // then copies string and size
91:   String& String::operator=(const String & rhs)
92:   {
```

Listing 16.9   continued

```
93:        if (this == &rhs)
94:            return *this;
95:        delete [] itsString;
96:        itsLen=rhs.GetLen();
97:        itsString = new char[itsLen+1];
98:        for (int i = 0; i<itsLen;i++)
99:            itsString[i] = rhs[i];
100:       itsString[itsLen] = '\0';
101:       return *this;
102:       // cout << "\tString operator=" << endl;
103:   }
104:
105:   //non constant offset operator, returns
106:   // reference to character so it can be
107:   // changed!
108:   char & String::operator[](int offset)
109:   {
110:       if (offset > itsLen)
111:           return itsString[itsLen-1];
112:       else
113:           return itsString[offset];
114:   }
115:
116:   // constant offset operator for use
117:   // on const objects (see copy constructor!)
118:   char String::operator[](int offset) const
119:   {
120:       if (offset > itsLen)
121:           return itsString[itsLen-1];
122:       else
123:           return itsString[offset];
124:   }
125:
126:   // creates a new string by adding current
127:   // string to rhs
128:   String String::operator+(const String& rhs)
129:   {
130:       int  totalLen = itsLen + rhs.GetLen();
131:       String temp(totalLen);
132:       int i, j;
133:       for (i = 0; i<itsLen; i++)
134:           temp[i] = itsString[i];
135:       for (j = 0; j<rhs.GetLen(); j++, i++)
136:           temp[i] = rhs[j];
137:       temp[totalLen]='\0';
138:       return temp;
139:   }
140:
141:   // changes current string, returns nothing
142:   void String::operator+=(const String& rhs)
```

LISTING 16.9 continued

```
143:   {
144:       unsigned short rhsLen = rhs.GetLen();
145:       unsigned short totalLen = itsLen + rhsLen;
146:       String  temp(totalLen);
147:       int i, j;
148:       for (i = 0; i<itsLen; i++)
149:           temp[i] = itsString[i];
150:       for (j = 0, i = 0; j<rhs.GetLen(); j++, i++)
151:           temp[i] = rhs[i-itsLen];
152:       temp[totalLen]='\0';
153:       *this = temp;
154:   }
155:
156:   // int String::ConstructorCount =
157:   ostream& operator<< ( ostream& theStream,String& theString)
158:   {
159:       theStream << theString.itsString;
160:       return theStream;
161:   }
162:
163:   int main()
164:   {
165:       String theString("Hello world.");
166:       cout << theString;
167:       return 0;
168:   }
```

OUTPUT

Hello world.

ANALYSIS
On lines 21–22, operator<< is declared to be a friend function that takes an ostream reference and a String reference and then returns an ostream reference. Note that this is not a member function of String. It returns a reference to an ostream so that you can concatenate calls to operator<<, such as this:

```
cout << "myAge: " << itsAge << " years.";
```

The implementation of this friend function is on lines 157–161. All this really does is hide the implementation details of feeding the string to the ostream, and that is just as it should be. You'll see more about overloading this operator and operator>> on Day 17.

Summary

Today, you saw how to delegate functionality to an aggregated object. You also saw how to implement one class in terms of another by using either aggregation or private inheritance. Aggregation is restricted in that the new class does not have access to the protected members of the aggregated class, and it cannot override the member functions of the aggregated object. Aggregation is simpler to use than inheritance, and should be used when possible.

You also saw how to declare both friend classes and friend functions. Using a friend function, you saw how to overload the extraction operator, to allow your new classes to use cout the same as the built-in classes do.

Remember that public inheritance expresses *is-a*, aggregation expresses *has-a*, and private inheritance expresses *implemented in terms of*. The relationship *delegates-to* can be expressed using either aggregation or private inheritance, although aggregation is more common.

Q&A

Q Why is it so important to distinguish between *is-a*, *has-a*, and *implemented in terms of*?

A The point of C++ is to implement well-designed, object-oriented programs. Keeping these relationships straight helps to ensure that your design corresponds to the reality of what you are modeling. Furthermore, a well-understood design will more likely be reflected in well-designed code.

Q What is containment?

A Containment is another word for aggregation.

Q Why is aggregation preferred over private inheritance?

A The challenge in modern programming is to cope with complexity. The more you can use objects as black boxes, the fewer details you have to worry about and the more complexity you can manage. Aggregated classes hide their details; private inheritance exposes the implementation details. To some extent, this is also true for conventional public inheritance, which is sometimes used when aggregation would be a better solution.

Q Why not make all classes friends of all the classes they use?

A Making one class a friend of another exposes the implementation details and reduces encapsulation. The idea is to keep as many of the details of each class hidden from all other classes as possible.

Q If a function is overloaded, do I need to declare each form of the function to be a friend?

A Yes, if you overload a function and declare it to be a friend of another class, you must declare a friend for each form to which you want to grant this access.

Workshop

The Workshop contains quiz questions to help solidify your understanding of the material covered and exercises to provide you with experience in using what you've learned. Try to answer the quiz and exercise questions before checking the answers in Appendix D, and be certain you understand the answers before going to tomorrow's lesson.

Quiz

1. How do you establish an *is-a* relationship?

2. How do you establish a *has-a* relationship?

3. What is the difference between aggregation and delegation?

4. What is the difference between delegation and *implemented in terms of*?

5. What is a friend function?

6. What is a friend class?

7. If `Dog` is a friend of `Boy`, is `Boy` a friend of `Dog`?

8. If `Dog` is a friend of `Boy`, and `Terrier` derives from `Dog`, is `Terrier` a friend of `Boy`?

9. If `Dog` is a friend of `Boy` and `Boy` is a friend of `House`, is `Dog` a friend of `House`?

10. Where must the declaration of a friend function appear?

Exercises

1. Show the declaration of a class, `Animal`, that contains a data member that is a `String` object.

2. Show the declaration of a class, `BoundedArray`, that is an array.

3. Show the declaration of a class, `Set`, that is declared in terms of an array.

4. Modify Listing 16.1 to provide the `String` class with an extraction operator (`>>`).

5. **BUG BUSTERS:** What is wrong with this program?

```
0:     Bug Busters
1:     #include <iostream>
2:     using namespace std;
3:     class Animal;
4:
5:     void setValue(Animal& , int);
6:
7:     class Animal
8:     {
9:        public:
10:          int GetWeight()const { return itsWeight; }
11:          int GetAge() const { return itsAge; }
12:       private:
13:          int itsWeight;
14:          int itsAge;
```

```
15:     };
16:
17:     void setValue(Animal& theAnimal, int theWeight)
18:     {
19:        friend class Animal;
20:        theAnimal.itsWeight = theWeight;
21:     }
22:
23:     int main()
24:     {
25:        Animal peppy;
26:        setValue(peppy,5);
27:        return 0;
28:     }
```

6. Fix the listing in Exercise 5 so that it compiles.

7. **BUG BUSTERS:** What is wrong with this code?

```
0:     // Bug Busters
1:     #include <iostream>
2:     using namespace std;
3:     class Animal;
4:
5:     void setValue(Animal& , int);
6:     void setValue(Animal& ,int, int);
7:
8:     class Animal
9:     {
10:        friend void setValue(Animal& ,int); // here's the change!
11:        private:
12:          int itsWeight;
13:          int itsAge;
14:     };
15:
16:     void setValue(Animal& theAnimal, int theWeight)
17:     {
18:        theAnimal.itsWeight = theWeight;
19:     }
20:
21:     void setValue(Animal& theAnimal, int theWeight, int theAge)
22:     {
23:        theAnimal.itsWeight = theWeight;
24:        theAnimal.itsAge = theAge;
25:     }
26:
27:     int main()
28:     {
29:        Animal peppy;
30:        setValue(peppy,5);
31:        setValue(peppy,7,9);
32:        return 0;
33:     }
```

8. Fix Exercise 7 so that it compiles.

DAY 17

Working with Streams

Until now, you've been using `cout` to write to the screen and `cin` to read from the keyboard, without a full understanding of how they work. Today, you will learn all about both of these.

Today, you will also learn

- What streams are and how they are used
- How to manage input and output using streams
- How to write to and read from files using streams

Overview of Streams

C++ does not define how data is written to the screen or to a file, nor how data is read into a program. These are clearly essential parts of working with C++, however, and the standard C++ library includes the `iostream` library, which facilitates input and output (I/O).

The advantage of having the input and output kept apart from the language and handled in libraries is that it is easier to make the language "platform-independent." That is, you can write C++ programs on a PC and then recompile them and run them on a Sun Workstation, or you can take code created using a Windows C++ compiler and recompile and run it on Linux. The compiler manufacturer supplies the right library, and everything works. At least that's the theory.

> A library is a collection of object (.obj or .o) files that can be linked to your program to provide additional functionality. This is the most basic form of code reuse and has been around since ancient programmers chiseled 1s and 0s into the walls of caves.

Today, streams are generally less important for C++ programming—except, perhaps, for flat file input. C++ programs have evolved to use operating system or compiler vendor-provided graphical user interface (GUI) libraries for working with the screen, files, and the user. This includes Windows libraries, X Windows libraries, and Borland's Kylix abstraction of both the Windows and X Windows user interfaces. Because these libraries are specialized to the operating system and are not part of the C++ standard, they are not discussed in this book.

Because streams are a part of the C++ standard, they are discussed today. In addition, it is good to understand streams in order to understand the inner workings of input and output. You should, however, quickly move to learning your operating system or vendor-supplied GUI library as well.

Encapsulation of Data Flow

Text input and output can be accomplished using the iostream classes. The iostream classes view the flow of data as being a *stream* of data, one byte following another. If the destination of the stream is a file or the console screen, the source of the data that will be flowing is usually some part of your program. If the stream is reversed, the data can come from the keyboard or a disk file and can be "poured" into your data variables.

One principal goal of streams is to encapsulate the problems of getting the data to and from the disk or the console screen. After a stream is created, your program works with the stream and the stream takes care of the details. Figure 17.1 illustrates this fundamental idea.

Understanding Buffering

Writing to the disk (and to a lesser extent the console screen) is very "expensive." It takes a long time (relatively speaking) to write data to the disk or to read data from the disk, and execution of the program can be blocked by disk writes and reads. To solve this problem, streams provide "buffering." When buffering is used, data is written into the stream, but is not written back out to the disk immediately. Instead, the stream's buffer fills and fills, and when it is full, it writes to the disk all at once.

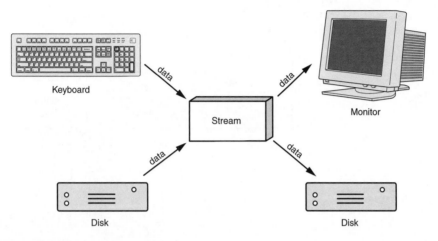

FIGURE 17.1 *Encapsulation through streams.*

NOTE

Although data is technically a plural noun, we treat it as singular, as do nearly all native speakers of English.

Picture water trickling into the top of a tank and the tank filling and filling, but no water running out of the bottom. Figure 17.2 illustrates this idea.

FIGURE 17.2

Filling the buffer.

When the water (data) reaches the top, the valve opens and all the water flows out in a rush. Figure 17.3 illustrates this.

FIGURE 17.3

Emptying the buffer.

After the buffer is empty, the bottom valve closes, the top valve opens, and more water flows into the buffer tank. Figure 17.4 illustrates this.

FIGURE 17.4

Refilling the buffer.

Every once in a while, you need to get the water out of the tank even before it is full. This is called "flushing the buffer." Figure 17.5 illustrates this idea.

You should be aware that one of the risks of using buffering is the possibility that the program will crash while data is still in the buffers. If this occurs, you might lose that data.

FIGURE 17.5

Flushing the buffer.

17

Streams and Buffers

As you might expect, C++ takes an object-oriented view toward implementing streams and buffers. It does this with the use of a number of classes and objects:

- The streambuf class manages the buffer, and its member functions provide the capability to fill, empty, flush, and otherwise manipulate the buffer.

- The ios class is the base class to the input and output stream classes. The ios class has a streambuf object as a member variable.

- The istream and ostream classes derive from the ios class and specialize input and output stream behavior, respectively.

- The iostream class is derived from both the istream and the ostream classes and provides input and output methods for writing to the screen.

- The fstream classes provide input and output from files.

You'll learn more about these classes throughout the rest of today's lesson.

Standard I/O Objects

When a C++ program that includes the iostream classes starts, four objects are created and initialized:

NOTE

> The iostream class library is added automatically to your program by the
> compiler. All you need to do to use these functions is to put the appropriate
> include statement at the top of your program listing:
>
> #include <iostream>
>
> This is something you have been doing in your programs already.

- cin (pronounced "see-in") handles input from the standard input, the keyboard.
- cout (pronounced "see-out") handles output to the standard output, the console screen.
- cerr (pronounced "see-err") handles unbuffered output to the standard error device, the console screen. Because this is unbuffered, everything sent to cerr is written to the standard error device immediately, without waiting for the buffer to fill or for a flush command to be received.
- clog (pronounced "see-log") handles buffered error messages that are output to the standard error device, the console screen. It is common for this to be "redirected" to a log file, as described in the following section.

Redirection of the Standard Streams

Each of the standard devices, input, output, and error, can be redirected to other devices. The standard error stream (cerr) is often redirected to a file, and standard input (cin) and output (cout) can be piped to files using operating system commands.

Redirecting refers to sending output (or input) to a place different than the default. Redirection is more a function of the operating system than of the iostream libraries. C++ just provides access to the four standard devices; it is up to the user to redirect the devices to whatever alternatives are needed.

The redirection operators for DOS, the Windows command prompt, and Unix are (<) redirect input and (>) redirect output. Unix provides more advanced redirection capabilities than DOS or the standard Windows command prompt; however, the general idea is the same: Take the output intended for the console screen and write it to a file, or pipe it into another program. Alternatively, the input for a program can be extracted from a file rather than from the keyboard.

NOTE

> Piping refers to using the output of one program as the input of another.

Input Using `cin`

The global object `cin` is responsible for input and is made available to your program when you include `iostream`. In previous examples, you used the overloaded extraction operator (>>) to put data into your program's variables. How does this work? The syntax, as you might remember, is as follows:

```
int someVariable;
cout << "Enter a number: ";
cin >> someVariable;
```

The global object `cout` is discussed later today; for now, focus on the third line, `cin >> someVariable;`. What can you guess about `cin`?

Clearly, it must be a global object because you didn't define it in your own code. You know from previous operator experience that `cin` has overloaded the extraction operator (>>) and that the effect is to write whatever data `cin` has in its buffer into your local variable, `someVariable`.

What might not be immediately obvious is that `cin` has overloaded the extraction operator for a great variety of parameters, among them `int&`, `short&`, `long&`, `double&`, `float&`, `char&`, `char*`, and so forth. When you write `cin >> someVariable;`, the type of `someVariable` is assessed. In the preceding example, `someVariable` is an integer, so the following function is called:

```
istream & operator>> (int &)
```

Note that because the parameter is passed by reference, the extraction operator is able to act on the original variable. Listing 17.1 illustrates the use of `cin`.

LISTING 17.1   `cin` Handles Different Data Types

```
0:  //Listing 17.1 - character strings and cin
1:
2:  #include <iostream>
3:  using namespace std;
4:
5:  int main()
6:  {
7:      int myInt;
8:      long myLong;
9:      double myDouble;
10:     float myFloat;
11:     unsigned int myUnsigned;
12:
13:     cout << "Int: ";
14:     cin >> myInt;
```

17

LISTING 17.1 continued

```
15:     cout << "Long: ";
16:     cin >> myLong;
17:     cout << "Double: ";
18:     cin >> myDouble;
19:     cout << "Float: ";
20:     cin >> myFloat;
21:     cout << "Unsigned: ";
22:     cin >> myUnsigned;
23:
24:     cout << "\n\nInt:\t" << myInt << endl;
25:     cout << "Long:\t" << myLong << endl;
26:     cout << "Double:\t" << myDouble << endl;
27:     cout << "Float:\t" << myFloat << endl;
28:     cout << "Unsigned:\t" << myUnsigned << endl;
29:     return 0;
30: }
```

OUTPUT
```
int: 2
Long: 70000
Double: 987654321
Float: 3.33
Unsigned: 25

Int:     2
Long:    70000
Double: 9.87654e+008
Float:  3.33
Unsigned:         25
```

ANALYSIS   On lines 7–11, variables of various types are declared. On lines 13–22, the user
is prompted to enter values for these variables, and the results are printed (using
cout) on lines 24–28.

The output reflects that the variables were put into the right "kinds" of variables, and the
program works as you might expect.

Inputting Strings

cin can also handle character pointer (char*) arguments; thus, you can create a character
buffer and use cin to fill it. For example, you can write the following:

```
char YourName[50]
cout << "Enter your name: ";
cin >> YourName;
```

If you enter Jesse, the variable YourName is filled with the characters J, e, s, s, e, \0. The
last character is a null; cin automatically ends the string with a null character, and you

must have enough room in the buffer to allow for the entire string plus the null. The null signals the "end of string" to the cin object.

String Problems

After all this success with cin, you might be surprised when you try to enter a full name into a string. cin has trouble getting the full name because it believes that any white-space is a separator. When it sees a space or a new line, it assumes the input for the parameter is complete, and in the case of strings, it adds a null character right then and there. Listing 17.2 illustrates this problem.

LISTING 17.2 Trying to Write More Than One Word to cin

```
0:  //Listing 17.2 - character strings and cin
1:
2:  #include <iostream>
3:
4:  int main()
5:  {
6:      char YourName[50];
7:      std::cout << "Your first name: ";
8:      std::cin >> YourName;
9:      std::cout << "Here it is: " << YourName << std::endl;
10:     std::cout << "Your entire name: ";
11:     std::cin >> YourName;
12:     std::cout << "Here it is: " << YourName << std::endl;
13:     return 0;
14: }
```

OUTPUT

```
Your first name: Jesse
Here it is: Jesse
Your entire name: Jesse Liberty
Here it is: Jesse
```

ANALYSIS On line 6, a character array called YourName is created to hold the user's input. On line 7, the user is prompted to enter one name, and that name is stored properly, as shown in the output.

On line 10, the user is again prompted, this time for a full name. cin reads the input, and when it sees the space between the names, it puts a null character after the first word and terminates input. This is not exactly what was intended.

To understand why this works this way, examine Listing 17.3, which shows input for several fields.

LISTING 17.3   Multiple Input

```
0:  //Listing 17.3 - character strings and cin
1:
2:  #include <iostream>
3:  using namespace std;
4:
5:  int main()
6:  {
7:      int myInt;
8:      long myLong;
9:      double myDouble;
10:     float myFloat;
11:     unsigned int myUnsigned;
12:     char myWord[50];
13:
14:     cout << "int: ";
15:     cin >> myInt;
16:     cout << "Long: ";
17:     cin >> myLong;
18:     cout << "Double: ";
19:     cin >> myDouble;
20:     cout << "Float: ";
21:     cin >> myFloat;
22:     cout << "Word: ";
23:     cin >> myWord;
24:     cout << "Unsigned: ";
25:     cin >> myUnsigned;
26:
27:     cout << "\n\nInt:\t" << myInt << endl;
28:     cout << "Long:\t" << myLong << endl;
29:     cout << "Double:\t" << myDouble << endl;
30:     cout << "Float:\t" << myFloat << endl;
31:     cout << "Word: \t" << myWord << endl;
32:     cout << "Unsigned:\t" << myUnsigned << endl;
33:
34:     cout << "\n\nInt, Long, Double, Float, Word, Unsigned: ";
35:     cin >> myInt >> myLong >> myDouble;
36:     cin >> myFloat >> myWord >> myUnsigned;
37:     cout << "\n\nInt:\t" << myInt << endl;
38:     cout << "Long:\t" << myLong << endl;
39:     cout << "Double:\t" << myDouble << endl;
40:     cout << "Float:\t" << myFloat << endl;
41:     cout << "Word: \t" << myWord << endl;
42:     cout << "Unsigned:\t" << myUnsigned << endl;
43:
44:     return 0;
45: }
```

OUTPUT

```
Int: 2
Long: 30303
Double: 393939397834
Float: 3.33
Word: Hello
Unsigned: 85

Int:    2
Long:   30303
Double: 3.93939e+011
Float:  3.33
Word:   Hello
Unsigned:        85

Int, Long, Double, Float, Word, Unsigned: 3 304938 393847473 6.66 bye -2

Int:    3
Long:   304938
Double: 3.93847e+008
Float:  6.66
Word:   bye
Unsigned: 4294967294
```

17

ANALYSIS Again, several variables are created, this time including a char array. The user is prompted for input and the output is faithfully printed.

On line 34, the user is prompted for all the input at once, and then each "word" of input is assigned to the appropriate variable. It is to facilitate this kind of multiple assignment that cin must consider each word in the input to be the full input for each variable. If cin was to consider the entire input to be part of one variable's input, this kind of concatenated input would be impossible.

Note that on line 42, the last object requested was an unsigned integer, but the user entered -2. Because cin believes it is writing to an unsigned integer, the bit pattern of -2 was evaluated as an unsigned integer, and when written out by cout, the value 4294967294 was displayed. The unsigned value 4294967294 has the exact bit pattern of the signed value -2.

Later today, you will see how to enter an entire string into a buffer, including multiple words. For now, the question arises, "How does the extraction operator manage this trick of concatenation?"

The cin Return Value

The return value of cin is a reference to an istream object. Because cin itself is an istream object, the return value of one extraction operation can be the input to the next extraction.

```
int varOne, varTwo, varThree;
cout << "Enter three numbers: "
cin >> varOne >> varTwo >> varThree;
```

When you write cin >> varOne >> varTwo >> varThree;, the first extraction is evaluated (cin >> varOne). The return value from this is another istream object, and that object's extraction operator gets the variable varTwo. It is as if you had written this:

```
((cin >> varOne) >> varTwo) >> varThree;
```

You'll see this technique repeated later when cout is discussed.

Other Member Functions of cin

In addition to overloading operator>>, cin has a number of other member functions. These are used when finer control over the input is required. These functions allow you to do the following:

- Get a single character
- Get strings
- Ignore input
- Look at the next character in the buffer
- Put data back into the buffer

Single Character Input

operator>> taking a character reference can be used to get a single character from the standard input. The member function get() can also be used to obtain a single character, and can do so in two ways: get() can be used with no parameters, in which case the return value is used, or it can be used with a reference to a character.

Using get() with No Parameters

The first form of get() is without parameters. This returns the value of the character found and returns EOF (end of file) if the end of the file is reached. get() with no parameters is not often used.

Unlike using cin to get multiple values, it is not possible to concatenate this use of get() for multiple input because the return value is not an iostream object. Thus, the following doesn't work:

```
cin.get() >>myVarOne >> myVarTwo; //   illegal
```

The return value of cin.get() >> myVarOne is actually an integer, not an iostream object.

A common use of `get()` with no parameters is illustrated in Listing 17.4.

LISTING 17.4 Using `get()` with No Parameters

```
0: // Listing 17.4 - Using get() with no parameters
1:
2: #include <iostream>
3:
4: int main()
5: {
6:     char ch;
7:     while ( (ch = std::cin.get()) != EOF)
8:         {
9:         std::cout << "ch: " << ch << std::endl;
10:         }
11:     std::cout << "\nDone!\n";
12:     return 0;
13: }
```

TIP

To exit this program, you must send end of file from the keyboard. On DOS computers, use Ctrl+Z; on Unix workstations, use Ctrl+D.

OUTPUT

```
Hello
ch: H
ch: e
ch: l
ch: l
ch: o
ch:

World
ch: W
ch: o
ch: r
ch: l
ch: d
ch:

^Z (ctrl-z)

Done!
```

ANALYSIS On line 6, a local character variable, `ch`, is declared. The `while` loop assigns the input received from `cin.get()` to `ch`, and if it is not `EOF`, the string is printed out.

This output is buffered until an end of line is read, however. When EOF is encountered (by pressing Ctrl+Z on a DOS machine, or Ctrl+D on a Unix machine), the loop exits.

Note that not every implementation of istream supports this version of get(), although it is now part of the ANSI/ISO standard.

Using get() with a Character Reference Parameter

When a character variable is passed as input to get(), that character variable is filled with the next character in the input stream. The return value is an iostream object, and so this form of get() can be concatenated, as illustrated in Listing 17.5.

LISTING 17.5 Using get() with Parameters

```
0:   // Listing 17.5 - Using get() with parameters
1:
2:   #include <iostream>
3:
4:   int main()
5:   {
6:       char a, b, c;
7:
8:       std::cout << "Enter three letters: ";
9:
10:      std::cin.get(a).get(b).get(c);
11:
12:      std::cout << "a: " << a << "\nb: ";
13:      std::cout << b << "\nc: " << c << std::endl;
14:      return 0;
15:  }
```

OUTPUT
```
Enter three letters: one
a: o
b: n
c: e
```

ANALYSIS On line 6, three character variables, a, b, and c, are created. On line 10, cin.get() is called three times, concatenated. First, cin.get(a) is called. This puts the first letter into a and returns cin so that when it is done, cin.get(b) is called, putting the next letter into b. Finally, cin.get(c) is called and the third letter is put in c.

Because cin.get(a) evaluates to cin, you could have written this:

cin.get(a) >> b;

In this form, cin.get(a) evaluates to cin, so the second phrase is cin >> b;.

Do	**Don't**
DO use the extraction operator (>>) when you need to skip over whitespace. **DO** use get() with a character parameter when you need to examine every character, including whitespace.	**DON'T** stack cin statements to get multiple input if it isn't clear what you are doing. It is better to use multiple commands that are easier to understand than to use one long command.

Getting Strings from Standard Input

The extraction operator (>>) can be used to fill a character array, as can the third version of the member functions get() and the member function getline().

This form of get() takes three parameters:

```
get( pCharArray, StreamSize, TermChar );
```

The first parameter (*pCharArray*) is a pointer to a character array, the second parameter (*StreamSize*) is the maximum number of characters to read plus one, and the third parameter (*TermChar*) is the termination character.

If you enter 20 as the second parameter, get() reads 19 characters and then null-terminates the string, which it stores in the first parameter. The third parameter, the termination character, defaults to newline ('\n'). If a termination character is reached before the maximum number of characters is read, a null is written and the termination character is left in the buffer.

Listing 17.6 illustrates the use of this form of get().

LISTING 17.6 Using get() with a Character Array

```
0:   // Listing 17.6 - Using get() with a character array
1:
2:   #include <iostream>
3:   using namespace std;
4:
5:   int main()
6:   {
7:      char stringOne[256];
8:      char stringTwo[256];
9:
10:     cout << "Enter string one: ";
11:     cin.get(stringOne,256);
12:     cout << "stringOne: " << stringOne << endl;
13:
```

17

LISTING 17.6 continued

```
14:     cout << "Enter string two: ";
15:     cin >> stringTwo;
16:     cout << "StringTwo: " << stringTwo << endl;
17:     return 0;
18:  }
```

OUTPUT

```
Enter string one: Now is the time
stringOne: Now is the time
Enter string two: For all good
StringTwo: For
```

ANALYSIS

On lines 7 and 8, two character arrays are created. On line 10, the user is prompted to enter a string, and cin.get() is called on line 11. The first parameter is the buffer to fill, and the second is one more than the maximum number for get() to accept (the extra position being given to the null character, ['\0']). There is not a third parameter shown; however, this is defaulted. The defaulted third parameter is a newline.

The user enters "Now is the time." Because the user ends the phrase with a newline, that phrase is put into stringOne, followed by a terminating null.

The user is prompted for another string on line 14, and this time the extraction operator is used. Because the extraction operator takes everything up to the first whitespace, only the string For, with a terminating null character, is stored in the second string, which, of course, is not what was intended.

Using get() with the three parameters is perfectly valid for obtaining strings; however, it is not the only solution. Another way to solve this problem is to use getline(), as illustrated in Listing 17.7.

LISTING 17.7 Using getline()

```
0:  // Listing 17.7 - Using getline()
1:
2:  #include <iostream>
3:  using namespace std;
4:
5:  int main()
6:  {
7:     char stringOne[256];
8:     char stringTwo[256];
9:     char stringThree[256];
10:
11:     cout << "Enter string one: ";
12:     cin.getline(stringOne,256);
```

LISTING 17.7   continued

```
13:      cout << "stringOne: " << stringOne << endl;
14:
15:      cout << "Enter string two: ";
16:      cin >> stringTwo;
17:      cout << "stringTwo: " << stringTwo << endl;
18:
19:      cout << "Enter string three: ";
20:      cin.getline(stringThree,256);
21:      cout << "stringThree: " << stringThree << endl;
22:      return 0;
23:  }
```

OUTPUT

```
Enter string one: one two three
stringOne: one two three
Enter string two: four five six
stringTwo: four
Enter string three: stringThree: five six
```

ANALYSIS   This example warrants careful examination; some potential surprises exist. On lines 7–9, three character arrays are declared this time.

On line 11, the user is prompted to enter a string, and that string is read by using get-line(). Like get(), getline() takes a buffer and a maximum number of characters. Unlike get(), however, the terminating newline is read and thrown away. With get(), the terminating newline is not thrown away. It is left in the input buffer.

On line 15, the user is prompted for the second time, and this time the extraction operator is used. In the sample output, you can see that the user enters four five six; however, only the first word, four, is put in stringTwo. The string for the third prompt, Enter string three, is then displayed, and getline() is called again. Because five six is still in the input buffer, it is immediately read up to the newline; getline() terminates and the string in stringThree is printed on line 21.

The user has no chance to enter the third string because the input buffer contained data that fulfilled the request this prompt was making.

The call to cin on line 16 did not use everything that was in the input buffer. The extraction operator (>>) on line 16 reads up to the first whitespace and puts the word into the character array.

17

> ### get() and getline()
>
> The member function get() is overloaded. In one version, it takes no parameters and returns the value of the character it receives. In the second version, it takes a single character reference and returns the istream object by reference.
>
> In the third and final version, get() takes a character array, a number of characters to get, and a termination character (which defaults to newline). This version of get() reads characters into the array until it gets to one fewer than its maximum number of characters or it encounters the termination character, whichever comes first. If get() encounters the termination character, it leaves that character in the input buffer and stops reading characters.
>
> The member function getline() also takes three parameters: the buffer to fill, one more than the maximum number of characters to get, and the termination character. getline() functions the same as get() does with these parameters, except getline() throws away the terminating character.

Using cin.ignore()

At times, you want to ignore the remaining characters on a line until you hit either end of line (EOL) or end of file (EOF). The member function ignore() serves this purpose. ignore() takes two parameters: the maximum number of characters to ignore and the termination character. If you write ignore(80,'\n'), up to 80 characters will be thrown away until a newline character is found. The newline is then thrown away and the ignore() statement ends. Listing 17.8 illustrates the use of ignore().

LISTING **17.8**   Using ignore()

```
0:  // Listing 17.8 - Using ignore()
1:  #include <iostream>
2:  using namespace std;
3:
4:  int main()
5:  {
6:      char stringOne[255];
7:      char stringTwo[255];
8:
9:      cout << "Enter string one:";
10:     cin.get(stringOne,255);
11:     cout << "String one: " << stringOne << endl;
12:
13:     cout << "Enter string two: ";
14:     cin.getline(stringTwo,255);
15:     cout << "String two: " << stringTwo << endl;
16:
```

LISTING 17.8   continued

```
17:     cout << "\n\nNow try again...\n";
18:
19:     cout << "Enter string one: ";
20:     cin.get(stringOne,255);
21:     cout << "String one: " << stringOne<< endl;
22:
23:     cin.ignore(255,'\n');
24:
25:     cout << "Enter string two: ";
26:     cin.getline(stringTwo,255);
27:     cout << "String Two: " << stringTwo<< endl;
28:     return 0;
29:  }
```

17

OUTPUT
```
Enter string one:once upon a time
String one: once upon a time
Enter string two: String two:

Now try again...
Enter string one: once upon a time
String one: once upon a time
Enter string two: there was a
String Two: there was a
```

ANALYSIS   On lines 6 and 7, two character arrays are created. On line 9, the user is prompted for input and types once upon a time, followed by pressing the Enter key. On line 10, get() is used to read this string. get() fills stringOne and terminates on the newline, but leaves the newline character in the input buffer.

On line 13, the user is prompted again, but the getline() on line 14 reads the input buffer up to the newline. Because a newline was left in the buffer by the call to get(), line 14 terminates immediately, before the user can enter any new input.

On line 19, the user is prompted again and puts in the same first line of input. This time, however, on line 23, ignore() is used to empty the input stream by "eating" the newline character. Thus, when the getline() call on line 26 is reached, the input buffer is empty, and the user can input the next line of the story.

Peeking at and Returning Characters: peek() and putback()

The input object cin has two additional methods that can come in rather handy: peek(), which looks at but does not extract the next character, and putback(), which inserts a character into the input stream. Listing 17.9 illustrates how these might be used.

LISTING **17.9**   Using peek() and putback()

```
0:   // Listing 17.9 - Using peek() and putback()
1:   #include <iostream>
2:   using namespace std;
3:
4:   int main()
5:   {
6:       char ch;
7:       cout << "enter a phrase: ";
8:       while ( cin.get(ch) != 0 )
9:       {
10:         if (ch == '!')
11:             cin.putback('$');
12:         else
13:             cout << ch;
14:         while (cin.peek() == '#')
15:             cin.ignore(1,'#');
16:      }
17:      return 0;
18:  }
```

OUTPUT

enter a phrase: **Now!is#the!time#for!fun#!**
Now$isthe$timeforfun

ANALYSIS   On line 6, a character variable, ch, is declared, and on line 7, the user is
prompted to enter a phrase. The purpose of this program is to turn any exclama-
tion marks (!) into dollar signs ($) and to remove any pound symbols (#).

The program loops on lines 8–16 as long as it is getting characters other than the end of
file (Ctrl+C on Windows machines, Ctrl+Z or Ctrl+D on other operating systems).
(Remember that cin.get() returns 0 for end of file.) If the current character is an excla-
mation point, it is thrown away and the $ symbol is put back into the input buffer. This $
symbol is then read the next time through the loop. If the current item is not an exclama-
tion point, it is printed on line 13.

On line 14, the next character is "peeked" at, and when pound symbols are found, they
are removed using the ignore() method, as shown on line 15.

This is not the most efficient way to do either of these things (and it won't find a pound
symbol if it is the first character), but it does illustrate how these methods work.

TIP

peek() and putback() are typically used for parsing strings and other data,
such as when writing a compiler.

Outputting with cout

You have used cout along with the overloaded insertion operator (<<) to write strings, integers, and other numeric data to the screen. It is also possible to format the data, aligning columns and writing numeric data in decimal and hexadecimal. This section shows you how.

Flushing the Output

You've already seen that using endl writes a newline and then flushes the output buffer. endl calls cout's member function flush(), which writes all the data it is buffering. You can also call the flush() method directly, either by calling the flush() member method or by writing the following:

```
cout << flush();
```

This can be convenient when you need to ensure that the output buffer is emptied and that the contents are written to the screen.

Functions for Doing Output

Just as the extraction operator can be supplemented with get() and getline(), the insertion operator can be supplemented with put() and write().

Writing Characters with put()

The function put() is used to write a single character to the output device. Because put() returns an ostream reference and because cout is an ostream object, you can concatenate put() the same as you can stack the insertion operator. Listing 17.10 illustrates this idea.

LISTING 17.10   Using put()

```
0:   // Listing 17.10 - Using put()
1:
2:   #include <iostream>
3:
4:   int main()
5:   {
6:       std::cout.put('H').put('e').put('l').put('l').put('o').put('\n');
7:       return 0;
8:   }
```

OUTPUT   Hello

Some nonstandard compilers have trouble printing using this code. If your compiler does not print the word Hello, you might want to skip this listing.

ANALYSIS Line 6 is evaluated like this: std::cout.put('H') writes the letter "H" to the screen and returns a cout object. This leaves the following:

```
cout.put('e').put('l').put('l').put('o').put('\n');
```

The letter "e" is written, and, again, a cout object is returned leaving:

```
cout.put('l').put('l').put('o').put('\n');
```

This process repeats, each letter being written and the cout object returned until the final character ('\n') is written and the function returns.

Writing More with write()

The function write() works the same as the insertion operator (<<), except that it takes a parameter that tells the function the maximum number of characters to write:

```
cout.write(Text, Size)
```

As you can see, the first parameter for write() is the text that will be printed. The second parameter, Size, is the number of characters that will be printed from Text. Note that this number might be smaller or larger than the actual size of the Text. If it is larger, you will output the values that reside in memory after the Text value. Listing 17.11 illustrates its use.

LISTING 17.11 Using write()

```
 0:  // Listing 17.11 - Using write()
 1:  #include <iostream>
 2:  #include <string.h>
 3:  using namespace std;
 4:
 5:  int main()
 6:  {
 7:      char One[] = "One if by land";
 8:
 9:      int fullLength = strlen(One);
10:      int tooShort = fullLength -4;
11:      int tooLong = fullLength + 6;
12:
13:      cout.write(One,fullLength) << endl;
14:      cout.write(One,tooShort) << endl;
15:      cout.write(One,tooLong) << endl;
16:      return 0;
17:  }
```

OUTPUT

```
One if by land
One if by
One if by land i?!
```

NOTE   The final line of output might look different on your computer because it accesses memory that is not part of an initialized variable.

ANALYSIS   This listing prints from a phrase. Each time it prints a different amount of the phrase. On line 7, one phrase is created. On line 9, the integer `fullLength` is set to the length of the phrase using a global `strlen()` method that was included with the string directive on line 2. Also set are two other length values that will be used; `tooShort` is set to the length of the phrase (`fullLength`) minus four, and `tooLong` is set to the length of the phrase plus six.

On line 13, the complete phrase is printed using `write()`. The length is set to the actual length of the phrase, and the correct phrase is printed.

On line 14, the phrase is printed again, but it is four characters shorter than the full phrase, and that is reflected in the output.

On line 15, the phrase is printed again, but this time `write()` is instructed to write an extra six characters. After the phrase is written, the next six bytes of contiguous memory are written. Anything could be in this memory, so your output might vary from what is shown previously.

Manipulators, Flags, and Formatting Instructions

The output stream maintains a number of state flags, determining which base (decimal or hexadecimal) to use, how wide to make the fields, and what character to use to fill in fields. A state flag is a byte whose individual bits are each assigned a special meaning. Manipulating bits in this way is discussed on Day 21, "What's Next." Each of `ostream`'s flags can be set using member functions and manipulators.

Using `cout.width()`

The default width of your output will be just enough space to print the number, character, or string in the output buffer. You can change this by using `width()`.

Because `width()` is a member function, it must be invoked with a `cout` object. It only changes the width of the very next output field and then immediately reverts to the default. Listing 17.12 illustrates its use.

LISTING 17.12   Adjusting the Width of Output

```
0:   // Listing 17.12 - Adjusting the width of output
1:   #include <iostream>
2:   using namespace std;
3:
4:   int main()
5:   {
6:      cout << "Start >";
7:      cout.width(25);
8:      cout << 123 << "< End\n";
9:
10:     cout << "Start >";
11:     cout.width(25);
12:     cout << 123<< "< Next >";
13:     cout << 456 << "< End\n";
14:
15:     cout << "Start >";
16:     cout.width(4);
17:     cout << 123456 << "< End\n";
18:
19:     return 0;
20:  }
```

OUTPUT
```
Start >                        123< End
Start >                        123< Next >456< End
Start >123456< End
```

ANALYSIS   The first output, on lines 6–8, prints the number 123 within a field whose width is set to 25 on line 7. This is reflected in the first line of output.

The second line of output first prints the value 123 in the same field whose width is set to 25, and then prints the value 456. Note that 456 is printed in a field whose width is reset to just large enough; as stated, the effect of width() lasts only as long as the very next output.

The final output reflects that setting a width that is smaller than the output is the same as setting a width that is just large enough. A width that is too small will not truncate what is being displayed.

Setting the Fill Characters

Normally, cout fills the empty field created by a call to width() with spaces, as shown previously. At times, you might want to fill the area with other characters, such as asterisks. To do this, you call fill() and pass in as a parameter the character you want used as a fill character. Listing 17.13 illustrates this.

LISTING 17.13 Using `fill()`

```
0:   // Listing 17.13 - fill()
1:
2:   #include <iostream>
3:   using namespace std;
4:
5:   int main()
6:   {
7:      cout << "Start >";
8:      cout.width(25);
9:      cout << 123 << "< End\n";
10:
11:     cout << "Start >";
12:     cout.width(25);
13:     cout.fill('*');
14:     cout << 123 << "< End\n";
15:
16:     cout << "Start >";
17:     cout.width(25);
18:     cout << 456 << "< End\n";
19:
20:     return 0;
21: }
```

OUTPUT

```
Start >                  123< End
Start >******************123< End
Start >******************456< End
```

ANALYSIS Lines 7–9 repeat the functionality from the previous example by printing the value 123 in a width area of 25. Lines 11–14 repeat this again, but this time, on line 13, the fill character is set to an asterisk, as reflected in the output. You should notice that unlike the `width()` function, which only applies to the next output, the new `fill()` character remains until you change it. You see this verified with the output from lines 16–18.

Managing the State of Output: Set Flags

Objects are said to have state when some or all of their data represents a condition that can change during the course of the program. For example, you can set whether to show trailing zeros (so that 20.00 is not truncated to 20).

The `iostream` objects keep track of their state by using flags. You can set these flags by calling `setf()` and passing in one of the predefined enumerated constants. For example, to turn trailing zeros on, you call `setf(ios::showpoint)`.

The enumerated constants are scoped to the `iostream` class (`ios`) and thus when used with `setf()`, they are called with the full qualification `ios::`*flagname*, such as ios::showpoint. TABLE 17.1 shows some of the flags you can use. When using these flags, you need to include iostream in your listing. In addition, for those flags that require parameters, you need to include iomanip.

TABLE 17.1   Some of the iostream Set Flags

Flag	Purpose
showpoint	Displays a decimal point and trailing zeros as required by precision
showpos	Turns on the plus sign (+) before positive numbers
left	Aligns output to the left
right	Aligns output to the right
internal	Aligns the sign for a number to the left and aligns the value to the right
showpoint	Adds trailing zeros as required by the precision
showpos	Displays a plus sign (+) if the number is positive
scientific	Shows floating-point values in scientific notation
fixed	Shows floating-point numbers in decimal notation
showbase	Adds "0x" in front of hexadecimal numbers to indicate that it is a hexadecimal value
Uppercase	Shows hexadecimal and scientific numbers in uppercase
dec	Sets the base of the numbers for display to decimal
oct	Sets the base of the numbers for display to octal—base 8
hex	Sets the base of the numbers for display to hexadecimal—base 16

The flags in Table 17.1 can also be concatenated into the insertion operator. Listing 17.14 illustrates these settings. As a bonus, Listing 17.14 also introduces the setw manipulator, which sets the width but can also be concatenated with the insertion operator.

LISTING 17.14   Using setf

```
0:  // Listing 17.14 - Using setf
1:  #include <iostream>
2:  #include <iomanip>
3:  using namespace std;
4:
5:  int main()
6:  {
7:     const int number = 185;
8:     cout << "The number is " << number << endl;
9:
10:    cout << "The number is " << hex <<  number << endl;
```

LISTING 17.4   continued

```
11:
12:       cout.setf(ios::showbase);
13:       cout << "The number is " << hex <<  number << endl;
14:
15:       cout << "The number is " ;
16:       cout.width(10);
17:       cout << hex << number << endl;
18:
19:       cout << "The number is " ;
20:       cout.width(10);
21:       cout.setf(ios::left);
22:       cout << hex << number << endl;
23:
24:       cout << "The number is " ;
25:       cout.width(10);
26:       cout.setf(ios::internal);
27:       cout << hex << number << endl;
28:
29:       cout << "The number is " << setw(10) << hex << number << endl;
30:       return 0;
31:  }
```

OUTPUT
```
The number is 185
The number is b9
The number is 0xb9
The number is           0xb9
The number is 0xb9
The number is 0x        b9
The number is:0x        b9
```

ANALYSIS   On line 7, the constant int number is initialized to the value 185. This is displayed normally on line 8.

The value is displayed again on line 10, but this time the manipulator hex is concatenated, causing the value to be displayed in hexadecimal as b9.

NOTE
> The value b in hexadecimal represents 11. Eleven times 16 equals 176; add the 9 for a total of 185.

On line 12, the flag showbase is set. This causes the prefix 0x to be added to all hexadecimal numbers, as reflected in the output.

On line 16, the width is set to 10, and by default, the value is pushed to the extreme right. On line 20, the width is again set to 10, but this time the alignment is set to the left, and the number is printed flush left this time.

On line 25, again the width is set to 10, but this time the alignment is internal. Thus, the 0x is printed flush left, but the value, b9, is printed flush right.

Finally, on line 29, the concatenation operator setw() is used to set the width to 10, and the value is printed again.

You should notice in this listing that if the flags are used within the cout list that they do not need to be qualified; hex can be passed as hex. When you use the setf() function, you need to qualify the flags to the class; hex is passed as ios::hex. You see this difference on line 17 versus 21.

Streams Versus the printf() Function

Most C++ implementations also provide the standard C I/O libraries, including the printf() statement. Although printf() is in some ways easier to use than cout, it is much less desirable.

printf() does not provide type safety, so it is easy to inadvertently tell it to display an integer as if it were a character, and vice versa. printf() also does not support classes, and so it is not possible to teach it how to print your class data; you must feed each class member to printf() one by one.

Because there is a lot of legacy code using printf(), this section briefly reviews how printf() is used. It is not, however, recommended that you use this function in your C++ programs.

To use printf(), be certain to include the stdio.h header file. In its simplest form, printf() takes a formatting string as its first parameter and then a series of values as its remaining parameters.

The formatting string is a quoted string of text and conversion specifiers. All conversion specifiers must begin with the percent symbol (%). The common conversion specifiers are presented in Table 17.2.

TABLE 17.2 The Common Conversion Specifiers

Specifier	Used For
%s	strings
%d	integers

TABLE 17.2 continued

%1	long integer
%ld	double
%f	float

Each of the conversion specifiers can also provide a width statement and a precision statement, expressed as a float, where the digits to the left of the decimal are used for the total width, and the digits to the right of the decimal provide the precision for floats. Thus, %5d is the specifier for a 5-digit-wide integer, and %15.5f is the specifier for a 15-digit-wide float, of which the final five digits are dedicated to the decimal portion. Listing 17.15 illustrates various uses of printf().

LISTING 17.15 Printing with printf()

```
0:  //17.15 Printing with printf()
1:  #include <stdio.h>
2:
3:  int main()
4:  {
5:      printf("%s","hello world\n");
6:
7:      char *phrase = "Hello again!\n";
8:      printf("%s",phrase);
9:
10:     int x = 5;
11:     printf("%d\n",x);
12:
13:     char *phraseTwo = "Here's some values: ";
14:     char *phraseThree = " and also these: ";
15:     int y = 7, z = 35;
16:     long longVar = 98456;
17:     float floatVar =  8.8f;
18:
19:     printf("%s %d %d", phraseTwo, y, z);
20:     printf("%s %ld %f\n",phraseThree,longVar,floatVar);
21:
22:     char *phraseFour = "Formatted: ";
23:     printf("%s %5d %10d  %10.5f\n",phraseFour,y,z,floatVar);
24:
25:     return 0;
26:  }
```

17

OUTPUT

```
hello world
Hello again!
5
Here's some values: 7 35  and also these: 98456 8.800000
Formatted:       7       35     8.800000
```

ANALYSIS The first `printf()` statement, on line 5, uses the standard form: the term `printf`, followed by a quoted string with a conversion specifier (in this case `%s`), followed by a value to insert into the conversion specifier.

The `%s` indicates that this is a string, and the value for the string is, in this case, the quoted string "hello world."

The second `printf()` statement on line 8 is the same as the first, but this time a char pointer is used, rather than quoting the string right in place in the `printf()` statement. The result, however, is the same.

The third `printf()`, on line 11, uses the integer conversion specifier (`%d`), and for its value the integer variable x is used. The fourth `printf()` statement, on line 19, is more complex. Here, three values are concatenated. Each conversion specifier is supplied, and then the values are provided, separated by commas. Line 20 is similar to line 19; however, different specifiers and values are used.

Finally, on line 23, format specifications are used to set the width and precision. As you can see, all this is somewhat easier than using manipulators.

As stated previously, however, the limitation here is that no type checking occurs and `printf()` cannot be declared a friend or member function of a class. So, if you want to print the various member data of a class, you must call each accessor method in the argument list sent to the `printf()` statement.

FAQ

Can you summarize how to manipulate output?

Answer: (with special thanks to Robert Francis) To format output in C++, you use a combination of special characters, output manipulators, and flags.

The following special characters are included in an output string being sent to cout using the insertion operator:

\n—Newline

\r—Carriage return

\t—Tab

\\—Backslash

\ddd (octal number)—ASCII character

\a—Alarm (ring bell)

For example,

```
cout << "\aAn error occured\t"
```

rings the bell, prints an error message, and moves to the next tab stop. Manipulators are used with the cout operator. Those manipulators that take arguments require that you include iomanip in your file.

The following is a list of manipulators that do *not* require iomanip:

flush—Flushes the output buffer

endl—Inserts newline and flushes the output buffer

oct—Sets output base to octal

dec—Sets output base to decimal

hex—Sets output base to hexadecimal

The following is a list of manipulators that *do* require iomanip:

setbase (base)—Sets output base (0 = decimal, 8 = octal, 10 = decimal, 16 = hex)

setw (width)—Sets minimum output field width

setfill (ch)—Fills character to be used when width is defined

setprecision (p)—Sets precision for floating-point numbers

setiosflags (f)—Sets one or more ios flags

resetiosflags (f)—Resets one or more ios flags

For example,

```
cout << setw(12) << setfill('#') << hex << x << endl;
```

sets the field width to 12, sets the fill character to '#', specifies hex output, prints the value of 'x', puts a newline in the buffer, and flushes the buffer. All the manipulators except flush, endl, and setw remain in effect until changed or until the end of the program. setw returns to the default after the current cout.

A number of flags can be used with the setiosflags and resetiosflags manipulators. These were listed in Table 17.1 earlier.

Additional information can be obtained from file ios and from your compiler's documentation.

17

File Input and Output

Streams provide a uniform way of dealing with data coming from the keyboard or the hard disk and going out to the console screen or hard disk. In either case, you can use the insertion and extraction operators or the other related functions and manipulators. To open and close files, you create `ifstream` and `ofstream` objects as described in the next few sections.

Using the `ofstream`

The particular objects used to read from or write to files are called `ofstream` objects. These are derived from the `iostream` objects you've been using so far.

To get started with writing to a file, you must first create an `ofstream` object, and then associate that object with a particular file on your disk. To use `ofstream` objects, you must be certain to include `fstream` in your program.

> **NOTE** Because `fstream` includes `iostream`, you do not need to include `iostream` explicitly.

Condition States

The `iostream` objects maintain flags that report on the state of your input and output. You can check each of these flags using the Boolean functions `eof()`, `bad()`, `fail()`, and `good()`. The function `eof()` returns `true` if the `iostream` object has encountered EOF, end of file. The function `bad()` returns `true` if you attempt an invalid operation. The function `fail()` returns `true` anytime `bad()` is true or an operation fails. Finally, the function `good()` returns `true` anytime all three of the other functions are `false`.

Opening Files for Input and Output

To use a file, you must first open it. To open the file `myfile.cpp` with an `ofstream` object, declare an instance of an `ofstream` object and pass in the filename as a parameter:

```
ofstream fout("myfile.cpp");
```

This attempts to open the file, `myfile.cpp`, for output. Opening this file for input works the same way, except that it uses an `ifstream` object:

```
ifstream fin("myfile.cpp");
```

Note that `fout` and `fin` are names you define; here, `fout` has been used to reflect its similarity to `cout`, and `fin` has been used to reflect its similarity to `cin`. These could also be given names that reflect what is in the file they are accessing.

One important file stream function that you will need right away is close(). Every file stream object you create opens a file for reading (input), writing (output), or both. It is important to close() the file after you finish reading or writing; this ensures that the file won't be corrupted and that the data you've written is flushed to the disk.

After the stream objects are associated with files, they can be used the same as any other stream objects. Listing 17.16 illustrates this.

LISTING 17.16   Opening Files for Read and Write

```
0:   //Listing 17.16 Opening Files for Read and Write
1:   #include <fstream>
2:   #include <iostream>
3:   using namespace std;
4:
5:   int main()
6:   {
7:       char fileName[80];
8:       char buffer[255];     // for user input
9:       cout << "File name: ";
10:      cin >> fileName;
11:
12:      ofstream fout(fileName);  // open for writing
13:      fout << "This line written directly to the file...\n";
14:      cout << "Enter text for the file: ";
15:      cin.ignore(1,'\n');  // eat the newline after the file name
16:      cin.getline(buffer,255);  // get the user's input
17:      fout << buffer << "\n";   // and write it to the file
18:      fout.close();             // close the file, ready for reopen
19:
20:      ifstream fin(fileName);    // reopen for reading
21:      cout << "Here's the contents of the file:\n";
22:      char ch;
23:      while (fin.get(ch))
24:         cout << ch;
25:
26:      cout << "\n***End of file contents.***\n";
27:
28:      fin.close();              // always pays to be tidy
29:      return 0;
30:  }
```

OUTPUT

```
File name: test1
Enter text for the file: This text is written to the file!
Here's the contents of the file:
This line written directly to the file...
This text is written to the file!

***End of file contents.***
```

ANALYSIS On line 7, a buffer is created for the filename, and on line 8, another buffer is set aside for user input. The user is prompted to enter a filename on line 9, and this response is written to the `fileName` buffer. On line 12, an `ofstream` object is created, `fout`, which is associated with the new filename. This opens the file; if the file already exists, its contents are thrown away.

On line 13, a string of text is written directly to the file. On line 14, the user is prompted for input. The newline character left over from the user's input of the filename is eaten on line 15 by using the `ignore()` function you learned about earlier. The user's input for the file is stored into `buffer` on line 16. That input is written to the file along with a newline character on line 17, and then the file is closed on line 18.

On line 20, the file is reopened, this time in input mode by using the `ifstream`. The contents are then read one character at a time on lines 23 and 24.

Changing the Default Behavior of `ofstream` on Open

The default behavior upon opening a file is to create the file if it doesn't yet exist and to truncate the file (that is, delete all its contents) if it does exist. If you don't want this default behavior, you can explicitly provide a second argument to the constructor of your `ofstream` object.

Valid values for the second argument include

- `ios::app`—Appends to the end of existing files rather than truncating them.
- `ios::ate`—Places you at the end of the file, but you can write data anywhere in the file.
- `ios::trunc`—Causes existing files to be truncated; the default.
- `ios::nocreate`—If the file does not exist, the open fails.
- `ios::noreplace`—If the file does already exist, the open fails.

Note that `app` is short for append, `ate` is short for at end, and `trunc` is short for truncate. Listing 17.17 illustrates using append by reopening the file from Listing 17.16 and appending to it.

LISTING 17.17 Appending to the End of a File

```
0:  //Listing 17.17 Appending to the End of a File
1:  #include <fstream>
2:  #include <iostream>
3:  using namespace std;
4:
5:  int main()    // returns 1 on error
```

LISTING 17.17   continued

```
 6:   {
 7:      char fileName[80];
 8:      char buffer[255];
 9:      cout << "Please reenter the file name: ";
10:      cin >> fileName;
11:
12:      ifstream fin(fileName);
13:      if (fin)                  // already exists?
14:      {
15:         cout << "Current file contents:\n";
16:         char ch;
17:         while (fin.get(ch))
18:            cout << ch;
19:         cout << "\n***End of file contents.***\n";
20:      }
21:      fin.close();
22:
23:      cout << "\nOpening " << fileName << " in append mode...\n";
24:
25:      ofstream fout(fileName,ios::app);
26:      if (!fout)
27:      {
28:         cout << "Unable to open " << fileName << " for appending.\n";
29:         return(1);
30:      }
31:
32:      cout << "\nEnter text for the file: ";
33:      cin.ignore(1,'\n');
34:      cin.getline(buffer,255);
35:      fout << buffer << "\n";
36:      fout.close();
37:
38:      fin.open(fileName);  // reassign existing fin object!
39:      if (!fin)
40:      {
41:         cout << "Unable to open " << fileName << " for reading.\n";
42:         return(1);
43:      }
44:      cout << "\nHere's the contents of the file:\n";
45:      char ch;
46:      while (fin.get(ch))
47:         cout << ch;
48:      cout << "\n***End of file contents.***\n";
49:      fin.close();
50:      return 0;
51:   }
```

17

OUTPUT

```
Please reenter the file name: test1
Current file contents:
This line written directly to the file...
This text is written to the file!

***End of file contents.***

Opening test1 in append mode...

Enter text for the file: More text for the file!

Here's the contents of the file:
This line written directly to the file...
This text is written to the file!
More text for the file!

***End of file contents.***
```

ANALYSIS

Like the preceding listing, the user is again prompted to enter the filename on lines 9 and 10. This time, an input file stream object is created on line 12. That open is tested on line 13, and if the file already exists, its contents are printed on lines 15–19. Note that if(fin) is synonymous with if (fin.good()).

The input file is then closed, and the same file is reopened, this time in append mode, on line 25. After this open (and every open), the file is tested to ensure that the file was opened properly. Note that if(!fout) is the same as testing if (fout.fail()). If the file didn't open, an error message is printed on line 28 and the program ends with the return statement. If the open is successful, the user is then prompted to enter text, and the file is closed again on line 36.

Finally, as in Listing 17.16, the file is reopened in read mode; however, this time fin does not need to be redeclared. It is just reassigned to the same filename. Again, the open is tested, on line 39, and if all is well, the contents of the file are printed to the screen and the file is closed for the final time.

Do	**Don't**
DO test each open of a file to ensure that it opened successfully.	**DON'T** try to close or reassign cin or cout.
DO reuse existing ifstream and ofstream objects.	**DON'T** use printf() in your C++ programs if you don't need to.
DO close all fstream objects when you are done using them.	

Binary Versus Text Files

Some operating systems distinguish between text files and binary files. Text files store everything as text (as you might have guessed), so large numbers such as 54,325 are stored as a string of numerals ('5', '4', ',', '3', '2', '5'). This can be inefficient, but has the advantage that the text can be read using simple programs such as the DOS and Windows command-line program type.

To help the file system distinguish between text and binary files, C++ provides the ios::binary flag. On many systems, this flag is ignored because all data is stored in binary format. On some rather prudish systems, the ios::binary flag is illegal and doesn't even compile!

Binary files can store not only integers and strings, but also entire data structures. You can write all the data at one time by using the write() method of fstream.

If you use write(), you can recover the data using read(). Each of these functions expects a pointer to character, however, so you must cast the address of your class to be a pointer to character.

The second argument to these functions is the number of characters expected to be read or written, which you can determine using sizeof(). Note that what is being written is the data, not the methods. What is recovered is only data. Listing 17.18 illustrates writing the contents of an object to a file.

LISTING 17.18 Writing a Class to a File

```
0:  //Listing 17.18 Writing a Class to a File
1:  #include <fstream>
2:  #include <iostream>
3:  using namespace std;
4:
5:  class Animal
6:  {
7:    public:
8:        Animal(int weight,long days):itsWeight(weight),DaysAlive(days){}
9:        ~Animal(){}
10:
11:       int GetWeight()const { return itsWeight; }
12:       void SetWeight(int weight) { itsWeight = weight; }
13:
14:       long GetDaysAlive()const { return DaysAlive; }
15:       void SetDaysAlive(long days) { DaysAlive = days; }
16:
17:    private:
18:        int itsWeight;
```

LISTING 17.18 continued

```
19:        long DaysAlive;
20:    };
21:
22:    int main()    // returns 1 on error
23:    {
24:        char fileName[80];
25:
26:
27:        cout << "Please enter the file name: ";
28:        cin >> fileName;
29:        ofstream fout(fileName,ios::binary);
30:        if (!fout)
31:        {
32:            cout << "Unable to open " << fileName << " for writing.\n";
33:            return(1);
34:        }
35:
36:        Animal Bear(50,100);
37:        fout.write((char*) &Bear,sizeof Bear);
38:
39:        fout.close();
40:
41:        ifstream fin(fileName,ios::binary);
42:        if (!fin)
43:        {
44:            cout << "Unable to open " << fileName << " for reading.\n";
45:            return(1);
46:        }
47:
48:        Animal BearTwo(1,1);
49:
50:        cout << "BearTwo weight: " << BearTwo.GetWeight() << endl;
51:        cout << "BearTwo days: " << BearTwo.GetDaysAlive() << endl;
52:
53:        fin.read((char*) &BearTwo, sizeof BearTwo);
54:
55:        cout << "BearTwo weight: " << BearTwo.GetWeight() << endl;
56:        cout << "BearTwo days: " << BearTwo.GetDaysAlive() << endl;
57:        fin.close();
58:        return 0;
59:    }
```

OUTPUT

```
Please enter the file name: Animals
BearTwo weight: 1
BearTwo days: 1
BearTwo weight: 50
BearTwo days: 100
```

ANALYSIS   On lines 5–20, a stripped-down `Animal` class is declared. On lines 24–34, a file is created and opened for output in binary mode. An animal whose weight is 50 and who is 100 days old is created on line 36, and its data is written to the file on line 37.

The file is closed on line 39 and reopened for reading in binary mode on line 41. A second animal is created, on line 48, whose weight is 1 and who is only one day old. The data from the file is read into the new animal object on line 53, wiping out the existing data and replacing it with the data from the file. The output confirms this.

Command-line Processing

Many operating systems, such as DOS and Unix, enable the user to pass parameters to your program when the program starts. These are called command-line options and are typically separated by spaces on the command line. For example,

```
SomeProgram Param1 Param2 Param3
```

These parameters are not passed to `main()` directly. Instead, every program's `main()` function is passed two parameters. The first is an integer count of the number of arguments on the command line. The program name itself is counted, so every program has at least one parameter. The sample command line shown previously has four. (The name `SomeProgram` plus the three parameters make a total of four command-line arguments.)

The second parameter passed to `main()` is an array of pointers to character strings. Because an array name is a constant pointer to the first element of the array, you can declare this argument to be a pointer to a pointer to `char`, a pointer to an array of `char`, or an array of arrays of `char`.

Typically, the first argument is called `argc` (argument count), but you can call it anything you like. The second argument is often called `argv` (argument vector), but again this is just a convention.

It is common to test `argc` to ensure you've received the expected number of arguments and to use `argv` to access the strings themselves. Note that `argv[0]` is the name of the program, and `argv[1]` is the first parameter to the program, represented as a string. If your program takes two numbers as arguments, you need to translate these numbers to strings. On Day 21, you will see how to use the Standard Library conversions. Listing 17.19 illustrates how to use the command-line arguments.

17

LISTING 17.19 Using Command-line Arguments

```
0:  //Listing 17.19 Using Command-line Arguments
1:  #include <iostream>
2:  int main(int argc, char **argv)
3:  {
4:      std::cout << "Received " << argc << " arguments...\n";
5:      for (int i=0; i<argc; i++)
6:          std::cout << "argument " << i << ": " << argv[i] << std::endl;
7:      return 0;
8:  }
```

OUTPUT

```
TestProgram  Teach Yourself C++ In 21 Days
Received 7 arguments...
argumnet 0: TestProgram
argument 1: Teach
argument 2: Yourself
argument 3: C++
argument 4: In
argument 5: 21
argument 6: Days
```

NOTE   You must either run this code from the command line (that is, from a DOS box) or you must set the command-line parameters in your compiler (see your compiler documentation).

ANALYSIS   The function main() declares two arguments: argc is an integer that contains the count of command-line arguments, and argv is a pointer to the array of strings. Each string in the array pointed to by argv is a command-line argument. Note that argv could just as easily have been declared as char *argv[] or char argv[][]. It is a matter of programming style how you declare argv; even though this program declared it as a pointer to a pointer, array offsets were still used to access the individual strings.

On line 4, argc is used to print the number of command-line arguments: seven in all, counting the program name itself.

On lines 5 and 6, each of the command-line arguments is printed, passing the null-terminated strings to cout by indexing into the array of strings.

A more common use of command-line arguments is illustrated by modifying Listing 17.18 to take the filename as a command-line argument, as shown in Listing 17.20.

LISTING **17.20** Using Command-line Arguments To Get a Filename

```
0:   //Listing 17.20 Using Command-line Arguments
1:   #include <fstream>
2:   #include <iostream>
3:   using namespace std;
4:
5:   class Animal
6:   {
7:     public:
8:        Animal(int weight,long days):itsWeight(weight),DaysAlive(days){}
9:        ~Animal(){}
10:
11:       int GetWeight()const { return itsWeight; }
12:       void SetWeight(int weight) { itsWeight = weight; }
13:
14:       long GetDaysAlive()const { return  DaysAlive; }
15:       void SetDaysAlive(long days) { DaysAlive = days; }
16:
17:     private:
18:       int itsWeight;
19:       long DaysAlive;
20:   };
21:
22:   int main(int argc, char *argv[])    // returns 1 on error
23:   {
24:     if (argc != 2)
25:     {
26:        cout << "Usage: " << argv[0] << " <filename>" << endl;
27:        return(1);
28:     }
29:
30:     ofstream fout(argv[1],ios::binary);
31:     if (!fout)
32:     {
33:        cout << "Unable to open " << argv[1] << " for writing.\n";
34:        return(1);
35:     }
36:
37:     Animal Bear(50,100);
38:     fout.write((char*) &Bear,sizeof Bear);
39:
40:     fout.close();
41:
42:     ifstream fin(argv[1],ios::binary);
43:     if (!fin)
44:     {
45:        cout << "Unable to open " << argv[1] << " for reading.\n";
46:        return(1);
47:     }
48:
```

17

LISTING 17.20   continued

```
49:       Animal BearTwo(1,1);
50:
51:       cout << "BearTwo weight: " << BearTwo.GetWeight() << endl;
52:       cout << "BearTwo days: " << BearTwo.GetDaysAlive() << endl;
53:
54:       fin.read((char*) &BearTwo, sizeof BearTwo);
55:
56:       cout << "BearTwo weight: " << BearTwo.GetWeight() << endl;
57:       cout << "BearTwo days: " << BearTwo.GetDaysAlive() << endl;
58:       fin.close();
59:       return 0;
60:   }
```

OUTPUT
```
BearTwo weight: 1
BearTwo days: 1
BearTwo weight: 50
BearTwo days: 100
```

ANALYSIS   The declaration of the Animal class is the same as in Listing 17.18. This time, however, rather than prompting the user for the filename, command-line arguments are used. On line 22, main() is declared to take two parameters: the count of the command-line arguments and a pointer to the array of command-line argument strings.

On lines 24–28 the program ensures that the expected number of arguments (exactly two) is received. If the user fails to supply a single filename, an error message is printed:

```
Usage TestProgram <filename>
```

Then, the program exits. Note that by using argv[0] rather than hard-coding a program name, you can compile this program to have any name, and this usage statement works automatically. You can even rename the executable after it was compiled and the usage statement will still be correct!

On line 30, the program attempts to open the supplied filename for binary output. No reason exists to copy the filename into a local temporary buffer. It can be used directly by accessing argv[1].

This technique is repeated on line 42 when the same file is reopened for input, and it is used in the error condition statements when the files cannot be opened, on lines 33 and 45.

Summary

Today, streams were introduced, and the global objects cout and cin were described. The goal of the istream and ostream objects is to encapsulate the work of writing to device drivers and buffering input and output.

Four standard stream objects are created in every program: cout, cin, cerr, and clog. Each of these can be "redirected" by many operating systems.

The istream object cin is used for input, and its most common use is with the overloaded extraction operator (>>). The ostream object cout is used for output, and its most common use is with the overloaded insertion operator (<<).

Each of these objects has a number of other member functions, such as get() and put(). Because the common forms of each of these methods returns a reference to a stream object, it is easy to concatenate each of these operators and functions.

The state of the stream objects can be changed by using manipulators. These can set the formatting and display characteristics and various other attributes of the stream objects.

File I/O can be accomplished by using the fstream classes, which derive from the stream classes. In addition to supporting the normal insertion and extraction operators, these objects also support read() and write() for storing and retrieving large binary objects.

17

Q&A

Q How do I know when to use the insertion and extraction operators and when to use the other member functions of the stream classes?

A In general, it is easier to use the insertion and extraction operators, and they are preferred when their behavior is what is needed. In those unusual circumstances when these operators don't do the job (such as reading in a string of words), the other functions can be used.

Q What is the difference between cerr and clog?

A cerr is not buffered. Everything written to cerr is immediately written out. This is fine for errors to be written to the console screen, but might have too high a performance cost for writing logs to disk. clog buffers its output, and thus can be more efficient, at the risk of losing part of the log if the program crashes.

Q Why were streams created if printf() works well?

A printf() does not support the strong type system of C++, and it does not support user-defined classes. Support for printf() is really just a carryover from the C programming language.

Q When would I ever use putback()?

A When one read operation is used to determine whether a character is valid, but a different read operation (perhaps by a different object) needs the character to be in the buffer. This is most often used when parsing a file; for example, the C++ compiler might use putback().

Q **My friends use `printf()` in their C++ programs. Can I?**

A No. At this point, `printf()` should properly be considered obsolete.

Workshop

The Workshop contains quiz questions to help solidify your understanding of the material covered and exercises to provide you with experience in using what you've learned. Try to answer the quiz and exercise questions before checking the answers in Appendix D, and be certain you understand the answers before going to tomorrow's lesson.

Quiz

1. What is the insertion operator, and what does it do?
2. What is the extraction operator, and what does it do?
3. What are the three forms of `cin.get()`, and what are their differences?
4. What is the difference between `cin.read()` and `cin.getline()`?
5. What is the default width for outputting a `long` integer using the insertion operator?
6. What is the return value of the insertion operator?
7. What parameter does the constructor to an `ofstream` object take?
8. What does the `ios::ate` argument do?

Exercises

1. Write a program that writes to the four standard iostream objects: `cin`, `cout`, `cerr`, and `clog`.
2. Write a program that prompts the user to enter her full name and then displays it on the screen.
3. Rewrite Listing 17.9 to do the same thing, but without using `putback()` or `ignore()`.
4. Write a program that takes a filename as a parameter and opens the file for reading. Read every character of the file and display only the letters and punctuation to the screen. (Ignore all nonprinting characters.) Then close the file and exit.
5. Write a program that displays its command-line arguments in reverse order and does not display the program name.

DAY **18**

Creating and Using Namespaces

Namespaces can be used to help you organize your classes. More importantly, namespaces help programmers avoid name clashes when using more than one library.

Today, you will learn

- How functions and classes are resolved by name
- How to create a namespace
- How to use a namespace
- How to use the standard namespace `std`

Getting Started

Name conflicts have been a source of aggravation to both C and C++ developers. A name clash happens when a duplicate name with matching scope is found in two parts of your program. The most common occurrence can be found in different library packages. For example, a container class library will almost certainly declare and implement a List class. (You'll learn more about container classes when you learn about templates on Day 19, "Templates.")

It is not a surprise to find a List class also being used in a windowing library. Suppose that you want to maintain a list of windows for your application. Further assume that you are using the List class found in the container class library. You declare an instance of the window library's List to hold your windows, and you discover that the member functions you want to call are not available. The compiler has matched your List declaration to the List container in the Standard Library, but what you really wanted is the List found in the vendor-specific window library.

Namespaces are used to reduce the chance of name conflicts. Namespaces are similar in some ways to classes, and the syntax is very similar.

Items declared within the namespace are owned by the namespace. All items within a namespace have public visibility. Namespaces can be nested within other namespaces. Functions can be defined within the body of the namespace or defined outside the body of the namespace. If a function is defined outside the body of the namespace, it must be qualified by the namespace's name or the calling program must have imported the namespace into its global namespace.

Resolving Functions and Classes by Name

As the compiler parses source code and builds a list of function and variable names, it also checks for name conflicts. Those conflicts that it can't resolve are left for the linker to resolve.

The compiler cannot check for name clashes across object files or other translation units; that is the purpose of the linker. Thus, the compiler does not even offer a warning in those cases.

It is not uncommon for the linker to fail with the message

```
Identifier multiply defined
```

where *identifier* is some named type. You see this linker message if you have defined the same name with the same scope in different translation units. You get a compiler error if you redefine a name within a single file having the same scope. Listing 18.1a and Listing 18.1b are an example, when compiled and linked together, that produces an error message by the linker.

LISTING **18.1A**   First Listing Using `integerValue`

```
0:  // file first.cpp
1:  int integerValue = 0 ;
2:  int main( ) {
3:      int integerValue = 0 ;
4:      // . . .
5:      return 0 ;
6:  } ;
```

LISTING **18.1B**   Second Listing Using `integerValue`

```
0:  // file second.cpp
1:  int integerValue = 0 ;
2:  // end of second.cpp
```

ANALYSIS My linker announces the following diagnostic:

```
in second.obj: integerValue already defined in first.obj.
```

If these names were in a different scope, the compiler and linker would not complain about the duplication.

It is also possible to receive a warning from the compiler concerning *identifier hiding*. The compiler should warn, in `first.cpp` in Listing 18.1a, that `integerValue` in `main()` is *hiding* the global variable with the same name.

To use the `integerValue` declared outside `main()`, you must explicitly scope the variable to global scope. Consider this example in Listings 18.2a and 18.2b, which assigns the value `10` to the `integerValue` outside `main()` and not to the `integerValue` declared within `main()`.

LISTING **18.2A**   First Listing for Identifier Hiding

```
0:  // file first.cpp
1:  int integerValue = 0 ;
2:  int main( )
3:  {
4:      int integerValue = 0 ;
5:      ::integerValue = 10 ; //assign to global "integerValue"
6:      // . . .
7:      return 0 ;
8:  } ;
```

18

Listing 18.2b Second Listing for Identifier Hiding

```
0:  // file second.cpp
1:  int integerValue = 0 ;
2:  // end of second.cpp
```

NOTE

> Note the use of the scope resolution operator ::, indicating that the
> integerValue being referred to is global, not local.

ANALYSIS The problem with the two global integers defined outside of any functions is that
they have the same name and visibility, and, thus, cause a linker error.

Visibility of Variables

The term *visibility* is used to designate the scope of a defined object, whether it is a variable, a class, or a function. Although this was covered on Day 5, "Organizing into Functions," it is worth covering again here briefly.

As an example, a variable declared and defined outside any function has *file*, or *global*, scope. The visibility of this variable is from the point of its definition through the end of the file. A variable having a *block*, or *local*, scope is found within a block structure. The most common examples are variables defined within functions. Listing 18.3 shows the scope of variables.

Listing 18.3 Working Variable Scope

```
0:  // Listing 18.3
1:  int globalScopeInt  = 5 ;
2:  void f( )
3:  {
4:      int localScopeInt = 10 ;
5:  }
6:  int main( )
7:  {
8:      int localScopeInt = 15 ;
9:      {
10:         int anotherLocal = 20 ;
11:         int localScopeInt = 30 ;
12:     }
13:     return 0 ;
14: }
```

ANALYSIS The first int definition, globalScopeInt, on line 1 is visible within the functions f() and main(). The next definition is found on line 4 within the function f() and is named localScopeInt. This variable has local scope, meaning that it is visible only within the block defining it.

The main() function cannot access f()'s localScopeInt. When the f() function returns, localScopeInt goes out of scope. The third definition, also named localScopeInt, is found on line 8 of the main() function. This variable has block scope.

Note that main()'s localScopeInt does not conflict with f()'s localScopeInt. The next two definitions on lines 10 and 11, anotherLocal and localScopeInt, both have block scope. As soon as the closing brace is reached on line 12, these two variables lose their visibility.

Notice that this localScopeInt is hiding the localScopeInt defined just before the opening brace (the second localScopeInt defined in the program). When the program moves past the closing brace, the second localScopeInt defined resumes visibility. Any changes made to the localScopeInt defined within the braces does not affect the contents of the outer localScopeInt.

Linkage

Names can have *internal* and *external linkage*. These two terms refer to the use or availability of a name across multiple translation units or within a single translation unit. Any name having *internal* linkage can only be referred to within the translation unit in which it is defined. For example, a variable defined to have internal linkage can be shared by functions within the same translation unit. Names having *external* linkage are available to other translation units. Listings 18.4a and 18.4b demonstrate internal and external linkage.

LISTING 18.4A Internal and External Linking

```
0:  // file: first.cpp
1:  int externalInt = 5 ;
2:  const int j = 10 ;
3:  int main()
4:  {
5:      return 0 ;
6:  }
```

LISTING 18.4B Internal and External Linking

```
0:  // file: second.cpp
1:  extern int externalInt ;
2:  int anExternalInt = 10 ;
3:  const int j = 10 ;
```

18

ANALYSIS The `externalInt` variable defined on line 1 of `first.cpp` (Listing 18.4a) has external linkage. Although it is defined in `first.cpp`, `second.cpp` can also access it. The two `j`s found in both files are `const`, which, by default, have internal linkage. You can override the `const` default by providing an explicit declaration, as shown in Listings 18.5a and 18.5b.

LISTING 18.5A   Overriding the const Default

```
0:  // file: first.cpp
1:  extern const int j = 10 ;
```

LISTING 18.5B   Overriding the const Default

```
0:  // file: second.cpp
1:  extern const int j ;
2:  #include <iostream>
3:  int main()
4:  {
5:      std::cout << "j is " << j << std::endl ;
6:      return 0 ;
7:  }
```

Note that `cout` is called on line 5 with the namespace designation of `std`. When built, this example displays the following:

```
j is 10
```

Static Global Variables

The standards committee has deprecated the use of static global variables. Static global variables are declared as follows:

```
static int staticInt = 10 ;
int main()
{
    //...
}
```

The use of `static` to limit the scope of external variables is no longer recommended and might become illegal in the future. You should now use namespaces instead of `static`. Of course, to do this, you need to know how to create one.

Do	Don't
DO use namespaces instead of static global variables.	**DON'T** apply the `static` keyword to a variable defined at file scope.

Creating a Namespace

The syntax for a namespace declaration is similar to the syntax for a `struct` or class declaration: First apply the keyword `namespace` followed by an optional namespace name, and then an opening curly brace. The namespace is concluded with a closing brace but no terminating semicolon.

For example:

```
namespace Window
{
    void move( int x, int y) ;

    class List
    {
        // ...
    }
}
```

The name `Window` uniquely identifies the namespace. You can have many occurrences of a named namespace. These multiple occurrences can occur within a single file or across multiple translation units. When this occurs, the separate instances are merged together by the compiler into a single namespace. The C++ Standard Library namespace, `std`, is a prime example of this feature. This makes sense because the Standard Library is a logical grouping of functionality, but it is too large and complex to be kept in a single file.

The main concept behind namespaces is to group related items into a specified (named) area. Listings 18.6a and 18.6b provide a brief example of a namespace that spans multiple header files.

LISTING 18.6A Grouping Related Items

```
0: // header1.h
1: namespace Window
2: {
3:     void move( int x, int y) ;
4: }
```

LISTING 18.6B   Grouping Related Items

```
0:   // header2.h
1:   namespace Window
2:   {
3:       void resize( int x, int y ) ;
4:   }
```

ANALYSIS   As you can see, the Window namespace is spread across both header files. The compiler treats both the move() function and the resize() function as part of the Window namespace.

Declaring and Defining Types

You can declare and define types and functions within namespaces. Of course, this is a design and maintenance issue. Good design dictates that you should separate interface from implementation. You should follow this principle not only with classes but also with namespaces. The following example demonstrates a cluttered and poorly defined namespace:

```
namespace Window {
    // . . . other declarations and variable definitions.
    void move( int x, int y) ; // declarations
    void resize( int x, int y ) ;
    // . . . other declarations and variable definitions.

    void move( int x, int y )
    {
        if( x < MAX_SCREEN_X  && x > 0 )
            if( y < MAX_SCREEN_Y  && y > 0 )
                platform.move( x, y ) ; // specific routine
    }

    void resize( int x, int y )
    {
        if( x < MAX_SIZE_X  && x > 0 )
            if( y < MAX_SIZE_Y  && y > 0 )
                platform.resize( x, y ) ; // specific routine
    }
    // . . . definitions continue
}
```

You can see how quickly the namespace becomes cluttered! The previous example is approximately 20 lines in length; imagine if this namespace were four times longer.

Defining Functions Outside a Namespace

You should define namespace functions outside the namespace body. Doing so illustrates a clear separation of the declaration of the function and its definition—and also keeps the namespace body uncluttered. Separating the function definition from the namespace also enables you to put the namespace and its embodied declarations within a header file; the definitions can be placed into an implementation file. Listings 18.7a and 18.7b illustrate this separation.

LISTING 18.7A   Declaring a Header in a Namespace

```
0:   // file header.h
1:   namespace Window {
2:       void move( int x, int y) ;
3:       // other declarations ...
4:   }
```

LISTING 18.7B   Declaring the Implementation in the Source File

```
0:   // file impl.cpp
1:   void Window::move( int x, int y )
2:   {
3:       // code to move the window
4:   }
```

18

Adding New Members

New members can be added to a namespace only within the namespace's body. You cannot define new members using qualifier syntax. The most you can expect from this style of definition is a complaint from your compiler. The following example demonstrates this error:

```
namespace Window
{
    // lots of declarations
}
//...some code
int Window::newIntegerInNamespace ; // sorry, can't do this
```

The preceding line of code is illegal. Your (conforming) compiler issues a diagnostic reflecting the error. To correct the error—or avoid it altogether—move the declaration within the namespace body.

When you add new members, you do not want to include access modifiers, such as public or private. All members encased within a namespace are public. The following code does not compile because you cannot specify private:

```
namespace Window
{
    private:
        void move( int x, int y ) ;
}
```

Nesting Namespaces

A namespace can be nested within another namespace. The reason they can be nested is because the definition of a namespace is also a declaration. As with any other namespace, you must qualify a name using the enclosing namespace. If you have nested namespaces, you must qualify each namespace in turn. For example, the following shows a named namespace nested within another named namespace:

```
namespace Window
{
    namespace Pane
{
        void size( int x, int y ) ;
    }
}
```

To access the function size() outside of the Window namespace, you must qualify the function with both enclosing namespace names. In this case, you need to use the following line to access size:

```
Window::Pane::size( 10, 20 ) ;
```

Using a Namespace

Let's take a look at an example of using a namespace and the associated use of the scope resolution operator. In the example, all types and functions for use within the namespace Window are declared. After everything required is defined, any member functions that were declared are defined. These member functions are defined outside of the namespace; the names are explicitly identified using the scope resolution operator. Listing 18.8 illustrates using a namespace.

LISTING 18.8   Using a Namespace

```
0:  #include <iostream>
1:  // Using a Namespace
2:
3:  namespace Window
```

LISTING 18.8 continued

```
 4:  {
 5:      const int MAX_X = 30 ;
 6:      const int MAX_Y = 40 ;
 7:      class Pane
 8:      {
 9:         public:
10:            Pane() ;
11:            ~Pane() ;
12:            void size( int x, int y ) ;
13:            void move( int x, int y ) ;
14:            void show( ) ;
15:         private:
16:            static int count ;
17:            int x ;
18:            int y ;
19:      };
20:  }
21:
22:  int Window::Pane::count = 0 ;
23:  Window::Pane::Pane() : x(0), y(0) { }
24:  Window::Pane::~Pane() { }
25:
26:  void Window::Pane::size( int x, int y )
27:  {
28:      if( x < Window::MAX_X  &&  x > 0 )
29:          Pane::x = x ;
30:      if( y < Window::MAX_Y  &&  y > 0 )
31:          Pane::y = y ;
32:  }
33:  void Window::Pane::move( int x, int y )
34:  {
35:      if( x < Window::MAX_X  &&  x > 0 )
36:          Pane::x = x ;
37:      if( y < Window::MAX_Y  &&  y > 0 )
38:          Pane::y = y ;
39:  }
40:  void Window::Pane::show( )
41:  {
42:      std::cout << "x " << Pane::x ;
43:      std::cout << " y " << Pane::y << std::endl ;
44:  }
45:
46:  int main( )
47:  {
48:      Window::Pane pane ;
49:
50:      pane.move( 20, 20 ) ;
51:      pane.show( ) ;
52:
53:      return 0 ;
54:  }
```

18

OUTPUT   x 20 y 20

ANALYSIS   Note that class `Pane` on lines 7–19 is nested inside the namespace `Window`, which is on lines 3–20. This is the reason you have to qualify the name `Pane` with the `Window::` qualifier.

The static variable `count`, which is declared in `Pane` on line 16, is defined as usual. Within the function `Pane::size()` on lines 26–32, notice that `MAX_X` and `MAX_Y` are fully qualified. This is because `Pane` is in scope; otherwise, the compiler issues an error diagnostic. This also holds true for the function `Pane::move()`.

Also interesting is the qualification of `Pane::x` and `Pane::y` inside both function definitions. Why is this needed? Well, if the function `Pane::move()` were written like this, you would have a problem:

```
void Window::Pane::move( int x, int y )
{
    if( x < Window::MAX_X  &&  x > 0 )
        x = x ;
    if( y < Window::MAX_Y  &&  y > 0 )
        y = y ;
    Platform::move( x, y ) ;
}
```

Can you spot the issue? You probably won't get much of an answer from your compiler; some don't issue any kind of diagnostic message at all.

The source of the problem is the function's arguments. Arguments x and y hide the private x and y instance variables declared within class `Pane`. Effectively, the statements assign both x and y to itself:

```
x = x ;
y = y ;
```

The using Keyword

The `using` keyword is used for both the `using` directive and the `using` declaration. The syntax of the `using` keyword determines whether the context is a directive or a declaration.

The using Directive

The `using` directive effectively exposes all names declared in a namespace to be in the current scope. You can refer to the names without qualifying them with their respective namespace name. The following example shows the `using` directive:

```
namespace Window
{
    int value1 = 20 ;
    int value2 = 40 ;
}
. . .
Window::value1 = 10 ;

using namespace Window ;
value2 = 30 ;
```

The scope of the `using` directive begins at its declaration and continues on to the end of the current scope. Notice that `value1` must be qualified to reference it. The variable `value2` does not require the qualification because the directive introduces all names in a namespace into the current scope.

The `using` directive can be used at any level of scope. This enables you to use the directive within block scope; when that block goes out of scope, so do all the names within the namespace. The following example shows this behavior:

```
namespace Window
{
    int value1 = 20 ;
    int value2 = 40 ;
}
//. . .
void f()
{
    {
        using namespace Window ;
        value2 = 30 ;
    }
    value2 = 20 ; //error!
}
```

The final line of code in `f()`, `value2 = 20 ;` is an error because `value2` is not defined. The name is accessible in the previous block because the directive pulls the name into that block. When that block goes out of scope, so do the names in namespace `Window`. For `value2` to work in the final line, you need to fully qualify it:

```
    Window::value2 = 20 ;
```

Variable names declared within a local scope hide any namespace names introduced in that scope. This behavior is similar to how a local variable hides a global variable. Even if you introduce a namespace after a local variable, that local variable hides the namespace name. Consider the following example:

```
namespace Window
{
```

```
    int value1 = 20 ;
    int value2 = 40 ;
}
//. . .
void f()
{
   int value2 = 10 ;
   using namespace Window ;
   std::cout << value2 << std::endl  ;
}
```

The output of this function is 10, not 40. The value2 in namespace Window is hidden by the value2 in f(). If you need to use a name within a namespace, you must qualify the name with the namespace name.

An ambiguity can arise using a name that is both globally defined and defined within a namespace. The ambiguity surfaces only if the name is used, not just when a namespace is introduced. This is demonstrated with the following code fragment:

```
namespace Window
{
    int value1 = 20 ;
}
//. . .
using namespace Window ;
int value1 = 10 ;
void f( )
{
   value1 = 10 ;
}
```

The ambiguity occurs within function f(). The directive effectively brings Window::value1 into the global namespace; because a value1 is already globally defined, the use of value1 in f() is an error. Note that if the line of code in f() were removed, no error would exist.

The using Declaration

The using declaration is similar to the using directive except that the declaration provides a finer level of control. More specifically, the using declaration is used to declare a specific name (from a namespace) to be in the current scope. You can then refer to the specified object by its name only. The following example demonstrates the use of the using declaration:

```
namespace Window
{
    int value1 = 20 ;
    int value2 = 40 ;
```

```
      int value3 = 60 ;
}
//. . .
using Window::value2 ; //bring value2 into current scope
Window::value1 = 10 ;  //value1 must be qualified
value2 = 30 ;
Window::value3 = 10 ;  //value3 must be qualified
```

The using declaration adds the specified name to the current scope. The declaration does not affect the other names within the namespace. In the previous example, value2 is referenced without qualification, but value1 and value3 require qualification. The using declaration provides more control over namespace names that you bring into scope. This is in contrast with the directive that brings all names in a namespace into scope.

After a name is brought into a scope, it is visible until the end of that scope. This behavior is the same as any other declaration. A using declaration can be used in the global namespace or within any local scope.

It is an error to introduce a duplicate name into a local scope in which a namespace name has been declared. The reverse is also true. The following example shows this:

```
namespace Window
{
    int value1 = 20 ;
    int value2 = 40 ;
}
//. . .
void f()
{
    int value2 = 10 ;
    using Window::value2 ; // multiple declaration
    std::cout << value2 << std::endl ;
}
```

The second line in function f() produces a compiler error because the name value2 is already defined. The same error occurs if the using declaration is introduced before the definition of the local value2.

Any name introduced at local scope with a using declaration hides any name outside that scope. Consider the following code snippet:

```
namespace Window
{
    int value1 = 20 ;
    int value2 = 40 ;
}
int value2 = 10 ;
//. . .
void f()
```

18

```
{
    using Window::value2 ;
    std::cout << value2 << std::endl  ;
}
```

The `using` declaration in `f()` hides the `value2` defined in the global namespace.

As mentioned before, a `using` *declaration* gives you finer control over the names introduced from a namespace. A `using` *directive* brings all names from a namespace into the current scope. It is preferable to use a declaration over a directive because a directive effectively defeats the purpose of the namespace mechanism. A declaration is more definitive because you are explicitly identifying the names you want to introduce into a scope. A `using` declaration does not pollute the global namespace, as is the case with a `using` directive (unless, of course, you declare all names found in the namespace). Name hiding, global namespace pollution, and ambiguity all are reduced to a more manageable level by using the `using` declaration.

The Namespace Alias

A namespace *alias* is designed to provide another name for a named namespace. An alias provides a shorthand term for you to use to refer to a namespace. This is especially true if a namespace name is very long; creating an alias can help cut down on lengthy, repetitive typing. Consider the following code:

```
namespace the_software_company
{
    int value ;
    // . . .
}
the_software_company::value = 10 ;
. . .
namespace TSC = the_software_company ;
TSC::value = 20 ;
```

A drawback, of course, is that your alias might collide with an existing name. If this is the case, the compiler catches the conflict and you can resolve it by renaming the alias.

The Unnamed Namespace

An unnamed namespace is simply that—a namespace that does not have a name. A common use of unnamed spaces is to shield global data from potential name clashes between object files and other translation units. Every translation unit has a unique, unnamed namespace. All names defined within the unnamed namespace (within each translation unit) can be referred to without explicit qualification. Listings 18.9a and 18.9b are examples of two unnamed namespaces found in two separate files.

LISTING 18.9A An Unnamed Namespace

```
0:  // file: one.cpp
1:  namespace
2:  {
3:      int value ;
4:      char p( char *p ) ;
5:      //. . .
6:  }
```

LISTING 18.9B A Second Unnamed Namespace

```
0:  // file: two.cpp
1:  namespace
2:  {
3:      int value ;
4:      char p( char *p ) ;
5:      //. . .
6:  }
7:  int main( )
8:  {
9:      char c = p( char * ptr ) ;
10: }
```

18

ANALYSIS In the case in which these two listings are compiled into the same executable, each of the names, value and function p(), is distinct to its respective file. To refer to a (unnamed namespace) name within a translation unit, use the name without qualification. This usage is demonstrated in the previous example with the call to function p() within each file.

This use implies a using directive for objects referred to from an unnamed namespace. Because of this, you cannot access members of an unnamed namespace in another translation unit.

The behavior of an unnamed namespace is the same as a static object having external linkage. Consider this example:

```
static int value = 10 ;
```

Remember that this use of the static keyword is deprecated by the standards committee. Namespaces now exist to replace code as this static declaration. Another way to think of unnamed namespaces is that they are global variables with internal linkage.

The Standard Namespace `std`

The best example of namespaces is found in the C++ Standard Library. The Standard Library is completely encased within the namespace named `std`. All functions, classes, objects, and templates are declared within the namespace `std`.

You have seen code such as the following:

```
#include <iostream>
using namespace std ;
```

Now, you know that when you use the `using` directive in this manner that it is pulling everything in from the named namespace.

Going forward, you should consider it bad form to employ the `using` directive when using the Standard Library. Why? Because doing so pollutes the global namespace of your applications with all the names found in the header. Keep in mind that all header files use the namespace feature, so if you include multiple standard header files and specify the `using` directive, then everything declared in the headers is in the global namespace.

You might be noting that most of the examples in this book violate this rule; this action is not an intent to advocate violating the rule, but it is used for brevity of the examples. You should use the `using` declaration instead, as in Listing 18.10.

LISTING 18.10 The Correct Way to Use `std` Namespace Items

```
0:  #include <iostream>
1:  using std::cin ;
2:  using std::cout ;
3:  using std::endl ;
4:  int main( )
5:  {
6:      int value = 0 ;
7:      cout << "So, how many eggs did you say you wanted?" << endl ;
8:      cin >> value ;
9:      cout << value << " eggs, sunny-side up!" << endl ;
10:     return( 0 ) ;
11: }
```

OUTPUT
```
So, how many eggs did you say you wanted?
4
4 eggs, sunny-side up!
```

ANALYSIS As you can see, three items from the `std` namespace are used. These are declared on lines 1–3.

As an alternative, you could fully qualify the names that you use, as in Listing 18.11.

LISTING 18.11 Qualifying Namespace Items Inline

```
0:  #include <iostream>
1:  int main( )
2:  {
3:      int value = 0 ;
4:      std::cout << "How many eggs did you want?" << std::endl ;
5:      std::cin >> value ;
6:      std::cout << value << " eggs, sunny-side up!" << std::endl ;
7:      return( 0 ) ;
8:  }
```

OUTPUT

```
How many eggs did you want?
4
4 eggs, sunny-side up!
```

ANALYSIS Qualifying namespace items inline might be appropriate for shorter programs but can become quite cumbersome for any significant amount of code. Imagine having to prefix `std::` for every name you use that is found in the Standard Library!

Summary

Today's lesson expanded on information you have been previously exposed to throughout this book.

Creating a namespace is very similar to a class declaration. A couple of differences are worth noting. First, a semicolon does not follow a namespace's closing brace. Second, a namespace is open, whereas a class is closed. This means that you can continue to define the namespace in other files or in separate sections of a single file.

Anything that can be declared can be inserted into a namespace. If you are designing classes for a reusable library, you should be using the namespace feature. Functions declared within a namespace should be defined outside of that namespace's body. This promotes a separation of interface from implementation and also keeps the namespace from becoming cluttered.

The using *directive* is used to expose all names in a namespace into the current scope. This effectively fills the global namespace with all names found in the named namespace. It is generally bad practice to use the using directive, especially with respect to the Standard Library. Use using *declarations* instead.

A using declaration is used to expose a specific namespace item into the current scope. This allows you to refer to the object by its name only.

A namespace alias is similar in nature to a `typedef`. A namespace alias enables you to create another name for a named namespace. This can be quite useful when you are using a namespace with a long name or nested namespaces.

Every file can contain an unnamed namespace. An unnamed namespace, as its name implies, is a namespace without a name. An unnamed namespace allows you to use the names within the namespace without qualification. It keeps the namespace names local to the translation unit. Unnamed namespaces are the same as declaring a global variable with the `static` keyword.

Q&A

Q Do I have to use namespaces?

A No, you can write simple programs and ignore namespaces altogether. Be certain to use the old Standard Libraries (for example, `#include <string.h>`) rather than the new libraries (for example, `#include <cstring>`. Because of the reasons you learned in today's lesson, it is recommended that you do use namespaces.

Q Is C++ the only language that uses namespaces?

A No. Other languages also use namespaces to help organize and separate values. This includes languages such as Visual Basic 7 (.NET), C#, and more. Other languages have similar concepts. For example, Java has packages.

Q What are the unnamed namespaces? Why do I need unnamed namespaces?

A Unnamed namespaces are namespaces without names. They are used to wrap a collection of declarations against possible name clashes. Names in an unnamed namespace cannot be used outside of the translation unit where the namespace is declared.

Workshop

The Workshop contains quiz questions to help solidify your understanding of the material covered and exercises to provide you with experience in using what you've learned. Try to answer the quiz and exercise questions before checking the answers in Appendix D, and be certain you understand the answers before going to tomorrow's lesson.

Quiz

1. How do you access the function `MyFunc()` if it is in the `Inner` namespace within the `Outer` namespace?

```
Outer::Inner::MyFunc();
```

2. Consider the following code:

```
int x = 4;
int main()
{
    for( y = 1; y < 10; y++)
    {
        cout << y << ":" << endl;
        {
            int x = 10 * y;
            cout << "X = " << x << endl
        }
    }
    // *** HERE ***
}
```

What is the value of X when this program reaches "HERE" in the listing?

3. Can I use names defined in a namespace without using the using keyword?

4. What are the major differences between normal and unnamed namespaces?

5. What are the two forms of statements with the using keyword? What are the differences between those two forms?

6. What are the unnamed namespaces? Why do we need unnamed namespaces?

7. What is the standard namespace?

Exercises

1. **BUG BUSTERS:** What is wrong in this program?

```
0:  #include <iostream>
1:  int main()
2:  {
3:      cout << "Hello world!" << endl;
4:      return 0;
5:  }
```

2. List three ways of fixing the problem found in Exercise 1.

3. Show the code for declaring a namespace called MyStuff. This namespace should contain a class called MyClass.

DAY 19

Templates

A powerful tool for C++ programmers is "parameterized types" or *templates*. Templates are so useful that a library containing a number of routines using templates has been adopted into the definition of the C++ language.

Today, you will learn

- What a template is and how templates can be used
- How to create class templates
- How to create function templates
- What the Standard Template Library (STL) is and how to use some of the templates within it

What Are Templates?

At the end of Week 2, you saw how to build a `PartsList` object and how to use it to create a `PartsCatalog`. If you want to build on the `PartsList` object to make a list of cats, you have a problem: `PartsList` only knows about parts.

To solve this problem, you can create a `List` base class. You could then cut and paste much of the `PartsList` class into the new `CatsList` declaration. Later, when you want to make a list of Car objects, you would then have to make a new class, and again you would cut and paste.

Needless to say, this is not a satisfactory solution. Over time, you can expect the List class and its derived classes will need to be extended. The task of making certain that all the needed changes are propagated to all the related classes could quickly become a nightmare.

Alternatively, you could inherit Cat from Part, so that a cat could fit into the parts inheritance hierarchy, and so that a collection of parts could hold cats as well. Obviously, this is a problem in terms of keeping a cleanly conceptual class hierarchy because cats are not normally parts.

You could also create a List class that would contain something like "Object" and inherit all objects from this base class. However, this relaxes strong typing and makes it harder to have the compiler enforce correctness in your program. What you really want is a way to create a family of related classes, whose only difference is the type of the thing that they operate on; and you want to have only one place to make changes to that class so that your maintenance effort can be kept low.

The creation and use of templates can solve these problems. Although templates were not a part of the original C++ language, they are now a part of the standard and an integral part of the language. Like all of C++, they are type-safe and very flexible. They can, however, be intimidating to the newer C++ programmer. After you understand them, however, you will see that they are a powerful feature of the language.

Templates enable you to create a class that can have the type of the things it works on be changed. For example, you can use them to show the compiler how to make a list of any type of thing, rather than creating a set of type-specific lists—a PartsList is a list of parts; a CatsList is a list of cats. The only way in which they differ is the *type* of the thing on the list. With templates, the *type* of the thing on the list becomes a parameter to the definition of the class. You can create a family of classes from the template, each of which is set up to work on a different type of thing.

A common component of virtually all C++ libraries is an array class. You know it would be tedious and inefficient to create one array class for integers, another for doubles, and yet another for an array of Animals. Templates let you declare a single, parameterized array class. You can then specify the type that the object will be for each instance of the array.

Although the Standard Template Library provides a standardized set of *container* classes, including arrays, lists, and so forth, the best way to learn about templates is to create your own! In the next few sections, you'll explore what it takes to write your template class so that you fully understand how templates work. In a commercial program, however, you would almost certainly use the STL classes for this purpose rather than creating your own. On the other hand, you will want to create templates for your own applications and leverage this powerful capability.

Instantiation is the act of creating a specific type from a template. The individual classes are called instances of the template.

Parameterized templates provide you with the ability to create a general class and pass types as parameters to that class to build specific instances.

Before you can instantiate a template, however, you need to define one.

Building a Template Definition

You begin the basic declaration of a template using the `template` keyword followed by a parameter for the type. The format of this is:

```
template <class T>
```

In this case, `template` and `class` are keywords that you use. `T` is a placeholder—like a variable name. As such, it can be any name you desire; however, either `T` or `Type` is generally used. The value of `T` will be a data type.

Because the keyword `class` can be confusing when used in this context, you can alternatively use the keyword `typename`:

```
template <typename T>
```

In today's lesson, you will see the keyword `class` used because it is what you will see more often in programs that have already been created. The keyword `typename`, however, is clearer at indicating what you are defining when the parameter is a primitive type rather than a class.

Going back to the example of creating your own array list, you can use the template statement to declare a parameterized type for the `Array` class—you can use this to create a template for an array as shown here:

19

```
template <class T>     // declare the template and the parameter
class Array            // the class being parameterized
{
    public:
      Array();
   // full class declaration here
};
```

This code is the basics for declaring a template class called `Array`. The keyword `template` is used at the beginning of every declaration and definition of a `template` class. The parameters of the template are after the keyword `template`. Like with functions, the parameters are the things that will change with each instance. In the array template being created in the preceding example, you want the type of the objects stored in the array to be changeable. One instance might store an array of integers and another might store an array of `Animals`.

In this example, the keyword `class` is used, followed by the identifier `T`. As stated before, the keyword `class` indicates that this parameter is a type. The identifier `T` is used throughout the rest of the template definition to refer to the parameterized type. Because this class is now a template, one instance could substitute `int` for `T` and one could substitute the type `Cat`. If written correctly, the template should be able to accept any valid data type (or class) as the value for `T`.

You set the type for your template when you declare a variable that will be an instance of it. This can be done using the following format:

```
className<type> instance;
```

In this case, *className* is the name of your template class. *instance* is the name of the instance, or object, you are creating. *type* is exactly that—the data type you want to use for the instance you are creating.

For example, to declare an `int` and an `Animals` instance of the parameterized `Array` class, you would write:

```
Array<int> anIntArray;
Array<Animal> anAnimalArray;
```

The object `anIntArray` is of the type *array of integers*; the object `anAnimalArray` is of the type *array of Animals*. You can now use the type `Array<int>` anywhere you would normally use a type—as the return value from a function, as a parameter to a function, and so forth. To help bring some this together for you, Listing 19.1 provides the full declaration of the stripped-down `Array` template. Be aware that this isn't a complete program, rather a listing focused on how the template is defined.

LISTING 19.1 A Template of an Array Class

```
0:  //Listing 19.1 A template of an array class
1:  #include <iostream>
2:  using namespace std;
3:  const int DefaultSize = 10;
4:
5:  template <class T>  // declare the template and the parameter
6:  class Array          // the class being parameterized
7:  {
8:    public:
9:        // constructors
10:       Array(int itsSize = DefaultSize);
11:       Array(const Array &rhs);
12:       ~Array() { delete [] pType; }
13:
14:       // operators
15:       Array& operator=(const Array&);
16:       T& operator[](int offSet) { return pType[offSet]; }
17:
18:       // accessors
19:       int getSize() { return itsSize; }
20:
21:    private:
22:       T *pType;
23:       int  itsSize;
24:  };
```

There is no output, because this is not a complete program. Rather, this is the definition of a scaled-down template.

ANALYSIS   The declaration of the template begins on line 5 with the keyword `template` followed by the parameter. In this case, the parameter is identified to be a type by the keyword `class`, and the identifier T is used to represent the parameterized type. As mentioned earlier, you could also have used the word `typename` instead of `class`:

```
5:  template <typename T>  // declare the template and the parameter
```

You should use whichever word is clearer for you, although, it is recommended to use `class` when the type is a class and `typename` when it is not a class.

From line 6 until the end of the template on line 24, the rest of the declaration is like any other class declaration. The only difference is that wherever the type of the object would normally appear, the identifier T is used instead. For example, `operator[]` would be expected to return a reference to an object in the array, and, in fact, it is declared to return a reference to a T.

19

When an instance of an integer array is defined, T is replaced with an integer, so the operator= that is provided to that array returns a reference to an integer. This is equivalent to the following:

```
int& operator[](int offSet) { return pType[offSet]; }
```

When an instance of an Animal array is declared, the operator= provided to the Animal array returns a reference to an Animal:

```
Animal& operator[](int offSet) { return pType[offSet]; }
```

In a way, this is very much like how a macro works, and, in fact, templates were created to reduce the need for macros in C++.

Using the Name

Within the class declaration, the word Array can be used without further qualification. Elsewhere in the program, this class is referred to as Array<T>. For example, if you do not write the constructor within the class declaration, then when you declare this function, you must write

```
template <class T>
Array<T>::Array(int size):
itsSize = size
{
    pType = new T[size];
    for (int i = 0; i < size; i++)
    pType[i] = 0;
}
```

Because this is part of a template, the declaration on the first line of this code fragment is required to identify the type for the function (class T). On the second line, you see that the template name is Array<T>, and the function name is Array(int size). In addition, you see that the function takes an integer parameter.

The remainder of the function is the same as it would be for a nontemplate function, except that anywhere the array type would be used, the parameter T is used. You see this on the line declaring a new array (new T[size]).

TIP

It is a common and preferred method to get the class and its functions working as a simple declaration before turning it into a template. This simplifies development, allowing you first to concentrate on the programming objective, and then later to generalize the solution with templates.

Also, you must define template functions in the file where the template is declared. Unlike other classes, where the declaration of a class and its

> member functions and the necessary member function definitions can be split between a header and a .cpp file, templates require both to be in either a header or .cpp file. If you are sharing the template with other parts of your project, it is common to either define the member function inline to the template class declaration, or to define them below the class declaration in the header file.

Implementing the Template

After you have a template defined, you'll want to use it. The full implementation of the Array template class requires implementation of the copy constructor, operator=, and so forth. Listing 19.2 provides the code for your Array template as well as a simple driver program that uses the template.

NOTE

> Some older compilers do not support templates. Templates are, however, part of the ANSI C++ standard. All major compiler vendors support templates in their current versions. If you have a very old compiler, you won't be able to compile and run the exercises in today's lesson. It's still a good idea to read through the entire lesson, however, and return to this material when you upgrade your compiler.

LISTING 19.2   The Implementation of the Template Array

19

```
0:  //Listing 19.2 The Implementation of the Template Array
1:  #include <iostream>
2:
3:  const int DefaultSize = 10;
4:
5:  // declare a simple Animal class so that we can
6:  // create an array of animals
7:
8:  class Animal
9:  {
10:    public:
11:      Animal(int);
12:      Animal();
13:      ~Animal() {}
14:      int GetWeight() const { return itsWeight; }
15:      void Display() const { std::cout << itsWeight; }
16:    private:
17:      int itsWeight;
18:  };
```

LISTING **19.2**   continued

```
19:
20: Animal::Animal(int weight):
21:     itsWeight(weight)
22: {}
23:
24: Animal::Animal():
25:     itsWeight(0)
26: {}
27:
28:
29: template <class T>    // declare the template and the parameter
30: class Array           // the class being parameterized
31: {
32:   public:
33:     // constructors
34:     Array(int itsSize = DefaultSize);
35:     Array(const Array &rhs);
36:     ~Array() { delete [] pType; }
37:
38:     // operators
39:     Array& operator=(const Array&);
40:     T& operator[](int offSet) { return pType[offSet]; }
41:     const T& operator[](int offSet) const
42:       { return pType[offSet]; }
43:     // accessors
44:     int GetSize() const { return itsSize; }
45:
46:   private:
47:     T *pType;
48:     int  itsSize;
49: };
50:
51: // implementations follow...
52:
53: // implement the Constructor
54: template <class T>
55: Array<T>::Array(int size):
56: itsSize(size)
57: {
58:    pType = new T[size];
59:    // the constructors of the type you are creating
60:    // should set a default value
61: }
62:
63: // copy constructor
64: template <class T>
65: Array<T>::Array(const Array &rhs)
66: {
```

LISTING 19.2   continued

```
67:      itsSize = rhs.GetSize();
68:      pType = new T[itsSize];
69:      for (int i = 0; i<itsSize; i++)
70:          pType[i] = rhs[i];
71:  }
72:
73:  // operator=
74:  template <class T>
75:  Array<T>& Array<T>::operator=(const Array &rhs)
76:  {
77:      if (this == &rhs)
78:          return *this;
79:      delete [] pType;
80:      itsSize = rhs.GetSize();
81:      pType = new T[itsSize];
82:      for (int i = 0; i<itsSize; i++)
83:          pType[i] = rhs[i];
84:      return *this;
85:  }
86:
87:  // driver program
88:  int main()
89:  {
90:      Array<int> theArray;        // an array of integers
91:      Array<Animal> theZoo;       // an array of Animals
92:      Animal *pAnimal;
93:
94:      // fill the arrays
95:      for (int i = 0; i < theArray.GetSize(); i++)
96:      {
97:          theArray[i] = i*2;
98:          pAnimal = new Animal(i*3);
99:          theZoo[i] = *pAnimal;
100:          delete pAnimal;
101:      }
102:      // print the contents of the arrays
103:      for (int j = 0; j < theArray.GetSize(); j++)
104:      {
105:          std::cout << "theArray[" << j << "]:\t";
106:          std::cout << theArray[j] << "\t\t";
107:          std::cout << "theZoo[" << j << "]:\t";
108:          theZoo[j].Display();
109:          std::cout << std::endl;
110:      }
111:
112:      return 0;
113:  }
```

19

```
theArray[0]:     0      theZoo[0]:     0
theArray[1]:     2      theZoo[1]:     3
theArray[2]:     4      theZoo[2]:     6
theArray[3]:     6      theZoo[3]:     9
theArray[4]:     8      theZoo[4]:    12
theArray[5]:    10      theZoo[5]:    15
theArray[6]:    12      theZoo[6]:    18
theArray[7]:    14      theZoo[7]:    21
theArray[8]:    16      theZoo[8]:    24
theArray[9]:    18      theZoo[9]:    27
```

ANALYSIS This is a pretty basic program; however, it illustrates creating and using a template. In this case, an Array template is defined and then used to instantiate to Array objects of types int and Animal. The integer array is filled with integers that are twice the value of the index to the array. The Array made of Animal objects is called theZoo. It is filled with values that are equal to three times the index value.

Digging into the code, you see that lines 8–26 provide a stripped-down Animal class, created here so that objects of a user-defined type are available to add to the array.

The statement on line 29 declares that what follows is a template and that the parameter to the template is a type, designated as T. As previously mentioned, this line could have also been declared using typename instead of class.

You can see on lines 34 and 35 that the Array template class has two constructors as shown. The first takes a size and defaults to the constant integer DefaultSize.

The assignment and offset operators are declared, with the latter declaring both a const and a non-const variant. The only accessor provided is GetSize() on line 44, which returns the size of the array.

You can certainly imagine a fuller interface, and, for any serious Array program, what has been supplied here would be inadequate. At a minimum, operators to remove elements, to expand the array, to pack the array, and so forth would be required. If you were to use the Array class from the Standard Template Library, you would find that all this functionality has been provided. You'll learn more about that later in today's lesson.

The private data in the Array template class consists of the size of the array and a pointer to the actual in-memory array of objects.

Starting on line 53, you can see the code for the implementation of some of the member functions from your template class. Because these are defined outside of the primary class definition, you must once again state that these are a part of the template. You do this with the same statement you placed before the class. You see this on line 54. You also indicate that the Array is a template class by then including the type parameter after the class name. You have declared your type parameter to be `T` on line 53, so for the `Array` class, you use `Array<T>` with your member functions. You see this on line 55.

Within the member function, you can then use the `T` parameter anywhere you would have ordinarily used the type of the array. For example, on line 58 the class' pointer, `pType`, is set to point to a new array of items. The items will be of type `T`, which is the type you declare when instantiating an object with this template class. When each item of a given type is created, its construction should initialize it.

You see this same process repeated with the declaration of the copy constructor on lines 64–71 and the overloading of the equals operator on lines 74–85.

Your `Array` template class is actually used on lines 90 and 91. On line 90, it is used to instantiate an object called `theArray` that uses the template with `int`s. On line 91, `theZoo` is instantiated to be an `Array` of type `Animal`.

The rest of the listing does what was described earlier and is pretty easy to follow.

Passing Instantiated Template Objects to Functions

If you want to pass an `Array` object to a normal function, you must pass a particular instance of the array, not a template. To create a function that can receive a specific instance of an `Array`, you declare the type as follows:

```
void SomeFunction(Array<theType>&);
```

where `SomeFunction` is the name of the function you are passing the `Array` object to, and `theType` is the type of the object you are creating. Therefore, if `SomeFunction()` takes an integer array as a parameter, you can write

```
void SomeFunction(Array<int>&);     // ok
```

but you cannot write

```
void SomeFunction(Array<T>&);     // error!
```

because there is no way to know what a `T&` is. You also cannot write

```
void SomeFunction(Array &);     // error!
```

because there is no class `Array`—only the template and the instances.

To create nonmember functions that have some of the advantages of templates, you can declare a template function. This is accomplished in a similar manner to declaring a

19

template class and defining a template member function. First, you indicate that your function is a template, and then you use the template parameter where you otherwise would have used a type or class name:

```
template <class T>
void MyTemplateFunction(Array<T>&);    // ok
```

In this example, the function MyTemplateFunction() is declared to be a template function by the declaration on the top line. Note that template functions can have any name, the same as other functions can.

Template functions can also take instances of the template in addition to the parameterized form. The following is an example:

```
template <class T>
void MyOtherFunction(Array<T>&, Array<int>&);    // ok
```

Note that this function takes two arrays: a parameterized array and an array of integers. The former can be an array of any object, but the latter is always an array of integers. A little bit later today, you will see a template function in action.

Templates and Friends

You learned about friends on Day 16, "Advanced Inheritance." Template classes can declare three types of friends:

- A nontemplate friend class or function
- A general template friend class or function
- A type-specific template friend class or function

The following sections cover the first two of these.

Nontemplate Friend Classes and Functions

It is possible to declare any class or function to be a friend to your template class. Each instance of the class will treat the friend properly, as if the declaration of friendship had been made in that particular instance.

Listing 19.3 adds a trivial friend function, Intrude(), to the template definition of the Array class. The driver program then invokes Intrude().

Because Intrude() is a friend, it can then access the private data of the Array. Because Intrude() is not a template function, it can only be passed Arrays of type int.

LISTING **19.3** Nontemplate Friend Function

```
0:   // Listing 19.3 - Type specific friend functions in templates
1:
2:   #include <iostream>
3:   using namespace std;
4:
5:   const int DefaultSize = 10;
6:
7:   // declare a simple Animal class so that we can
8:   // create an array of animals
9:
10:  class Animal
11:  {
12:    public:
13:      Animal(int);
14:      Animal();
15:      ~Animal() {}
16:      int GetWeight() const { return itsWeight; }
17:      void Display() const { cout << itsWeight; }
18:    private:
19:      int itsWeight;
20:  };
21:
22:  Animal::Animal(int weight):
23:      itsWeight(weight)
24:  {}
25:
26:  Animal::Animal():
27:      itsWeight(0)
28:  {}
29:
30:  template <class T>  // declare the template and the parameter
31:  class Array          // the class being parameterized
32:  {
33:    public:
34:      // constructors
35:      Array(int itsSize = DefaultSize);
36:      Array(const Array &rhs);
37:      ~Array() { delete [] pType; }
38:
39:      // operators
40:      Array& operator=(const Array&);
41:      T& operator[](int offSet) { return pType[offSet]; }
42:      const T& operator[](int offSet) const
43:      { return pType[offSet]; }
44:      // accessors
45:      int GetSize() const { return itsSize; }
46:
47:      // friend function
```

19

LISTING 19.3   continued

```
48:        friend void Intrude(Array<int>);
49:
50:    private:
51:       T *pType;
52:       int  itsSize;
53:  };
54:
55:  // friend function. Not a template, can only be used
56:  // with int arrays! Intrudes into private data.
57:  void Intrude(Array<int> theArray)
58:  {
59:     cout << endl << "*** Intrude ***" << endl;
60:     for (int i = 0; i < theArray.itsSize; i++)
61:        cout << "i: " <<    theArray.pType[i] << endl;
62:     cout << endl;
63:  }
64:
65:  // implementations follow...
66:
67:  // implement the Constructor
68:  template <class T>
69:  Array<T>::Array(int size):
70:     itsSize(size)
71:  {
72:     pType = new T[size];
73:     // the constructors of the type you are creating
74:     // should set a default value
75:  }
76:
77:  // copy constructor
78:  template <class T>
79:  Array<T>::Array(const Array &rhs)
80:  {
81:     itsSize = rhs.GetSize();
82:     pType = new T[itsSize];
83:     for (int i = 0; i < itsSize; i++)
84:        pType[i] = rhs[i];
85:  }
86:
87:  // operator=
88:  template <class T>
89:  Array<T>& Array<T>::operator=(const Array &rhs)
90:  {
91:     if (this == &rhs)
92:        return *this;
93:     delete [] pType;
94:     itsSize = rhs.GetSize();
95:     pType = new T[itsSize];
```

LISTING 19.3 continued

```
96:     for (int i = 0; i < itsSize; i++)
97:         pType[i] = rhs[i];
98:     return *this;
99: }
100:
101: // driver program
102: int main()
103: {
104:     Array<int> theArray;        // an array of integers
105:     Array<Animal> theZoo;       // an array of Animals
106:     Animal *pAnimal;
107:
108:     // fill the arrays
109:     for (int i = 0; i < theArray.GetSize(); i++)
110:     {
111:         theArray[i] = i*2;
112:         pAnimal = new Animal(i*3);
113:         theZoo[i] = *pAnimal;
114:     }
115:
116:     int j;
117:     for (j = 0; j < theArray.GetSize(); j++)
118:     {
119:         cout << "theZoo[" << j << "]:\t";
120:         theZoo[j].Display();
121:         cout << endl;
122:     }
123:     cout << "Now use the friend function to ";
124:     cout << "find the members of Array<int>";
125:     Intrude(theArray);
126:
127:     cout << endl <<"Done." << endl;
128:     return 0;
129: }
```

19

OUTPUT

```
theZoo[0]:      0
theZoo[1]:      3
theZoo[2]:      6
theZoo[3]:      9
theZoo[4]:      12
theZoo[5]:      15
theZoo[6]:      18
theZoo[7]:      21
theZoo[8]:      24
theZoo[9]:      27
Now use the friend function to find the members of Array<int>
*** Intrude ***
```

```
i: 0
i: 2
i: 4
i: 6
i: 8
i: 10
i: 12
i: 14
i: 16
i: 18

Done.
```

ANALYSIS The declaration of the Array template has been extended to include the friend function Intrude(). This addition on line 48 declares that every instance of an int Array considers Intrude() to be a friend function; thus, Intrude() has access to the private member data and functions of the Array instance.

The Intrude() function is defined on lines 57–63. On line 60, Intrude() accesses itsSize directly, and on line 61, it accesses pType directly. This trivial use of these members was unnecessary because the Array class provides public accessors for this data, but it serves to demonstrate how friend functions can be declared with templates.

General Template Friend Class or Function

It would be helpful to add a display operator to the Array class so that values could be sent to an output steam and treated appropriately based on their type. One approach is to declare a display operator for each possible type of Array, but this undermines the whole point of having made Array a template.

What is needed is an insertion operator that works for any possible type of Array:

```
ostream& operator<< (ostream&, Array<T>&);
```

To make this work, operator<< needs to be declared to be a template function:

```
template <class T>
ostream& operator<< (ostream&, Array<T>&)
```

Now that operator<< is a template function, you need only to provide an implementation. Listing 19.4 shows the Array template extended to include this declaration and provides the implementation for the operator<<.

LISTING 19.4   Using Operator ostream

```
0:  //Listing 19.4 Using Operator ostream
1:  #include <iostream>
2:  using namespace std;
```

LISTING 19.4 continued

```
 3:
 4:   const int DefaultSize = 10;
 5:
 6:   class Animal
 7:   {
 8:     public:
 9:        Animal(int);
10:        Animal();
11:        ~Animal() {}
12:        int GetWeight() const { return itsWeight; }
13:        void Display() const { cout << itsWeight; }
14:     private:
15:        int itsWeight;
16:   };
17:
18:   Animal::Animal(int weight):
19:      itsWeight(weight)
20:   {}
21:
22:   Animal::Animal():
23:      itsWeight(0)
24:   {}
25:
26:   template <class T>     // declare the template and the parameter
27:   class Array            // the class being parameterized
28:   {
29:     public:
30:        // constructors
31:        Array(int itsSize = DefaultSize);
32:        Array(const Array &rhs);
33:        ~Array() { delete [] pType; }
34:
35:        // operators
36:        Array& operator=(const Array&);
37:        T& operator[](int offSet) { return pType[offSet]; }
38:        const T& operator[](int offSet) const
39:           { return pType[offSet]; }
40:        // accessors
41:        int GetSize() const { return itsSize; }
42:        // template <class T>
43:        friend ostream& operator<< (ostream&, Array<T>&);
44:
45:     private:
46:        T *pType;
47:        int  itsSize;
48:   };
49:
50:   template <class T>
51:   ostream& operator<< (ostream& output, Array<T>& theArray)
```

LISTING 19.4   continued

```
52:  {
53:      for (int i = 0; i < theArray.itsSize; i++)
54:          output << "[" << i << "] " << theArray[i] << endl;
55:      return output;
56:  }
57:
58:  // implementations follow...
59:
60:  // implement the Constructor
61:  template <class T>
62:  Array<T>::Array(int size):
63:      itsSize(size)
64:  {
65:      pType = new T[size];
66:      for (int i = 0; i < size; i++)
67:          pType[i] = 0;
68:  }
69:
70:  // copy constructor
71:  template <class T>
72:  Array<T>::Array(const Array &rhs)
73:  {
74:      itsSize = rhs.GetSize();
75:      pType = new T[itsSize];
76:      for (int i = 0; i < itsSize; i++)
77:          pType[i] = rhs[i];
78:  }
79:
80:  // operator=
81:  template <class T>
82:  Array<T>& Array<T>::operator=(const Array &rhs)
83:  {
84:      if (this == &rhs)
85:          return *this;
86:      delete [] pType;
87:      itsSize = rhs.GetSize();
88:      pType = new T[itsSize];
89:      for (int i = 0; i < itsSize; i++)
90:          pType[i] = rhs[i];
91:      return *this;
92:  }
93:
94:  int main()
95:  {
96:      bool Stop = false;        // flag for looping
97:      int offset, value;
98:      Array<int> theArray;
99:
100:     while (Stop == false)
```

LISTING 19.4   continued

```
101:    {
102:        cout << "Enter an offset (0-9) ";
103:        cout << "and a value. (-1 to stop): ";
104:        cin >> offset >> value;
105:
106:        if (offset < 0)
107:            break;
108:
109:        if (offset > 9)
110:        {
111:            cout << "***Please use values between 0 and 9.***\n";
112:            continue;
113:        }
114:
115:        theArray[offset] = value;
116:    }
117:
118:    cout << "\nHere's the entire array:\n";
119:    cout << theArray << endl;
120:    return 0;
121: }
```

NOTE   If you are using a Microsoft compiler, uncomment line 42. Based on the C++ standards, this line should not be necessary; however, it is needed to compile with the Microsoft C++ compiler.

19

OUTPUT

```
Enter an offset (0-9) and a value. (-1 to stop): 1 10
Enter an offset (0-9) and a value. (-1 to stop): 2 20
Enter an offset (0-9) and a value. (-1 to stop): 3 30
Enter an offset (0-9) and a value. (-1 to stop): 4 40
Enter an offset (0-9) and a value. (-1 to stop): 5 50
Enter an offset (0-9) and a value. (-1 to stop): 6 60
Enter an offset (0-9) and a value. (-1 to stop): 7 70
Enter an offset (0-9) and a value. (-1 to stop): 8 80
Enter an offset (0-9) and a value. (-1 to stop): 9 90
Enter an offset (0-9) and a value. (-1 to stop): 10 10
***Please use values between 0 and 9.***
Enter an offset (0-9) and a value. (-1 to stop): -1 -1

Here's the entire array:
[0] 0
[1] 10
[2] 20
[3] 30
[4] 40
```

```
[5] 50
[6] 60
[7] 70
[8] 80
[9] 90
```

ANALYSIS On line 43, the function template `operator<<()` is declared to be a friend of the Array class template. Because `operator<<()` is implemented as a template function, every instance of this parameterized array type automatically has an `operator<<()`.

The implementation for this operator starts on line 50. Using a simple loop on lines 53 and 54, every member of an array is called in turn. This only works if an `operator<<()` is defined for every type of object stored in the array.

It is worth pointing out that this listing also required that the overloading of `operator[]`. You can see on line 37 that this was done using the template type as well.

Using Template Items

You can treat template items as you would any other type. You can pass them as parameters, either by reference or by value, and you can return them as the return values of functions, also by value or by reference. Listing 19.5 demonstrates how to pass template objects.

LISTING 19.5 Passing Template Objects to and from Functions

```
0:  //Listing 19.5 Passing Template Objects to and from Functions
1:  #include <iostream>
2:  using namespace std;
3:
4:  const int DefaultSize = 10;
5:
6:  // A trivial class for adding to arrays
7:  class Animal
8:  {
9:    public:
10:       // constructors
11:       Animal(int);
12:       Animal();
13:       ~Animal();
14:
15:       // accessors
16:       int GetWeight() const { return itsWeight; }
17:       void SetWeight(int theWeight) { itsWeight = theWeight; }
18:
19:       // friend operators
20:       friend ostream& operator<< (ostream&, const Animal&);
```

LISTING 19.5   continued

```
21:
22:    private:
23:      int itsWeight;
24:  };
25:
26:  // extraction operator for printing animals
27:  ostream& operator<<
28:  (ostream& theStream, const Animal& theAnimal)
29:  {
30:     theStream << theAnimal.GetWeight();
31:     return theStream;
32:  }
33:
34:  Animal::Animal(int weight):
35:  itsWeight(weight)
36:  {
37:     // cout << "Animal(int)" << endl;
38:  }
39:
40:  Animal::Animal():
41:  itsWeight(0)
42:  {
43:     // cout << "Animal()" << endl;
44:  }
45:
46:  Animal::~Animal()
47:  {
48:     // cout << "Destroyed an animal..." << endl;
49:  }
50:
51:  template <class T>   // declare the template and the parameter
52:  class Array          // the class being parameterized
53:  {
54:    public:
55:      Array(int itsSize = DefaultSize);
56:      Array(const Array &rhs);
57:      ~Array() { delete [] pType; }
58:
59:      Array& operator=(const Array&);
60:      T& operator[](int offSet) { return pType[offSet]; }
61:      const T& operator[](int offSet) const
62:         { return pType[offSet]; }
63:      int GetSize() const { return itsSize; }
64:      // friend function:
65:      // template <class T>
66:      friend ostream& operator<< (ostream&, const Array<T>&);
67:
68:    private:
69:      T *pType;
```

19

LISTING **19.5**   continued

```
70:      int  itsSize;
71:  };
72:
73:  template <class T>
74:  ostream& operator<< (ostream& output, const Array<T>& theArray)
75:  {
76:     for (int i = 0; i < theArray.itsSize; i++)
77:         output << "[" << i << "] " << theArray[i] << endl;
78:     return output;
79:  }
80:
81:  // implementations follow...
82:
83:  // implement the Constructor
84:  template <class T>
85:  Array<T>::Array(int size):
86:  itsSize(size)
87:  {
88:     pType = new T[size];
89:     for (int i = 0; i < size; i++)
90:         pType[i] = 0;
91:  }
92:
93:  // copy constructor
94:  template <class T>
95:  Array<T>::Array(const Array &rhs)
96:  {
97:     itsSize = rhs.GetSize();
98:     pType = new T[itsSize];
99:     for (int i = 0; i < itsSize; i++)
100:         pType[i] = rhs[i];
101:  }
102:
103:  void IntFillFunction(Array<int>& theArray);
104:  void AnimalFillFunction(Array<Animal>& theArray);
105:
106:  int main()
107:  {
108:     Array<int> intArray;
109:     Array<Animal> animalArray;
110:     IntFillFunction(intArray);
111:     AnimalFillFunction(animalArray);
112:     cout << "intArray...\n" << intArray;
113:     cout << "\nanimalArray...\n" << animalArray << endl;
114:     return 0;
115:  }
116:
117:  void IntFillFunction(Array<int>& theArray)
118:  {
```

LISTING 19.5   continued

```
119:     bool Stop = false;
120:     int offset, value;
121:     while (Stop == false)
122:     {
123:        cout << "Enter an offset (0-9) ";
124:        cout << "and a value. (-1 to stop): " ;
125:        cin >> offset >> value;
126:        if (offset < 0)
127:           break;
128:        if (offset > 9)
129:        {
130:           cout << "***Please use values between 0 and 9.***\n";
131:           continue;
132:        }
133:        theArray[offset] = value;
134:     }
135: }
136:
137:
138: void AnimalFillFunction(Array<Animal>& theArray)
139: {
140:     Animal * pAnimal;
141:     for (int i = 0; i < theArray.GetSize(); i++)
142:     {
143:        pAnimal = new Animal;
144:        pAnimal->SetWeight(i*100);
145:        theArray[i] = *pAnimal;
146:        delete pAnimal;  // a copy was put in the array
147:     }
148: }
```

19

NOTE   If you are using a Microsoft compiler, uncomment line 65. Based on the C++ standards, this line should not be necessary; however, it is needed to compile with the Microsoft compiler.

OUTPUT
```
Enter an offset (0-9) and a value. (-1 to stop): 1 10
Enter an offset (0-9) and a value. (-1 to stop): 2 20
Enter an offset (0-9) and a value. (-1 to stop): 3 30
Enter an offset (0-9) and a value. (-1 to stop): 4 40
Enter an offset (0-9) and a value. (-1 to stop): 5 50
Enter an offset (0-9) and a value. (-1 to stop): 6 60
Enter an offset (0-9) and a value. (-1 to stop): 7 70
Enter an offset (0-9) and a value. (-1 to stop): 8 80
Enter an offset (0-9) and a value. (-1 to stop): 9 90
Enter an offset (0-9) and a value. (-1 to stop): 10 10
```

```
***Please use values between 0 and 9.***
Enter an offset (0-9) and a value. (-1 to stop): -1 -1

intArray:...
[0] 0
[1] 10
[2] 20
[3] 30
[4] 40
[5] 50
[6] 60
[7] 70
[8] 80
[9] 90

animalArray:...
[0] 0
[1] 100
[2] 200
[3] 300
[4] 400
[5] 500
[6] 600
[7] 700
[8] 800
[9] 900
```

ANALYSIS Most of the Array class implementation is left out to save space. The Animal class is declared on lines 7–24. Although this is a stripped-down and simplified class, it does provide its own insertion operator (<<) to allow the printing of Animals. As you can see in the definition of the insertion operator on lines 27–32, printing simply prints the current weight of the Animal.

Note that Animal has a default constructor. This is necessary because, when you add an object to an array, the object's default constructor is used to create the object. This creates some difficulties, as you'll see.

On line 103, the function IntFillFunction() is declared. The prototype indicates that this function takes an integer Array. Note that this is not a template function. IntFillFunction() expects only one type of an Array—an integer array. Similarly, on line 104, AnimalFillFunction() is declared to take an Array of Animal.

The implementations for these functions are different from one another because filling an array of integers does not have to be accomplished in the same way as filling an array of Animals.

Using Specialized Functions

If you uncomment the print statements in Animal's constructors and destructor in Listing 19.5, you'll find unanticipated extra constructions and destructions of Animals.

When an object is added to an array, the object's default constructor is called. The Array constructor, however, goes on to assign 0 to the value of each member of the array, as shown on lines 89 and 90 of Listing 19.5.

When you write someAnimal = (Animal) 0;, you call the default operator= for Animal. This causes a temporary Animal object to be created, using the constructor, which takes an integer (zero). That temporary is used as the right-hand side of the operator= and then is destroyed.

This is an unfortunate waste of time because the Animal object was already properly initialized. However, you can't remove this line because integers are not automatically initialized to a value of 0. The solution is to teach the template not to use this constructor for Animals, but to use a special Animal constructor.

You can provide an explicit implementation for the Animal class, as indicated in Listing 19.6. This type of specification is called *specialization* of the template.

LISTING 19.6 Specializing Template Implementations

```
0:   #include <iostream>
1:   using namespace std;
2:
3:   const int DefaultSize = 3;
4:
5:   // A trivial class for adding to arrays
6:   class Animal
7:   {
8:     public:
9:        // constructors
10:       Animal(int);
11:       Animal();
12:       ~Animal();
13:
14:       // accessors
15:       int GetWeight() const { return itsWeight; }
16:       void SetWeight(int theWeight) { itsWeight = theWeight; }
17:
18:       // friend operators
19:       friend ostream& operator<< (ostream&, const Animal&);
20:
21:     private:
22:       int itsWeight;
```

19

LISTING 19.6   continued

```
23:  };
24:
25:  // extraction operator for printing animals
26:  ostream& operator<<
27:  (ostream& theStream, const Animal& theAnimal)
28:  {
29:     theStream << theAnimal.GetWeight();
30:     return theStream;
31:  }
32:
33:  Animal::Animal(int weight):
34:  itsWeight(weight)
35:  {
36:     cout << "animal(int) ";
37:  }
38:
39:  Animal::Animal():
40:  itsWeight(0)
41:  {
42:     cout << "animal() ";
43:  }
44:
45:  Animal::~Animal()
46:  {
47:     cout << "Destroyed an animal...";
48:  }
49:
50:  template <class T>   // declare the template and the parameter
51:  class Array          // the class being parameterized
52:  {
53:    public:
54:      Array(int itsSize = ::DefaultSize);
55:      Array(const Array &rhs);
56:      ~Array() { delete [] pType; }
57:
58:      // operators
59:      Array& operator=(const Array&);
60:      T& operator[](int offSet) { return pType[offSet]; }
61:      const T& operator[](int offSet) const
62:      { return pType[offSet]; }
63:
64:      // accessors
65:      int GetSize() const { return itsSize; }
66:      // friend function
67:      // template <class T>
68:      friend ostream& operator<< (ostream&, const Array<T>&);
69:
70:    private:
71:      T *pType;
```

LISTING 19.6 continued

```
72:        int  itsSize;
73:    };
74:
75:    template <class T>
76:    Array<T>::Array(int size = DefaultSize):
77:    itsSize(size)
78:    {
79:       pType = new T[size];
80:       for (int i = 0; i < size; i++)
81:          pType[i] = (T)0;
82:    }
83:
84:    template <class T>
85:    Array<T>& Array<T>::operator=(const Array &rhs)
86:    {
87:       if (this == &rhs)
88:          return *this;
89:       delete [] pType;
90:       itsSize = rhs.GetSize();
91:       pType = new T[itsSize];
92:       for (int i = 0; i < itsSize; i++)
93:          pType[i] = rhs[i];
94:       return *this;
95:    }
96:
97:    template <class T>
98:    Array<T>::Array(const Array &rhs)
99:    {
100:       itsSize = rhs.GetSize();
101:       pType = new T[itsSize];
102:       for (int i = 0; i < itsSize; i++)
103:          pType[i] = rhs[i];
104:    }
105:
106:
107:    template <class T>
108:    ostream& operator<< (ostream& output, const Array<T>& theArray)
109:    {
110:       for (int i = 0; i<theArray.GetSize(); i++)
111:          output << "[" << i << "] " << theArray[i] << endl;
112:       return output;
113:    }
114:
115:
116:    Array<Animal>::Array(int AnimalArraySize):
117:    itsSize(AnimalArraySize)
118:    {
119:       pType = new Animal[AnimalArraySize];
120:    }
```

19

LISTING 19.6   continued

```
121:
122:
123:   void IntFillFunction(Array<int>& theArray);
124:   void AnimalFillFunction(Array<Animal>& theArray);
125:
126:   int main()
127:   {
128:      Array<int> intArray;
129:      Array<Animal> animalArray;
130:      IntFillFunction(intArray);
131:      AnimalFillFunction(animalArray);
132:      cout << "intArray...\n" << intArray;
133:      cout << "\nanimalArray...\n" << animalArray << endl;
134:      return 0;
135:   }
136:
137:   void IntFillFunction(Array<int>& theArray)
138:   {
139:      bool Stop = false;
140:      int offset, value;
141:      while (Stop == false)
142:      {
143:         cout << "Enter an offset (0-2) and a value. ";
144:         cout << "(-1 to stop): " ;
145:         cin >> offset >> value;
146:         if (offset < 0)
147:            break;
148:         if (offset > 2)
149:         {
150:            cout << "***Please use values between 0 and 2.***\n";
151:            continue;
152:         }
153:         theArray[offset] = value;
154:      }
155:   }
156:
157:
158:   void AnimalFillFunction(Array<Animal>& theArray)
159:   {
160:      Animal * pAnimal;
161:      for (int i = 0; i<theArray.GetSize(); i++)
162:      {
163:         pAnimal = new Animal(i*10);
164:         theArray[i] = *pAnimal;
165:         delete pAnimal;
166:      }
167:   }
```

NOTE

> If you are using a Microsoft compiler, uncomment line 67. Based on the C++ standards, this line should not be necessary; however, it is needed to compile with the Microsoft compiler.

NOTE

> Line numbers have been added to the output to make analysis easier. Line numbers will not appear in your output.

OUTPUT

First run

```
1:  animal() animal() animal() Enter an offset (0-2) and a value.
    ➥(-1 to stop): 0 0
2:  Enter an offset (0-2) and a value. (-1 to stop): 0 1
3:  Enter an offset (0-2) and a value. (-1 to stop): 1 2
4:  Enter an offset (0-2) and a value. (-1 to stop): 2 3
5:  Enter an offset (0-2) and a value. (-1 to stop): -1 -1
6:  animal(int) Destroyed an animal...animal(int) Destroyed an
    ➥animal...animal(int) Destroyed an animal...initArray...
7:  [0] 0
8:  [1] 1
9:  [2] 2
10:
11: animal array...
12: [0] 0
13: [1] 10
14: [2] 20
15:
16: Destroyed an animal...Destroyed an animal...Destroyed an animal...
```

Second run

```
1:  animal(int)   Destroyed an animal...
2:  animal(int)   Destroyed an animal...
3:  animal(int)   Destroyed an animal...
4:  Enter an offset (0-9) and a value. (-1 to stop): 0 0
5:  Enter an offset (0-9) and a value. (-1 to stop): 1 1
6:  Enter an offset (0-9) and a value. (-1 to stop): 2 2
7:  Enter an offset (0-9) and a value. (-1 to stop): 3 3
8:  animal(int)
9:  Destroyed an animal...
10: animal(int)
11: Destroyed an animal...
12: animal(int)
13: Destroyed an animal...
14: initArray...
```

19

```
15:    [0] 0
16:    [1] 1
17:    [2] 2
18:
19:    animal array...
20:    [0] 0
21:    [1] 10
22:    [2] 20
23:
24:    Destroyed an animal...
25:    Destroyed an animal...
26:    Destroyed an animal...
```

ANALYSIS Listing 19.6 reproduces both classes in their entirety so that you can see the creation and destruction of temporary `Animal` objects. The value of `DefaultSize` has been reduced from 10 to 3 to simplify the output.

The `Animal` constructors and destructors on lines 33–48 each print a statement indicating that they are called.

On lines 75–82, the template behavior of an `Array` constructor is declared. On lines 116–120, the specialized constructor for an `Array` of `Animals` is demonstrated. Note that in this special constructor, the default constructor is allowed to set the initial value for each `Animal`, and no explicit assignment is done.

The first time this program is run, the first set of output is shown. Line 1 of the output shows the three default constructors called by creating the array. The user enters four numbers for the array, and these are entered into the integer array.

Execution jumps to `AnimalFillFunction()`. Here, a temporary `Animal` object is created on the heap on line 163, and its value is used to modify the `Animal` object in the array on line 164. On line 165, the temporary `Animal` is destroyed. This is repeated for each member of the array and is reflected in the output on line 6.

At the end of the program, the arrays are destroyed, and when their destructors are called, all their objects are destroyed as well. This is reflected in the output on line 16.

For the second set of output, the special implementation of the array of character constructor, shown on lines 116–120 of the program, is commented out. When the program is run again, the template constructor, shown on lines 75–82 of the program, is run when the `Animal` array is constructed. This causes temporary `Animal` objects to be called for each member of the array on lines 80 and 81 of the program, and is reflected in the second set of output on lines 1–3.

In all other respects, the output for the two runs is identical, as you would expect.

Static Members and Templates

A template can declare static data members. A unique set of static data is created for each class type that can be created from the template. That is, if you add a static member to the `Array` class (for example, a counter of how many arrays have been created), you have one such member per type: one for all the arrays of `Animals` and another for all the arrays of integers. Listing 19.7 adds a static member and a static function to the `Array` class.

LISTING 19.7   Using Static Member Data and Functions with Templates

```
0:  #include <iostream>
1:  using namespace std;
2:
3:  const int DefaultSize = 3;
4:
5:  // A trivial class for adding to arrays
6:  class Animal
7:  {
8:    public:
9:        // constructors
10:       Animal(int);
11:       Animal();
12:       ~Animal();
13:
14:       // accessors
15:       int GetWeight() const { return itsWeight; }
16:       void SetWeight(int theWeight) { itsWeight = theWeight; }
17:
18:       // friend operators
19:       friend ostream& operator<< (ostream&, const Animal&);
20:
21:    private:
22:        int itsWeight;
23:  };
24:
25:  // extraction operator for printing animals
26:  ostream& operator<<
27:     (ostream& theStream, const Animal& theAnimal)
28:  {
29:     theStream << theAnimal.GetWeight();
30:     return theStream;
31:  }
32:
33:  Animal::Animal(int weight):
34:     itsWeight(weight)
35:  {
```

19

LISTING 19.7   continued

```
36:      //cout << "animal(int) ";
37:  }
38:
39:  Animal::Animal():
40:      itsWeight(0)
41:  {
42:      //cout << "animal() ";
43:  }
44:
45:  Animal::~Animal()
46:  {
47:      //cout << "Destroyed an animal...";
48:  }
49:
50:  template <class T>    // declare the template and the parameter
51:  class Array           // the class being parameterized
52:  {
53:    public:
54:      // constructors
55:      Array(int itsSize = DefaultSize);
56:      Array(const Array &rhs);
57:      ~Array() { delete [] pType;    itsNumberArrays--; }
58:
59:      // operators
60:      Array& operator=(const Array&);
61:      T& operator[](int offSet) { return pType[offSet]; }
62:      const T& operator[](int offSet) const
63:      { return pType[offSet]; }
64:      // accessors
65:      int GetSize() const { return itsSize; }
66:      static int GetNumberArrays() { return itsNumberArrays; }
67:
68:      // friend function
69:      friend ostream& operator<< (ostream&, const Array<T>&);
70:
71:    private:
72:      T *pType;
73:      int  itsSize;
74:      static int itsNumberArrays;
75:  };
76:
77:  template <class T>
78:  int Array<T>::itsNumberArrays = 0;
79:
80:  template <class T>
81:  Array<T>::Array(int size = DefaultSize):
82:      itsSize(size)
83:  {
```

LISTING 19.7 continued

```
84:      pType = new T[size];
85:      for (int i = 0; i < size; i++)
86:         pType[i] = (T)0;
87:      itsNumberArrays++;
88:   }
89:
90:   template <class T>
91:   Array<T>& Array<T>::operator=(const Array &rhs)
92:   {
93:      if (this == &rhs)
94:         return *this;
95:      delete [] pType;
96:      itsSize = rhs.GetSize();
97:      pType = new T[itsSize];
98:      for (int i = 0; i < itsSize; i++)
99:         pType[i] = rhs[i];
100:  }
101:
102:  template <class T>
103:  Array<T>::Array(const Array &rhs)
104:  {
105:     itsSize = rhs.GetSize();
106:     pType = new T[itsSize];
107:     for (int i = 0; i < itsSize; i++)
108:        pType[i] = rhs[i];
109:     itsNumberArrays++;
110:  }
111:
112:  template <class T>
113:  ostream& operator<< (ostream& output, const Array<T>& theArray)
114:  {
115:     for (int i = 0; i < theArray.GetSize(); i++)
116:        output << "[" << i << "] " << theArray[i] << endl;
117:     return output;
118:  }
119:
120:  int main()
121:  {
122:     cout << Array<int>::GetNumberArrays() << " integer arrays\n";
123:     cout << Array<Animal>::GetNumberArrays();
124:     cout << " animal arrays" << endl << endl;
125:     Array<int> intArray;
126:     Array<Animal> animalArray;
127:
128:     cout << intArray.GetNumberArrays() << " integer arrays\n";
129:     cout << animalArray.GetNumberArrays();
130:     cout << " animal arrays" << endl << endl;
131:
```

19

LISTING 19.7 continued

```
132:      Array<int> *pIntArray = new Array<int>;
133:
134:      cout << Array<int>::GetNumberArrays() << " integer arrays\n";
135:      cout << Array<Animal>::GetNumberArrays();
136:      cout << " animal arrays" << endl << endl;
137:
138:      delete pIntArray;
139:
140:      cout << Array<int>::GetNumberArrays() << " integer arrays\n";
141:      cout << Array<Animal>::GetNumberArrays();
142:      cout << " animal arrays" << endl << endl;
143:      return 0;
144:   }
```

OUTPUT
```
0 integer arrays
0 animal arrays

1 integer arrays
1 animal arrays

2 integer arrays
1 animal arrays

1 integer arrays
1 animal arrays
```

ANALYSIS The Array class has added the static variable tsNumberArrays on line 74, and because this data is private, the static public accessor GetNumberArrays() was added on line 66.

Initialization of the static data is accomplished with a full template qualification, as shown on lines 77 and 78. The constructors of Array and the destructor are each modified to keep track of how many arrays exist at any moment.

Accessing the static members is the same as accessing the static members of any class: You can do so with an existing object, as shown on lines 134 and 135, or by using the full class specification, as shown on lines 128 and 129. Note that you must use a specific type of array when accessing the static data. One variable exists for each type.

Do	Don't
DO use templates whenever you have a concept that can operate across objects of different classes or across different primitive data types.	**DON'T** stop learning about templates. Today's lesson has covered only some of what you can do with templates. Detailed coverage of templates is beyond the scope of this book.
DO use the parameters to template functions to narrow their instances to be type-safe.	
DO use statics with templates as needed.	**DON'T** fret if you don't yet fully understand how to create your own templates. It is more immediately important to know how to use them. As you'll see in the next section, there are lots of existing templates for you to use in the STL.
DO specialize template behavior by overriding template functions by type.	

The Standard Template Library

As it is said, there is no point in reinventing the wheel. The same is true in creating programs with C++. This is why the Standard Template Library (STL) became popular. As with other components of the Standard C++ Library, the STL is portable between various operating systems.

All the major compiler vendors now offer the STL as part of their compilers. The STL is a library of template-based container classes, including vectors, lists, queues, and stacks. The STL also includes a number of common algorithms, including sorting and searching.

The goal of the STL is to give you an alternative to reinventing the wheel for these common requirements. The STL is tested and debugged, offers high performance, and is free. Most important, the STL is reusable; after you understand how to use an STL container, you can use it in all your programs without reinventing it.

19

Using Containers

A *container* is an object that holds other objects. The Standard C++ Library provides a series of container classes that are powerful tools that help C++ developers handle common programming tasks.

Two types of Standard Template Library container classes are sequence and associative. *Sequence* containers are designed to provide sequential and random access to their members, or *elements*. *Associative* containers are optimized to access their elements by key values. All of the STL container classes are defined in `namespace std`.

Understanding Sequence Containers

The Standard Template Library sequence containers provide efficient sequential access to a list of objects. The Standard C++ Library provides five sequence containers: `vector`, `list`, `stack`, `deque`, and `queue`.

The Vector Container

You often use arrays to store and access a number of elements. Elements in an array are of the same type and are accessed with an index. The STL provides a container class `vector` that behaves like an array but that is more powerful and safer to use than the standard C++ array.

A *vector* is a container optimized to provide fast access to its elements by an index. The container class `vector` is defined in the header file `<vector>` in `namespace std` (see Day 18, "Creating and Using Namespaces," for more information on the use of namespaces).

A vector can grow itself as necessary. Suppose that you have created a vector to contain 10 elements. After you have filled the vector with 10 objects, the vector is full. If you then add another object to the vector, the vector automatically increases its capacity so that it can accommodate the eleventh object. Here is how the `vector` class is defined:

```
template <class T, class Allocator = allocator<T>> class vector
{
    // class members
};
```

The first argument (`class T`) is the type of the elements in the vector. The second argument (`class Allocator`) is an allocator class. *Allocators* are memory managers responsible for the memory allocation and deallocation of elements for the containers. The concept and implementation of allocators are advanced topics that are beyond the scope of this book.

By default, elements are created using the operator `new()` and are freed using the operator `delete()`. That is, the default constructor of class `T` is called to create a new element. This provides another argument in favor of explicitly defining a default constructor for your own classes. If you do not, you cannot use the standard vector container to hold a set of instances of your class.

You can define vectors that hold integers and floats as follows:

```
vector<int>      vInts;        // vector holding int elements
vector<float>    vFloats;      // vector holding float elements
```

Usually, you would have some idea as to how many elements a vector will contain. For instance, suppose that in your school, the maximum number of students is 50. To create a vector of students in a class, you will want the vector to be large enough to contain 50 elements. The standard vector class provides a constructor that accepts the number of elements as its parameter. So, a vector of 50 students can be defined as follows:

```
vector<Student> MathClass(50);
```

A compiler allocates enough memory spaces for 50 `Students`; each element is created using the default constructor `Student::Student()`.

The number of elements in a vector can be retrieved using a member function `size()`. For the `Student` vector `MathClass` that was just defined, `Student.size()`returns `50`.

Another member function `capacity()` tells us exactly how many elements a vector can accommodate before its size needs to be increased. You will see more on this later.

A vector is said to be empty if no element is in a vector; that is, the vector's size is zero. To make it easier to test whether a vector is empty, the `vector` class provides a member function `empty()` that evaluates to true if the vector is empty.

To assign a `Student` object `Harry` to the `MathClass`, the subscripting operator `[]` is used:

```
MathClass[5] = Harry;
```

The subscript starts at `0`. As you might have noticed, the overloaded assignment operator of the `Student` class is used here to assign `Harry` to the sixth element in `MathClass`. Similarly, to find out `Harry`'s age, access his record using:

```
MathClass[5].GetAge();
```

As mentioned earlier, vectors can grow automatically when you add more elements than they can handle. For instance, suppose one class in your school has become so popular that the number of students exceeds 50. Well, it might not happen to our math class, but who knows, strange things do happen. When the fifty-first student, `Sally`, is added to the `MathClass`, the vector can expand to accommodate her.

You can add an element into a vector in several ways; one of them is `push_back()`:

```
MathClass.push_back(Sally);
```

This member function appends the new `Student` object `Sally` to the end of the vector `MathClass`. Now, `MathClass` has 51 elements, and `Sally` is placed at `MathClass[50]`.

For this function to work, our `Student` class must define a copy constructor. Otherwise, this `push_back()` function will not be able to make a copy of object `Sally`.

STL does not specify the maximum number of elements in a vector; the compiler vendors are in better positions to make this decision. The `vector` class provides a member function that tells you what this magic number is in your compiler: `max_size()`.

19

Listing 19.8 demonstrates the members of the vector class that have been discussed so far. You will see that the standard string class is used in this listing to simplify the handling of strings. For more details about the string class, check your compiler's documentation.

LISTING **19.8**   Vector Creation and Element Access

```cpp
0:  #include <iostream>
1:  #include <string>
2:  #include <vector>
3:  using namespace std;
4:
5:  class Student
6:  {
7:    public:
8:      Student();
9:      Student(const string& name, const int age);
10:     Student(const Student& rhs);
11:     ~Student();
12:
13:     void     SetName(const string& name);
14:     string   GetName()   const;
15:     void     SetAge(const int age);
16:     int      GetAge()   const;
17:
18:     Student& operator=(const Student& rhs);
19:
20:   private:
21:     string itsName;
22:     int itsAge;
23:  };
24:
25:  Student::Student()
26:  : itsName("New Student"), itsAge(16)
27:  {}
28:
29:  Student::Student(const string& name, const int age)
30:  : itsName(name), itsAge(age)
31:  {}
32:
33:  Student::Student(const Student& rhs)
34:  : itsName(rhs.GetName()), itsAge(rhs.GetAge())
35:  {}
36:
37:  Student::~Student()
38:  {}
39:
40:  void Student::SetName(const string& name)
41:  {
```

LISTING **19.8** continued

```
42:       itsName = name;
43:   }
44:
45:   string Student::GetName() const
46:   {
47:       return itsName;
48:   }
49:
50:   void Student::SetAge(const int age)
51:   {
52:       itsAge = age;
53:   }
54:
55:   int Student::GetAge() const
56:   {
57:       return itsAge;
58:   }
59:
60:   Student& Student::operator=(const Student& rhs)
61:   {
62:       itsName = rhs.GetName();
63:       itsAge = rhs.GetAge();
64:       return *this;
65:   }
66:
67:   ostream& operator<<(ostream& os, const Student& rhs)
68:   {
69:       os << rhs.GetName() << " is " << rhs.GetAge() << " years old";
70:       return os;
71:   }
72:
73:   template<class T>
74:   // display vector properties
75:   void ShowVector(const vector<T>& v);
76:
77:   typedef vector<Student>   SchoolClass;
78:
79:   int main()
80:   {
81:       Student Harry;
82:       Student Sally("Sally", 15);
83:       Student Bill("Bill", 17);
84:       Student Peter("Peter", 16);
85:
86:       SchoolClass   EmptyClass;
87:       cout << "EmptyClass:" << endl;
88:       ShowVector(EmptyClass);
89:
90:       SchoolClass GrowingClass(3);
```

19

LISTING 19.8   continued

```
91:     cout << "GrowingClass(3):" << endl;
92:     ShowVector(GrowingClass);
93:
94:     GrowingClass[0] = Harry;
95:     GrowingClass[1] = Sally;
96:     GrowingClass[2] = Bill;
97:     cout << "GrowingClass(3) after assigning students:" << endl;
98:     ShowVector(GrowingClass);
99:
100:    GrowingClass.push_back(Peter);
101:    cout << "GrowingClass() after added 4th student:" << endl;
102:    ShowVector(GrowingClass);
103:
104:    GrowingClass[0].SetName("Harry");
105:    GrowingClass[0].SetAge(18);
106:    cout << "GrowingClass() after Set\n:";
107:    ShowVector(GrowingClass);
108:
109:    return 0;
110: }
111:
112: //
113: // Display vector properties
114: //
115: template<class T>
116: void ShowVector(const vector<T>& v)
117: {
118:    cout << "max_size() = " << v.max_size();
119:    cout << "\tsize() = " << v.size();
120:    cout << "\tcapacity() = " << v.capacity();
121:    cout << "\t" << (v.empty()? "empty": "not empty");
122:    cout << endl;
123:
124:    for (int i = 0; i < v.size(); ++i)
125:       cout << v[i] << endl;
126:
127:    cout << endl;
128: }
```

OUTPUT

```
EmptyClass:
max_size() = 214748364  size() = 0       capacity() = 0  empty

GrowingClass(3):
max_size() = 214748364  size() = 3       capacity() = 3  not empty
New Student is 16 years old
New Student is 16 years old
New Student is 16 years old
```

```
GrowingClass(3) after assigning students:
max_size() = 214748364  size() = 3      capacity() = 3  not empty
New Student is 16 years old
Sally is 15 years old
Bill is 17 years old

GrowingClass() after added 4th student:
max_size() = 214748364  size() = 4      capacity() = 6  not empty
New Student is 16 years old
Sally is 15 years old
Bill is 17 years old
Peter is 16 years old

GrowingClass() after Set:
max_size() = 214748364 size() = 4       capacity() = 6  not empty
Harry is 18 years old
Sally is 15 years old
Bill is 17 years old
Peter is 16 years old
```

ANALYSIS Our `Student` class is defined on lines 5–23. Its member function implementations are on lines 25–65. It is simple and vector-container friendly. For the reasons discussed earlier, a default constructor, a copy constructor, and an overloaded assignment operator are all defined. Note that its member variable `itsName` is defined as an instance of the `string` class. As you can see here, it is much easier to work with a STL C++ string than with a C-style string `char*`.

The template function `ShowVector()` is declared on lines 73 and 75 and defined on lines 115–128. It demonstrates the usage of some of the vector member functions: `max_size()`, `size()`, `capacity()`, and `empty()`. As you can see from the output, the maximum number of `Student` objects a vector can accommodate is 214,748,364 in Visual C++. This number might be different for other types of elements. For instance, a vector of integers can have up to 1,073,741,823 elements. If you are using other compilers, you might have a different value for the maximum number of elements.

On lines 124 and 125, the value of each element in the vector is displayed using the overloaded insertion operator <<, which is defined on lines 67–71.

In the main routine for this program, four students are created on lines 81–84. On line 86, an empty vector, properly named `EmptyClass`, is defined using the default constructor of the `vector` class. When a vector is created in this way, no space is allocated for it by the compiler. As you can see in the output produced by `ShowVector(EmptyClass)`, its size and capacity are both zero.

19

On line 90, a vector of three `Student` objects is defined. Its size and capacity are both three. Elements in the `GrowingClass` are assigned with the `Student` objects on lines 94–96 using the subscripting operator `[]`.

The fourth student, `Peter`, is added to the vector on line 100. This increases the size of the vector to four. Interestingly, its capacity is now set to six. This means that the compiler has allocated enough space for up to six `Student` objects.

Because vectors must be allocated to a continuous block of memory, expanding them requires a set of operations. First, a new block of memory large enough for all four `Student` objects is allocated. Second, the three elements are copied to this newly allocated memory and the fourth element is appended after the third element. Finally, the original memory block is returned to the memory. When a large number of elements are in a vector, this deallocation and reallocation process can be time-consuming. Therefore, the compiler employs an optimization strategy to reduce the possibility of such expensive operations. In this example, if you append one or two more objects to the vector, no need exists to deallocate and reallocate memory.

On lines 104 and 105, the subscripting operator `[]` is again used to change the member variables for the first object in the `GrowingClass`.

Do	**Don't**
DO define a default constructor for a class if its instances are likely to be held in a vector.	**DON'T** create your own vector class! You can use the one in the STL. Because this is a part of the C++ standard, any standard compliant compiler should have this class!
DO define a copy constructor for such a class.	
DO define an overloaded assignment operator for such a class.	

The `vector` container class has other member functions. The `front()` function returns a reference to the first element in a list. The `back()` function returns a reference to the last element. The `at()` function works like the subscript operator `[]`. It is safer than the vector implementation of `[]` because it checks whether the subscript passed to it is within the range of available elements (although, of course, you could code a subscript operator to perform the same check). If the index is out of range, it throws an `out_of_range` exception. (Exceptions are covered tomorrow.)

The `insert()` function inserts one or more nodes into a given position in a vector. The `pop_back()` function removes the last element from a vector. And finally, a `remove()` function removes one or more elements from a vector.

The List Container

A list is a container designed to be optimal when you are frequently inserting and deleting elements. The `list` STL container class is defined in the header file `<list>` in the namespace `std`. The `list` class is implemented as a doubly-linked list, where each node has links to both the previous node and the next node in the list.

The `list` class has all the member functions provided by the `vector` class. As you have seen in "Week 2 in Review," you can traverse a list by following the links provided in each node. Typically, the links are implemented using pointers. The standard `list` container class uses a mechanism called the iterator for the same purpose.

An iterator is a generalization of a pointer and attempts to avoid some of the dangers of a pointer.

You can dereference an iterator to retrieve the node to which it points. Listing 19.9 demonstrates the use of iterators in accessing nodes in a list.

LISTING 19.9 Traverse a List Using an Iterator

```
0:  #include <iostream>
1:  #include <list>
2:  using namespace std;
3:
4:  typedef list<int> IntegerList;
5:
6:  int main()
7:  {
8:      IntegerList   intList;
9:
10:     for (int i = 1; i <= 10; ++i)
11:         intList.push_back(i * 2);
12:
13:     for (IntegerList::const_iterator ci = intList.begin();
14:                     ci != intList.end(); ++ci)
15:         cout << *ci << " ";
16:
17:     return 0;
18: }
```

OUTPUT 2 4 6 8 10 12 14 16 18 20

ANALYSIS Listing 19.9 uses the STL's list template. On line 1, the necessary include file is `#include`d. This pulls in the code for the list template from the STL.

On line 4, you see the use of the `typedef` commend. In this case, instead of using `list<int>` throughout the listing, the `typedef` lets you use `IntegerList`. This is much easier to read.

On line 8, `intList` is defined as a list of integers using the `typedef` that was just created. The first 10 positive even numbers are added to the list using the `push_back()` function on lines 10 and 11.

On lines 13–15, each node in the list is accessed using a constant iterator. This indicates that there is no intent to change the nodes with this iterator. If you want to change a node pointed to be an iterator, you need to use a non-`const` iterator instead:

```
intList::iterator
```

The `begin()` member function returns an iterator pointing to the first node of the list. As can be seen here, the increment operator ++ can be used to point an iterator to the next node. The `end()` member function is kind of strange—it returns an iterator pointing to one-pass-last node of a list. You must be certain that your iterator doesn't reach `end()`!

The iterator is dereferenced the same as a pointer, to return the node pointed to, as shown on line 15.

Although iterators are introduced here with the `list` class, the `vector` class also provides iterators. In addition to functions introduced in the `vector` class, the `list` class also provides the `push_front()` and `pop_front()` functions that work just like `push_back()` and `pop_back()`. Instead of adding and removing elements at the back of the list, they add and remove elements in the front of the list.

The Stacks Container

One of the most commonly used data structures in computer programming is the stack. The stack, however, is not implemented as an independent container class. Instead, it is implemented as a wrapper of a container. The template class `stack` is defined in the header file `<stack>` in the `namespace std`.

A *stack* is a continuously allocated block that can grow or shrink at the back end. Elements in a stack can only be accessed or removed from the back. You have seen similar characteristics in the sequence containers, notably `vector` and `deque`. In fact, any sequence container that supports the `back()`, `push_back()`, and `pop_back()` operations can be used to implement a stack. Most of the other container methods are not required for the stack and are, therefore, not exposed by the stack.

The STL `stack` template class is designed to contain any type of objects. The only restriction is that all elements must be of the same type.

A stack is a *LIFO* (*last in, first out*) structure. The classic analogy for a stack is this: A stack is like a stack of dishes at a salad bar. You add to the stack by placing a dish on top (pushing the stack down), and you take from the stack by "popping" the top dish (the one most recently added to the stack) off the top.

By convention, the open end of a stack is often called the *top* of the stack, and operations carried out to a stack are often called *push* and *pop*. The stack class inherits these conventional terms.

NOTE

> The STL stack class is not the same as the stack mechanism used by compilers and operating systems, in which stacks can contain different types of objects. The underlying functionality, however, is very similar.

The Deque Container

A deque is like a double-ended vector—it inherits the vector container class's efficiency in sequential read and write operations. But, in addition, the deque container class provides optimized front-end and back-end operations. These operations are implemented similarly to the list container class, where memory allocations are engaged only for new elements. This feature of the deque class eliminates the need to reallocate the whole container to a new memory location, as the vector class has to do. Therefore, deques are ideally suited for applications in which insertions and deletions take place at either one or both ends, and for which sequential access of elements is important. An example of such an application is a train-assembly simulator, in which carriages can join the train at both ends.

The Queues Container

A *queue* is another commonly used data structure in computer programming. Elements are added to the queue at one end and taken out at the other.

A queue is like a line at the theater. You enter the queue at the back, and you leave the queue at the front. This is known as a *FIFO* (first in, first out) structure; a stack is a *LIFO* (last in, first out) structure. Of course, every once in a while, you're second-to-last in a long line at the supermarket when someone opens a new register and grabs the last person in line—turning what should be a FIFO queue into a LIFO stack, and making you grind your teeth in frustration.

Like the stack, the queue is implemented as a wrapper class to a container. The container must support front(), back(), push_back(), and pop_front() operations.

19

Understanding Associative Containers

You have seen that a vector is like an enhanced version of an array. It has all the characteristics of an array and some additional features. Unfortunately, the vector also suffers from one of the significant weaknesses of arrays: You cannot find an element using any index other than its offset in the container. Associative containers, on the other hand, provide fast random access based on *keys* that are associated with *values*.

The sequence containers are designed for sequential and random access of elements using the index or an iterator, the associative containers are designed for fast random access of elements using keys. The Standard C++ Library provides five associative containers: map, multimap, set, multiset, and bitset.

The Map Container

The first associate container you will learn about is the map. The name comes from the idea that they contain "maps," which are the key to the associated value, just as a point on a paper map corresponds to a real place on earth. In the following example (Listing 19.10), a map is used to implement the school class example shown in Listing 19.8.

LISTING **19.10**   A Map Container Class

```
0:   #include <iostream>
1:   #include <string>
2:   #include <map>
3:   using namespace std;
4:
5:   class Student
6:   {
7:     public:
8:        Student();
9:        Student(const string& name, const int age);
10:       Student(const Student& rhs);
11:       ~Student();
12:
13:       void    SetName(const string& name);
14:       string  GetName()   const;
15:       void    SetAge(const int age);
16:       int     GetAge()    const;
17:
18:       Student& operator=(const Student& rhs);
19:
20:     private:
21:        string itsName;
22:        int itsAge;
23:   };
24:
```

LISTING 19.10 continued

```
25:    Student::Student()
26:    : itsName("New Student"), itsAge(16)
27:    {}
28:
29:    Student::Student(const string& name, const int age)
30:    : itsName(name), itsAge(age)
31:    {}
32:
33:    Student::Student(const Student& rhs)
34:    : itsName(rhs.GetName()), itsAge(rhs.GetAge())
35:    {}
36:
37:    Student::~Student()
38:    {}
39:
40:    void Student::SetName(const string& name)
41:    {
42:        itsName = name;
43:    }
44:
45:    string Student::GetName() const
46:    {
47:        return itsName;
48:    }
49:
50:    void Student::SetAge(const int age)
51:    {
52:        itsAge = age;
53:    }
54:
55:    int Student::GetAge() const
56:    {
57:        return itsAge;
58:    }
59:
60:    Student& Student::operator=(const Student& rhs)
61:    {
62:        itsName = rhs.GetName();
63:        itsAge = rhs.GetAge();
64:        return *this;
65:    }
66:
67:    ostream& operator<<(ostream& os, const Student& rhs)
68:    {
69:        os << rhs.GetName() << " is " << rhs.GetAge() << " years old";
70:        return os;
71:    }
72:
73:    template<class T, class A>
```

19

LISTING **19.10**   continued

```
74:    void ShowMap(const map<T, A>& v);      // display map properties
75:
76:    typedef map<string, Student>   SchoolClass;
77:
78:    int main()
79:    {
80:       Student Harry("Harry", 18);
81:       Student Sally("Sally", 15);
82:       Student Bill("Bill", 17);
83:       Student Peter("Peter", 16);
84:
85:       SchoolClass    MathClass;
86:       MathClass[Harry.GetName()] = Harry;
87:       MathClass[Sally.GetName()] = Sally;
88:       MathClass[Bill.GetName()] = Bill;
89:       MathClass[Peter.GetName()] = Peter;
90:
91:       cout << "MathClass:" << endl;
92:       ShowMap(MathClass);
93:
94:       cout << "We know that " << MathClass["Bill"].GetName()
95:            << " is " << MathClass["Bill"].GetAge()
96:            << " years old" << endl;
97:       return 0;
98:    }
99:
100:   //
101:   // Display map properties
102:   //
103:   template<class T, class A>
104:   void ShowMap(const map<T, A>& v)
105:   {
106:      for (map<T, A>::const_iterator ci = v.begin();
107:                  ci != v.end(); ++ci)
108:        cout << ci->first << ": " << ci->second << endl;
109:
110:      cout << endl;
111:   }
```

OUTPUT

```
MathClass:
Bill: Bill is 17 years old
Harry: Harry is 18 years old
Peter: Peter is 16 years old
Sally: Sally is 15 years old

We know that Bill is 17 years old
```

ANALYSIS In this example, a class is created and four students are added. The list of students is then printed. After printing this list, Bill is printed along with his age; however, rather than using a numeric indexer like previous example, Bill's name is used to find his age. This is made possible using the map template.

Digging into the code, you see that most of the listing is the Student class. This is code you should be able to understand at this point.

The unique items in this listing start on line 2, where the header file <map> is included because the standard map container class is being used. On line 73, you can see that a prototype is provided for the ShowMap function. You can also see that this is a template function. It is used to display the elements in a map.

On line 76, typedef is used to define SchoolClass as a map of elements; each consists of a (key, value) pair. The first value in the pair is a string that is the key value. In this example, for SchoolClass, the students' names are this key value. The key value of elements in the map container must be unique; that is, no two elements can have the same key value. The second value in the pair is the actual object, a Student object in the example. The pair data type is implemented in the STL as a struct of two members: namely, first and second. These members can be used to access a node's key and value.

You can take a look at the ShowMap() function on lines 103–111. The ShowMap() function uses a constant iterator to access a map object. On line 108, ci->first points to the key, or a student's name. ci->second points to the Student object.

All that remains to review in this listing is the main() function on lines 78–98. Back on lines 80–83, four Student objects are created. The MathClass is defined as an instance of our SchoolClass on line 85. On lines 86–89, the four students (actually the Student objects) are added to the MathClass using the following syntax:

```
map_object[key_value] = object_value;
```

On line 86, you can see that the *key_value* being used is the name from a Student object. This name is obtained using the GetName() method from the Student object. The *object_value* is a Student object.

The push_back() or insert() functions could also have been used to add a (key, value) pair to the map; you can look up your compiler's documentation for more details.

After all Student objects have been added to the map, you can access any of them using their key values. On lines 94–96, MathClass["Bill"] is used to retrieve Bill's record. Bill is the key value. You could just as easily have used any of the other student's names to access their records.

19

Other Associative Containers

The `multimap` container class is a `map` class without the restriction of unique keys. More than one element can have the same key value.

The `set` container class is also similar to the `map` class. The only difference is that its elements are not (key, value) pairs. An element is only the key. The `multiset` container class is a `set` class that allows duplex key values.

Finally, the `bitset` container class is a template for storing a sequence of bits.

Working with the Algorithm Classes

A container is a useful place to store a sequence of elements. All standard containers define operations that manipulate the containers and their elements. Implementing all these operations in your own sequences, however, can be laborious and prone to error. Because most of those operations are likely to be the same in most sequences, a set of generic algorithms can reduce the need to write your own operations for each new container. The standard library provides approximately 60 standard algorithms that perform the most basic and commonly used operations of containers.

Standard algorithms are defined in `<algorithm>` in namespace `std`.

To understand how the standard algorithms work, you need to understand the concept of function objects. A function object is an instance of a class that defines the overloaded `operator()`. Therefore, it can be called as a function. Listing 19.11 demonstrates a function object.

LISTING 19.11   A Function Object

```
0:  #include <iostream>
1:  using namespace std;
2:
3:  template<class T>
4:  class Print
5:  {
6:    public:
7:        void operator()(const T& t)
8:        {
9:            cout << t << " ";
10:       }
11: };
12:
13: int main()
14: {
15:     Print<int> DoPrint;
16:     for (int i = 0; i < 5; ++i)
```

LISTING 19.11 continued

```
17:            DoPrint(i);
18:        return 0;
19:  }
```

OUTPUT   0 1 2 3 4

ANALYSIS On lines 3–11, a template class named Print is defined. As you can see, this is a standard template class. On lines 6–9, the operator () is overloaded to take an object and outputs it to the standard output. On line 15, DoPrint is defined as an instance of the Print class using an int value. With this, you can now use DoPrint just like a function to print any integer values, as shown on line 17. The standard algorithm classes work just like DoPrint. They have overloaded the operator() so you can use them like functions.

Nonmutating Sequence Operations

Nonmutating sequence operations are components from the algorithm library that perform operations that don't change the elements in a sequence. These include operators such as for_each(), find(), search(), and count(). Listing 19.12 shows how to use a function object and the for_each algorithm to print elements in a vector.

LISTING 19.12 Using the for_each() Algorithm

```
0:  #include <iostream>
1:  #include <vector>
2:  #include <algorithm>
3:  using namespace std;
4:
5:  template<class T>
6:  class Print
7:  {
8:    public:
9:       void operator()(const T& t)
10:      {
11:         cout << t << " ";
12:      }
13:  };
14:
15:  int main()
16:  {
17:     Print<int>   DoPrint;
18:     vector<int>  vInt(5);
19:
20:     for (int i = 0; i < 5; ++i)
```

19

LISTING **19.12** continued

```
21:          vInt[i] = i * 3;
22:
23:     cout << "for_each()" << endl;
24:     for_each(vInt.begin(), vInt.end(), DoPrint);
25:     cout << endl;
26:
27:     return 0;
28:   }
```

OUTPUT

```
for_each()
0 3 6 9 12
```

ANALYSIS Note that all C++ standard algorithms are defined in `<algorithm>`, so it is included on line 2 of the listing. Although most of the program should be easy for you, one line, however, is worth reviewing. On line 24, the `for_each()` function is called to go through each element in the vector `vInt`. For each element in the vector, it invokes the `DoPrint` function object and passes the element to `DoPrint.operator()`. This results in the value of the element to be printed on the screen.

Mutating Sequence Operations

Mutating sequence operations perform operations that change the elements in a sequence, including operations that fill or reorder collections. Listing 19.13 shows the `fill()` algorithm.

LISTING 19.13 A Mutating Sequence Algorithm

```
0:  #include <iostream>
1:  #include <vector>
2:  #include <algorithm>
3:  using namespace std;
4:
5:  template<class T>
6:  class Print
7:  {
8:    public:
9:       void operator()(const T& t)
10:       {
11:          cout << t << " ";
12:       }
13:  };
14:
15:  int main()
16:  {
17:     Print<int>   DoPrint;
18:     vector<int>  vInt(10);
```

LISTING 19.13 continued

```
19:
20:     fill(vInt.begin(), vInt.begin() + 5, 1);
21:     fill(vInt.begin() + 5, vInt.end(), 2);
22:
23:     for_each(vInt.begin(), vInt.end(), DoPrint);
24:     cout << endl << endl;
25:
26:     return 0;
27: }
```

OUTPUT   1 1 1 1 1 2 2 2 2 2

ANALYSIS   The only new content in this listing is on lines 20 and 21, where the `fill()` algorithm is used. The fill algorithm fills the elements in a sequence with a given value. On line 20, it assigns an integer value 1 to the first five elements in `vInt`. The last five elements of `vInt` are assigned with integer 2 on line 21.

Sorting and Related Operations

The third category of algorithms is the sorting and related operations subclass. Within this set of operations, you find merging, partial sorts, partial sorts with copying, binary searches, lower and upper bounds checks, set intersections, set differencing, minimums, maximums, permutations, and more. You can check your compiler's documentation or the C++ standards documentation for specific information on each of these operations.

NOTE

> It is beyond the scope of this book to go into details on all the operations in the algorithm and other Standard Template Library classes. You can check your compiler's documentation or the C++ standards to get more details on the classes and operations available as well as the details on their parameters and usage. In addition, entire books are available on the STL and its usage.

19

Summary

Today, you learned how to create and use templates. Templates are a key part of the C++ standard and a built-in facility of C++. Templates are used to create parameterized types—types that change their behavior based on parameters passed in at creation. They are a way to reuse code safely and effectively.

The definition of the template determines the parameterized type. Each instance of the template is an actual object, which can be used like any other object—as a parameter to a function, as a return value, and so forth.

Template classes can also declare three types of friend functions: nontemplate, general template, and type-specific template. A template can declare static data members, in which case each instance of the template has its own set of static data.

If you need to specialize behavior for some template functions based on the actual type, you can override a template function with a particular type. This works for member functions as well.

In the second half of today's lesson, you learned that the C++ standard includes information on the Standard Template Library (STL). The STL includes numerous template and operations for you to use.

Q&A

Q Why use templates when macros will do?

A Templates are type-safe and built in to the language, so they are checked by the compiler—at least when you instantiate the class to create a particular variable.

Q What is the difference between the parameterized type of a template function and the parameters to a normal function?

A A regular function (nontemplate) takes parameters on which it can take action. A template function enables you to parameterize the type of a particular parameter to the function. That is, you can pass an Array of Type to a function and then have the Type determined by the definition of the variable that is an instance of the class for a specific type.

Q When do I use templates and when do I use inheritance?

A Use templates when all the behavior, or virtually all the behavior, is unchanged, except in regard to the type of the item on which your class acts. If you find yourself copying a class and changing only the type of one or more of its members, it might be time to consider using a template. Also, use a template when you are tempted to change a class to operate on a higher-level ancestor class (reducing type-safety) of its operands, or to make two unrelated classes share a common ancestor so that your class can work with both of them (again, reducing type-safety).

Q When do I use general template friend classes?

A When every instance, regardless of type, should be a friend to this class or function.

Q When do I use type-specific template friend classes or functions?

A When you want to establish a one-to-one relationship between two classes. For example, `array<int>` should match `iterator<int>`, but not `iterator<Animal>`.

Workshop

The Workshop provides quiz questions to help you solidify your understanding of the material covered and exercises to provide you with experience in using what you've learned. Try to answer the quiz and exercise questions before checking the answers in Appendix D, and be certain you understand the answers before continuing to tomorrow's lesson.

Quiz

1. What is the difference between a template and a macro?
2. What is the difference between the parameter in a template and the parameter in a function?
3. What is the difference between a type-specific template friend class and a general template friend class?
4. Is it possible to provide special behavior for one instance of a template but not for other instances?
5. How many static variables are created if you put one static member into a template class definition?
6. What attributes must your class have to be used with the standard containers?
7. What does STL stand for and why is the STL important?

Exercises

1. Create a template based on this `List` class:
```
class List
{
  private:

  public:
    List():head(0),tail(0),theCount(0) {}
    virtual ~List();
    void insert( int value );
```

19

```
      void append( int value );
      int is_present( int value ) const;
      int is_empty() const { return head == 0; }
      int count() const { return theCount; }
   private:
      class ListCell
      {
      public:
          ListCell( int value, ListCell *cell = 0):val(value),
                    next(cell){}
          int val;
          ListCell *next;
      };
      ListCell *head;
      ListCell *tail;
      int theCount;
};
```

2. Write the implementation for the List class (nontemplate) version.

3. Write the template version of the implementations.

4. Declare three list objects: a list of Strings, a list of Cats, and a list of ints.

5. **BUG BUSTERS:** What is wrong with the following code? (Assume the List template is defined and Cat is the class defined earlier in the book.)

```
List<Cat> Cat_List;
Cat Felix;
CatList.append( Felix );
cout << "Felix is "
     << ( Cat_List.is_present( Felix ) ) ? "" : "not "
     << "present" << endl;
```

   Hint (this is tough): What makes Cat different from int?

6. Declare friend operator== for List.

7. Implement friend operator== for List.

8. Does operator== have the same problem as in Exercise 5?

9. Implement a template function for swap that exchanges two variables.

DAY **20**

Handling Errors and Exceptions

The code you've seen in this book has been created for illustration purposes. It has not dealt with errors so that you would not be distracted from the central issues being presented. Real-world programs must take error conditions into consideration.

Today, you will learn

- What exceptions are
- How exceptions are used and what issues they raise
- How to build exception hierarchies
- How exceptions fit into an overall error-handling approach
- What a debugger is

Bugs, Errors, Mistakes, and Code Rot

It is rare for a real-world-sized program not to have some sort of error, or bug. The bigger the program, the more likely there will be bugs. In fact, in larger programs, it is often the case that many bugs actually "get out the door" and into final, released software. That this is true does not make it okay. Making robust, bug-free programs should be the number-one priority of anyone serious about programming.

The single biggest problem in the software industry is buggy, unstable code. One of the biggest expenses in many major programming efforts is testing and fixing. The person who solves the problem of producing good, solid, bulletproof programs at low cost and on time will revolutionize the software industry.

A number of discrete kinds of errors can trouble a program. The first is poor logic: The program does just what you asked, but you haven't thought through the algorithms properly. The second is syntactic: You used the wrong idiom, function, or structure. These two are the most common, and they are the ones most programmers are on the lookout for.

Research and real-world experience have shown that the later in the development process you find a logic problem, the more it costs to fix it. The least expensive problems or bugs to fix are the ones you manage to avoid creating. The next cheapest are those spotted by the compiler. The C++ standards force compilers to put a lot of energy into making more and more bugs show up at compile time.

Errors that get compiled in your program, but are caught at the first test—those that crash every time—are less expensive to find and fix than those that are flaky and only crash once in a while.

A more common runtime problem than logic or syntactic bugs is fragility: Your program works just fine if the user enters a number when you ask for one, but it crashes if the user enters letters. Other programs crash if they run out of memory, if the floppy disk is left out of the drive, or if an Internet connection is lost.

To combat this kind of fragility, programmers strive to make their programs bulletproof. A *bulletproof* program is one that can handle anything that comes up at runtime, from bizarre user input to running out of memory.

It is important to distinguish between bugs, which arise because the programmer made a mistake; logic errors, which arise because the programmer misunderstood the problem or how to solve it; and exceptions, which arise because of unusual but predictable problems such as running out of resources (memory or disk space).

Exceptional Circumstances

You can't eliminate exceptional circumstances; you can only prepare for them. What happens if your program requests memory to dynamically allocate an object, and there isn't any available? How will your program respond? Or, what will your program do if you cause one of the most common math errors by dividing by zero? Your choices include

- Crash.

- Inform the user and exit gracefully.

- Inform the user and allow the user to try to recover and continue.

- Take corrective action and continue without disturbing the user.

Consider Listing 20.1, which is extremely simple and ready to crash; however, it illustrates a problem that makes it into many programs and that is extremely serious!

LISTING 20.1   Creating an Exceptional Situation

```
0:  // This program will crash
1:  #include <iostream>
2:  using namespace std;
3:
4:  const int DefaultSize = 10;
5:
6:  int main()
7:  {
8:      int top = 90;
9:      int bottom = 0;
10:
11:     cout << "top / 2 = " << (top/ 2) << endl;
12:
13:     cout << "top divided by bottom = ";
14:     cout << (top / bottom) << endl;
15:
16:     cout << "top / 3 = " << (top/ 3) << endl;
17:
18:     cout << "Done." << endl;
19:     return 0;
20: }
```

OUTPUT

```
top / 2 = 45
top divided by bottom =
```

20

> **CAUTION** This program might display the preceding output to the console; however, it will most likely immediately crash afterward.

ANALYSIS Listing 20.1 was actually designed to crash; however, if you had asked the user to enter two numbers, he could have encountered the same results.

In lines 8 and 9, two integer variables are declared and given values. You could just as easily have prompted the user for these two numbers or read them from a file. In lines 11, 14, and 16, these numbers are used in math operations. Specifically, they are used for division. In lines 11 and 16, there are no issues; however, line 14 has a serious problem. Division by zero causes an exceptional problem to occur—a crash. The program ends and most likely an exception is displayed by the operating system.

Although it is not always necessary (or even desirable) to automatically and silently recover from all exceptional circumstances, it is clear that you must do better than this program. You can't simply let your program crash.

C++ exception handling provides a type-safe, integrated method for coping with the predictable but unusual conditions that arise while running a program.

The Idea Behind Exceptions

The basic idea behind exceptions is fairly straightforward:

- The computer tries to run a piece of code. This code might try to allocate resources such as memory, might try to lock a file, or any of a variety of tasks.

- Logic (code) is included to be prepared in case the code you are trying to execute fails for some exceptional reason. For example, you would include code to catch any issues, such as memory not being allocated, a file being unable to be locked, or any of a variety of other issues.

- In case your code is being used by other code (for instance, one function calling another), you also need a mechanism to pass information about any problems (exceptions) from your level, up to the next. There should be a path from the code where an issue occurs to the code that can handle the error condition. If intervening layers of functions exist, they should be given an opportunity to clean the issue but should not be required to include code whose only purpose is to pass along the error condition.

Exception handling makes all three of these points come together, and they do it in a relatively straightforward manner.

The Parts of Exception Handling

To handle exceptions, you have to first identify that you want a particular piece of code to be watched for any exceptions. This is accomplished by using a `try` block.

You should create a `try` block around any area of code that you believe has the potential to cause a problem. The basic format of the `try` block is:

```
try
{
    SomeDangerousFunction();
}
catch (...)
{
}
```

In this case, when `SomeDangerousFunction()` executes, if any exception occurs, it is noted and caught. Adding the keyword `try` and the braces is all that is required to have your program start watching for exceptions. Of course, if an exception occurs, then you need to act upon it.

When the code within a `try` block is executed, if an exception occurs, the exception is said to be "thrown." Thrown exceptions can then be caught, and as shown previously, you *catch* an exception with a `catch` block! When an exception is thrown, control transfers to the appropriate `catch` block following the current `try` block. In the previous example, the ellipse (...) refers to any exception. But you can also catch specific types of exceptions. To do this, you use one or more `catch` blocks following your `try` block. For example,

```
try
{
    SomeDangerousFunction();
}
catch(OutOfMemory)
{
    // take some actions
}
catch(FileNotFound)
{
    // take other action
}
catch (...)
{
}
```

In this example, when `SomeDangerousFunction()` is executed, there will be handling in case there is an exception. If an exception is thrown, it is sent to the first `catch` block immediately following the `try` block. If that `catch` block has a type parameter, like those

20

in the previous example, the exception is checked to see if it matches the indicated type. If not, the next catch statement is checked, and so on, until either a match is found or something other than a catch block is found. When the first match is found, that catch block is executed. Unless you really intended to let other types of exceptions through, it is always a good idea to have the last catch use the ellipse parameter.

> **NOTE**   A catch block is also called a handler because it can handle an exception.

> **NOTE**   You can look at the catch blocks as being like overloaded functions. When the matching signature is found, that function is executed.

The basic steps in handling exceptions are

1. Identify those areas of the program in which you begin an operation that might raise an exception, and put them in try blocks.

2. Create catch blocks to catch the exceptions if they are thrown. You can either create a catch for a specific type of exception (by specifying a typed parameter for the catch block) or all exceptions (by using an ellipses (. . .) as the parameter).

Listing 20.2 adds basic exception handling to Listing 20.1. You can see this with the use of both a try block and a catch block.

> **NOTE**   Some very old compilers do not support exceptions. Exceptions are part of the ANSI C++ standard, however, and every compiler vendor's latest edition fully supports exceptions. If you have an older compiler, you won't be able to compile and run the exercises in today's lesson. It's still a good idea to read through the entire chapter, however, and return to this material when you upgrade your compiler.

LISTING 20.2   Catching an Exception

```
0:   // trying and catching
1:   #include <iostream>
2:   using namespace std;
3:
4:   const int DefaultSize = 10;
5:
```

LISTING 20.2   continued

```
 6:  int main()
 7:  {
 8:      int top = 90;
 9:      int bottom = 0;
10:
11:      try
12:      {
13:          cout << "top / 2 = " << (top/ 2) << endl;
14:
15:          cout << "top divided by bottom = ";
16:          cout << (top / bottom) << endl;
17:
18:          cout << "top / 3 = " << (top/ 3) << endl;
19:      }
20:      catch(...)
21:      {
22:          cout << "something has gone wrong!" << endl;
23:      }
24:
25:      cout << "Done." << endl;
26:      return 0;
27:  }
```

OUTPUT
```
top / 2 = 45
top divided by bottom = something has gone wrong!
Done.
```

ANALYSIS   Unlike the prior listing, executing Listing 20.2 doesn't cause a crash. Rather, the program is able to report an issue and exit gracefully.

This time, a try block was added around the code where a potential issue could occur. In this case, it is around the division operations (lines 11 to 19). In case an exception does occur, a catch block is included in lines 20–23 after the try block.

The catch on line 20 contains three dots, or an ellipsis. As mentioned previously, this is a special case for catch, and indicates that all exceptions that occur in the preceding try's code should be handled by this catch statement, unless a prior catch block handled the exception. In this listing, that will most likely only be a division by zero error. As you will see later, it is often better to look for more specific types of exceptions so that you can customize the handling of each.

You should notice that this listing does not crash when it is run. In addition, you can see from the output that the program continued to line 25 right after the catch statement. This is confirmed by the fact that the word "Done" was printed to the console.

20

> ### *try* Blocks
>
> A try block is a series of statements that begins with the keyword try; it is followed by an opening brace and ends with a closing brace.
>
> **Example**
>
> ```
> try
> {
>     Function();
> };
> ```

> ### *catch* Blocks
>
> A catch block is a piece of code that begins with the keyword catch, followed by an exception type in parentheses, followed by an opening brace, and ending with a closing brace. catch blocks are only allowed to follow a try block.
>
> **Example**
>
> ```
> try
> {
>     Function();
> };
> catch (OutOfMemory)
> {
>     // take action
> }
> ```

Causing Your Own Exceptions

Listing 20.2 illustrated two of the aspects of exception handling—marking the code to be watched and specifying how the exception is to be handled. However, only predefined exceptions were handled. The third part of exception handling is the ability for you to create your own types of exceptions to be handled. By creating your own exceptions, you gain the ability to have customized handlers (catch blocks) for exceptions that are meaningful to your application.

To create an exception that causes the try statement to react, the keyword, throw, is used. In essence, you *throw* the exception and, hopefully, a handler (catch block) catches it. The basic format of the throw statement is:

```
throw exception;
```

With this statement, *exception* is thrown. This causes control to be passed to a handler. If a handler can't be found, the program terminates.

The value that you throw in the exception can be of virtually any type. As mentioned earlier, you can set up corresponding handlers for each different type of object your program might throw. Listing 20.3 illustrates how to throw a basic exception by modifying Listing 20.2.

LISTING 20.3 Throwing an Exception

```
0:   //Throwing
1:   #include <iostream>
2:
3:   using namespace std;
4:
5:   const int DefaultSize = 10;
6:
7:   int main()
8:   {
9:        int top = 90;
10:      int bottom = 0;
11:
12:      try
13:      {
14:        cout << "top / 2 = " << (top/ 2) << endl;
15:
16:         cout << "top divided by bottom = ";
17:         if ( bottom == 0 )
18:            throw "Division by zero!";
19:
20:         cout << (top / bottom) << endl;
21:
22:         cout << "top / 3 = " << (top/ 3) << endl;
23:      }
24:      catch( const char * ex )
25:      {
26:         cout << "\n*** " << ex << " ***" << endl;
27:      }
28:
29:      cout << "Done." << endl;
30:      return 0;
31:  }
```

OUTPUT

```
top / 2 = 45
top divided by bottom = *** Division by zero! ***
Done.
```

20

ANALYSIS Unlike the prior listing, this listing takes more control of its exceptions. Although this isn't the best use of exceptions, it clearly illustrates using the throw statement.

In line 17, a check is done to see if the value of bottom is equal to zero. If it is, an exception is thrown. In this case, the exception is a string value.

On line 24, a catch statement starts a handler. This handler is looking for a constant character pointer. With exceptions, strings are matched to a constant character pointer, so the handler starting in line 24 catches the throw in line 18. In line 26, the string that was passed is displayed between asterisks. Line 27 is the closing brace, which indicates the end of the handler, so control goes to the first line following the catch statements and the program continues to the end.

If your exception had been a more serious problem, you could have exited the application after printing the message in line 26. If you throw your exception in a function that was called by another function, you could have passed the exception up. To pass on an exception, you can simply call the throw command without any parameter. This causes the existing exception to be rethrown from the current location.

Creating an Exception Class

You can create much more complex classes for throwing an exception. Listing 20.4 presents a somewhat stripped-down Array class, based on the template developed on Day 19, "Templates."

LISTING 20.4 Throwing an Exception

```
0:  #include <iostream>
1:  using namespace std;
2:
3:  const int DefaultSize = 10;
4:
5:  class Array
6:  {
7:    public:
8:      // constructors
9:      Array(int itsSize = DefaultSize);
10:     Array(const Array &rhs);
11:     ~Array() { delete [] pType;}
12:
13:     // operators
14:     Array& operator=(const Array&);
15:     int& operator[](int offSet);
16:     const int& operator[](int offSet) const;
17:
```

LISTING 20.4 continued

```
18:        // accessors
19:        int GetitsSize() const { return itsSize; }
20:
21:        // friend function
22:        friend ostream& operator<< (ostream&, const Array&);
23:
24:        class xBoundary {};   // define the exception class
25:
26:      private:
27:        int *pType;
28:        int  itsSize;
29:    };
30:
31:    Array::Array(int size):
32:       itsSize(size)
33:    {
34:       pType = new int[size];
35:       for (int i = 0; i < size; i++)
36:          pType[i] = 0;
37:    }
38:
39:    Array& Array::operator=(const Array &rhs)
40:    {
41:       if (this == &rhs)
42:          return *this;
43:       delete [] pType;
44:       itsSize = rhs.GetitsSize();
45:       pType = new int[itsSize];
46:       for (int i = 0; i < itsSize; i++)
47:       {
48:          pType[i] = rhs[i];
49:       }
50:       return *this;
51:    }
52:
53:    Array::Array(const Array &rhs)
54:    {
55:       itsSize = rhs.GetitsSize();
56:       pType = new int[itsSize];
57:       for (int i = 0; i < itsSize; i++)
58:       {
59:          pType[i] = rhs[i];
60:       }
61:    }
62:
63:    int& Array::operator[](int offSet)
64:    {
65:       int size = GetitsSize();
```

20

LISTING 20.4 continued

```
66:        if (offSet >= 0 && offSet < GetitsSize())
67:           return pType[offSet];
68:        throw xBoundary();
69:        return pType[0]; // appease MSC
70:    }
71:
72:    const int& Array::operator[](int offSet) const
73:    {
74:       int mysize = GetitsSize();
75:       if (offSet >= 0 && offSet < GetitsSize())
76:          return pType[offSet];
77:       throw xBoundary();
78:       return pType[0]; // appease MSC
79:    }
80:
81:    ostream& operator<< (ostream& output, const Array& theArray)
82:    {
83:       for (int i = 0; i<theArray.GetitsSize(); i++)
84:          output << "[" << i << "] " << theArray[i] << endl;
85:       return output;
86:    }
87:
88:    int main()
89:    {
90:       Array intArray(20);
91:       try
92:       {
93:          for (int j = 0; j< 100; j++)
94:          {
95:             intArray[j] = j;
96:             cout << "intArray[" << j << "] okay..." << endl;
97:          }
98:       }
99:       catch (Array::xBoundary)
100:      {
101:         cout << "Unable to process your input!" << endl;
102:      }
103:      cout << "Done." << endl;
104:      return 0;
105: }
```

OUTPUT

```
intArray[0] okay...
intArray[1] okay...
intArray[2] okay...
intArray[3] okay...
intArray[4] okay...
intArray[5] okay...
intArray[6] okay...
```

```
intArray[7] okay...
intArray[8] okay...
intArray[9] okay...
intArray[10] okay...
intArray[11] okay...
intArray[12] okay...
intArray[13] okay...
intArray[14] okay...
intArray[15] okay...
intArray[16] okay...
intArray[17] okay...
intArray[18] okay...
intArray[19] okay...
Unable to process your input!
Done.
```

ANALYSIS Listing 20.4 presents a somewhat stripped-down `Array` class; however, this time exception handling is added in case the array goes out of bounds.

On line 24, a new class, `xBoundary`, is declared within the declaration of the outer class `Array`.

This new class is not in any way distinguished as an exception class. It is just a class the same as any other. This particular class is incredibly simple; it has no data and no methods. Nonetheless, it is a valid class in every way.

In fact, it is incorrect to say it has no methods because the compiler automatically assigns it a default constructor, destructor, copy constructor, and the assignment operator (operator equals); so it actually has four class functions, but no data.

Note that declaring it from within `Array` serves only to couple the two classes together. As discussed on Day 16, "Advanced Inheritance," `Array` has no special access to `xBoundary`, nor does `xBoundary` have preferential access to the members of `Array`.

On lines 63–70 and 72–79, the offset operators are modified to examine the offset requested, and if it is out of range, to throw the `xBoundary` class as an exception. The parentheses are required to distinguish between this call to the `xBoundary` constructor and the use of an enumerated constant.

In line 90, the main part of the program starts by declaring an `Array` object that can hold 20 values. On line 91, the keyword `try` begins a `try` block that ends on line 98. Within that `try` block, 101 integers are added to the array that was declared on line 90.

On line 99, the `handler` has been declared to catch any `xBoundary` exceptions.

In the driver program on lines 88–105, a `try` block is created in which each member of the array is initialized. When j (line 93) is incremented to 20, the member at offset 20 is

20

accessed. This causes the test on line 66 to fail, and operator[] raises an xBoundary exception on line 67.

Program control switches to the catch block on line 99, and the exception is caught or handled by the catch on the same line, which prints an error message. Program flow drops through to the end of the catch block on line 102.

Placing try Blocks and catch Blocks

Figuring out where to put your try blocks can be hard: It is not always obvious which actions might raise an exception. The next question is where to catch the exception. It might be that you'll want to throw all memory exceptions where the memory is allocated, but you'll want to catch the exceptions high in the program where you deal with the user interface.

When trying to determine try block locations, look to where you allocate memory or use resources. Other things to look for are out-of-bounds errors, illegal input, and so forth. At the very least, put a try/catch around all of the code in main(). try/catch usually belongs in high-level functions, particularly those that know about the program's user interface. For instance, a utility class should not generally catch exceptions that need to be reported to the user because it might be used in windowed programs or console programs, or even in programs that communicate with users via the Web or messaging.

How Catching Exceptions Work

Here's how it works: When an exception is thrown, the call stack is examined. The call stack is the list of function calls created when one part of the program invokes another function.

The call stack tracks the execution path. If main() calls the function Animal::GetFavoriteFood(), and GetFavoriteFood() calls Animal::LookupPreferences(), which, in turn, calls fstream::operator>>(), all these are on the call stack. A recursive function might be on the call stack many times.

The exception is passed up the call stack to each enclosing block. This is called "unwinding the stack." As the stack is unwound, the destructors for local objects on the stack are invoked, and the objects are destroyed.

One or more catch statements follow each try block. If the exception matches one of the catch statements, it is considered to be handled by having that statement execute. If it doesn't match any, the unwinding of the stack continues.

If the exception reaches all the way to the beginning of the program (main()) and is still not caught, a built-in handler is called that terminates the program.

It is important to note that the exception unwinding of the stack is a one-way street. As it progresses, the stack is unwound and objects on the stack are destroyed. There is no going back: After the exception is handled, the program continues after the try block of the catch statement that handled the exception.

Thus, in Listing 20.4, execution continues on line 101, the first line after the try block of the catch statement that handled the xBoundary exception. Remember that when an exception is raised, program flow continues after the catch block, not after the point where the exception was thrown.

Using More Than One catch Specification

It is possible for more than one condition to cause an exception. In this case, the catch statements can be lined up one after another, much like the conditions in a switch statement. The equivalent to the default statement is the "catch everything" statement, indicated by catch(...). Listing 20.5 illustrates multiple exception conditions.

LISTING 20.5   Multiple Exceptions

```
0:  #include <iostream>
1:  using namespace std;
2:
3:  const int DefaultSize = 10;
4:
5:  class Array
6:  {
7:    public:
8:       // constructors
9:       Array(int itsSize = DefaultSize);
10:       Array(const Array &rhs);
11:       ~Array() { delete [] pType;}
12:
13:       // operators
14:       Array& operator=(const Array&);
15:       int& operator[](int offSet);
16:       const int& operator[](int offSet) const;
17:
18:       // accessors
19:       int GetitsSize() const { return itsSize; }
20:
21:       // friend function
22:       friend ostream& operator<< (ostream&, const Array&);
23:
24:       // define the exception classes
```

20

LISTING 20.5 continued

```
25:       class xBoundary {};
26:       class xTooBig {};
27:       class xTooSmall{};
28:       class xZero {};
29:       class xNegative {};
30:    private:
31:       int *pType;
32:       int  itsSize;
33:  };
34:
35:  int& Array::operator[](int offSet)
36:  {
37:     int size = GetitsSize();
38:     if (offSet >= 0 && offSet < GetitsSize())
39:        return pType[offSet];
40:     throw xBoundary();
41:     return pType[0];  // appease MFC
42:  }
43:
44:
45:  const int& Array::operator[](int offSet) const
46:  {
47:     int mysize = GetitsSize();
48:     if (offSet >= 0 && offSet < GetitsSize())
49:        return pType[offSet];
50:     throw xBoundary();
51:
52:     return pType[0];  // appease MFC
53:  }
54:
55:
56:  Array::Array(int size):
57:     itsSize(size)
58:  {
59:     if (size == 0)
60:        throw xZero();
61:     if (size < 10)
62:        throw xTooSmall();
63:     if (size > 30000)
64:        throw xTooBig();
65:     if (size < 1)
66:        throw xNegative();
67:
68:     pType = new int[size];
69:     for (int i = 0; i < size; i++)
70:        pType[i] = 0;
71:  }
72:
```

LISTING 20.5 continued

```
73:  int main()
74:  {
75:      try
76:      {
77:          Array intArray(0);
78:          for (int j = 0; j < 100; j++)
79:          {
80:              intArray[j] = j;
81:              cout << "intArray[" << j << "] okay..." << endl;
82:          }
83:      }
84:      catch (Array::xBoundary)
85:      {
86:          cout << "Unable to process your input!" << endl;
87:      }
88:      catch (Array::xTooBig)
89:      {
90:          cout << "This array is too big..." << endl;
91:      }
92:      catch (Array::xTooSmall)
93:      {
94:          cout << "This array is too small..." << endl;
95:      }
96:      catch (Array::xZero)
97:      {
98:          cout << "You asked for an array";
99:          cout << " of zero objects!" << endl;
100:     }
101:     catch (...)
102:     {
103:         cout << "Something went wrong!" << endl;
104:     }
105:     cout << "Done." << endl;
106:     return 0;
107: }
```

OUTPUT

```
You asked for an array of zero objects!
Done.
```

ANALYSIS Four new classes are created in lines 25–29: xTooBig, xTooSmall, xZero, and xNegative. In the constructor, on lines 56–71, the size passed to the constructor is examined. If it's too big, too small, negative, or zero, an exception is thrown.

The try block is changed to include catch statements for each condition other than negative, which is caught by the "catch everything" statement catch(...), shown on line 101.

20

Try this with a number of values for the size of the array. Then try putting in –5. You
might have expected xNegative to be called, but the order of the tests in the constructor
prevented this: size < 10 was evaluated before size < 1. To fix this, swap lines 61 and
62 with lines 65 and 66 and recompile.

> **TIP**
>
> After the constructor has been invoked, memory has been allocated for the
> object. Therefore, throwing any exception from the constructor can leave
> the object allocated but unusable. Generally, you should wrap the construc-
> tor in a try/catch, and if an exception occurs, mark the object (internally) as
> unusable. Each member function should check this "valid" flag to be certain
> additional errors won't occur when someone uses an object whose initializa-
> tion was interrupted.

Exception Hierarchies

Exceptions are classes, and as such, they can be derived from. It might be advantageous
to create a class xSize, and to derive from it xZero, xTooSmall, xTooBig, and
xNegative. Thus, some functions might just catch xSize errors, and other functions
might catch the specific type of xSize error. Listing 20.6 illustrates this idea.

LISTING 20.6   Class Hierarchies and Exceptions

```
0:  #include <iostream>
1:  using namespace std;
2:
3:  const int DefaultSize = 10;
4:
5:  class Array
6:  {
7:    public:
8:      // constructors
9:      Array(int itsSize = DefaultSize);
10:     Array(const Array &rhs);
11:     ~Array() { delete [] pType;}
12:
13:     // operators
14:     Array& operator=(const Array&);
15:     int& operator[](int offSet);
16:     const int& operator[](int offSet) const;
17:
18:     // accessors
19:     int GetitsSize() const { return itsSize; }
20:
```

LISTING 20.6   continued

```
21:      // friend function
22:      friend ostream& operator<< (ostream&, const Array&);
23:
24:      // define the exception classes
25:      class xBoundary {};
26:      class xSize {};
27:      class xTooBig : public xSize {};
28:      class xTooSmall : public xSize {};
29:      class xZero  : public xTooSmall {};
30:      class xNegative  : public xSize {};
31:   private:
32:      int *pType;
33:      int  itsSize;
34:   };
35:
36:
37:   Array::Array(int size):
38:      itsSize(size)
39:   {
40:      if (size == 0)
41:         throw xZero();
42:      if (size > 30000)
43:         throw xTooBig();
44:      if (size <1)
45:         throw xNegative();
46:      if (size < 10)
47:         throw xTooSmall();
48:
49:      pType = new int[size];
50:      for (int i = 0; i < size; i++)
51:         pType[i] = 0;
52:   }
53:
54:   int& Array::operator[](int offSet)
55:   {
56:      int size = GetitsSize();
57:      if (offSet >= 0 && offSet < GetitsSize())
58:         return pType[offSet];
59:      throw xBoundary();
60:      return pType[0];   // appease MFC
61:   }
62:
63:   const int& Array::operator[](int offSet) const
64:   {
65:      int mysize = GetitsSize();
66:
67:      if (offSet >= 0 && offSet < GetitsSize())
68:         return pType[offSet];
69:      throw xBoundary();
```

20

LISTING 20.6   continued

```
70:
71:      return pType[0];  // appease MFC
72:  }
73:
74:  int main()
75:  {
76:     try
77:     {
78:        Array intArray(0);
79:        for (int j = 0; j < 100; j++)
80:        {
81:           intArray[j] = j;
82:           cout << "intArray[" << j << "] okay..." << endl;
83:        }
84:     }
85:     catch (Array::xBoundary)
86:     {
87:        cout << "Unable to process your input!" << endl;
88:     }
89:     catch (Array::xTooBig)
90:     {
91:        cout << "This array is too big..." << endl;
92:     }
93:
94:     catch (Array::xTooSmall)
95:     {
96:        cout << "This array is too small..." << endl;
97:     }
98:     catch (Array::xZero)
99:     {
100:         cout << "You asked for an array";
101:         cout << " of zero objects!" << endl;
102:      }
103:      catch (...)
104:      {
105:         cout << "Something went wrong!" << endl;
106:      }
107:      cout << "Done." << endl;
108:      return 0;
109:  }
```

OUTPUT   This array is too small...
Done.

ANALYSIS   The significant change is on lines 27–30, where the class hierarchy is established. Classes xTooBig, xTooSmall, and xNegative are derived from xSize, and
xZero is derived from xTooSmall.

The Array is created with size zero, but what's this? The wrong exception appears to be caught! Examine the catch block carefully, however, and you will find that it looks for an exception of type xTooSmall before it looks for an exception of type xZero. Because an xZero object is thrown and an xZero object is an xTooSmall object, it is caught by the handler for xTooSmall. After being handled, the exception is not passed on to the other handlers, so the handler for xZero is never called.

The solution to this problem is to carefully order the handlers so that the most specific handlers come first and the less specific handlers come later. In this particular example, switching the placement of the two handlers xZero and xTooSmall fixes the problem.

Data in Exceptions and Naming Exception Objects

Often, you will want to know more than just what type of exception was thrown so you can respond properly to the error. Exception classes are the same as any other class. You are free to provide data, initialize that data in the constructor, and read that data at any time. Listing 20.7 illustrates how to do this.

LISTING 20.7   Getting Data Out of an Exception Object

```
0:   #include <iostream>
1:   using namespace std;
2:
3:   const int DefaultSize = 10;
4:
5:   class Array
6:   {
7:     public:
8:       // constructors
9:       Array(int itsSize = DefaultSize);
10:      Array(const Array &rhs);
11:      ~Array() { delete [] pType;}
12:
13:      // operators
14:      Array& operator=(const Array&);
15:      int& operator[](int offSet);
16:      const int& operator[](int offSet) const;
17:
18:      // accessors
19:      int GetitsSize() const { return itsSize; }
20:
21:      // friend function
22:      friend ostream& operator<< (ostream&, const Array&);
```

20

LISTING 20.7   continued

```
23:
24:        // define the exception classes
25:        class xBoundary {};
26:        class xSize
27:        {
28:          public:
29:            xSize(int size):itsSize(size) {}
30:            ~xSize(){}
31:            int GetSize() { return itsSize; }
32:          private:
33:            int itsSize;
34:        };
35:
36:        class xTooBig : public xSize
37:        {
38:          public:
39:            xTooBig(int size):xSize(size){}
40:        };
41:
42:        class xTooSmall : public xSize
43:        {
44:          public:
45:            xTooSmall(int size):xSize(size){}
46:        };
47:
48:        class xZero  : public xTooSmall
49:        {
50:          public:
51:            xZero(int size):xTooSmall(size){}
52:        };
53:
54:        class xNegative : public xSize
55:        {
56:          public:
57:            xNegative(int size):xSize(size){}
58:        };
59:
60:     private:
61:        int *pType;
62:        int  itsSize;
63:    };
64:
65:
66: Array::Array(int size):
67: itsSize(size)
68: {
69:    if (size == 0)
70:        throw xZero(size);
```

LISTING 20.7   continued

```
71:        if (size > 30000)
72:            throw xTooBig(size);
73:        if (size < 1)
74:            throw xNegative(size);
75:        if (size < 10)
76:            throw xTooSmall(size);
77:
78:        pType = new int[size];
79:        for (int i = 0; i < size; i++)
80:            pType[i] = 0;
81:    }
82:
83:
84:    int& Array::operator[] (int offSet)
85:    {
86:        int size = GetitsSize();
87:        if (offSet >= 0 && offSet < size)
88:            return pType[offSet];
89:        throw xBoundary();
90:        return pType[0];
91:    }
92:
93:    const int& Array::operator[] (int offSet) const
94:    {
95:        int size = GetitsSize();
96:        if (offSet >= 0 && offSet < size)
97:            return pType[offSet];
98:        throw xBoundary();
99:        return pType[0];
100:   }
101:
102:   int main()
103:   {
104:       try
105:       {
106:           Array intArray(9);
107:           for (int j = 0; j < 100; j++)
108:           {
109:               intArray[j] = j;
110:               cout << "intArray[" << j << "] okay..." << endl;
111:           }
112:       }
113:       catch (Array::xBoundary)
114:       {
115:           cout << "Unable to process your input!" << endl;
116:       }
117:       catch (Array::xZero theException)
118:       {
```

20

LISTING 20.7   continued

```
119:          cout << "You asked for an Array of zero objects!" << endl;
120:          cout << "Received " << theException.GetSize() << endl;
121:        }
122:      catch (Array::xTooBig theException)
123:        {
124:          cout << "This Array is too big..." << endl;
125:          cout << "Received " << theException.GetSize() << endl;
126:        }
127:      catch (Array::xTooSmall theException)
128:        {
129:          cout << "This Array is too small..." << endl;
130:          cout << "Received " << theException.GetSize() << endl;
131:        }
132:      catch (...)
133:        {
134:          cout << "Something went wrong, but I've no idea what!\n";
135:        }
136:      cout << "Done." << endl;
137:      return 0;
138:    }
```

OUTPUT
```
This array is too small...
Received 9
Done.
```

ANALYSIS   The declaration of xSize has been modified to include a member variable, itsSize, on line 33 and a member function, GetSize(), on line 31. In addition, a constructor has been added that takes an integer and initializes the member variable, as shown on line 29.

The derived classes declare a constructor that does nothing but initialize the base class. No other functions were declared, in part to save space in the listing.

The catch statements on lines 113–135 are modified to name the exception they catch, theException, and to use this object to access the data stored in itsSize.

NOTE

Keep in mind that if you are constructing an exception, it is because an exception has been raised: Something has gone wrong, and your exception should be careful not to kick off the same problem. Therefore, if you are creating an OutOfMemory exception, you probably don't want to allocate memory in its constructor.

It is tedious and error-prone to have each of these `catch` statements individually print the appropriate message. This job belongs to the object, which knows what type of object it is and what value it received. Listing 20.8 takes a more object-oriented approach to this problem, using virtual functions so that each exception "does the right thing."

LISTING 20.8 Passing by Reference and Using Virtual Functions in Exceptions

```
0:   #include <iostream>
1:   using namespace std;
2:
3:   const int DefaultSize = 10;
4:
5:   class Array
6:   {
7:     public:
8:     // constructors
9:       Array(int itsSize = DefaultSize);
10:      Array(const Array &rhs);
11:      ~Array() { delete [] pType;}
12:
13:      // operators
14:      Array& operator=(const Array&);
15:      int& operator[](int offSet);
16:      const int& operator[](int offSet) const;
17:
18:      // accessors
19:      int GetitsSize() const { return itsSize; }
20:
21:      // friend function
22:      friend ostream& operator<<
23:      (ostream&, const Array&);
24:
25:      // define the exception classes
26:      class xBoundary {};
27:      class xSize
28:      {
29:        public:
30:          xSize(int size):itsSize(size) {}
31:          ~xSize(){}
32:          virtual int GetSize() { return itsSize; }
33:          virtual void PrintError()
34:          {
35:             cout << "Size error. Received: ";
36:             cout << itsSize << endl;
37:          }
38:        protected:
39:           int itsSize;
40:      };
41:
```

20

LISTING 20.8   continued

```
42:        class xTooBig : public xSize
43:        {
44:          public:
45:            xTooBig(int size):xSize(size){}
46:            virtual void PrintError()
47:            {
48:                cout << "Too big! Received: ";
49:                cout << xSize::itsSize << endl;
50:            }
51:        };
52:
53:        class xTooSmall : public xSize
54:        {
55:          public:
56:            xTooSmall(int size):xSize(size){}
57:            virtual void PrintError()
58:            {
59:                cout << "Too small! Received: ";
60:                cout << xSize::itsSize << endl;
61:            }
62:        };
63:
64:        class xZero  : public xTooSmall
65:        {
66:          public:
67:            xZero(int size):xTooSmall(size){}
68:            virtual void PrintError()
69:            {
70:                cout << "Zero!!. Received: " ;
71:                cout << xSize::itsSize << endl;
72:            }
73:        };
74:
75:        class xNegative : public xSize
76:        {
77:          public:
78:            xNegative(int size):xSize(size){}
79:            virtual void PrintError()
80:            {
81:                cout << "Negative! Received: ";
82:                cout << xSize::itsSize << endl;
83:            }
84:        };
85:
86:    private:
87:      int *pType;
88:      int  itsSize;
89:    };
```

LISTING 20.8 continued

```
90:
91:   Array::Array(int size):
92:      itsSize(size)
93:   {
94:      if (size == 0)
95:         throw xZero(size);
96:      if (size > 30000)
97:         throw xTooBig(size);
98:      if (size < 0)
99:         throw xNegative(size);
100:     if (size < 10)
101:        throw xTooSmall(size);
102:
103:     pType = new int[size];
104:     for (int i = 0; i < size; i++)
105:        pType[i] = 0;
106:  }
107:
108:  int& Array::operator[] (int offSet)
109:  {
110:     int size = GetitsSize();
111:     if (offSet >= 0 && offSet < GetitsSize())
112:        return pType[offSet];
113:     throw xBoundary();
114:     return pType[0];
115:  }
116:
117:  const int& Array::operator[] (int offSet) const
118:  {
119:     int size = GetitsSize();
120:     if (offSet >= 0 && offSet < GetitsSize())
121:        return pType[offSet];
122:     throw xBoundary();
123:     return pType[0];
124:  }
125:
126:  int main()
127:  {
128:     try
129:     {
130:        Array intArray(9);
131:        for (int j = 0; j < 100; j++)
132:        {
133:           intArray[j] = j;
134:           cout << "intArray[" << j << "] okay..." << endl;
135:        }
136:     }
137:     catch (Array::xBoundary)
```

20

LISTING 20.8   continued

```
138:      {
139:          cout << "Unable to process your input!" << endl;
140:      }
141:      catch (Array::xSize& theException)
142:      {
143:          theException.PrintError();
144:      }
145:      catch (...)
146:      {
147:          cout << "Something went wrong!" << endl;
148:      }
149:      cout << "Done." << endl;
150:      return 0;
151: }
```

OUTPUT

```
Too small! Received: 9
Done.
```

ANALYSIS Listing 20.8 declares a virtual method on lines 33–37 in the xSize class,
PrintError(), that prints an error message and the actual size of the class. This
is overridden in each of the derived classes.

On line 141 in the exception handler, the exception object is declared to be a reference.
When PrintError() is called with a reference to an object, polymorphism causes the
correct version of PrintError() to be invoked. The code is cleaner, easier to understand,
and easier to maintain.

Exceptions and Templates

When creating exceptions to work with templates, you have a choice: You can create an
exception for each instance of the template, or you can use exception classes declared
outside the template declaration. Listing 20.9 illustrates both approaches.

LISTING 20.9   Using Exceptions with Templates

```
0:  #include <iostream>
1:  using namespace std;
2:
3:  const int DefaultSize = 10;
4:  class xBoundary {};
5:
6:  template <class T>
7:  class Array
8:  {
```

LISTING 20.9   continued

```
 9:    public:
10:       // constructors
11:       Array(int itsSize = DefaultSize);
12:       Array(const Array &rhs);
13:       ~Array() { delete [] pType;}
14:
15:       // operators
16:       Array& operator=(const Array<T>&);
17:       T& operator[](int offSet);
18:       const T& operator[](int offSet) const;
19:
20:       // accessors
21:       int GetitsSize() const { return itsSize; }
22:
23:       // friend function
24:       friend ostream& operator<< (ostream&, const Array<T>&);
25:
26:       // define the exception classes
27:
28:       class xSize {};
29:
30:    private:
31:       int *pType;
32:       int  itsSize;
33: };
34:
35: template <class T>
36: Array<T>::Array(int size):
37:    itsSize(size)
38: {
39:    if (size <10 || size > 30000)
40:       throw xSize();
41:    pType = new T[size];
42:    for (int i = 0; i<size; i++)
43:       pType[i] = 0;
44: }
45:
46: template <class T>
47: Array<T>& Array<T>::operator=(const Array<T> &rhs)
48: {
49:    if (this == &rhs)
50:       return *this;
51:    delete [] pType;
52:    itsSize = rhs.GetitsSize();
53:    pType = new T[itsSize];
54:    for (int i = 0; i < itsSize; i++)
55:       pType[i] = rhs[i];
56: }
```

20

LISTING 20.9 continued

```
57:   template <class T>
58:   Array<T>::Array(const Array<T> &rhs)
59:   {
60:      itsSize = rhs.GetitsSize();
61:      pType = new T[itsSize];
62:      for (int i = 0; i < itsSize; i++)
63:          pType[i] = rhs[i];
64:   }
65:
66:   template <class T>
67:   T& Array<T>::operator[](int offSet)
68:   {
69:      int size = GetitsSize();
70:      if (offSet >= 0 && offSet < GetitsSize())
71:          return pType[offSet];
72:      throw xBoundary();
73:      return pType[0];
74:   }
75:
76:   template <class T>
77:   const T& Array<T>::operator[](int offSet) const
78:   {
79:      int mysize = GetitsSize();
80:      if (offSet >= 0 && offSet < GetitsSize())
81:          return pType[offSet];
82:      throw xBoundary();
83:   }
84:
85:   template <class T>
86:   ostream& operator<< (ostream& output, const Array<T>& theArray)
87:   {
88:      for (int i = 0; i < theArray.GetitsSize(); i++)
89:          output << "[" << i << "] " << theArray[i] << endl;
90:      return output;
91:   }
92:
93:
94:   int main()
95:   {
96:      try
97:      {
98:          Array<int> intArray(9);
99:          for (int j = 0; j < 100; j++)
100:         {
101:             intArray[j] = j;
102:             cout << "intArray[" << j << "] okay..." << endl;
103:         }
104:      }
```

LISTING 20.9 continued

```
105:     catch (xBoundary)
106:     {
107:        cout << "Unable to process your input!" << endl;
108:     }
109:     catch (Array<int>::xSize)
110:     {
111:        cout << "Bad Size!" << endl;
112:     }
113:
114:     cout << "Done." << endl;
115:     return 0;
116: }
```

OUTPUT

```
Bad Size!
Done.
```

ANALYSIS The first exception, xBoundary, is declared outside the template definition on line 4. The second exception, xSize, is declared from within the definition of the template on line 28.

The exception xBoundary is not tied to the template class, but it can be used the same as any other class. xSize is tied to the template and must be called based on the instantiated Array. You can see the difference in the syntax for the two catch statements. Line 105 shows catch (xBoundary), but line 109 shows catch (Array<int>::xSize). The latter is tied to the instantiation of an integer Array.

Exceptions Without Errors

When C++ programmers get together for a virtual beer in the cyberspace bar after work, talk often turns to whether exceptions should be used for routine conditions. Some maintain that by their nature, exceptions should be reserved for those predictable but exceptional circumstances (hence the name!) that a programmer must anticipate, but that are not part of the routine processing of the code.

Others point out that exceptions offer a powerful and clean way to return through many layers of function calls without danger of memory leaks. A frequent example is this: The user requests an action in a graphical user interface (GUI) environment. The part of the code that catches the request must call a member function on a dialog manager, which, in turn, calls code that processes the request, which calls code that decides which dialog box to use, which, in turn, calls code to put up the dialog box, which finally calls code that processes the user's input. If the user clicks Cancel, the code must return to the very first calling method where the original request was handled.

20

One approach to this problem is to put a `try` block around the original call and catch `CancelDialog` as an exception, which can be raised by the handler for the Cancel button. This is safe and effective, but clicking Cancel is a routine circumstance, not an exceptional one.

This frequently becomes something of a religious argument, but a reasonable way to decide the question is to ask the following: Does use of exceptions in this way make the code easier or harder to understand? Are there fewer risks of errors and memory leaks, or more? Will it be harder or easier to maintain this code? These decisions, like so many others, require an analysis of the trade-offs; no single, obvious right answer exists.

A Word About Code Rot

Code rot is a well-known phenomenon in which software deteriorates due to being neglected. A perfectly well-written, fully debugged program will turn bad on your customer's shelf just weeks after you deliver it. After a few months, your customer will notice that a green mold has covered your logic, and many of your objects have begun to flake apart.

Besides shipping your source code in air-tight containers, your only protection is to write your programs so that when you go back to fix the spoilage, you can quickly and easily identify where the problems are.

NOTE

> Code rot is a programmer's joke, which teaches an important lesson. Programs are enormously complex, and bugs, errors, and mistakes can hide for a long time before turning up. Protect yourself by writing easy-to-maintain code.

This means that your code must be written to be understood, and commented where tricky. Six months after you deliver your code, you will read it with the eyes of a total stranger, bewildered by how anyone could ever have written such convoluted and twisty logic.

Bugs and Debugging

Nearly all modern development environments include one or more high-powered debuggers. The essential idea of using a debugger is this: You run the debugger, which loads your source code, and then you run your program from within the debugger. This enables you to see each instruction in your program as it executes and to examine your variables as they change during the life of your program.

All compilers let you compile with or without symbols. Compiling with symbols tells the compiler to create the necessary mapping between your source code and the generated program; the debugger uses this to point to the line of source code that corresponds to the next action in the program.

Full-screen symbolic debuggers make this chore a delight. When you load your debugger, it reads through all your source code and shows the code in a window. You can step over function calls or direct the debugger to step into the function, line by line.

With most debuggers, you can switch between the source code and the output to see the results of each executed statement. More powerfully, you can examine the current state of each variable, look at complex data structures, examine the value of member data within classes, and look at the actual values in memory of various pointers and other memory locations. You can execute several types of control within a debugger that include setting breakpoints, setting watch points, examining memory, and looking at the assembler code.

Breakpoints

Breakpoints are instructions to the debugger that when a particular line of code is ready to be executed, the program should stop. This allows you to run your program unimpeded until the line in question is reached. Breakpoints help you analyze the current condition of variables just before and after a critical line of code.

Watch Points

It is possible to tell the debugger to show you the value of a particular variable or to break when a particular variable is read or written to. Watch points enable you to set these conditions, and, at times, even to modify the value of a variable while the program is running.

Examining Memory

At times, it is important to see the actual values held in memory. Modern debuggers can show values in the form of the actual variable; that is, strings can be shown as characters, longs as numbers rather than as four bytes, and so forth. Sophisticated C++ debuggers can even show complete classes and provide the current value of all the member variables, including the `this` pointer.

Assembler

Although reading through the source can be all that is required to find a bug, when all else fails, it is possible to instruct the debugger to show you the actual assembly code

20

generated for each line of your source code. You can examine the memory registers and flags, and generally delve as deep into the inner workings of your program as required.

Learn to use your debugger. It can be the most powerful weapon in your holy war against bugs. Runtime bugs are the hardest to find and squash, and a powerful debugger can make it possible, if not easy, to find nearly all of them.

Summary

Today, you learned the basics for creating and using exceptions. Exceptions are objects that can be created and thrown at points in the program where the executing code cannot handle the error or other exceptional condition that has arisen. Other parts of the program, higher in the call stack, implement catch blocks that catch the exception and take appropriate action.

Exceptions are normal, user-created objects, and as such can be passed by value or by reference. They can contain data and methods, and the catch block can use that data to decide how to deal with the exception.

It is possible to create multiple catch blocks, but after an exception matches a catch block's signature, it is considered to be handled and is not given to the subsequent catch blocks. It is important to order the catch blocks appropriately so that more specific catch blocks have first chance, and more general catch blocks handle those not otherwise handled.

Today's lesson also mentioned the fundamentals of symbolic debuggers, including using watch points, breakpoints, and so forth. These tools can help you zero in on the part of your program that is causing the error and let you see the value of variables as they change during the course of the execution of the program.

Q&A

Q Why bother with raising exceptions? Why not handle the error right where it happens?

A Often, the same error can be generated in different parts of the code. Exceptions let you centralize the handling of errors. In addition, the part of the code that generates the error might not be the best place to determine how to handle the error.

Q Why generate an object? Why not just pass an error code?

A Objects are more flexible and powerful than error codes. They can convey more information, and the constructor/destructor mechanisms can be used for the creation and removal of resources that might be required to properly handle the exceptional condition.

Q Why not use exceptions for nonerror conditions? Isn't it convenient to be able to express-train back to previous areas of the code, even when nonexceptional conditions exist?

A Yes, some C++ programmers use exceptions for just that purpose. The danger is that exceptions might create memory leaks as the stack is unwound and some objects are inadvertently left in the free store. With careful programming techniques and a good compiler, this can usually be avoided. Otherwise, it is a matter of personal aesthetic; some programmers feel that, by their nature, exceptions should not be used for routine conditions.

Q Does an exception have to be caught in the same place where the `try` block created the exception?

A No, it is possible to catch an exception anywhere in the call stack. As the stack is unwound, the exception is passed up the stack until it is handled.

Q Why use a debugger when I can use `cout` and other such statements?

A The debugger provides a much more powerful mechanism for stepping through your code and watching values change without having to clutter your code with thousands of debugging statements. In addition, there is a significant risk each time you add or remove lines from your code. If you have just removed problems by debugging, and you accidentally delete a real code line when deleting your use of `cout`, you haven't helped the situation.

Workshop

The Workshop contains quiz questions to help solidify your understanding of the material covered and exercises to provide you with experience in using what you've learned. Try to answer the quiz and exercise questions before checking the answers in Appendix D, and be certain you understand the answers before going to tomorrow's lesson.

20

Quiz

1. What is an exception?
2. What is a `try` block?
3. What is a `catch` statement?
4. What information can an exception contain?
5. When are exception objects created?

6. Should you pass exceptions by value or by reference?

7. Will a catch statement catch a derived exception if it is looking for the base class?

8. If two catch statements are used, one for base and one for derived, which should come first?

9. What does catch(...) mean?

10. What is a breakpoint?

Exercises

1. Create a try block, a catch statement, and a simple exception.

2. Modify the answer from Exercise 1, put data into the exception along with an accessor function, and use it in the catch block.

3. Modify the class from Exercise 2 to be a hierarchy of exceptions. Modify the catch block to use the derived objects and the base objects.

4. Modify the program from Exercise 3 to have three levels of function calls.

5. **BUG BUSTERS:** What is wrong with the following code?

```
#include "stringc.h"          // our string class

class xOutOfMemory
{
  public:
     xOutOfMemory( const String& where ) : location( where ){}
     ~xOutOfMemory(){}
     virtual String where(){ return location };
  private:
     String location;
}

int main()
{
    try
    {
        char *var = new char;
        if ( var == 0 )
            throw xOutOfMemory();
    }
    catch( xOutOfMemory& theException )
    {
        cout << "Out of memory at " << theException.location() << endl;
    }
    return 0;
}
```

This listing shows exception handling for handling an out-of-memory error.

DAY 21

What's Next

Congratulations! You are nearly done with a full three-week intensive introduction to C++. By now, you should have a solid understanding of C++, but in modern programming there is always more to learn. This final day's lesson fills in some missing details and then sets the course for continued study.

Most of what you write in your source code files is C++. This is interpreted by the compiler and turned into your program. Before the compiler runs, however, the preprocessor runs, and this provides an opportunity for conditional compilation.

Today, you will learn

- What conditional compilation is and how to manage it
- How to write macros using the preprocessor
- How to use the preprocessor in finding bugs
- How to manipulate individual bits and use them as flags
- What the next steps are in learning to use C++ effectively

The Preprocessor and the Compiler

Every time you run your compiler, your preprocessor runs first. The preprocessor looks for preprocessor instructions, each of which begins with a pound symbol (#). The effect of each of these instructions is a change to the text of the source code. The result is a new source code file—a temporary file that you normally don't see, but that you can instruct the compiler to save so you can examine it if you want to.

The compiler does not read your original source code file; it reads the output of the preprocessor and compiles that file. You've seen the effect of this already with the #include directive. This instructs the preprocessor to find the file whose name follows the #include directive and to write it into the intermediate file at that location. It is as if you had typed that entire file right into your source code, and by the time the compiler sees the source code, the included file is there.

TIP

> Nearly every compiler has a switch that you can set either in the Integrated Development Environment (IDE) or at the command line, which instructs the compiler to save the intermediate file. Check your compiler manual for the right switches to set for your compiler if you want to examine this file.

The #define Preprocessor Directive

You can create string substitutions using the #define command you write

```
#define BIG 512
```

you have instructed the precompiler to substitute the string 512 wherever it sees the string BIG. This is not a string in the C++ sense. The characters "512" are substituted in your source code wherever the word "BIG" is seen. Thus, if you write

```
#define BIG 512
int myArray[BIG];
```

the intermediate file produced by the precompiler looks like this:

```
int myArray[512];
```

Note that the #define statement is gone. Precompiler statements are all removed from the intermediate file; they do not appear in the final source code at all.

Using #define for Constants

One way to use #define is as a substitute for constants. This is almost never a good idea, however, because #define merely makes a string substitution and does no type checking. As explained in the section on constants, tremendous advantages exist in using the const keyword rather than #define.

Using #define for Tests

A second way to use #define is simply to declare that a particular character string is defined. Therefore, you could write

```
#define DEBUG
```

Later in your listing, you can test to determine whether BIG has been defined and take action accordingly. To check if it is defined, you can use the preprocessor #if command followed by the defined command:

```
#if defined DEBUG
cout << Debug defined";
#endif
```

The defined expression evaluates to true if the name it tests—DEBUG in this case—has been defined already. Keep in mind that this happens in the preprocessor, not in the compiler or in the executing program.

When the preprocessor reads the #if defined, it checks a table it has built to see whether you've defined the value that follows. If you have, defined evaluates to true, and everything between the #if defined DEBUG and its #endif is written into the intermediate file for compiling. If it evaluates to false, nothing between #if defined DEBUG and #endif is written into the intermediate file; it is as if it were never in the source code in the first place.

A shortcut directive also exists for checking defined values. This is the #ifdef directive:

```
#ifdef DEBUG
cout << "Debug defined";
#endif
```

You can also test to see if a value is not defined. This is done by using the not operator with the defined directive:

```
#if !defined DEBUG
cout << "Debug is not defined";
#endif
```

There is also a shortcut version for this as well, #ifndef:

21

```
#ifndef DEBUG
cout << "Debug is not defined.";
#endif
```

Note that `#ifndef` is the logical reverse of `#ifdef`. `#ifndef` evaluates to true if the string has not been defined up to that point in the file.

You should notice that all of these checks required that `#endif` also be included to indicate the end of the code impacted by the check.

The `#else` Precompiler Command

As you might imagine, the term `#else` can be inserted between either `#ifdef` or `#ifndef` and the closing `#endif`. Listing 21.1 illustrates how these terms are used.

LISTING 21.1   Using `#define`

```
0:  #define DemoVersion
1:  #define SW_VERSION 5
2:  #include <iostream>
3:
4:  using std::endl;
5:  using std::cout;
6:
7:  int main()
8:  {
9:      cout << "Checking on the definitions of DemoVersion,";
10:     cout << "SW_VERSION, and WINDOWS_VERSION..." << endl;
11:
12:     #ifdef DemoVersion
13:         cout << "DemoVersion defined." << endl;
14:     #else
15:         cout << "DemoVersion not defined." << endl;
16:     #endif
17:
18:     #ifndef SW_VERSION
19:         cout << "SW_VERSION not defined!" << endl;
20:     #else
21:         cout << "SW_VERSION defined as: "
22:                 << SW_VERSION << endl;
23:     #endif
24:
25:     #ifdef WINDOWS_VERSION
26:         cout << "WINDOWS_VERSION defined!" << endl;
27:     #else
28:         cout << "WINDOWS_VERSION was not defined." << endl;
29:     #endif
30:
31:     cout << "Done."  << endl;
32:     return 0;
33:  }
```

OUTPUT

```
Checking on the definitions of DemoVersion, NT_VERSION,_and
WINDOWS_VERSION...
DemoVersion defined.
NT_VERSION defined as: 5
WINDOWS_VERSION was not defined.
Done.
```

ANALYSIS On lines 0 and 1, DemoVersion and NT_VERSION are defined, with SW_VERSION defined with the string 5. On line 12, the definition of DemoVersion is tested, and because DemoVersion is defined (albeit with no value), the test is true and the string on line 11 is printed.

On line 18 is the test that SW_VERSION is not defined. Because SW_VERSION is defined, this test fails and execution jumps to line 21. Here the string 5 is substituted for the word SW_VERSION; this is seen by the compiler as

```
cout << "SW_VERSION defined as: " << 5 << endl;
```

Note that the first word SW_VERSION is not substituted because it is in a quoted string. The second SW_VERSION is substituted, however, and thus the compiler sees 5 as if you had typed 5 there.

Finally, on line 25, the program tests for WINDOWS_VERSION. Because you did not define WINDOWS_VERSION, the test fails and the message on line 28 is printed.

Inclusion and Inclusion Guards

You will create projects with many different files. You will probably organize your directories so that each class has its own header file (for example, .hpp) with the class declaration and its own implementation file (for example, .cpp) with the source code for the class methods.

Your main() function will be in its own .cpp file, and all the .cpp files will be compiled into .obj files, which will then be linked into a single program by the linker.

Because your programs will use methods from many classes, many header files will be included in each file. Also, header files often need to include one another. For example, the header file for a derived class's declaration must include the header file for its base class.

Imagine that the Animal class is declared in the file ANIMAL.hpp. The Dog class (which derives from Animal) must include the file ANIMAL.hpp in DOG.hpp, or Dog will not be able to derive from Animal. The Cat header also includes ANIMAL.hpp for the same reason.

21

If you create a program that uses both a `Cat` and a `Dog`, you will be in danger of including `ANIMAL.hpp` twice. This generates a compile-time error because it is not legal to declare a class (`Animal`) twice, even though the declarations are identical.

You can solve this problem with inclusion guards. At the top of your `ANIMAL` header file, you write these lines:

```
#ifndef ANIMAL_HPP
#define ANIMAL_HPP
...                             // the whole file goes here
#endif
```

This says, if you haven't defined the term `ANIMAL_HPP`, go ahead and define it now. Between the `#define` statement and the closing `#endif` are the entire contents of the file.

The first time your program includes this file, it reads the first line and the test evaluates to true; that is, you have not yet defined `ANIMAL_HPP`. So, it defines it and then includes the entire file.

The second time your program includes the `ANIMAL.hpp` file, it reads the first line and the test evaluates to false because you have already included `ANIMAL.hpp`. The preprocessor, therefore, doesn't process any lines until it reaches the next `#else` (in this case, there isn't one) or the next `#endif` (at the end of the file). Thus, it skips the entire contents of the file, and the class is not declared twice.

The actual name of the defined symbol (`ANIMAL_HPP`) is not important, although it is customary to use the filename in all uppercase with the dot (`.`) changed to an underscore. This is purely convention; however, because you won't be able to give two files the same name, this convention works.

> **NOTE**   It never hurts to use inclusion guards. Often, they will save you hours of debugging time.

Macro Functions

The `#define` directive can also be used to create macro functions. A macro function is a symbol created using `#define` that takes an argument, much like a function does. The preprocessor substitutes the substitution string for whatever argument it is given. For example, you can define the macro `TWICE` as

```
#define TWICE(x) ( (x) * 2 )
```

and then in your code you write

```
TWICE(4)
```

The entire string TWICE(4) is removed, and the value ((4) * 2) is substituted. When the precompiler sees the 4, it substitutes ((4) * 2), which then evaluates to 4 * 2, or 8.

A macro can have more than one parameter, and each parameter can be used repeatedly in the replacement text. Two common macros are MAX and MIN:

```
#define MAX(x,y) ( (x) > (y) ? (x) : (y) )
#define MIN(x,y) ( (x) < (y) ? (x) : (y) )
```

Note that in a macro function definition, the opening parenthesis for the parameter list must immediately follow the macro name, with no spaces. The preprocessor is not as forgiving of whitespace as is the compiler. If there is a space, a standard substitution is used like you saw earlier in today's lesson.

For example, if you write:

```
#define MAX (x,y) ( (x) > (y) ? (x) : (y) )
```

and then try to use MAX like this:

```
int x = 5, y = 7, z;
z = MAX(x,y);
```

the intermediate code is

```
int x = 5, y = 7, z;
z = (x,y) ( (x) > (y) ? (x) : (y) )(x,y)
```

A simple text substitution is done, rather than invoking the macro function. Thus, the token MAX has substituted for it (x,y) ((x) > (y) ? (x) : (y)), and then that is followed by the (x,y), which follows MAX.

By removing the space between MAX and (x,y), however, the intermediate code becomes:

```
int x = 5, y = 7, z;
a = ( (5) > (7) ? (5) : (7) );
```

This, of course, then evaluates to 7.

Why All the Parentheses?

You might be wondering why so many parentheses are in many of the macros presented so far. The preprocessor does not demand that parentheses be placed around the arguments in the substitution string, but the parentheses help you to avoid unwanted side effects when you pass complicated values to a macro. For example, if you define MAX as

```
#define MAX(x,y) x > y ? x : y
```

21

and pass in the values 5 and 7, the macro works as intended. But, if you pass in a more complicated expression, you receive unintended results, as shown in Listing 21.2.

LISTING 21.2 Using Parentheses in Macros

```
0:  // Listing 21.2 Macro Expansion
1:  #include <iostream>
2:  using namespace std;
3:
4:  #define CUBE(a) ( (a) * (a) * (a) )
5:  #define THREE(a) a * a * a
6:
7:  int main()
8:  {
9:     long x = 5;
10:    long y = CUBE(x);
11:    long z = THREE(x);
12:
13:    cout << "y: " << y << endl;
14:    cout << "z: " << z << endl;
15:
16:    long a = 5, b = 7;
17:    y = CUBE(a+b);
18:    z = THREE(a+b);
19:
20:    cout << "y: " << y << endl;
21:    cout << "z: " << z << endl;
22:    return 0;
23: }
```

OUTPUT
```
y: 125
z: 125
y: 1728
z: 82
```

ANALYSIS On line 4, the macro CUBE is defined, with the argument x put into parentheses each time it is used. On line 5, the macro THREE is defined, without using parentheses.

In the first use of these macros on lines 10 and 11, the value 5 is given as the parameter, and both macros work fine. CUBE(5) expands to ((5) * (5) * (5)), which evaluates to 125, and THREE(5) expands to 5 * 5 * 5, which also evaluates to 125.

In the second use, on lines 16 to 18, the parameter is 5 + 7. In this case, CUBE(5+7) evaluates to

((5+7) * (5+7) * (5+7))

which evaluates to

```
( (12) * (12) * (12) )
```

which, in turn, evaluates to 1728. THREE(5+7), however, evaluates to

```
5 + 7 * 5 + 7 * 5 + 7
```

Because multiplication has a higher precedence than addition, this becomes

```
5 + (7 * 5) + (7 * 5) + 7
```

which evaluates to

```
5 + (35) + (35) + 7
```

which finally evaluates to 82. As you can see, without the parenthesis, an error occurs—three of 5+7 is really 36!

String Manipulation

The preprocessor provides two special operators for manipulating strings in macros. The stringizing operator (#) substitutes a quoted string for whatever follows the stringizing operator. The concatenation operator bonds two strings into one.

Stringizing

The stringizing operator puts quotes around any characters following the operator, up to the next whitespace. Thus, if you write

```
#define WRITESTRING(x) cout << #x
```

and then call

```
WRITESTRING(This is a string);
```

the precompiler turns it into

```
cout << "This is a string";
```

Note that the string This is a string is put into quotes, as required by cout.

Concatenation

The concatenation operator allows you to bond more than one term into a new word. The new word is actually a token that can be used as a class name, a variable name, an offset into an array, or anywhere else a series of letters might appear.

21

Assume for a moment that you have five functions named fOnePrint, fTwoPrint, fThreePrint, fFourPrint, and fFivePrint. You can then declare

```
#define fPRINT(x) f ## x ## Print
```

and then use it with fPRINT(Two) to generate fTwoPrint and with fPRINT(Three) to generate fThreePrint.

At the conclusion of Week 2, a PartsList class was developed. This list could only handle objects of type List. Suppose that this list works well, and you want to be able to make lists of animals, cars, computers, and so forth.

One approach is to create AnimalList, CarList, ComputerList, and so on, cutting and pasting the code in place. This quickly becomes a nightmare because every change to one list must be written to all the others.

An alternative is to use macros and the concatenation operator. For example, you could define

```
#define Listof(Type)  class Type##List \
{ \
public: \
Type##List(){} \
private:          \
int itsLength; \
};
```

This example is overly sparse, but the idea is to put in all the necessary methods and data. When you are ready to create an AnimalList, you write

```
Listof(Animal)
```

and this is turned into the declaration of the AnimalList class. Some problems occur with this approach, all of which were discussed in detail on Day 19, "Templates."

Predefined Macros

Many compilers predefine a number of useful macros, including __DATE__, __TIME__, __LINE__, and __FILE__. Each of these names is surrounded by two underscore characters to reduce the likelihood that the names will conflict with names you've used in your program.

When the precompiler sees one of these macros, it makes the appropriate substitutes. For __DATE__, the current date is substituted. For __TIME__, the current time is substituted. __LINE__ and __FILE__ are replaced with the source code line number and filename, respectively. You should note that this substitution is made when the source is precompiled, not when the program is run. If you ask the program to print __DATE__, you do not get the current date; instead, you receive the date the program was compiled. These defined macros are very useful in debugging, as mentioned on Day 20, "Handling Errors and Exceptions," during the discussion of exceptions.

The assert() Macro

Many compilers offer an assert() macro. The assert() macro returns true if its parameter evaluates to true and takes some kind of action if it evaluates false. Many compilers abort the program on an assert() that fails; others throw an exception (see Day 20).

The assert() macro is used for debugging your program before you release it. In fact, if DEBUG is not defined, the preprocessor collapses the assert() so that no code from it is included in the generated source for the compiler. This is a great help during development, and when the final product ships, there is no performance penalty or increase in the size of the executable version of the program.

Rather than depending on the compiler-provided assert(), you are free to write your own assert() macro. Listing 21.3 provides a simple custom assert() macro and shows its use.

LISTING 21.3   A Simple assert() Macro

```
0:  // Listing 21.3 ASSERTS
1:  #define DEBUG
2:  #include <iostream>
3:  using namespace std;
4:
5:  #ifndef DEBUG
6:      #define ASSERT(x)
7:  #else
8:      #define ASSERT(x) \
9:          if (! (x)) \
10:         { \
11:             cout << "ERROR!! Assert " << #x << " failed << endl; \
12:             cout << " on line " << __LINE__  << endl; \
13:             cout << " in file " << __FILE__ << endl;  \
14:         }
15: #endif
16:
17: int main()
18: {
19:     int x = 5;
20:     cout << "First assert: " << endl;
21:     ASSERT(x==5);
```

21

LISTING 21.3 continued

```
22:      cout << "\nSecond assert: " << endl;
23:      ASSERT(x != 5);
24:      cout << "\nDone. << endl";
25:      return 0;
26:  }
```

OUTPUT

First assert:

Second assert:
ERROR!! Assert x !=5 failed
 on line 24
 in file List2104.cpp

Done.

ANALYSIS On line 1, the term DEBUG is defined. Typically, this is done from the command line (or the IDE) at compile time, so you can turn this on and off at will. On lines 8–14, the ASSERT() macro is defined. Typically, this is done in a header file, and that header (assert.hpp) is included in all your implementation files.

On line 5, the term DEBUG is tested. If it is not defined, ASSERT() is defined to create no code at all. If DEBUG is defined, the functionality defined on lines 8–14 is applied.

The ASSERT() itself is one long statement split across seven source code lines as far as the precompiler is concerned. On line 9, the value passed in as a parameter is tested; if it evaluates false, the statements on lines 11–13 are invoked, printing an error message. If the value passed in evaluates true, no action is taken.

Debugging with assert()

When writing your program, you will often know deep down in your soul that something is true: A function has a certain value, a pointer is valid, and so forth. It is the nature of bugs that what you know to be true might not be so under some conditions. For example, you know that a pointer is valid, yet the program crashes. assert() can help you find this type of bug, but only if you make it a regular practice to use assert() liberally in your code. Every time you assign or are passed a pointer as a parameter or function return value, be certain to assert that the pointer is valid. Any time your code depends on a particular value being in a variable, assert() that that is true.

No penalty is assessed for frequent use of assert(); it is removed from the code when you undefine debugging. It also provides good internal documentation, reminding the reader of what you believe is true at any given moment in the flow of the code.

Using `assert()` Versus Exceptions

Yesterday, you saw how to work with exceptions to handle error conditions. It is important to note that `assert()` is not intended to handle runtime error conditions such as bad data, out-of-memory conditions, unable to open file, and so forth. `assert()` is created to catch programming errors only. That is, if an `assert()` "fires," you know you have a bug in your code.

This is critical because when you ship your code to your customers, instances of `assert()` are removed. You can't depend on an `assert()` to handle a runtime problem because the `assert()` won't be there.

It is a common mistake to use `assert()` to test the return value from a memory assignment:

```
Animal *pCat = new Cat;
Assert(pCat);    // bad use of assert
pCat->SomeFunction();
```

This is a classic programming error; every time the programmer runs the program, enough memory is available and the `assert()` never fires. After all, the programmer is running with lots of extra RAM to speed up the compiler, debugger, and so forth. The programmer then ships the executable, and the poor user, who has less memory, reaches this part of the program and the call to new fails and returns NULL. The `assert()`, however, is no longer in the code and nothing indicates that the pointer points to NULL. As soon as the statement `pCat->SomeFunction()` is reached, the program crashes.

Getting NULL back from a memory assignment is not a programming error, although it is an exceptional situation. Your program must be able to recover from this condition, if only by throwing an exception. Remember: The entire `assert()` statement is gone when DEBUG is undefined. Exceptions are covered in detail on Day 20.

Side Effects

It is not uncommon to find that a bug appears only after the instances of `assert()` are removed. This is almost always due to the program unintentionally depending on side effects of things done in `assert()` and other debug-only code. For example, if you write

```
ASSERT (x = 5)
```

when you mean to test whether x == 5, you create a particularly nasty bug.

Suppose that just prior to this `assert()`, you called a function that set x equal to 0. With this `assert()`, you think you are testing whether x is equal to 5; in fact, you are setting x equal to 5. The test returns true because x = 5 not only sets x to 5, but returns the value 5, and because 5 is nonzero, it evaluates as true.

21

When you pass the assert() statement, x really is equal to 5 (you just set it!). Your program runs just fine. You're ready to ship it, so you turn off debugging. Now, the assert() disappears, and you are no longer setting x to 5. Because x was set to 0 just before this, it remains at 0 and your program breaks.

In frustration, you turn debugging back on, but hey! Presto! The bug is gone. Again, this is rather funny to watch, but not to live through, so be very careful about side effects in debugging code. If you see a bug that only appears when debugging is turned off, take a look at your debugging code with an eye out for nasty side effects.

Class Invariants

Most classes have some conditions that should always be true whenever you are finished with a class member function. These class invariants are the sine qua non of your class. For example, it might be true that your CIRCLE object should never have a radius of zero or that your ANIMAL should always have an age greater than zero and less than 100.

It can be very helpful to declare an Invariants() method that returns true only if each of these conditions is still true. You can then ASSERT(Invariants()) at the start and at the completion of every class method. The exception would be that your Invariants() would not expect to return true before your constructor runs or after your destructor ends. Listing 21.4 demonstrates the use of the Invariants() method in a trivial class.

LISTING 21.4   Using Invariants()

```
0:  #define DEBUG
1:  #define SHOW_INVARIANTS
2:  #include <iostream>
3:  #include <string.h>
4:  using namespace std;
5:
6:  #ifndef DEBUG
7:      #define ASSERT(x)
8:  #else
9:      #define ASSERT(x) \
10:             if (! (x)) \
11:             { \
12:                 cout << "ERROR!! Assert " << #x << " failed" << endl; \
13:                 cout << " on line " << __LINE__ << endl; \
14:                 cout << " in file " << __FILE__ << endl; \
15:             }
16:  #endif
17:
18:
19:  const int FALSE = 0;
20:  const int TRUE = 1;
```

LISTING 21.4   continued

```
21:    typedef int BOOL;
22:
23:
24:    class String
25:    {
26:      public:
27:         // constructors
28:         String();
29:         String(const char *const);
30:         String(const String &);
31:         ~String();
32:
33:         char & operator[](int offset);
34:         char operator[](int offset) const;
35:
36:         String & operator= (const String &);
37:         int GetLen()const { return itsLen; }
38:         const char * GetString() const { return itsString; }
39:         BOOL Invariants() const;
40:
41:      private:
42:         String (int);          // private constructor
43:         char * itsString;
44:         // unsigned short itsLen;
45:         int itsLen;
46:    };
47:
48:    // default constructor creates string of 0 bytes
49:    String::String()
50:    {
51:         itsString = new char[1];
52:         itsString[0] = '\0';
53:         itsLen=0;
54:         ASSERT(Invariants());
55:    }
56:
57:    // private (helper) constructor, used only by
58:    // class methods for creating a new string of
59:    // required size.  Null filled.
60:    String::String(int len)
61:    {
62:         itsString = new char[len+1];
63:         for (int i = 0; i <= len; i++)
64:             itsString[i] = '\0';
65:         itsLen=len;
66:         ASSERT(Invariants());
67:    }
68:
```

21

LISTING 21.4 continued

```
69:  // Converts a character array to a String
70:  String::String(const char * const cString)
71:  {
72:     itsLen = strlen(cString);
73:     itsString = new char[itsLen+1];
74:     for (int i = 0; i < itsLen; i++)
75:        itsString[i] = cString[i];
76:     itsString[itsLen]='\0';
77:     ASSERT(Invariants());
78:  }
79:
80:  // copy constructor
81:  String::String (const String & rhs)
82:  {
83:     itsLen=rhs.GetLen();
84:     itsString = new char[itsLen+1];
85:     for (int i = 0; i < itsLen;i++)
86:        itsString[i] = rhs[i];
87:     itsString[itsLen] = '\0';
88:     ASSERT(Invariants());
89:  }
90:
91:  // destructor, frees allocated memory
92:  String::~String ()
93:  {
94:     ASSERT(Invariants());
95:     delete [] itsString;
96:     itsLen = 0;
97:  }
98:
99:  // operator equals, frees existing memory
100: // then copies string and size
101: String& String::operator=(const String & rhs)
102: {
103:    ASSERT(Invariants());
104:    if (this == &rhs)
105:       return *this;
106:    delete [] itsString;
107:    itsLen=rhs.GetLen();
108:    itsString = new char[itsLen+1];
109:    for (int i = 0; i < itsLen;i++)
110:       itsString[i] = rhs[i];
111:    itsString[itsLen] = '\0';
112:    ASSERT(Invariants());
113:    return *this;
114: }
115:
116: //non constant offset operator
```

LISTING 21.4 continued

```
117:  char & String::operator[](int offset)
118:  {
119:     ASSERT(Invariants());
120:     if (offset > itsLen)
121:     {
122:        ASSERT(Invariants());
123:        return itsString[itsLen-1];
124:     }
125:     else
126:     {
127:        ASSERT(Invariants());
128:        return itsString[offset];
129:     }
130:  }
131:
132:  // constant offset operator
133:  char String::operator[](int offset) const
134:  {
135:     ASSERT(Invariants());
136:     char retVal;
137:     if (offset > itsLen)
138:        retVal = itsString[itsLen-1];
139:     else
140:        retVal = itsString[offset];
141:     ASSERT(Invariants());
142:     return retVal;
143:  }
144:
145:  BOOL String::Invariants() const
146:  {
147:     #ifdef SHOW_INVARIANTS
148:        cout << "String Tested OK ";
149:     #endif
150:     return ( (itsLen && itsString) || (!itsLen && !itsString) );
151:  }
152:
153:  class Animal
154:  {
155:    public:
156:      Animal():itsAge(1),itsName("John Q. Animal")
157:         {ASSERT(Invariants());}
158:      Animal(int, const String&);
159:      ~Animal(){}
160:      int GetAge() {  ASSERT(Invariants()); return itsAge;}
161:      void SetAge(int Age)
162:      {
163:         ASSERT(Invariants());
164:         itsAge = Age;
```

21

LISTING 21.4   continued

```
165:         ASSERT(Invariants());
166:       }
167:       String& GetName()
168:       {
169:         ASSERT(Invariants());
170:         return itsName;
171:       }
172:       void SetName(const String& name)
173:       {
174:         ASSERT(Invariants());
175:         itsName = name;
176:         ASSERT(Invariants());
177:       }
178:       BOOL Invariants();
179:     private:
180:       int itsAge;
181:       String itsName;
182: };
183:
184: Animal::Animal(int age, const String& name):
185:     itsAge(age),
186:     itsName(name)
187: {
188:     ASSERT(Invariants());
189: }
190:
191: BOOL Animal::Invariants()
192: {
193:     #ifdef SHOW_INVARIANTS
194:        cout << "Animal Tested OK";
195:     #endif
196:        return (itsAge > 0 && itsName.GetLen());
197: }
198:
199: int main()
200: {
201:     Animal sparky(5,"Sparky");
202:     cout << endl << sparky.GetName().GetString() << " is ";
203:     cout << sparky.GetAge() << " years old.";
204:     sparky.SetAge(8);
205:     cout << endl << sparky.GetName().GetString() << " is ";
206:     cout << sparky.GetAge() << " years old.";
207:     return 0;
208: }
```

OUTPUT

```
String Tested OK String Tested OK String Tested OK String Tested OK
String Tested OK String Tested OK String Tested OK String Tested OK
String Tested OK StringTested OK String Tested OK String Tested OK
String Tested OK String Tested OK Animal Tested OK String Tested OK
Animal Tested OK
Sparky is Animal Tested OK 5 years old.Animal Tested OK Animal Tested OK
Animal
Tested OK
Sparky is Animal Tested OK 8 years old.String Tested OK
```

ANALYSIS On lines 9–15, the ASSERT() macro is defined. If DEBUG is defined, this writes out an error message when the ASSERT() macro evaluates false.

On line 39, the String class member function Invariants() is declared; it is defined on lines 143–150. The constructor is declared on lines 49–55; on line 54, after the object is fully constructed, Invariants() is called to confirm proper construction.

This pattern is repeated for the other constructors, and the destructor calls Invariants() only before it sets out to destroy the object. The remaining class functions call Invariants() before taking any action and then again before returning. This both affirms and validates a fundamental principle of C++: Member functions other than constructors and destructors should work on valid objects and should leave them in a valid state.

On line 176, class Animal declares its own Invariants() method, implemented on lines 189–195. Note on lines 155, 158, 161, and 163 that inline functions can call the Invariants() method.

Printing Interim Values

In addition to asserting that something is true using the ASSERT() macro, you might want to print the current value of pointers, variables, and strings. This can be very helpful in checking your assumptions about the progress of your program and in locating off-by-one bugs in loops. Listing 21.5 illustrates this idea.

LISTING 21.5 Printing Values in DEBUG Mode

```
0:  // Listing 21.5 - Printing values in DEBUG mode
1:  #include <iostream>
2:  using namespace std;
3:  #define DEBUG
4:
5:  #ifndef DEBUG
6:     #define PRINT(x)
```

21

LISTING 21.5 continued

```
 7:  #else
 8:    #define PRINT(x) \
 9:        cout << #x << ":\t" << x << endl;
10:  #endif
11:
12:  enum BOOL { FALSE, TRUE } ;
13:
14:  int main()
15:  {
16:     int x = 5;
17:     long y = 738981;
18:     PRINT(x);
19:     for (int i = 0; i < x; i++)
20:     {
21:        PRINT(i);
22:     }
23:
24:     PRINT (y);
25:     PRINT("Hi.");
26:     int *px = &x;
27:     PRINT(px);
28:     PRINT (*px);
29:     return 0;
30:  }
```

OUTPUT

```
x:      5
i:      0
i:      1
i:      2
i:      3
i:      4
y:      73898
"Hi.":  Hi.
px:         0012FEDC
*px:    5
```

ANALYSIS The PRINT() macro on lines 6 and 8–9 provides printing of the current value of the supplied parameter. Note that the first thing fed to cout on line 9 is the stringized version of the parameter; that is, if you pass in x, cout receives "x".

Next, cout receives the quoted string ":\t", which prints a colon and then a tab. Third, cout receives the value of the parameter (x), and then finally, endl, which writes a new line and flushes the buffer.

Note that you might receive a value other than 0012FEDC.

Macros Versus Functions and Templates

Macros suffer from four problems in C++. The first is that they can be confusing if they get large because all macros must be defined on one line. You can extend that line by using the backslash character (\), but large macros quickly become difficult to manage.

The second problem is that macros are expanded inline each time they are used. This means that if a macro is used a dozen times, the substitution appears a dozen times in your program, rather than appearing once as a function call does. On the other hand, they are usually quicker than a function call because the overhead of a function call is avoided.

The fact that they are expanded inline leads to the third problem, which is that the macro does not appear in the intermediate source code used by the compiler; therefore, it is unavailable in most debuggers. This makes debugging macros tricky.

The final problem, however, is the biggest: Macros are not type-safe. Although it is convenient that absolutely any argument can be used with a macro, this completely undermines the strong typing of C++ and so is an anathema to C++ programmers. Of course, the right way to solve this is with templates, as you saw on Day 19.

Inline Functions

It is often possible to declare an inline function rather than a macro. For example, Listing 21.6 creates an inline Cube() function, which accomplishes the same thing as the CUBE macro in Listing 21.2, but it does so in a type-safe way.

LISTING 21.6   Using Inline Rather than a Macro

```
0:  #include <iostream>
1:  using namespace std;
2:
3:  inline unsigned long Square(unsigned long a) { return a * a; }
4:  inline unsigned long Cube(unsigned long a)
5:      { return a * a * a; }
6:  int main()
7:  {
8:      unsigned long x=1 ;
9:      for (;;)
10:     {
11:         cout << "Enter a number (0 to quit): ";
12:         cin >> x;
13:         if (x == 0)
14:             break;
15:         cout << "You entered: " << x;
```

21

LISTING 21.6   continued

```
16:          cout << ".  Square(" << x << "): ";
17:          cout  << Square(x);
18:          cout<< ". Cube(" << x << "): ";
19:          cout << Cube(x) << "." << endl;
20:     }
21:     return 0;
22: }
```

OUTPUT

```
Enter a number (0 to quit): 1
You entered: 1.  Square(1): 1. Cube(1): 1.
Enter a number (0 to quit): 2
You entered: 2.  Square(2): 4. Cube(2): 8.
Enter a number (0 to quit): 3
You entered: 3.  Square(3): 9. Cube(3): 27.
Enter a number (0 to quit): 4
You entered: 4.  Square(4): 16. Cube(4): 64.
Enter a number (0 to quit): 5
You entered: 5.  Square(5): 25. Cube(5): 125.
Enter a number (0 to quit): 6
You entered: 6.  Square(6): 36. Cube(6): 216.
```

ANALYSIS   On lines 3 and 4, two inline functions are defined: Square() and Cube(). Each is declared to be inline, so like a macro function, these are expanded in place for each call, and no function call overhead occurs.

As a reminder, expanded inline means that the content of the function is placed into the code wherever the function call is made (for example, on line 17). Because the function call is never made, there is no overhead of putting the return address and the parameters on the stack.

On line 17, the function Square is called, as is the function Cube on line 19. Again, because these are inline functions, it is exactly as if this line had been written like this:

```
16:          cout << ".  Square(" << x << "): "  ;
17:          cout << x * x ;
18:          cout << ". Cube(" << x << "): "  ;
19:          cout << x * x * x << "." << endl;
```

Do	**Don't**
DO use CAPITALS for your macro names. This is a pervasive convention, and other programmers will be confused if you don't. **DO** surround all arguments with parentheses in macro functions.	**DON'T** allow your macros to have side effects. Don't increment variables or assign values from within a macro. **DON'T** use #define values when a constant variable will work.

Bit Twiddling

Often, you will want to set flags in your objects to keep track of the state of your object. (Is it in AlarmState? Has this been initialized yet? Are you coming or going?)

You can do this with user-defined Booleans, but some applications—particularly those with low-level drivers and hardware devices—require you to be able to use the individual bits of a variable as flags.

Each byte has eight bits, so in a four-byte long you can hold 32 separate flags. A bit is said to be "set" if its value is 1 and clear if its value is 0. When you set a bit, you make its value 1, and when you clear it, you make its value 0. (Set and clear are both adjectives and verbs.) You can set and clear bits by changing the value of the long, but that can be tedious and confusing.

> **NOTE**
>
> Appendix A, "Working with Numbers: Binary and Hexadecimal," provides valuable additional information about binary and hexadecimal manipulation.

C++ provides bitwise operators that act upon the individual bits of a variable. These look like, but are different from, the logical operators, so many novice programmers confuse them. The bitwise operators are presented in Table 21.1.

TABLE 21.1   The Bitwise Operators

Symbol	Operator
&	AND
|	OR
^	exclusive OR
~	complement

Operator AND

The AND operator (&) is a single ampersand, in contrast to the logical AND, which is two ampersands. When you AND two bits, the result is 1 if both bits are 1, but 0 if either or both bits are 0. The way to think of this is the following: The result is 1 if bit 1 is set and if bit 2 is set; otherwise, the result is 0.

21

Operator OR

The second bitwise operator is OR (|). Again, this is a single vertical bar, in contrast to the logical OR, which is two vertical bars. When you OR two bits, the result is 1 if either bit is set or if both are. If neither bit is set, the value is 0.

Operator Exclusive OR

The third bitwise operator is exclusive OR (^). When you exclusive OR two bits, the result is 1 if the two bits are different. The result is 0 if both bits are the same—if both bits are set or neither bit is set.

The Complement Operator

The complement operator (~) clears every bit in a number that is set and sets every bit that is clear. If the current value of the number is 1010 0011, the complement of that number is 0101 1100.

Setting Bits

When you want to set or clear a particular bit, you use masking operations. If you have a four-byte flag and you want to set bit 8 so that it is true (on), you need to OR the flag with the value 128.

Why? 128 is 1000 0000 in binary; thus, the value of the eighth bit is 128. Whatever the current value of that bit (set or clear), if you OR it with the value 128, you will set that bit and not change any of the other bits. Assume that the current value of the eight bits is 1010 0110 0010 0110. ORing 128 to it looks like this:

```
        9 8765 4321
   1010 0110 0010 0110    // bit 8 is clear
|  0000 0000 1000 0000    // 128
   _ _ _ _ _ _ _ _ _ _
   1010 0110 1010 0110    // bit 8 is set
```

You should note a few more things. First, as usual, bits are counted from right to left. Second, the value 128 is all zeros except for bit 8, the bit you want to set. Third, the starting number 1010 0110 0010 0110 is left unchanged by the OR operation, except that bit 8 was set. Had bit 8 already been set, it would have remained set, which is what you want.

Clearing Bits

If you want to clear bit 8, you can AND the bit with the complement of 128. The complement of 128 is the number you get when you take the bit pattern of 128 (1000 0000), set every bit that is clear, and clear every bit that is set (0111 1111). When you AND these numbers, the original number is unchanged, except for the eighth bit, which is forced to zero.

```
  1010 0110 1010 0110  // bit 8 is set
& 1111 1111 0111 1111  // ~128
  -------------------
  1010 0110 0010 0110  // bit 8 cleared
```

To fully understand this solution, do the math yourself. Each time both bits are 1, write 1 in the answer. If either bit is 0, write 0 in the answer. Compare the answer with the original number. It should be the same except that bit 8 was cleared.

Flipping Bits

Finally, if you want to flip bit 8, no matter what its state, you exclusive OR the number with 128. If you do this twice, you end up back with the original setting. Thus,

```
  1010 0110 1010 0110  // number
^ 0000 0000 1000 0000  // 128
  -------------------
  1010 0110 0010 0110  // bit flipped
^ 0000 0000 1000 0000  // 128
  -------------------
  1010 0110 1010 0110  // flipped back
```

Do	Don't
DO set bits by using masks and the OR operator.	**DON'T** confuse the different bit operators.
DO clear bits by using masks and the AND operator.	**DON'T** forget to consider bits to the left of the bit(s) you are flipping. One byte is eight bits; you need to know how many bytes are in the variable you are using.
DO flip bits using masks and the exclusive OR operator.	

Bit Fields

Under some circumstances, every byte counts, and saving six or eight bytes in a class can make all the difference. If your class or structure has a series of Boolean variables or variables that can have only a very small number of possible values, you might save some room using bit fields.

Using the standard C++ data types, the smallest type you can use in your class is a type char, which might be just one byte. You will usually end up using an int, which is most

21

often four bytes on a machine with a 32-bit processor. By using bit fields, you can store eight binary values in a char and 32 such values in a four-byte integer.

Here's how bit fields work: Bit fields are named and accessed the same as any class member. Their type is always declared to be unsigned int. After the bit field name, write a colon followed by a number.

The number is an instruction to the compiler as to how many bits to assign to this variable. If you write 1, the bit represents either the value 0 or 1. If you write 2, two bits are used to represent numbers; thus, the field would be able to represent 0, 1, 2, or 3, a total of four values. A three-bit field can represent eight values, and so forth. Appendix A reviews binary numbers. Listing 21.7 illustrates the use of bit fields.

LISTING 21.7 Using Bit Fields

```
0:  #include <iostream>
1:  using namespace std;
2:  #include <string.h>
3:
4:  enum STATUS { FullTime, PartTime } ;
5:  enum GRADLEVEL { UnderGrad, Grad } ;
6:  enum HOUSING { Dorm, OffCampus };
7:  enum FOODPLAN { OneMeal, AllMeals, WeekEnds, NoMeals };
8:
9:  class student
10: {
11:    public:
12:      student():
13:          myStatus(FullTime),
14:          myGradLevel(UnderGrad),
15:          myHousing(Dorm),
16:          myFoodPlan(NoMeals)
17:      {}
18:      ~student(){}
19:      STATUS GetStatus();
20:      void SetStatus(STATUS);
21:      unsigned GetPlan() { return myFoodPlan; }
22:
23:    private:
24:      unsigned myStatus : 1;
25:      unsigned myGradLevel: 1;
26:      unsigned myHousing : 1;
27:      unsigned myFoodPlan : 2;
28: };
29:
30: STATUS student::GetStatus()
31: {
32:    if (myStatus)
```

LISTING 21.7   continued

```
33:          return FullTime;
34:      else
35:          return PartTime;
36:  }
37:
38:  void student::SetStatus(STATUS theStatus)
39:  {
40:      myStatus = theStatus;
41:  }
42:
43:  int main()
44:  {
45:      student Jim;
46:
47:      if (Jim.GetStatus()== PartTime)
48:          cout << "Jim is part-time" << endl;
49:      else
50:          cout << "Jim is full-time" << endl;
51:
52:      Jim.SetStatus(PartTime);
53:
54:      if (Jim.GetStatus())
55:          cout << "Jim is part-time" << endl;
56:      else
57:          cout << "Jim is full-time" << endl;
58:
59:      cout << "Jim is on the " ;
60:
61:      char Plan[80];
62:      switch (Jim.GetPlan())
63:      {
64:        case OneMeal:  strcpy(Plan,"One meal"); break;
65:        case AllMeals: strcpy(Plan,"All meals"); break;
66:        case WeekEnds: strcpy(Plan,"Weekend meals"); break;
67:        case NoMeals:  strcpy(Plan,"No Meals");break;
68:        default :    cout << "Something bad went wrong! "<< endl;
69:                     break;
70:      }
71:      cout << Plan << " food plan." << endl;
72:      return 0;
73:  }
```

OUTPUT

```
Jim is part-time
Jim is full-time
Jim is on the No Meals food plan.
```

21

ANALYSIS   On lines 4–7, several enumerated types are defined. These serve to define the possible values for the bit fields within the student class.

student is declared on lines 9–28. Although this is a trivial class, it is interesting because all the data is packed into five bits on lines 24–27. The first bit on line 24 represents the student's status, full-time or part-time. The second bit on line 25 represents whether this is an undergraduate. The third bit on line 25 represents whether the student lives in a dorm. The final two bits represent the four possible food plans.

The class methods are written as for any other class and are in no way affected by the fact that these are bit fields and not integers or enumerated types.

The member function GetStatus() on lines 30–36 reads the Boolean bit and returns an enumerated type, but this is not necessary. It could just as easily have been written to return the value of the bit field directly. The compiler would have done the translation.

To prove that to yourself, replace the GetStatus() implementation with this code:

```
STATUS student::GetStatus()
{
    return myStatus;
}
```

No change whatsoever should occur in the functioning of the program. It is a matter of clarity when reading the code; the compiler isn't particular.

Note that the code on line 47 must check the status and then print the meaningful message. It is tempting to write this:

```
cout << "Jim is " << Jim.GetStatus() << endl;
```

that simply prints this:

```
Jim is 0
```

The compiler has no way to translate the enumerated constant PartTime into meaningful text.

On line 62, the program switches on the food plan, and for each possible value, it puts a reasonable message into the buffer, which is then printed on line 71. Note again that the switch statement could have been written as follows:

```
case  0: strcpy(Plan,"One meal"); break;
case  1: strcpy(Plan,"All meals"); break;
case  2: strcpy(Plan,"Weekend meals"); break;
case  3: strcpy(Plan,"No Meals");break;
```

The most important thing about using bit fields is that the client of the class need not worry about the data storage implementation. Because the bit fields are private, you can feel free to change them later and the interface will not need to change.

Programming Style

As stated elsewhere in this book, it is important to adopt a consistent coding style, although in many ways it doesn't matter which style you adopt. A consistent style makes it easier to guess what you meant by a particular part of the code, and you avoid having to look up whether you spelled the function with an initial cap the last time you invoked it.

The following guidelines are arbitrary; they are based on the guidelines used in projects done in the past, and they've worked well. You can just as easily make up your own, but these will get you started.

As Emerson said, "Foolish consistency is the hobgoblin of small minds," but having some consistency in your code is a good thing. Make up your own, but then treat it as if it were dispensed by the programming gods.

Indenting

If you use tabs, they should be three spaces. Be certain your editor converts each tab to three spaces.

Braces

How to align braces can be the most controversial topic between C++ programmers. Here are a few suggested tips:

- Matching braces should be aligned vertically.

- The outermost set of braces in a definition or declaration should be at the left margin. Statements within should be indented. All other sets of braces should be in line with their leading statements.

- No code should appear on the same line as a brace. For example,

```
if (condition==true)
{
   j = k;
   SomeFunction();
}
m++;
```

> **NOTE**
>
> As stated, the alignment of braces can be controversial. Many C++ programmers believe you should put the opening brace on the same line as the command it is associated with and the closing brace lines up with the command:

21

```
if (condition==true) {
    j = k;
    SomeFunction();
}
```

This format is considered harder to read because the braces don't line up.

Long Lines and Function Length

Keep lines to the width displayable on a single screen. Code that is off to the right is easily overlooked, and scrolling horizontally is annoying.

When a line is broken, indent the following lines. Try to break the line at a reasonable place, and try to leave the intervening operator at the end of the previous line (instead of at the beginning of the following line) so that it is clear that the line does not stand alone and that more is coming.

In C++, functions tend to be much shorter than they were in C, but the old, sound advice still applies. Try to keep your functions short enough to print the entire function on one page.

Structuring `switch` Statements

Indent switches as follows to conserve horizontal space:

```
switch(variable)
{
    case ValueOne:
        ActionOne();
        break;
    case ValueTwo:
        ActionTwo();
        break;
    default:
        assert("bad Action");
        break;
}
```

As you can see, the case statements are slightly indented and lined up. In addition, the statements within each case are lined up. With this layout, it is generally easy to find a case statement and easy to then follow its code.

Program Text

You can use several tips to create code that is easy to read. Code that is easy to read is generally easier to maintain.

- Use whitespace to help readability.

- Don't use spaces between object and array names and their operators (`.`, `->`, `[ ]`).

- Unary operators are associated with their operands, so don't put a space between them. Do put a space on the side away from the operand. Unary operators include `!`, `~`, `++`, `--`, `-`, `*` (for pointers), `&` (casts), and `sizeof`.

- Binary operators should have spaces on both sides: `+`, `=`, `*`, `/`, `%`, `>>`, `<<`, `<`, `>`, `==`, `!=`, `&`, `|`, `&&`, `||`, `?:`, `=`, `+=`, and so on.

- Don't use lack of spaces to indicate precedence:

   (4+ 3*2).

- Put a space after commas and semicolons, not before.

- Parentheses should not have spaces on either side.

- Keywords, such as `if`, should be set off by a space: `if (a == b)`.

- The body of a single-line comment should be set off from the `//` with a space.

- Place the pointer or reference indicator next to the type name, not the variable name:
   ```
   char* foo;
   int& theInt;
   ```
   rather than
   ```
   char *foo;
   int &theInt;
   ```

- Do not declare more than one variable on the same line.

Naming Identifiers

The following are guidelines for working with identifier names:

- Identifier names should be long enough to be descriptive.

- Avoid cryptic abbreviations.

- Take the time and energy to spell things out.

- Do not use Hungarian notation. C++ is strongly typed and there is no reason to put the type into the variable name. With user-defined types (classes), Hungarian notation quickly breaks down. The exceptions to this might be to use a prefix for pointers (p) and references (r), as well as for class member variables (its).

- Short names (i, p, x, and so on) should be used only where their brevity makes the code more readable and where the usage is so obvious that a descriptive name is not needed. In general, however, you should avoid this. Also, avoid the use of the letters i, l, and o as variable names because they are easy to confuse with numbers.

21

- The length of a variable's name should be proportional to its scope.
- Be certain identifiers look and sound different from one another to minimize confusion.
- Function (or method) names are usually verbs or verb-noun phrases: `Search()`, `Reset()`, `FindParagraph()`, `ShowCursor()`. Variable names are usually abstract nouns, possibly with an additional noun: `count`, `state`, `windSpeed`, `windowHeight`. Boolean variables should be named appropriately: `windowIconized`, `fileIsOpen`.

Spelling and Capitalization of Names

Spelling and capitalization should not be overlooked when creating your own style. Some tips for these areas include the following:

- Use all uppercase and underscore to separate the logical words of `#defined` names, such as `SOURCE_FILE_TEMPLATE`. Note, however, that these are rare in C++. Consider using constants and templates in most cases.
- All other identifiers should use mixed case—no underscores. Function names, methods, class, typedef, and struct names should begin with a capitalized letter. Elements such as data members or locals should begin with a lowercase letter.
- Enumerated constants should begin with a few lowercase letters as an abbreviation for the enum. For example,

```
enum TextStyle
{
    tsPlain,
    tsBold,
    tsItalic,
    tsUnderscore,
};
```

Comments

Comments can make it much easier to understand a program. Sometimes, you will not work on a program for several days or even months. In that time, you can forget what certain code does or why it has been included. Problems in understanding code can also occur when someone else reads your code. Comments that are applied in a consistent, well-thought-out style can be well worth the effort. Several tips to remember concerning comments include the following:

- Wherever possible, use C++ single-line `//` comments rather than the `/* */` style. Reserve the multiline style (`/* */`) for commenting out blocks of code that might include C++ single-line comments.

- Higher-level comments are infinitely more important than process details. Add value; do not merely restate the code.

```
n++; // n is incremented by one
```

This comment isn't worth the time it takes to type it in. Concentrate on the semantics of functions and blocks of code. Say what a function does. Indicate side effects, types of parameters, and return values. Describe all assumptions that are made (or not made), such as "assumes n is nonnegative" or "will return –1 if x is invalid." Within complex logic, use comments to indicate the conditions that exist at that point in the code.

- Use complete English sentences with appropriate punctuation and capitalization. The extra typing is worth it. Don't be overly cryptic and don't abbreviate. What seems exceedingly clear to you as you write code will be amazingly obtuse in a few months.

- Use blank lines freely to help the reader understand what is going on. Separate statements into logical groups.

Setting Up Access

The way you access portions of your program should also be consistent. Some tips for access include the following:

- Always use `public:`, `private:`, and `protected:` labels; don't rely on the defaults.

- List the public members first, then protected, then private. List the data members in a group after the methods.

- Put the constructor(s) first in the appropriate section, followed by the destructor. List overloaded methods with the same name adjacent to each other. Group accessor functions together whenever possible.

- Consider alphabetizing the method names within each group and alphabetizing the member variables. Be certain to alphabetize the filenames in `include` statements.

- Even though the use of the `virtual` keyword is optional when overriding, use it anyway; it helps to remind you that it is virtual, and it also keeps the declaration consistent.

Class Definitions

Try to keep the definitions of methods in the same order as the declarations. It makes things easier to find.

When defining a function, place the return type and all other modifiers on a previous line so that the class name and function name begin at the left margin. This makes it much easier to find functions.

21

`include` Files

Try as hard as you can to minimize the use of `#include`, and thus minimize the number of files being included in header files. The ideal minimum is the header file for the class from which this one derives. Other mandatory includes are those for objects that are members of the class being declared. Classes that are merely pointed to or referenced only need forward references of the form.

Don't leave out an include file in a header just because you assume that whatever `.cpp` file includes this one will also have the needed include. And don't add extra ones to try to "help out" other included files.

> **TIP**
>
> All header files should use inclusion guards.

Using `assert()`

You learned about `assert()` earlier today. Use `assert()` freely. It helps find errors, but it also greatly helps a reader by making it clear what the assumptions are. It also helps to focus the writer's thoughts around what is valid and what isn't.

Making Items Constant with `const`

Use `const` wherever appropriate: for parameters, variables, and methods. Often, there is a need for both a `const` and a non-`const` version of a method; don't use this as an excuse to leave one out. Be very careful when explicitly casting from `const` to non-`const` and vice versa (at times, this is the only way to do something), but be certain that it makes sense, and include a comment.

Next Steps in Your C++ Development

You've spent three long, hard weeks working at C++, and you are likely to have the basics needed to be a competent C++ programmer, but you are by no means finished. There is much more to learn and many more places you can get valuable information as you move from novice C++ programmer to expert.

The following sections recommend a number of specific sources of information, and these recommendations reflect only personal experience and opinions. Dozens of books and thousands of articles are available on each of these topics, however, so be certain to get other opinions before purchasing.

Where to Get Help and Advice

The very first thing you will want to do as a C++ programmer will be to tap into one or more of the C++ communities on the Internet. These groups supply immediate contact with hundreds or thousands of C++ programmers who can answer your questions, offer advice, and provide a sounding board for your ideas.

The C++ Internet newsgroups (comp.lang.c++ and comp.lang.c++.moderated) are recommended as excellent sources of information and support. There are also sites such as http://www.CodeGuru.com and http://www.CodeProject.com. These two sites have hundreds of thousands of C++ developers come to them every month. They offer resources such as articles, tutorials, news, and discussions on C++. Numerous other such communities are available as well.

Also, you might want to look for local user groups. Many cities have C++ interest groups where you can meet other programmers and exchange ideas.

Finally, compiler vendors such as Borland and Microsoft have newsgroups that can be invaluable sources of information about their development environments and the C++ language.

Related C++ Topics: Managed C++, C#, and Microsoft's .NET

Microsoft's new .NET platform is radically changing the way many of us develop for the Internet. A key component of .NET is the new language, C#, as well as a number of serious extensions to C++ called Managed Extensions.

C# is a natural extension of C++, and is an easy bridge to .NET for C++ programmers. A number of good books on C# are available, including *Programming C#* (O'Reilly Press), and of course, there is *Sams Teach Yourself the C# Language in 21 Days*, which follows a similar structure to the one used in this book.

As a programming language, C# has some differences from C++. For example, multiple inheritance is not allowed in C#; though the use of interfaces provides similar capabilities. In addition, C# avoids the use of pointers. This removes issues with dangling pointers and other such problems, at the price of making the language less capable of low-level, real-time programming. The final item worth mentioning on C# is that it uses a runtime and a garbage collector (GC). The GC takes care of freeing resources when they are needed so you, the programmer, don't have to.

Managed C++ is also from Microsoft and a part of .NET. In very simple terms, this is an extension to C++ that gives C++ the ability to use all the features of .NET, including the garbage collector and more.

21

Staying in Touch

If you have comments, suggestions, or ideas about this book or other books, I'd love to hear them. Please contact me through my Web site: www.libertyassociates.com. I look forward to hearing from you.

Do	Don't
DO look at other books. There's plenty to learn and no single book can teach you everything you need to know. **DO** join a good C++ user group.	**DON'T** just read code! The best way to learn C++ is to write C++ programs.

Summary

Today, you learned more details about working with the preprocessor. Each time you run the compiler, the preprocessor runs first and translates your preprocessor directives such as `#define` and `#ifdef`.

The preprocessor does text substitution, although with the use of macros these can be somewhat complex. By using `#ifdef`, `#else`, and `#ifndef`, you can accomplish conditional compilation, compiling in some statements under one set of conditions and in another set of statements under other conditions. This can assist in writing programs for more than one platform and is often used to conditionally include debugging information.

Macro functions provide complex text substitution based on arguments passed at compile time to the macro. It is important to put parentheses around every argument in the macro to ensure the correct substitution takes place.

Macro functions, and the preprocessor in general, are less important in C++ than they were in C. C++ provides a number of language features, such as `const` variables and templates, that offer superior alternatives to use of the preprocessor.

You also learned how to set and test individual bits and how to allocate a limited number of bits to class members.

Finally, C++ style issues were addressed, and resources were provided for further study.

Q&A

Q **If C++ offers better alternatives than the preprocessor, why is this option still available?**

A First, C++ is backward-compatible with C, and all significant parts of C must be supported in C++. Second, some uses of the preprocessor are still used frequently in C++, such as inclusion guards.

Q **Why use macro functions when I can use a regular function?**

A Macro functions are expanded inline and are used as a substitute for repeatedly typing the same commands with minor variations. Again, however, templates usually offer a better alternative.

Q **How do I know when to use a macro versus an inline function?**

A Use inline functions whenever possible. Although macros offer character substitution, stringizing, and concatenation, they are not type-safe and can make code that is more difficult to maintain.

Q **What is the alternative to using the preprocessor to print interim values during debugging?**

A The best alternative is to use `watch` statements within a debugger. For information on `watch` statements, consult your compiler or debugger documentation.

Q **How do I decide when to use an `assert()` and when to throw an exception?**

A If the situation you're testing can be true without your having committed a programming error, use an exception. If the only reason for this situation to ever be true is a bug in your program, use an `assert()`.

Q **When would I use bit structures rather than simply using integers?**

A When the size of the object is crucial. If you are working with limited memory or with communications software, you might find that the savings offered by these structures is essential to the success of your product.

Q **Can I assign a pointer to a bit field?**

A No. Memory addresses usually point to the beginning of a byte. A bit field might be in the middle of a byte.

Q **Why do style wars generate so much emotion?**

A Programmers become very attached to their habits. If you are used to the following indentation:

```
if (SomeCondition){
    // statements
}    // closing brace
```

21

it is a difficult transition to give it up. New styles look wrong and create confusion. If you get bored, try logging in to a popular online service and asking which indentation style works best, which editor is best for C++, or which product is the best word processor. Then sit back and watch as ten thousand messages are generated, all contradicting one another.

Q Is that it?

A Yes! You've learned C++, but... there is always more to learn! Ten years ago, it was possible for one person to learn all there was to know about a computer programming language, or at least to feel pretty confident about being close. Today, it is out of the question. You can't possibly catch up, and even as you try, the industry is changing. Be certain to keep reading, and stay in touch with the resources—magazines and online services—that will keep you current with the latest changes.

Workshop

The Workshop provides quiz questions to help you solidify your understanding of the material covered and exercises to provide you with experience in using what you've learned. Try to answer the quiz and exercise questions before checking the answers in Appendix D, and be certain you understand the answers before continuing to the final Week in Review.

Quiz

1. What is an inclusion guard?
2. How do you instruct your compiler to print the contents of the intermediate file showing the effects of the preprocessor?
3. What is the difference between `#define debug 0` and `#undef debug`?
4. Consider the following macro:

   `#define HALVE(x) x / 2`

   What is the result if this is called with 4?
5. What is the result if the HALVE macro in Question 5 is called with `10+10`?
6. How would you modify the HALVE macro to avoid erroneous results?
7. How many bit values could be stored in a two-byte variable?
8. How many values can be stored in five bits?
9. What is the result of 0011 1100 | 1111 1111?
10. What is the result of 0011 1100 & 1111 1111?

Exercises

1. Write the inclusion guard statements for the header file STRING.H.

2. Write an assert() macro that prints an error message and the file and line number if debug level is 2, that prints a message (without file and line number) if the level is 1, and that does nothing if the level is 0.

3. Write a macro DPrint that tests whether DEBUG is defined and, if it is, prints the value passed in as a parameter.

4. Write the declaration for creating a month, day, and year variable all stored within a single unsigned int variable.

21

WEEK 3

In Review

The following program (as shown in Listing R3.1) brings together many of the advanced techniques you've learned during the past three weeks of hard work. Week 3 in Review provides a template-based linked list with exception handling. Examine it in detail; if you understand it fully, you are a C++ programmer.

CAUTION	If your compiler does not support templates, or if your compiler does not support try and catch, you will not be able to compile or run this listing.

LISTING R3.1   Week 3 in Review Listing

```
0:  // **************************************************
1:  //
2:  // Title:      Week 3 in Review
3:  //
4:  // File:       Week3
5:  //
6:  // Description:  Provide a template-based linked list
7:  //                demonstration program with exception handling
8:  //
9:  // Classes:    PART - holds part numbers and potentially other
10: //                information about parts. This will be the
11: //                example class for the list to hold.
12: //                Note use of operator<< to print the
13: //                information about a part based on its
14: //                runtime type.
15: //
16: //               Node - acts as a node in a List
17: //
18: //               List - template-based list that provides the
19: //                mechanisms for a linked list
20: //
21: //
22: // Author:     Jesse Liberty (jl)
23: //
24: // Developed:  Pentium 200 Pro. 128MB RAM MVC 5.0
25: //
26: // Target:     Platform independent
27: //
28: // Rev History: 9/94 - First release (jl)
29: //               4/97 - Updated (jl)
30: //               9/04 – Updated (blj)
31: // **************************************************
```

DAY 21

```
32: #include <iostream>
```

DAY 18

```
33: using namespace std;
34:
35: // exception classes
```

DAY 20

```
36: class Exception {};
37: class OutOfMemory :   public Exception{};
38: class NullNode :    public Exception{};
39: class EmptyList :    public Exception {};
40: class BoundsError :   public Exception {};
41:
42:
```

LISTING R3.1 continued

```
43:  // **************** Part ************
44:  // Abstract base class of parts
45:  class Part
46:  {
47:    public:
48:      Part():itsObjectNumber(1) {}
49:      Part(int ObjectNumber):itsObjectNumber(ObjectNumber){}
50:      virtual ~Part(){};
51:      int GetObjectNumber() const { return itsObjectNumber; }
52:      virtual void Display() const =0;  // must be overridden
53:
54:    private:
55:      int itsObjectNumber;
56:  };
57:
58:  // implementation of pure virtual function so that
59:  // derived classes can chain up
60:  void Part::Display() const
61:  {
62:    cout << "\nPart Number: " << itsObjectNumber << endl;
63:  }
64:
65:  // this one operator<< will be called for all part objects.
66:  // It need not be a friend as it does not access private data
67:  // It calls Display(), which uses the required polymorphism
68:  // We'd like to be able to override this based on the real type
69:  // of thePart, but C++ does not support contravariance
```

DAY 17

```
70:  ostream& operator<<( ostream& theStream,Part& thePart)
71:  {
72:    thePart.Display();  // virtual contravariance!
```

DAY 20

```
73:    return theStream;
74:  }
75:
76:  // **************** Car Part ************
77:  class CarPart : public Part
78:  {
79:    public:
80:      CarPart():itsModelYear(94){}
81:      CarPart(int year, int partNumber);
82:      int GetModelYear() const { return itsModelYear; }
83:      virtual void Display() const;
84:    private:
85:      int itsModelYear;
86:  };
87:
88:  CarPart::CarPart(int year, int partNumber):
```

LISTING R3.1   continued

```
 89:      itsModelYear(year),
 90:      Part(partNumber)
 91:  {}
 92:
 93:  void CarPart::Display() const
 94:  {
 95:    Part::Display();
 96:    cout << "Model Year: " << itsModelYear << endl;
 97:  }
 98:
 99:  // *************** AirPlane Part ***********
100:  class AirPlanePart : public Part
101:  {
102:    public:
103:      AirPlanePart():itsEngineNumber(1){};
104:      AirPlanePart(int EngineNumber, int PartNumber);
105:      virtual void Display() const;
106:      int GetEngineNumber()const { return itsEngineNumber; }
107:    private:
108:      int itsEngineNumber;
109:  };
110:
111:  AirPlanePart::AirPlanePart(int EngineNumber, int PartNumber):
112:      itsEngineNumber(EngineNumber),
113:      Part(PartNumber)
114:  {}
115:
116:  void AirPlanePart::Display() const
117:  {
118:      Part::Display();
119:      cout << "Engine No.: " << itsEngineNumber << endl;
120:  }
121:
122:  // forward declaration of class List
123:  template <class T>
124:  class List;
125:
126:  // *************** Node ***********
127:  // Generic node, can be added to a list
128:  // *********************************
129:
```

DAY 19

```
130:  template <class T>
131:  class Node
132:  {
133:    public:
```

LISTING R3.1   continued

DAY 16

```
134:     friend class List<T>;
135:     Node (T*);
136:     ~Node();
137:     void SetNext(Node * node) { itsNext = node; }
138:     Node * GetNext() const;
```

DAY 19

```
139:      T * GetObject() const;
140:   private:
141:      T* itsObject;
142:      Node * itsNext;
143:  };
144:
145:  // Node Implementations...
146:
```

DAY 19

```
147:   template <class T>
148:   Node<T>::Node(T* pOjbect):
149:      itsObject(pOjbect),
150:      itsNext(0)
151:   {}
152:
153:   template <class T>
154:   Node<T>::~Node()
155:   {
156:      delete itsObject;
157:      itsObject = 0;
158:      delete itsNext;
159:      itsNext = 0;
160:   }
161:
162:   // Returns NULL if no next Node
163:   template <class T>
164:   Node<T> * Node<T>::GetNext() const
165:   {
166:      return itsNext;
167:   }
168:
```

DAY 19

```
169:   template <class T>
170:   T * Node<T>::GetObject() const
171:   {
172:      if (itsObject)
173:         return itsObject;
174:      else
175:         throw NullNode();
```

LISTING R3.1   continued

```
176:  }
177:
178:  // ****************  List ************
179:  // Generic list template
180:  // Works with any numbered object
181:  // **********************************
182:  template <class T>
183:  class List
184:  {
185:    public:
186:      List();
187:      ~List();
188:
```

DAY 19

```
189:      T*        Find(int & position, int ObjectNumber)  const;
190:      T*        GetFirst() const;
191:      void      Insert(T *);
192:      T*        operator[](int) const;
193:      int       GetCount() const { return itsCount; }
194:    private:
```

DAY 19

```
195:      Node<T> * pHead;
196:      int       itsCount;
197:  };
198:
199:  // Implementations for Lists...
200:  template <class T>
201:  List<T>::List():
202:    pHead(0),
203:    itsCount(0)
204:  {}
205:
```

DAY 19

```
206:  template <class T>
207:  List<T>::~List()
208:  {
209:    delete pHead;
210:  }
211:
212:  template <class T>
213:  T*  List<T>::GetFirst() const
214:  {
215:    if (pHead)
216:        return pHead->itsObject;
```

```
217:    else
218:        throw EmptyList();
219: }
220:
```

DAY 19

```
221: template <class T>
222: T *  List<T>::operator[](int offSet) const
223: {
224:    Node<T>* pNode = pHead;
225:
226:    if (!pHead)
227:        throw EmptyList();
228:
229:    if (offSet > itsCount)
230:        throw BoundsError();
231:
232:    for (int i=0;i<offSet; i++)
233:        pNode = pNode->itsNext;
234:
235:    return   pNode->itsObject;
236: }
237:
238: // find a given object in list based on its unique number (id)
```

DAY 19

```
239: template <class T>
240: T*   List<T>::Find(int & position, int ObjectNumber)  const
241: {
242:    Node<T> * pNode = 0;
243:    for (pNode = pHead, position = 0;
244:         pNode!=NULL;
245:         pNode = pNode->itsNext, position++)
246:    {
247:        if (pNode->itsObject->GetObjectNumber() == ObjectNumber)
248:          break;
249:    }
250:    if (pNode == NULL)
251:        return NULL;
252:    else
253:        return pNode->itsObject;
254: }
255:
256: // insert if the number of the object is unique
```

DAY 19

```
257: template <class T>
258: void List<T>::Insert(T* pObject)
259: {
260:    Node<T> * pNode = new Node<T>(pObject);
```

```
261:    Node<T> * pCurrent = pHead;
262:    Node<T> * pNext = 0;
263:
264:    int New =  pObject->GetObjectNumber();
265:    int Next = 0;
266:    itsCount++;
267:
268:    if (!pHead)
269:    {
270:       pHead = pNode;
271:       return;
272:    }
273:
274:    // if this one is smaller than head
275:    // this one is the new head
276:    if (pHead->itsObject->GetObjectNumber() > New)
277:    {
278:       pNode->itsNext = pHead;
279:       pHead = pNode;
280:       return;
281:    }
282:
283:    for (;;)
284:    {
285:       // if there is no next, append this new one
286:       if (!pCurrent->itsNext)
287:       {
288:          pCurrent->itsNext = pNode;
289:          return;
290:       }
291:
292:       // if this goes after this one and before the next
293:       // then insert it here, otherwise get the next
294:       pNext = pCurrent->itsNext;
295:       Next = pNext->itsObject->GetObjectNumber();
296:       if (Next > New)
297:       {
298:          pCurrent->itsNext = pNode;
299:          pNode->itsNext = pNext;
300:          return;
301:       }
302:       pCurrent = pNext;
303:    }
304: }
305:
306:
307: int main()
308: {
```

LISTING R3.1   continued

DAY 19

```
309:     List<Part> theList;
310:     int choice = 99;
311:     int ObjectNumber;
312:     int value;
313:     Part * pPart;
314:     while (choice != 0)
315:     {
316:        cout << "(0)Quit (1)Car (2)Plane: ";
317:        cin >> choice;
318:
319:        if (choice != 0)
320:        {
321:
322:           cout << "New PartNumber?: ";
323:           cin >>  ObjectNumber;
324:
325:           if (choice == 1)
326:           {
327:             cout << "Model Year?: ";
328:             cin >> value;
```

DAY 20

```
329:             try
330:             {
331:               pPart = new CarPart(value,ObjectNumber);
332:             }
```

DAY 20

```
333:             catch (OutOfMemory)
334:             {
335:               cout << "Not enough memory; Exiting..." << endl;
336:               return 1;
337:             }
338:           }
339:           else
340:           {
341:             cout << "Engine Number?: ";
342:             cin >> value;
```

DAY 20

```
343:             try
344:             {
345:               pPart = new AirPlanePart(value,ObjectNumber);
346:             }
```

DAY 20

LISTING R3.1   continued

```
347:               catch (OutOfMemory)
348:               {
349:                 cout << "Not enough memory; Exiting..." << endl;
350:                 return 1;
351:               }
352:             }
```

DAY 20

```
353:           try
354:           {
355:             theList.Insert(pPart);
356:           }
```

DAY 20

```
357:           catch (NullNode)
358:           {
359:             cout << "The list is broken, and the node is null!" << endl;
360:             return 1;
361:           }
```

DAY 20

```
362:           catch (EmptyList)
363:           {
364:             cout << "The list is empty!" << endl;
365:             return 1;
366:           }
367:         }
368:     }
```

DAY 20

```
369:     try
370:     {
371:       for (int i = 0; i < theList.GetCount(); i++ )
372:         cout << *(theList[i]);
373:     }
```

DAY 20

```
374:     catch (NullNode)
375:     {
376:       cout << "The list is broken, and the node is null!" << endl;
377:       return 1;
378:     }
```

DAY 20

LISTING R3.1   continued

```
379:        catch (EmptyList)
380:        {
381:          cout << "The list is empty!" << endl;
382:          return 1;
383:        }
```

DAY 20

```
384:        catch (BoundsError)
385:        {
386:          cout << "Tried to read beyond the end of the list!" << endl;
387:          return 1;
388:        }
389:      return 0;
390:    }
```

OUTPUT

```
(0)Quit (1)Car (2)Plane: 1
New PartNumber?: 2837
Model Year? 90

 (0)Quit (1)Car (2)Plane: 2
New PartNumber?: 378
Engine Number?: 4938

 (0)Quit (1)Car (2)Plane: 1
New PartNumber?: 4499
Model Year? 94

 (0)Quit (1)Car (2)Plane: 1
New PartNumber?: 3000
Model Year? 93

 (0)Quit (1)Car (2)Plane: 0

Part Number: 378
Engine No. 4938

Part Number: 2837
Model Year: 90

Part Number: 3000
Model Year: 93

Part Number 4499
Model Year: 94
```

ANALYSIS   The Week 3 in Review listing modifies the program provided in Week 2 to add templates, ostream processing, and exception handling. The output is identical.

On lines 36–40, a number of exception classes are declared. In the somewhat primitive exception handling provided by this program, no data or methods are required of these exceptions; they serve as flags to the catch statements, which print out a very simple warning and then exit. A more robust program might pass these exceptions by reference and then extract context or other data from the exception objects in an attempt to recover from the problem.

On line 45, the abstract base class Part is declared exactly as it was in Week 2. The only interesting change here is in the nonclass member operator<<(), which is declared on lines 70–74. Note that this is neither a member of Part nor a friend of Part, it simply takes a Part reference as one of its arguments.

You might want to have operator<< take a CarPart and an AirPlanePart in the hopes that the correct operator<< would be called, based on whether a car part or an airplane part is passed. Because the program passes a pointer to a part, however, and not a pointer to a car part or an airplane part, C++ would have to call the right function based on the real type of one of the arguments to the function. This is called contravariance and is not supported in C++.

You can only achieve polymorphism in C++ in two ways: function polymorphism and virtual functions. Function polymorphism won't work here because in every case you are matching the same signature: the one taking a reference to a Part.

Virtual functions won't work here because operator<< is not a member function of Part. You can't make operator<< a member function of Part because you want to invoke

```
cout << thePart
```

and that means that the actual call would be to cout.operator<<(Part&), and cout does not have a version of operator<< that takes a Part reference!

To get around this limitation, the Week 3 program uses just one operator<<, taking a reference to a Part. This then calls Display(), which is a virtual member function, and thus the right version is called.

On lines 130–143, Node is defined as a template. It serves the same function as Node did in the Week 2 Review program, but this version of Node is not tied to a Part object. It can, in fact, be the node for any type of object.

Note that if you try to get the object from Node, and there is no object, this is considered an exception, and the exception is thrown on line 175.

On lines 182 and 183, a generic List class template is defined. This List class can hold nodes of any objects that have unique identification numbers, and it keeps them sorted in ascending order. Each of the list functions checks for exceptional circumstances and throws the appropriate exceptions as required.

On lines 307 and 308, the driver program creates a list of two types of `Part` objects and then prints out the values of the objects in the list by using the standard streams mechanism.

FAQ

In the comment above line 70, you mention that C++ does not support contravariance. What is contravariance?

Answer: Contravariance is the ability to assign a pointer to a base class to a pointer to a derived class.

If C++ did support contravariance, you could override the function based on the real type of the object at runtime. Listing R3.2 won't compile in C++, but if it supported contravariance, it would…

CAUTION   This listing will not compile!

LISTING R3.2 Contravariance

```
0:  #include <iostream>
1:  using namespace std;
2:  class Animal
3:  {
4:    public:
5:       virtual void Speak()
6:           { cout << "Animal  Speaks" << endl; }
7:  };
8:
9:  class Dog : public Animal
10: {
11:   public:
12:      void Speak() { cout << "Dog Speaks" << endl; }
13: };
14:
15:
16: class Cat : public Animal
17: {
18:   public:
19:      void Speak() { cout << "Cat Speaks" << endl; }
```

LISTING R3.2   continued

```
20:  };
21:
22:  void DoIt(Cat*);
23:  void DoIt(Dog*);
24:
25:  int main()
26:  {
27:     Animal * pA = new Dog;
28:     DoIt(pA);
29:     return 0;
30:  }
31:
32:  void DoIt(Cat * c)
33:  {
34:     cout << "They passed a cat!" << endl << endl;
35:     c->Speak();
36:  }
37:
38:  void DoIt(Dog * d)
39:  {
40:     cout << "They passed a dog!" << endl << endl;
41:     d->Speak();
42:  }
```

What you can do, of course, is to use a virtual function as shown in Listing R3.3, which partially solves the problem.

LISTING R3.3   Using Virtual Functions

```
0:  #include<iostream>
1:  using namespace std;
2:
3:  class Animal
4:  {
5:    public:
6:      virtual void Speak() { cout << "Animal Speaks" << endl; }
7:  };
8:
9:  class Dog : public Animal
10: {
11:   public:
12:      void Speak() { cout << "Dog Speaks" << endl; }
13: };
14:
15:
16:  class Cat : public Animal
```

LISTING R3.3 continued

```
17:  {
18:    public:
19:      void Speak() { cout << "Cat Speaks" << endl; }
20:  };
21:
22:  void DoIt(Animal*);
23:
24:  int main()
25:  {
26:
27:      Animal * pA = new Dog;
28:      DoIt(pA);
29:      return 0;
30:  }
31:
32:  void DoIt(Animal * c)
33:  {
34:      cout << "They passed some kind of  animal" << endl << endl;
35:      c->Speak();
36:  }
```

APPENDIX A

Working with Numbers: Binary and Hexadecimal

You learned the fundamentals of arithmetic so long ago, it is hard to imagine what it would be like without that knowledge. When you look at the number 145, you instantly see "one hundred forty-five" without much reflection.

You generally see numbers in what is called the decimal format. There are, however, other formats that can be used for numbering. When working with computers, the two systems that come up the most are binary and hexadecimal. Understanding binary and hexadecimal requires that you reexamine the number 145 and see it not as a number, but as a code for a number.

Start small: Examine the relationship between the number three and "3." The numeral "3" is a squiggle on a piece of paper; the number three is an idea. The numeral is used to represent the number.

The distinction can be made clear by realizing that three, 3, |||, III, and *** all can be used to represent the same idea of three.

In base 10 (decimal) math, you use ten symbols—the numerals 0, 1, 2, 3, 4, 5, 6, 7, 8, and 9—to represent all numbers. How is the number ten represented?

You can imagine that a strategy could have evolved of using the letter A to represent ten; or IIIIIIIII could have been used to represent that idea. The Romans used X. The Arabic system, which we use, makes use of position in conjunction with numerals to represent values. The first (rightmost) column is used for ones, and the next column (to the left) is used for tens. Thus, the number fifteen is represented as 15 (read "one, five"); that is, 1 ten and 5 ones.

Certain rules emerge, from which some generalizations can be made:

1. Base 10 uses ten digits—the digits 0–9.
2. The columns are powers of ten: 1s, 10s, 100s, and so on.
3. If the third column is 100, the largest number you can make with two columns is 99. More generally, with n columns you can represent from 0 to (10^n-1). Thus, with three columns, you can represent from 0 to (10^3-1) or 0-999.

Using Other Bases

It is not a coincidence that we use base 10; we have 10 fingers. You can imagine a different base, however. Using the rules found in base 10, you can describe base 8:

1. There are eight digits used in base 8—the digits 0–7.
2. The columns are powers of 8: 1s, 8s, 64s, and so on.
3. With n columns, you can represent 0 to 8^n-1.

To distinguish numbers written in each base, write the base as a subscript next to the number. The number fifteen in base 10 would be written as 15_{10} and read as "one, five, base ten."

Thus, to represent the number 15_{10} in base 8, you would write 17_8. This is read "one, seven, base eight." Note that it can also be read "fifteen" as that is the number it continues to represent.

Why 17? The 1 means 1 eight, and the 7 means 7 ones. One eight plus seven ones equals fifteen. Consider fifteen asterisks:

```
**********     *****
```

The natural tendency is to make two groups, a group of ten asterisks and another of five. This would be represented in decimal as 15 (1 ten and 5 ones). You can also group the asterisks as

```
********      *******
```

A

That is, eight asterisks and seven. That would be represented in base 8 as 17_8. That is, one eight and seven ones.

Converting to Different Bases

You can represent the number fifteen in base 10 as 15, in base 9 as 16_9, in base 8 as 17_8, in base 7 as 21_7. Why 21_7? In base 7, there is no numeral 8. To represent fifteen, you need two sevens and one 1.

How do you generalize the process? To convert a base 10 number to base 7, think about the columns: In base 7 they are ones, sevens, forty-nines, three-hundred forty-threes, and so on. Why these columns? They represent 7^0, 7^1, 7^2, 7^4, and so forth.

Remember, any number to the 0th power (for example, 7^0) is 1, any number to the first power (for example, 7^1) is the number itself, any number to the second power is that number times itself ($7^2 = 7*7 = 49$), and any number to the third power is that number times itself and then times itself again ($7^3 = 7*7*7 = 343$).

Create a table for yourself:

Column	4	3	2	1
Power	7^3	7^2	7^1	7^0
Value	343	49	7	1

The first row represents the column number. The second row represents the power of 7. The third row represents the decimal value of each number in that row.

To convert from a decimal value to base 7, here is the procedure: Examine the number and decide which column to use first. If the number is 200, for example, you know that column 4 (343) is 0, and you don't have to worry about it.

To find out how many 49s there are, divide 200 by 49. The answer is 4, so put 4 in column 3 and examine the remainder: 4. There are no 7s in 4, so put a zero in the 7s column. There are 4 ones in 4, so put a 4 in the 1s column. The answer is 404_7.

Column	4	3	2	1
Power	7^3	7^2	7^1	7^0
Value	343	49	7	1
200 in base 7	0	4	0	4
Decimal value	0	4*49 = 196	0	4*1 = 4

In this example, the 4 in the third column represents the decimal value 196, and the 4 in the first column represents the value 4. 196+4 = 200. Thus, $404_7 = 200_{10}$.

Try another example. Convert the number 968 to base 6:

Column	5	4	3	2	1
Power	6^4	6^3	6^2	6^1	6^0
Value	1296	216	36	6	1

Be certain you are comfortable with why these are the column values. Remember that $6^3 = 6*6*6 = 216$.

To determine the base 6 representation of 968, you start at column 5. How many 1296s are there in 968? There are none, so column 5 has 0. Dividing 968 by 216 yields 4 with a remainder of 104. Column 4 is 4. That is, column 4 represents 4*216 (864).

You must now represent the remaining value (968-864 = 104). Dividing 104 by 36 yields 2 with a remainder of 32. Column 3 is 2. Dividing 32 by 6 yields 5 with a remainder of 2. The answer therefore is 4252_6.

Column	5	4	3	2	1
Power	6^4	6^3	6^2	6^1	6^0
Value	1296	216	36	6	1
968 in base 6	0	4	2	5	2
Decimal value	0	4*216=864	2*36=72	5*6=30	2*1=2

864+72+30+2 = 968.

Binary

Base 2 is the ultimate extension of this idea. In base 2, also called binary, there are only two digits: 0 and 1. The columns are

Column	8	7	6	5	4	3	2	1
Power	2^7	2^6	2^5	2^4	2^3	2^2	2^1	2^0
Value	128	64	32	16	8	4	2	1

To convert the number 88 to base 2, you follow the same procedure: There are no 128s, so column 8 is 0.

A

There is one 64 in 88, so column 7 is 1 and 24 is the remainder. There are no 32s in 24 so column 6 is 0.

There is one 16 in 24 so column 5 is 1. The remainder is 8. There is one 8 in 8, and so column 4 is 1. There is no remainder, so the rest of the columns are 0.

Column	8	7	6	5	4	3	2	1
Power	2^7	2^6	2^5	2^4	2^3	2^2	2^1	2^0
Value	128	64	32	16	8	4	2	1
88_2	0	1	0	1	1	0	0	0
Value	0	64	0	16	8	0	0	0

To test this answer, convert it back:

```
1 * 64 =  64
0 * 32 =   0
1 * 16 =  16
1 *  8 =   8
0 *  4 =   0
0 *  2 =   0
0 *  1 =   0
          88
```

Why Base 2?

Base 2 is important in programming because it corresponds so cleanly to what a computer needs to represent. Computers do not really know anything at all about letters, numerals, instructions, or programs. At their core they are just circuitry, and at a given juncture there either is a lot of power or there is very little.

To keep the logic clean, engineers do not treat this as a relative scale (a little power, some power, more power, lots of power, tons of power), but rather as a binary scale ("enough power" or "not enough power"). Rather than saying "enough" or "not enough," they simplify it to "yes" or "no." Yes or no, or true or false, can be represented as 1 or 0. By convention, 1 means true or Yes, but that is just a convention; it could just as easily have meant false or no.

After you make this great leap of intuition, the power of binary becomes clear: With 1s and 0s, you can represent the fundamental truth of every circuit (there is power or there isn't). All a computer ever knows is, "Is you is, or is you ain't?" Is you is = 1; is you ain't = 0.

Bits, Bytes, and Nybbles

After the decision is made to represent truth and falsehood with 1s and 0s, *bi*nary dig*its* (or bits) become very important. Because early computers could send eight bits at a time, it was natural to start writing code using 8-bit numbers—called bytes.

NOTE

> Half a byte (4 bits) is called a nybble!

With eight binary digits, you can represent up to 256 different values. Why? Examine the columns: If all 8 bits are set (1), the value is 255. (128+64+32+16+8+4+2+1) If none is set (all the bits are clear or zero), the value is 0. 0–255 is 256 possible states.

What's a KB?

It turns out that 2^{10} (1,024) is roughly equal to 10^3 (1,000). This coincidence was too good to miss, so computer scientists started referring to 2^{10} bytes as 1K or 1 kilobyte, based on the scientific prefix of kilo for thousand.

Similarly, 1024*1024 (1,048,576) is close enough to one million to receive the designation 1MB or 1 megabyte, and 1,024 megabytes is called 1 gigabyte (giga implies thousand-million or billion). Finally, 1,024 gigabytes is called a *terabyte*.

Binary Numbers

Computers use patterns of 1s and 0s to encode everything they do. Machine instructions are encoded as a series of 1s and 0s and interpreted by the fundamental circuitry. Arbitrary sets of 1s and 0s can be translated back into numbers by computer scientists, but it would be a mistake to think that these numbers have intrinsic meaning.

For example, the Intel 8086 chipset interprets the bit pattern 1001 0101 as an instruction. You certainly can translate this into decimal (149), but that number per se has no meaning.

Sometimes, the numbers are instructions, sometimes they are values, and sometimes they are codes. One important standardized code set is ASCII. In ASCII, every letter and punctuation is given a seven-digit binary representation. For example, the lowercase letter "a" is represented by 0110 0001. This is not a number, although you can translate it to the number 97 in base 10 (64+32+1). It is in this sense that people say that the letter "a" is represented by 97 in ASCII; but the truth is that the binary representation of 97, 01100001, is the encoding of the letter "a," and the decimal value 97 is a human convenience.

Hexadecimal

Because binary numbers are difficult to read, a simpler way to represent the same values is sought. Translating from binary to base 10 involves a fair bit of manipulation of numbers; but it turns out that translating from base 2 to base 16 is very simple, because there is a very good shortcut.

A

To understand this, you must first understand base 16, which is known as hexadecimal. In base 16, there are sixteen numerals: 0, 1, 2, 3, 4, 5, 6, 7, 8, 9, A, B, C, D, E, and F. The last six are arbitrary; the letters A–F were chosen because they are easy to represent on a keyboard. The columns in hexadecimal are

Column	4	3	2	1
Power	16^3	16^2	16^1	16^0
Value	4096	256	16	1

To translate from hexadecimal to decimal, you can multiply. Thus, the number F8C represents:

```
F * 256 = 15 * 256 = 3840
8 * 16 =          128
C * 1 = 12 * 1 =    12
3980
```

(Remember that F in Hexadecimal is equal to 15_{10}.)

Translating the number FC to binary is best done by translating first to base 10, and then to binary:

```
F * 16 = 15 * 16 =  240
C * 1 = 12 * 1 =     12
252
```

Converting 252_{10} to binary requires the chart:

Column	9	8	7	6	5	4	3	2	1
Power	2^8	2^7	2^6	2^5	2^4	2^3	2^2	2^1	2^0
Value	256	128	64	32	16	8	4	2	1

There are no 256s.

1*128 = 128. 252-128 = 124

1*64 = 64. 124-64 = 60

1*32 = 32. 60-32 = 28

1*16 = 16. 28-16 = 12

1*8 = 8. 12-8 = 4

1*4 = 4. 4-4 = 0

0*2 = 0

0*1 = 0

124+60+28+12+4 = 252.

Thus, the answer in binary is 11111100.

Now, it turns out that if you treat this binary number as two sets of four digits (1111 1100), you can do a magical transformation.

The right set is 1100. In decimal that is 12, or in hexadecimal it is C. (1*8 + 1*4 + 0*2 + 0*1)

The left set is 1111, which in base 10 is 15, or in hex is F.

Thus, you have:

```
1111 1100
F    C
```

Putting the two hex numbers together is FC, which is the real value of 1111 1100. This shortcut always works! You can take any binary number of any length, and reduce it to sets of four, translate each set of four to hex, and put the hex numbers together to get the result in hex. Here's a much larger number:

```
1011 0001 1101 0111
```

To check this assumption, first convert this number to decimal.

You can find the value of the columns by doubling. The rightmost column is 1, the next is 2, then 4, 8, 16, and so forth.

Start with the rightmost column, which is worth 1 in decimal. You have a 1 there so that column is worth 1. The next column to the left is 2. Again, you have a 1 in that column, so add 2 and for a total of 3.

The next column to the left is worth 4 (you double for each column). Thus, you have 4+2+1 = 7.

Continue this for each column:

1×1	1
1×2	2
1×4	4
0×8	0
1×16	16
0×32	0
1×64	64
1×128	128
1×256	256
0×512	0
0×1024	0
0×2048	0
1×4096	4,096
1×8192	8,192
0×16384	0
1×32768	32,768
Total	**45,527**

Converting this to hexadecimal requires a chart with the hexadecimal values.

Column	5	4	3	2	1
Power	16^4	16^3	16^2	16^1	16^0
Value	**65536**	4096	256	16	1

The number is less than 65,536, so you can start with the fourth column. There are eleven 4096s (45,056), with a remainder of 471. There is one 256 in 471 with a remainder of 215. There are thirteen 16s (208) in 215 with a remainder of 7. Thus, the hexadecimal number is B1D7.

Checking the math:

```
B (11) * 4096 =    45,056
1 * 256 =             256
D (13) * 16 =         208
7 * 1 =                 7
Total              45,527
```

The shortcut version is to take the original binary number, 1011000111010111, and break it into groups of four: 1011 0001 1101 0111. Each of the four then is evaluated as a hexadecimal number:

```
1011 =
1 x 1 =    1
1 x 2 =    2
0 x 4 =    0
1 x 8 =    8
Total     11
Hex:       B

0001 =
1 x 1 =    1
0 x 2 =    0
0 x 4 =    0
0 x 8 =    0
Total      1
Hex:       1

1101 =
1 x 1 =    1
0 x 2 =    0
1 x 4 =    4
1 x 8 =    8
Total     13
Hex =      D

0111 =
1 x 1 =    1
1 x 2 =    2
1 x 4 =    4
0 x 8 =    0
Total      7
Hex:       7
```

Total Hex: B1D7

Hey! Presto! The shortcut conversion from binary to hexadecimal gives us the same answer as the longer version.

You will find that programmers use hexadecimal fairly frequently in advanced programming; but you'll also find that you can work quite effectively in programming for a long time without ever using any of this!

NOTE

One common place to see the use of hexadecimal is when working with color values. This is true in your C++ programs or even in other areas such as HTML.

APPENDIX B

C++ Keywords

Keywords are reserved to the compiler for use by the language. You cannot define classes, variables, or functions that have these keywords as their names.

asm	false	sizeof
auto	float	static
bool	for	static_cast
break	friend	struct
case	goto	switch
catch	if	template
char	inline	this
class	int	throw
const	long	true
const_cast	mutable	try
continue	namespace	typedef
default	new	typeid
delete	operator	typename
do	private	union
double	protected	unsigned
dynamic_cast	public	using
else	register	virtual
enum	reinterpret_cast	void
explicit	return	volatile
export	short	wchar_t
extern	signed	while

In addition, the following words are reserved:

and	compl	or_eq
and_eq	not	xor
bitand	not_eq	xor_eq
bitor	or	

APPENDIX C

Operator Precedence

It is important to understand that operators have a precedence, but it is not essential to memorize the precedence.

Precedence is the order in which a program performs the operations in a formula. If one operator has precedence over another operator, it is evaluated first.

Higher precedence operators "bind tighter" than lower precedence operators; thus, higher precedence operators are evaluated first. The lower the rank in Table C.1, the higher the precedence.

TABLE C.1 The Precedence of Operators

Rank	Name	Operator
1	Scope resolution	`::`
2	Member selection, subscripting, function calls, postfix increment and decrement	`. ->` `()` `++ --`
3	`Sizeof`, prefix increment and decrement, complement, and, not, unary minus and plus, address-of and dereference, `new`, `new[]`, `delete`, `delete[]`, casting, `sizeof()`	`++ --` `^ !` `- +` `& *` `()`
4	Member selection for pointer	`.* ->*`
5	Multiply, divide, modulo	`* / %`
6	Add, subtract	`+ -`
7	Shift (shift left, shift right)	`<< >>`
8	Inequality relational	`< <= > >=`
9	Equality, inequality	`== !=`
10	Bitwise AND	`&`
11	Bitwise exclusive OR	`^`
12	Bitwise OR	`|`
13	Logical AND	`&&`
14	Logical OR	`||`
15	Conditional	`?:`
16	Assignment operators	`= *= /= %=` `+= -= <<=` `>>=` `&= |= ^=`
17	Comma	`,`

APPENDIX D

Answers

Day 1

Quiz

1. Interpreters read through source code and translate a program, turning the programmer's "code," or program instructions, directly into actions. Compilers translate source code into an executable program that can be run at a later time.

2. Every compiler is different. Be certain to check the documentation that came with your compiler.

3. The linker's job is to tie together your compiled code with the libraries supplied by your compiler vendor and other sources. The linker lets you build your program in "pieces" and then link together the pieces into one big program.

4. Edit source code, compile, link, test (run), repeat if necessary.

Exercises

1. This program initializes two integer variables (numbers) and then prints out their sum, 12, and their product, 35.

2. See your compiler manual.

3. You must put a # symbol before the word `include` on the first line.

4. This program prints the words `Hello World` to the console, followed by a new line (carriage return).

Day 2

Quiz

1. Each time you run your compiler, the preprocessor runs first. It reads through your source code and includes the files you've asked for, and performs other housekeeping chores. The compiler is then run to convert your preprocessed source code to object code.

2. `main()` is special because it is called automatically each time your program is executed. It might not be called by any other function and it must exist in every program.

3. C++-style, single-line comments are started with two slashes (`//`) and they comment out any text until the end of the line. Multiline, or C-style, comments are identified with marker pairs (`/* */`), and everything between the matching pairs is commented out. You must be careful to ensure you have matched pairs.

4. C++-style, single-line comments can be nested within multiline, C-style comments:

```
/* This marker starts a comment. Everything including
// this single line comment,
is ignored as a comment until the end marker */
```

You can, in fact, nest slash-star style comments within double-slash, C++-style comments as long as you remember that the C++-style comments end at the end of the line.

5. Multiline, C-style comments can be longer than one line. If you want to extend C++-style, single-line comments to a second line, you must put another set of double slashes (`//`).

Exercises

1. The following is one possible answer:

```
1: #include <iostream>
2: using namespace std;
3: int main()
4: {
5:     cout << "I love C++\n";
6:     return 0;
7: }
```

2. The following program contains a `main()` function that does nothing. This is, however, a complete program that can be compiled, linked, and run. When run, it appears that nothing happens because the program does nothing!

```
int main(){}
```

3. Line 4 is missing an opening quote for the string.

4. The following is the corrected program:

```
1: #include <iostream>
2: main()
3: {
4:     std::cout << "Is there a bug here?";
5: }
```

This listing prints the following to the screen:

```
Is there a bug here?
```

5. The following is one possible solution:

```
 1:  #include <iostream>
 2:  int Add (int first, int second)
 3:  {
 4:      std::cout << "In Add(), received " << first << " and " << second
         ↩<< "\n";
 5:      return (first + second);
 6:  }
 7:
 8:  int Subtract (int first, int second)
 9:  {
10:      std::cout << "In Subtract(), received " << first << " and "
         ↩<< second << "\n";
11:      return (first - second);
12:  }
13:
14:  int main()
15:  {
16:      using std::cout;
17:      using std::cin;
18:
19:      cout << "I'm in main()!\n";
```

```
20:        int a, b, c;
21:        cout << "Enter two numbers: ";
22:        cin >> a;
23:        cin >> b;
24:
25:        cout << "\nCalling Add()\n";
26:        c=Add(a,b);
27:        cout << "\nBack in main().\n";
28:        cout << "c was set to " << c;
29:
30:        cout << "\n\nCalling Subtract()\n";
31:        c=Subtract(a,b);
32:        cout << "\nBack in main().\n";
33:        cout << "c was set to " << c;
34:
35:        cout << "\nExiting...\n\n";
36:        return 0;
37:    }
```

Day 3

Quiz

1. Integer variables are whole numbers; floating-point variables are "reals" and have a "floating" decimal point. Floating-point numbers can be represented using a mantissa and exponent.

2. The keyword `unsigned` means that the integer will hold only positive numbers. On most computers with 32-bit processors, `short` integers are two bytes and `long` integers are four. The only guarantee, however, is that a `long` integer is at least as big or bigger than a regular integer, which is at least as big as a `short` integer. Generally, a `long` integer is twice as large as a `short` integer.

3. A symbolic constant explains itself; the name of the constant tells what it is for. Also, symbolic constants can be redefined at one location in the source code, rather than the programmer having to edit the code everywhere the literal is used.

4. `const` variables are "typed," and, thus, the compiler can check for errors in how they are used. Also, they survive the preprocessor, and, thus, the name is available in the debugger. Most importantly, using `#define` to declare constants is no longer supported by the C++ standard.

5. A good variable name tells you what the variable is for; a bad variable name has no information. `myAge` and `PeopleOnTheBus` are good variable names, but `x`, `xjk`, and `prndl` are probably less useful.

6. `BLUE` = 102

7.   a. Good

b. Not legal

c. Legal, but a bad choice

d. Good

e. Legal, but a bad choice

Exercises

1. The following are appropriate answers for each:

   a. `unsigned short int`

   b. `unsigned long int` or `unsigned float`

   c. `unsigned double`

   d. `unsigned short int`

2. The following are possible answers:

   a. `myAge`

   b. `backYardArea`

   c. `StarsInGalaxy`

   d. `averageRainFall`

3. The following is a declaration for pi:

   `const float PI = 3.14159;`

4. The following declares and initializes the variable:

   `float myPi = PI;`

Day 4

Quiz

1. An expression is any statement that returns a value.

2. Yes, x = 5 + 7 is an expression with a value of 12.

3. The value of 201 / 4 is 50.

4. The value of 201 % 4 is 1.

5. Their values are myAge: 41, a: 39, b: 41.

6. The value of 8+2*3 is 14.

7. `if(x = 3)` assigns 3 to x and returns the value 3, which is interpreted as true.
   `if(x == 3)` tests whether x is equal to 3; it returns true if the value of x is equal to 3 and false if it is not.

D

8. The answers are

    a. False

    b. True

    c. True

    d. False

    e. True

Exercises

1. The following is one possible answer:

```
if (x > y)
    x = y;
else            // y > x || y == x
    y = x;
```

2. See exercise 3.

3. Entering **20**, **10**, **50** gives back a: 20, b: 30, c: 10.

   Line 14 is assigning, not testing for equality.

4. See Exercise 5.

5. Because line 6 is assigning the value of a-b to c, the value of the assignment is a (2) minus b (2), or 0. Because 0 is evaluated as false, the if fails and nothing is printed.

Day 5

Quiz

1. The function prototype declares the function; the definition defines it. The prototype ends with a semicolon; the definition need not. The declaration can include the keyword inline and default values for the parameters; the definition cannot. The declaration need not include names for the parameters; the definition must.

2. No. All parameters are identified by position, not name.

3. Declare the function to return void.

4. Any function that does not explicitly declare a return type returns int. You should always declare the return type as a matter of good programming practice.

5. A local variable is a variable passed into or declared within a block, typically a function. It is visible only within the block.

6. Scope refers to the visibility and lifetime of local and global variables. Scope is usually established by a set of braces.

7. Recursion generally refers to the ability of a function to call itself.

8. Global variables are typically used when many functions need access to the same data. Global variables are very rare in C++; after you know how to create static class variables, you will almost never create global variables.

9. Function overloading is the ability to write more than one function with the same name, distinguished by the number or type of the parameters.

Exercises

1. `unsigned long int Perimeter(unsigned short int, unsigned short int);`

2. The following is one possible answer:
```
unsigned long int Perimeter(unsigned short int length, unsigned short int
➥width)
{
   return (2*length) + (2*width);
}
```

3. The function tries to return a value even though it is declared to return `void` and, thus, cannot return a value.

4. The function would be fine, but there is a semicolon at the end of the `myFunc()` function's definition header.

5. The following is one possible answer:
```
short int Divider(unsigned short int valOne, unsigned short int valTwo)
{
    if (valTwo == 0)
        return -1;
    else
        return valOne / valTwo;
}
```

6. The following is one possible solution:
```
1:  #include <iostream>
2:  using namespace std;
3:
4:  short int Divider(
5:          unsigned short int valone,
6:          unsigned short int valtwo);
7:
8:  int main()
9:  {
10:      unsigned short int one, two;
11:      short int answer;
```

D

```
12:     cout << "Enter two numbers.\n Number one: ";
13:     cin >> one;
14:     cout << "Number two: ";
15:     cin >> two;
16:     answer = Divider(one, two);
17:     if (answer > -1)
18:         cout << "Answer: " << answer;
19:     else
20:         cout << "Error, can't divide by zero!";
21:     return 0;
22: }
23:
24: short int Divider(unsigned short int valOne, unsigned short int
    ➥valTwo)
25: {
26:     if (valTwo == 0)
27:         return -1;
28:     else
29:         return valOne / valTwo;
30: }
```

7. The following is one possible solution:

```
1:  #include <iostream>
2:  using namespace std;
3:  typedef unsigned short USHORT;
4:  typedef unsigned long ULONG;
5:
6:  ULONG GetPower(USHORT n, USHORT power);
7:
8:  int main()
9:  {
10:     USHORT number, power;
11:     ULONG answer;
12:     cout << "Enter a number: ";
13:     cin >> number;
14:     cout << "To what power? ";
15:     cin >> power;
16:     answer = GetPower(number,power);
17:     cout << number << " to the " << power << "th power is " <<
18:       answer << endl;
19:     return 0;
20: }
21:
22: ULONG GetPower(USHORT n, USHORT power)
23: {
24:     if(power == 1)
25:         return n;
26:     else
27:         return (n * GetPower(n,power-1));
28: }
```

Day 6

Quiz

1. The dot operator is the period (.). It is used to access the members of a class or structure.

2. Definitions of variables set aside memory. Declarations of classes don't set aside memory.

3. The declaration of a class is its interface; it tells clients of the class how to interact with the class. The implementation of the class is the set of member functions—usually in a related CPP file.

4. Public data members can be accessed by clients of the class. Private data members can be accessed only by member functions of the class.

5. Yes, member functions can be private. Although not shown in this chapter, a member function can be private. Only other member functions of the class will be able to use the private function.

6. Although member data can be public, it is good programming practice to make it private and to provide public accessor functions to the data.

7. Yes. Each object of a class has its own data members.

8. Declarations end with a semicolon after the closing brace; function definitions do not.

9. The header for a `Cat` function, `Meow()`, that takes no parameters and returns `void` looks like this:

```
void Cat::Meow()
```

10. The constructor is called to initialize a class. This special function has the same name as the class.

Exercises

1. The following is one possible solution:

```
class Employee
{
    int Age;
    int YearsOfService;
    int Salary;
};
```

2. The following is one possible answer. Notice that the `Get...` accessor methods were also made constant because they won't change anything in the class.

```
// Employee.hpp
class Employee
{
  public:
    int  GetAge() const;
    void SetAge(int age);
    int  GetYearsOfService() const;
    void SetYearsOfService(int years);
    int  GetSalary() const;
    void SetSalary(int salary);

  private:
    int itsAge;
    int itsYearsOfService;
    int itsSalary;
};
```

3. The following is one possible solution:

```
 1:  // Employee.cpp
 2:  #include <iostream>
 3:  #include "Employee.hpp"
 4:
 5:  int  Employee::GetAge() const
 6:  {
 7:      return itsAge;
 8:  }
 9:  void Employee::SetAge(int age)
10:  {
11:      itsAge = age;
12:  }
13:  int  Employee::GetYearsOfService() const
14:  {
15:      return itsYearsOfService;
16:  }
17:  void Employee::SetYearsOfService(int years)
18:  {
19:      itsYearsOfService = years;
20:  }
21:  int  Employee::GetSalary()const
22:  {
23:      return itsSalary;
24:  }
25:  void Employee::SetSalary(int salary)
26:  {
27:      itsSalary = salary;
28:  }
29:
30:  int main()
31:  {
32:      using namespace std;
33:
```

```
34:        Employee John;
35:        Employee Sally;
36:
37:        John.SetAge(30);
38:        John.SetYearsOfService(5);
39:        John.SetSalary(50000);
40:
41:        Sally.SetAge(32);
42:        Sally.SetYearsOfService(8);
43:        Sally.SetSalary(40000);
44:
45:        cout << "At AcmeSexist company, John and Sally have ";
46:        cout << "the same job.\n\n";
47:
48:        cout << "John is " << John.GetAge() << " years old." << endl;
49:        cout << "John has been with the firm for " ;
50:        cout << John.GetYearsOfService() << " years." << endl;
51:        cout << "John earns $" << John.GetSalary();
52:        cout << " dollars per year.\n\n";
53:
54:        cout << "Sally, on the other hand is " << Sally.GetAge();
55:        cout << " years old and has been with the company ";
56:        cout << Sally.GetYearsOfService();
57:        cout << " years. Yet Sally only makes $" << Sally.GetSalary();
58:        cout << " dollars per year! Something here is unfair.";
59:   }
```

4. The following is one possible answer:

```
float Employee::GetRoundedThousands() const
{
    return Salary / 1000;
}
```

5. The following is one possible answer:

```
class Employee
{
  public:

    Employee(int age, int years, int salary);
    int  GetAge() const;
    void SetAge(int age);
    int  GetYearsOfService() const;
    void SetYearsOfService(int years);
    int  GetSalary() const;
    void SetSalary(int salary);

  private:
    int itsAge;
    int itsYearsOfService;
    int itsSalary;
};
```

D

6. Class declarations must end with a semicolon.

7. The accessor `GetAge()` is private. Remember: All class members are private unless you say otherwise.

8. You can't access `itsStation` directly. It is private.

    You can't call `SetStation()` on the class. You can call `SetStation()` only on objects.

    You can't initialize `myOtherTV` because there is no matching constructor.

Day 7

Quiz

1. Separate the initializations with commas, such as

   ```
   for (x = 0, y = 10; x < 100; x++, y++).
   ```

2. `goto` jumps in any direction to any arbitrary line of code. This makes for source code that is difficult to understand and, therefore, difficult to maintain.

3. Yes, if the condition is false after the initialization, the body of the `for` loop will never execute. Here's an example:

   ```
   for (int x = 100; x < 100; x++)
   ```

4. The variable x is out of scope; thus, it has no valid value.

5. Yes. Any loop can be nested within any other loop.

6. Yes. Following are examples for both a `for` loop and a `while` loop:

   ```
   for(;;)
   {
       // This for loop never ends!
   }
   while(true)
   {
       // This while loop never ends!
   }
   ```

7. Your program appears to "hang" because it never quits running. This causes you to have to reboot the computer or to use advanced features of your operating system to end the task.

Exercises

1. The following is one possible answer:

   ```
   for (int i = 0; i< 10; i++)
   {
       for ( int j = 0; j< 10; j++)
   ```

```
        cout << "0";
    cout << endl;
}
```

2. The following is one possible answer:

```
for (int x = 100; x<=200; x+=2)
```

3. The following is one possible answer:

```
int x = 100;
while (x <= 200)
    x+= 2;
```

4. The following is one possible answer:

```
int x = 100;
do
{
    x+=2;
} while (x <= 200);
```

5. `counter` is never incremented and the `while` loop will never terminate.

6. There is a semicolon after the loop and the loop does nothing. The programmer might have intended this, but if `counter` was supposed to print each value, it won't. Rather, it will only print out the value of the counter after the `for` loop has completed.

7. `counter` is initialized to 100, but the test condition is that if it is less than 10, the test will fail and the body will never be executed. If line 1 were changed to `int counter = 5;`, the loop would not terminate until it had counted down past the smallest possible int. Because `int` is `signed` by default, this would not be what was intended.

8. `Case 0` probably needs a `break` statement. If not, it should be documented with a comment.

Day 8

Quiz

1. The address-of operator (&) is used to determine the address of any variable.

2. The dereference operator (*) is used to access the value at an address in a pointer.

3. A pointer is a variable that holds the address of another variable.

4. The address stored in the pointer is the address of another variable. The value stored at that address is any value stored in any variable. The indirection operator (*) returns the value stored at the address, which itself is stored in the pointer.

D

5. The indirection operator returns the value at the address stored in a pointer. The address-of operator (&) returns the memory address of the variable.

6. The `const int * ptrOne` declares that `ptrOne` is a pointer to a constant integer. The integer itself cannot be changed using this pointer.

   The `int * const ptrTwo` declares that `ptrTwo` is a constant pointer to integer. After it is initialized, this pointer cannot be reassigned.

Exercises

1. a. `int * pOne;` declares a pointer to an integer.

   b. `int vTwo;` declares an integer variable.

   c. `int * pThree = &vTwo;` declares a pointer to an integer and initializes it with the address of another variable, `vTwo`.

2. `unsigned short *pAge = &yourAge;`

3. `*pAge = 50;`

4. The following is one possible answer:

```
1:   #include <iostream>
2:
3:   int main()
4:   {
5:       int theInteger;
6:       int *pInteger = &theInteger;
7:       *pInteger = 5;
8:
9:       std::cout << "The Integer: "
10:                 << *pInteger << std::endl;
11:
12:      return 0;
13:  }
```

5. `pInt` should have been initialized. More importantly, because it was not initialized and was not assigned the address of any memory, it points to a random place in memory. Assigning a literal (9) to that random place is a dangerous bug.

6. Presumably, the programmer meant to assign 9 to the value at `pVar`, which would be an assignment to `SomeVariable`. Unfortunately, 9 was assigned to be the value of `pVar` because the indirection operator (*) was left off. This will lead to disaster if `pVar` is used to assign a value because it is pointing to whatever is at the address of 9 and not at `SomeVariable`.

Day 9

Quiz

1. A reference is an alias, and a pointer is a variable that holds an address. References cannot be null and cannot be assigned to.

2. When you need to reassign what is pointed to, or when the pointer might be null.

3. A null pointer (0).

4. This is a shorthand way of saying a reference to a constant object.

5. Passing *by* reference means not making a local copy. It can be accomplished by passing a reference or by passing a pointer.

6. All three are correct; however, you should pick one style and then use it consistently.

Exercises

1. The following is one possible answer:

```
1:  //Exercise 9.1 -
2:  #include <iostream>
3:
4:  int main()
5:  {
6:     int  varOne = 1;      // sets varOne to 1
7:     int& rVar = varOne;
8:     int* pVar = &varOne;
9:     rVar = 5;             // sets varOne to 5
10:     *pVar = 7;            // sets varOne to 7
11:
12:     // All three of the following will print 7:
13:     std::cout << "variable:  " << varOne << std::endl;
14:     std::cout << "reference: " << rVar   << std::endl;
15:     std::cout << "pointer:   " << *pVar  << std::endl;
16:
17:     return 0;
18:  }
```

2. The following is one possible answer.

```
1:  int main()
2:  {
3:     int varOne;
4:     const int * const pVar = &varOne;
5:     varOne = 6;
6:     *pVar = 7;
7:     int varTwo;
8:     pVar = &varTwo;
9:     return 0;
10:  }
```

3. You can't assign a value to a constant object, and you can't reassign a constant pointer. This means that lines 6 and 8 are problems.

4. The following is one possible answer. Note that this is a dangerous program to run because of the stray pointer.

```
1:  int main()
2:  {
3:      int * pVar;
4:      *pVar = 9;
5:      return 0;
6:  }
```

5. The following is one possible answer:

```
1:  int main()
2:  {
3:      int VarOne;
4:      int * pVar = &varOne;
5:      *pVar = 9;
6:      return 0;
7:  }
```

6. The following is one possible answer. Note that you should avoid memory leaks in your programs.

```
1:  #include <iostream>
2:  int FuncOne();
3:  int main()
4:  {
5:      int localVar = FunOne();
6:      std::cout << "The value of localVar is: " << localVar;
7:      return 0;
8:  }
9:
10: int FuncOne()
11: {
12:     int * pVar = new int (5);
13:     return *pVar;
14: }
```

7. The following is one possible answer:

```
1:  #include <iostream>
2:  void FuncOne();
3:  int main()
4:  {
5:      FuncOne();
6:      return 0;
7:  }
8:
9:  void FuncOne()
10: {
```

```
11:    int * pVar = new int (5);
12:    std::cout << "The value of *pVar is: " << *pVar ;
13:    delete pVar;
14: }
```

8. MakeCat returns a reference to the CAT created on the free store. There is no way to free that memory, and this produces a memory leak.

9. The following is one possible answer:

```
1:    #include <iostream>
2:    using namespace std;
3:    class CAT
4:    {
5:       public:
6:          CAT(int age) { itsAge = age; }
7:          ~CAT(){}
8:          int GetAge() const { return itsAge;}
9:       private:
10:          int itsAge;
11:    };
12:
13:    CAT * MakeCat(int age);
14:    int main()
15:    {
16:       int age = 7;
17:       CAT * Boots = MakeCat(age);
18:       cout << "Boots is " << Boots->GetAge() << " years old";
19:       delete Boots;
20:     return 0;
21:    }
22:
23:    CAT * MakeCat(int age)
24:    {
25:       return new CAT(age);
26:    }
```

Day 10

Quiz

1. Overloaded member functions are functions in a class that share a name but differ in the number or type of their parameters.

2. A definition sets aside memory; a declaration does not. Almost all declarations are definitions; the major exceptions are class declarations, function prototypes, and typedef statements.

3. Whenever a temporary copy of an object is created. This also happens every time an object is passed by value.

4. The destructor is called each time an object is destroyed, either because it goes out of scope or because you call `delete` on a pointer pointing to it.

5. The assignment operator acts on an existing object; the copy constructor creates a new one.

6. The `this` pointer is a hidden parameter in every member function that points to the object itself.

7. The prefix operator takes no parameters. The postfix operator takes a single `int` parameter, which is used as a signal to the compiler that this is the postfix variant.

8. No, you cannot overload any operator for built-in types.

9. It is legal, but it is a bad idea. Operators should be overloaded in a way that is likely to be readily understood by anyone reading your code.

10. None. Like constructors and destructors, they have no return values.

Exercises

1. The following is one possible answer:

```
class SimpleCircle
{
    public:
      SimpleCircle();
      ~SimpleCircle();
      void SetRadius(int);
      int GetRadius();
    private:
      int itsRadius;
};
```

2. The following is one possible answer:

```
SimpleCircle::SimpleCircle():
itsRadius(5)
{}
```

3. The following is one possible answer:

```
SimpleCircle::SimpleCircle(int radius):
itsRadius(radius)
{}
```

4. The following is one possible answer:

```
const SimpleCircle& SimpleCircle::operator++()
{
    ++(itsRadius);
    return *this;
}

// Operator ++(int) postfix.
```

```
// Fetch then increment
const SimpleCircle SimpleCircle::operator++ (int)
{
    // declare local SimpleCircle and initialize to value of *this
    SimpleCircle temp(*this);
    ++(itsRadius);
    return temp;
}
```

5. The following is one possible answer:

```
class SimpleCircle
{
    public:
      SimpleCircle();
      SimpleCircle(int);
      ~SimpleCircle();
      void SetRadius(int);
      int GetRadius();
      const SimpleCircle& operator++();
      const SimpleCircle operator++(int);
    private:
      int *itsRadius;
};


SimpleCircle::SimpleCircle()
{
    itsRadius = new int(5);
}

SimpleCircle::SimpleCircle(int radius)
{
    itsRadius = new int(radius);
}

const SimpleCircle& SimpleCircle::operator++()
{
    ++(*itsRadius);
    return *this;
}

// Operator ++(int) postfix.
// Fetch then increment
const SimpleCircle SimpleCircle::operator++ (int)
{
    // declare local SimpleCircle and initialize to value of *this
➥SimpleCircle temp(*this);
    ++(*itsRadius);
    return temp;
}
```

D

6. The following is one possible answer:

```
SimpleCircle::SimpleCircle(const SimpleCircle & rhs)
{
    int val = rhs.GetRadius();
    itsRadius = new int(val);
}
```

7. The following is one possible answer:

```
SimpleCircle& SimpleCircle::operator=(const SimpleCircle & rhs)
{
    if (this == &rhs)
        return *this;
    delete itsRadius;
    itsRadius = new int;
    *itsRadius = rhs.GetRadius();
    return *this;
}
```

8. The following is one possible answer:

```
1:  #include <iostream>
2:  using namespace std;
3:
4:  class SimpleCircle
5:  {
6:    public:
7:        // constructors
8:        SimpleCircle();
9:        SimpleCircle(int);
10:       SimpleCircle(const SimpleCircle &);
11:       ~SimpleCircle() {}
12:
13:       // accessor functions
14:       void SetRadius(int);
15:       int GetRadius()const;
16:
17:       // operators
18:       const SimpleCircle& operator++();
19:       const SimpleCircle operator++(int);
20:       SimpleCircle& operator=(const SimpleCircle &);
21:
22:    private:
23:        int *itsRadius;
24:  };
25:
26:
27:  SimpleCircle::SimpleCircle()
28:  {itsRadius = new int(5);}
29:
30:  SimpleCircle::SimpleCircle(int radius)
31:  {itsRadius = new int(radius);}
```

```
32:
33:    SimpleCircle::SimpleCircle(const SimpleCircle & rhs)
34:    {
35:        int val = rhs.GetRadius();
36:        itsRadius = new int(val);
37:    }
38:
39:    SimpleCircle& SimpleCircle::operator=(const SimpleCircle & rhs)
40:    {
41:        if (this == &rhs)
42:            return *this;
43:        *itsRadius = rhs.GetRadius();
44:        return *this;
45:    }
46:
47:    const SimpleCircle& SimpleCircle::operator++()
48:    {
49:        ++(*itsRadius);
50:        return *this;
51:    }
52:
53:    // Operator ++(int) postfix.
54:    // Fetch then increment
55:    const SimpleCircle SimpleCircle::operator++ (int)
56:    {
57:        // declare local SimpleCircle and initialize to value of *this
58:        SimpleCircle temp(*this);
59:        ++(*itsRadius);
60:        return temp;
61:    }
62:    int SimpleCircle::GetRadius() const
63:    {
64:        return *itsRadius;
65:    }
66:    int main()
67:    {
68:        SimpleCircle CircleOne, CircleTwo(9);
69:        CircleOne++;
70:        ++CircleTwo;
71:        cout << "CircleOne: " << CircleOne.GetRadius() << endl;
72:        cout << "CircleTwo: " << CircleTwo.GetRadius() << endl;
73:        CircleOne = CircleTwo;
74:        cout << "CircleOne: " << CircleOne.GetRadius() << endl;
75:        cout << "CircleTwo: " << CircleTwo.GetRadius() << endl;
76:        return 0;
77:    }
```

9. You must check to see whether rhs equals this, or the call to a = a will crash
   your program.

D

10. This `operator+` is changing the value in one of the operands, rather than creating a new `VeryShort` object with the sum. The correct way to do this is as follows:

```
VeryShort  VeryShort::operator+ (const VeryShort& rhs)
{
    return VeryShort(itsVal + rhs.GetItsVal());
}
```

Day 11

Quiz

1. Procedural programming focuses on functions separate from data. Object-oriented programming ties data and functionality together into objects, and focuses on the interaction among the objects.

2. The phases of object-oriented analysis and design include conceptualization, which is the single sentence that describes the great idea; analysis, which is the process of understanding the requirements; and design, which is the process of creating the model of your classes, from which you will generate your code.

   These are followed by implementation, testing, and rollout.

3. Encapsulation refers to the (desirable) trait of bringing together in one class all the data and functionality of one discrete entity.

4. A domain is an area of the business for which you are creating a product.

5. An actor is any person or system that is external to the system you are developing and interacts with the system you are developing.

6. A use case is a description of how the software will be used. It is a description of an interaction between an actor and the system itself.

7. A is true and B is not.

Exercises

1. The following diagram provides one possible answer:

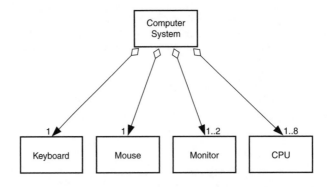

2. Cars, motorcycles, trucks, bicycles, pedestrians, and emergency vehicles all use the intersection. In addition, there is a traffic signal with Walk/Don't Walk lights.

Should the road surface be included in the simulation? Certainly, road quality can have an effect on the traffic, but for a first design, it might be simpler to leave this consideration aside.

The first object is probably the intersection itself. Perhaps the intersection object maintains lists of cars waiting to pass through the signal in each direction, as well as lists of people waiting to cross at the crosswalks. It will need methods to choose which and how many cars and people go through the intersection.

There will only be one intersection, so you might want to consider how you will ensure that only one object is instantiated. (*Hint:* Think about static methods and protected access.)

People and cars are both clients of the intersection. They share a number of characteristics: They can appear at any time, there can be any number of them, and they both wait at the signal (although in different lines). This suggests that you will want to consider a common base class for pedestrians and cars.

The classes could, therefore, include the following:

```
class Entity;            // a client of the intersection
class Vehicle : Entity ...;         // the root of
➥all cars, trucks, bicycles and emergency vehicles.
class Pedestrian : Entity...;   // the root of all People
class Car : public Vehicle...;
class Truck : public Vehicle...;
class Motorcycle : public Vehicle...;
class Bicycle : public Vehicle...;
class Emergency_Vehicle : public Vehicle...;
class Intersection;         // contains lists of
➥cars and people waiting to pass
```

3. Two discrete programs could be written for this project: the client, which the users run, and the server, which would run on a separate machine. In addition, the client machine would have an administrative component to enable a system administrator to add new people and rooms.

If you decide to implement this as a client/server model, the client would accept input from users and generate a request to the server. The server would service the request and send back the results to the client. With this model, many people can schedule meetings at the same time.

On the client's side, there are two major subsystems in addition to the administrative module: the user interface and the communications subsystem. The server's side consists of three main subsystems: communications, scheduling, and a mail interface, which would announce to the user when changes have occurred in the schedule.

4. A meeting is defined as a group of people reserving a room for a certain amount of time. The person making the schedule might desire a specific room, or a specified time; however, the scheduler must always be told how long the meeting will last and who is required.

The objects will probably include the users of the system as well as the conference rooms. Remember to include classes for the calendar, and perhaps a class Meeting that encapsulates all that is known about a particular event.

The prototypes for the classes might include

```
class Calendar_Class;          // forward reference
class Meeting;                 // forward reference
class Configuration
{
  public:
     Configuration();
     ~Configuration();
     Meeting Schedule( ListOfPerson&,
                       Delta Time duration );
     Meeting Schedule( ListOfPerson&,
                       Delta Time duration, Time );
     Meeting Schedule( ListOfPerson&,
                       Delta Time duration, Room );
     ListOfPerson&    People();  // public accessors
     ListOfRoom&      Rooms();   // public accessors
  protected:
     ListOfRoom     rooms;
     ListOfPerson    people;
};
typedef long       Room_ID;
class Room
{
  public:
     Room( String name, Room_ID id, int capacity,
String directions = "", String description = "" );
     ~Room();
     Calendar_Class Calendar();

  protected:
     Calendar_Class    calendar;
     int            capacity;
     Room_ID     id;
     String         name;
     String         directions;       // where is this room?
     String         description;
};
typedef long Person_ID;
class Person
```

```
{
  public:
    Person( String name, Person_ID id );
    ~Person();
    Calendar_Class Calendar();         // the access point to add
➥meetings
  protected:
    Calendar_Class     calendar;
    Person_ID      id;
    String             name;
};
class Calendar_Class
{
  public:
    Calendar_Class();
    ~Calendar_Class();

    void Add( const Meeting& );      // add a meeting to the calendar
    void Delete( const Meeting& );
    Meeting* Lookup( Time );         // see if there is a meeting at the
                                     // given time

    Block( Time, Duration, String reason = "" );
// allocate time to yourself...

  protected:
    OrderedListOfMeeting meetings;
};
class Meeting
{
  public:
    Meeting( ListOfPerson&, Room room,
        Time when, Duration duration, String purpose
= "" );
    ~Meeting();
  protected:
    ListOfPerson    people;
    Room            room;
    Time            when;
    Duration        duration;
    String          purpose;
};
```

You might have used private instead of protected. Protected members are covered on Day 12, "Implementing Inheritance."

Day 12

Quiz

1. A v-table, or virtual function table, is a common way for compilers to manage virtual functions in C++. The table keeps a list of the addresses of all the virtual functions, and depending on the runtime type of the object pointed to, invokes the right function.

2. A destructor of any class can be declared to be virtual. When the pointer is deleted, the runtime type of the object will be assessed and the correct derived destructor invoked.

3. This was a trick question—there are no virtual constructors.

4. By creating a virtual method in your class, which itself calls the copy constructor.

5. `Base::FunctionName();`

6. `FunctionName();`

7. Yes, the virtuality is inherited and *cannot* be turned off.

8. `protected` members are accessible to the member functions of derived objects.

Exercises

1. `virtual void SomeFunction(int);`

2. Because you are showing a declaration of `Square`, you don't need to worry about `Shape`. `Shape` is automatically included as a part of `Rectangle`.
   ```
   class Square : public Rectangle
   {};
   ```

3. Just as with Exercise 2, you don't need to worry about `Shape`.
   ```
   Square::Square(int length):
       Rectangle(length, width){}
   ```

4. The following is one possible answer:
   ```
   class Square
   {
       public:
           // ...
           virtual Square * clone() const { return new Square(*this); }
           // ...
   };
   ```

5. Perhaps nothing. `SomeFunction` expects a `Shape` object. You've passed it a `Rectangle` "sliced" down to a `Shape`. As long as you don't need any of the

Rectangle parts, this will be fine. If you do need the Rectangle parts, you'll need to change SomeFunction to take a pointer or a reference to a Shape.

6. You can't declare a copy constructor to be virtual.

Day 13

Quiz

1. SomeArray[0], SomeArray[24]

2. Write a set of subscripts for each dimension. For example, SomeArray[2][3][2] is a three-dimensional array. The first dimension has two elements, the second has three, and the third has two.

3. SomeArray[2][3][2] = { { {1,2},{3,4},{5,6} } , { {7,8},{9,10},{11,12} ➥} };

4. 10*5*20=1,000

5. Both arrays and linked lists are containers for storing information; however, linked lists are designed to link together as needed.

6. This string contains 16 characters—the fifteen you see and the null character that ends the string.

7. The null character.

Exercises

1. The following is one possible solution. Your array might have a different name, but should be followed by [3][3] in order to hold a 3 by 3 board.

```
int GameBoard[3][3];
```

2. `int GameBoard[3][3] = { {0,0,0},{0,0,0},{0,0,0} }`

3. The following is one possible solution. This uses the strcpy() and strlen() functions.

```
#include <iostream>
#include <string.h>
using namespace std;

int main()
{
    char firstname[] = "Alfred";
    char middlename[] = "E";
    char lastname[] = "Numan";
    char fullname[80];
    int  offset = 0;
```

```
strcpy(fullname,firstname);
offset = strlen(firstname);
strcpy(fullname+offset," ");
offset += 1;
strcpy(fullname+offset,middlename);
offset += strlen(middlename);
strcpy(fullname+offset,". ");
offset += 2;
strcpy(fullname+offset,lastname);

cout << firstname << "-" << middlename << "-"
    << lastname << endl;
cout << "Fullname: " << fullname << endl;

return 0;
}
```

4. The array is five elements by four elements, but the code initializes 4×5.

5. You wanted to write i<5, but you wrote i<=5 instead. The code will run when i == 5 and j == 4, but there is no such element as SomeArray[5][4].

Day 14

Quiz

1. A down cast (also called "casting down") is a declaration that a pointer to a base class is to be treated as a pointer to a derived class.

2. This refers to the idea of moving shared functionality upward into a common base class. If more than one class shares a function, it is desirable to find a common base class in which that function can be stored.

3. If neither class inherits using the keyword virtual, two Shapes are created, one for Rectangle and one for Shape. If the keyword virtual is used for both classes, only one shared Shape is created.

4. Both Horse and Bird initialize their base class, Animal, in their constructors. Pegasus does as well, and when a Pegasus is created, the Horse and Bird initializations of Animal are ignored.

5. The following is one possible answer:

```
class Vehicle
{
    virtual void Move() = 0;
}
```

6. None must be overridden unless you want to make the class nonabstract, in which case all three must be overridden.

Exercises

1. `class JetPlane : public Rocket, public Airplane`

2. `class Seven47: public JetPlane`

3. The following is one possible answer:
   ```
   class Vehicle
   {
       virtual void Move() = 0;
       virtual void Haul() = 0;
   };

   class Car : public Vehicle
   {
       virtual void Move();
       virtual void Haul();
   };

   class Bus : public Vehicle
   {
       virtual void Move();
       virtual void Haul();
   };
   ```

4. The following is one possible answer:
   ```
   class Vehicle
   {
       virtual void Move() = 0;
       virtual void Haul() = 0;
   };

   class Car : public Vehicle
   {
       virtual void Move();
   };

   class Bus : public Vehicle
   {
       virtual void Move();
       virtual void Haul();
   };

   class SportsCar : public Car
   {
       virtual void Haul();
   };

   class Coupe : public Car
   {
       virtual void Haul();
   };
   ```

D

Day 15

Quiz

1. Yes. They are member variables and their access can be controlled like any other. If they are private, they can be accessed only by using member functions or, more commonly, static member functions.

2. ```
   static int itsStatic;
   ```

3. ```
   static int SomeFunction();
   ```

4. ```
   long (* function)(int);
   ```

5. ```
   long ( Car::*function)(int);
   ```

6. ```
   long ( Car::*function)(int) theArray [10];
   ```

Exercises

1. The following is one possible answer:

```
0:      // Ex1501.cpp
1:      class myClass
2:      {
3:         public:
4:           myClass();
5:           ~myClass();
6:         private:
7:           int itsMember;
8:           static int itsStatic;
9:      };
10:
11:     myClass::myClass():
12:      itsMember(1)
13:     {
14:        itsStatic++;
15:     }
16:
17:     myClass::~myClass()
18:     {
19:        itsStatic--;
20:     }
21:
22:     int myClass::itsStatic = 0;
23:
24:     int main()
25:     {
26:        // do something
27:        return 0;
28:     }
```
```

2. The following is one possible answer:

```
0:    // Ex1502.cpp
1:    #include <iostream>
2:    using namespace std;
3:    class myClass
4:    {
5:      public:
6:        myClass();
7:        ~myClass();
8:        void ShowMember();
9:        void ShowStatic();
10:     private:
11:        int itsMember;
12:        static int itsStatic;
13:   };
14:
15:   myClass::myClass():
16:      itsMember(1)
17:   {
18:      itsStatic++;
19:   }
20:
21:   myClass::~myClass()
22:   {
23:      itsStatic--;
24:      cout << "In destructor. ItsStatic: " << itsStatic << endl;
25:   }
26:
27:   void myClass::ShowMember()
28:   {
29:      cout << "itsMember: " << itsMember << endl;
30:   }
31:
32:   void myClass::ShowStatic()
33:   {
34:      cout << "itsStatic: " << itsStatic << endl;
35:   }
36:   int myClass::itsStatic = 0;
37:
38:   int main()
39:   {
40:      myClass obj1;
41:      obj1.ShowMember();
42:      obj1.ShowStatic();
43:
44:      myClass obj2;
45:      obj2.ShowMember();
46:      obj2.ShowStatic();
47:
48:      myClass obj3;
```

D

```
49:        obj3.ShowMember();
50:        obj3.ShowStatic();
51:     return 0;
52:     }
```

3. The following is one possible answer:

```
0:    // Ex1503.cpp
1:    #include <iostream>
2:    using namespace std;
3:    class myClass
4:    {
5:       public:
6:         myClass();
7:         ~myClass();
8:         void ShowMember();
9:         static int GetStatic();
10:      private:
11:         int itsMember;
12:         static int itsStatic;
13:    };
14:
15:    myClass::myClass():
16:       itsMember(1)
17:    {
18:       itsStatic++;
19:    }
20:
21:    myClass::~myClass()
22:    {
23:       itsStatic--;
24:       cout << "In destructor. ItsStatic: " << itsStatic << endl;
25:    }
26:
27:    void myClass::ShowMember()
28:    {
29:       cout << "itsMember: " << itsMember << endl;
30:    }
31:
32:    int myClass::itsStatic = 0;
33:
34:    int myClass::GetStatic()
35:    {
36:       return itsStatic;
37:    }
38:
39:    int main()
40:    {
41:       myClass obj1;
42:       obj1.ShowMember();
43:       cout << "Static: " << myClass::GetStatic() << endl;
44:
```

```
45:        myClass obj2;
46:        obj2.ShowMember();
47:        cout << "Static: " << myClass::GetStatic() << endl;
48:
49:        myClass obj3;
50:        obj3.ShowMember();
51:        cout << "Static: " << myClass::GetStatic() << endl;
52:        return 0;
53:    }
```

4. The following is one possible answer:

```
0:     // Ex1504.cpp
1:     #include <iostream>
2:     using namespace std;
3:     class myClass
4:     {
5:       public:
6:         myClass();
7:         ~myClass();
8:         void ShowMember();
9:         static int GetStatic();
10:      private:
11:        int itsMember;
12:        static int itsStatic;
13:     };
14:
15:     myClass::myClass():
16:       itsMember(1)
17:     {
18:        itsStatic++;
19:     }
20:
21:     myClass::~myClass()
22:     {
23:        itsStatic--;
24:        cout << "In destructor. ItsStatic: " << itsStatic << endl;
25:     }
26:
27:     void myClass::ShowMember()
28:     {
29:        cout << "itsMember: " << itsMember << endl;
30:     }
31:
32:     int myClass::itsStatic = 0;
33:
34:     int myClass::GetStatic()
35:     {
36:        return itsStatic;
37:     }
38:
39:     int main()
```

D

```
40:    {
41:        void (myClass::*PMF) ();
42:
43:        PMF=myClass::ShowMember;
44:
45:        myClass obj1;
46:        (obj1.*PMF)();
47:        cout << "Static: " << myClass::GetStatic() << endl;
48:
49:        myClass obj2;
50:        (obj2.*PMF)();
51:        cout << "Static: " << myClass::GetStatic() << endl;
52:
53:        myClass obj3;
54:        (obj3.*PMF)();
55:        cout << "Static: " << myClass::GetStatic() << endl;
56:        return 0;
57:    }
```

5. The following is one possible answer:

```
0:    // Ex1505.cpp
1:    #include <iostream>
2:    using namespace std;
3:    class myClass
4:    {
5:        public:
6:            myClass();
7:            ~myClass();
8:            void ShowMember();
9:            void ShowSecond();
10:           void ShowThird();
11:           static int GetStatic();
12:        private:
13:            int itsMember;
14:            int itsSecond;
15:            int itsThird;
16:            static int itsStatic;
17:    };
18:
19:    myClass::myClass():
20:        itsMember(1),
21:        itsSecond(2),
22:        itsThird(3)
23:    {
24:        itsStatic++;
25:    }
26:
27:    myClass::~myClass()
28:    {
29:        itsStatic--;
30:        cout << "In destructor. ItsStatic: " << itsStatic << endl;
```

```
31:    }
32:
33:    void myClass::ShowMember()
34:    {
35:        cout << "itsMember: " << itsMember << endl;
36:    }
37:
38:    void myClass::ShowSecond()
39:    {
40:        cout << "itsSecond: " << itsSecond << endl;
41:    }
42:
43:    void myClass::ShowThird()
44:    {
45:        cout << "itsThird: " << itsThird << endl;
46:    }
47:    int myClass::itsStatic = 0;
48:
49:    int myClass::GetStatic()
50:    {
51:        return itsStatic;
52:    }
53:
54:    int main()
55:    {
56:        void (myClass::*PMF) ();
57:
58:        myClass obj1;
59:        PMF=myClass::ShowMember;
60:        (obj1.*PMF)();
61:        PMF=myClass::ShowSecond;
62:        (obj1.*PMF)();
63:        PMF=myClass::ShowThird;
64:        (obj1.*PMF)();
65:        cout << "Static: " << myClass::GetStatic() << endl;
66:
67:        myClass obj2;
68:        PMF=myClass::ShowMember;
69:        (obj2.*PMF)();
70:        PMF=myClass::ShowSecond;
71:        (obj2.*PMF)();
72:        PMF=myClass::ShowThird;
73:        (obj2.*PMF)();
74:        cout << "Static: " << myClass::GetStatic() << endl;
75:
76:        myClass obj3;
77:        PMF=myClass::ShowMember;
78:        (obj3.*PMF)();
79:        PMF=myClass::ShowSecond;
80:        (obj3.*PMF)();
81:        PMF=myClass::ShowThird;
```

D

```
82:          (obj3.*PMF)();
83:          cout << "Static: " << myClass::GetStatic() << endl;
84:
85:          return 0;
86:      }
```

Day 16

Quiz

1. An *is-a* relationship is established with public inheritance.

2. A *has-a* relationship is established with aggregation (containment); that is, one class has a member that is an object of another type.

3. Aggregation describes the idea of one class having a data member that is an object of another type. Delegation expresses the idea that one class uses another class to accomplish a task or goal.

4. Delegation expresses the idea that one class uses another class to accomplish a task or goal. *Implemented in terms of* expresses the idea of inheriting implementation from another class.

5. A friend function is a function declared to have access to the protected and private members of your class.

6. A friend class is a class declared so that all of its member functions are friend functions of your class.

7. No, friendship is not commutative.

8. No, friendship is not inherited.

9. No, friendship is not associative.

10. A declaration for a friend function can appear anywhere within the class declaration. It makes no difference whether you put the declaration within the `public:`, `protected:`, or `private:` access areas.

Exercises

1. The following is one possible answer:
```
class Animal:
{
   private:
       String itsName;
};
```

2. The following is one possible answer:
```
class boundedArray : public Array
{
    //...
}
```

3. The following is one possible answer:
```
class Set : private Array
{
    // ...
}
```

4. The following is one possible answer:
```
0:      #include <iostream.h>
1:      #include <string.h>
2:
3:      class String
4:      {
5:         public:
6:            // constructors
7:             String();
8:             String(const char *const);
9:             String(const String &);
10:            ~String();
11:
12:            // overloaded operators
13:            char & operator[](int offset);
14:            char operator[](int offset) const;
15:            String operator+(const String&);
16:            void operator+=(const String&);
17:            String & operator= (const String &);
18:            friend ostream& operator<<( ostream&
19:                          theStream,String& theString);
20:            friend istream& operator>>( istream&
21:                theStream,String& theString);
22:            // General accessors
23:            int GetLen()const { return itsLen; }
24:            const char * GetString() const { return itsString; }
25:            // static int ConstructorCount;
26:
27:         private:
28:            String (int);         // private constructor
29:            char * itsString;
30:            unsigned short itsLen;
31:
32:      };
33:
34:      ostream& operator<<( ostream& theStream,String& theString)
35:      {
36:           theStream << theString.GetString();
```

```
37:          return theStream;
38:      }
39:
40:      istream& operator>>( istream& theStream,String& theString)
41:      {
42:          theStream >> theString.GetString();
43:          return theStream;
44:      }
45:
46:      int main()
47:      {
48:          String theString("Hello world.");
49:          cout << theString;
50:          return 0;
51:      }
```

5. You can't put the `friend` declaration into the function. You must declare the function to be a friend in the class.

6. The following is the fixed listing:

```
0:      Bug Busters
1:      #include <iostream>
2:      using namespace std;
3:      class Animal;
4:
5:      void setValue(Animal& , int);
6:
7:      class Animal
8:      {
9:        public:
10:          friend void setValue(Animal&, int);
11:          int GetWeight()const { return itsWeight; }
12:          int GetAge() const { return itsAge; }
13:        private:
14:          int itsWeight;
15:          int itsAge;
16:      };
17:
18:      void setValue(Animal& theAnimal, int theWeight)
19:      {
20:          theAnimal.itsWeight = theWeight;
21:      }
22:
23:      int main()
24:      {
25:          Animal peppy;
26:          setValue(peppy,5);
27:          return 0;
28:      }
```

7. The function setValue(Animal&,int) was declared to be a friend, but the overloaded function setValue(Animal&,int,int) was not declared to be a friend.

8. The following is the fixed listing:

```
0:     // Bug Busters
1:     #include <iostream>
2:     using namespace std;
3:     class Animal;
4:
5:     void setValue(Animal& , int);
6:     void setValue(Animal& ,int,int); // here's the change!
7:
8:     class Animal
9:     {
10:      friend void setValue(Animal& ,int);
11:      friend void setValue(Animal& ,int,int);
12:      private:
13:         int itsWeight;
14:         int itsAge;
15:     };
16:
17:     void setValue(Animal& theAnimal, int theWeight)
18:     {
19:         theAnimal.itsWeight = theWeight;
20:     }
21:
22:     void setValue(Animal& theAnimal, int theWeight, int theAge)
23:     {
24:        theAnimal.itsWeight = theWeight;
25:        theAnimal.itsAge = theAge;
26:     }
27:
28:     int main()
29:     {
30:         Animal peppy;
31:         setValue(peppy,5);
32:         setValue(peppy,7,9);
33:         return 0;
34:     }
```

Day 17

Quiz

1. The insertion operator (<<) is a member operator of the ostream object and is used for writing to the output device.

2. The extraction operator (>>) is a member operator of the istream object and is used for writing to your program's variables.

3. The first form of get() is without parameters. This returns the value of the character found, and will return EOF (end of file) if the end of the file is reached.

The second form of get() takes a character reference as its parameter; that character is filled with the next character in the input stream. The return value is an iostream object.

The third form of get() takes an array, a maximum number of characters to get, and a terminating character. This form of get() fills the array with up to one fewer characters than the maximum (appending null) unless it reads the terminating character, in which case it immediately writes a null and leaves the terminating character in the buffer.

4. cin.read() is used for reading binary data structures.

getline() is used to read from the istream's buffer.

5. Wide enough to display the entire number.

6. A reference to an istream object.

7. The filename to be opened.

8. ios::ate places you at the end of the file, but you can write data anywhere in the file.

Exercises

1. The following is one possible solution:

```
0:    // Ex1701.cpp
1:    #include <iostream>
2:    int main()
3:    {
4:        int x;
5:        std::cout << "Enter a number: ";
6:        std::cin >> x;
7:        std::cout << "You entered: " << x << std::endl;
8:        std::cerr << "Uh oh, this to cerr!" << std::endl;
9:        std::clog << "Uh oh, this to clog!" << std::endl;
10:       return 0;
11:   }
```

2. The following is one possible solution:

```
0:    // Ex1702.cpp
1:    #include <iostream>
2:    int main()
3:    {
4:        char name[80];
5:        std::cout << "Enter your full name: ";
6:        std::cin.getline(name,80);
7:        std::cout << "\nYou entered: " << name << std::endl;
8:        return 0;
9:    }
```

3. The following is one possible solution:

```
0:    // Ex1703.cpp
1:    #include <iostream>
2:    using namespace std;
3:
4:    int main()
5:    {
6:       char ch;
7:       cout << "enter a phrase: ";
8:       while ( cin.get(ch) )
9:       {
10:          switch (ch)
11:          {
12:            case '!':
13:               cout << '$';
14:               break;
15:            case '#':
16:               break;
17:            default:
18:               cout << ch;
19:               break;
20:          }
21:       }
22:       return 0;
23:    }
```

D

4. The following is one possible solution:

```
0:    // Ex1704.cpp
1:    #include <fstream>
2:    #include <iostream>
3:    using namespace std;
4:
5:    int main(int argc, char**argv)    // returns 1 on error
6:    {
7:       if (argc != 2)
8:       {
9:          cout << "Usage: argv[0] <infile>\n";
10:          return(1);
11:       }
12:
13:       // open the input stream
14:       ifstream fin (argv[1],ios::binary);
15:       if (!fin)
16:       {
17:          cout << "Unable to open " << argv[1] <<" for reading.\n";
18:          return(1);
19:       }
20:
21:       char ch;
22:       while ( fin.get(ch))
```

```
23:          if ((ch > 32 && ch < 127) || ch == '\n'|| ch == '\t')
24:              cout << ch;
25:       fin.close();
26:    }
```

5. The following is one possible solution:

```
0:  // Ex1705.cpp
1:  #include <iostream>
2:
3:  int main(int argc, char**argv)    // returns 1 on error
4:  {
5:     for (int ctr = argc-1; ctr>0 ; ctr--)
6:         std::cout << argv[ctr] << " ";
7:  }
```

Day 18

Quiz

1. `Outer::Inner::MyFunc();`

2. At the point the listing reaches HERE, the global version of X will be used, so it will be 4.

3. Yes, you can use names defined in a namespace by prefixing them with the namespace qualifier.

4. Names in a normal namespace can be used outside of the translation unit where the namespace is declared. Names in an unnamed namespace can only be used within the translation unit where the namespace is declared.

5. The using keyword can be used for the using directives and the using declarations. A using directive allows all names in a namespace to be used as if they are normal names. A using declaration, on the other hand, enables the program to use an individual name from a namespace without qualifying it with the namespace qualifier.

6. Unnamed namespaces are namespaces without names. They are used to wrap a collection of declarations against possible name clashes. Names in an unnamed namespace cannot be used outside of the translation unit where the namespace is declared.

7. The standard namespace std is defined by the C++ Standard Library. It includes declarations of all names in the Standard Library.

Exercises

1. The C++ standard `iostream` header file declares `cout` and `endl` in namespace `std`. They cannot be used outside of the standard namespace `std` without a namespace qualifier.

2. You can add the following line between lines 0 and 1.

   ```
   using namespace std;
   ```

   You can add the following two lines between 0 and 1:

   ```
   using std::cout;
        using std::endl;
   ```

   You can change line 3 to the following:

   ```
   std::cout << "Hello world!" << std::endl;
   ```

3. The following is one possible answer:

   ```
   Namespace MyStuff
   {
      class MyClass
      {
         //MyClass stuff
      }
   }
   ```

Day 19

Quiz

1. Templates are built in to the C++ language and are type-safe. Macros are implemented by the preprocessor and are not type-safe.

2. The parameter to the template creates an instance of the template for each type. If you create six template instances, six different classes or functions are created. The parameters to the function change the behavior or data of the function, but only one function is created.

3. The general template friend function creates one function for every type of the parameterized class; the type-specific function creates a type-specific instance for each instance of the parameterized class.

4. Yes, create a specialized function for the particular instance. In addition to creating `Array<t>::SomeFunction()`, also create `Array<int>::SomeFunction()` to change the behavior for integer arrays.

5. One for each instance type of the class.

6. The class must define a default constructor, a copy constructor, and an overloaded assignment operator.

7. STL stands for the Standard Template Library. This library is important because it contains a number of template classes that have already been created and are ready for you to use. Because these are a part of the C++ standard, any compiler supporting the standard will also support these classes. This means you don't have to "reinvent the wheel!"

Exercises

1. One way to implement this template:

```
0:   //Exercise 19.1
1:   template <class Type>
2:   class List
3:   {
4:
5:     public:
6:         List():head(0),tail(0),theCount(0) { }
7:         virtual ~List();
8:
9:         void insert( Type value );
10:        void append( Type value );
11:        int is_present( Type value ) const;
12:        int is_empty() const { return head == 0; }
13:        int count() const { return theCount; }
14:
15:     private:
16:        class ListCell
17:        {
18:          public:
19:            ListCell(Type value, ListCell *cell =
                 ➥0):val(value),next(cell){}
20:            Type val;
21:            ListCell *next;
22:        };
23:
24:        ListCell *head;
25:        ListCell *tail;
26:        int theCount;
27:   };
```

2. The following is one possible answer:

```
0:   // Exercise 19.2
1:   void List::insert(int value)
2:   {
3:       ListCell *pt = new ListCell( value, head );
4:
```

```
 5:        // this line added to handle tail
 6:        if ( head == 0 ) tail = pt;
 7:
 8:        head = pt;
 9:        theCount++;
10:   }
11:
12:   void List::append( int value )
13:   {
14:        ListCell *pt = new ListCell( value );
15:        if ( head == 0 )
16:            head = pt;
17:        else
18:            tail->next = pt;
19:
20:        tail = pt;
21:        theCount++;
22:   }
23:
24:   int List::is_present( int value ) const
25:   {
26:        if ( head == 0 ) return 0;
27:        if ( head->val == value || tail->val == value )
28:            return 1;
29:
30:         ListCell *pt = head->next;
31:        for (; pt != tail; pt = pt->next)
32:            if ( pt->val == value )
33:                return 1;
34:
35:        return 0;
36:   }
```

3. The following is one possible answer:

```
 0:   // Exercise 19.3
 1:   template <class Type>
 2:   List<Type>::~List()
 3:   {
 4:        ListCell *pt = head;
 5:
 6:        while ( pt )
 7:        {
 8:            ListCell *tmp = pt;
 9:            pt = pt->next;
10:            delete tmp;
11:        }
12:        head = tail = 0;
13:   }
14:
15:   template <class Type>
```

```
16:   void List<Type>::insert(Type value)
17:   {
18:        ListCell *pt = new ListCell( value, head );
19:        assert (pt != 0);
20:
21:        // this line added to handle tail
22:        if ( head == 0 ) tail = pt;
23:
24:        head = pt;
25:        theCount++;
26:   }
27:
28:   template <class Type>
29:   void List<Type>::append( Type value )
30:   {
31:        ListCell *pt = new ListCell( value );
32:        if ( head == 0 )
33:             head = pt;
34:        else
35:             tail->next = pt;
36:
37:        tail = pt;
38:        theCount++;
39:   }
40:
41:   template <class Type>
42:   int List<Type>::is_present( Type value ) const
43:   {
44:        if ( head == 0 ) return 0;
45:        if ( head->val == value || tail->val == value )
46:             return 1;
47:
48:        ListCell *pt = head->next;
49:        for (; pt != tail; pt = pt->next)
50:             if ( pt->val == value )
51:                  return 1;
52:
53:        return 0;
54:   }
```

4. The following declare the three objects:

```
List<String> string_list;
List<Cat> Cat_List;
List<int> int_List;
```

5. Cat doesn't have operator == defined; all operations that compare the values in the List cells, such as is_present, will result in compiler errors. To reduce the chance of this, put copious comments before the template definition stating what operations must be defined for the instantiation to compile.

6. The following is one possible answer:

```
friend int operator==( const Type& lhs, const Type& rhs );
```

7. The following is one possible answer:

```
0:   Exercise 19.7
1:   template <class Type>
2:   int List<Type>::operator==( const Type& lhs, const Type& rhs )
3:   {
4:        // compare lengths first
5:        if ( lhs.theCount != rhs.theCount )
6:            return 0;      // lengths differ
7:
8:        ListCell *lh = lhs.head;
9:        ListCell *rh = rhs.head;
10:
11:       for(; lh != 0; lh = lh.next, rh = rh.next )
12:            if ( lh.value != rh.value )
13:                return 0;
14:
15:       return 1;          // if they don't differ, they must match
16:  }
```

8. Yes, because comparing the array involves comparing the elements, `operator!=` must be defined for the elements as well.

9. The following is one possible answer:

```
0:   // Exercise 19.9
1:   // template swap:
2:   // must have assignment and the copy constructor defined for the Type.
3:   template <class Type>
4:   void swap( Type& lhs, Type& rhs)
5:   {
6:        Type temp( lhs );
7:        lhs = rhs;
8:        rhs = temp;
9:   }
```

Day 20

Quiz

1. An exception is an object that is created as a result of invoking the keyword `throw`. It is used to signal an exceptional condition, and is passed up the call stack to the first `catch` statement that handles its type.

2. A `try` block is a set of statements that might generate an exception.

3. A `catch` statement is a routine that has a signature of the type of exception it handles. It follows a `try` block and acts as the receiver of exceptions raised within the `try` block.

4. An exception is an object and can contain any information that can be defined within a user-created class.

5. Exception objects are created when the program invokes the keyword `throw`.

6. In general, exceptions should be passed by reference. If you don't intend to modify the contents of the exception object, you should pass a `const` reference.

7. Yes, if you pass the exception by reference.

8. `catch` statements are examined in the order they appear in the source code. The first `catch` statement whose signature matches the exception is used. In general, it is best to start with the most specific exception and work toward the most general.

9. `catch(...)` catches any exception of any type.

10. A breakpoint is a place in the code where the debugger stops execution.

Exercises

1. The following is one possible answer:

```
0:  #include <iostream>
1:  using namespace std;
2:  class OutOfMemory {};
3:  int main()
4:  {
5:      try
6:      {
7:          int *myInt = new int;
8:          if (myInt == 0)
9:              throw OutOfMemory();
10:     }
11:     catch (OutOfMemory)
12:     {
13:         cout << "Unable to allocate memory!" << endl;
14:     }
15:     return 0;
16: }
```

2. The following is one possible answer:

```
1:  #include <iostream>
2:  #include <stdio.h>
3:  #include <string.h>
4:  using namespace std;
5:  class OutOfMemory
6:  {
7:    public:
8:        OutOfMemory(char *);
```

```
 9:        char* GetString() { return itsString; }
10:    private:
11:        char* itsString;
12: };
13:
14: OutOfMemory::OutOfMemory(char * theType)
15: {
16:        itsString = new char[80];
17:        char warning[] = "Out Of Memory! Can't allocate room for: ";
18:        strncpy(itsString,warning,60);
19:        strncat(itsString,theType,19);
20: }
21:
22: int main()
23: {
24:        try
25:        {
26:            int *myInt = new int;
27:            if (myInt == 0)
28:                throw OutOfMemory("int");
29:        }
30:        catch (OutOfMemory& theException)
31:        {
32:            cout << theException.GetString();
33:        }
34:        return 0;
35: }
```

3. The following is one possible answer:

```
0:     // Exercise 20.3
1:     #include <iostream>
2:     using namespace std;
3:     // Abstract exception data type
4:     class Exception
5:     {
6:        public:
7:          Exception(){}
8:          virtual ~Exception(){}
9:          virtual void PrintError() = 0;
10:    };
11:
12:    // Derived class to handle memory problems.
13:    // Note no allocation of memory in this class!
14:    class OutOfMemory : public Exception
15:    {
16:       public:
17:         OutOfMemory(){}
18:         ~OutOfMemory(){}
19:         virtual void PrintError();
20:       private:
21:    };
```

D

```
22:
23:     void OutOfMemory::PrintError()
24:     {
25:        cout << "Out of Memory!!" << endl;
26:     }
27:
28:     // Derived class to handle bad numbers
29:     class RangeError : public Exception
30:     {
31:       public:
32:         RangeError(unsigned long number){badNumber = number;}
33:         ~RangeError(){}
34:         virtual void PrintError();
35:         virtual unsigned long GetNumber() { return badNumber; }
36:         virtual void SetNumber(unsigned long number) {badNumber =
        ➥number;}
37:       private:
38:         unsigned long badNumber;
39:     };
40:
41:     void RangeError::PrintError()
42:     {
43:        cout << "Number out of range. You used " ;
44:        cout << GetNumber() << "!!" << endl;
45:     }
46:
47:     void MyFunction();   // func. prototype
48:
49:     int main()
50:     {
51:        try
52:        {
53:           MyFunction();
54:        }
55:        // Only one catch required, use virtual functions to do the
56:        // right thing.
57:        catch (Exception& theException)
58:        {
59:           theException.PrintError();
60:        }
61:        return 0;
62:     }
63:
64:     void MyFunction()
65:     {
66:           unsigned int *myInt = new unsigned int;
67:           long testNumber;
68:
69:           if (myInt == 0)
70:               throw OutOfMemory();
71:
```

```
72:              cout << "Enter an int: ";
73:              cin >> testNumber;
74:
75:              // this weird test should be replaced by a series
76:              // of tests to complain about bad user input
77:
78:              if (testNumber > 3768 || testNumber < 0)
79:                  throw RangeError(testNumber);
80:
81:              *myInt = testNumber;
82:              cout << "Ok. myInt: " << *myInt;
83:              delete myInt;
84:      }
```

4. The following is one possible answer:

```
0:      // Exercise 20.4
1:      #include <iostream>
2:      using namespace std;
3:      // Abstract exception data type
4:      class Exception
5:      {
6:        public:
7:          Exception(){}
8:          virtual ~Exception(){}
9:          virtual void PrintError() = 0;
10:     };
11:
12:     // Derived class to handle memory problems.
13:     // Note no allocation of memory in this class!
14:     class OutOfMemory : public Exception
15:     {
16:       public:
17:         OutOfMemory(){}
18:         ~OutOfMemory(){}
19:         virtual void PrintError();
20:       private:
21:     };
22:
23:     void OutOfMemory::PrintError()
24:     {
25:        cout << "Out of Memory!!\n";
26:     }
27:
28:     // Derived class to handle bad numbers
29:     class RangeError : public Exception
30:     {
31:       public:
32:         RangeError(unsigned long number){badNumber = number;}
33:         ~RangeError(){}
34:         virtual void PrintError();
35:         virtual unsigned long GetNumber() { return badNumber; }
```

D

```
36:        virtual void SetNumber(unsigned long number) {badNumber =
           ➥number;}
37:     private:
38:        unsigned long badNumber;
39:     };
40:
41:     void RangeError::PrintError()
42:     {
43:        cout << "Number out of range. You used ";
44:        cout << GetNumber() << "!!" << endl;
45:     }
46:
47:     // func. prototypes
48:     void MyFunction();
49:     unsigned int * FunctionTwo();
50:     void FunctionThree(unsigned int *);
51:
52:     int main()
53:     {
54:        try
55:        {
56:           MyFunction();
57:        }
58:        // Only one catch required, use virtual functions to do the
59:        // right thing.
60:        catch (Exception& theException)
61:        {
62:           theException.PrintError();
63:        }
64:        return 0;
65:      }
66:
67:     unsigned int * FunctionTwo()
68:     {
69:        unsigned int *myInt = new unsigned int;
70:        if (myInt == 0)
71:          throw OutOfMemory();
72:        return myInt;
73:     }
74:
75:     void MyFunction()
76:     {
77:           unsigned int *myInt = FunctionTwo();
78:           FunctionThree(myInt);
79:           cout << "Ok. myInt: " << *myInt;
80:           delete myInt;
81:     }
82:
83:     void FunctionThree(unsigned int *ptr)
84:     {
85:           long testNumber;
86:           cout << "Enter an int: ";
```

```
87:            cin >> testNumber;
88:            // this weird test should be replaced by a series
89:            // of tests to complain about bad user input
90:            if (testNumber > 3768 || testNumber < 0)
91:                throw RangeError(testNumber);
92:            *ptr = testNumber;
93:    }
```

5. In the process of handling an "out of memory" condition, a string object is created by the constructor of xOutOfMemory. This exception can only be raised when the program is out of memory, and so this allocation must fail.

It is possible that trying to create this string will raise the same exception, creating an infinite loop until the program crashes. If this string is really required, you can allocate the space in a static buffer before beginning the program, and then use it as needed when the exception is thrown.

You can test this program by changing the line if (var == 0) to if (1), which forces the exception to be thrown.

Day 21

Quiz

1. Inclusion guards are used to protect a header file from being included into a program more than once.

2. This quiz question must be answered by you, depending on the compiler you are using.

3. #define debug 0 defines the term debug to equal 0 (zero). Everywhere the word "debug" is found, the character 0 is substituted. #undef debug removes any definition of debug; when the word debug is found in the file, it is left unchanged.

4. The answer is 4 / 2, which is 2.

5. The result is 10 + 10 / 2, which is 10 + 5, or 15. This is obviously not the result desired.

6. You should add parentheses:

   HALVE (x) ((x)/2)

7. Two bytes is 16 bits, so up to 16 bit values could be stored.

8. Five bits can hold 32 values (0 to 31).

9. The result is 1111 1111.

10. The result is 0011 1100.

Exercises

1. The inclusion guard statements for the header file `STRING.H` would be:

```
#ifndef STRING_H
#define STRING_H
...
#endif
```

2. The following is one possible answer:

```
0:     #include <iostream>
1:
2:     using namespace std;
3:     #ifndef DEBUG
4:     #define ASSERT(x)
5:     #elif DEBUG == 1
6:     #define ASSERT(x) \
7:                 if (! (x)) \
8:                 { \
9:         cout << "ERROR!! Assert " << #x << " failed" << endl; \
10:                 }
11:    #elif DEBUG == 2
12:    #define ASSERT(x) \
13:                 if (! (x) ) \
14:                 { \
15:         cout << "ERROR!! Assert " << #x << " failed" << endl; \
16:         cout << " on line " << __LINE__ << endl; \
17:         cout << " in file " << __FILE__ << endl;  \
18:                 }
19:    #endif
```

3. The following is one possible answer:

```
#ifndef DEBUG
#define DPRINT(string)
#else
#define DPRINT(STRING) cout << #STRING ;
#endif
```

4. The following is one possible answer:

```
class myDate
{
  public:
    // stuff here...
  private:
    unsigned int Month : 4;
    unsigned int Day   : 8;
    unsigned int Year  : 12;
}
```

APPENDIX E

A Look at Linked Lists

On Day 13, "Managing Arrays and Strings," you learned about arrays. You also learned what a linked list is. A linked list is a data structure that consists of small containers that are designed to link together as needed. The idea is to write a class that holds one object of your data that can point at the next container of the same type. You create one container for each object that you need to store, and you chain them together as needed.

The containers are called nodes. The first node in the list is called the head, and the last node in the list is called the tail.

Lists come in three fundamental forms. From simplest to most complex, they are

- Singly linked
- Doubly linked
- Trees

In a singly linked list, each node points forward to the next one, but not backward. To find a particular node, start at the top and go from node to node, as in a treasure hunt ("The next node is under the sofa"). A doubly linked list enables you to move backward and forward in the chain. A tree is a complex structure built from nodes, each of which can point in two or more directions. Figure E.1 shows these three fundamental structures.

FIGURE E.1

Linked lists.

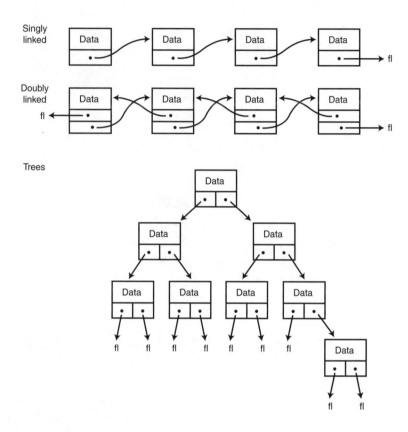

In this appendix, you examine a linked list in detail as a case study of how you create complex structures and, more importantly, how you use them.

The Component Parts of Your Linked List

The linked lists you create will consist of nodes. The node class itself will be abstract; you'll use three subtypes to accomplish the work. There will be a head node whose job is to manage the head of the list, a tail node (guess what its job is!), and zero or more internal nodes. The internal nodes will keep track of the actual data to be held in the list.

Note that the data and the list are quite distinct. You can, in theory, save any type of data you like in a list. It isn't the data that is linked together; it is the node that *holds* the data.

The driver program doesn't know about the nodes; it works with the list. The list, however, does little work; it simply delegates to the nodes.

Listing E.1 shows the code; you'll examine it in excruciating detail in the rest of this appendix.

LISTING E.1 Linked List

```
 1:  // ************************************************
 2:  //    FILE:        Listing E.1
 3:  //    PURPOSE:     Demonstrate a linked list
 4:  //    NOTES:
 5:  //
 6:  //  COPYRIGHT:  Copyright (C) 2000-04 Liberty Associates, Inc.
 7:  //                  All Rights Reserved
 8:  //
 9:  // Demonstrates an object-oriented approach to
10:  // linked lists. The list delegates to the node.
11:  // The node is an abstract data type. Three types of
12:  // nodes are used, head nodes, tail nodes and internal
13:  // nodes. Only the internal nodes hold data.
14:  //
15:  // The Data class is created to serve as an object to
16:  // hold in the linked list.
17:  //
18:  // ************************************************
19:
20:
21:  #include <iostream>
22:  using namespace std;
23:
24:  enum { kIsSmaller, kIsLarger, kIsSame};
25:
26:  // Data class to put into the linked list
27:  // Any class in this linked list must support two methods:
28:  // Show (displays the value) and
29:  // Compare (returns relative position)
30:  class Data
31:  {
32:    public:
33:      Data(int val):myValue(val){}
34:      ~Data(){}
35:      int Compare(const Data &);
36:      void Show() { cout << myValue << endl; }
37:    private:
38:      int myValue;
39:  };
40:
41:  // Compare is used to decide where in the list
42:  // a particular object belongs.
43:  int Data::Compare(const Data & theOtherData)
44:  {
45:     if (myValue < theOtherData.myValue)
46:        return kIsSmaller;
47:     if (myValue > theOtherData.myValue)
48:        return kIsLarger;
```

E

```
49:      else
50:          return kIsSame;
51:  }
52:
53:  // forward declarations
54:  class Node;
55:  class HeadNode;
56:  class TailNode;
57:  class InternalNode;
58:
59:  // ADT representing the node object in the list
60:  // Every derived class must override Insert and Show
61:  class Node
62:  {
63:    public:
64:      Node(){}
65:      virtual ~Node(){}
66:      virtual Node * Insert(Data * theData)=0;
67:      virtual void Show() = 0;
68:    private:
69:  };
70:
71:  // This is the node that holds the actual object
72:  // In this case the object is of type Data
73:  // We'll see how to make this more general when
74:  // we cover templates
75:  class InternalNode: public Node
76:  {
77:    public:
78:      InternalNode(Data * theData, Node * next);
79:      ~InternalNode(){ delete myNext; delete myData; }
80:      virtual Node * Insert(Data * theData);
81:      // delegate!
82:      virtual void Show() { myData->Show(); myNext->Show(); }
83:
84:    private:
85:      Data * myData;  // the data itself
86:      Node * myNext;    // points to next node in the linked list
87:  };
88:
89:  // All the constructor does is to initialize
90:  InternalNode::InternalNode(Data * theData, Node * next):
91:  myData(theData),myNext(next)
92:  {
93:  }
94:
95:  // the meat of the list
96:  // When you put a new object into the list
```

LISTING E.1   continued

```
 97:    // it is passed to the node, which figures out
 98:    // where it goes and inserts it into the list
 99:    Node * InternalNode::Insert(Data * theData)
100:    {
101:
102:        // is the new guy bigger or smaller than me?
103:        int result = myData->Compare(*theData);
104:
105:
106:        switch(result)
107:        {
108:        // by convention if it is the same as me it comes first
109:        case kIsSame:         // fall through
110:        case kIsLarger:    // new data comes before me
111:            {
112:                InternalNode * dataNode = new InternalNode(theData, this);
113:                return dataNode;
114:            }
115:
116:        // it is bigger than I am so pass it on to the next
117:        // node and let HIM handle it.
118:        case kIsSmaller:
119:            myNext = myNext->Insert(theData);
120:            return this;
121:        }
122:        return this;  // appease MSC
123:    }
124:
125:
126:    // Tail node is just a sentinel
127:
128:    class TailNode : public Node
129:    {
130:      public:
131:        TailNode(){}
132:        ~TailNode(){}
133:        virtual Node * Insert(Data * theData);
134:        virtual void Show() { }
135:
136:      private:
137:
138:    };
139:
140:    // If data comes to me, it must be inserted before me
141:    // as I am the tail and NOTHING comes after me
142:    Node * TailNode::Insert(Data * theData)
143:    {
144:        InternalNode * dataNode = new InternalNode(theData, this);
145:        return dataNode;
146:    }
147:
```

E

LISTING E.1   continued

```
148:  // Head node has no data, it just points
149:  // to the very beginning of the list
150:  class HeadNode : public Node
151:  {
152:    public:
153:      HeadNode();
154:      ~HeadNode() { delete myNext; }
155:      virtual Node * Insert(Data * theData);
156:      virtual void Show() { myNext->Show(); }
157:    private:
158:      Node * myNext;
159:  };
160:
161:  // As soon as the head is created
162:  // it creates the tail
163:  HeadNode::HeadNode()
164:  {
165:      myNext = new TailNode;
166:  }
167:
168:  // Nothing comes before the head so just
169:  // pass the data on to the next node
170:  Node * HeadNode::Insert(Data * theData)
171:  {
172:     myNext = myNext->Insert(theData);
173:     return this;
174:  }
175:
176:  // I get all the credit and do none of the work
177:  class LinkedList
178:  {
179:    public:
180:      LinkedList();
181:      ~LinkedList() { delete myHead; }
182:      void Insert(Data * theData);
183:      void ShowAll() { myHead->Show(); }
184:    private:
185:      HeadNode * myHead;
186:  };
187:
188:  // At birth, I create the head node
189:  // It creates the tail node
190:  // So an empty list points to the head which
191:  // points to the tail and has nothing between
192:  LinkedList::LinkedList()
193:  {
194:      myHead = new HeadNode;
195:  }
```

LISTING E.1   continued

```
196:
197:    // Delegate, delegate, delegate
198:    void LinkedList::Insert(Data * pData)
199:    {
200:        myHead->Insert(pData);
201:    }
202:
203:    // test driver program
204:    int main()
205:    {
206:        Data * pData;
207:        int val;
208:        LinkedList ll;
209:
210:        // ask the user to produce some values
211:        // put them in the list
212:        for (;;)
213:        {
214:            cout << "What value? (0 to stop): ";
215:            cin >> val;
216:            if (val == 0)
217:                break;
218:            pData = new Data(val);
219:            ll.Insert(pData);
220:        }
221:
222:        // now walk the list and show the data
223:        ll.ShowAll();
224:        return 0;   // ll falls out of scope and is destroyed!
225:    }
```

OUTPUT

```
What value? (0 to stop): 5
What value? (0 to stop): 8
What value? (0 to stop): 3
What value? (0 to stop): 9
What value? (0 to stop): 2
What value? (0 to stop): 10
What value? (0 to stop): 0
2
3
5
8
9
10
```

ANALYSIS   The first thing to note is the enumerated constant defined on line 24, which provides three constant values: kIsSmaller, kIsLarger, and kIsSame. Every object that might be held in this linked list must support a Compare() method. These constants will be the result value returned by the Compare() method.

For illustration purposes, the class Data is created on lines 30–39, and the Compare() method is implemented on lines 43–51. A Data object holds a value and can compare itself with other Data objects. It also supports a Show() method to display the value of the Data object.

The easiest way to understand the workings of the linked list is to step through an example of using one. On line 203, a driver program is declared; on line 206, a pointer to a Data object is declared; and on line 208, a local linked list is defined.

You can see the LinkList class on lines 177–186. When the linked list is created, the constructor on line 192 is called. The only work done in the constructor is to allocate a HeadNode object and to assign that object's address to the pointer held in the linked list on line 185.

This allocation of a HeadNode invokes the HeadNode constructor shown on lines 163–166. This, in turn, allocates a TailNode and assigns its address to the head node's myNext pointer. The creation of the TailNode calls the TailNode constructor shown on line 131, which is inline and which does nothing.

Thus, by the simple act of allocating a linked list on the stack, the list is created, a head and a tail node are created, and their relationship is established, as illustrated in Figure E.2.

FIGURE E.2

The linked list after it is created.

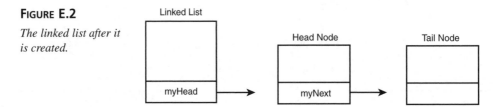

Back in the driver program, line 212 begins an infinite loop. The user is prompted for values to add to the linked list. He can add as many values as he likes, entering 0 when he is finished. The code on line 216 evaluates the value entered; if it is 0, it breaks out of the loop.

If the value is not 0, a new Data object is created on line 218, and that is inserted into the list on line 219. For illustration purposes, assume the user enters the value 15. This invokes the Insert method on line 198.

The linked list immediately delegates responsibility for inserting the object to its head node. This invokes the method Insert on line 170. The head node immediately passes the responsibility to whatever node its myNext is pointing to. In this (first) case, it is pointing to the tail node (remember, when the head node was born, it created a link to a tail node). This, therefore, invokes the method Insert on line 142.

`TailNode::Insert` knows that the object it has been handed must be inserted immediately before itself—that is, the new object will be in the list right before the tail node. Therefore, on line 144 it creates a new `InternalNode` object, passing in the data and a pointer to itself. This invokes the constructor for the `InternalNode` object, shown on line 90.

The `InternalNode` constructor does nothing more than initialize its `Data` pointer with the address of the `Data` object it was passed and its `myNext` pointer with the node's address it was passed. In this case, the node it points to is the tail node (remember, the tail node passed in its own `this` pointer).

Now that the `InternalNode` has been created, the address of that internal node is assigned to the pointer `dataNode` on line 144, and that address is in turn returned from the `TailNode::Insert()` method. This returns us to `HeadNode::Insert()`, where the address of the `InternalNode` is assigned to the `HeadNode`'s `myNext` pointer (on line 172). Finally, the `HeadNode`'s address is returned to the linked list where, on line 200, it is thrown away (nothing is done with it because the linked list already knows the address of the head node).

Why bother returning the address if it is not used? `Insert` is declared in the base class, `Node`. The return value is needed by the other implementations. If you change the return value of `HeadNode::Insert()`, you receive a compiler error; it is simpler just to return the `HeadNode` and let the linked list throw its address on the floor.

So what happened? The data was inserted into the list. The list passed it to the head. The head, blindly, passed the data to whatever the head happened to be pointing to. In this (first) case, the head was pointing to the tail. The tail immediately created a new internal node, initializing the new node to point to the tail. The tail then returned the address of the new node to the head, which reassigned its `myNext` pointer to point to the new node. Hey! Presto! The data is in the list in the right place, as illustrated in Figure E.3.

E

FIGURE E.3

The linked list after the first node is inserted.

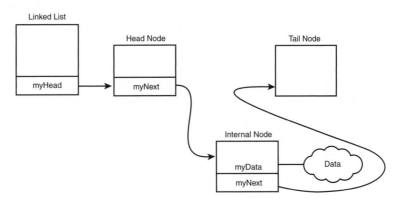

After inserting the first node, program control resumes at line 214. Once again, the value is evaluated. For illustration purposes, assume that the value 3 is entered. This causes a new Data object to be created on line 218 and to be inserted into the list on line 219.

Once again, on line 200, the list passes the data to its HeadNode. The HeadNode::Insert() method, in turn, passes the new value to whatever its myNext happens to be pointing to. As you know, it is now pointing to the node that contains the Data object whose value is 15. This invokes the InternalNode::Insert() method on line 99.

On line 103, the InternalNode uses its myData pointer to tell its Data object (the one whose value is 15) to call its Compare() method, passing in the new Data object (whose value is 3). This invokes the Compare() method shown on line 43.

The two values are compared, and, because myValue will be 15 and theOtherData.myValue will be 3, the returned value will be kIsLarger. This causes program flow to jump to the kIsLarger case on line 110.

A new InternalNode is created for the new Data object. The new node points to the current InternalNode object, and the new InternalNode's address is returned from the InternalNode::Insert() method to the HeadNode. Thus, the new node, whose object's value is smaller than the current node's object's value, is inserted into the list, and the list now looks like Figure E.4.

FIGURE E.4

The linked list after the second node is inserted.

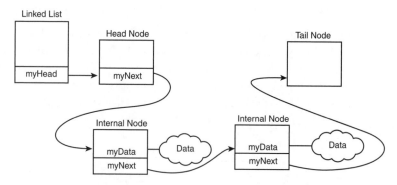

In the third invocation of the loop, the customer adds the value 8. This is larger than 3 but smaller than 15, and so it should be inserted between the two existing nodes. Progress is like the previous example, except that when the node whose object's value is 3 does the compare, rather than returning kIsLarger, it returns kIsSmaller (meaning that the object whose value is 3 is smaller than the new object, whose value is 8). This causes the InternalNode::Insert() method to branch to the kIsSmaller case on line 118. Rather than creating a new node and inserting it, the InternalNode just passes the new data on to the Insert method of whatever its myNext pointer happens to be pointing to. In this case, it invokes InsertNode on the InternalNode whose Data object's value is 15.

The comparison is done again, and a new `InternalNode` is created. This new `InternalNode` points to the `InternalNode` whose `Data` object's value is 15, and its address is passed back to the `InternalNode` whose `Data` object's value is 3, as shown on line 119.

The net effect is that the new node is inserted into the list at the right location.

If at all possible, you'll want to step through the insertion of a number of nodes in your debugger. You should be able to watch these methods invoke one another and the pointers be properly adjusted.

What Have You Learned?

In a well-designed object-oriented program, *no one* is in charge. Each object does its own little job, and the net effect is a well-running machine.

The linked list has the single job of maintaining the head node. The head node immediately passes new data to whatever it points to, without regard to what that might be.

The tail node creates a new node and inserts it whenever it is handed data. It knows only one thing: If this came to me, it gets inserted right before me.

Internal nodes are marginally more complicated; they ask their existing object to compare itself with the new object. Depending on the result, they then insert or they just pass it along.

Note that the internal node (`InternalNode` in the preceding listing) has *no idea* how to do the comparison; that is properly left to the object itself. All the internal node knows is to ask the objects to compare themselves and to expect one of three possible answers. Given one answer, it inserts; otherwise, it just passes it along, not knowing or caring where it will end up.

E

INDEX

collaboration diagrams, 364
combining
  arrays, 446
  math operators with
    assignment operators,
    73-74
  references and pointers,
    280
command-line
  processing, 631-634
comments, 32-33, 38
  /* (C-style), 33
  // (C++-style), 33
  cautions, 34
  example, 33-34
  readability, 782-783
  writing, 39
Compare( ) method, 881
compile time, 22
compile-time errors, 162
compilers, 6, 19, 752
  assert( ) macro, 761-762
  compiling with symbols,
    747
  errors, 20-21
  intermediate files, saving,
    752
  troubleshooting, 20
compiling
  errors, 20-21
  Hello World program,
    17-18
  source code, 15
  with symbols, 747
complement operator, 774
compound statements, 68-69
concatenating
  strings, 759-760
  values, 30
concatenation operator,
  759-760
conditional operator,
  94-95
conflict resolution, 637-642
const default, overriding,
  642

const methods, 158-159,
  249-251
const pointers, 248-251
  declaring, 248-249
  methods, 249-250
  passing, 274-277
const statement, 60, 158,
  172-173, 784
const this pointers, 251
constants, 59. *See also*
  variables
  in arrays, 415
  changing, 60
  defining, 60
  enumerated, 61-63
  literals, 59
  substitutions, 753
  symbolic, 59-60, 64
constructors, 154
  base constructors,
    passing arguments to,
    381-385
  contained classes, 546-549
  copy constructors,
    298-302
    deep copies, 298,
      301-302
    member-wise copies,
      298
    parameters, 298
    virtual, 400-403
  defaults, 154-158, 295
  inheritance, 378-381
  initializing, 297
  member variables, 297
  multiple constructors,
    calling, 460-463
  overloading, 294-296, 381,
    384
  specialized, 688
containment, 342-343, 537,
  693
  compared to delegation,
    553-561
  compared to private
    inheritance, 590

contained classes
  accessing members of,
    545
  class design, 358-359
  compared to
    delegation, 553-561
  constructors, 546-549
  costs, 546-549
  Employee class,
    542-544
  filtering access to, 545
  implementing, 552-553
  passing by value,
    549-552
  String class, 538-542
  costs, 546-549
  implementing, 552-553
continue statements,
  180-182
contravariance, 803-804
conversion operators
  creating, 321-323
  sample program, 323-324
conversion specifiers,
  620-621
Convert( ) function, 106
converting
  base 10 to base 6, 810
  base 10 to base 7, 809-810
  base 10 to binary, 810-811
  data types, 320-324
  decimals to binary,
    813-814
  Fahrenheit/Celsius, 106
copy constructors, 298-302
  deep copies, 298, 301-302
  member-wise copies, 298
  parameters, 298
  virtual, 400-403
copying strings, 435-436
Counter class
  Counter object
    converting int to,
      321-322
    converting to unsigned
      short, 324

overloading

compared to overriding, 387

functions/methods, 118-121

constructors, 294-296, 381, 384

example, 289-292

when to use, 294

operators, 302-303

addition, 314-316

friend functions, 580-585

guidelines, 317

insertion, 585-589

limitations, 316-317

postfix, 311

prefix, 304-306

temporary objects, 306-309

this pointer, 309-310

overriding

compared to hiding, 389

compared to over-loading, 387

const default, 642

methods, 385-387

ownership of pointers, 285

P

p( ) function, 653

packages, 347

Pane class, 648

parameterized templates, 661

parameterized types.
See **templates**

parameters, 36, 101, 113

command-line processing, 631-634

copy constructors, 298

defaults, 116-118

get( ) method, 606

macros, 757

passing

to base constructors, 381-385

by reference, 262-265, 271-274

by value, 109-110, 134, 263-264, 549-552

parentheses ( ), 96

macro syntax, 757-759

nesting, 78

parsing character strings, 423-425

partitioning RAM (random access memory), 130-132

PartsList class, 554-561

passing

exceptions, 739-742

objects, 397-399

parameters

by reference, 262-265, 271-274

by value, 109-110, 134, 263-264, 549-552

to base constructors, 381-385

pointers

const pointers, 274-277

pointers to functions, 523-525

references to objects, 277-279

template objects, 678-682

peek( ) method, 611-612

percolating shared functions, 452

period (.), 150, 239

persistence of variables, 233

pipe character (|), 91

piping, 598

plus sign (+)

addition operator, 314-316

increment operator, 74-76

prefix operator, 304-306, 311-313

Point class, 166-167

pointers, 221-224, 227-228

advantages, 232

allocating, 236

arrays, 421-423, 426-428

combining with references, 280

compared to references, 279-280

const, 248-251

declaring, 248-249

methods, 249-250

passing, 274-277

const this, 251

current values, printing, 769-771

data manipulation, 228-229

as data members on free store, 241-243

declaring, 224, 231

deleting, 235-236

dereferencing, 226, 232

function pointers

advantages, 517-520

arrays, 521-523

assigning, 517

declaring, 514

dereferencing, 520

example, 514-517

passing, 523-525

typedef statement, 525-528

indirection, 225

initializing, 224, 232

memory addresses

assigning, 224-225

examining, 229-231

retrieving, 226

memory leaks, 237

method pointers

arrays, 531-532

declaring, 528

example, 528-530

invoking, 528

naming, 224

null, 224, 248, 262

How can we make this index more useful? Email us at indexes@samspublishing.com

Operator precedence and associativity

Level	Operators	Evaluation Order
1 (high)	( ) . [ ] -> ::	left-to-right
2	* & ! ~ ++ -- + - sizeof new delete	right-to-left
3	.* -> *	left-to-right
4	* / %	left-to-right
5	+ -	left-to-right
6	<< >>	left-to-right
7	< <= > >=	left-to-right
8	== !=	left-to-right
9	&	left-to-right
10	^	left-to-right
11	|	left-to-right
12	&&	left-to-right
13	||	left-to-right
14	?:	right-to-left
15	= *= /= += -= %= <<= >>= &= ^= |=	right-to-left
16 (low)	,	left-to-right

Operators at the top of the table have higher precedence than operators below. In expressions beginning with arguments in the innermost set of parentheses (if any), programs evaluate operators of higher precedence before evaluating operators of lower precedence.

Unary plus (+) and unary minus (–) are at level 2, and have precedence over arithmetic plus and minus at level 5. The & symbol at level 2 is the address-of operator; the & symbol at level 9 is the bitwise AND operator. The * symbol at level 2 is the pointer-dereference operator; the * symbol at level 4 is the multiplication operator. In the absence of clarifying parentheses, operators on the same level are evaluated according to their left-to-right or right-to-left evaluation order.

Operators that may be overloaded

*	/	+	-	%	^	&	|	~	!	,	=	<	>
<=	>=	++	--	<<	>>	==	!=	&&	||	*=	/=	%=	^=
&=	|=	+=	-=	<<=	>>=	->	->*	[]	()	new	delete		

Operators +, -, *, and & may be overloaded for binary and unary expressions. Operators ., .*, ::, ?:, and sizeof may not be overloaded. In addition, =, ( ), [ ], and -> must be implemented as nonstatic member functions.

Visual database components

TDBCheckBox	A data-aware TCheckBox component.
TDBComboBox	A data-aware TComboBox component.
TDBEdit	A data-aware TEdit single-line text entry component.
SSView	A data-aware text-only TGrid component.
TDBImage	A data-aware graphical TImage component.
TDBListBox	A data-aware TListBox component.
TDBLookupCombo	A data-aware TComboBox component with the capability to search a lookup table.
TDBLookupList	A data-aware TListBox component with the capability to search a lookup table.
TDBMemo	A data-aware TMemo multiple-line text-entry component.
TDBNavigator	A sophisticated database browsing and editing tool. This component is to database programming what a remote control is to a video recorder. Users click the control's buttons to move through database records, insert new records, delete records, and perform other navigational operations.
TDBRadioGroup	A data-aware TRadioGroup component.
TDBText	A data-aware read-only text component for displaying database information that you don't want users to be able to edit.

Nonvisual database components

TBatchMove	Performs operations on records and tables, such as updating all records that match a specified argument.
TBlobField	A field of indefinite size of a record in a dataset that consists of an arbitrary set of bytes—typically a graphical image such as a bitmap.
TDatabase	Provides additional database services such as server log-ins and local aliases.
TDataSet	The immediate ancestor of TDBDataSet.
TDataSource	Connects dataset components such as TTable and TQuery with data-aware components such as TDBEdit and TDBMenu. Every database application needs at least one TDataSource object.
TDBDataSet	The direct ancestor of TTable, TQuery, and TStoredProc. Most applications use the derived classes TTable, TQuery, and TStoredProc for dataset access rather than TDBDataSet. However, functions may pass parameters of this type to operate on all types of datasets and the results of queries.
TField	Provides access to fields in a record.
TFieldDef	Defines the structure of physical fields in records. All TField objects do not necessarily have corresponding TFieldDef objects. For example, calculated TField objects have no physical record fields, and therefore no TFieldDef objects.
TFieldDefs	Holds the TFieldDef objects that define the physical fields in a data set.
TIndexDef	Describes the index of a table.
TIndexDefs	Holds the set of all TIndexDef objects for a table.
TParam	Defines parameters for TQuery and TStoredProc objects.
TParams	Holds all parameters for TQuery and TStoredProc objects.